xford excellence for the Caribbean

Book 3

STP Caribbean Mathematics

FOURTH EDITION

Chandler
Smith
Chan-Tack
R Griffith
D Holder
Bostock
Shepherd

OXFORD
UNIVERSITY PRESS

OXFORD
UNIVERSITY PRESS

Great Clarendon Street, Oxford, OX2 6DP, United Kingdom

Oxford University Press is a department of the University of Oxford. It furthers the University's objective of excellence in research, scholarship, and education by publishing worldwide. Oxford is a registered trade mark of Oxford University Press in the UK and in certain other countries

The Publisher would like to acknowledge the contributions of Karyl Chan-Tack, Wendy Griffith and Kenneth Holder to this series.

First published in 1987

Second edition published by Stanley Thornes (Publishers) Ltd in 1997

Third edition published by Nelson Thornes Ltd in 2005

This edition published by Oxford University Press in 2019

British Library Cataloguing in Publication Data
Data available

978-0-19-842657-8

10 9 8 7

Paper used in the production of this book is a natural, recyclable product made from wood grown in sustainable forests.
The manufacturing process conforms to the environmental regulations of the country of origin.

Printed in India by Multivista Global Pvt. Ltd

Acknowledgements
The publishers would like to thank the following for permissions to use copyright material:

Cover image: Radachynskyi/iStock

Artwork by Thomson Digital

Contents

Introduction

To the student

This new edition of *STP Caribbean Mathematics Student Book 3* attempts to meet your needs as you begin your study of Mathematics at the Secondary school level. Your learning experiences at this stage lay the foundation for future achievement in CSEC Mathematics and beyond. We are very conscious of your need for success and enjoyment in doing Mathematics, which comes from solving problems correctly. With this in mind, we have divided most of the exercises into three types of question:

Type 1 questions

These are identified by numbers written in bold print, e.g. **12**. They help you to see if you understand the topic being discussed and should be attempted in every chapter you study.

Type 2 questions

These are identified by a single underline under the bold print, e.g. **12**. They are extra questions for you to do and are not more difficult. They should be attempted if you need extra practice or want to do revision at a later time.

Type 3 questions

These are identified by a double underline under the bold print, e.g. **12**. They are for those of you who completed Type 1 questions fairly easily and want to attempt questions that are more challenging.

Multiple choice questions

Multiple choice questions have been used throughout the book to help you become more familiar with the format of your assessments at CSEC.

Mixed exercises

Most chapters end with Mixed exercises to help you advance your critical thinking, problem-solving and computational skills. These exercises will also help you revise what you have done, either when you have finished the chapter or as you prepare for examinations.

Use of calculator

You should be able to use a calculator accurately before you leave school. We suggest that you use a calculator mainly to check your answers. Whether you use a calculator or do the computations yourself, always estimate your answer first and always ask the question, 'Does my answer make sense?'

Suggestions for use of student book

- Break up the material in a chapter into manageable parts.
- Have paper and a pencil with you always when you are studying mathematics.
- Write down and look up the meaning of all new vocabulary you encounter.
- Read all questions carefully and rephrase them in your own words.
- Remember that each question contains all the information you need to solve the problem. Do not look only at the numbers that are given.
- Practise your mathematics. This will ensure your success!

You are therefore advised to try to solve as many problems as you can.
Above all, don't be afraid to make mistakes as you are learning. The greatest mathematicians all made many mistakes as they tried to solve problems.

You are now on your way to success in mathematics – GOOD LUCK!

To the teacher

In writing this series, the authors attempted to present the topics in such a way that students will understand the connections among topics in mathematics, and be encouraged to see and use mathematics as a means to make sense of the real world. The exercises have been carefully graded to make the content more accessible to students.

This new edition is designed to:

1 Assist you in helping students to

- attain important mathematical skills
- connect mathematics to their everyday lives and understand its role in the development of our contemporary society
- see the importance of critical thinking skills in everyday problems
- discover the fun of doing mathematics both individually and collaboratively
- develop a positive attitude towards doing mathematics.

2 Encourage you to include historical information about mathematics in your teaching.

Topics from the history of mathematics have been incorporated to ensure that mathematics is not dissociated from its past. This should lead to an increase in the level of enthusiasm, interest and fascination among students, thus enriching the teaching and learning experiences in the mathematics lessons.

Investigations

'Investigation' is included in this revised STP Caribbean Mathematics series. This is in keeping with the requirements of the latest Lower and Secondary and CSEC syllabuses in the region.

Investigations are used to provide students with the opportunity to explore hands-on and minds-on mathematics. At the same time, teachers are presented with open-ended explorations to enhance their mathematical instruction.

It is expected that the tasks will

- encourage problem solving and reasoning
- develop communication skills and the ability to work collaboratively
- connect various mathematical concepts and theories.

Suggestions

1 At the start of each lesson, give a brief outline of the topic to be covered in the lesson. As examples are given, refer back to the outline to show how the example fits into it.

2 List terms that you consider new to the students and solicit additional words from them. Encourage students to read from the text and make their own vocabulary list. Remember that mathematics is a foreign language. The ability to communicate mathematically must involve the careful use of the correct terminology.

3 Have students construct different ways to phrase questions. This helps students to see mathematics as a language. Students, especially in the junior classes, tend to concentrate on the numerical or 'maths' part of the question and pay little attention to the information that is required to solve the problem.

4 When solving problems, have students identify their own problem-solving strategies and listen to the strategies of others. This practice should create an atmosphere of discussion in the class centred on different approaches to solving the same problem.

   As the students try to solve problems on their own they will make mistakes. This is expected, as this was the experience of the inventors of mathematics: they tried, guessed, made many mistakes and worked for hours, days and sometimes years before reaching a solution.

   There are enough problems in the exercises to allow the students to try and try again. The excitement, disappointment and struggle with a problem until a solution is found will create rewarding mathematical experiences.

1 Making sure of arithmetic

At the end of this chapter you should be able to...

1. remember how to identify prime numbers and write a number as a product of primes
2. remember how to write a set of multiples of a number and identify square numbers
3. distinguish between different types of number and understand the relationship between them
4. recall what the reciprocal of a number is
5. interchange decimals and fractions
6. use the dot notation to write recurring decimals
7. recall the laws of indices and understand the meaning of zero and negative indices
8. understand and use standard form
9. multiply and divide decimals and approximate a number to a given number of decimal places or significant figures
10. add and subtract base two and base three numbers.

Did you know?

Did you know that the ancient Greeks did not think of unity as a number? To them 3 was the first odd number.

You need to know...

- ✔ how to add, subtract, multiply and divide whole numbers
- ✔ how to use set notation and the meaning of a subset
- ✔ the meaning of the complement of a set
- ✔ the meaning of mixed fractions and improper fractions
- ✔ how to add, subtract and multiply decimals.

Key words

base 3 numbers, binary numbers, common fraction, decimal fraction, denary numbers, denominator, equivalent fraction, factor, improper fraction, index (plural indices), integer, irrational number, lowest common multiple (LCM), mixed number, multiple, natural number, numerator, perfect cube, perfect square, prime number, rational number, real number, reciprocal, recurring decimal, set, significant figures, standard form

Prime numbers

A number greater than 1 that can be divided exactly only by itself and 1 is called a *prime number*; for example, 7 is a prime number (as 7 can only be 7×1) but 6 is not a prime number (because $6 = 6 \times 1$ or 3×2).

The smallest prime number is 2.

Did you know?

The Greek mathematician Euclid (born about 300 BCE) showed that the number of primes is infinite.

In December 2018, the number $2^{82\,589\,933} - 1$ was found to be a prime number, the largest discovered so far. This number has 24 862 048 digits.

Factors

A *factor* of a number divides exactly into that number, for example, 2 is a factor of 10 because 2 divides into 10 exactly 5 times.

On the other hand 3 is not a factor of 10 because 3 does not divide exactly into 10.

Exercise 1a

1 Write the prime numbers that are less than 10.

2 Write the prime numbers that are between 10 and 20.

3 In the set {5, 7, 9, 11, 13, 15}, which members are prime numbers?

4 In the set {20, 21, 22, 23, 24, 25}, which members are prime numbers?

5 Write those members of the set {8, 16, 40, 35, 41, 81, 206, 515} for which

a 2 is a factor **b** 5 is a factor **c** 3 is a factor.

Write all the factors of 12.

1, 2, 3, 4, 6, 12 are all factors of 12.

(Note that factors of a number are not always prime.)

Write all the factors of:

6 6 **8** 9 **10** 21

7 8 **9** 18 **11** 26

Prime factors

Sometimes we need to know just the prime factors of a number and to be able to express the number as the product of its prime factors.

For example, the prime factors of 6 are 2 and 3

and $6 = 2 \times 3$

For larger numbers we need a more systematic approach.
Consider the number 84.

We start with the smallest prime factor of 84, which is 2,
so we divide 2 into 84 $84 \div 2 = 42$

We then repeat the process with 42 $42 \div 2 = 21$

We repeat the process with 21
but 3 is the lowest prime factor of 21 $21 \div 3 = 7$

Repeating the process again $7 \div 7 = 1$

Therefore the prime factors of 84 are 2, 2, 3 and 7.

It is easier to keep track of the prime factors if the division is set out like this:

$$\begin{array}{r|l} 2 & 84 \\ 2 & 42 \\ 3 & 21 \\ 7 & 7 \\ & 1 \end{array}$$

Now we can see that $84 = 2 \times 2 \times 3 \times 7$

Exercise 1b

Express the following numbers as products of their prime factors.

1 10	**4** 12	**7** 60	**10** 66
2 21	**5** 8	**8** 50	**11** 126
3 35	**6** 28	**9** 36	**12** 108

Multiples

If a number divides exactly into a second number, the second number is a *multiple* of the first.

For example, the first six multiples of 3 are 3, 6, 9, 12, 15, 18.

Exercise 1c

1 From the set
{2, 3, 5, 6, 8, 10, 12, 14, 15, 16, 18, 20}
write the members that are

a multiples of 2 **c** multiples of 4 **e** multiples of 6
b multiples of 3 **d** multiples of 5 **f** multiples of 8.

2 Write the multiples of 9 between 50 and 100.

3 Write the multiples of 7 between 10 and 50.

Investigation

Sieve of Eratosthenes

This is a way of finding prime numbers.

Start with an array of whole numbers:

~~1~~	2	3	4	5	~~6~~	7	8	9	10
11	~~12~~	13	14	~~15~~	16	17	18	19	20
~~21~~	22	23	~~24~~	25	26	27	28	29	30
31	32	~~33~~	34	35	36	37	38	39	40
41	~~42~~	43	44	45	46	47	48	49	50
~~51~~	52	53	54	55	56	57	58	59	60
61	62	63	64	65	66	67	68	69	70
71	72	73	74	75	76	77	78	79	80
81	82	83	84	85	86	87	88	89	90
91	92	93	94	95	96	97	98	99	100

1 is not a prime number – cross it out.

Cross out all numbers, apart from 2, that are divisible by 2 (some have been done).

Then cross out all numbers, apart from 3, that are divisible by 3 (some have been done).

4 has already been crossed out. The next number is 5. Cross out all numbers apart from 5 that are divisible by 5, and so on for 7, 11, etc.

The numbers that are left are the prime numbers less than 100.

Extend this idea to find the prime numbers between 100 and 200.

Squares

A square number, or a *perfect square*, can be written as the product of two equal numbers.

For example, 16 is a perfect square because $16 = 4 \times 4$.

Exercise 1d

1 Write the perfect squares between 2 and 10.

2 Write the perfect squares between 10 and 101.

3 In the set {2, 4, 6, 8, 10, 12, 16, 18, 20}, which members are perfect squares?

4 In the set {3, 9, 27, 81}, which members are perfect squares?

5 A *perfect cube* is the product of three equal numbers, e.g. $27 = 3 \times 3 \times 3$.
Find the prime factors of each number in the set {6, 8, 25, 64, 81, 125}.
Hence write down those members of the set that are perfect cubes.

Multiplying a string of numbers

Consider $2 \times 3 \times 6$; this means multiply 2 by 3 and then multiply the result by 6,

therefore $$2 \times 3 \times 6 = 6 \times 6 = 36$$

Similarly $2 \times 3 \times 4 \times 5 = 6 \times 4 \times 5 = 24 \times 5 = 120$

Mixed operations

When a calculation involves a mixture of addition, subtraction, multiplication and division, we do the multiplication and division first.

For example, $3+4\times2=3+8=11$

It helps if brackets are put round the parts that are to be done first.

In this case we would write $3+(4\times2)=3+8=11$

Exercise 1e

Calculate:

1 $2\times4\times3$

2 $3\times2\times5$

3 $5\times4\times2$

4 $3\times5\times2$

5 $4\times5\times3$

6 $6\times2\times3$

7 $2\times5\times2\times3$

8 $4\times2\times4\times3$

9 $3\times7\times1\times5$

Calculate:

10 $8-2\times2$

11 $3\times4-6$

12 $12\div4+3$

13 $5+2\times3$

14 $3\times7-8$

15 $10\div2+2$

16 $3-4\div2$

17 $8+2\times2$

<u>18</u> $16-3\times2$

<u>19</u> $7+12\div2$

<u>20</u> $24\div8-2$

21 $3+4-6\div3$

22 $2\times7+8\div4$

23 $3+2\times4-5$

Put brackets round the multiplications and the divisions.

24 $7-10\div2+3$

25 $5\times2-3+1$

26 $18\div3+6\div2$

Names for numbers

As young children we start learning about numbers by counting objects: 1, 2, 3, ... 10, ...

The numbers that we use for counting are called the *natural numbers* and we use the symbol $\mathbb{N}$ for the set of natural numbers.

The natural numbers, together with 0, i.e. 0, 1, 2, ..., are called *whole numbers* and are denoted by $\mathbb{W}$.

Later we learn about negative numbers. The numbers ..., −3, −2, −1, 0, 1, 2, 3, ... are called *integers*. The set of integers is denoted by the symbol $\mathbb{Z}$, so $\mathbb{Z} = \{..., -2, -1, 0, 1, 2, ...\}$. Notice that $\mathbb{N}$ is a subset of $\mathbb{Z}$.

We next learn that whole objects can be divided into parts, or fractions, for example, half an orange, one and a half bars of chocolate.

We use *common fractions*, e.g. $\frac{1}{2}, \frac{3}{4}, \frac{3}{2}, ...$, to describe the size of the part. The *denominator* (bottom number) describes the number of equal parts of the object and the *numerator* (top number) tells us how many parts we have. For example, $\frac{3}{4}$ means that we have 3 of the 4 equal parts of the whole object.

A fraction such as $\frac{3}{2}$, where the numerator is bigger than the denominator, is called an *improper fraction*. The improper fraction $\frac{3}{2}$ can be written as $1\frac{1}{2}$ and in this form it is called a *mixed number*. Note that $1\frac{1}{2}$ means $1 + \frac{1}{2}$.

Any number that can be written as $\frac{a}{b}$ where a and b are integers is called a *rational number*, and we use the symbol $\mathbb{Q}$ for the set of rational numbers.

Any integer can be written as a common fraction, e.g. $4 = \frac{4}{1}$ and $-3 = \frac{-3}{1}$, so the set of rational numbers includes the integers, i.e. $\mathbb{Z} \subset \mathbb{Q}$.

Later we learn that there are other numbers, such as π and $\sqrt{2}$, that cannot be written exactly as common fractions. These numbers are called *irrational numbers* and when they are added to the set of rational numbers, we have all the possible types of number that can be shown as points on a number line. The set of all possible numbers that can be shown on a number line is called the set of *real numbers* and is denoted by $\mathbb{R}$.

It follows from this that $\mathbb{N}$, $\mathbb{W}$, $\mathbb{Z}$ and $\mathbb{Q}$ are all subsets of $\mathbb{R}$, as illustrated by this Venn diagram.

The set of irrational numbers is $\mathbb{R} \cap \mathbb{Q}'$.

This is the shaded section in the diagram.

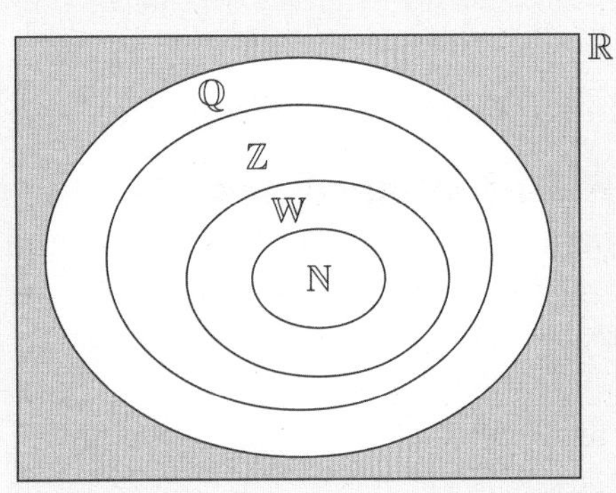

Exercise 1f

1 3 and 2 are both members of $\mathbb{N}$. Which of the following are members of $\mathbb{N}$?

Explain your answers.

a $3+2$ b 3×2 c $3\div 2$ d $3-2$ e $2-3$

2 $2, -5, \frac{3}{4}, \pi$

Choose one of this list of numbers to complete the following.

Use each number once only.

a $\in\mathbb{Q}$ b $\in\mathbb{Z}$ c $\in\mathbb{N}$ d $\in\mathbb{R}$

3 Describe the set given by $\mathbb{Z}\cap\mathbb{N}$.

4 $A=\{2, 4, 6, 8, 10, ...\}$ and $B=\{1, 3, 5, 7, 9, ...\}$ Describe the set $A\cup B$.

5 Describe the set $\mathbb{R}\cap\mathbb{Q}'$.

Addition and subtraction of fractions

We cannot add apples to oranges unless we reclassify them both as, say, fruit. In much the same way, we cannot add tenths to quarters unless we change them both into the same kind of fraction, i.e. change them so that both have the same, or common, denominator. To do this we use the following fact.

The value of a fraction is unaltered if both numerator and denominator are multiplied by the same number.

To find a common denominator for, say, $\frac{1}{4}$ and $\frac{3}{10}$, we look for the lowest number that both 4 and 10 divide into exactly. This number is called the *lowest common multiple* (LCM) of 4 and 10 and in this case it is 20.

Then, as $20=4\times 5$ we have $\frac{1}{4}=\frac{1\times 5}{4\times 5}=\frac{5}{20}$

and as $20=10\times 2$ we have $\frac{3}{10}=\frac{3\times 2}{10\times 2}=\frac{6}{20}$

Therefore $\frac{1}{4}+\frac{3}{10}=\frac{5}{20}+\frac{6}{20}=\frac{11}{20}$

Exercise 1g

Find the LCM of the following sets of numbers:

1 3, 7

2 2, 9

3 3, 4, 6

4 2, 6, 3

5 4, 6

6 3, 5, 12

7 18, 6, 9

8 12, 36, 8

Find $\frac{5}{11}+\frac{2}{5}+\frac{7}{10}$.

You must write each fraction as an equivalent fraction with the LCM of 11, 5 and 10 as the denominator, which is 110.

$$\frac{5}{11}=\frac{5\times 10}{11\times 10}=\frac{50}{110},\ \frac{2}{5}=\frac{2\times 22}{5\times 22}=\frac{44}{110}\ \text{and}\ \frac{7}{10}=\frac{7\times 11}{10\times 11}=\frac{77}{110}$$

so

$$\frac{5}{11}+\frac{2}{5}+\frac{7}{10}=\frac{50+44+77}{110}$$

$$=\frac{171}{110}$$

$$=\frac{110+61}{110}$$

$$=1\frac{61}{110}$$

Find:

9 $\frac{2}{3}+\frac{7}{8}$

10 $\frac{3}{5}+\frac{3}{10}$

11 $\frac{3}{5}+\frac{5}{8}+\frac{1}{2}$

12 $\frac{2}{7}+\frac{1}{2}+\frac{3}{14}$

13 $\frac{3}{16}+\frac{3}{4}+\frac{5}{12}$

14 $\frac{1}{4}+\frac{2}{3}$

Find $\frac{7}{15}-\frac{5}{12}$.

60 is the LCM of 15 and 12 so express each fraction as an equivalent fraction with a denominator of 60.

$$\frac{7}{15}=\frac{7\times 4}{15\times 4}=\frac{28}{60}\ \text{and}\ \frac{5}{12}=\frac{5\times 5}{12\times 5}=\frac{25}{60}$$

so

$$\frac{7}{15}-\frac{5}{12}=\frac{28}{60}-\frac{25}{60}=\frac{28-25}{60}$$

$$=\frac{3}{60}=\frac{1}{20}$$

15 $\frac{7}{9}-\frac{5}{12}$

16 $\frac{1}{4}-\frac{2}{9}$

17 $\frac{3}{10}-\frac{1}{15}$

18 $\frac{1}{10}-\frac{1}{20}$

Find: **a** $1\frac{2}{3}+\frac{1}{6}+2\frac{1}{2}$ **b** $2\frac{1}{4}-\frac{3}{5}$

a $1\frac{2}{3}+\frac{1}{6}+2\frac{1}{2}=3+\frac{2}{3}+\frac{1}{6}+\frac{1}{2}$ (adding whole numbers)

$=3+\frac{4+1+3}{6}$ (expressing the fractions as equivalent fractions with a denominator of 6)

$=3+\frac{8}{6}$

$=3+1\frac{1}{3}=4\frac{1}{3}$

b $2\frac{1}{4}-\frac{3}{5}=2+\frac{5-12}{20}$

$=1+\frac{20+5-12}{20}$ (changing 1 unit into $\frac{20}{20}$)

$=1+\frac{13}{20}=1\frac{13}{20}$

Find:

19 $2\frac{3}{5}+1\frac{1}{8}$

20 $4\frac{2}{9}-3\frac{5}{6}$

21 $2\frac{1}{5}-4\frac{1}{8}+1\frac{7}{10}$

22 $2\frac{3}{4}+1\frac{1}{2}-\frac{1}{3}$

23 $3\frac{1}{8}-2\frac{3}{4}+4\frac{1}{2}$

24 $1\frac{3}{10}-\frac{9}{20}$

Multiplication of fractions

Remember that $\frac{2}{3}\times\frac{1}{5}$ means $\frac{2}{3}$ of $\frac{1}{5}$.

Now $\frac{1}{3}$ of $\frac{1}{5}$ is $\frac{1}{15}$, so $\frac{2}{3}$ of $\frac{1}{5}$ is $\frac{2}{15}$,

i.e. $\frac{2}{3}\times\frac{1}{5}=\frac{2\times1}{3\times5}=\frac{2}{15}$

To multiply fractions, multiply the numerators together and multiply the denominators together.

Any mixed numbers must be changed into improper fractions, and factors that are common to the numerator and denominator should be cancelled before multiplication.

Exercise 1h

Find $2\frac{1}{2} \times \frac{3}{15}$.

$$2\frac{1}{2} \times \frac{3}{15} = \frac{5}{2} \times \frac{3}{15} \quad \text{(writing } 2\tfrac{1}{2} \text{ as an improper fraction)}$$

$$= \frac{\cancel{5}^{1} \times \cancel{3}^{1}}{2 \times \cancel{15}_{1}} \quad \text{(cancelling common factors)}$$

$$= \frac{1}{2}$$

Find:

1 $\frac{2}{3} \times \frac{5}{6}$

2 $1\frac{1}{2} \times \frac{8}{9}$

3 $4 \times \frac{3}{8}$

4 $\frac{2}{3} \times \frac{1}{4} \times \frac{3}{5}$

5 $1\frac{1}{3} \times \frac{1}{2} \times \frac{5}{7}$

6 $\frac{3}{4} \times \frac{2}{5}$

Write $1\frac{1}{2}$ as an improper fraction first.

Write 4 as $\frac{4}{1}$.

In questions **7** to **12** find the missing numbers:

7 $\frac{3}{4} \times \frac{-}{6} = \frac{1}{4}$

8 $\frac{1}{3} \times \frac{-}{2} = \frac{1}{2}$

9 $\frac{2}{-} \times \frac{1}{4} = \frac{1}{6}$

10 $- \times \frac{2}{3} = 1$

11 $\frac{3}{4} \times - = 1$

12 $- \times \frac{7}{8} = 1$

The denominator is 6 times too big. What is the missing number for the numerator to be 6 times too big?

Reciprocals

If the product of two numbers is 1 then each number is called the reciprocal of the other.

We know that $\frac{1}{3} \times 3 = 1$ so

$\frac{1}{3}$ is the reciprocal of 3 and 3 is the reciprocal of $\frac{1}{3}$.

To find the reciprocal of $\frac{3}{4}$ we require the number which, when multiplied by $\frac{3}{4}$, gives 1.

Now $\frac{4}{3} \times \frac{3}{4} = 1$ so

$\frac{4}{3}$ is the reciprocal of $\frac{3}{4}$.

In all cases the reciprocal of a fraction is obtained by turning the fraction upside down.

Any number can be written as a fraction, e.g. $3 = \frac{3}{1}$, $2.5 = \frac{2.5}{1}$, ...

so the reciprocal of $\frac{3}{1}$ is $\frac{1}{3}$ or $1 \div 3$,

the reciprocal of $\frac{2.5}{1}$ is $\frac{1}{2.5}$ or $1 \div 2.5$

Alternatively, as $2.5 = 2\frac{1}{2} = \frac{5}{2}$, the reciprocal of 2.5 is $1 \div \frac{5}{2} = \frac{2}{5} = 0.4$.

> The reciprocal of a number is 1 divided by that number.

Division by a fraction

Consider $\frac{2}{5} \div \frac{3}{7}$.

This can be interpreted as $\frac{2}{5} \times 1 \div \frac{3}{7} = \frac{2}{5} \times \left(1 \div \frac{3}{7}\right)$

Now $1 \div \frac{3}{7}$ is the reciprocal of $\frac{3}{7}$, i.e. $\frac{7}{3}$.

Therefore $\frac{2}{5} \div \frac{3}{7} = \frac{2}{5} \times \frac{7}{3} = \frac{14}{15}$

i.e. to divide by a fraction we multiply by its reciprocal.

Exercise 1i

Write the reciprocals of the following numbers.

1 4

2 $\frac{1}{2}$

3 $\frac{2}{5}$

4 10

5 $\frac{3}{11}$

<u>6</u> 100

<u>7</u> $\frac{2}{9}$

<u>8</u> $\frac{15}{4}$

9 $2\frac{1}{4}$

10 $3\frac{2}{5}$

11 $1\frac{4}{7}$

The reciprocal of a number is 1 divided by that number.

The reciprocal of a fraction is the fraction turned upside down.

Find $3\frac{1}{2} \div \frac{7}{8}$.

(Before multiplying or dividing, mixed numbers must be changed into improper fractions.)

$$3\frac{1}{2} \div \frac{7}{8} = \frac{7}{2} \div \frac{7}{8}$$

$$= \frac{\cancel{7}^{1}}{\cancel{2}_{1}} \times \frac{\cancel{8}^{4}}{\cancel{7}_{1}} = 4$$

Find:

12 $\frac{2}{3} \div \frac{1}{2}$

13 $1\frac{2}{3} \div \frac{5}{6}$

14 $2\frac{1}{2} \div 4$

15 $5 \div \frac{4}{5}$

16 $\frac{2}{9} \div 1\frac{2}{7}$

17 $\frac{3}{7} \div 1\frac{3}{4}$

18 $\frac{5}{9} \div 10$

19 $3 \div \frac{2}{3}$

Multiply $\frac{2}{3}$ by the reciprocal of $\frac{1}{2}$.

Change $1\frac{2}{3}$ to an improper fraction first.

Find $2\frac{1}{2} + \frac{3}{5} \div 1\frac{1}{2} - \frac{1}{2}\left(\frac{3}{5} + \frac{1}{3}\right)$.

(Remember that brackets are worked out first, then multiplication and division and lastly addition and subtraction.)

$$2\frac{1}{2} + \frac{3}{5} \div 1\frac{1}{2} - \frac{1}{2}\left(\frac{3}{5} + \frac{1}{3}\right) = 2\frac{1}{2} + \frac{3}{5} \div 1\frac{1}{2} - \frac{1}{2}\left(\frac{9+5}{15}\right)$$

$$= 2\frac{1}{2} + \frac{3}{5} \div \frac{3}{2} - \frac{1}{2} \times \frac{14}{15}$$

$$= 2\frac{1}{2} + \frac{\cancel{3}^{1}}{5} \times \frac{2}{\cancel{3}_{1}} - \frac{1}{\cancel{2}_{1}} \times \frac{\cancel{14}^{7}}{15}$$

$$= 2\frac{1}{2} + \frac{2}{5} - \frac{7}{15}$$

$$= 2 + \frac{15 + 12 - 14}{30} \quad \text{(the LCM of 2, 5 and 15 is 30)}$$

$$= 2 + \frac{13}{30} = 2\frac{13}{30}$$

Find:

20 $1\frac{2}{3} \times \frac{1}{2} - \frac{2}{5}$

Remember: multiplication before subtraction.

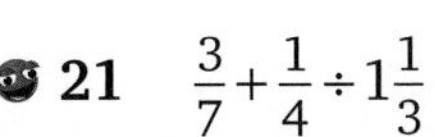

21 $\frac{3}{7} + \frac{1}{4} \div 1\frac{1}{3}$

Remember: division before addition.

22 $\frac{2}{5} \div \left(\frac{1}{2} + \frac{3}{4}\right)$

25 $\frac{9}{11} - \frac{2}{5} \times \frac{3}{4}$

Work out the brackets first.

23 $5\frac{1}{2} \div 3 + \frac{2}{9}$

26 $2\frac{1}{2} \div \frac{7}{9} + 1\frac{1}{3}$

24 $\frac{4}{5} \div \frac{1}{6} + \frac{1}{3} \times 1\frac{1}{2}$

Find:

27 $\dfrac{\frac{1}{3} + \frac{1}{4}}{\frac{5}{6} - \frac{3}{4}}$

29 $\dfrac{\frac{9}{10}}{\frac{5}{6}}$

Get a single fraction on top and a single fraction on the bottom before dividing the top by the bottom.

28 $\dfrac{1\frac{1}{5} - \frac{3}{4}}{2\frac{1}{2}}$

30 $\frac{2}{3} \times \frac{6}{7} - \frac{5}{8} \div 1\frac{1}{4}$

31 $\dfrac{\frac{7}{8}}{3\frac{1}{2} - \frac{2}{3}}$

32 $\dfrac{3\frac{1}{4}}{2\frac{3}{5}}$

33 $\dfrac{\frac{2}{3} \times \frac{3}{4}}{\frac{5}{6} \times \frac{3}{10}}$

Decimal fractions

Long after meeting common fractions, we learn that we can represent fractions of an object by placing a point after the units and continuing to add digits to the right. The first digit after the decimal point is the number of tenths, the next digit is the number of hundredths, and so on.

For example, 0.75 is 7 tenths plus 5 hundredths.

Fractions written this way are called *decimal fractions.*

Usually we refer to common fractions simply as fractions and to decimal fractions simply as decimals.

Interchanging decimals and fractions

Exercise 1j

Express 0.705 as a fraction.

$$0.705 = \frac{7}{10} + \frac{5}{1000} \quad \text{(this step is usually omitted)}$$

$$= \frac{\cancel{705}^{141}}{\cancel{1000}_{200}} \quad \text{(divide top and bottom by 5)}$$

$$= \frac{141}{200}$$

Express the following decimals as fractions:

1 0.35
2 0.216
3 0.204
4 1.36
5 0.03
6 0.012
7 0.005
8 1.01

Express $\frac{7}{8}$ as a decimal.

To express a fraction as a decimal, divide the top by the bottom.

$\frac{7}{8} = 0.875$ $\qquad 8\overline{)7.000}$ gives 0.875 Add zeros for the extra decimal places.

Express the following fractions as decimals:

9 $\frac{3}{20}$
10 $\frac{1}{8}$
11 $\frac{3}{5}$
12 $\frac{6}{25}$
13 $\frac{1}{16}$
14 $\frac{27}{50}$
15 $1\frac{3}{4}$
16 $\frac{5}{32}$

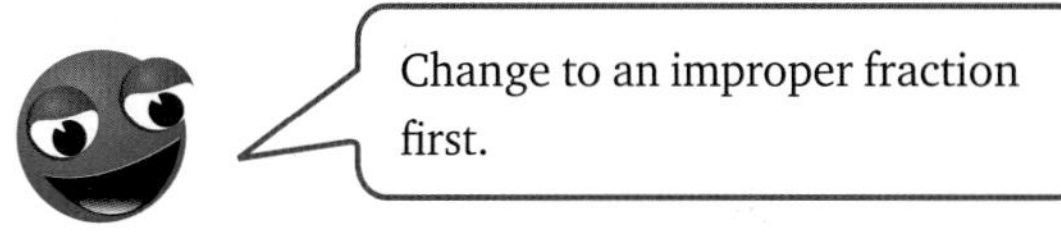
Change to an improper fraction first.

Recurring decimals

If we try to change $\frac{1}{6}$ to a decimal, i.e. $6\overline{)1.0000\ldots}$ giving $0.1666\ldots$ we discover that

a we cannot write $\frac{1}{6}$ as an exact decimal

b from the second decimal place, the 6 recurs for as long as we have the patience to continue the division.

Similarly if we convert $\frac{2}{11}$ to a decimal by dividing 2 by 11, we get 0.18181818 ... and we see that

a $\frac{2}{11}$ cannot be expressed as an exact decimal

b the pair of figures '18' recurs indefinitely.

Decimals like these are called *recurring decimals*. To save time and space we place a dot over the figure that recurs. In the case of a group of figures recurring we place a dot over the first and last figure in the group.

Therefore we write 0.166666 ... as $0.1\dot{6}$

and we write 0.181818 ... as $0.\dot{1}\dot{8}$

Similarly we write 0.316316316 ... as $0.\dot{3}1\dot{6}$

Exercise 1k

Use the dot notation to write the following fractions as decimals:

1	$\frac{1}{3}$	**4**	$\frac{1}{15}$	**7**	$\frac{1}{11}$	**10**	$\frac{1}{14}$
2	$\frac{2}{9}$	**5**	$\frac{1}{7}$	**8**	$\frac{1}{18}$	**11**	$\frac{7}{30}$
3	$\frac{5}{6}$	**6**	$\frac{1}{12}$	**9**	$\frac{5}{12}$	**12**	$\frac{1}{13}$

Addition and subtraction of decimals

Decimals are added and subtracted in the same way as whole numbers. It is sensible to write them in a column so that the decimal points are in a vertical line. This ensures that units are added to units, tenths are added to tenths, and so on.

Multiplication of decimals

To multiply decimals we can first convert them to fractions.

For example,
$$\underset{(2\text{ d.p.})}{0.05} \times \underset{(2\text{ d.p.})}{1.04} = \frac{5}{100} \times \frac{104}{100}$$
$$= \frac{520}{10\,000}$$
$$= \underset{(4\text{ d.p.})}{0.0520}$$

From such examples we deduce the following rule.

First ignore the decimal points and multiply the numbers together. Then the sum of the number of decimal places in the original numbers gives the number of decimal places in the answer (including any zeros at the end).

Division by decimals

To divide a decimal by a whole number, proceed as with whole numbers, adding zeros after the point when necessary. For example, to find $3.14 \div 5$ we have

$$5\overline{)3.140}\quad = 0.628$$

(Make sure that the decimal points are in a vertical line.)

Therefore $\quad 3.14 \div 5 = 0.628$

To divide by a decimal we use the fact that the top and bottom of a fraction can be multiplied by the same number without altering the value of the fraction. Division by a decimal can therefore be converted to division by a whole number.

For example,

$$\begin{aligned} 3.14 \div 0.5 &= \frac{3.14}{0.5} \\ &= \frac{31.4}{5} \qquad \left(\frac{3.14\times 10}{0.5\times 10}\right) \\ &= 6.28 \end{aligned}$$

Exercise 1I

Calculate, without using a calculator:

1 $1.26 + 3.75$

2 $12.4 + 6.7$

3 $5.82 + 0.35$

4 $0.04 + 8.76$

5 $1.8 + 0.02$

6 $25 + 1.36$

7 $4.002 + 0.83$

8 $0.016 + 1.09$

9 $0.000\,32 + 0.0017$

10 $5.3 - 2.1$

11 $8.2 - 4.9$

12 $0.16 - 0.08$

13 1.2×0.8

14 0.7×0.06

15 0.4×0.02

16 $0.36 \div 1.2$

17 $1.08 \div 0.4$

For addition and subtraction write the numbers as you would for whole numbers but with the decimal points one under the other.

Evaluate:

18 $2.6 - 1.4 \div 0.7$

19 $200 \times 0.04 - 0.2$

20 $(1.2 - 0.8) \div 0.8$

21 $4.3 \times 2.1 \div 0.07$

22 $3.2(0.6 - 0.09) + 10.25$

23 $2.73 \div 0.9 \times 1.02$

24 $(20 \times 0.06) \div (3.1 - 1.9)$

Remember, do × and ÷ before + and –

25 $(2.5 + 1.3) \div (2.06 - 0.16)$

26 $\dfrac{2.4 + 0.98}{1.78 + 0.22}$

27 $\dfrac{0.04 \times 1.02}{3.4 \times 0.06}$

Relative sizes

Before we can compare the sizes of a set of numbers we must either change them all into decimals or change them all into fractions with the same denominator. Choose whichever method is easier.

Exercise 1m

Place > or < between the two numbers $\frac{3}{5}$, 0.67.

(Remember that > means 'is greater than' and < means 'is less than'.)

Convert each to a fraction or to a decimal. It is easier to convert $\frac{3}{5}$ to a decimal.

$$\frac{3}{5} = 0.6$$

Comparing 0.6 and 0.67 we see that $0.6 < 0.67$

$\therefore$ $$\frac{3}{5} < 0.67$$

Place > or < between each of the following pairs of numbers:

1 $\frac{5}{8}$, 0.63

2 0.16, $\frac{3}{20}$

3 $\frac{9}{11}$, 0.9

4 $\frac{1}{16}$, 0.07

5 $\frac{2}{7}$, 0.16

6 0.48, $\frac{4}{9}$

7 0.33, $\frac{7}{25}$

8 $\frac{3}{11}$, 0.25

9 $\frac{2}{3}$, 0.66

Arrange the following numbers in ascending order (i.e. the smallest first):

$$\frac{1}{2}, 0.52, \frac{11}{20}, 0.51$$

Writing them all as fractions with denominator 100 gives

$$\frac{1}{2} = \frac{50}{100}, \quad 0.52 = \frac{52}{100}, \quad \frac{11}{20} = \frac{55}{100}, \quad 0.51 = \frac{51}{100}$$

Therefore the required order is $\frac{1}{2}$, 0.51, 0.52, $\frac{11}{20}$.

In each of the following questions arrange the numbers in ascending order of size:

10 $\frac{2}{3}$, 0.6, $\frac{4}{5}$

11 0.85, $\frac{4}{5}$, 0.79

12 $\frac{2}{7}$, 0.3, $\frac{1}{5}$

13 0.75, $\frac{5}{7}$, 0.875, $\frac{7}{9}$

14 0.16, $\frac{3}{20}$, 0.2, $\frac{6}{25}$

15 $1\frac{1}{5}$, 1.3, 1.24, $1\frac{1}{8}$

Convert $\frac{2}{3}$ and $\frac{4}{5}$ to decimals.

Indices

In the number 2^3, the 3 is called the *index* or *power* and 2^3 means $2 \times 2 \times 2$. Thus, indices are a kind of shorthand notation. All other forms of indices are derived from this.

Did you know?

Did you know that an index or power was first used by the Greek mathematician Hippocrates of Chios in the fifth century BCE?

Exercise 1n

Find the value of: **a** $2^2 \times 3^3$ **b** $(3^3)^2$

a $2^2 \times 3^3 = 2 \times 2 \times 3 \times 3 \times 3$
$= 4 \times 27$
$= 108$

b $(3^3)^2 = (27)^2$
$= 27 \times 27$
$= 729$

Find the value of:

1 5^2

2 3^4

3 5^3

4 4^3

5 $2^4 \times 3^2$

6 $8^2 \times 5^2$

7 $6^3 \times 2^2$

8 3.25×10^2

9 8.01×10^3

Remember that we can multiply one number to a power by the *same* number to another power by adding the indices.

Where possible write as a single number in index form:

a $5^2 \times 5^4$ **b** $3^2 \times 2^3$

a $5^2 \times 5^4 = 5^6$

($5^2 \times 5^4 = 5 \times 5 \times 5 \times 5 \times 5 \times 5 = 5^6$, i.e. you can add the indices)

b $3^2 \times 2^3$ cannot be written as a single number in index form

($3^2 \times 2^3 = 3 \times 3 \times 2 \times 2 \times 2$)

Write the following, where possible, as a single number in index form:

10 $2^3 \times 2^4$

11 $3^2 \times 3^5$

12 $5^2 \times 3^5$

13 2×2^4

14 $a^2 \times a^3$

15 $a^2 \times b^3$

To multiply powers of the same number you can add the indices.

We can also divide one number to a power by the *same* number to another power by subtracting the indices.

Where possible write as a single number in index form:

a $2^5 \div 2^2$ **b** $3^3 \div 5^3$

a $2^5 \div 2^2 = 2^3$

$$\left(2^5 \div 2^2 = \frac{\not{2}^1 \times \not{2}^1 \times 2 \times 2 \times 2}{\not{2}_1 \times \not{2}_1} = 2^3\right)$$

b $3^3 \div 5^3$ cannot be simplified into a single number in index form.

$$\left(3^3 \div 5^3 = \frac{3 \times 3 \times 3}{5 \times 5 \times 5}\right)$$

Write the following, where possible, as a single number in index form:

16 $2^4 \div 2^2$

17 $7^3 \div 7^2$

18 $4^5 \div 4^2$

19 $3^4 \div 3$

20 $a^8 \div a^4$

21 $a^3 \div b^2$

Laws of indices

We already know the first two laws, namely $a^m \times a^n = a^{m+n}$

and $a^m \div a^n = a^{m-n}$

Now consider $(a^4)^2$; this means $a^4 \times a^4$ which, using the first law is a^8,

i.e. $(a^4)^2 = a^{4 \times 2}$.

This gives the third law: $(a^m)^n = a^{mn}$

Exercise 1p

1 Write each as a single number in index form.

$(2^3)^2 = (2^3) \times (2^3)$

a $(2^3)^2$ **b** $(3^2)^2$ **c** $(5^2)^2$

Simplify $2(a^3b^2)^3$.

Notice that only the items in the bracket are cubed, so

$$2(a^3b^2)^3 = 2 \times (a^3)^3 \times (b^2)^3$$
$$= 2 \times a^9 \times b^6 = 2a^9b^6$$

2 Simplify:

a $3(t^3)^5$ **b** $(2d^5)^3$ **c** $2(a^2)^3$ **d** $(5p^3)^3$

3 Find the value of:

a $3(2^2)^3$ **c** $10(3^2)^2$

b $(5 \times 2^4)^2$ **d** $2(3^2 - 2^2)^2$

4 Simplify:

a $3(x^3y)^3$ **b** $5(ab^3)^4$ **c** $(4u^2v)^3$ **d** $2p^2(p^3q)^2$

Zero and negative indices

Consider $a^3 \div a^3$.

Subtracting indices gives $a^3 \div a^3 = a^0$

Dividing gives $a^3 \div a^3 = 1$

$$a^0 = 1 \quad \text{i.e. (any number)}^0 = 1$$

For example, 2^0, 10^0, 200^0 all equal 1.

Now consider $a^3 \div a^5$.

Subtracting indices gives $a^3 \div a^5 = a^{-2}$

Dividing gives $\frac{a^3}{a^5} = \frac{a \times a \times a}{a \times a \times a \times a \times a} = \frac{1}{a^2}$

Therefore a^{-2} means $\frac{1}{a^2}$.

A negative sign in front of the index means 'the reciprocal of'

i.e. $$a^{-b} = \frac{1}{a^b}$$

For example, $2^{-1} = \frac{1}{2}$, $10^{-1} = \frac{1}{10}$.

Exercise 1q

Find the value of 3^{-1}.

$$3^{-1}=\frac{1}{3^1}=\frac{1}{3}$$

Find the value of:

1 2^{-1} **2** 10^{-1} **3** 5^{-1} **4** 7^{-1} **5** 8^{-1} **6** 4^{-1} **7** a^{-1} **8** x^{-1}

Find the value of:

a $\left(\frac{1}{2}\right)^{-1}$ **b** $\left(\frac{2}{5}\right)^{-1}$

a $\left(\frac{1}{2}\right)^{-1}=\left(\frac{2}{1}\right)^1=2$ **b** $\left(\frac{2}{5}\right)^{-1}=\left(1\div\frac{2}{5}\right)^1=\left(1\times\frac{5}{2}\right)^1=\left(\frac{5}{2}\right)^1=2\frac{1}{2}$

Find the value of:

9 $\left(\frac{1}{3}\right)^{-1}$ **10** $\left(\frac{2}{3}\right)^{-1}$ **11** $\left(\frac{1}{4}\right)^{-1}$ **12** $\left(\frac{3}{4}\right)^{-1}$ **13** $\left(\frac{1}{5}\right)^{-1}$ **14** $\left(\frac{4}{5}\right)^{-1}$ **15** $\left(\frac{1}{a}\right)^{-1}$ **16** $\left(\frac{x}{y}\right)^{-1}$

Find the value of 3^{-2}.

$$3^{-2}=\frac{1}{3^2}=\frac{1}{9}$$

Find the value of:

17 2^{-3} **18** 5^{-2} **19** 10^{-3} **20** 6^{-2} **21** 2^{-5} **22** 10^{-4} **23** 10^{-2} **24** 4^{-3}

Find the value of $\left(\frac{1}{3}\right)^{-2}$.

$$\left(\frac{1}{3}\right)^{-2}=\left(1\div\frac{1}{3}\right)^2$$

$$=\left(1\times\frac{3}{1}\right)^2=3^2=9$$

Find the value of:

25 $\left(\frac{1}{5}\right)^{-3}$ **27** $\left(\frac{1}{2}\right)^{-5}$ **29** $\left(\frac{1}{8}\right)^{-3}$ **31** $\left(\frac{1}{2}\right)^{-3}$

26 $\left(\frac{1}{4}\right)^{-2}$ **28** $\left(\frac{1}{3}\right)^{-4}$ **30** $\left(\frac{1}{10}\right)^{-4}$ **32** $\left(\frac{1}{6}\right)^{-2}$

Find the value of $\left(\frac{2}{5}\right)^{-3}$.

$$\left(\frac{2}{5}\right)^{-3} = \left(\frac{5}{2}\right)^{3}$$

$$= \frac{5^3}{2^3} = \frac{125}{8} = 15\frac{5}{8}$$

Find the value of:

33 $\left(\frac{3}{4}\right)^{-2}$ **35** $\left(\frac{4}{9}\right)^{-2}$ **37** $\left(\frac{2}{3}\right)^{-4}$ **39** $\left(\frac{3}{10}\right)^{-4}$

34 $\left(\frac{2}{3}\right)^{-3}$ **36** $\left(\frac{2}{7}\right)^{-2}$ **38** $\left(\frac{3}{5}\right)^{-2}$ **40** $\left(\frac{5}{8}\right)^{-2}$

Find the value of:

41 $\left(\frac{1}{8}\right)^{-1}$ **46** $\left(\frac{2}{3}\right)^{0}$ **<u>51</u>** $\left(\frac{3}{4}\right)^{-3}$ **<u>56</u>** $\left(\frac{4}{5}\right)^{3}$

42 $\left(\frac{2}{5}\right)^{-2}$ **47** 5^3 **<u>52</u>** $\left(\frac{2}{7}\right)^{-1}$ **<u>57</u>** 12^{-1}

43 4^{-2} **48** 9^{-1} **<u>53</u>** 5^0 **<u>58</u>** 9^3

44 8^2 **49** $\left(\frac{1}{2}\right)^{-4}$ **<u>54</u>** $\left(\frac{7}{10}\right)^{-3}$ **<u>59</u>** $\left(\frac{1}{4}\right)^{-3}$

45 $\left(\frac{1}{2}\right)^{0}$ **50** 6^0 **<u>55</u>** 2^{-2} **<u>60</u>** $\left(\frac{3}{7}\right)^{0}$

? Puzzle

Replace the stars with digits to complete this addition so that every digit from 1 to 9 is used once.

```
  * 6 *
  * 1 * +
  -----
  * 8 *
```

Standard form (scientific notation)

Very large or very small numbers are more briefly written in *standard form*. It is easier to compare sizes of numbers written in standard form.

Standard form is a number between 1 and 10 multiplied by the appropriate power of 10.

Exercise 1r

The following numbers are given in standard form. Write them as ordinary numbers.

1 3.45×10^2

2 1.2×10^3

3 5.01×10^{-2}

4 4.7×10^{-3}

5 2.8×10^2

6 7.3×10^{-1}

7 9.02×10^5

8 6.37×10^{-4}

9 8.72×10^6

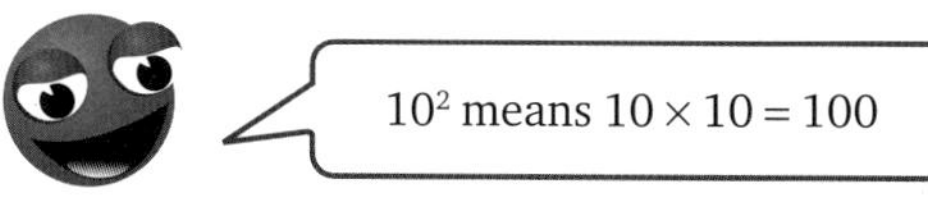

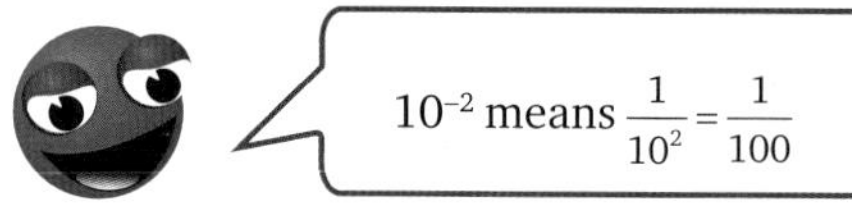

10^2 means $10 \times 10 = 100$

10^{-2} means $\frac{1}{10^2} = \frac{1}{100}$

Write the following numbers in standard form:

a 3840 b 0.0025

(First, write the given digits as a number between 1 and 10 and then decide what power of 10 to multiply the number by to bring it back to the correct size.)

a $3840 = 3.84 \times 10^3$ (The decimal point has been moved 3 places to the left so the index of 10 is 3.)

b $0.0025 = 2.5 \times 10^{-3}$ (The decimal point has been moved 3 places to the right so the index of 10 is –3.)

Write the following numbers in standard form:

10 265

11 0.18

12 3020

13 0.019

14 76 700

15 390 000

16 0.000 85

17 7000

18 0.004

19 58 700

20 2600

21 450 000

22 0.000 007

23 0.8

24 0.000 56

25 24 000

26 39 000 000

27 0.000 000 000 08

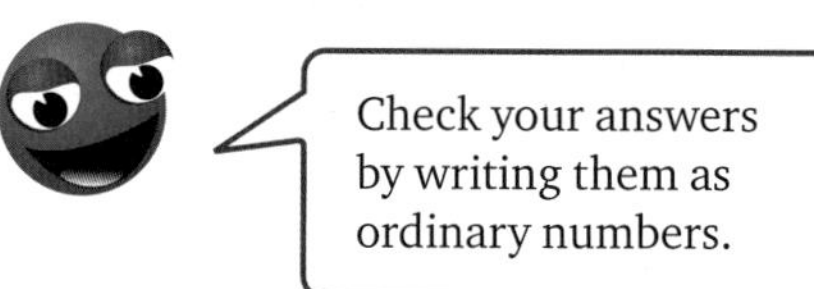

Check your answers by writing them as ordinary numbers.

Activity

If you have a scientific calculator, it will display very large or very small numbers in scientific notation.

Try this: enter 0.000 05, then press $\boxed{x^2}$ and press $\boxed{x^2}$ again.

The display will read 6.25×10^{-18}.

Use your calculator to find the value of

1 $(250\,000)^2$ 2 $(257\,000)^2$ 3 $(0.000\,008)^2$ 4 $(0.000\,007)^2$

Approximations (decimal places and significant figures)

We have seen that it is sometimes unnecessary and often impossible to give exact values. In the case of measurements this is particularly true. However, we do need to know the degree of accuracy of an answer. For example, if a manufacturer is asked to make screws that are about $12\frac{1}{2}$ cm long, he does not know what is acceptable as being 'about $12\frac{1}{2}$ cm long'! But if he is asked to make them 12.5 cm long correct to one decimal place, he knows what tolerances to work to.

Decimal places

To correct 0.078 22 to *two* decimal places (d.p.) we look at the *third* decimal place. If it is 5 or larger, we add 1 to the digit in the second decimal place. If it is less than 5, we do not alter the digit in the second decimal place.

In this example, the digit in the third decimal place is 8,

so $0.07\,822 = 0.08$ correct to 2 d.p.

Significant figures

To determine the first *significant figure* (s.f.) in a number, find the first non-zero digit from the left. The second significant figure is the next digit to the right, zero or otherwise.

For example, $0.0\,7\,0\,2\,5 = 7.0\,2\,5 \times 10^{-2}$

(In 0.07025: 7 is the 1st s.f., 0 is the 2nd s.f., 2 is the 3rd s.f. In 7.025×10^{-2}: 7 is the 1st s.f., 0 is the 2nd s.f., 2 is the 3rd s.f.)

To correct 0.078 22 to two significant figures we look at the third significant figure; in this case it is 2.

Therefore $\quad 0.078\,22 = 0.078$ correct to 2 s.f.

Exercise 1s

Give 0.070 25 correct to: **a** 3 d.p. **b** 3 s.f.

a $0.070\,25 = 0.070$ correct to 3 d.p. (2 is less than 5 so the zero after the 7 is unchanged.)

(We leave the zero at the end of the corrected answer to indicate that the third decimal place is zero.)

b $0.070\,25 = 0.0703$ correct to 3 s.f.

Give each of the following numbers correct to:

a three decimal places **b** three significant figures.

1 2.7846

2 0.1572

3 3.2094

4 0.073 25

5 0.150 76

6 0.020 39

7 0.000 925 8

8 7.8196

9 0.009 638

Estimate a rough value for 0.826×38.3 by correcting each number to 1 significant figure. Then use your calculator to give the answer correct to 3 significant figures.

$0.826 \times 38.3 \approx 0.8 \times 40 = 32 \approx 30$

(For 0.826 the first significant figure is 8 and the second significant figure is less than 5 so the 8 is not changed. For 38.3 the second significant figure is greater than 5 so the first significant figure is increased by 1.)

$0.826 \times 38.3 = 31.6$ correct to 3 s.f.

First estimate a rough value for each of the following calculations, then use your calculator to give the answer correct to three significant figures.

10 0.035×1.098

11 258×184

12 0.0932×0.48

13 18.27×3.82

<u>14</u> 1250×532

15 $86.27 \div 39.8$

16 $204 \div 942$

17 $0.827 \div 0.093$

<u>18</u> $0.0026 \div 0.0378$

<u>19</u> $(3.827)^3$

<u>20</u> $\dfrac{3.257}{83.6}$

<u>21</u> $0.532 \times 3.621 \times 36$

22 $(0.32)^3$ **23** $\dfrac{2.27 \times 3.84}{5.01}$ **24** $\dfrac{0.016 \times 5.82}{2.31}$

Base 2 and base 3 numbers

We met numbers written in different bases in Book 2. Here is a quick reminder.

Denary numbers are base 10 numbers where each place value is a power of 10. They use the digits 0 to 9. These are the numbers we use every day.

Base 2 numbers are called *binary numbers*. Each place value is a power of 2 and they use only the digits 0 and 1.

To convert 1101_2 into a denary number, we can write the number in a table showing the place values.

Place value	2^5	2^4	2^3	2^2	2^1	2^0
			1	1	0	1

This shows that 1101_2 is $(1 \times 2^3) + (1 \times 2^2) + (0 \times 2^1) + (1 \times 2^0) = 8 + 4 + 0 + 1 = 13$

To add or subtract binary numbers we can convert them to base 10, do the addition or subtraction and convert them back again. This can be time consuming so it is quicker to work with them in binary form.

To calculate $1101_2 + 110_2$, write the numbers in columns.

2^4	2^3	2^2	2^1	2^0	
$^{+1}$	1^{+1}	1	0	1	
		1	1	0	+
1	0	0	1	1	
	②	②			

Working from right to left:
$1 + 0 = 1$, $0 + 1 = 1$, $1 + 1 = 2$ so one 2 is carried to the next column then $1 + 1 = 2$, so again 1 is carried to the next column.

Therefore $1101_2 + 110_2 = 10011_2$
(*Check*: $1101_2 = 13$, $110_2 = 6$, $13 + 6 = 19$ and $10011_2 = 2^4 + 2 + 1 = 19$)

To calculate $1101_2 - 110_2$, again write the numbers in columns.

2^4	2^3	2^2	2^1	2^0	
	1^{-1}	1^{-1+2}	0^{+2}	1	
		1	1	0	−
	0	1	1	1	

Working from right to left:
$1 - 0 = 1$, $0 - 1$ cannot be done, so take one 2 from the next column then $2 - 1 = 1$. In the 3rd column, $1 - 1 = 0$, so as $0 - 1$ cannot be done bring in a 2 from the 4th column. There is now zero in the 4th column.

Therefore $1101_2 - 110_2 = 111_2$
(*Check*: $1101_2 - 110_2 = 13 - 6 = 7$, and $111_2 = 2^2 + 2 + 1 = 7$)

For base 3 numbers, the place values are powers of 3 and only the digits 0, 1 and 2 are used.

Place value	3^5	3^4	3^3	3^2	3^1	3^0
			1	1	0	1

This shows that $1101_3 = 3^3 + 3^2 + 1 = 27 + 9 + 1 = 37$

Base 3 numbers can also be added and subtracted by a similar method used for binary numbers.

To calculate $1101_3 + 221_3$ write the numbers in columns.

3^4	3^3	3^2	3^1	3^0	
	1^{+1}	1	0	1	
		2	2	1	+
	2	0	2	2	
	(3)				

Working from right to left:
$1 + 1 = 2$, $0 + 2 = 2$, $1 + 2 = 3$ so one 3 is carried to the next column.

Therefore $1101_3 + 221_3 = 2022_3$
(*Check*: $1101_3 = 37$, $221_3 = 2 \times 3^2 + 2 \times 3 + 1 = 25$, $37 + 25 = 62$
$2022_3 = 2 \times 3^3 + 2 \times 3 + 2 = 62$)
To calculate $1101_3 - 221_3$ again write the numbers in columns.

3^4	3^3	3^2	3^1	3^0	
	1^{-1}	1^{-1+3}	0^{+3}	1	
		2	2	1	−
	0	1	1	0	

Working from right to left:
$1 - 1 = 0$, $0 - 2 = 2$ cannot be done so take 3 from the next column.
Then in the 3rd column $0 - 2$ cannot be done so take the 3 from the 4th column.

Therefore $1101_3 - 221_3 = 110_3$
(*Check*: $1101_3 - 221_3 = 37 - 25 = 12$ and $110_3 = 3^2 + 3 = 12$)

Exercise 1t

Write as denary numbers:

1 **a** 101_2 **b** 110_2 **c** 10101_2 **d** 111011_2

2 **a** 11_3 **b** 200_3 **c** 120_3 **d** 112_3 **e** 2001_3 **f** 1122_3

Calculate:

3 **a** $101_2 + 11_2$ **b** $101_2 - 11_2$

4 **a** $111_2 + 10_2$ **b** $111_2 - 10_2$

5 a $1101_2 + 111_2$ b $1101_2 - 111_2$

6 a $1001_2 + 101_2$ b $1001_2 - 101_2$

7 a $10101_2 + 1101_2$ b $10101_2 - 1101_2$

8 a $110101_2 + 11101_2$ b $110101_2 - 11101_2$

9 a $21_3 + 12_3$ b $21_3 - 12_3$

10 a $22_3 + 2_3$ b $22_3 - 2_3$

11 a $121_3 + 12_3$ b $121_3 - 12_3$

12 a $211_3 + 22_3$ b $211_3 - 22_3$

13 a $1021_3 + 201_3$ b $1021_3 - 201_3$

Mixed exercises

Exercise 1u

Select the letter that gives the correct answer.

1 The prime numbers in the set {1, 2, 4, 7, 11, 15} are

A 2, 4 B 2, 7, 11 C 1, 2, 7, 11 D 2, 7, 11, 15

2 The value of $2 + 3 \times 2$ is

A 6 B 7 C 8 D 10

3 The square numbers (perfect squares) in the set {2, 4, 8, 9, 10, 16, 20} are

A 4, 9, 16 C 4, 8, 10, 16, 20

B 2, 4, 8, 9, 16 D 2, 4, 8, 10, 16, 20

4 The highest number which is a factor of both 4 and 6 is

A 1 B 2 C 4 D 12

5 The value of $\left(\frac{2}{3}\right)^{-2}$ is

A $\frac{4}{9}$ B $\frac{3}{4}$ C $2\frac{1}{4}$ D $3\frac{3}{4}$

6 Written in standard form, 0.00793 is

A 7.93×10^{-4} B 7.93×10^{-3} C 7.93×10^{-2} D 7.93×10^{-1}

7 $1101101_2 - 100111_2$

A 1000110_2 B 1001110_2 C 1001100_2 D 1010110_2

Exercise 1v

1 Calculate: a $1\frac{1}{3} \div \frac{8}{9}$ b $1\frac{1}{3} - \frac{8}{9}$

2 Calculate $\left(3\frac{1}{4} + 2\frac{1}{2}\right) \times \frac{2}{5}$

3 Find, without using a calculator:

a $3.27 + 0.09$ b 3.27×0.09 c $3.27 \div 0.03$

4 Find the value of:

a 2^4 b 2^0 c 2^{-4}

5 Write as a single number in index form:

a $5^6 \div 5^4$ b $5^{10} \times 5^2$

6 Write the following numbers in standard form:

a 2560 b 0.000 256

7 Find the LCM of:

a 3, 8 and 24 b 2, 3 and 5

8 Find the reciprocal of:

a $\frac{1}{5}$ b $1\frac{1}{2}$

9 Calculate: a $\frac{3}{5} \times 1\frac{1}{4}$ b $\frac{3}{5} + 1\frac{1}{4}$

10 Calculate $2\frac{1}{2} \times \frac{7}{10} + 1\frac{1}{3}$

11 Find, without using a calculator:

a $2.5 - 1.05$ b 2.5×1.05 c $1.05 \div 2.5$

12 Find the value of:

a $\left(\frac{1}{2}\right)^2$ b $\left(\frac{1}{2}\right)^0$ c $\left(\frac{1}{2}\right)^{-2}$

13 Write in standard form:

a 570 000 b 0.057

14 Calculate:

a $10011_2 - 1101_2$ b $120_3 + 211_3$

Investigation

How accurate are calculators?

1 Use your calculator to perform these instructions.

Enter 5×10^{-20} on your calculator. Now add 2. Next subtract 1.

Multiply the result by 10^{20}.

2 Repeat the instruction given in part **1** without using a calculator.

Comment on the results.

3 For this part, you will need to use a calculator on which you can enter more than 8 digits.

Find the value of $\sqrt{100\,000\,000} - \sqrt{99\,999\,999}$.

How many significant figures are there in your answer?

It is possible to use such a calculator to evaluate

$\sqrt{100\,000\,000} - \sqrt{99\,999\,999}$ to 11 significant figures. Can you discover how to do this?

4 A basic scientific calculator can be used to enter the numbers

$\sqrt{100\,000\,000\,000} - \sqrt{99\,999\,999\,999}$ by first writing them in another form. How can this be done? Try it and comment on the result.

Did you know?

Pythagoras once defined a friend as 'One who is the other I, such as 220 and 284'.

These two numbers are AMICABLE, because the proper divisors of one number add up to the other number.

Divisors of 284 are $\{1, 2, 4, 71, 142\}$.

Their sum is $1 + 2 + 4 + 71 + 142 = 220$.

Divisors of 220 are $\{1, 2, 4, 5, 10, 11, 20, 22, 44, 55, 110\}$.

Their sum is $1 + 2 + 4 + 5 + 10 + 11 + 20 + 22 + 44 + 55 + 110 = 284$.

The Hebrews believed that such numbers were good omens.

Today more than 600 pairs of friendly numbers are known.

In 1866 a sixteen-year-old Italian boy, Nicole Paganini, discovered the amicable numbers 1184 and 1210. Can you discover any?

In this chapter you have seen that...

- ✔ a prime number can be divided exactly only by 1 and itself
- ✔ an even number can be divided exactly by 2
- ✔ any number that ends in 5 or 0 can be divided exactly by 5
- ✔ any number can be divided exactly by 3 if the sum of its digits can be divided by 3
- ✔ fractions can be added and subtracted by expressing them as equivalent fractions with the same denominator
- ✔ fractions can be multiplied together by multiplying the numerators together and multiplying the denominators together
- ✔ the reciprocal of a number is 1 divided by that number, e.g. the reciprocal of $\frac{5}{7}$ is $\frac{7}{5}$ and the reciprocal of 6 is $\frac{1}{6}$
- ✔ to divide by a fraction you multiply by its reciprocal, e.g. $\frac{2}{3} \div \frac{4}{7} = \frac{2}{3} \times \frac{7}{4}$
- ✔ before multiplying or dividing by fractions, mixed numbers must be changed to improper fractions
- ✔ brackets are always worked out first, then multiplication and division, and lastly addition and subtraction
- ✔ a multiple of a number can be divided exactly by that number
- ✔ a perfect square is the product of two equal numbers
- ✔ when a calculation involves a mixture of operations, do the multiplication and division first
- ✔ some fractions, e.g. $\frac{1}{7} = 0.1428571428\ldots$ and $\frac{3}{11} = 0.272727\ldots$, cannot be expressed as exact decimals. They are called recurring decimals. The first can be written $0.\dot{1}4285\dot{7}$ and the second as $0.\dot{2}\dot{7}$
- ✔ numbers can be compared by converting all of them either into decimals or into fractions
- ✔ indices provide a shorthand notation for multiplying and dividing several of the same number.

  An index can be positive, negative or zero. Remember that $a^0 = 1$ and $a^{-2} = \frac{1}{a^2}$

  The laws of indices are $a^m \times a^n = a^{m+n}$, $a^m \div a^n = a^{m-n}$, $(a^m)^n = a^{mn}$
- ✔ any number can be written as a number between 1 and 10 multiplied by the appropriate power of 10. This is called standard form, e.g. $26\,700 = 2.67 \times 10^4$ and $0.0086 = 8.6 \times 10^{-3}$
- ✔ binary numbers use the digits 0 and 1; the place values are powers of 2
- ✔ base 3 numbers use the digits 0, 1 and 2; the place values are powers of 3.

2 Areas

At the end of this chapter you should be able to...

1 calculate the areas of triangles, rectangles and parallelograms

2 calculate the area of a polygon by subdividing it into triangles, rectangles or parallelograms

3 calculate the area of a trapezium given the lengths of its parallel sides and height

4 identify triangles or parallelograms that have equal area

5 state the ratio of the areas of two triangles that have equal heights (bases) but different bases (heights)

6 solve problems using the fact that triangles with equal heights (bases) have areas proportional to their bases (heights).

Did you know?

The word *trapezium* comes from the Greek word *trapeza* meaning 'table'. Since the sixteenth century its meaning has been 'a quadrilateral with one pair of opposite sides parallel' but originally it applied to any quadrilateral that was not a parallelogram.

You need to know...

- ✔ how to work with decimals
- ✔ the meaning of symmetry
- ✔ the meaning of ratios
- ✔ the properties of special quadrilaterals
- ✔ how to construct triangles and quadrilaterals.

Key words

kite, parallelogram, perpendicular height, ratio, rectangle, rhombus, slant height, symmetry, trapezium, triangle

Areas of familiar shapes

Rectangle

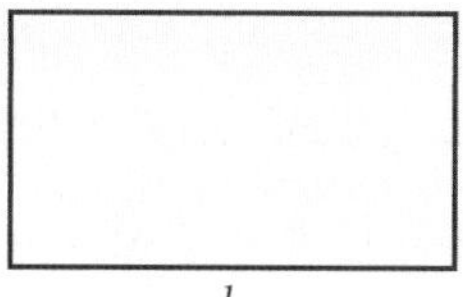

$A = lb$

Parallelogram

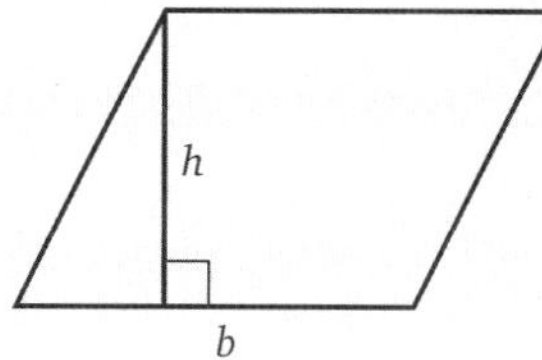

$A = bh$

Triangle

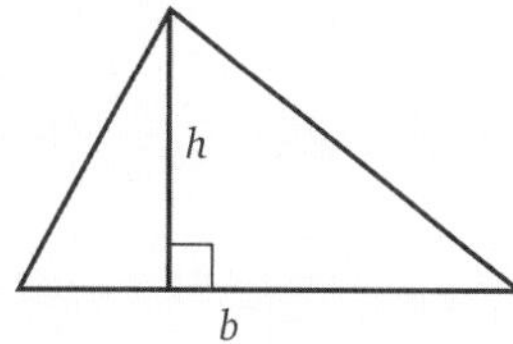

$A = \frac{1}{2}bh$

Remember that when we talk about the height of a figure we mean the *perpendicular height*, not the *slant height*.

Remember also that both the lengths we use must be measured in the *same* unit.

Exercise 2a

Find the areas of the following figures:

1

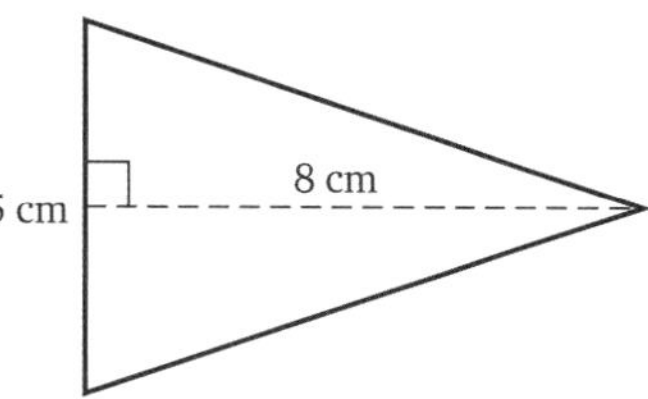

3

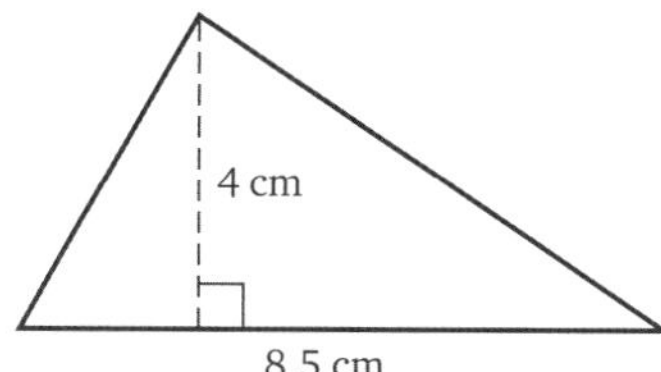

2

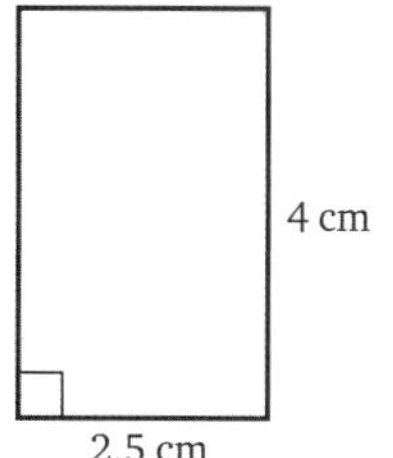

4

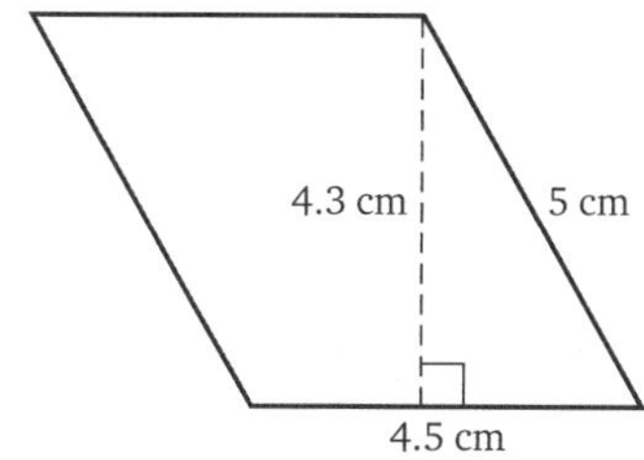

In questions **5** to **9** use square grid paper and draw axes for x and y in the ranges $-6 \leqslant x \leqslant 6$, $-6 \leqslant y \leqslant 6$ using 1 square to 1 unit. Draw the figure and find its area in square units.

5 Triangle ABC with A(0, 6), B(6, 6) and C(5, 2).

6 Parallelogram ABCD with A(0, 1), B(0, 6), C(6, 4) and D(6, −1).

7 Rectangle ABCD with A(−4, 2), B(0, 2) and C(0, −1).

8 Square ABCD with A(0, 0), B(0, 4) and C(4, 4).

9 Triangle ABC with A(−5, −4), B(2, −4), C(−2, 3).

For each of the figures described in the table, find the missing measurement. Draw a diagram in each case.

	Figure	Base	Height	Area
10	Triangle	8 cm		16 cm^2
11	Rectangle	3 cm	15 mm	
12	Parallelogram	4 cm		20 cm^2
13	Square	5 m		
14	Triangle	70 mm		14 cm^2

In questions **15** to **18** give answers correct to three significant figures where necessary.

15

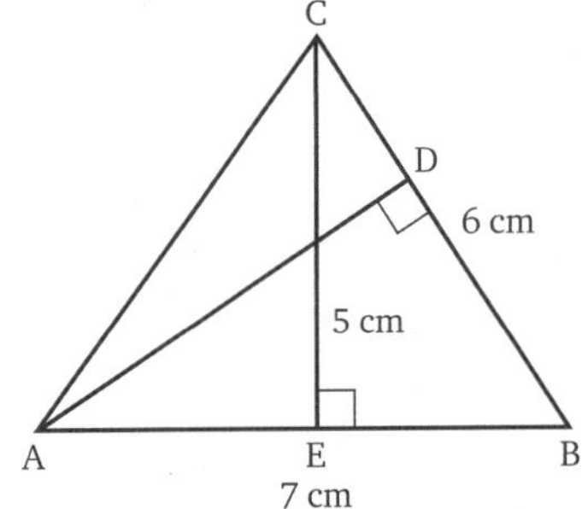

In △ABC, AB = 7 cm, CB = 6 cm and CE = 5 cm.
Find:

a the area of △ABC **b** the length of AD.

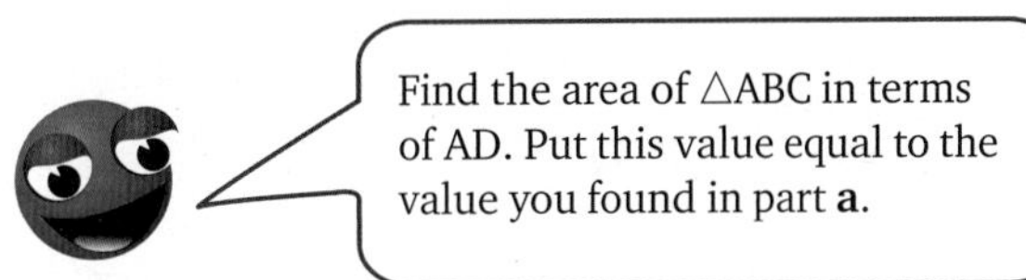

Find the area of △ABC in terms of AD. Put this value equal to the value you found in part **a**.

16

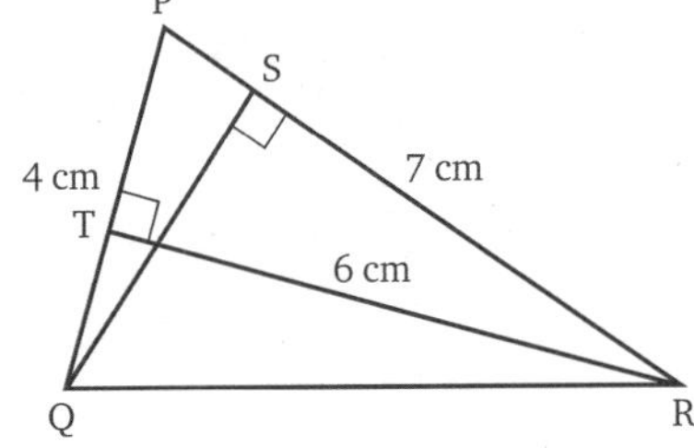

In △PQR, PQ = 4 cm, PR = 7 cm and RT = 6 cm.
Find:

a the area of △PQR **b** the length of QS.

17

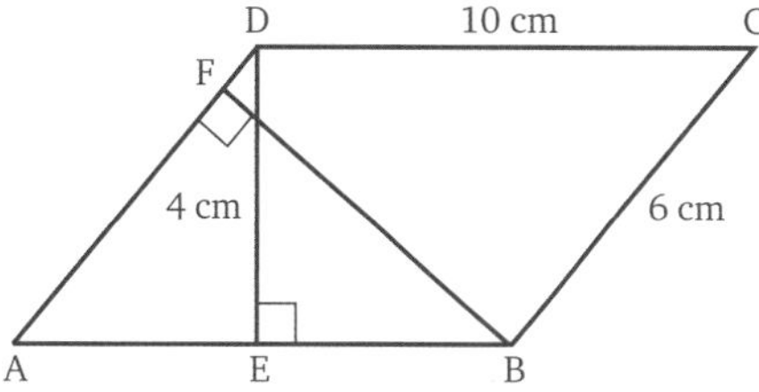

In parallelogram ABCD, DC = 10 cm, BC = 6 cm and DE = 4 cm. Find:

a the area of ABCD **b** the length of BF.

18

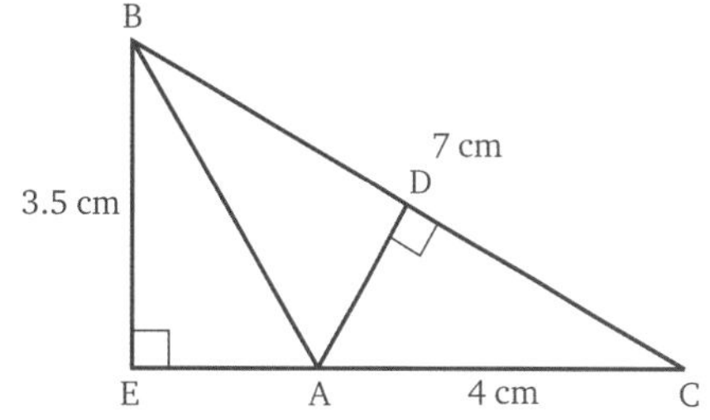

In △ABC, AC = 4 cm, BC = 7 cm and BE = 3.5 cm. Find:

a the area of △ABC **b** the length of AD.

Areas of compound shapes

Exercise 2b

ABCD is a *rhombus*. AC = 8 cm and BD = 12 cm.

Find the area of ABCD.

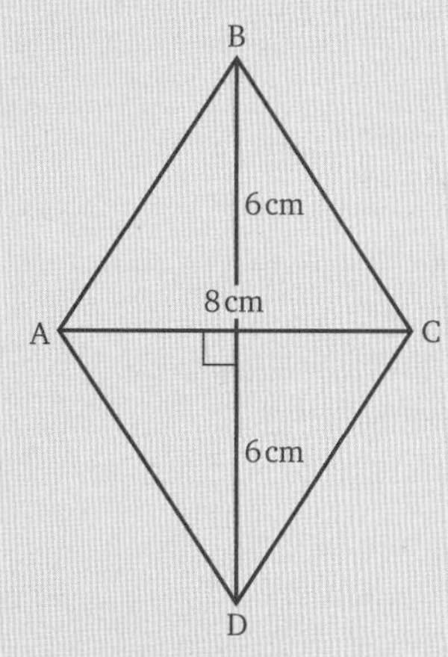

Split the rhombus into two triangles.

(The diagonals of a rhombus bisect each other at right angles.)

Area △ABC $= \frac{1}{2}$ base × height

$= \frac{1}{2} \times 8 \times 6\,\text{cm}^2$

$= 24\,\text{cm}^2$

Area △ACD = area △ABC

(AC is a line of symmetry)

∴ total area $= 48\,\text{cm}^2$

Find the area of each of the following shapes.

Draw a diagram for each question and mark in all the measurements. Then mark in any other facts that you know.

1

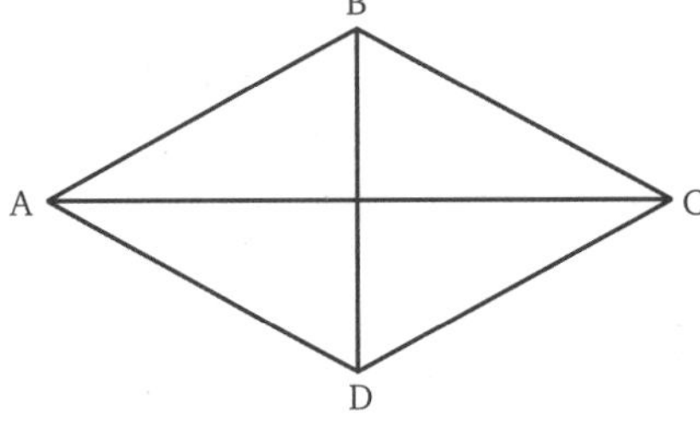

ABCD is a rhombus.
AC = 15 cm and BD = 8 cm

2

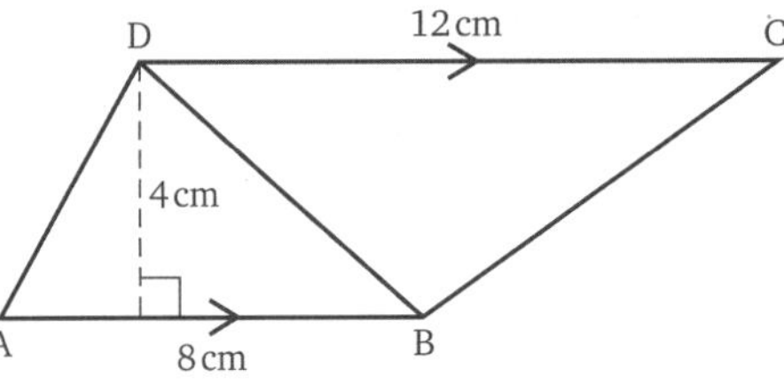

3

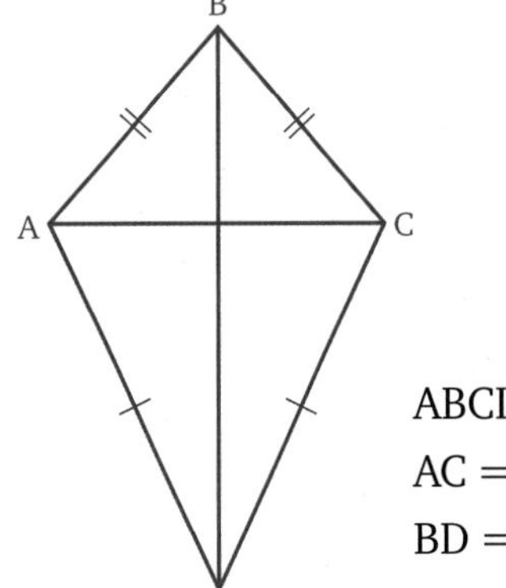

ABCD is a kite.
AC = 6 cm and
BD = 10 cm

4

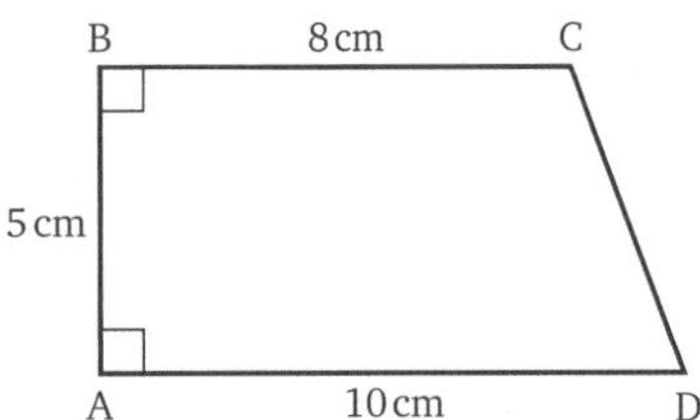

In questions **5** and **6**, find the area of the shaded figure (find the area of the complete figure, then subtract the areas of the unshaded parts).

5

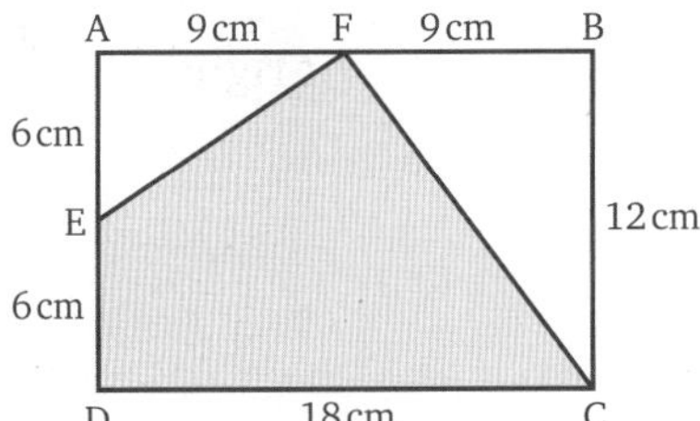

ABCD is a rectangle.

6

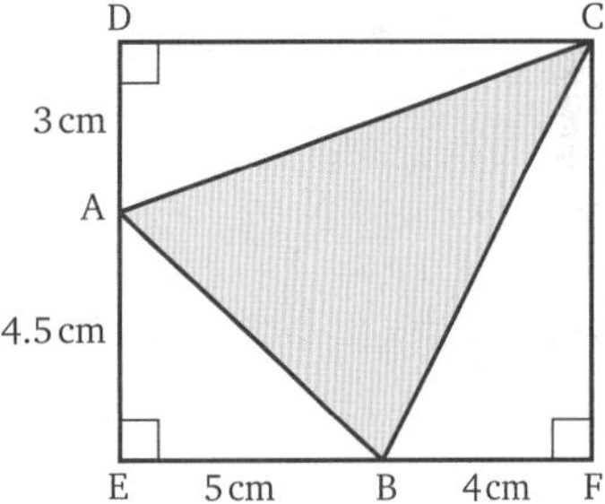

Puzzle

How many different rectangles can you find in this shape?

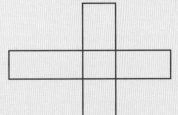

Area of a trapezium

In the last exercise we found the areas of several trapeziums. A trapezium is a shape that occurs often enough to justify finding a formula for its area.

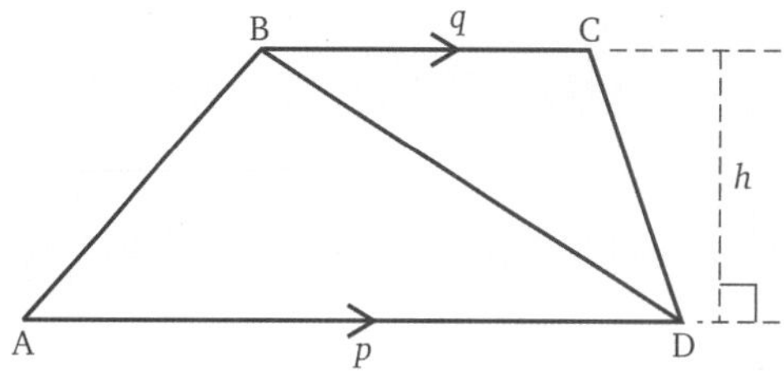

$$\text{Area of } \triangle\text{ABD} = \frac{1}{2}\text{ base} \times \text{height} = \frac{1}{2}p \times h$$

$$\text{Area of } \triangle\text{BCD} = \frac{1}{2}\text{ base} \times \text{height} = \frac{1}{2}q \times h$$

The perpendicular heights of both triangles are the same, as each is the distance between the parallel sides of the trapezium.

$\therefore$ total area of ABCD $= \frac{1}{2}ph + \frac{1}{2}qh = \frac{1}{2}(p+q) \times h$

i.e. the area of a trapezium is equal to

$\frac{1}{2}$ (sum of parallel sides) $\times$ (distance between them)

Exercise 2c

Find the area of the trapezium in the diagram.

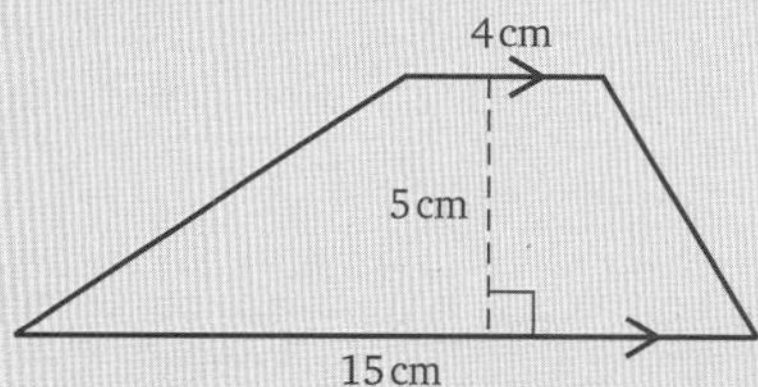

Area $= \frac{1}{2}$ (sum of parallel sides) $\times$ (distance between them)

$= \frac{1}{2}(4 + 15) \times 5\text{ cm}^2$

$= \frac{1}{2} \times 19 \times 5\text{ cm}^2$

$= 47.5\text{ cm}^2$

Find the area of each of the following trapeziums:

1

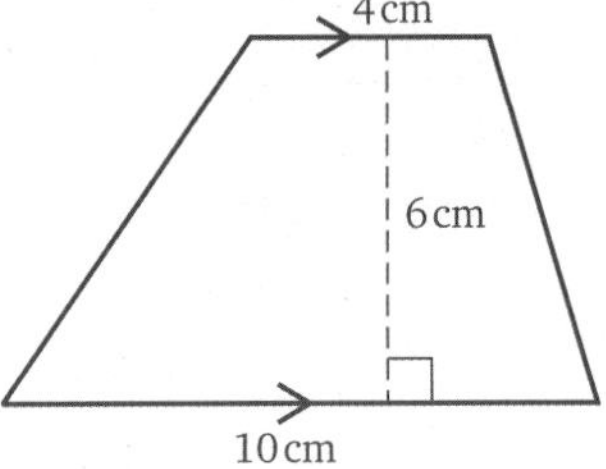

3

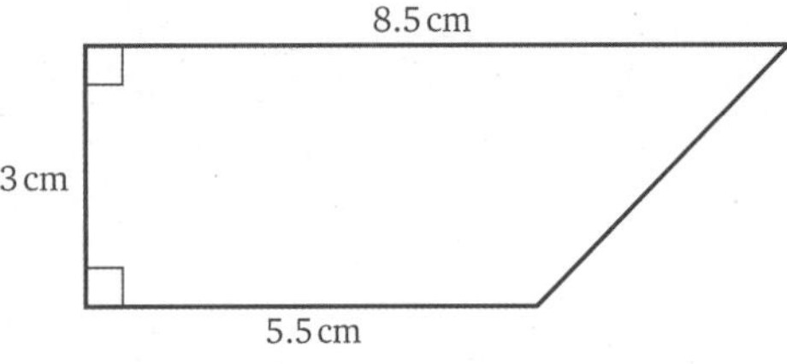

2

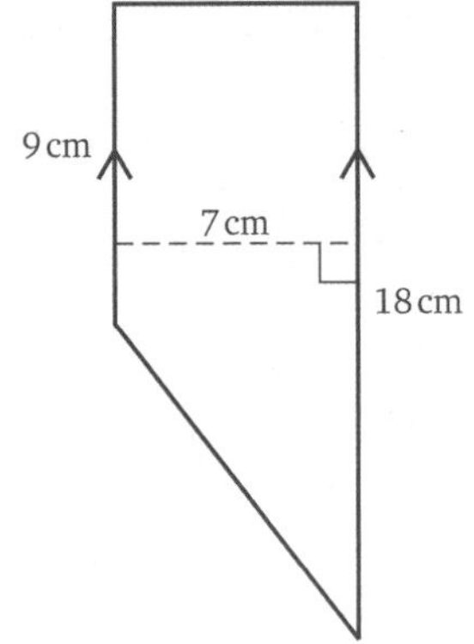

4

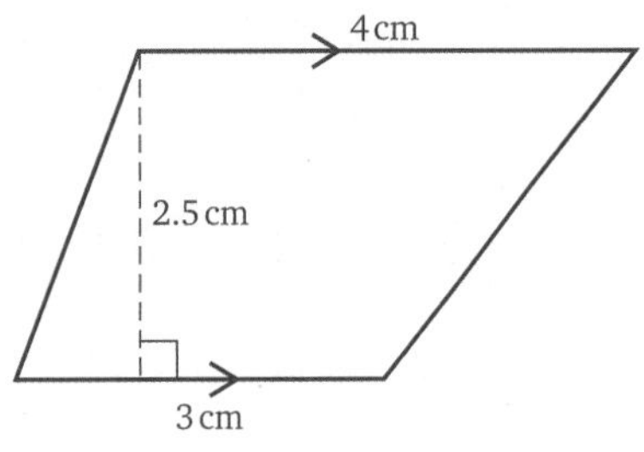

For questions **5** to **10** use square grid paper and draw axes for x and y using ranges $-6 \leqslant x \leqslant 6$ and $-6 \leqslant y \leqslant 6$ and a scale of one square to 1 unit. Plot the points and join them up in alphabetical order. Find, in square units, the area of the resulting shape.

5 A(6, 1), B(4, –3), C(–2, –3), D(–3, 1)

6 A(4, 4), B(–2, 2), C(–2, –2), D(4, –3)

7 A(3, 5), B(–4, 4), C(–4, –2), D(3, –5)

8 A(1, 0), B(5, 0), C(5, 3), D(3, 5), E(1, 3)

9 A(6, –4), B(6, 1), C(2, 5), D(–5, 3), E(–5, –4)

10 A(2, 0), B(6, 4), C(–4, 4), D(–4, –2), E(5, –2)

Shapes that have equal areas

Exercise 2d

1

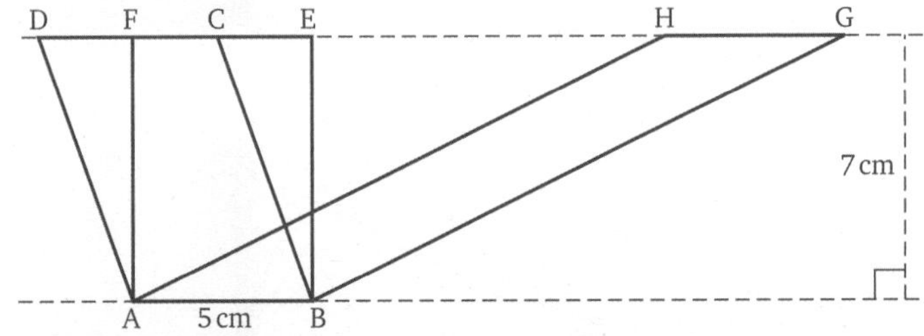

There are three parallelograms in the diagram. Write the area of each one.

2

Write the area of each of the three triangles ABC, ABD and ABE.

In questions **3** and **4**, take the side of a grid square as the unit of length.

3

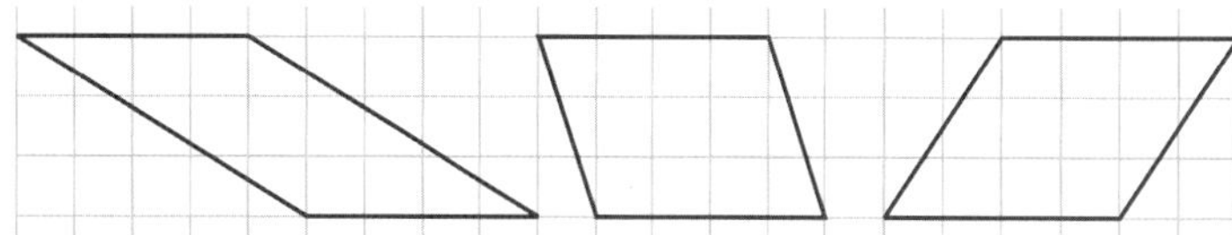

What is the length of the base and the height of each of these parallelograms? What can you conclude about the areas of the three parallelograms?

4

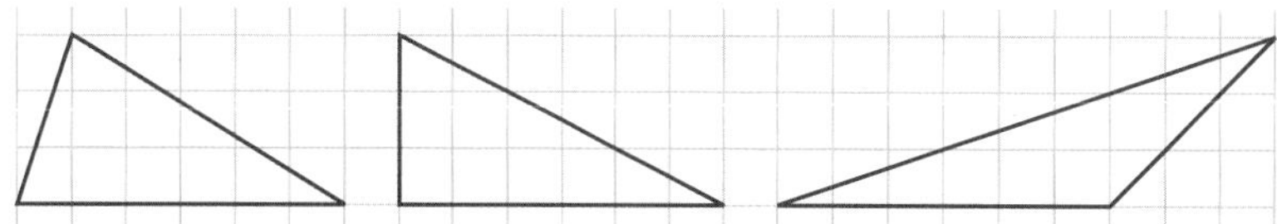

What is the length of the base and the height of each of these triangles? What can you conclude about the areas of the three triangles?

5 Using square grid paper draw x and y axes for $-8 \leqslant x \leqslant 8$ and $-4 \leqslant y \leqslant 12$. Draw parallelogram ABCD with A(2, 2), B(2, 7), C(7, 4) and D(7, −1). Using AB as the base in each case, draw three other parallelograms whose areas are equal to the area of ABCD.

6 Use another set of axes the same as you used for question **5**. Draw the triangle LMN with L(−6, 1), M(−1, 1) and N(−5, 5). Using LM as the base draw two other triangles whose areas are equal to the area of triangle LMN.

7 Draw again the diagram that you used for question **6**. Draw a triangle which is equal in area to triangle LMN and which has LN for one of its sides.

8 There are four triangles in the diagram all with the same base AB. Find, in ascending order, the ratio of their heights. Find, in ascending order, the ratio of their areas. Comment on your results.

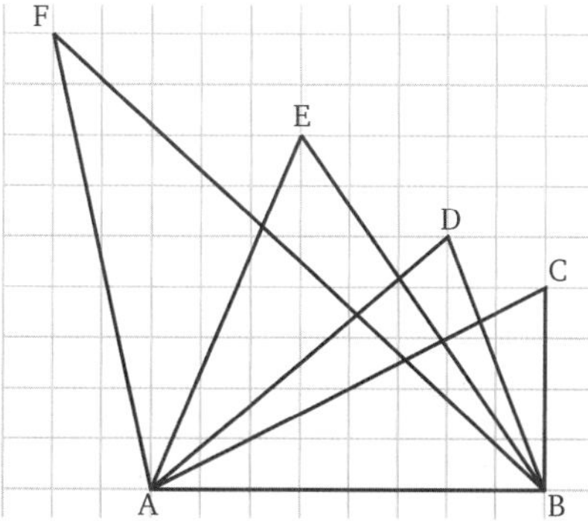

9 Using square grid paper draw x and y axes for $0 \leqslant x \leqslant 10$ and $0 \leqslant y \leqslant 12$. Plot the points A(2, 1), B(10, 1) and C(8, 5). Draw a triangle ABD whose area is twice that of triangle ABC. Give the y coordinate of D.

10 Using another set of axes the same as in question **9**, draw a triangle ABE whose area is half the area of $\triangle$ABC. Give the y-coordinate of E.

11 The triangles XAB, YBD, ZBC and ZCE all have equal heights of 5 units.

a Find the ratio of their bases.

b Find the ratio of their areas.

Comment on your results.

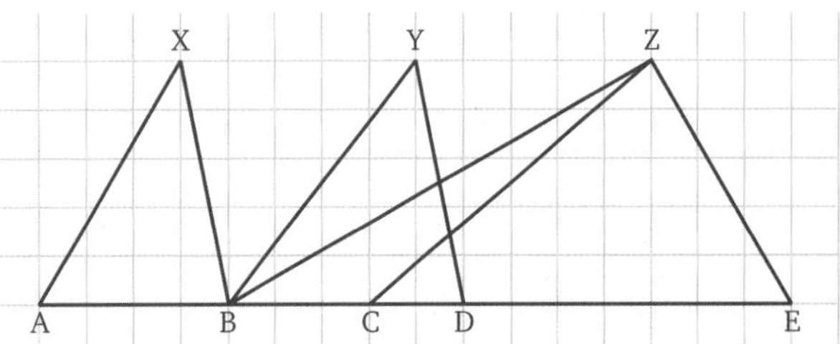

From the last exercise we see that:

Parallelograms with equal bases and equal heights have the same area.

Triangles with equal bases and equal heights have the same area.

Triangles on equal bases but with different heights have areas proportional to (i.e. in the same ratio as) their heights.

Triangles with equal heights but different bases have areas proportional to (i.e. in the same ratio as) their bases.

Exercise 2e

ABCD is a trapezium. Show that the blue triangles have the same area.

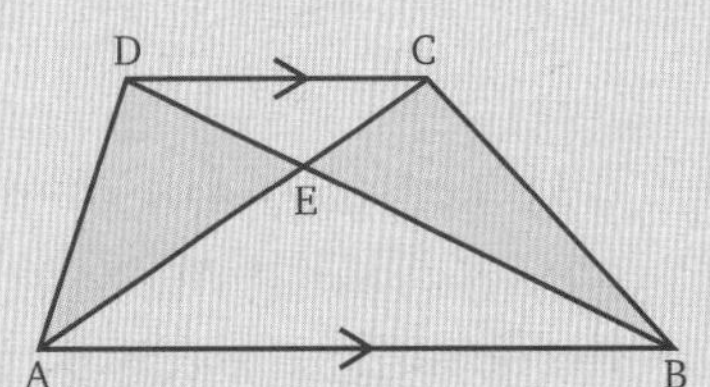

Area $\triangle$ADB = area $\triangle$ACB

(Same base AB and same height, as DC || AB.)

Area $\triangle$AEB is common to both $\triangle$ADB and $\triangle$ACB. Removing it from each triangle in turn leaves the shaded areas.

$\therefore$ area $\triangle$AED = area $\triangle$BEC

1

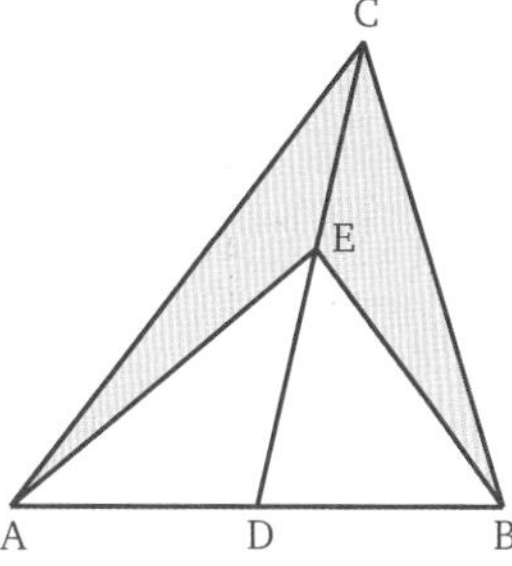

Triangles with the same base and height are equal in area.

D is the midpoint of AB. Show that the shaded triangles have the same area.

2

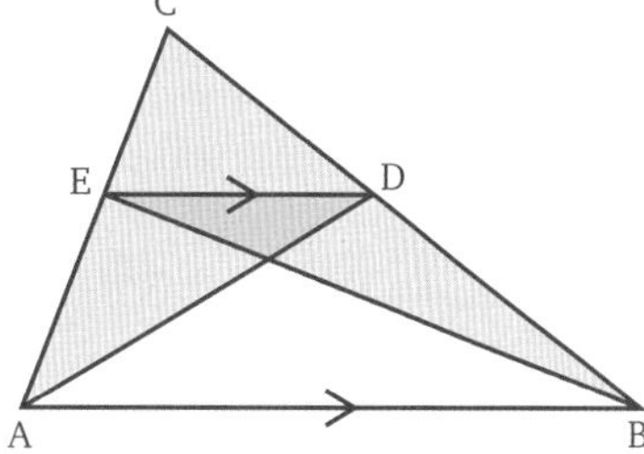

ED is parallel to AB. Show that area △ACD = area △BCE.

3

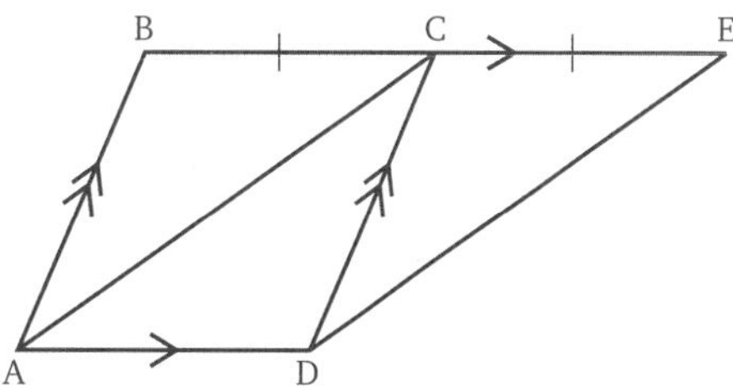

BC = CE, AB is parallel to DC and AD is parallel to BE. Show that area △ADC = area △DCE.

4

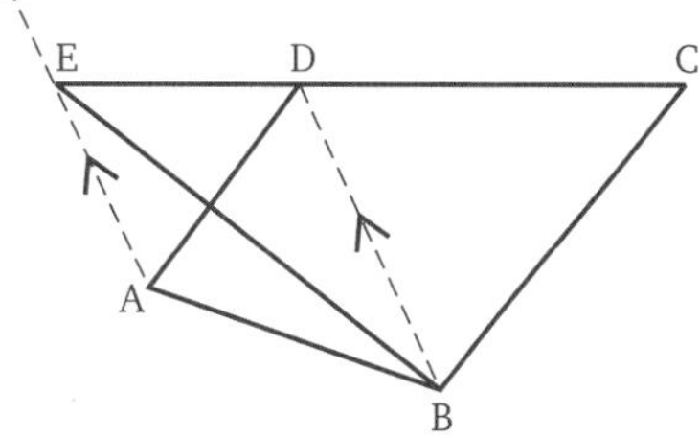

AE is parallel to BD. Show that the area of △BCE is equal to the area of the quadrilateral ABCD.

5

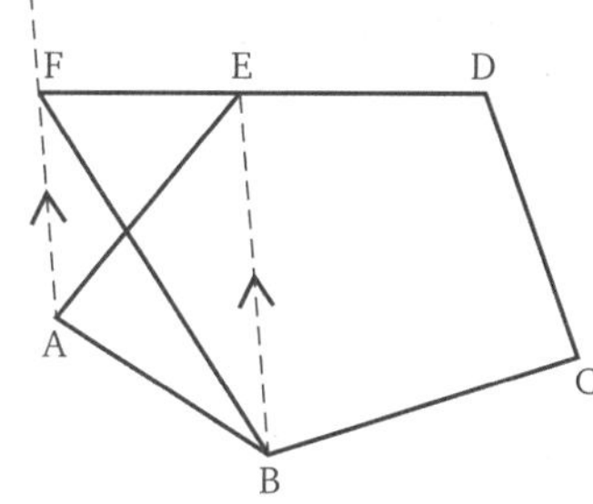

AF is parallel to BE. Show that the area of the pentagon ABCDE is equal to the area of the quadrilateral BCDF.

6

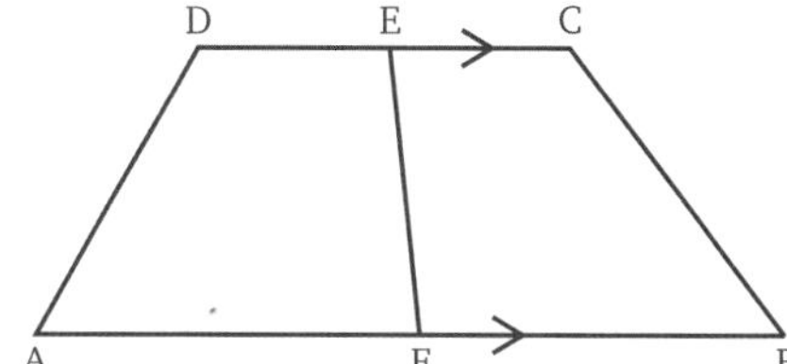

ABCD is a trapezium. E is the midpoint of DC and F is the midpoint of AB. Show that EF divides the area of ABCD into two equal parts.

ABCD is a rectangle.
The height of $\triangle ABE$ (i.e. the distance of E above AB) is two-thirds of the height, AD, of the rectangle.
The area of ABCD is $12\,\text{cm}^2$.
Find the area of $\triangle AEB$.

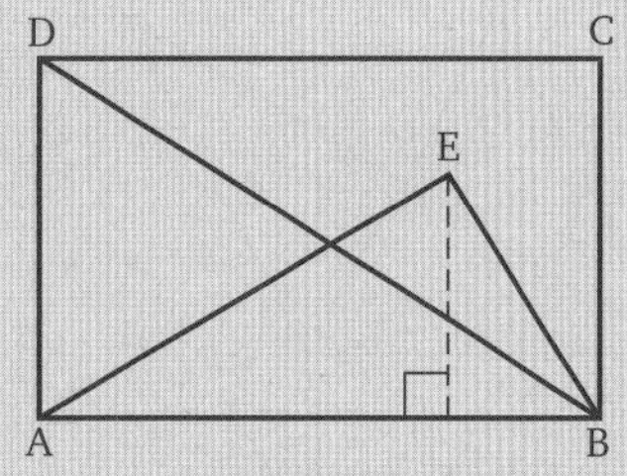

Area of $\triangle ADB = 6\,\text{cm}^2$ (half area of ABCD)

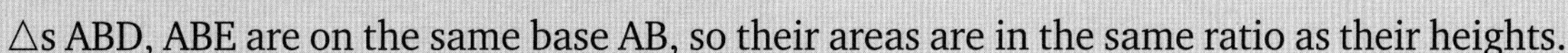
$\triangle$s ABD, ABE are on the same base AB, so their areas are in the same ratio as their heights.

$$\therefore \quad \frac{\text{area } \triangle ABE}{\text{area } \triangle ADB} = \frac{2}{3}$$

$$\frac{\text{area } \triangle ABE}{6\,\text{cm}^2} = \frac{2}{3}$$

$$\text{area } \triangle ABE = \frac{2}{3} \times 6\,\text{cm}^2 \text{ (multiply both sides by } 6\,\text{cm}^2\text{)}$$

$$\text{area } \triangle ABE = 4\,\text{cm}^2$$

7

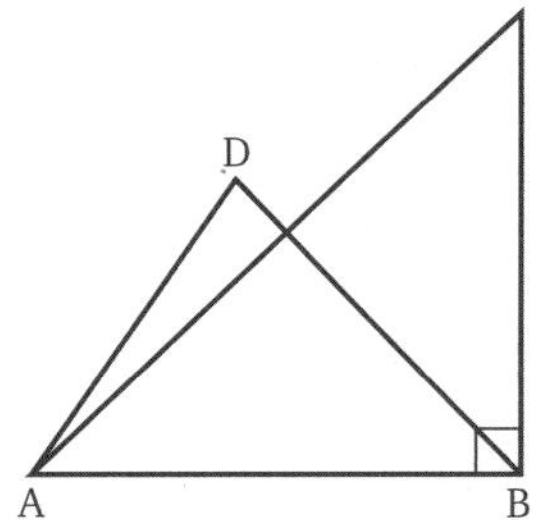

The area of $\triangle ABD$ is $\frac{3}{5}$ of the area of $\triangle ABC$. BC = 20 cm. Find the height of D above AB.

8

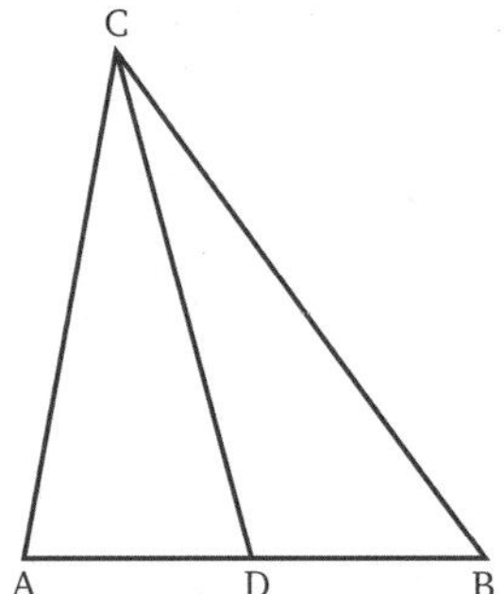

D is the midpoint of AB. Find the ratio of the area of $\triangle ABC$ to the area of $\triangle ADC$.

9

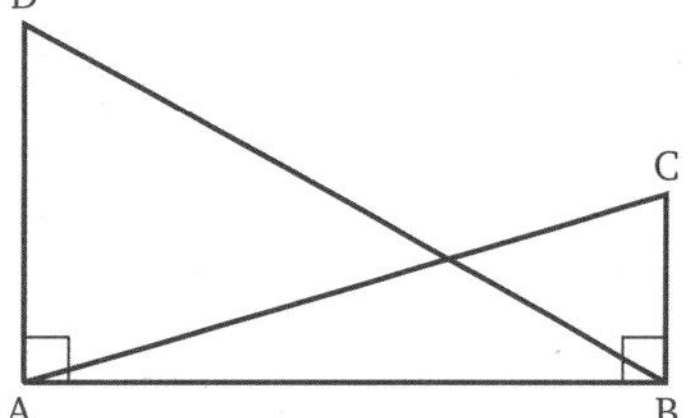

The area of $\triangle ABC = \frac{7}{12}$ of the area of $\triangle ADB$. AD = 24 cm.
Find the length of BC.

10

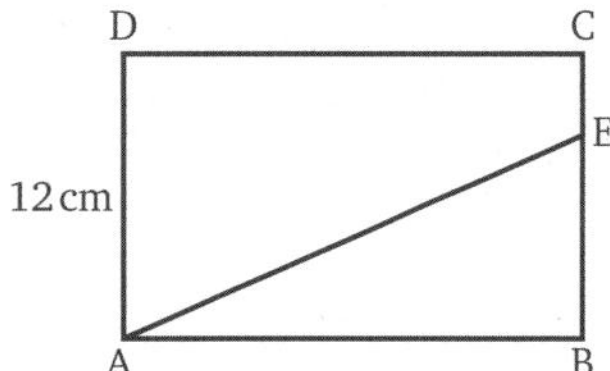

In the rectangle ABCD, E is a point on BC such that area of $\triangle ABE$ is $\frac{1}{3}$ of the area of the rectangle ABCD.
Find the length of BE.

11

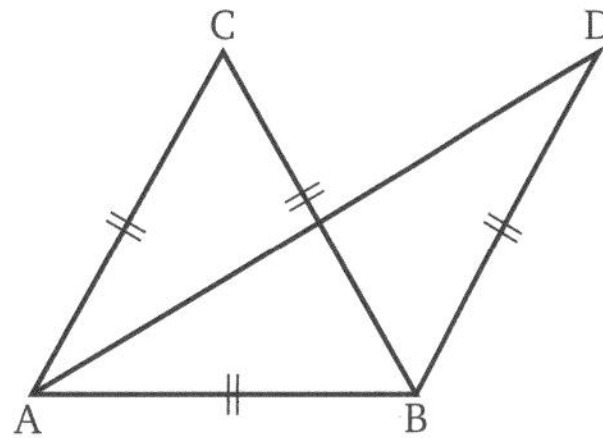

AB = AC = CB = BD.

Area △ABC = area △ABD

Find the size of $A\hat{D}B$.

12

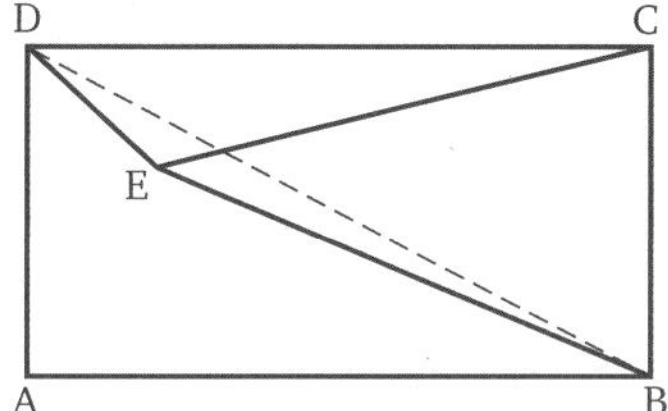

E is a point inside the rectangle ABCD such that the distance of E from BC is $\frac{3}{4}$ of the distance of A from BC and the distance of E from DC is $\frac{1}{3}$ of the distance of A from DC. The area of the rectangle ABCD is 72 cm^2.

Find the areas of △BEC and △DEC.

In questions **13** and **14**, before beginning the construction draw a rough sketch and on it mark any extra lines that you will need.

13 Construct a parallelogram ABCD with AB = 4 cm, BC = 6 cm and $A\hat{B}C = 60°$. Construct a parallelogram ABEF that is equal in area to ABCD such that BE = 7 cm, and such that E and D are on opposite sides of BC. Measure $A\hat{B}E$.

14 Construct △ABC with AB = 12 cm, $\hat{A} = 30°$ and $\hat{B} = 30°$. On AC as base, construct a triangle ADC that is equal in area to △ABC, such that $C\hat{A}D = 90°$. Measure AD.

15 In the △ABC, D is the midpoint of BC. E is a point on AD so that AE = $\frac{1}{4}$ AD. If BC = 16 cm and the area of △ABC = 96 cm^2, find the area of △DEC.

Puzzle

The sketch shows seventeen identical sticks laid out to form six equal squares.

Remove six sticks to leave two perfect squares.

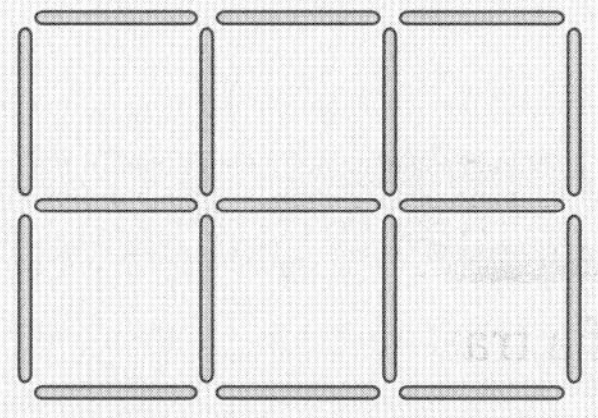

Activity

Did you know that if one rectangle measuring l cm by b cm overlaps another larger rectangle measuring L cm by B cm, the difference between the two shaded areas, P and Q, is always the same? This is quite easy to prove. Try it.

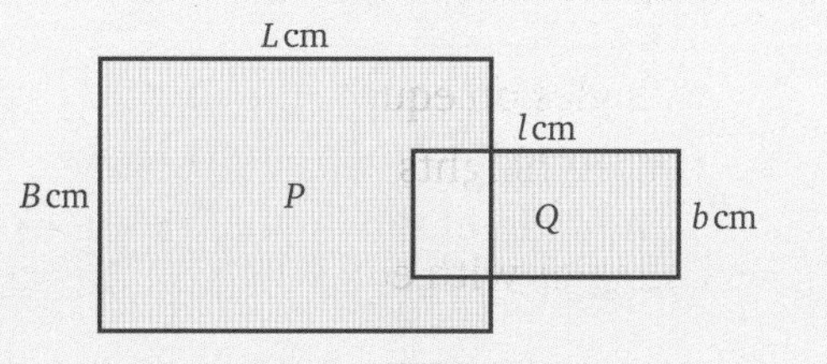

Exercise 2f

Select the letter that gives the correct answer.

1 The area of a rectangle measuring 3.5 cm by 5 cm is

A $14\,cm^2$ B $15\,cm^2$ C $17.5\,cm^2$ D $19.25\,cm^2$

2 The area of a triangle with a base of 6.5 cm and height 4 cm is

A $12\,cm^2$ B $13\,cm^2$ C $19.5\,cm^2$ D $26\,cm^2$

3 The area of this parallelogram is

A $18\,cm^2$

B $19\,cm^2$

C $21.8\,cm^2$

D $22.8\,cm^2$

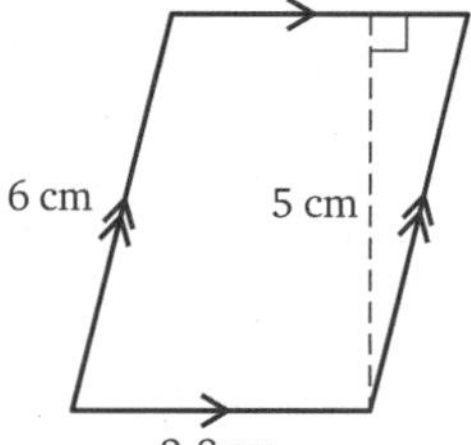

4 The area of this trapezium is

A $21.6\,cm^2$

B $26.4\,cm^2$

C $30.25\,cm^2$

D $31.2\,cm^2$

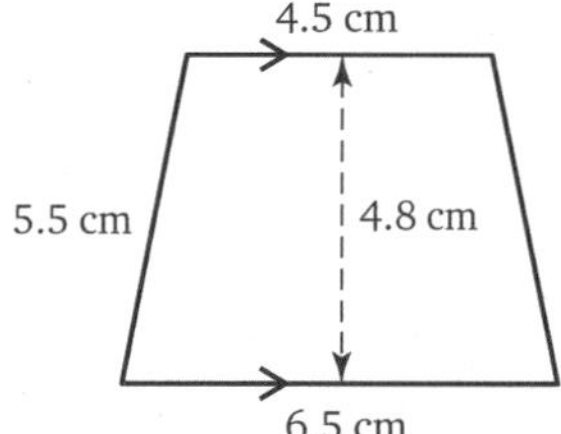

5 The area of a triangle is $23.8\,cm^2$. Its base is of length 6.8 cm. The height of the triangle is therefore

A 3.5 cm B 5 cm C 6.5 cm D 7 cm

6 A rectangle measures 9 cm by 4 cm. The side of a square of the same area is

A 5 cm B 5.5 cm C 6 cm D 6.6 cm

In this chapter you have seen that...

- ✔ the area of a trapezium is equal to

  $\frac{1}{2}$ (sum of the parallel sides) × (distance between them)
- ✔ parallelograms with equal bases and the same heights have the same area
- ✔ triangles with equal bases and equal heights have the same area
- ✔ triangles on equal bases but with different heights have areas proportional to their heights
- ✔ triangles with equal heights but different bases have areas proportional to their bases.

3 Arc length and area of the sector of a circle

At the end of this chapter you should be able to...

1 find the length of an arc of a circle, given the radius of the circle and the size of the angle at the centre of that circle
2 find the area of a sector of a circle given the radius and the angle at the centre
3 find the radius of a circle given the length of the arc and the angle at the centre
4 find the angle at the centre of a circle given the length of the arc and the radius of the circle
5 find the angle at the centre of a circle given the area of a sector and the radius of the circle
6 find the radius of a circle given the length of the arc and the area of the sector of the circle.

You need to know...

✔ the meaning of π

✔ the formula for the circumference of a circle

✔ the formula for the area of a circle.

Key words

arc, centre, chord, circumference, perimeter, radius, sector, subtend, trapezium

The length of an arc

A shape that frequently occurs in everyday life is a slice of a circle. It may be a slice of cake or a piece of wood cut from the trunk of a tree.

Part of a circle is called an *arc*.
The shape formed by two radii and an arc is called a *sector*.

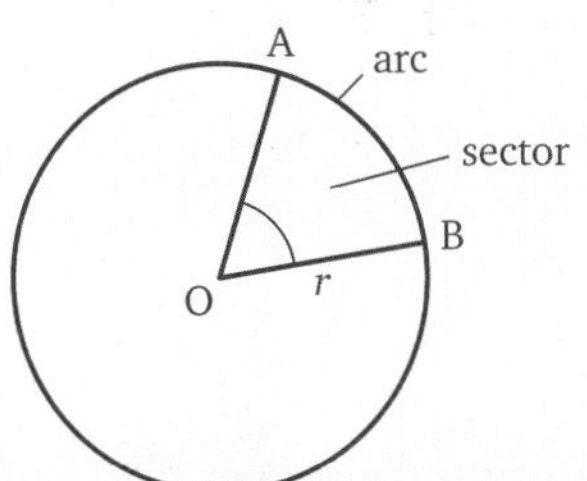

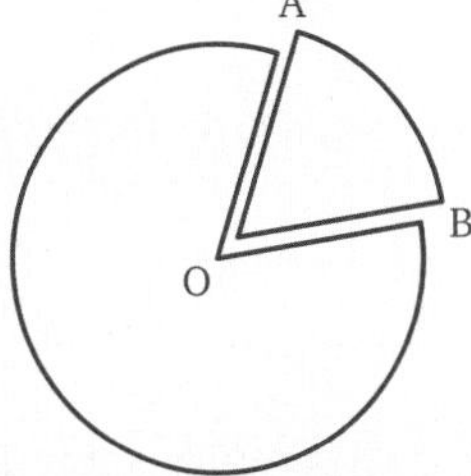

The length of an arc depends on the radius of the circle and the angle enclosed at the centre of the circle by the radii at the two ends of the arc. This angle is $\hat{AOB}$ in the diagram on page 46; it is called the angle *subtended* by the arc AB at the centre, O, of the circle.

The length of the arc AB as a fraction of the circumference of the circle is $\frac{\hat{AOB}}{360°}$,

i.e. length of arc AB $= \frac{\hat{AOB}}{360°}$ of the circumference.

The circumference of a circle is $2\pi r$, so

$$\text{length of arc AB is } \frac{\hat{AOB}}{360°} \times 2\pi r = \pi r \times \frac{\hat{AOB}}{180°}$$

Exercise 3a

An arc subtends an angle of 60° at the centre of a circle of radius 6 cm. Find the length of the arc:

a in terms of π

b correct to three significant figures.

a Arc length $= 6\pi \times \frac{60}{180}$ cm
$= 2\pi$ cm

b Arc length $= 2\pi$ cm
$= 2 \times 3.14...$ cm
$= 6.28$ cm

1 Find, in terms of π, the length of the arc that subtends an angle of 30° at the centre of a circle of radius 4 cm.

2 Find, in terms of π, the length of the arc that subtends an angle of 40° at the centre of a circle of radius 4 cm.

3 Find, in terms of π, the length of the arc that subtends an angle of 80° at the centre of a circle of radius 9 cm.

4 Find, in terms of π, the length of the arc that subtends an angle of 120° at the centre of a circle of radius 12 cm.

In questions **5** to **8** use the value of π on your calculator and give your answers correct to three significant figures.

5 Find the length of the arc that subtends an angle of 40° at the centre of a circle of radius 3.65 cm.

6 Find the length of the arc that subtends an angle of 65° at the centre of a circle of radius 7.43 cm.

7 Find the length of the arc that subtends an angle of 135° at the centre of a circle of radius 18.6 cm.

8 Find the length of the arc that subtends an angle of 100° at the centre of a circle of radius 48.5 cm.

Find the angle subtended at the centre of a circle of radius 8 cm by an arc of length 12 cm.

$$\text{Arc length} = \pi \times \text{radius} \times \frac{\text{angle subtended at centre of circle}}{180^\circ}$$

$$\text{Therefore } 12 = \pi \times 8 \times \frac{\text{angle subtended at centre of circle}}{180^\circ}$$

i.e. (angle subtended at centre of circle) $\times \pi \times 8 = 12 \times 180^\circ$

$$\therefore \text{ angle subtended at centre of circle} = \frac{12 \times 180^\circ}{8 \times \pi} = 85.9\ldots^\circ$$

$$= 86^\circ \text{ correct to the nearest degree.}$$

Give angles correct to the nearest degree and lengths correct to three significant figures.

9 Find the angle subtended at the centre of a circle of radius 5 cm by an arc of length 12 cm.

10 What is the size of the angle subtended at the centre of a circle of radius 65 mm by an arc of length 45 mm?

11 Find the radius of a circle in which an arc of length 15 cm subtends an angle of 66° at the centre.

12 The arc of a circle of length 34.5 cm subtends an angle of 110° at the centre of the circle. Find the radius of the circle.

13 Find the radius of a circle in which an arc of length 24 cm subtends an angle of 116° at the centre.

14 The arc of a circle of length 18.2 cm subtends an angle of 77° at the centre of the circle. Find the radius of the circle.

15 Find the radius of a circle in which an arc of length 44 cm subtends an angle of 96° at the centre.

16 A circle has a radius of 16.5 cm. An arc of this circle subtends an angle of 19° at its centre. Calculate the length of the arc.

17 An arc of length 15 cm subtends an angle of 45° at the centre of the circle. Find the radius of the circle.

18 Calculate the angle subtended at the centre of a circle of radius 2.7 cm by an arc of length 6.9 cm.

19 Find the angle subtended at the centre of a circle of radius a cm by an arc of length $2a$ cm.

20 Find the angle subtended at the centre of a circle of radius b cm by an arc of length $1.5b$ cm.

In questions **21** to **26** find the *perimeter* of each shape.

21

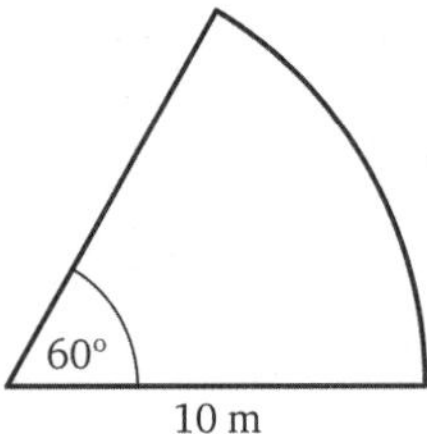

24

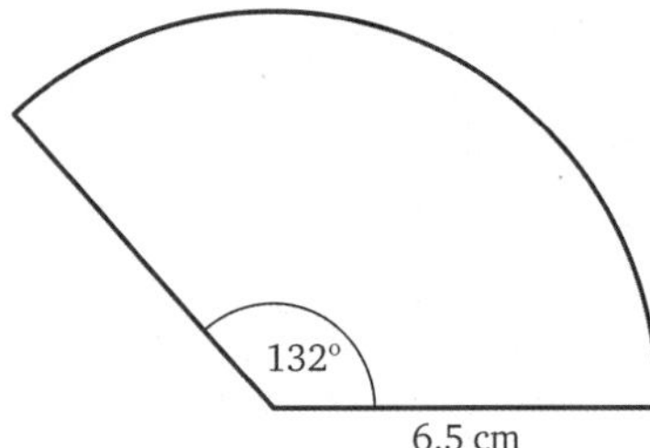

22

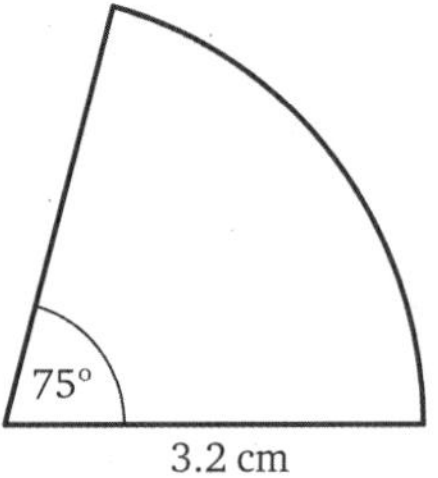

25

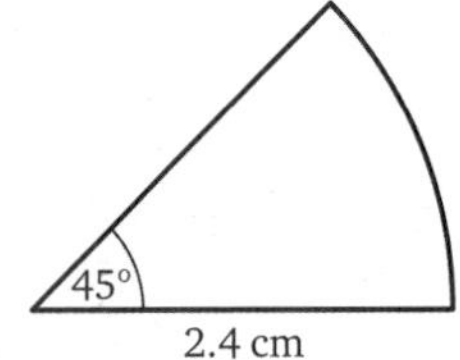

23

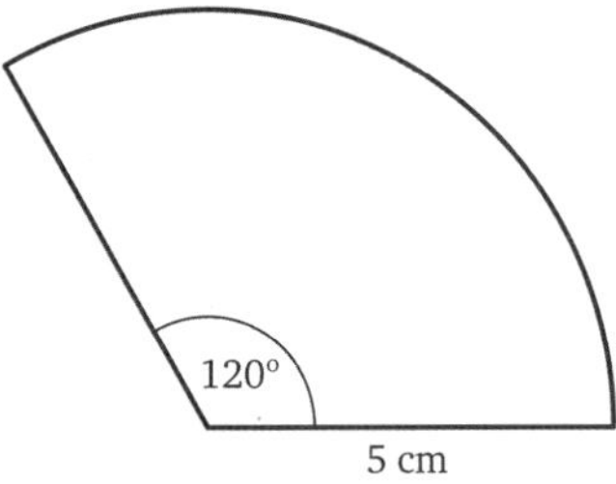

26

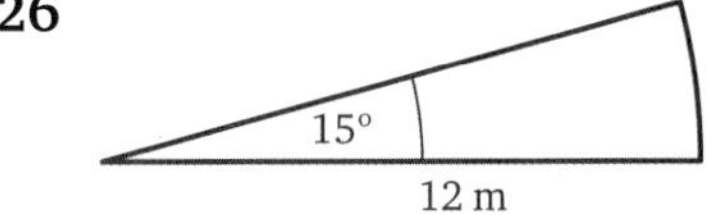

27 A company logo is made by removing a sector containing an angle of 67° from a circle of radius 25 mm. Find the perimeter of the logo.

28 A curve in the track of a railway line is a circular arc of length 400 m and radius 1200 m. Through what angle does the direction of the track turn?

The area of a sector of a circle

The slice enclosed by the arc and the radii is called a sector.

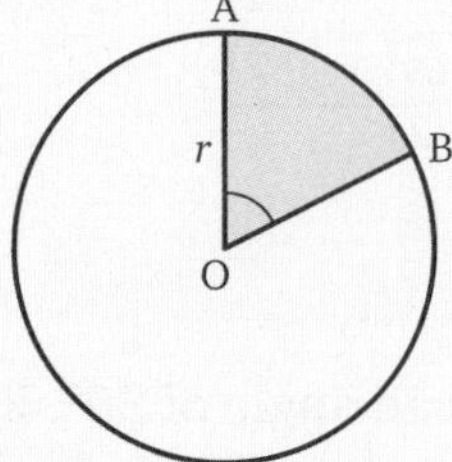

The area of the sector AOB as a fraction of the area of the circle is the same fraction as the arc is, i.e. $\frac{A\hat{O}B}{360°}$.

Therefore $\quad$ area of sector AOB $= \pi r^2 \times \frac{A\hat{O}B}{360°}$

Exercise 3b

Find the area of the shaded sector if angle AOB = 30°.

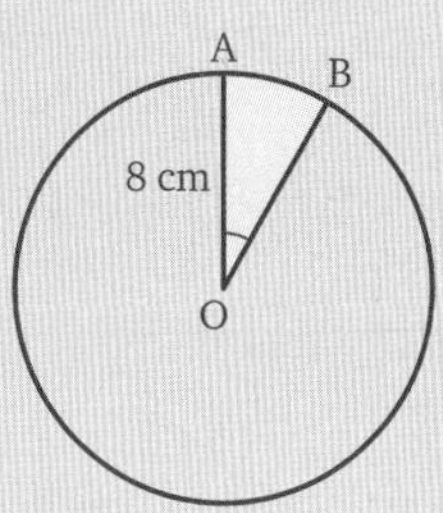

Area of sector $= \frac{30}{360} \times$ area of circle

$= \frac{30}{360} \times \pi \times 8^2 \text{ cm}^2$

$= 16.75... \text{ cm}^2$

The area of the sector is 16.8 cm² correct to three significant figures.

In questions **1** to **8** find the area of the sector. Give each answer correct to three significant figures.

1

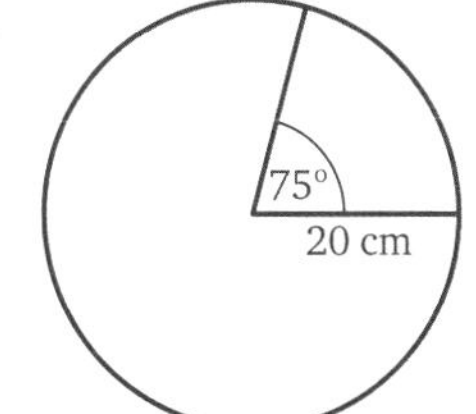

2

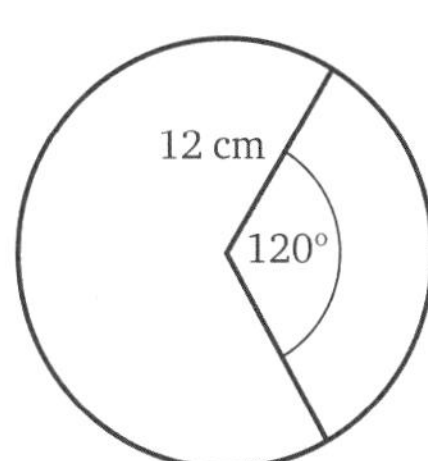

3

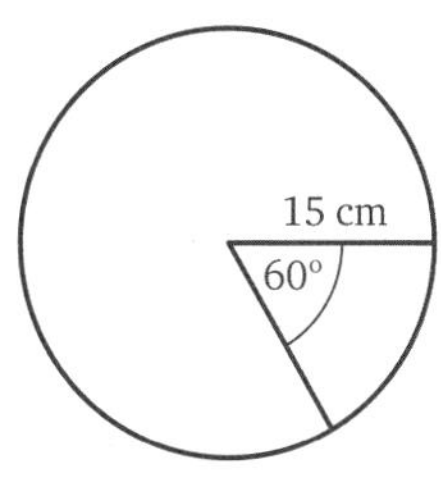

4

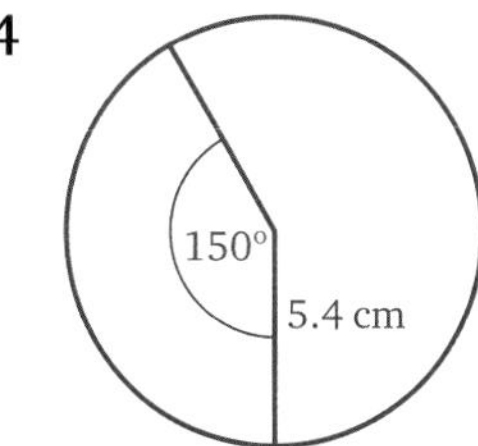

5

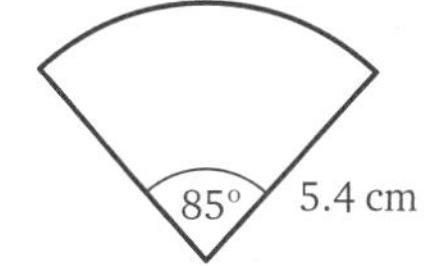

6

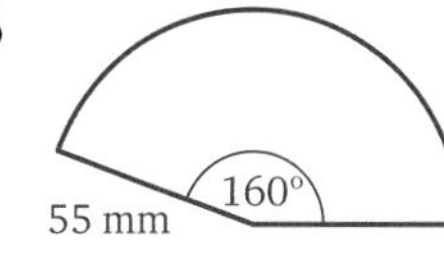

7

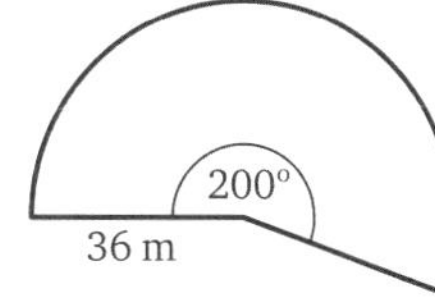

8

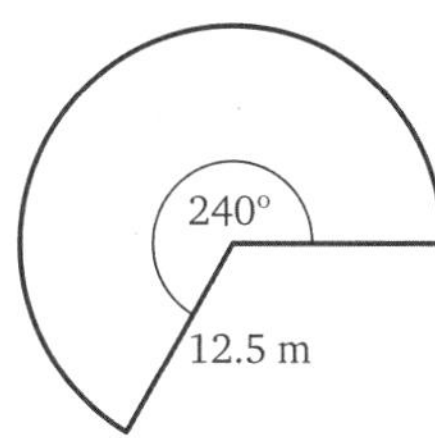

9 A sector of a circle of radius 4 cm contains an angle of 30°. Find the area of the sector.

10 A sector of a circle of radius 8 cm contains an angle of 135°. Find the area of the sector.

11 The area of a sector of a circle of radius 2 cm is π cm². Find the angle contained by the sector.

12 The area of a sector of a circle of radius 5 cm is $12\,\text{cm}^2$. Find the angle contained by the sector.

13 A sector of a circle of radius 10 cm contains an angle of 150°. Find the area of the sector.

14 A sector of a circle has an area of $3\pi\,\text{cm}^2$ and contains an angle of 30°. Find the radius of the circle.

15 A sector of a circle has an area of $6\pi\,\text{cm}^2$ and contains an angle of 45°. Find the radius of the circle.

16 An arc of a circle of radius 12 cm is of length π cm. Find:

a the angle subtended by the arc at the centre of the circle

b the area of the sector in terms of π.

17 Calculate the angle at the centre of a circle of radius 83 mm contained in a sector of area $974\,\text{mm}^2$.

18

A flower bed is a quadrant of a circle.

a Find the length of the edging needed for the curved edge of the bed.

b Find the area of the flower bed.

19 The diagram shows the plan of a herb garden. The beds are sectors of the circle, each one of which contains an angle of 40° at the centre. The radius of the circle is 0.9 m.

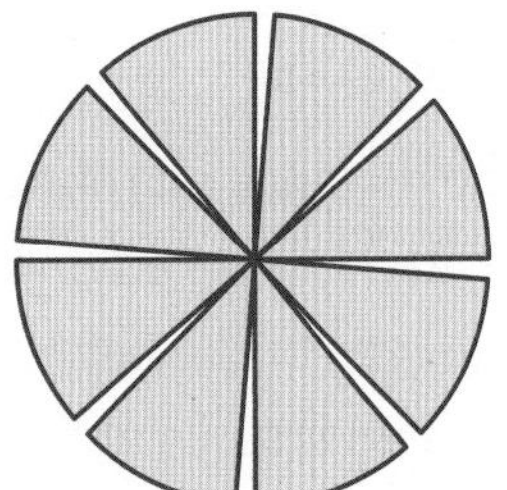

a What length of edging is required to surround all these beds?

b One handful of fertiliser covers one quarter of a square metre of soil.
How many handfuls are required to cover all the beds?

20 A silver earring pendant is part of a sector of a circle. Find the area of silver.

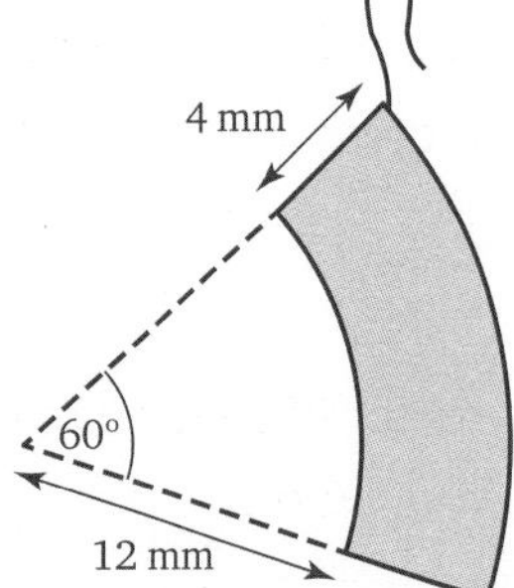

21 In this pattern, the blue sections are identical sectors of a circle of radius 9 cm and the grey sections are identical sectors of a circle of radius 7 cm. Which of the grey or blue sections of the pattern covers the greater area? Justify your answer.

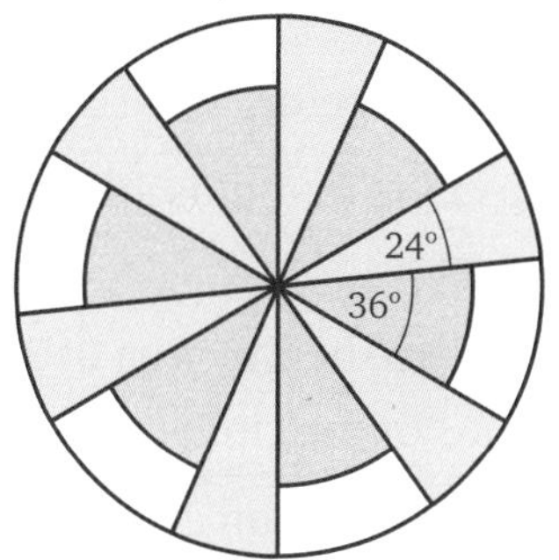

22 Harry is making a marquetry pattern. The diagram shows one of the pieces he has cut. The arcs are quadrants of circles.

Find:

a the perimeter of the piece

b its area.

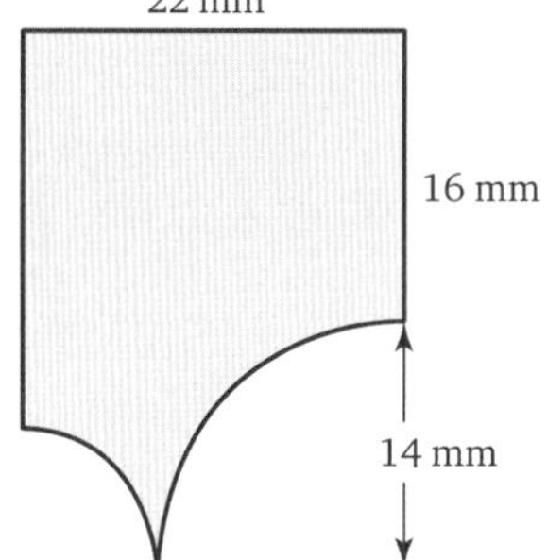

23 Mr Gardener has designed a lawn in the shape of a sector of a circle with radius 2.8 m, as shown in the diagram. He plans to edge the whole lawn with a flexible edging which is sold by the metre at $32.50 a metre.

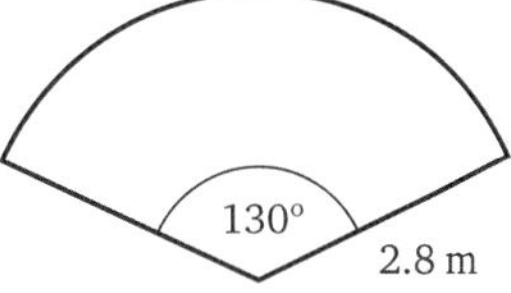

a Find the distance all round the edge of the lawn.

b What will the lawn edging cost?

c Find the area of the lawn.

d If grass seed is sown at 56 grams per square metre, find how much seed will be needed for the lawn.

24 The diagram shows the cross-section of a low boundary wall. The cross-section can be divided into a sector of a circle of radius 20 cm and two equal trapeziums.

Find each of the areas marked A, B and C, and the total area.

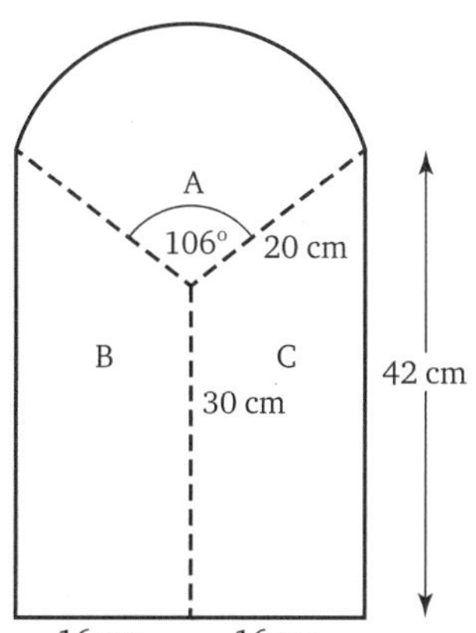

Exercise 3c

Select the letter that gives the correct answer.

1 The length of the arc, in terms of π, that subtends an angle of 50° at the centre of a circle of radius 6 cm is

A $\frac{5\pi}{6}$ cm B $\frac{7\pi}{6}$ cm C $\frac{4\pi}{3}$ cm D $\frac{5\pi}{3}$ cm

2 The size of the angle, correct to the nearest degree, subtended at the centre of a circle of radius 50 cm by an arc of length 80 cm is

A 88° B 90° C 92° D 95°

3 An arc of length 20 cm subtends an angle of 45° at the centre of the circle.

The radius of this circle, correct to the nearest whole number, is

A 20 cm B 22 cm C 24 cm D 25 cm

4 The area of this sector of radius 12 cm, correct to 3 s.f., is

A 37 cm^2
B 37.6 cm^2
C 37.7 cm^2
D 38 cm^2

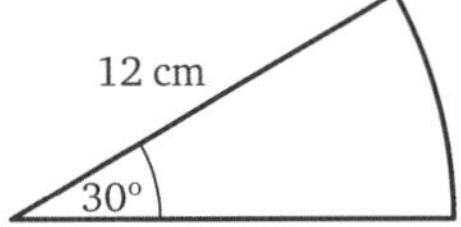

5 The area between these two circles is

A 2.25π cm^2
B 4π cm^2
C 5π cm^2
D 6.25π cm^2

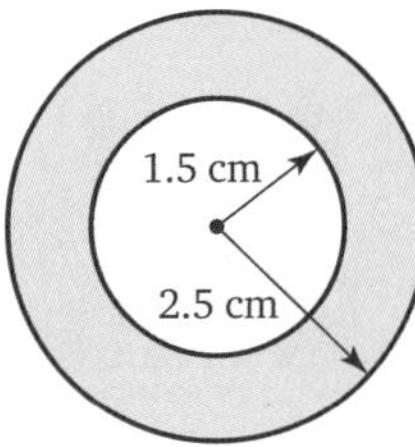

Puzzle

Place the numbers from 1 to 10, one in each square, so that the total in each of the three lines of four squares is the same.

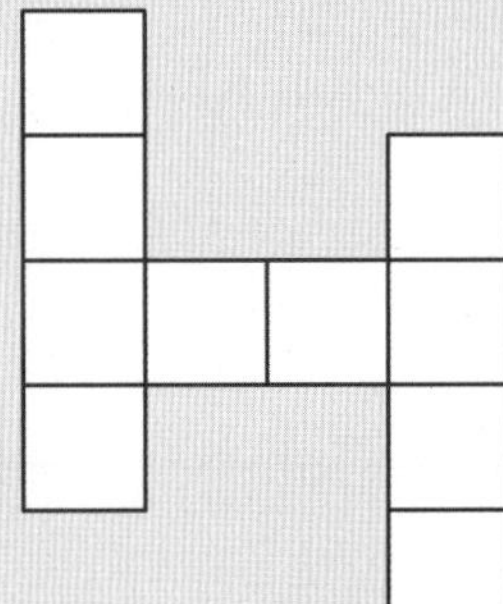

Did you know?

The number system used by the Mayans had only three symbols:

- a large dot ● represented one
- a bar ———— represented five
- a seashell represented zero.

Numbers 1 to 20 were written as:

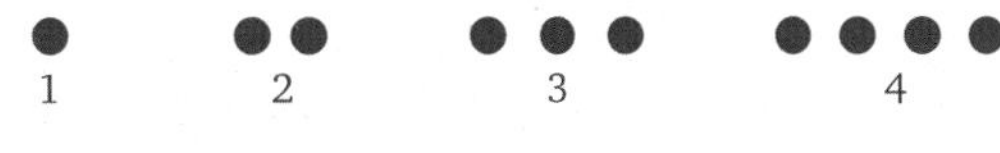

5 6 7

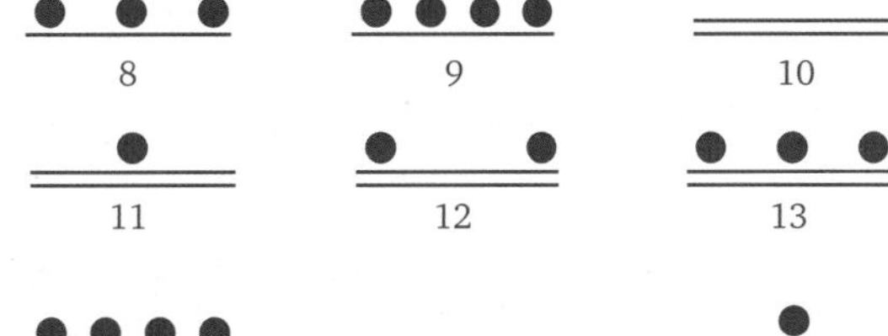

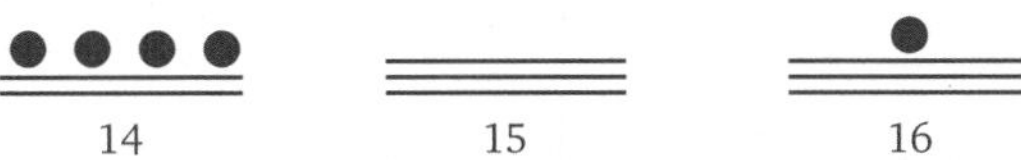

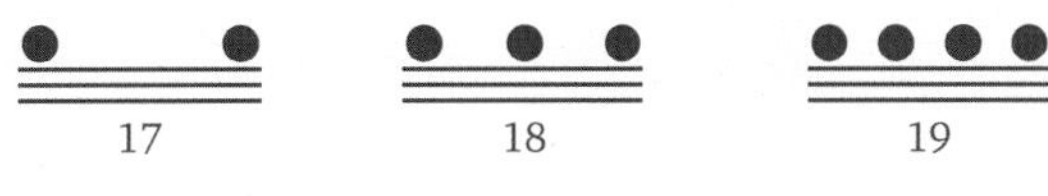

In this chapter you have seen that...

✔ for a circle, centre O, radius r, the length of the arc AB is $\pi r \times \frac{A\hat{O}B}{180°}$

✔ for a circle, centre O, radius r, the area of the sector AOB, formed by the arc AB and the radii OA and OB, is $\pi r^2 \times \frac{A\hat{O}B}{360°}$.

4 Prisms and pyramids

At the end of this chapter you should be able to...

1 make a prism or pyramid from a net
2 draw a net for various solids
3 calculate the volume and surface area of a prism
4 calculate the volume and surface area of a pyramid
5 calculate the volume and surface area of a cylinder
6 calculate the volume and surface area of a cone.

You need to know...

✔ how to multiply fractions and decimals
✔ how to find the area of a rectangle and a triangle
✔ how to find the area of a circle
✔ how to find the area of a parallelogram and a trapezium.

Key words

capacity, circumference, cone, conversely, cross-section, cube, cuboid, cylinder, diameter, dimensions, edge, face, frustum, isosceles, net, octahedron, polyhedron, prism, pyramid, right circular cone, right prism, right pyramid, surface area, tetrahedron, trapezium, triangle, uniform, volume

Making solids from nets

To make a solid object from a sheet of flat paper you need to construct a *net*. This is the shape that has to be cut out, folded and stuck together to make the solid. A net should be drawn as accurately as possible, otherwise you will find that the edges will not fit together properly.

Exercise 4a

Each solid in this exercise has flat faces (called plane faces) and is called a *polyhedron*. 'Poly' means 'many'.

1 *Cube*

This net will make a cube.

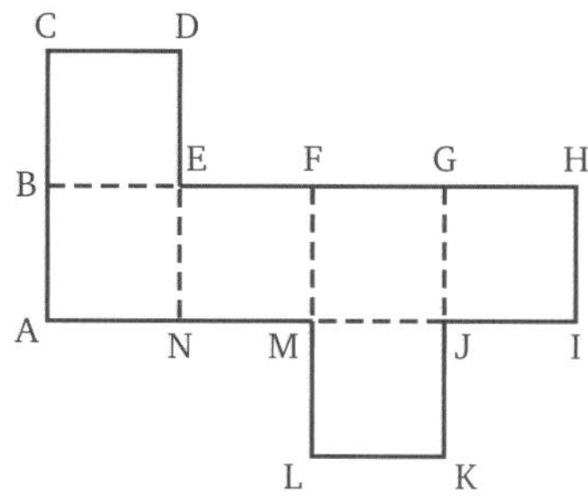

a Which edge meets AB?

b Which edge meets FG?

c Which other corners meet at N?

d Which other corners meet at H?

2 *Tetrahedron*

This net consists of four equilateral triangles. Construct the net accurately, making the sides of each triangle 5 cm long. Start by drawing an equilateral triangle of side 10 cm. Mark the midpoints of the sides and join them.

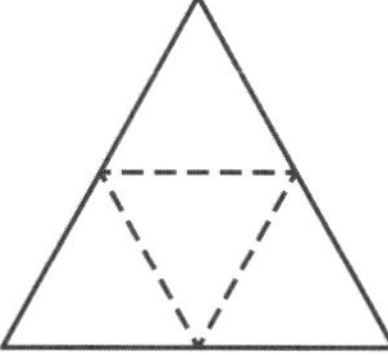

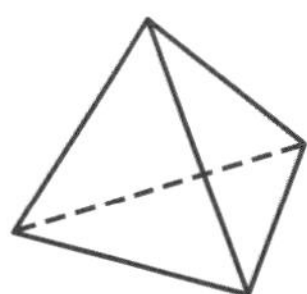

Cut out the net and fold the outer triangles up so that their vertices meet.

These shapes when painted make appealing decorations.

This solid is called a *regular tetrahedron*. All its faces are the same size and shape.

3 *Octahedron*

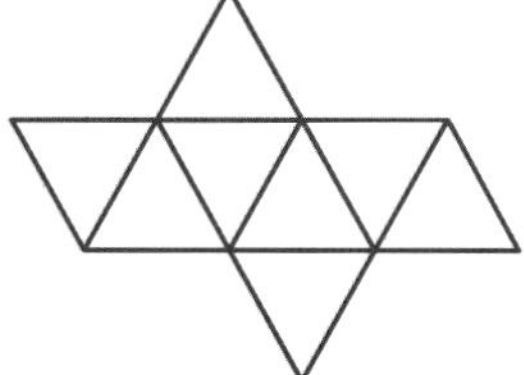

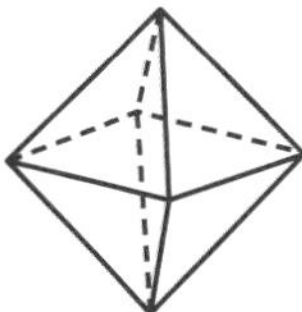

This net consists of 8 identical equilateral triangles. Make the sides of each triangle 3 cm long. Is this octahedron a regular solid?

4 *Square-based pyramid*

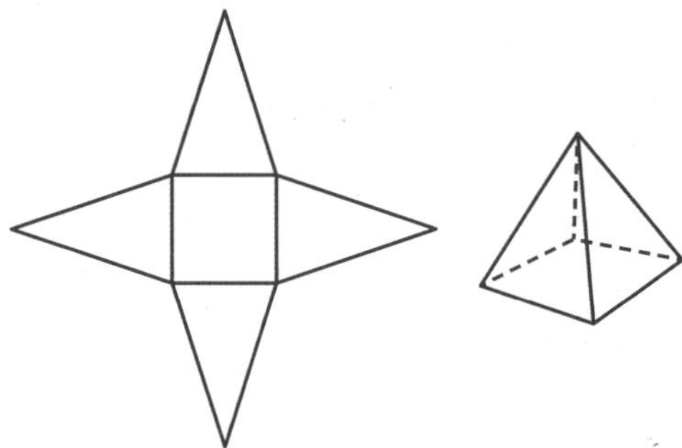

This net is a square with an isosceles triangle on each side of the square. Make the sides of the square 5 cm and the equal sides of the triangles 8 cm. Is this a regular solid?

5 *Prism* with a triangular cross-section

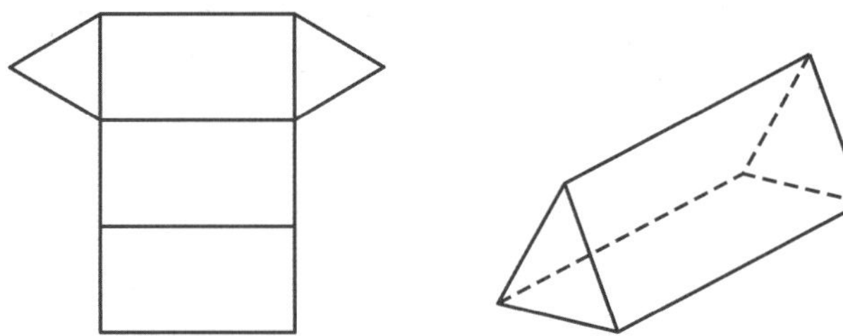

This net consists of 3 rectangles measuring 10 cm by 5 cm and 2 equilateral triangles of sides 5 cm.

In questions **6** and **7** sketch the cuboid given by the net. Show its dimensions on your sketch.

6

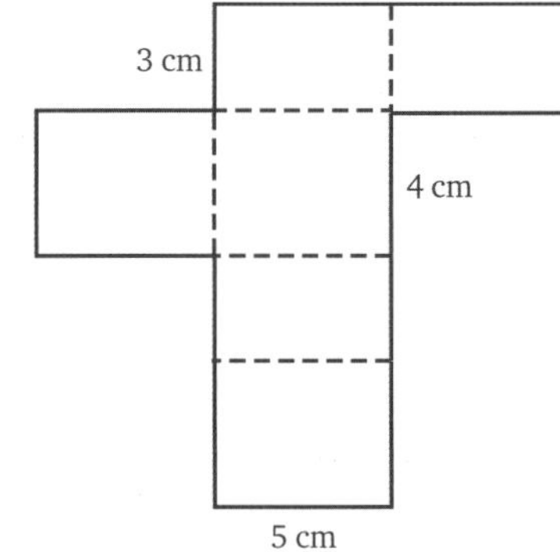

7

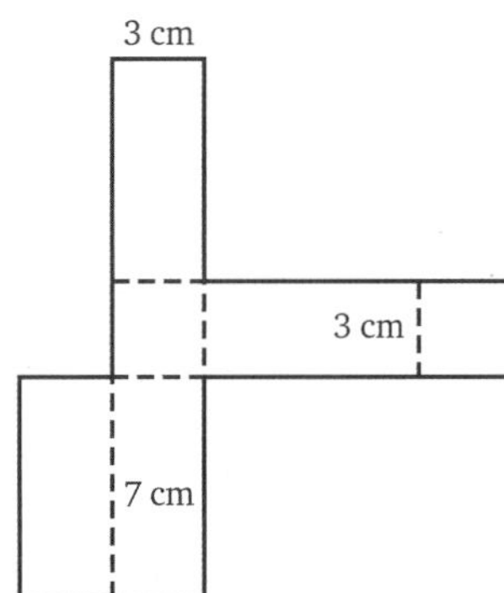

8 This net will make a cuboid.

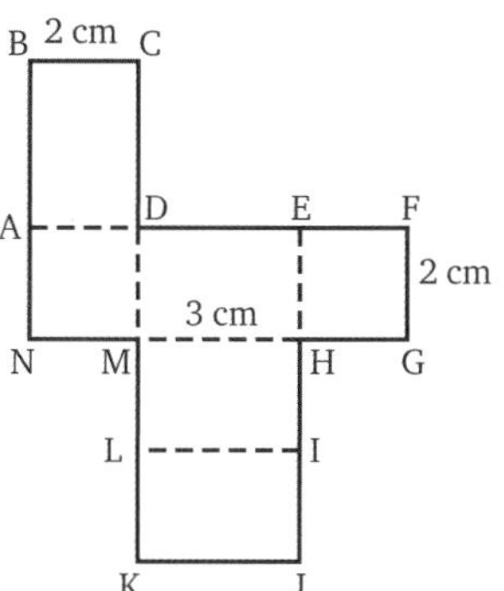

a Sketch the cuboid and mark its dimensions on the sketch.

b Which corners meets with B?

c Which edge joins with EF?

For questions **9** and **10**, choose the correct letters.

9 Which of these nets will make a cuboid?

A

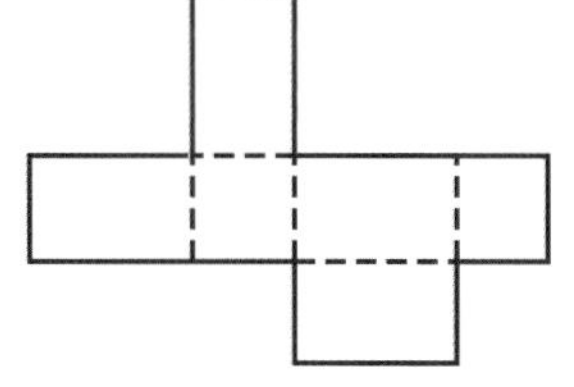

B

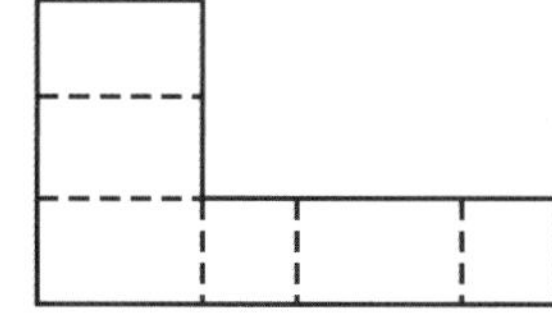

C

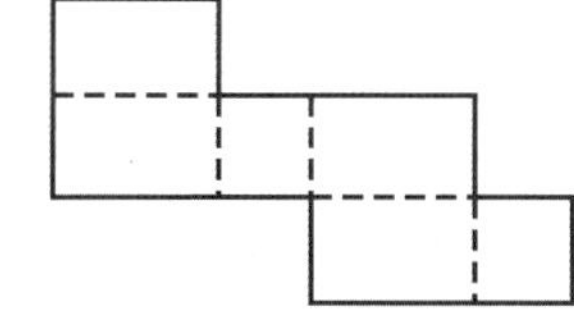

10 Which of these nets will fold to make a cube?

A

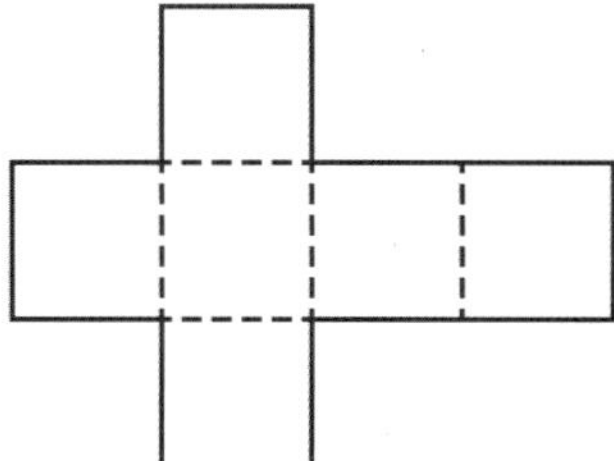

D

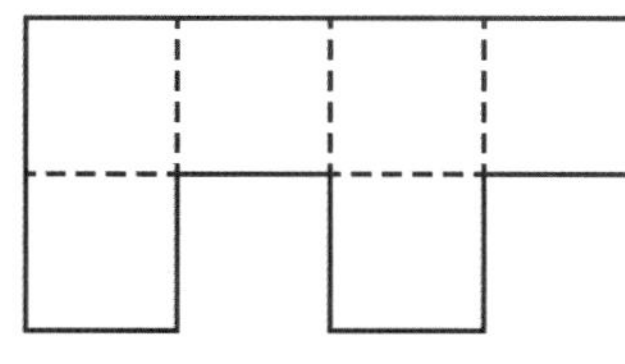

B

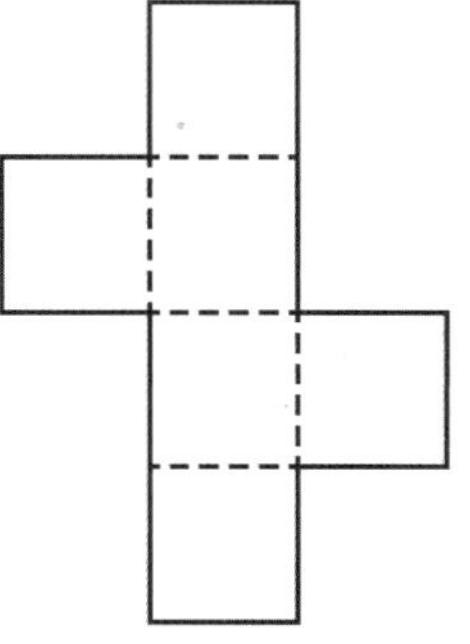

E

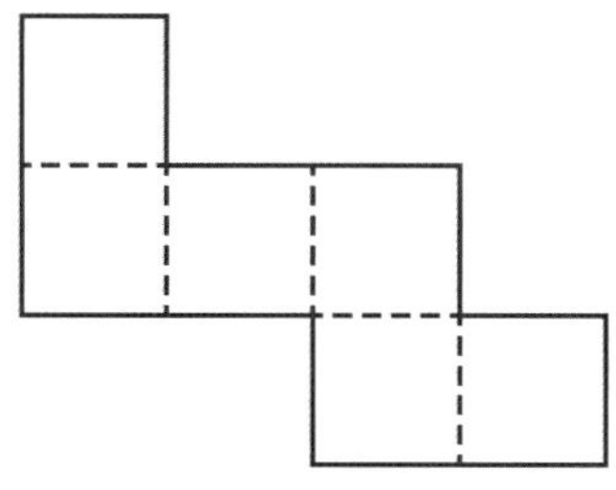

C

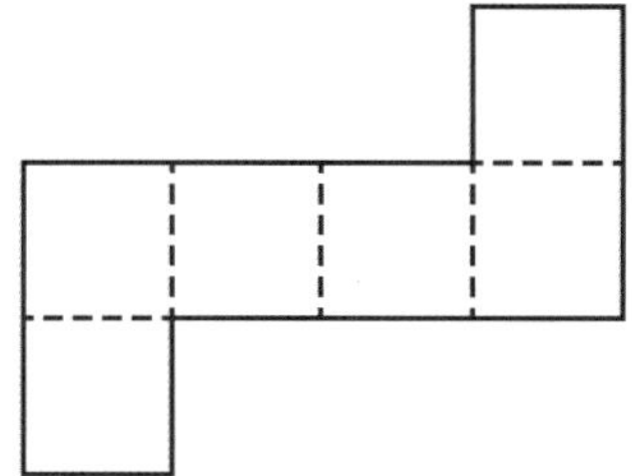

Questions **1** to **10** show how nets can be used to make solid shapes. Conversely, for any prism or pyramid we can draw its net.

11 Draw a net for this cuboid.

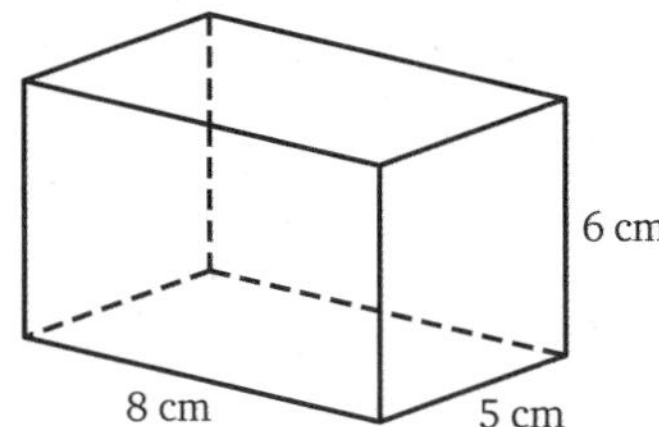

12 Draw a net for a cuboid measuring 5 cm by 4 cm by 3 cm.

In questions **13** and **14**, draw a net for each solid.

13 A cuboid measuring 7 cm by 4 cm by 3 cm.

14 A cuboid measuring 4 cm by 3.5 cm by 2.5 cm.

15 Draw as many different nets as you can for a cube with an edge of 3 cm. Each net should be in one piece.

16 Draw a net for this prism.
The cross-section is an equilateral triangle.

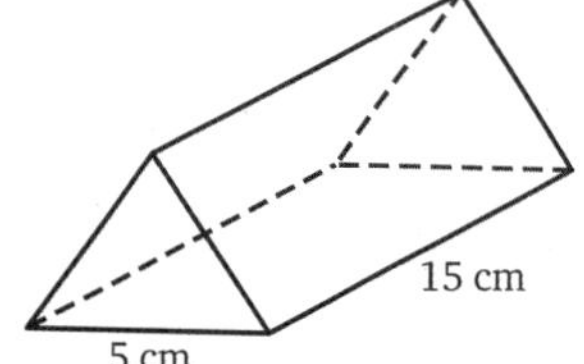

17 Show that you can draw at least two different nets for this prism.

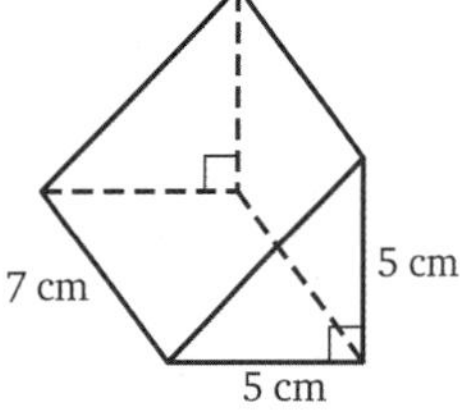

Prisms

First we revise the work we did in Book 2.

A *right prism* has two faces that are identical polygons. The other faces are rectangles.

When a right prism is cut parallel to one of its ends, we get the same shape as an end.

This shape is called the cross-section and is constant, i.e. it is the same throughout the prism.

Volume of a prism = area of cross-section × length.

∴ Volume of the prism shown in the diagram is given by

$$V = Al$$

Sometimes the prism is standing on the cross-section.
The length is then its height, so

$$V = Ah$$

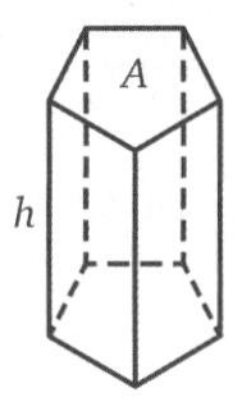

A cube is a right prism whose ends are squares and whose length is the same as its width. All the edges are the same length so the area of cross-section is a^2. The volume of a cube is given by $V = a^3$.

A cuboid is a right prism whose ends are squares or rectangles.
The volume of a cuboid is given by

$$V = lbh$$

Surface area of a prism

A cube of side a has 6 square faces. The area of each face is a^2 so the total surface area of a cube with side a is $6a^2$.

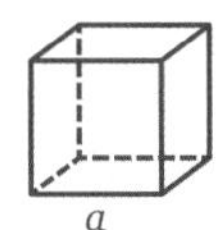

Similarly a cuboid has 6 faces.

This cuboid has two rectangular faces measuring $a \times b$
two measuring $b \times c$
and two measuring $a \times c$

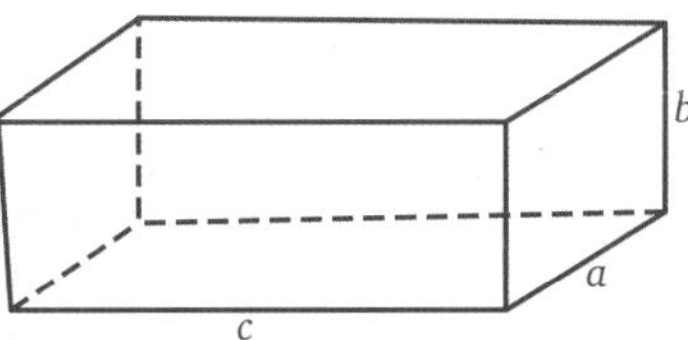

The total surface area of a cuboid is therefore

$$2(ab + bc + ac).$$

The surface area of a prism is the sum of the areas of all the faces.

Exercise 4b

This cuboid, which is not drawn to scale, represents an open box.

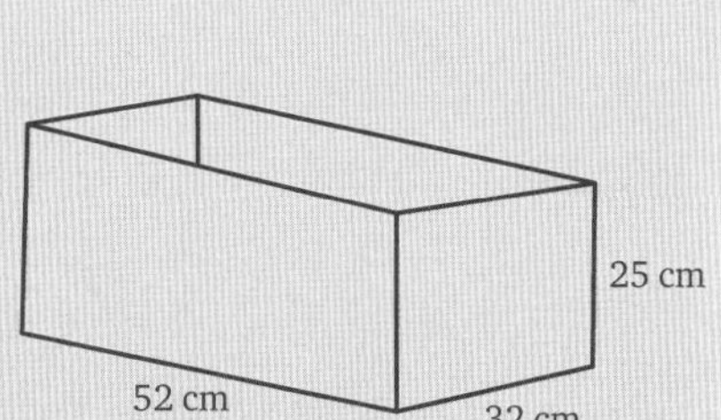

The internal dimensions are 52 cm by 32 cm by 25 cm.

a Find the total surface area of the inside of the box.

b Find the capacity of the box in litres.

a There are two rectangular faces measuring 52 cm by 25 cm, two measuring 32 cm by 25 cm, and the base measuring 52 cm by 32 cm.

The surface area of the inside of the box

$= 2(52 \times 25) + 2(32 \times 25) + 52 \times 32\,\text{cm}^2$

$= 5864\,\text{cm}^2$

b Internal volume of the box $= 52 \times 32 \times 25\,\text{cm}^3$

$= 41\,600\,\text{cm}^3$

$= 41.6$ litres (1 litre $= 1000\,\text{cm}^3$)

1 Find the surface area of a cube of side 3 cm.

2 Find the surface area of a cube of side 6 cm.

3 The total surface area of a cube is $150\,\text{cm}^2$. Find:

a the area of one face

b the length of an edge of the cube

c the volume of the cube.

4 The volume of a cube is $64\,\text{cm}^3$. Find:

a the length of an edge of the cube

b the area of one face

c the total surface area of the cube.

5 Find the total surface area of this cuboid.

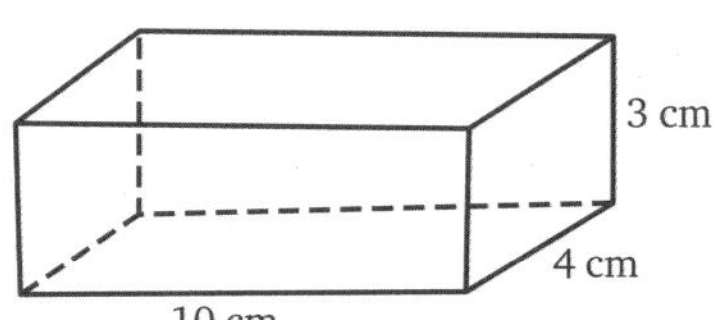

6 A cuboid measures 10 cm by 5 cm by 4 cm. Find:

a the area of one of the largest faces

b the area of one of the smallest faces

c its total surface area.

7 A prism with a rectangular cross-section measuring 5 cm by 6 cm, is 2.5 m long. Find:

a the area of cross-section

b the total surface of the prism

c its volume.

8 The diagram shows the cross-section of a water channel which is 15 m long and open at the top.

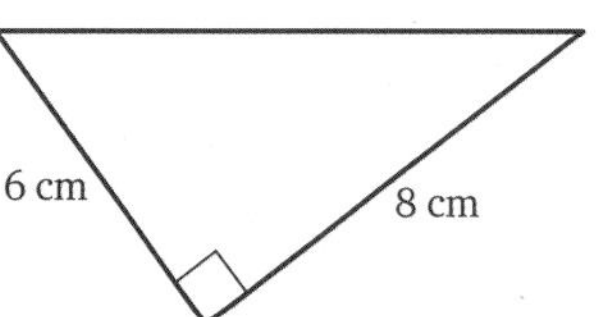

a How many litres of water will it hold when full?

b Find, in square metres:

the area of the channel in contact with the water

the area of water open to the elements.

9 The diagram shows the cross-section of a block of wood which is 12 cm long. Find:

a the area of cross-section

b the volume of the block.

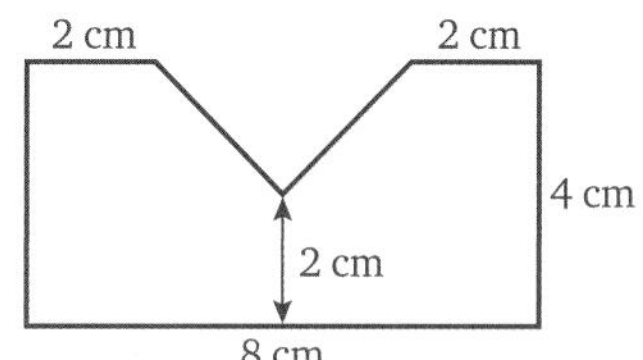

10 The diagram shows the roof-space of a workshop which is 8 m long. The sloping sides of the roof are at right angles. Find:

a the area of the cross-section

b the total area of the sloping faces

c the capacity of the roof-space.

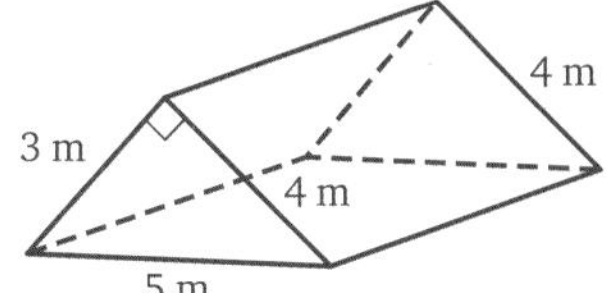

11 The cross-section of a building is a rectangle surmounted by a triangle. It is 6 m wide, 3 m high at the eaves and it is 4 m from the floor to the ridge.

a If the building is 7 m long, calculate its capacity in cubic metres.

b Find the surface area of the building excluding the floor and the roof.

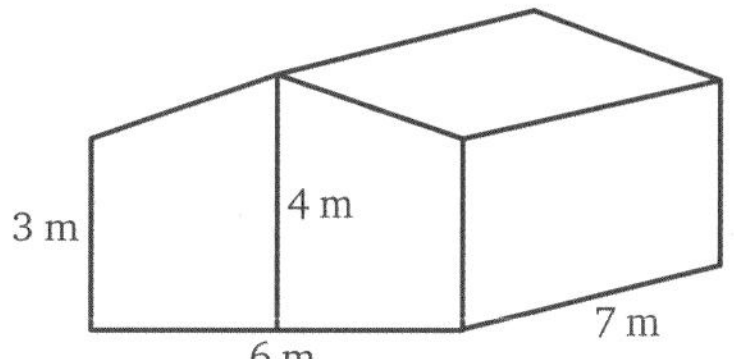

12 Use the measurements on the diagram to find

a the surface area of the solid

b the area of cross-section of the solid

c the volume of metal needed to make this shape.

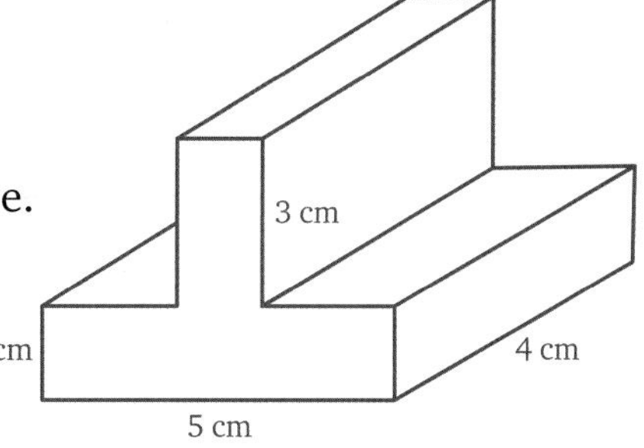

13 a Use the measurements on the diagram, which are given in centimetres, to find the volume of wood used to make this capital letter I.

b The solid is to be painted. One tin of spray covers $4\,m^2$. How many tins must be purchased to give enough paint for three coats?

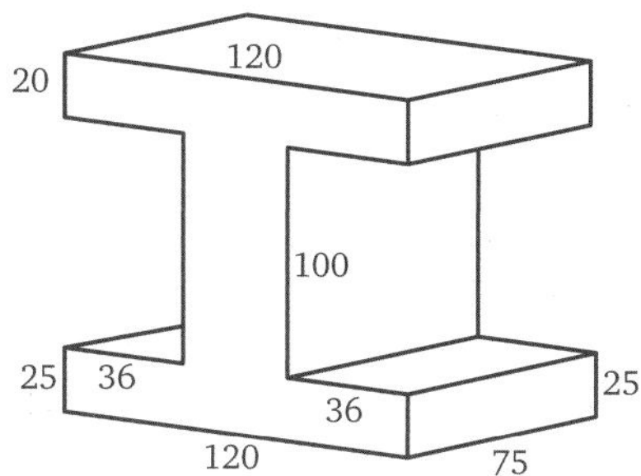

14 The diagram shows a food trough as used on a farm. The cross-section is a trapezium and the trough is 3 m long. Find:

a the area of the cross-section

b the capacity of the trough if filled with liquid.

Reminder: area of a trapezium is given by

$$A = \frac{1}{2}(a+b) \times h$$

where a and b are the lengths of the parallel sides and h is the distance between them.

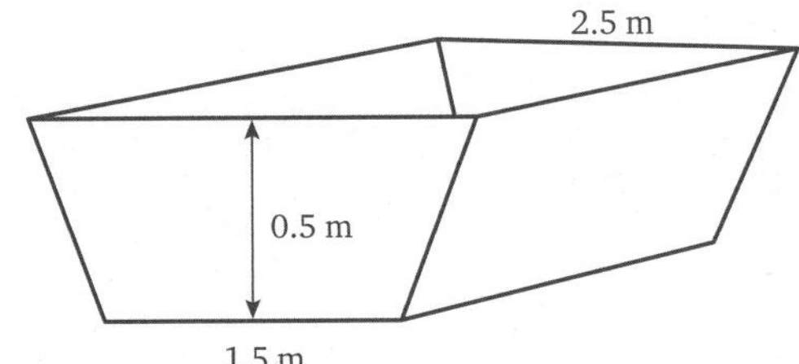

15 The diagram shows an open box. The cross-section is a hexagon ABCDEF, where all the edges are 5 cm. The line BE = 11 cm and divides the cross-section into two identical trapeziums such that CD and AF are 8 cm apart. If the box is 10 cm long, find

a the area of the cross-section

b the total external area of the box

c the capacity of the box.

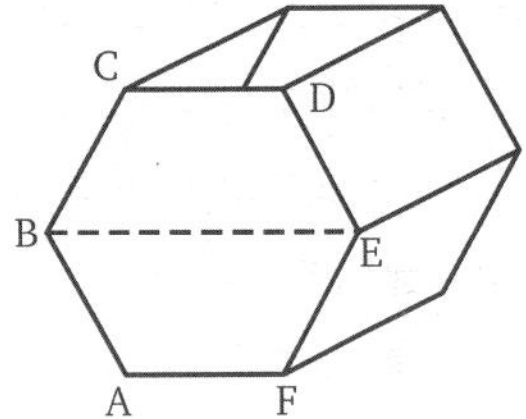

Pyramids

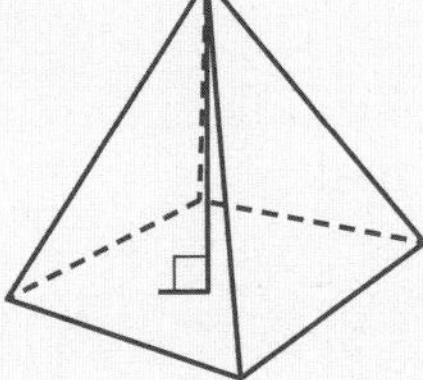

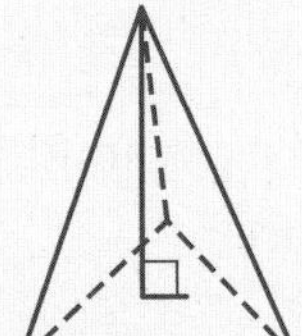

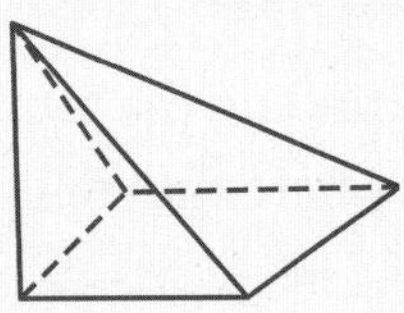

Each of these solids is a *pyramid*. Its shape is given by drawing lines from a single point to each corner of the base.

The first solid has a square base. It is called a square-based pyramid, and because the vertex is directly above the middle of the base it is called a *right pyramid*.

The second solid has a triangular base and is called a triangular pyramid. It is also called a *tetrahedron*, a special name that applies only to this shape.

The third solid is also a pyramid but not a right pyramid.

Net for a pyramid

The net for a right pyramid with a rectangular base is shown below. The equal sloping sides occur in pairs.

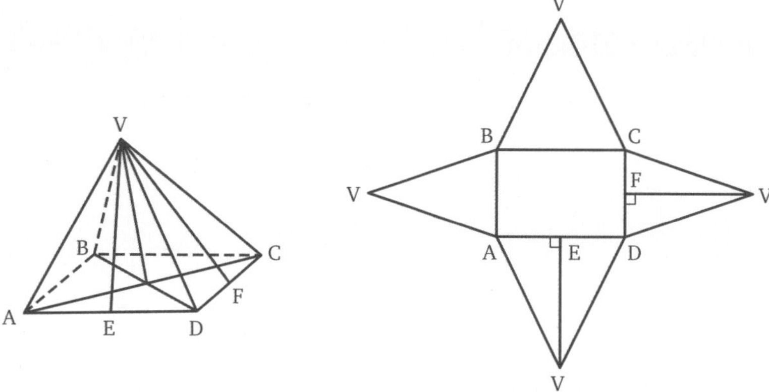

E is the midpoint of AD and F is the midpoint of DC.

Total surface area of pyramid = area ABCD + 2 × area △VAD + 2 × area △VDC

Volume of a pyramid

The volume of a pyramid is given by

$$\text{Volume} = \frac{1}{3}\,\text{area of base} \times \text{perpendicular height}$$

Surface area of a pyramid

The surface area of any pyramid is found by adding the area of the base to the sum of the areas of the sloping sides.

Drawing a net often helps in finding the total area of a pyramid. This makes distances clearer and shows where the right angles are.

Exercise 4c

The diagram shows a right pyramid VABCD with a square base ABCD of side 8 cm. The height of the pyramid is 3 cm and the distance from V to the midpoint of BC is 5 cm. Find

a the volume of the pyramid

b its total surface area.

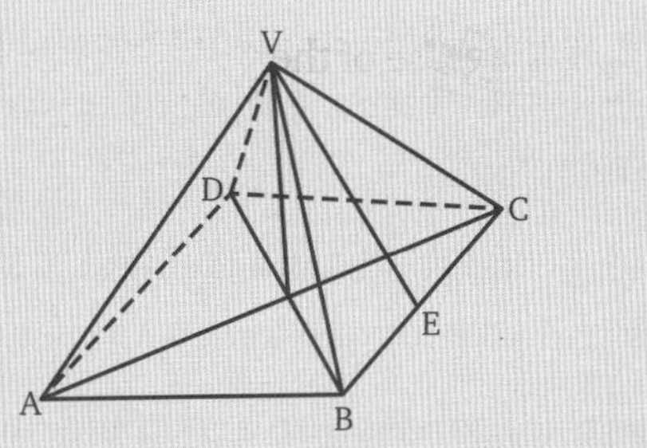

a

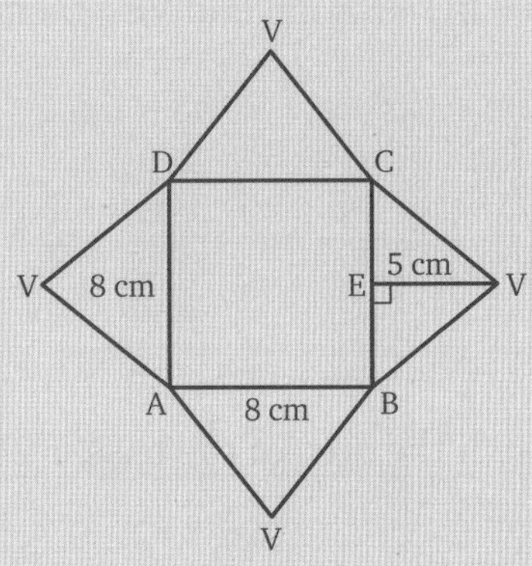

Area of base $= 8 \times 8\,\text{cm}^2$

$= 64\,\text{cm}^2$

Volume $= \frac{1}{3}$ area of base $\times$ perpendicular height

$= \left(\frac{1}{3} \times 64 \times 3\right)\text{cm}^3$

$= 64\,\text{cm}^3$

b Length of VE = 5 cm

Area of one sloping face $= \left(\frac{1}{2} \times 8 \times 5\right)\text{cm}^2$

$= 20\,\text{cm}^2$

$\therefore$ area of the four sloping faces $= 4 \times 20\,\text{cm}^2$

$= 80\,\text{cm}^2$

Total surface area of pyramid = area of base + area of the four sloping faces

$= (64 + 80)\,\text{cm}^2$

$= 144\,\text{cm}^2$

Find the volume of each pyramid in questions **1** to **4**.

1 The area of the base of a pyramid is $84\,\text{cm}^2$. The vertex of the pyramid is 7.5 cm above its base.

2 The base of the pyramid is a rectangle measuring 12 cm by 20 cm. Its perpendicular height is 8 cm.

3 The base of the pyramid is a rectangle. PQ = 15 cm, QR = 12 cm and TP = 9 cm.

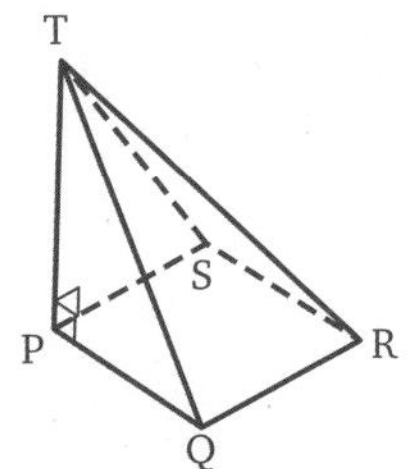

4 The base ABCD is a rectangle. AB = BC = 5.4 cm and VE = 7 cm.

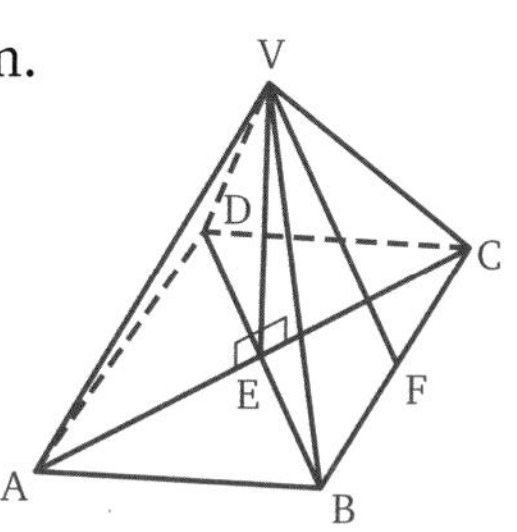

5 The volume of a pyramid is 56 cm³. If the area of the base is 24 cm², find its perpendicular height.

6 The volume of a pyramid is 240 cm³. If the area of the base is 18 cm², find its perpendicular height.

7 The volume of a pyramid is 63 cm³. It is 9 cm high. Find the area of the base.

8 The volume of a pyramid is 33.6 cm³. It is 8 cm high. Find the area of the base.

Volume of a cylinder

The formula for the volume of a cylinder is

$$V = \pi r^2 h$$

i.e. area of the circular cross-section × height, where V cubic units is the volume, r units is the radius of the circular cross-section and h units is its height or length.

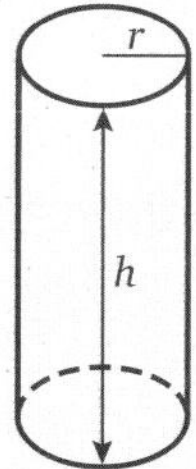

Exercise 4d

Find the radius of a cylinder of volume 64 cm³ and height 8 cm.

$$V = \pi r^2 h$$

Hence $64 = \pi \times r^2 \times 8$

$$\frac{64}{\pi \times 8} = r^2$$

$$r^2 = 2.546...$$

As r^2 means 'the same number multiplied by itself', that number, r, is called the square root of the number 2.546.... To find r use the [√] button on your calculator.

$$r = 1.595...$$

The radius is 1.60 cm correct to three significant figures.

In each of questions **1** to **10**, find the missing measurement of the cylinder.

Give your answers correct to three significant figures.

	Radius	Height	Volume
1	3 cm	6 cm	
2	0.4 m	2 m	
3	2.5 cm	3.2 cm	
4	11 cm		4560 cm^3
5	5.3 cm		582 cm^3
6		2 cm	804 cm^3
7		0.5 cm	0.565 cm^3
8	3.6 cm	7.2 cm	
9	0.3 cm		0.21 cm^3
10	0.4 m	22 cm	

11 The diameter of a cylinder is equal to its height. If the volume of the cylinder is 100 cm^3, find

a its radius **b** its height.

12 The radius of a cylinder is equal to its height. If the volume of the cylinder is 250 cm^3, find

a its radius **b** its height.

13 A 4-cylinder diesel engine has a bore (the diameter of each cylinder) of 89 mm and a stroke (the length of each piston) of 86.6 mm. Find, correct to three significant figures, the capacity of the engine in cubic centimetres.

14 Find the capacity of a 4-cylinder petrol engine which has a bore of 84 mm and a stroke of 75 mm. Give your answer correct to three significant figures.

15 Copper wire is circular in cross-section with a radius of 0.4 mm. Find, in cubic centimetres, the volume of copper in a 100 m length of this wire.

16 Wooden dowel, with a diameter of 1 cm, is made from lengths of timber with a square cross-section of side 1.2 cm. Find

a the area of cross-section of the original timber

b the area of cross-section of the dowel

c the percentage of wood wasted.

Curved surface area of a cylinder

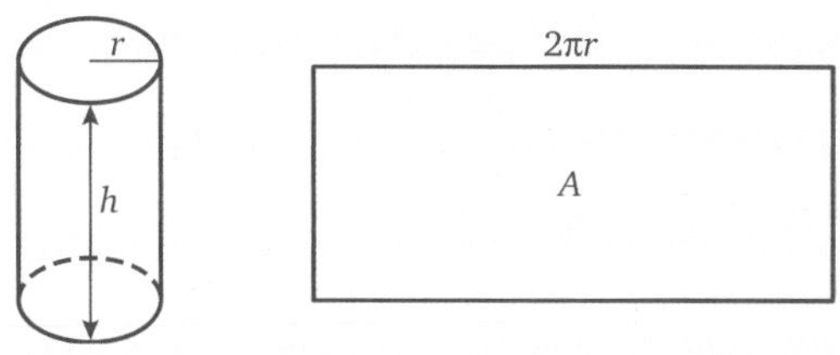

If we have a cylindrical tin with a paper label covering its curved surface, the label can be removed and laid flat to give a rectangle whose length is equal to the circumference of the tin.

Therefore the area A of the curved surface is given by $2\pi r \times h$, i.e.

$$A = 2\pi rh$$

The total surface area of a closed cylinder is given by

$$A = 2\pi rh + 2\pi r^2$$

Exercise 4e

In each of questions **1** to **8**, find the curved surface area of the cylinder whose measurements are given. Remember to make sure the units are compatible.

1 Radius 5 cm, height 6 cm

2 Radius 20 cm, height 4 cm

3 Radius 4.6 cm, height 7.3 cm

4 Radius 2 m, height 64 cm

5 Radius 0.4 m, height 52 cm

6 Radius 6.5 cm, height 8.7 cm

7 Radius 62.8 cm, height 40 cm

8 Radius 5.4 m, height 86 cm

9 A closed cylinder has radius 3.6 cm and height 4.4 cm. Find

a the area of its curved surface

b the area of its base

c the total surface area.

10 An open cylindrical tin has radius 6.5 cm and height 4.8 cm. Find

a the area of its curved surface

b the area of its base

c the total external surface area.

11 A closed cylinder has a radius of 3.3 cm and a height of 6.5 cm. Find

a the area of its curved surface

b the total surface area.

12 What area of sheet metal is needed to make a cylindrical tube of length 56 cm and radius 2.8 cm? The metal overlaps by 1 cm along its length.

13 Find the area of the paper label covering the side of a cylindrical tin of soup of height 10.5 cm and radius 3.6 cm. The label has an overlap of 1 cm.

14 Find the total area of card required to make a cylinder 7.4 cm high and radius 3.8 cm open at both ends.

15 A garden roller is in the form of a cylinder of radius 0.4 m and width 0.6 m. What area of lawn does the roller cover in 6 revolutions?

16 A cylindrical post box is 1.5 m high and has a diameter of 63 cm. Find, in square metres, the area that needs painting.

17 A coin is 1.5 mm thick and has a diameter of 2.5 cm. Find the total surface area of the coin.

Take care with the units.

18 A cylindrical breakfast cup has an internal radius of 4 cm and is 8 cm deep. Find the surface area of the cup in contact with tea when it is filled to a depth of 0.5 cm from the top.

75 litres of water are poured into a cylindrical tank of radius 0.4 m. Find the depth of the water in the tank in centimetres.

Volume of water = 75 litres

$= 75\,000\text{ cm}^3$

$V = 75\,000$, $r = 0.4 \times 100 = 40$ cm

$$V = \pi r^2 h$$

$$\therefore \quad 75\,000 = \pi \times 40^2 \times h$$

$$\frac{75\,000}{\pi \times 40^2} = h$$

$$h = 14.92...$$

The depth of water is 14.9 cm correct to three significant figures.

19 A cylindrical mug has a radius of 3 cm and will hold 283 cm^3 of milk. How deep is the mug?

20 A cylindrical cup is 8 cm deep and will hold 400 cm^3 of coffee. Find its diameter.

21 It takes 1500 litres of water to fill a drum of radius 60 cm. Find the depth of the drum.

22 Water from a full rectangular tank measuring 2 m by 1 m by 0.6 m is emptied into a cylindrical tank and fills it to a depth of 1.4 m. Find

a the volume of water involved

b the diameter of the cylindrical tank.

Volume of a cone

We have already seen that the volume of a pyramid is given by

$$\text{Volume} = \frac{1}{3} \text{ area of base} \times \text{perpendicular height}$$

where a pyramid is a solid with a polygon as a base that comes up to a point called the vertex.

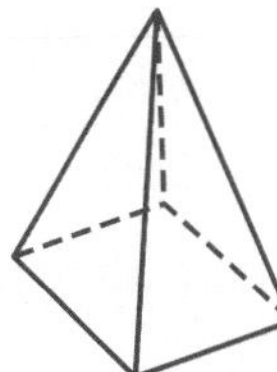
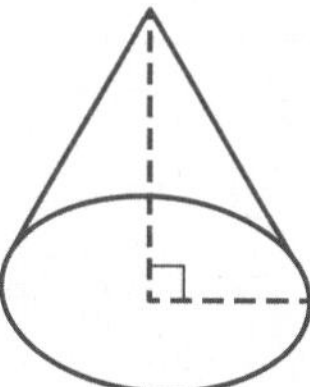

The formula for the volume of a pyramid also applies to a cone, so the volume of a cone is given by

$$\text{Volume} = \frac{1}{3} \text{ area of circular base} \times \text{perpendicular height}$$

i.e. $V = \frac{1}{3}\pi r^2 h$

A cone whose vertex is directly above the centre of the base is called a *right circular cone*; this is the only type of cone we study.

Exercise 4f

Find the volume of a cone of base radius 4.2 cm and height 9.5 cm.

$r = 4.2 \qquad h = 9.5 \qquad V = \frac{1}{3}\pi r^2 h$

$$= \frac{\pi \times (4.2)^2 \times 9.5}{3} = 175.48\ldots$$

The volume is 175 cm^3 to three significant figures.

In each of questions **1** to **6** find the volume of the cone whose dimensions are given:

1 base radius 8 cm, height 12 cm

2 base radius 2.4 cm, height 4.8 cm

3 base diameter 34.6 cm, height 84 cm

4 base diameter 14.5 cm, height 5.9 cm

5 base diameter 140 mm, height 6.5 cm

6 base radius 0.42 m, height 140 cm.

7 This salt cellar is in the form of a cylinder surmounted by a cone. The total height of the salt cellar is 7 cm, the common radius is 2 cm and the height of the cone is 2 cm. Find the volume of the salt cellar.

8

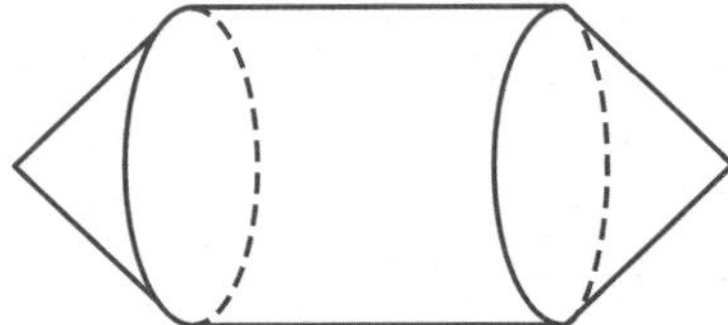

A spindle is made by attaching a cone to each end of a cylinder. The total length of the spindle is 24 cm, the common radius is 5 cm and the height of each cone is 6 cm. Find the volume of the spindle.

9 A frustum of a cone is formed by slicing the top off a cone. The section that remains, shown by solid lines, is the frustum. The original cone has base radius 8 cm and height 12 cm. The part cut off has radius 4 cm and height 6 cm. Find the volume of the frustum.

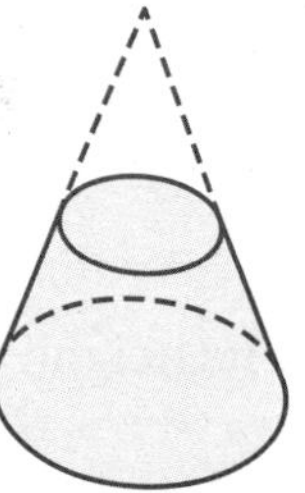

10 A cylindrical piece of wood of radius 4.5 cm and height 12 cm has a conical hole cut in it. The cone is the same radius and height as the cylinder. Find the volume of the solid.

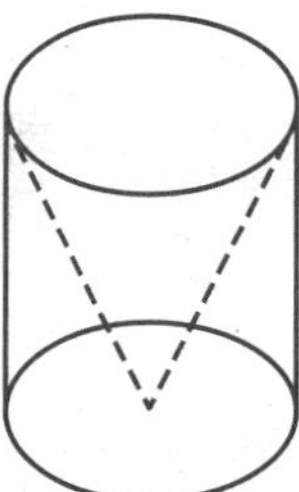

Surface area of a cone

The **curved** surface area of a cone is given by

$$A = \pi rl$$

where l units is the slant height.

The total surface area of a cone is given by

$$A = \pi r^2 + \pi rl$$

Exercise 4g

In each of questions **1** to **6** find the area of the curved surface of the cone whose measurements are given:

1 radius 5 cm, slant height 10 cm

2 radius 0.4 m, slant height 1.8 m

3 radius 45 mm, slant height 54 mm

4 radius 8.3 cm, slant height 12.5 cm

5 radius 34 mm, slant height 76 mm

6 radius 7.6 cm, slant height 10.6 cm.

7 Find the total surface area of a cone of base radius 6 cm and slant height 9 cm.

8 Find the total surface area of a cone of base radius 12 cm and slant height 15 cm.

9 The volume of a cone is 60 cm^3. If the radius of its base is 3 cm, find its height.

10 The volume of a cone is 100 cm^3. If the radius of its base is 4.5 cm, find its height.

Mixed exercise

Exercise 4h

Select the letter that gives the correct answer.

1 Which of the following shapes will this net fold up to give?

A a cuboid

B a prism

C a pyramid

D a tetrahedron

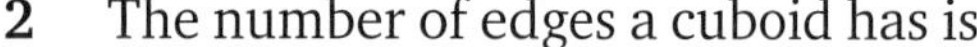

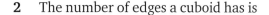

2 The number of edges a cuboid has is

A 8 **B** 10 **C** 12 **D** 16

3 The number of faces a regular tetrahedron has is

A 3 **B** 4 **C** 5 **D** 6

4 The number of corners a cube has is

A 4 B 6 C 8 D 10

5 The number of faces for a prism with a triangular cross-section is

A 3 B 4 C 5 D 6

6 This net will fold up to give a cube.

The volume of the cube is

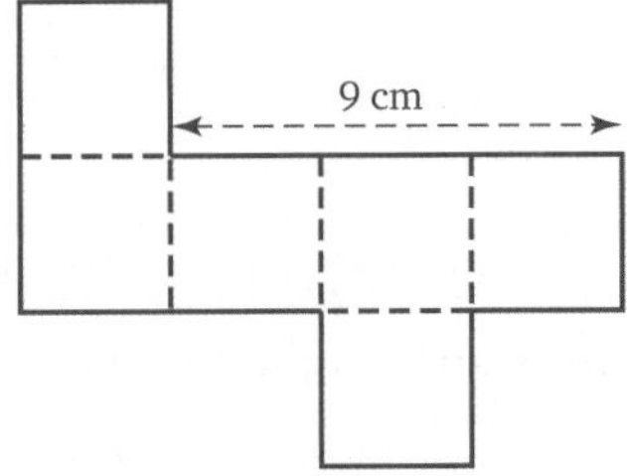

A $12\,cm^3$

B $18\,cm^3$

C $24\,cm^3$

D $27\,cm^3$

7 The volume, correct to 3 s.f., of a cylinder of radius 6 cm and height 15 cm, is

A $424\,cm^3$ B $540\,cm^3$ C $1250\,cm^3$ D $1700\,cm^3$

In this chapter you have seen that...

- ✔ a net is a flat shape that can be folded to make a solid
- ✔ the cross-section of a prism is constant, i.e. the same throughout its length
- ✔ the volume of a prism = area of cross-section × length (note that if the prism is standing on the cross-section then the length is the height)
- ✔ drawing a net for a pyramid makes it easier to find its surface area
- ✔ the volume of a pyramid is given by

$$\text{volume} = \frac{1}{3}\text{ area of base} \times \text{perpendicular height}$$

- ✔ the surface area of a pyramid is given by adding the area of the base to the sum of the areas of the sloping faces
- ✔ the volume of a cylinder is given by $V = \pi r^2 h$ and its curved surface area is $2\pi rh$
- ✔ the curved surface area of a cylinder is equivalent to a rectangle
- ✔ the formula for the volume of a cone is $V = \frac{1}{3}\pi r^2 h$
- ✔ the curved surface area of a cone is πrl where l is the slant height of the cone.

5 Enlargements

At the end of this chapter you should be able to...

1 find, by drawing, the centre of enlargement, given an object and its image
2 calculate the scale factor of an enlargement, given an object and its image
3 draw the image of a given figure, knowing the scale factor and the centre of enlargement
4 classify an image in terms of relative size and position, depending on whether the scale factor is greater than 1 or less than 1.

You need to know...

✔ the sum of the three angles in a triangle

✔ how to find one quantity as a fraction of another

✔ how to draw x and y axes and plot points.

Key words

centre of enlargement, enlargement, fractional scale factor, guideline, image, object, reflection, scale factor, translation

Enlargements

All the transformations we have used so far (i.e. reflections, translations and rotations) have moved the object and perhaps turned it over to produce the image, but its shape and size have not changed. Next we come to a transformation that keeps the shape but alters the size.

Think of the picture thrown on the screen when a projector is used.

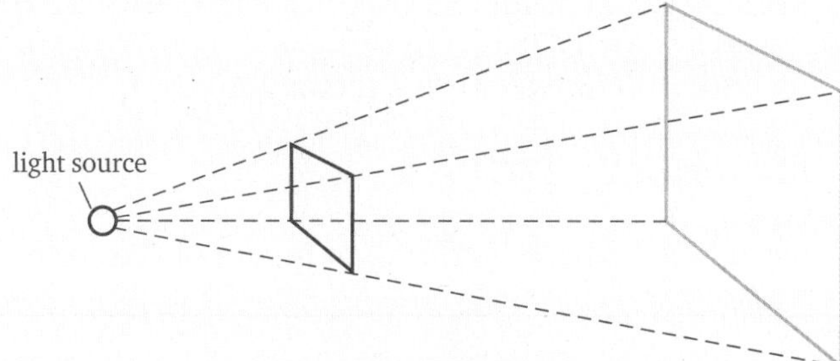

The picture on the screen is the same as the original picture but it is very much bigger.

We can use the same idea to enlarge any shape.

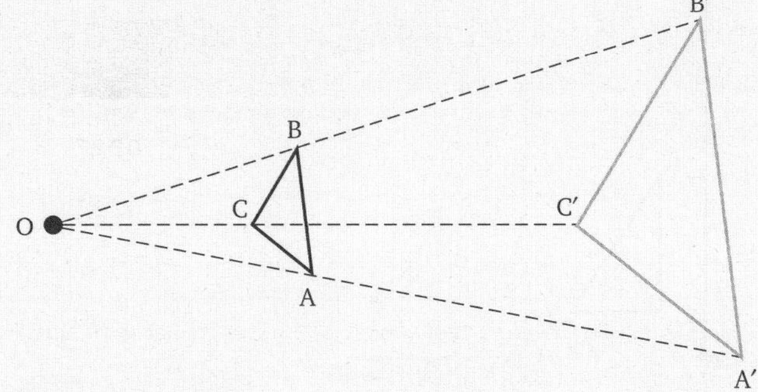

△A′B′C′ is the image of △ABC under an *enlargement, centre O*.

O is the *centre of enlargement*.

We call the dotted lines *guidelines*.

Centre of enlargement

In all the questions in Exercise 5a, one triangle is an enlargement of the other.

Exercise 5a

1 Copy the diagram using 1 cm to 1 unit. Draw P′P, Q′Q and R′R and continue all three lines until they meet.

The point where the lines meet is called the centre of enlargement.

Give the coordinates of the centre of enlargement.

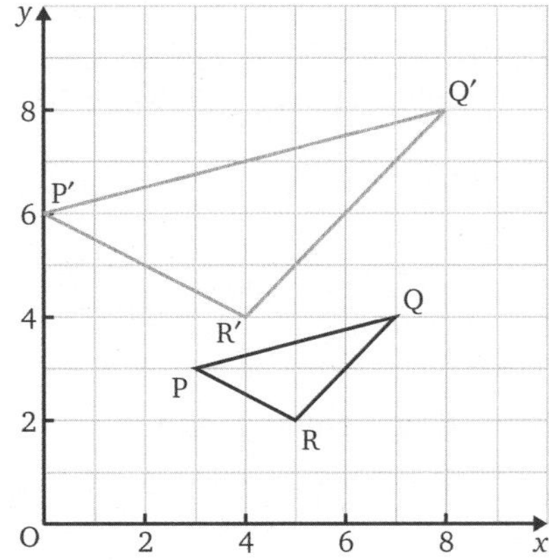

Repeat question **1** using the diagrams in questions **2** and **3**.

2

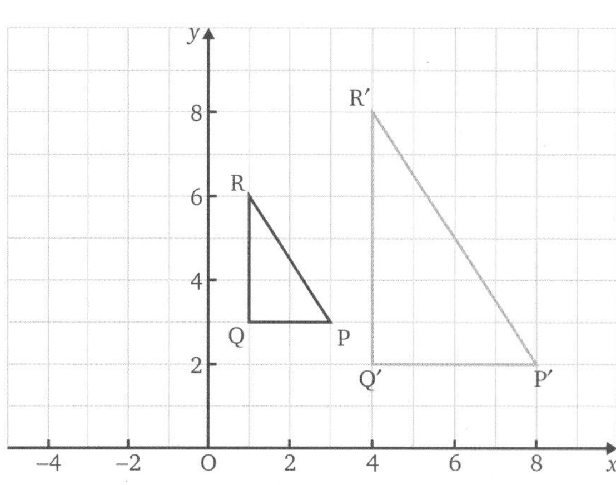

3

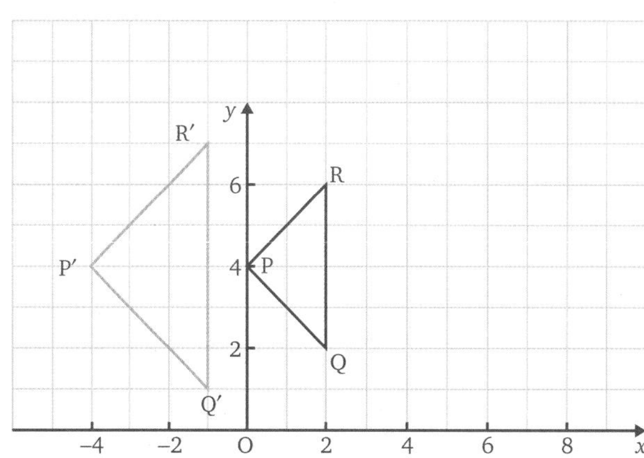

4 In questions **1** to **3**, name pairs of lines that are parallel.

5 Draw axes for x and y from 0 to 9 using 1 cm as 1 unit.

Draw △ABC: A(2, 3), B(4, 1), C(5, 4).

Draw △A′B′C′: A′(2, 5), B′(6, 1), C′(8, 7).

Draw A′A, B′B and C′C and extend these lines until they meet.

a Give the coordinates of the centre of enlargement.

b Measure the sides and angles of the two triangles. What do you notice?

6 Repeat question **5** with △ABC: A(8, 4), B(6, 6), C(6, 4) and △A′B′C′: A′(6, 2), B′(0, 8), C′(0, 2).

7 Draw axes for x and y from 0 to 10 using 1 cm as 1 unit.

Draw △XYZ with X(8, 2), Y(6, 6) and Z(5, 3) and △X′Y′Z′ with X′(6, 2), Y′(2, 10) and Z′(0, 4).

Find the centre of enlargement and label it P.

Measure PX, PX′, PY, PY′, PZ, PZ′. What do you notice?

The centre of enlargement can be anywhere, including a point inside the object or a point on the object.

The centres of enlargement in the diagrams below are marked with a cross.

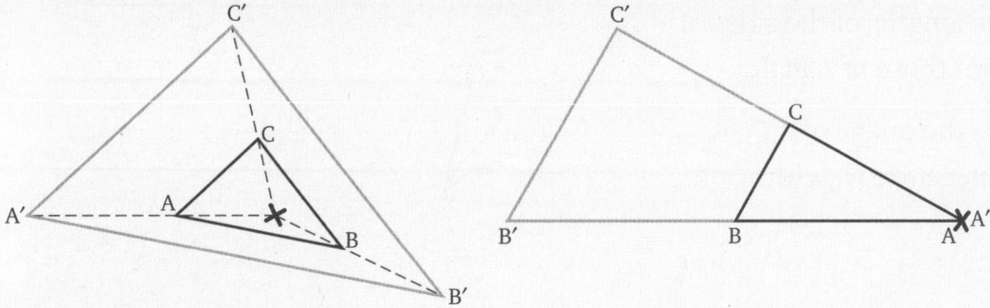

Exercise 5b

1 Copy the diagram using 1 cm as 1 unit. Draw A′A, B′B and C′C and extend the lines until they meet. Give the coordinates of the centre of enlargement.

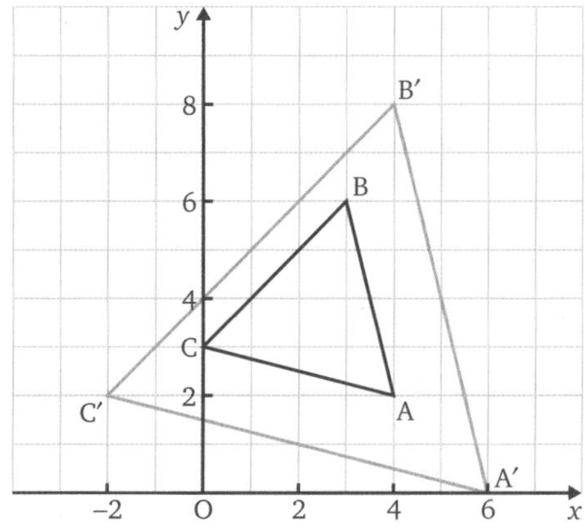

2 In the diagram below, which point is the centre of enlargement?

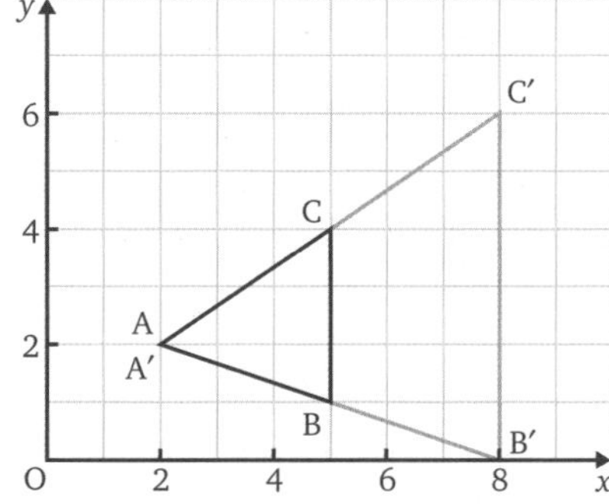

3 Draw axes for x and y from –3 to 10 using 1 cm as 1 unit. Draw △ABC with A(4, 0), B(4, 4) and C(0, 2). Draw △A′B′C′ with A′(5, –2), B′(5, 6) and C′(–3, 2). Find the coordinates of the centre of enlargement.

4 Repeat question **3** with A(1, 4), B(5, 2), C(5, 5) and A′(–3, 6), B′(9, 0), C′(9, 9).

Scale factors

If we measure the lengths of the sides of the two triangles PQR and P′Q′R′ and compare them, we find that the lengths of the sides of △P′Q′R′ are three times those of △PQR.

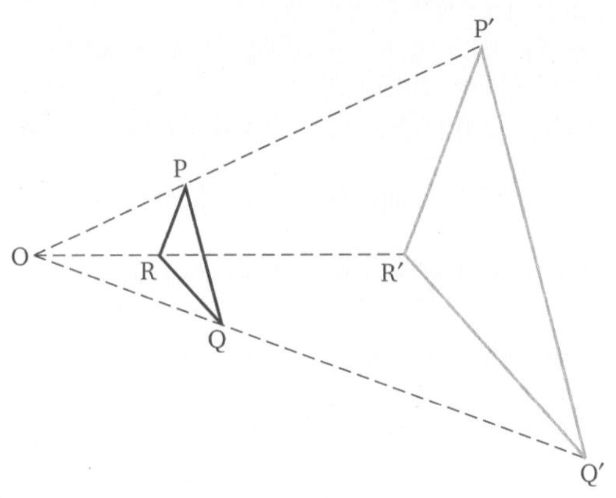

We say that △P′Q′R′ is the image of △PQR under an enlargement, centre O, with *scale factor 3*.

Finding an image under enlargement

If we measure OR and OR′ in the diagram above, we find R′ is three times as far from O as R is. This enables us to work out a method for enlarging an object with a given centre of enlargement (say O) and a given scale factor (say 3).

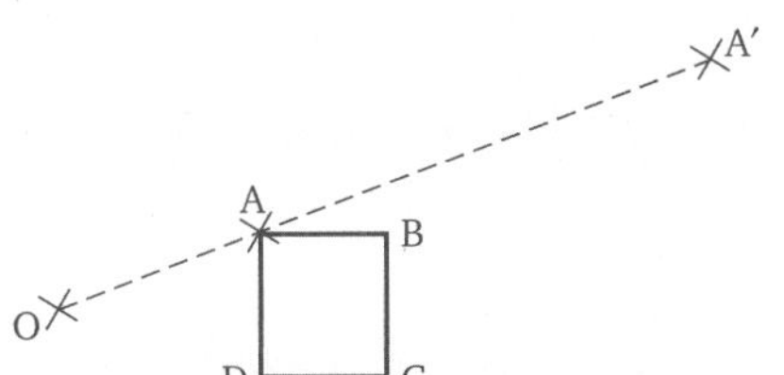

Measure OA. Multiply it by 3. Mark A′ on the guideline three times as far from O as A is.

$$OA' = 3 \times OA$$

Repeat for B and the other vertices of ABCD.

Then A′B′C′D′ is the image of ABCD. To check, measure A′B′ and AB. A′B′ should be three times as large as AB.

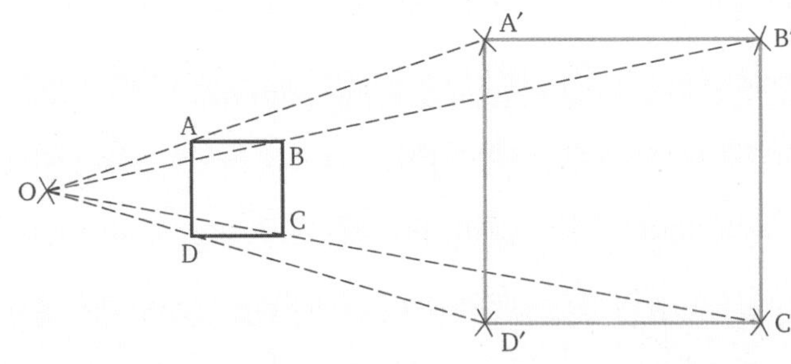

Exercise 5c

1 Copy the diagram using 1 cm as 1 unit. P is the centre of enlargement. Draw the image of △ABC under an enlargement scale factor 2.

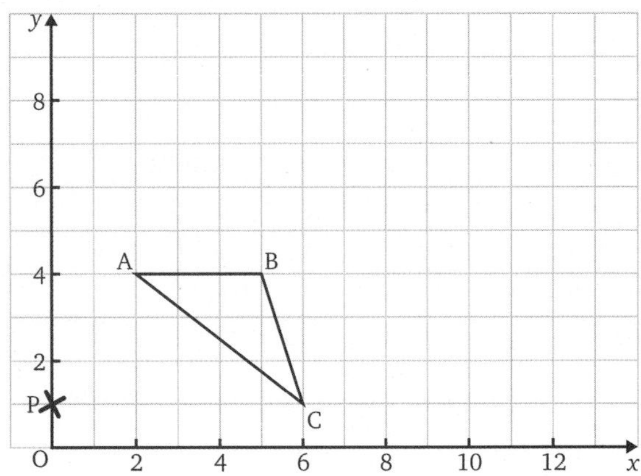

2 Repeat question **1** using this diagram.

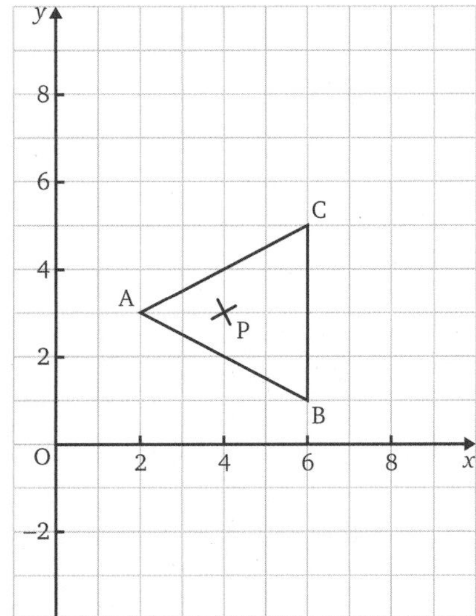

In questions **3** to **6**, draw axes for x and y from 0 to 10, using 1 cm as 1 unit. In each case, find the image A′B′C′ of △ABC using the given enlargement. Check by measuring the lengths of the sides of the two triangles.

3 △ABC: A(3, 3), B(6, 2), C(5, 6).

Enlargement with centre (5, 4) and scale factor 2.

4 △ABC: A(1, 2), B(3, 2), C(1, 5).

Enlargement with centre (0, 0) and scale factor 2.

What do you notice about the coordinates of A′ compared with those of A?

5 △ABC: A(2, 1), B(4, 1), C(3, 4).
Enlargement with centre (1, 1) and scale factor 3.

6 △ABC: A(1, 2), B(7, 2), C(1, 6).
Enlargement with centre (1, 2) and scale factor $1\frac{1}{2}$.

7 On plain paper, mark a point P near the left-hand edge. Draw a small object (a pin man perhaps, or a square house) between P and the middle of the page. Using the method of enlargement, draw the image of the object with centre P and scale factor 2.

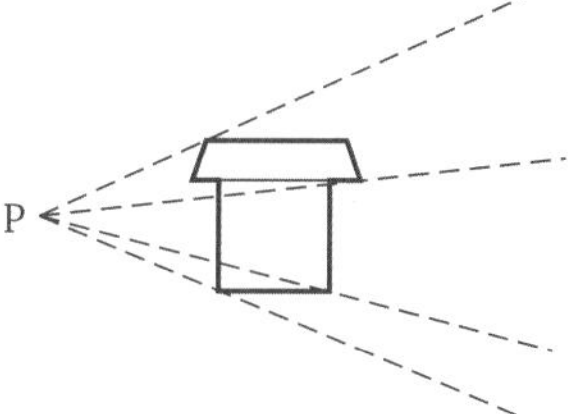

8 Repeat question **7** with other objects and other scale factors. Think carefully about the space you will need for the image.

9 Draw axes for x and y from 0 to 10 using 1 cm as 1 unit. Draw △ABC with A(2, 2), B(5, 1) and C(3, 4). Taking the origin as the centre of enlargement and a scale factor of 2, draw the image of △ABC by counting squares and without drawing the guidelines.

10 Draw axes for x and y from 0 to 8 using 1 cm as 1 unit. Draw △ABC with A(1, 2), B(5, 2) and C(2, 5). Taking (3, 2) as the centre of enlargement and a scale factor of 2, draw the image △ABC by counting squares and without drawing the guidelines.

Puzzle

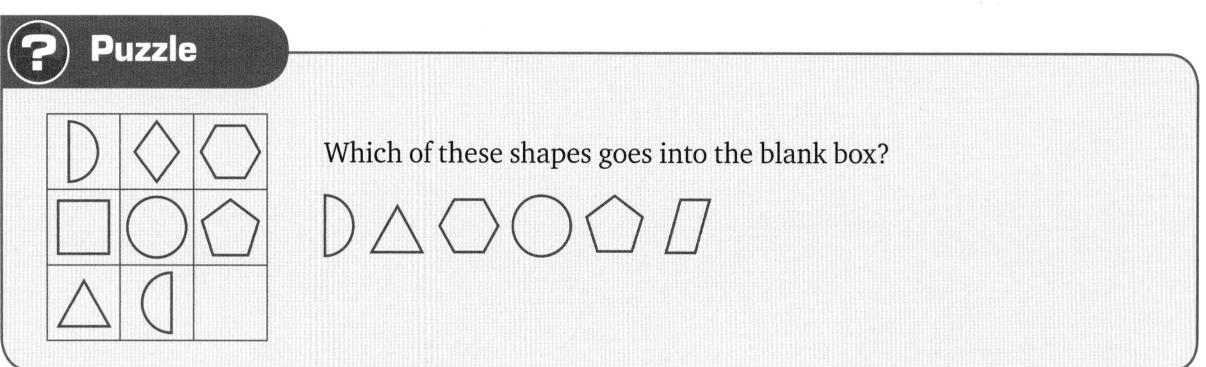

Which of these shapes goes into the blank box?

Fractional scale factors

We can reverse the process of enlargement and shrink or reduce the object, producing a smaller image. If the lengths of the image are one-third of the lengths of the object, then the scale factor is $\frac{1}{3}$.

There is no satisfactory word to cover both enlargement and shrinking (some people use 'dilation' and some 'scaling') so *enlargement* tends to be used for both. An enlargement may therefore be defined as a transformation which maps an object onto an image of similar shape. If the scale factor is less than 1, the image is smaller than the object. If the scale factor is greater than 1, the image is larger than the object.

Exercise 5d

In questions **1** to **4**, △A′B′C′ is the image of △ABC. Give the centre of enlargement and the scale factor.

1

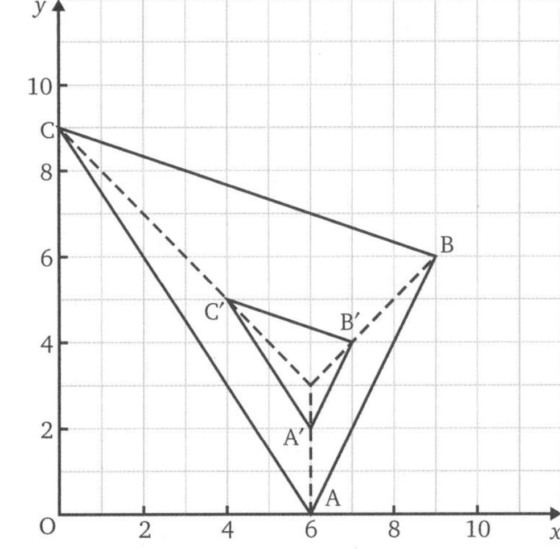

To find the scale factor, find the length of a side on the image as a fraction of the length of the corresponding side on the object.

2

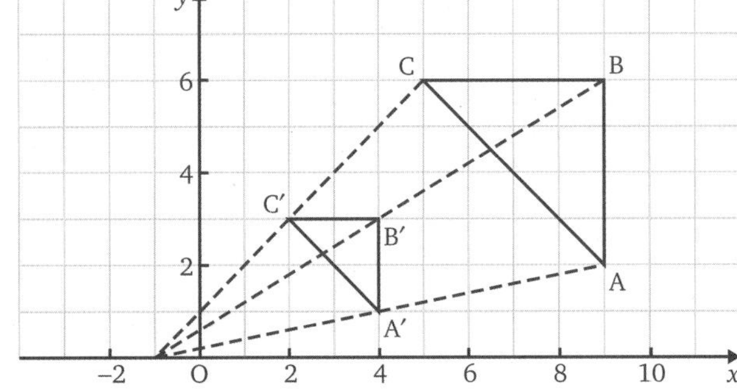

3 Draw axes for x and y from –2 to 8 using 1 cm as 1 unit. Draw △ABC with A(–1, 4), B(5, 1) and C(5, 7), and △A′B′C′ with A′(2, 4), B′(4, 3) and C′(4, 5).

4 Draw axes for x and y from 0 to 9 using 1 cm as 1 unit. Draw △ABC with A(1, 2), B(9, 2) and C(9, 6), and △A′B′C′ with A′(1, 2), B′(5, 2) and C′(5, 4).

In questions **5** and **6**, draw axes for x and y from -1 to 11 using 1 cm as 1 unit. Find the image of $\triangle$ABC under the given enlargement.

5 $\triangle$ABC: A(9, 1), B(11, 5), C(7, 7). Centre $(-1, 1)$, scale factor $\frac{1}{2}$.

6 $\triangle$ABC: A(4, 0), B(10, 9), C(1, 6). Centre (4, 3), scale factor $\frac{1}{3}$.

Exercise 5e

Select the letter that gives the correct answer.

Use this diagram for questions **1** and **2**.

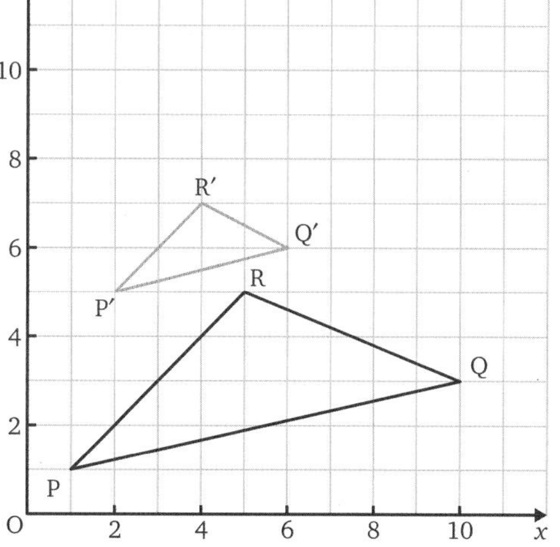

1 Triangle P′Q′R′ is the image of triangle PQR under an enlargement.

Join PP′, QQ′ and RR′. These lines show that the coordinates of the centre of enlargement are

A (3, 8) **C** (4, 8)

B (3, 9) **D** (4, 9)

2 The scale factor that enlarges triangle PQR to triangle P′Q′R′ is

A $\frac{1}{4}$ **B** $\frac{1}{3}$ **C** $\frac{1}{2}$ **D** $\frac{2}{3}$

Use this diagram for questions **3** and **4**.

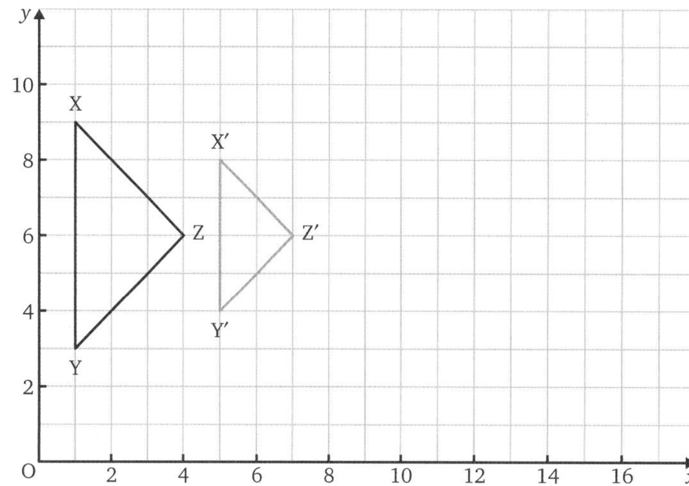

3 Triangle X′Y′Z′ is the image of triangle XYZ under an enlargement. The coordinates of the centre of enlargement are

A (12, 6) **B** (13, 6) **C** (14, 6) **D** (15, 6)

4 The scale factor that enlarges triangle XYZ to triangle X′Y′Z′ is

A $\frac{1}{3}$ **B** $\frac{1}{2}$ **C** $\frac{2}{3}$ **D** $\frac{3}{2}$

Investigation

Daniel designs packaging. The sketch shows a design that will fold to make a package suitable for sending books of various sizes by post. The design can be produced in several different sizes if it is enlarged by a given scale factor.

The basic rectangle is divided into six smaller rectangles, marked A, B, C, D, E and F on the sketch. It is cut along the heavy lines and fold marks are pressed into it along the broken lines.

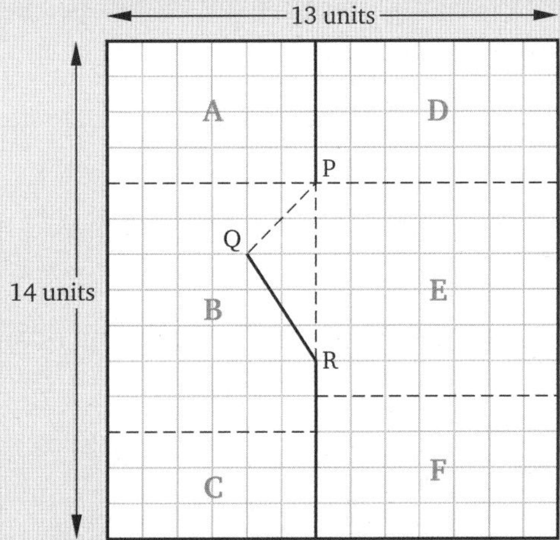

By folding along PQ and PR, you will find that rectangle B now fits over rectangle E and this acts as the base of the package. The remaining four rectangles fold up and over, allowing books of different thicknesses to be packed.

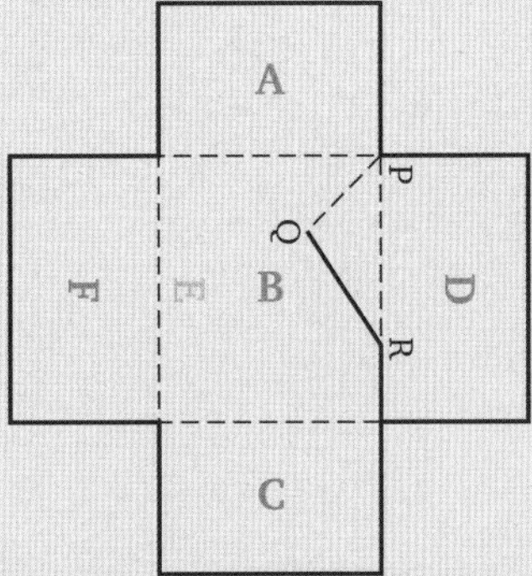

1 On 5 mm squared paper, draw an enlargement of the diagram with a scale factor of 2.

2 Cut it out and fold it to show how it is used.

3 If you have a much larger sheet of paper or card, repeat parts **1** and **2** using a larger scale factor, for example, 4.

4 **a** Can the fold PQ be drawn at any angle?

  b Can the cut QR be made at any angle?

  Give reasons for your answers.

5 What is the ratio of the length of the original rectangle to its breadth?

  If you alter this ratio, can you still make a satisfactory package?

  Investigate.

6 Can you improve on the design?

In this chapter you have seen that...

- ✔ to find the centre of enlargement, you can draw guidelines between corresponding points on the object and the image
- ✔ you can find the scale factor by comparing lengths of corresponding sides on the object and the image
- ✔ to find an image of a given shape under an enlargement you need the scale factor and centre of enlargement
- ✔ a scale factor less than 1 gives an image smaller than the object whereas a scale factor larger than 1 gives an image larger than the object.

6 Scale drawing

At the end of this chapter you should be able to...

1 draw a given shape to scale
2 identify angles of elevation or depression
3 make and use scale drawings to find distances or heights, given an angle of elevation or depression
4 understand the relationship between the scale factor and the effect on areas and volumes.

You need to know...

✔ how to use a ruler, a protractor and a pair of compasses
✔ the angle sum of a triangle
✔ the sum of angles round a point
✔ how to construct triangles, perpendicular lines and angles of 30°, 45°, 60° and 90°
✔ the meaning of scale factor
✔ how to convert between metric units of length, of area and of volume.

Key words

angle of depression, angle of elevation, protractor, rectangular, scale, scale drawing, triangular

Scale drawing

An architect uses a computer to make an accurate drawing of a building before it is built. Everything is shown much smaller than it will be in the completed building, but it is all carefully drawn to scale so that all the proportions are correct.

Likewise a motor engineer makes accurate drawings when he or she designs small parts for a new car. However, these drawings usually show small components much larger than they will be when they are made.

In these, as in many other occupations, *scale drawings* are essential to produce high-quality products.

Activity

This is a class discussion.

1 Discuss other occupations in which accurate drawings are used. Say whether each occupation tends to make scale drawings that show each object larger or smaller than the finished product.

2 If you had a map of your area within 20 miles of where you live, and the scale was not given, would you be able to decide how far one place was from another?

Would you give the same answer if the map was of a foreign country where you wanted to take a holiday?

3 What information do you think is needed on any scale drawing?

Accurate drawing with scaled down measurements

If you are asked to draw a parking lot that is a rectangle measuring 50 m by 25 m, you obviously cannot draw it full size. To fit it on to your page you will have to scale down the measurements. In this case you could use 1 cm to represent 5 m on the parking lot. This is called the *scale*; it is usually written as 1 cm ≡ 5 m, and must *always* be stated on any scale drawing.

Exercise 6a

Start by making a rough drawing of the object you are asked to draw to scale. Mark all the full-size measurements on your sketch. Next draw another sketch and put the scaled measurements on this one. Then do the accurate scale drawing. Always give the scale on your drawing.

The end wall of a bungalow is a rectangle with a triangular top. The rectangle measures 6 m wide by 3 m high. The base of the triangle is 6 m and the sloping sides are 4 m long. Using a scale of 1 cm to 1 m, make a scale drawing of this wall. Use your drawing to find, to the nearest tenth of a metre, the distance from the ground to the ridge of the roof.

Rough sketch of wall to give measurements

Rough sketch of scale drawing with scale measurements

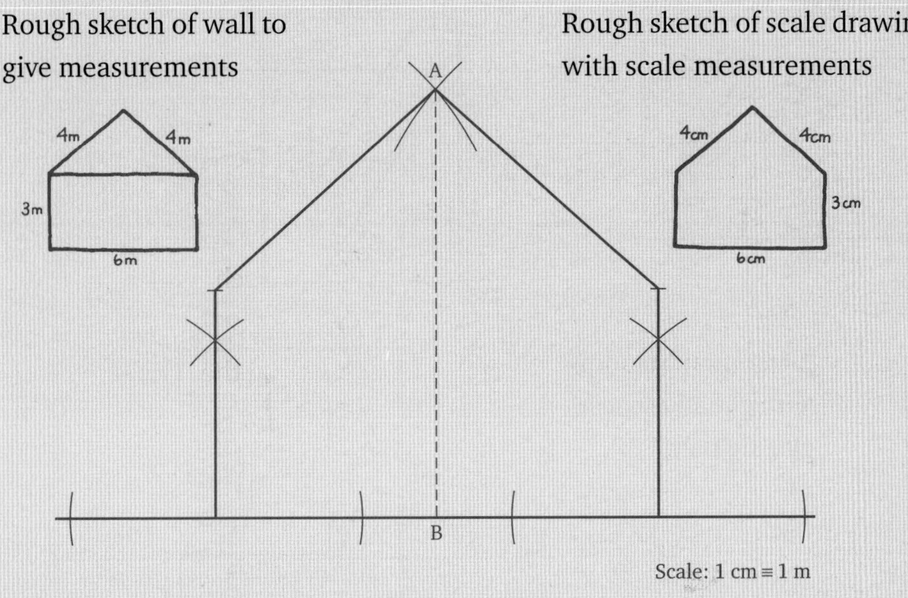

From the drawing, AB measures 5.6 cm.

So the height of the wall is $5.6 \times 1\text{ m} = 5.6\text{ m}$.

In questions **1** to **5**, use a scale of 1 cm to 1 m to make a scale drawing.

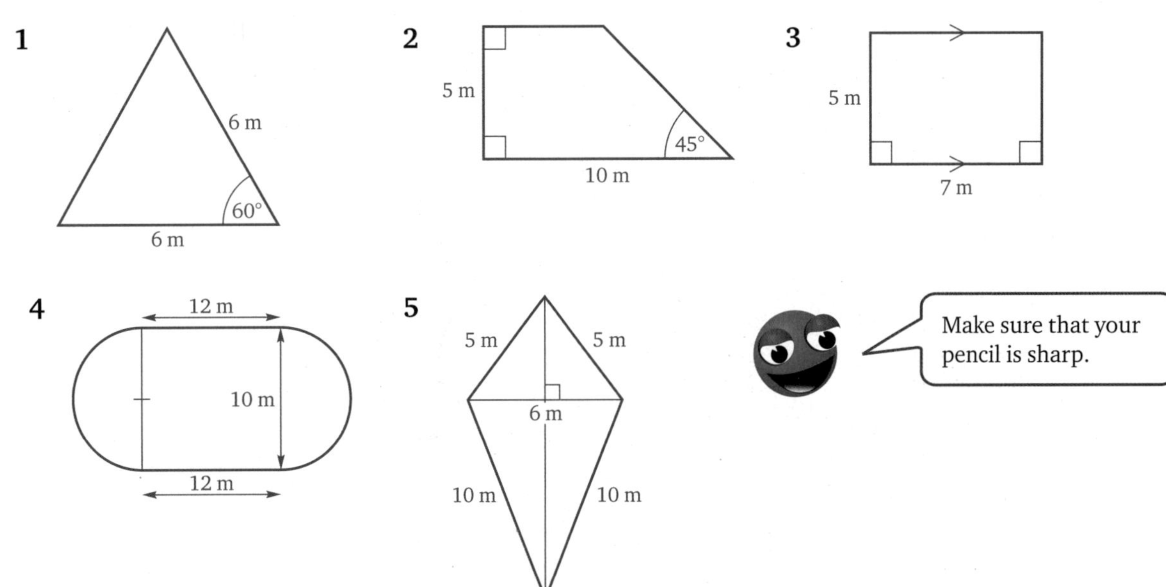

In questions **6** to **10**, choose your own scale.

Choose a scale that gives lines that are long enough to draw easily; in general, the lines on your drawing should be at least 5 cm long. Avoid scales that give lengths involving awkward fractions of a centimetre, such as thirds; $\frac{1}{3}$ cm cannot easily be read from your ruler.

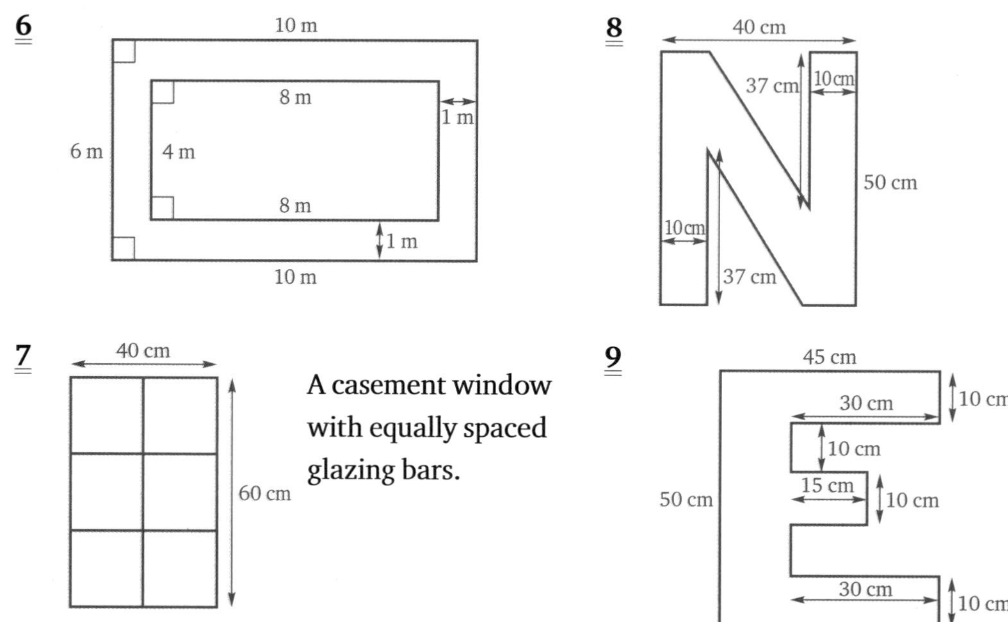

10 A rectangular door with four rectangular panels, each 35 cm by 70 cm, and 10 cm from the edges of the door.

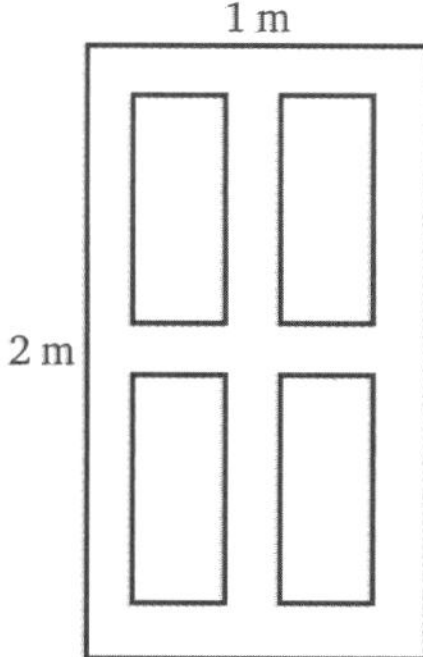

11 A field is rectangular in shape. It measures 300 m by 400 m. A land drain goes in a straight line from one corner of the field to the opposite corner. Using a scale of 1 cm to 50 m, make a scale drawing of the field and use it to find the length of the land drain.

12 The end wall of a ridge tent is a triangle. The base is 2 m and the sloping edges are each 2.5 m. Using a scale of 1 cm to 0.5 m, make a scale drawing of the triangular end of the tent and use it to find the height of the tent.

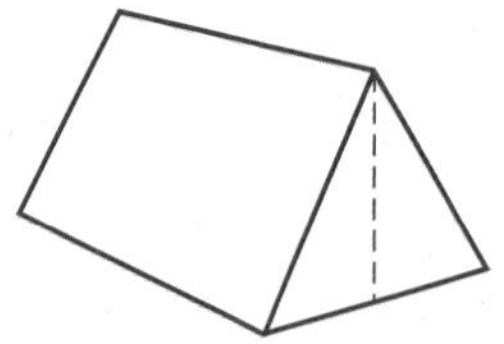

13 The surface of a swimming pool is a rectangle measuring 25 m by 10 m. Choose your own scale and make a scale drawing of the pool. Now compare and discuss your drawing with other pupils.

14 The whole class working together can collect the information for this question. Measure your classroom and make a rough sketch of the floor plan. Mark the position and width of doors and windows. Choosing a suitable scale, make an accurate scale drawing of the floor plan of your classroom.

Scale drawings without measurements

Exercise 6b

This is a scale drawing of Sally's kitchen.

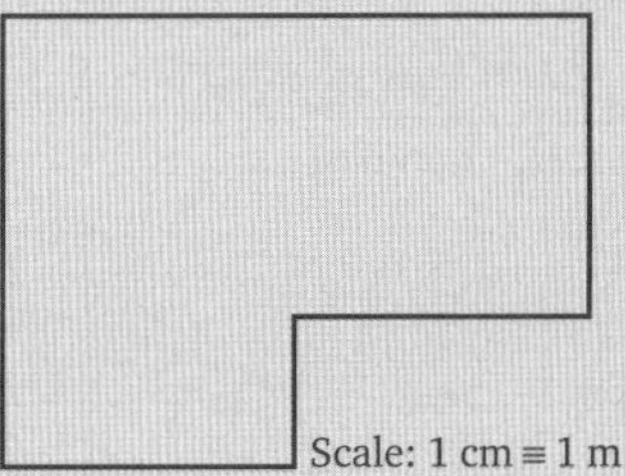

a How long, in centimetres, on the drawing, is Sally's kitchen?

b How long is the actual kitchen?

c How wide, in centimetres, on the drawing is the kitchen at its widest point?

d How wide is the actual kitchen?

a The length of the drawing of the kitchen is 4 cm.

b Since 1 cm represents 1 m, the length of the actual kitchen is 4×1 m, i.e. 4 m.

c The width of the kitchen in the drawing at its widest point is 3 cm.

d The width of the actual kitchen is $3 \times 1\text{ m} = 3\text{ m}$.

1 This is a scale drawing of Joe's lounge.

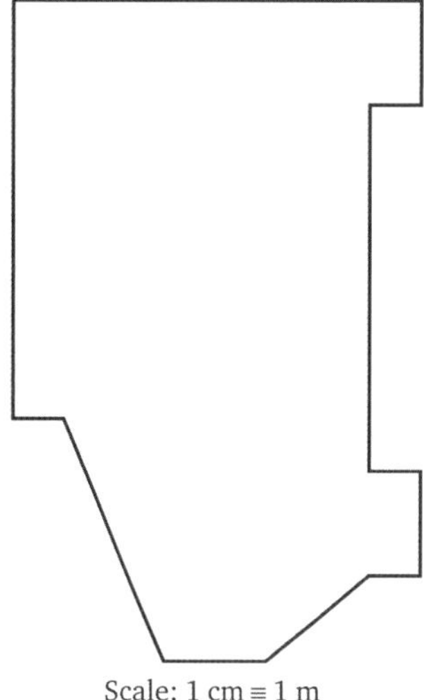

Scale: 1 cm ≡ 1 m

a On the drawing, how long is the room, in centimetres, from the back wall to the front of the bay window?

b How far is it in the actual room from the back wall to the front of the bay window?

c How wide is the room on the drawing at the widest point?

d What is the actual width of the room?

2 This is a scale drawing of one of the set of metal plates needed to manufacture an HK180 earth-moving machine.

What is the actual measurement of

a the length of the plate

b the diameter of one of the small holes

c the radius of the large hole?

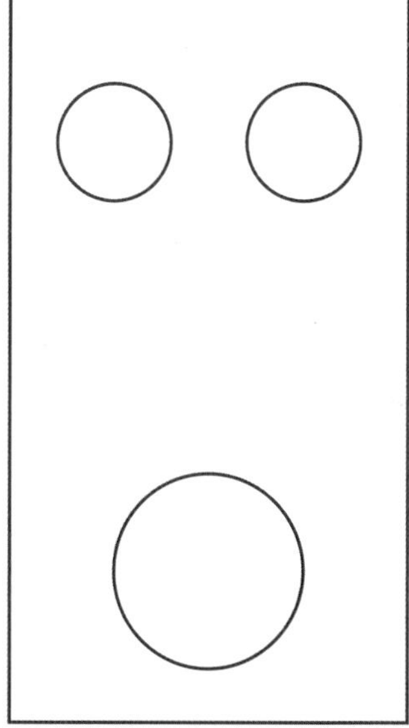

Scale: 1 cm ≡ 5 cm

3 These are scale drawings for the goalposts on the soccer and rugby pitches at Windford Recreation Ground.

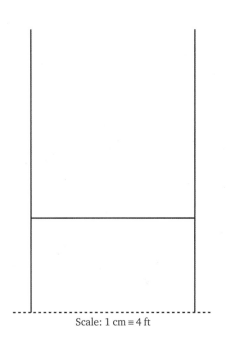

a On the drawing, how wide, in centimetres, are the goalposts for
   i soccer   ii rugby?

b How far apart are the actual posts for
   i soccer   ii rugby?

c How high is each crossbar actually above the ground?

d How high is one of the rugby posts at the Recreation Ground?

4

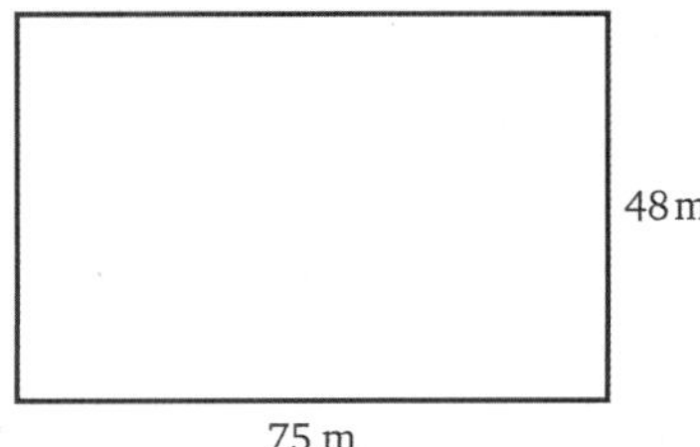

This sketch is of an area of ground that is to be laid with tarmac. It is required to make a scale drawing of the area using a scale of 1 cm to represent 5 m.

a How long should the rectangle be in the drawing?

b How wide should it be?

5 Given here is a scale drawing of the ground floor of a house. Each square of the grid has a side of 1 cm and represents 1 m.

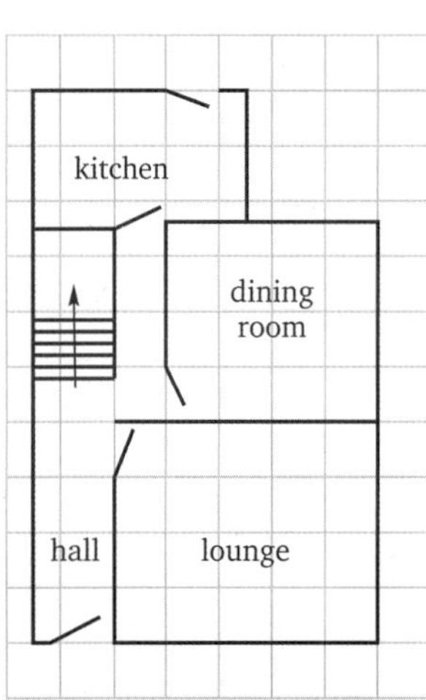

a Find the actual length and breadth of
   i the lounge   ii the dining room.

b How wide is the actual hall at its widest part?

c What is the actual area of the lounge?
   How much would it cost to carpet at $130 a square metre?

6

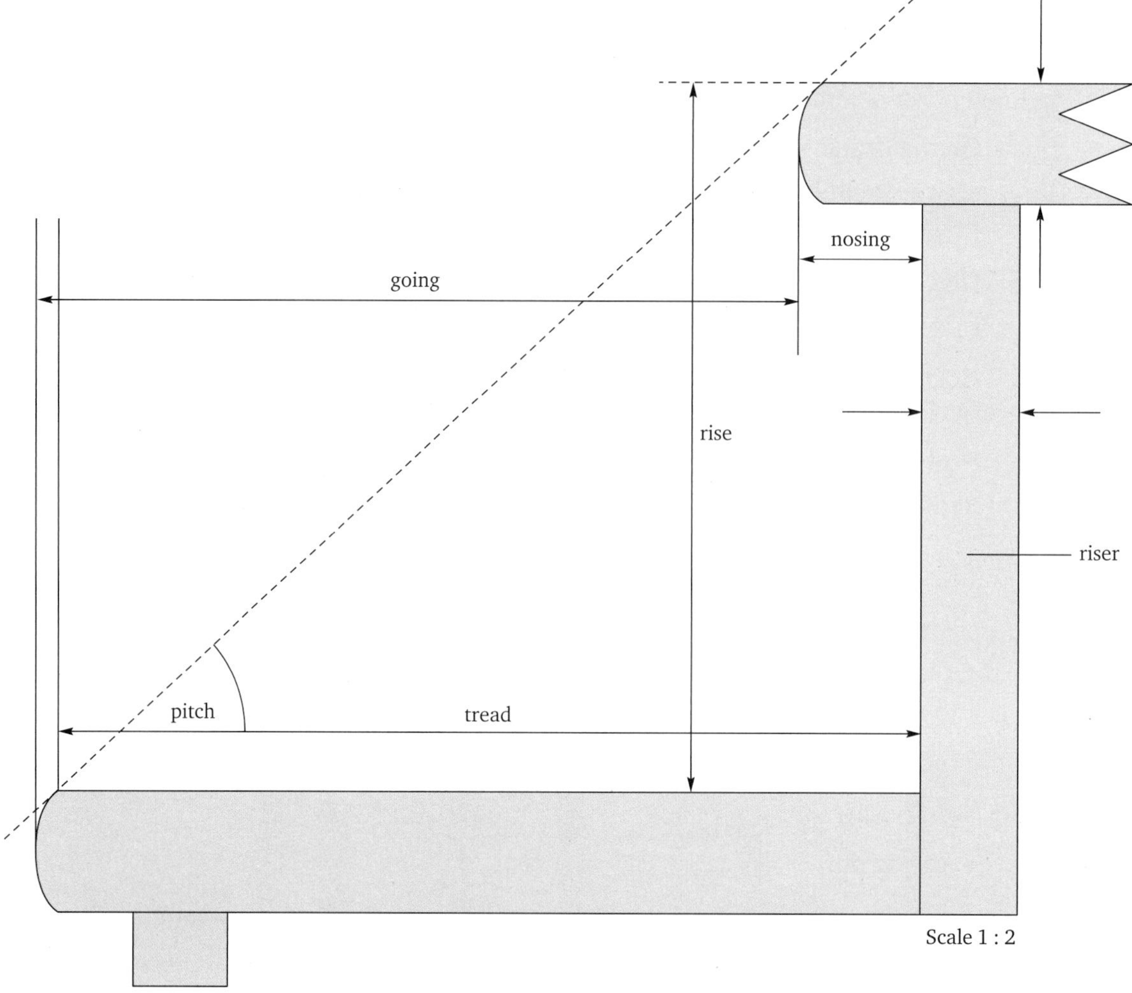

This is an accurate drawing, drawn half-size, of the cross-section of part of a domestic staircase.

a Use the drawing to find the actual length of

i the tread **ii** the rise **iii** the going **iv** the nosing.

b What thickness of timber has been used for

i the tread **ii** the riser?

c A safety regulation states that the sum of the going plus twice the rise must be more than 500 mm but less than 700 mm. Do these stairs satisfy this regulation?

d The maximum permitted pitch of a staircase is 42°. Use your protractor to check whether or not this staircase complies with the regulation.

Investigation

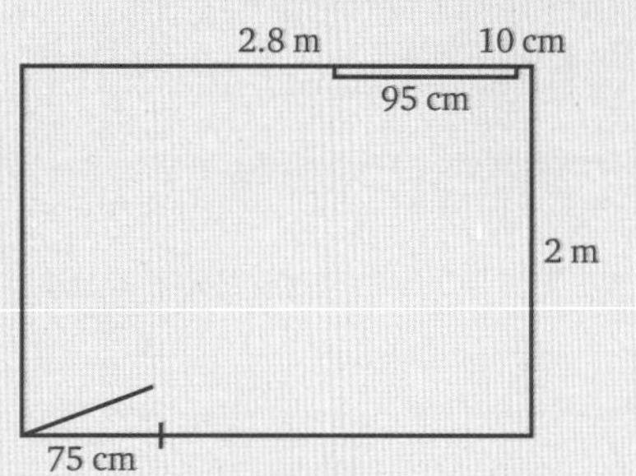

The sketch shows the measurements of Ken's bathroom. There is only one outside wall and the bottom of the window is 120 cm above the level of the floor. Draw an accurate diagram of the floor, using a scale of 1 cm to 10 cm.

Ken wants a new bathroom suite. The units he would like to install, together with their measurements, are:

- bath: 170 cm × 75 cm
- handbasin: 60 cm × 42 cm, the longest edge against a wall
- shower tray: 80 cm square
- toilet: 70 cm × 50 cm, the shorter measurement against a wall
- bidet: 55 cm × 35 cm, the shorter measurement against a wall.

Using the same scale make accurate drawings of the plans of these units, then cut them out and see if you can place them on your plan in acceptable positions.

If they will not all fit into the room, which unit(s) would you be prepared to do without? Give reasons for your answer.

Is it possible to arrange your chosen units so that all the plumbing is

1 against the outside wall

2 not on more than two walls at right angles, one of which is the outside wall?

Illustrate your answer with a diagram.

Map ratio (or representative fraction)

Remember that the map ratio of a map is the ratio of a length on the map to the length it represents on the ground. This ratio or fraction is given on most maps in addition to the scale.

Two towns are 40 km apart.

On a map this distance is 20 cm so the map ratio is

$$\begin{aligned} 20\,\text{cm} : 40\,\text{km} &= 20\,\text{cm} : 4\,000\,000\,\text{cm} \\ &= 1 : 200\,000 \end{aligned}$$

So the map ratio is 1 : 200 000.

Any length on the ground is 200 000 times the corresponding length on the map.

Exercise 6c

1

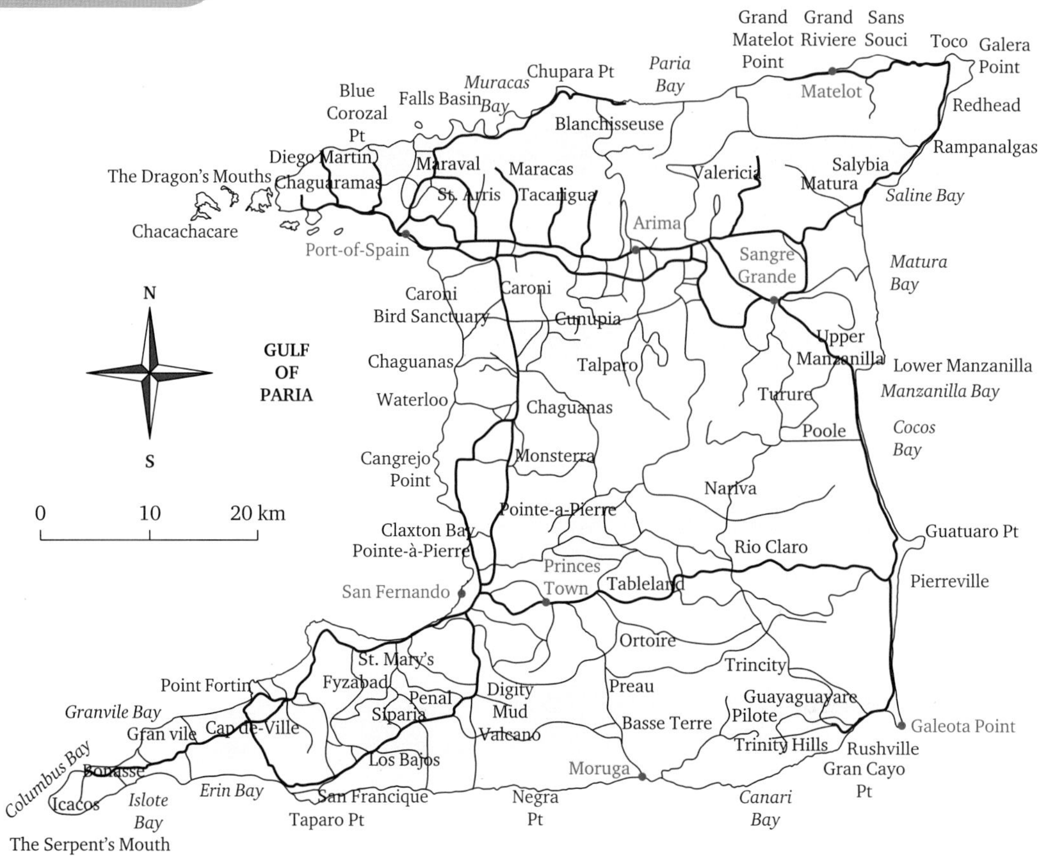

Use this map of Trinidad and the given scale to find

a the representative fraction for this map

b the distance from Port-of-Spain to Arima

c the distance from Princes Town to Port-of-Spain

d the distance from Galeota Point to Princes Town

e the distance from San Fernando to Sangre Grande.

On a map the area of a park is $2.4\,\text{cm}^2$. The scale of the map is $1:20\,000$.

Find the actual area of the park in hectares.

1 cm on the map represents 20 000 cm

so $1\,\text{cm}^2$ on the map represents $20\,000 \times 20\,000\,\text{cm}^2$ on the ground

$$1\,\text{cm}^2 = \frac{20\,000}{100} \times \frac{20\,000}{100}\,\text{m}^2$$

$$= 200 \times 200\,\text{m}^2$$

$$= 40\,000\,\text{m}^2$$

$$2.4\,\text{cm}^2 = 2.4 \times 40\,000\,\text{m}^2$$

$$= \frac{96\,000}{10\,000}\,\text{hectares} \qquad (1\text{ hectare} = 10\,000\,\text{m}^2)$$

$$= 9.6\,\text{hectares}$$

2 On a map the area of a piece of land is $7.2\,\text{cm}^2$. The scale of the map is $1:10\,000$. What is the actual area of the land in hectares?

3 The scale of the map is $1:50\,000$.

  a Find the actual distance between two places that are 15 cm apart on the map.

  b The area of a farm is 100 hectares. What is its area on the map?

4 The scale of the map is $1:50\,000$.

  a Find the actual distance between two places that are 4.8 cm apart on the map.

  b On the map the area of an airfield is $11.2\,\text{cm}^2$.

  Find, in square kilometres, the actual area of the airfield.

5 The scale of the model of a building is 5 cm to 150 metres.

  a Find this scale in the form $1:n$

  b How high is the building if the height of the model is 6.4 cm?

  c The area of one wall of the building is $1600\,\text{m}^2$.
  What is the area of this wall on the model?

Angles of elevation

If you are standing on level ground and can see a tall building, you will have to look up to see the top of that building.

If you start by looking straight ahead and then look up to the top of the building, the angle through which you raise your eyes is called the *angle of elevation* of the top of the building.

There are instruments for measuring angles of elevation. A simple one can be made from a large card protractor and a piece of string with a weight on the end.

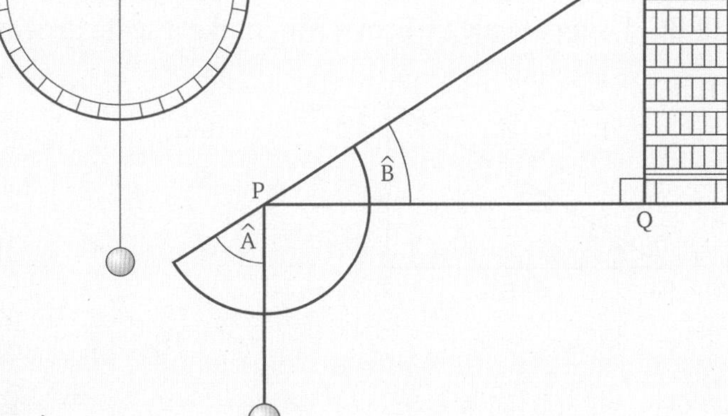

You can read the size of $\hat{A}$.

Then the angle of elevation, $\hat{B}$, is given by $\hat{B} = 90° - \hat{A}$.

(Note that this method is not very accurate.)

If your distance from the foot of the building and the angle of elevation of the top are both known, you can make a scale drawing of $\triangle PQR$.

This drawing can then be used to work out the height of the building.

Exercise 6d

From a point A on the ground, 50 m from the base of a tree, the angle of elevation of the top of the tree is 22°. Using a scale of 1 cm ≡ 5 m, make a scale drawing and use it to find the height of the tree.

Rough sketch to give actual measurements

Rough sketch of scale drawing with scale measurements

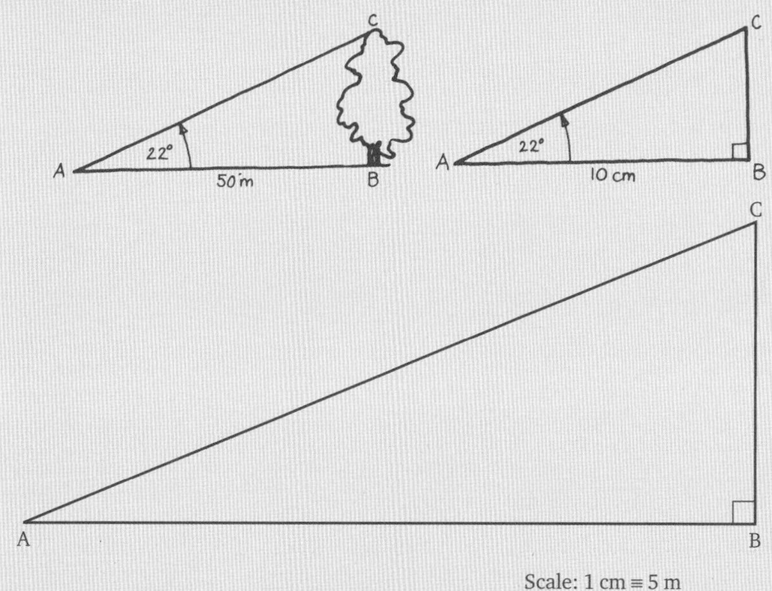

Scale: 1 cm ≡ 5 m

From the diagram, BC = 4 cm.

∴ the tree is 4 × 5 m = 20 m high.

In questions **1** to **4**, A is a place on the ground, $\hat{A}$ is the angle of elevation of C, the top of BC. Using a scale of 1 cm ≡ 5 m, make a scale drawing to find the height of BC.

1

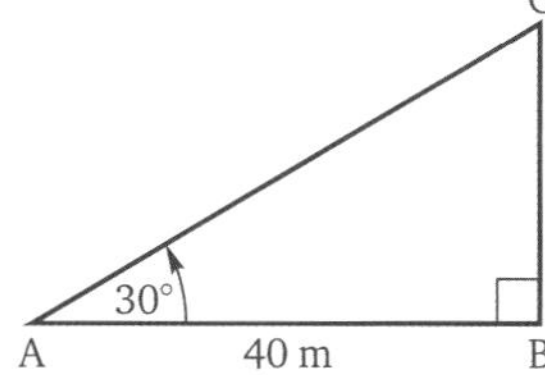

2

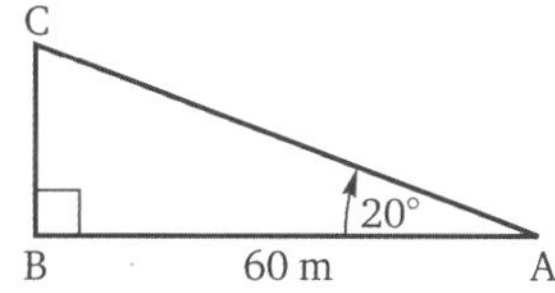

3

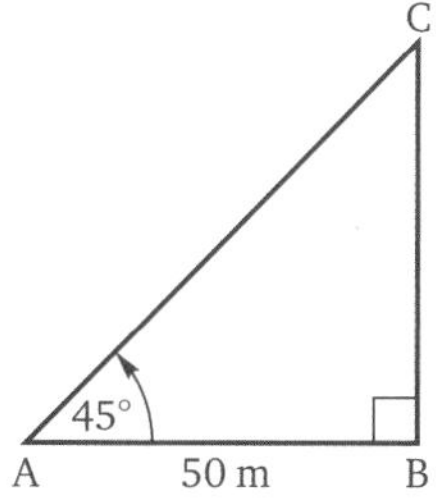

4

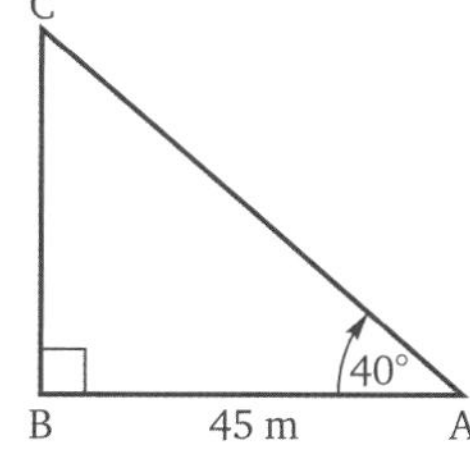

In questions **5** to **7**, use a scale of 1 cm ≡ 10 m.

5 From A, the angle of elevation of C is 35°. Find BC.

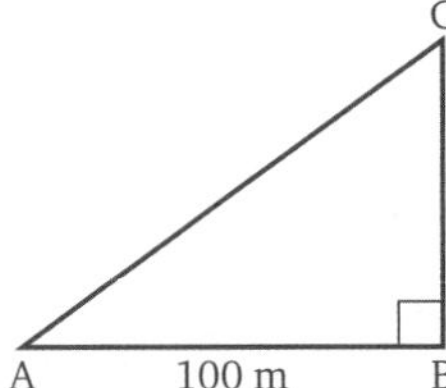

6 From P, the angle of elevation of R is 15°. Find QR.

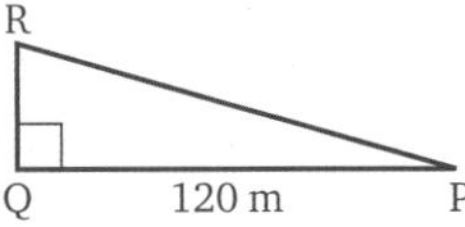

7 From N, the angle of elevation of L is 30°. Find ML.

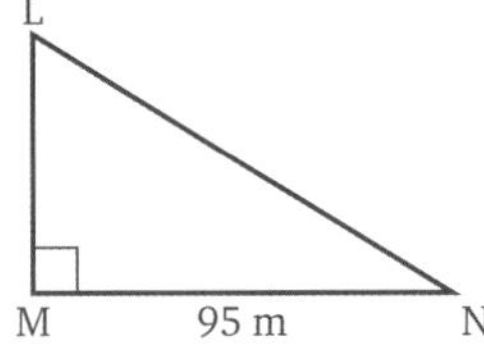

8 From a point D on the ground, 100 m from the foot of a church tower, the angle of elevation of the top of the tower is 30°. Use a scale of 1 cm to 10 m to make a scale drawing. Use your drawing to find the height of the tower.

9 From the opposite side of the road, the angle of elevation of the top of the roof of my house is 37°. The horizontal distance from the point where I measured the angle to the house is 12 m. Make a scale drawing, using a scale of 1 cm to 1 m, and use it to find the height of the top of the roof.

10 From a point P on the ground, 150 m from the base of the Barbados Central Bank, the angle of elevation of the top is 17°. Use a scale of 1 cm to 20 m to make a scale diagram and find the height of the Barbados Central Bank.

11 The top of a radio mast is 76 m from the ground. From a point, P, on the ground, the angle of elevation of the top of the mast is 40°. Use a scale of 1 cm to 10 m to make a scale drawing to find how far away P is from the mast.

You will need to do some calculations before you can do the scale drawing.

Angles of depression

An *angle of depression* is the angle between the line looking straight ahead and the line looking down at an object below you.

If, for example, you are standing on a cliff looking out to sea, the diagram shows the angle of depression of a boat.

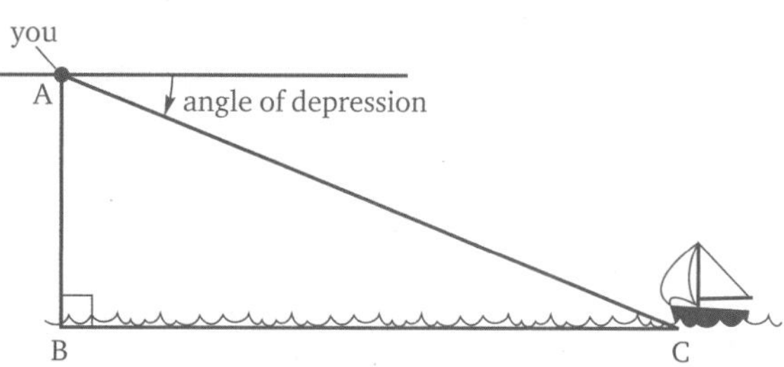

If the angle of depression and the height of the cliff are both known, you can make a scale drawing of △ABC. Then you can work out the distance of the boat from the foot of the cliff.

Exercise 6e

In questions **1** to **4**, use a scale of 1 cm ≡ 10 m to make a scale drawing.

Is your pencil sharp?

1 From A, the angle of depression of C is 25°. Find BC.

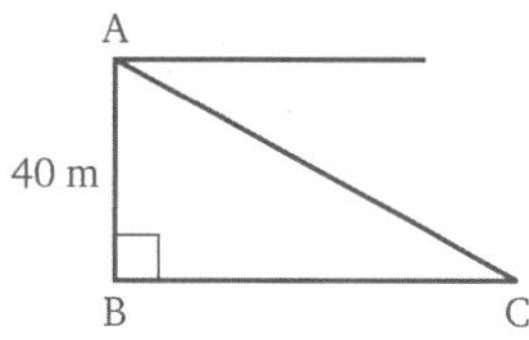

2 From L, the angle of depression of N is 40°. Find MN.

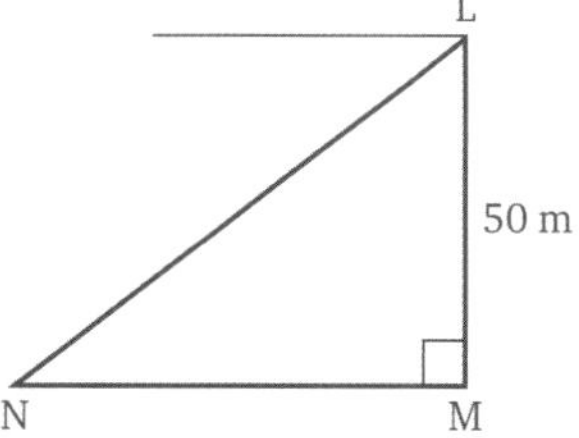

3 From P, the angle of depression of R is 35°. Find RQ.

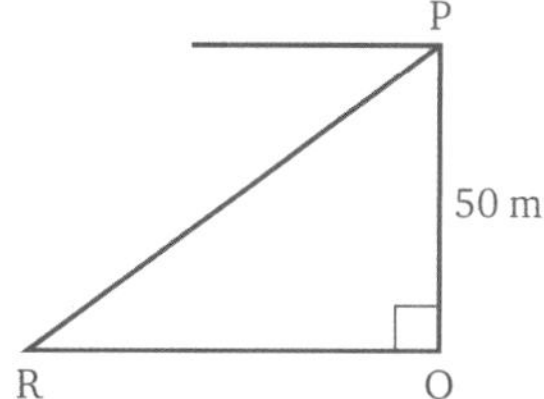

4 From Z, the angle of depression of X is 42°. Find XY.

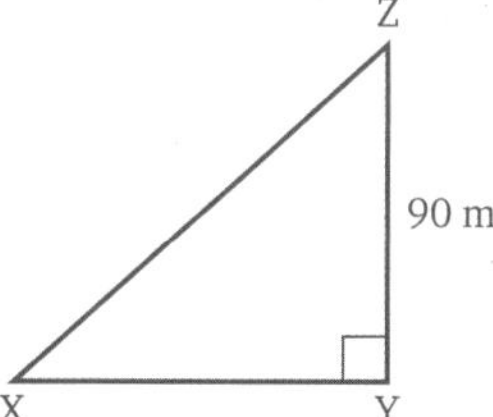

5 From the top of Blackpool Tower, which is in the UK and which is 158 m high, the angle of depression of a ship at sea is 25°. Use a scale of 1 cm to 50 m to make a scale drawing to find the distance of the ship from the base of the tower.

6 From the top of Hackelton's Cliff in Barbados, which is 300 m high, the angle of depression of a house is 20°. Use a scale of 1 cm to 50 m to make a scale drawing and find the distance of the house from the base of the cliff.

7 From the top of a vertical cliff, which is 30 m high, the angle of depression of a yacht is 15°. Using a scale of 1 cm to 5 m, make a scale drawing to find the distance of the yacht from the foot of the cliff.

8 An aircraft flying at a height of 300 m measures the angle of depression of the end of the runway as 18°. Using a scale of 1 cm to 100 m, make a scale diagram to find the horizontal distance of the aircraft from the runway.

9 The Sears Tower in Chicago is an office building and it is 443 m high. From the top of this tower, the angle of depression of a ship on a lake is 40°. How far away from the base of the building is the ship? Use a scale of 1 cm to 50 m to make your scale drawing.

For the remaining questions in this exercise, make a scale drawing choosing your own scale.

10 From a point on the ground 60 m away, the angle of elevation of the top of a factory chimney is 42°. Find the height of the chimney.

11 From the top of a hill, which is 400 m above sea level, the angle of depression of a boathouse is 20°. The boathouse is at sea level. Find the distance of the boathouse from the top of the hill.

12 An aircraft flying at 5000 m measures the angle of depression of a point on the coast as 30°. At the moment that it measures the angle, how much further has the plane to fly before passing over the coastline?

13 A vertical radio mast is 250 m high. From a point A on the ground, the angle of elevation of the top of the mast is 30°. How far is the point A from the foot of the mast?

14 An automatic lighthouse is stationed 500 m from a point, A, on the coast. There are high cliffs at A and from the top of these cliffs, the angle of depression of the lighthouse is 15°. How high are the cliffs?

15 An airport controller measures the angle of elevation of an approaching aircraft as 20°. If the aircraft is then 1.6 km from the control building, at what height is it flying?

16 A surveyor standing 400 m from the foot of a church tower, on level ground, measures the angle of elevation of the top of the tower. If this angle is 35° how high is the tower?

Puzzle

What number should go in the centre of the last cross?

	6	
6	25	4
	5	

	8	
7	18	3
	11	

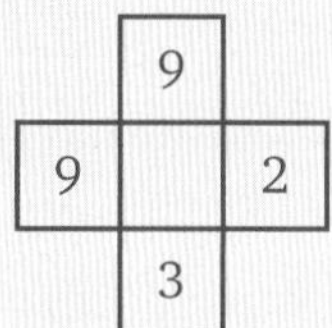

Enlargement and the effect on areas and volumes

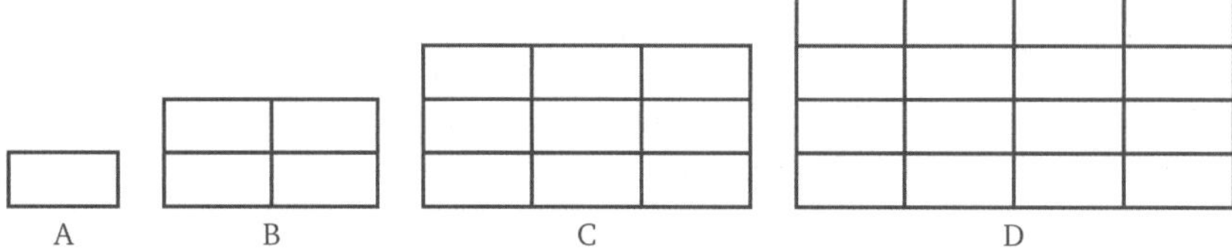

Look at these four rectangles. They are all exactly the same shape (we say they are similar).

The lengths of the sides of rectangle B are twice as long as those of rectangle A, so the scale factor to enlarge A to B is 2.

Comparing the areas of A and B, we can see that the area of B is 4 (i.e. 2^2) times the area of A.

Similarly, the scale factor to enlarge A to C is 3. The area of C is 9 (i.e. 3^2) times the area of A.

Also the scale factor to enlarge A to D is 4. The area of D is 16 (i.e. 4^2) times the area of A.

In general, when the scale factor to enlarge a shape is x, the area is enlarged by x^2.

Exercise 6f

Using the four rectangles A, B, C and D given above, write down the scale factor when

1 rectangle D is enlarged to be **a** A **b** C

2 rectangle B is enlarged to be **a** D **b** C

3 rectangle C is enlarged to be **a** A **b** B **c** D.

A rectangle R of length 5 cm is enlarged by a scale factor of $\frac{2}{3}$ to rectangle S.

The area of R is 9 cm². Find the area of S.

As the scale factor is $\frac{2}{3}$ the area of S is $\left(\frac{2}{3}\right)^2 \times 9\,\text{cm}^2$

$$= \frac{4}{9} \times \frac{9}{1}\,\text{cm}^2 = 4\,\text{cm}^2$$

In questions **4** to **7** write down the scale factor to enlarge the area of the first shape into the area of the second shape.

4

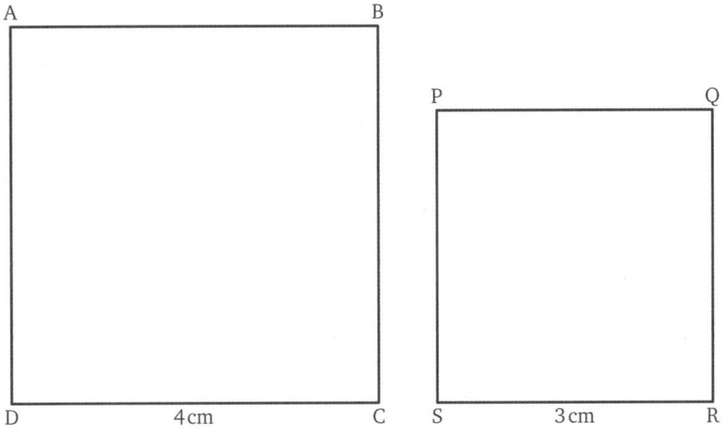

A B P Q

D 4 cm C S 3 cm R

5

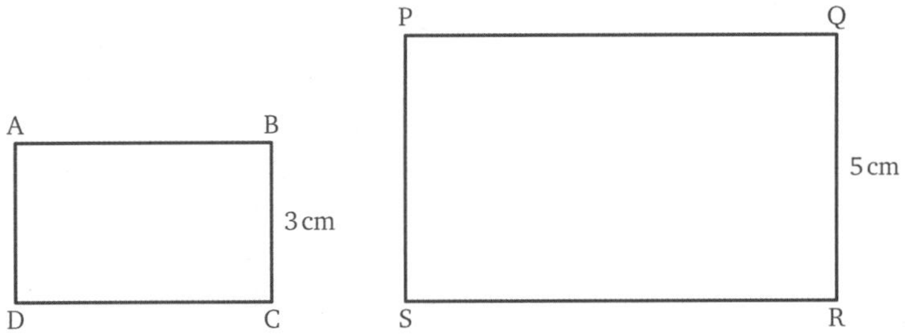

P Q

A B

5 cm

3 cm

D C S R

6

21 cm 14 cm

A B P Q

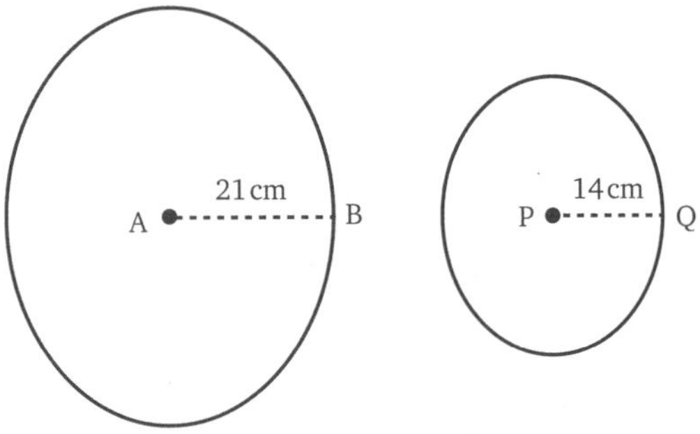

7

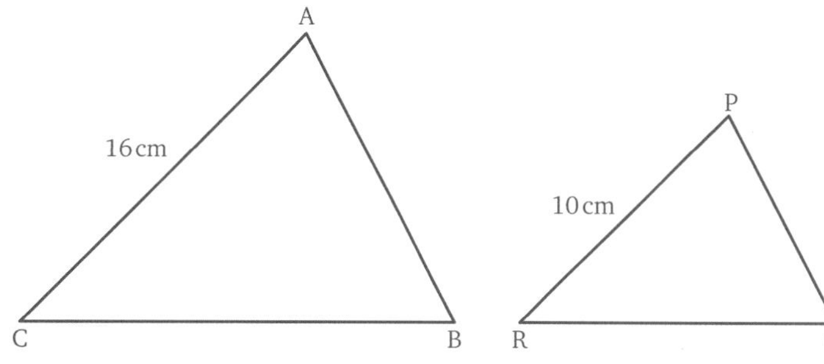

Exercise 6g

Find the scale factor that enlarges the area of ABCD into the area of PQRS.

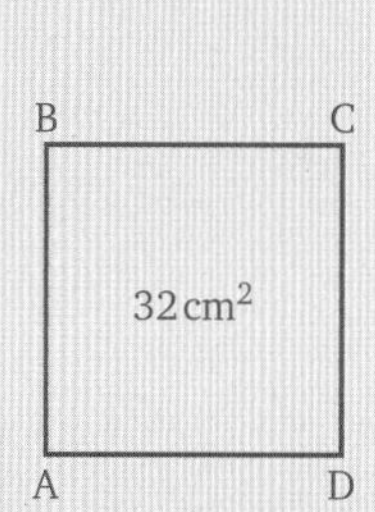

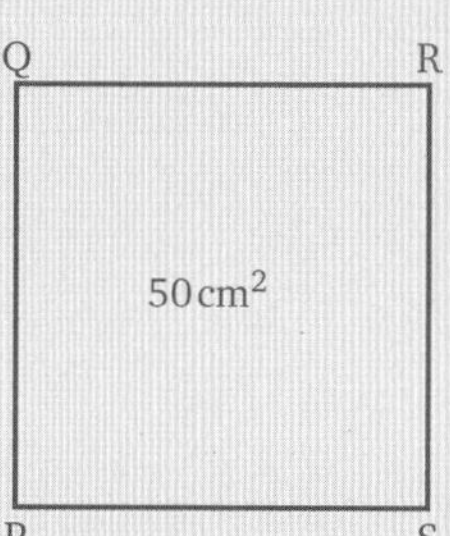

$$\frac{\text{area PQRS}}{\text{area ABCD}} = \frac{50}{32} = \frac{25}{16}$$

But $$\frac{\text{area PQRS}}{\text{area ABCD}} = \frac{PQ^2}{AB^2}$$

Therefore $$\frac{PQ^2}{AB^2} = \frac{25}{16} = \left(\frac{5}{4}\right)^2$$

so the scale factor is $\frac{5}{4}$.

Find the scale factor that enlarges the area of the first shape into the area of the second shape.

1

2

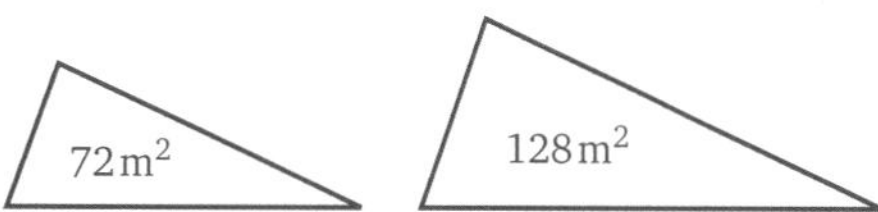

3

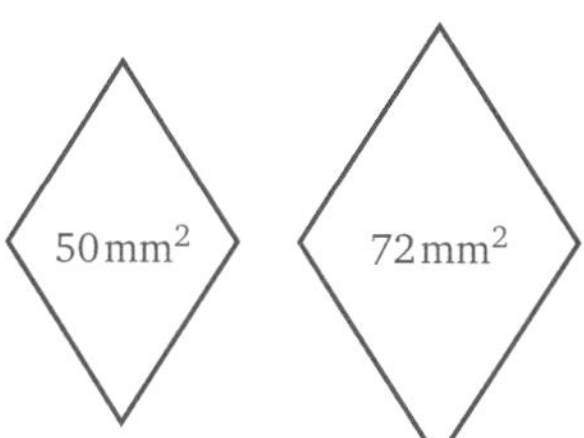

4

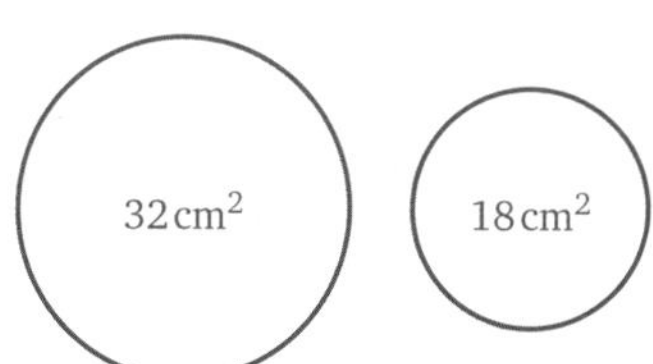

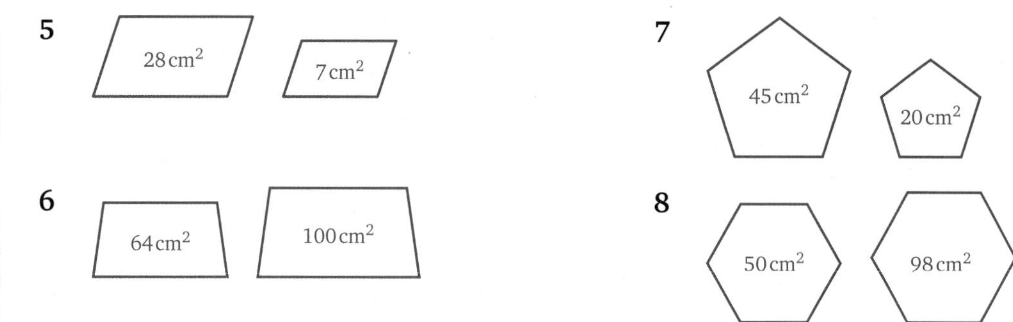

Volumes and scale factor

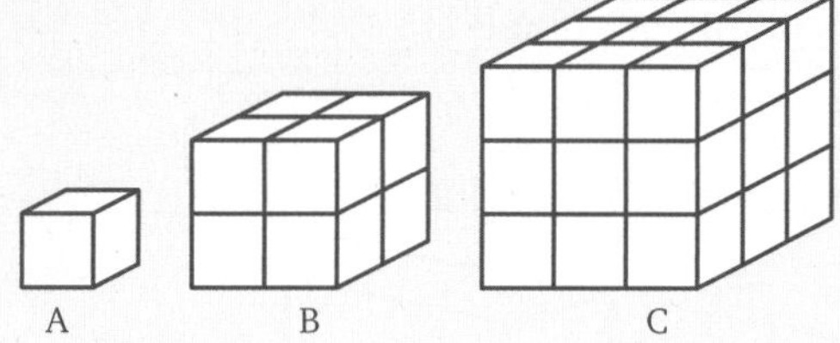

Look at these three cubes.

To enlarge cube A to cube B the edges have been increased by a factor of 2, i.e. the scale factor is 2.

To enlarge cube A to the size of cube B, 8 cubes are needed, so the volume of B is 8 or 2^3 times the volume of A.

Similarly, to enlarge from A to C the scale factor is 3.
The volume of C is 27, i.e. 3^3, times the volume of A.

Hence if one solid is an enlargement of another by a factor a, then the area of any face on the second solid is the area of the face on the first solid times a^2 and the volume the second solid is the volume of the first solid times a^3.

Exercise 6h

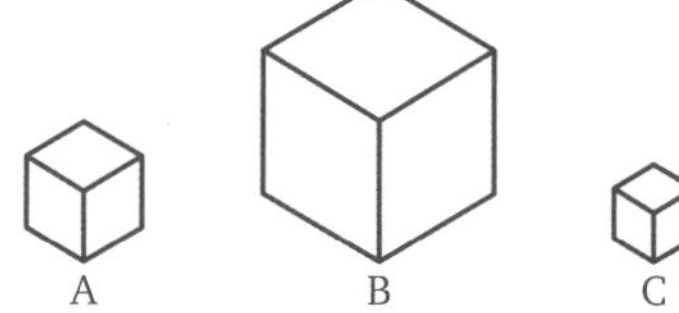

Questions **1** and **2** refer to the three cubes which are shown above.

1 If the scale factor to enlarge cube A to cube B is 2, find

a the length of an edge of B given that an edge of A is

i 2.5 cm **ii** 4 cm

b the area of a face of B given that the area of a face of A is

i $4\,cm^2$ ii $12\,cm^2$

c the volume of cube B if the volume of cube A is

i $9\,cm^3$ ii $20\,cm^3$.

2 The scale factor to enlarge cube B to cube C is $\frac{1}{3}$. Find

a the length of an edge of C given that an edge of B is

i 6 cm ii 8.4 cm

b the area of a face of cube C given that the area of a face of cube B is

i $18\,cm^2$ ii $108\,cm^2$

c the volume of cube C if the volume of cube B is

i $54\,cm^3$ ii $135\,cm^3$.

Questions **3** and **4** refer to the three cuboids P, Q and R.

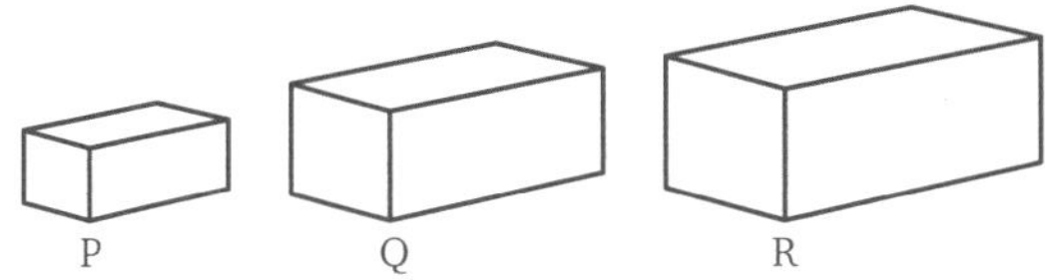

3 If the scale factor to enlarge cuboid P into cuboid Q is 3, find

a the length of the longest edge of cuboid Q given that the longest edge of cuboid P is

i 3 cm ii 20 mm

b the area of one of the smallest faces of cuboid Q given that the area of one of the smallest faces of cuboid P is

i $2\,cm^2$ ii $12\,cm^2$

c the volume of cuboid Q if the volume of cuboid P is

i $1\,cm^3$ ii $5\,cm^3$.

4 If the scale factor to enlarge cuboid R into cuboid P is $\frac{1}{4}$, find

a the length of the longest edge of cuboid P given that the longest edge of cuboid R is

i 9 cm ii 36 mm

b the area of one of the smallest faces of cuboid P given that the area of one of the smallest faces of cuboid R is

i $32\,cm^2$ ii $96\,cm^2$

c the volume of cuboid P if the volume of cuboid R is

i $128\,cm^3$ ii $160\,cm^3$.

5 The scale factor to enlarge cylinder A into cylinder B is $\frac{3}{2}$. Find

a the height of cylinder B if the height of cylinder A is 12 cm

b the height of cylinder A if the height of cylinder B is 24 cm

c the curved surface area of cylinder B if the curved surface area of cylinder A is 20 cm^2

d the area of the circular base of cylinder B if the area of the circular base of cylinder A is 28 cm^2.

6 The scale factor to enlarge cone D into cone E is $\frac{4}{3}$. Find

a the total surface area of cone E if the total surface area of cone D is

i 45 cm^2 ii 72 cm^2

b the volume of cone E if the volume of cone D is

i 54 cm^3 ii 9 m^3.

7 The total surface of a prism is 84 cm^2. The scale factor to enlarge this prism into a larger identically shaped prism is $\frac{5}{2}$. Find the total surface area of the larger prism.

8 A scale factor of a enlarges a prism of volume 80 cm^3 into a prism of volume 270 cm^3. Find the value of a, the scale factor.

9 Two solids with identical shapes have total surface areas of 48 cm^3 and 75 cm^3 respectively. Find the scale factor that enlarges

a the smaller solid into the larger solid

b the larger solid into the smaller solid.

10 Two identically shaped solids have volumes of 162 mm^3 and 48 mm^3. Find the scale factor that 'enlarges' the larger solid into the smaller solid.

Mixed exercises

Exercise 6i

1 Using a scale of 1 cm to 100 cm, make a scale drawing of the figure below. Use your drawing to find the length of the diagonal AC.

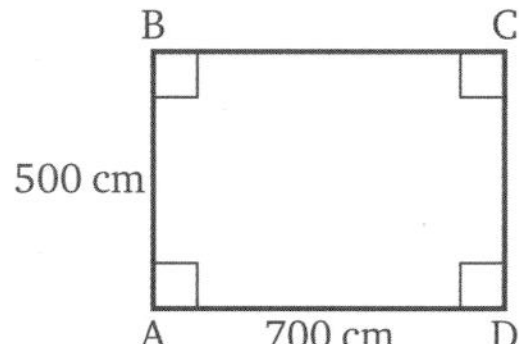

For each of the following questions, make a rough sketch to show all the given information.

2 From the top of a tower which is 150 m tall, the angle of depression of a house is 17°.

3 An aircraft is flying at a height of 2000 m. From a point on the ground its angle of elevation is 40°.

4 An aircraft is flying at a height of 500 m when it measures the angle of depression of the end of the runway as 30°.

Exercise 6j

1 Use a scale of 1 cm to 10 m to make a scale drawing of the figure below. Use your scale drawing to find the length of AC.

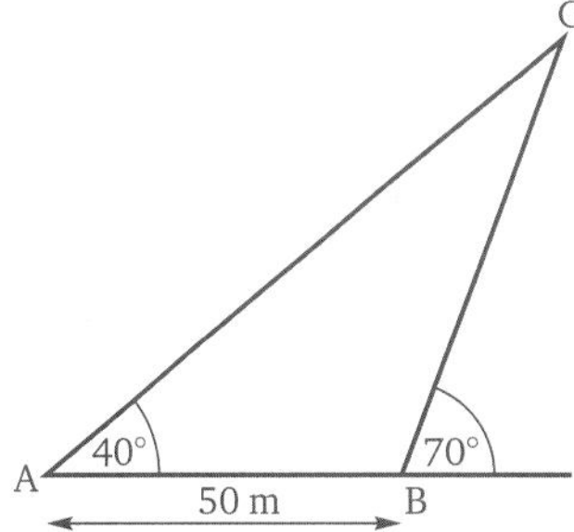

For each of the following questions, make a rough sketch showing all the given information.

2 From a position, A, on the ground, the angle of elevation of the top of an office block is 25°. The office block is 75 m tall.

3 From the top of a cliff which is 50 m high, the angle of depression of a boat is 34°.

4 The scale of a map is 1 : 500. A road on the map is 6 cm long and a field on the map has an area of 20 cm^2. Find the length of the actual road and the area of the actual field.

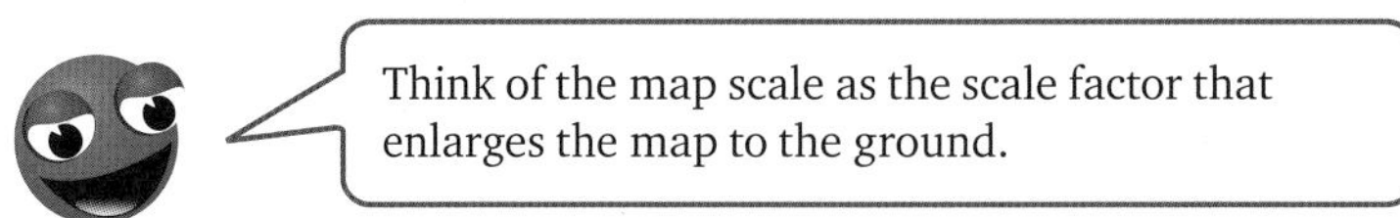

Think of the map scale as the scale factor that enlarges the map to the ground.

Exercise 6k

Select the letter that gives the correct answer.

Questions **1** to **3** refer to the scale drawing of the plan of a house where the scale is 1 cm ≡ 1 metre.

1 On the plan the length of the lounge is 4.5 cm. The actual length of the lounge is

A 2.25 m **B** 4 m **C** 4.5 m **D** 5 m

2 On the plan the width of the lounge is 3 cm. The actual width of the lounge is

A 2.5 m **B** 3 m **C** 3.5 m **D** 6 m

3 On the plan the length of the kitchen is 3.5 cm. The actual length of the kitchen is

A 1.5 m **B** 2.5 m **C** 3 m **D** 3.5 m

4 The map ratio of a map is 1 : 25 000. The distance between two villages that are 3.4 cm apart on the map is

A 2.5 km **B** 3.4 km **C** 3.8 km **D** 6.8 km

5 I am at the top of a cliff. The angle of depression of my brother George, who is standing on the beach below me, is 37°. The angle of elevation of me from where my brother is standing is

A 37° **B** 47° **C** 53° **D** 63°

6 The scale factor to enlarge rectangle A into rectangle B is 4.

How many times larger is the area of rectangle B than the area of rectangle A?

A 4 **B** 8 **C** 12 **D** 16

7 The scale factor to enlarge cube A to cube B is $\frac{1}{3}$. The length of an edge of cube A is 9 cm.

The length of an edge of cube B is

A 3 cm **B** 6 cm **C** 9 cm **D** 27 cm

8 A scale factor of a enlarges a prism of volume 270 cm^3 into a prism of volume 640 cm^3.

The value of a is

A $\frac{9}{16}$ **B** $\frac{3}{4}$ **C** $\frac{4}{3}$ **D** $\frac{16}{9}$

Puzzle

What is the smallest whole number that will divide exactly by every whole number from 2 to 12?

Did you know?

Up to the middle of the 18th century, because of the difficulty of measuring longitude, it was impossible to fix your exact position at sea. Because of this, thousands of sailors had perished. The problem was solved by John Harrison (1693–1776), a self-taught Yorkshire clockmaker, who spent 40 years designing and building a clock that would keep perfect time at sea. John Harrison's clock, tested on a journey from the UK to Jamaica, gave an error of 5 seconds or less than 1 nautical mile.

In this chapter you have seen that...

- ✔ the map ratio of a map is the ratio of a length on the map to the length it represents on the ground.
- ✔ you can use scale diagrams to find heights and distances
- ✔ the angle of elevation is the angle you turn your eyes through from the horizontal to look *up* to an object
- ✔ the angle of depression is the angle you turn your eyes through from the horizontal to look *down* at an object
- ✔ when an object is enlarged by a scale factor a
  - the area of the enlarged shape is the area of the first shape multiplied by the square of the scale factor, i.e. by a^2
  - the volume of the enlarged shape is the volume of the first shape multiplied by the cube of the scale factor, i.e. by a^3.

7 Congruent triangles

At the end of this chapter you should be able to...

1 identify congruent shapes
2 identify transformations under which shapes are congruent
3 state the necessary and sufficient conditions for triangles to be congruent
4 use the necessary and sufficient conditions for congruency to solve problems on congruent triangles
5 use conditions necessary for congruent triangles to prove properties of parallelograms
6 use conditions for congruence to investigate properties of special quadrilaterals.

You need to know...

✔ basic facts about angles
✔ the meaning of reflection, rotation, translation and enlargement
✔ how to describe a transformation
✔ how to draw an accurate copy of a triangle.

Key words

alternate angles, congruent, corresponding angles, corresponding sides, hypotenuse, included angle, interior angles, kite, parallelogram, rectangle, reflection, rhombus, rotation, similar, square, transformations, translation, vertically opposite angles

The basic facts

These facts were introduced earlier. They are revised here because they are needed for the exercises in this chapter:

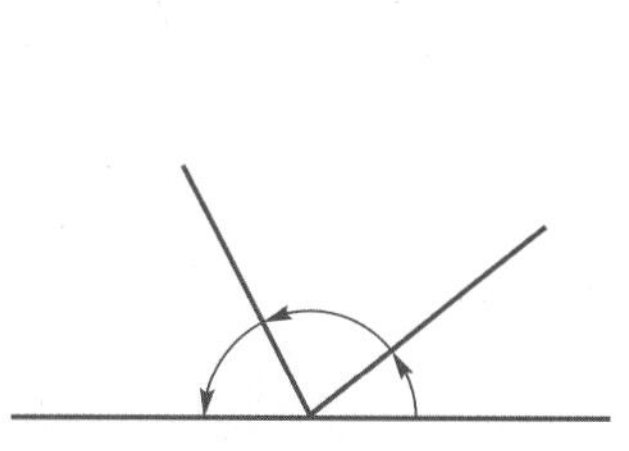

angles on a straight line add up to 180°

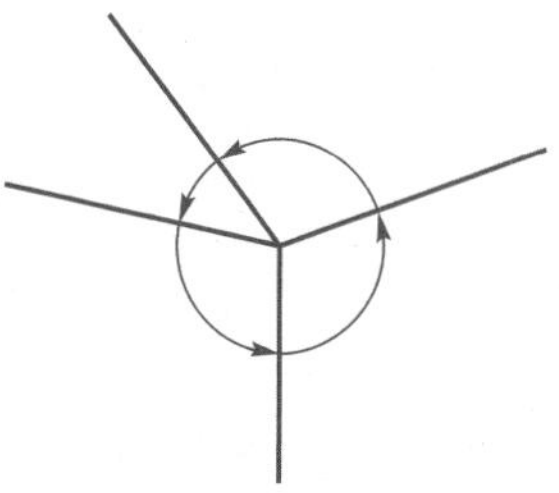

angles at a point add up to 360°

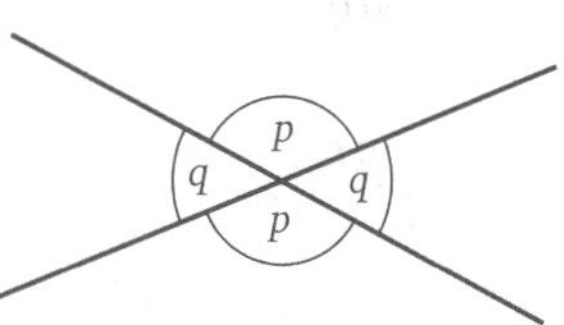

vertically opposite angles are equal.

When a transversal cuts a pair of parallel lines, various angles are formed and:

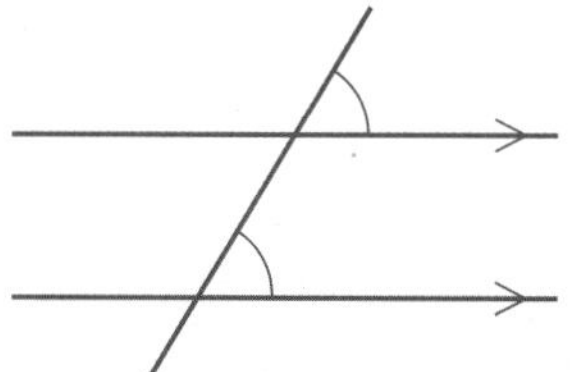

corresponding angles are equal

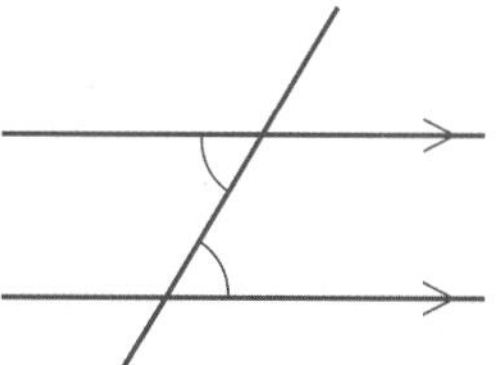

alternate angles are equal

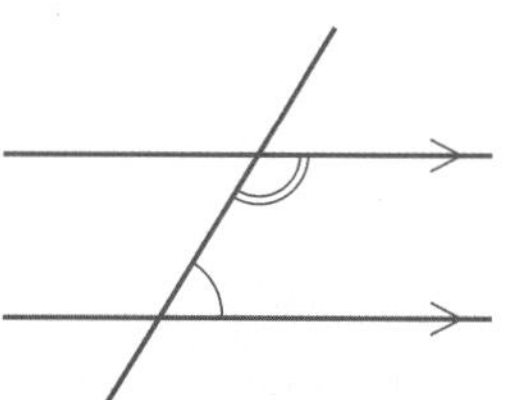

interior angles add up to 180°.

In *any* triangle, whatever its shape or size, the sum of the three angles is 180°, e.g.

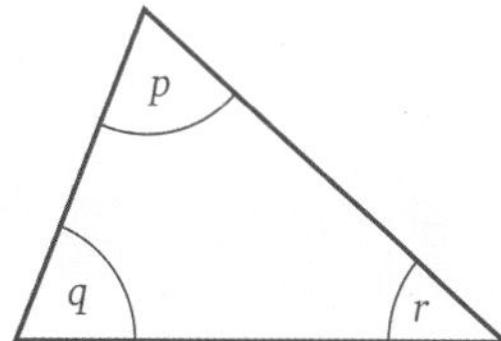

$$p + q + r = 180°$$

The exercise that follows will help you revise these facts. However, you must state which fact you have used as a reason for statements that you make. The facts do not have to be quoted in full but can be shortened using a number of standard abbreviations.

For example, if you state that $x = 60°$ and the reason is that x and 60° are vertically opposite angles then you could write

$$x = 60° \text{ (vert. opp. } \angle\text{s)}$$

Exercise 7a

Find the size of the angle marked x, giving brief reasons to justify your statements.

(Fill in the size of any angles that you find.)

From the diagram SP and QR are parallel

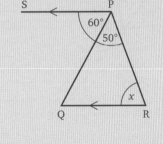

$$\text{so } P\hat{Q}R = 60^\circ \text{ (alt. } \angle\text{s)}$$

$$50^\circ + 60^\circ + x = 180^\circ \text{ (}\angle \text{ sum of } \triangle PQR\text{)}$$

$$\therefore \quad x = 70^\circ$$

In each of the following diagrams find the size of the angle marked x, giving brief reasons for your answer:

Draw a diagram. Mark in all the facts given and any other facts you know. This will help you to find the required angle.

1

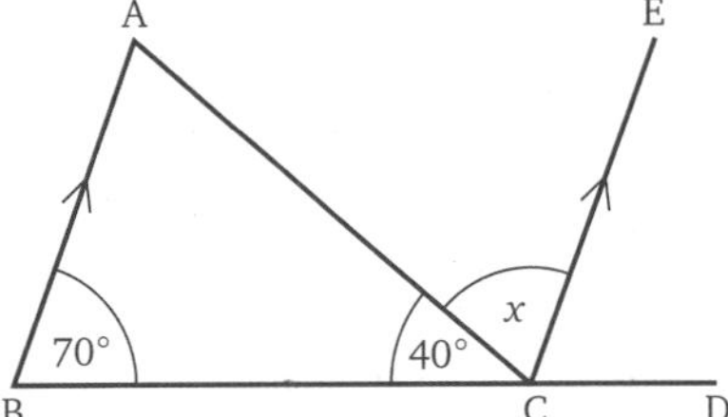

2

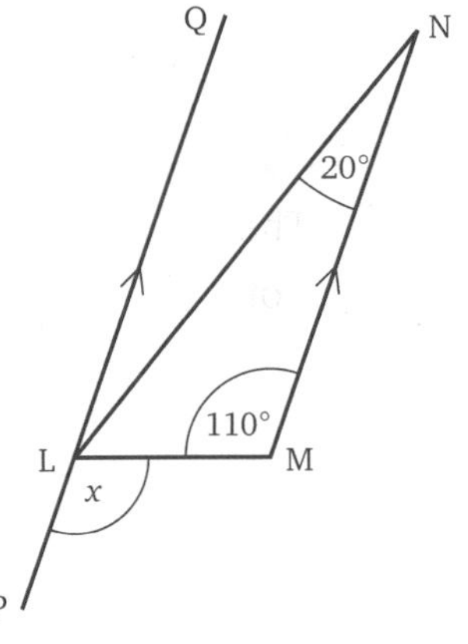

3

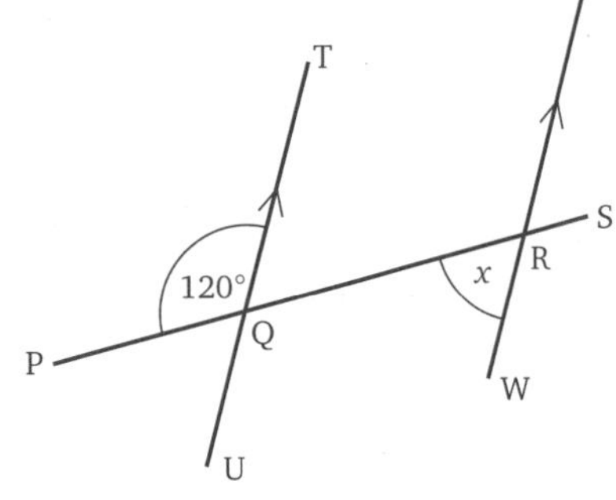

4

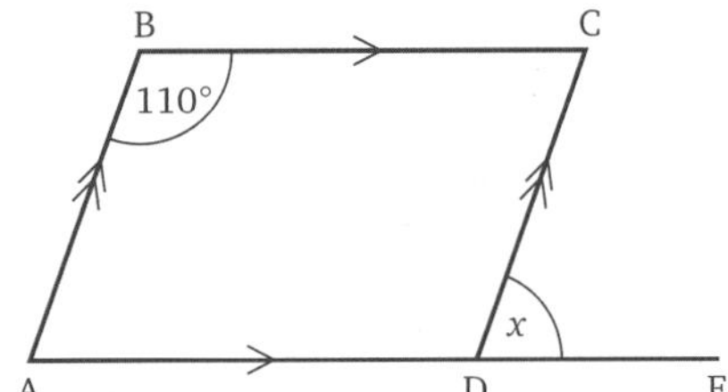

5

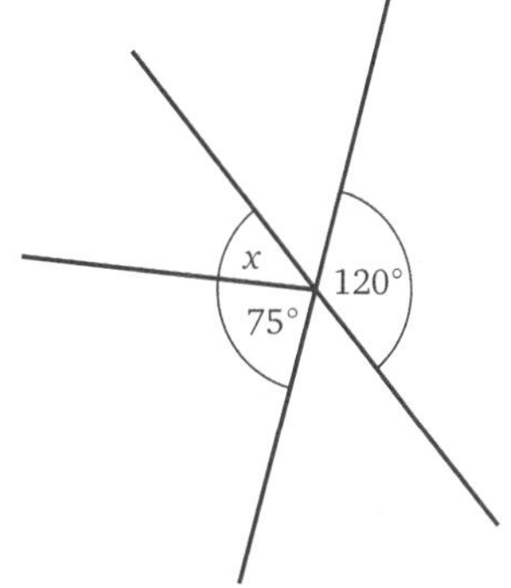

6

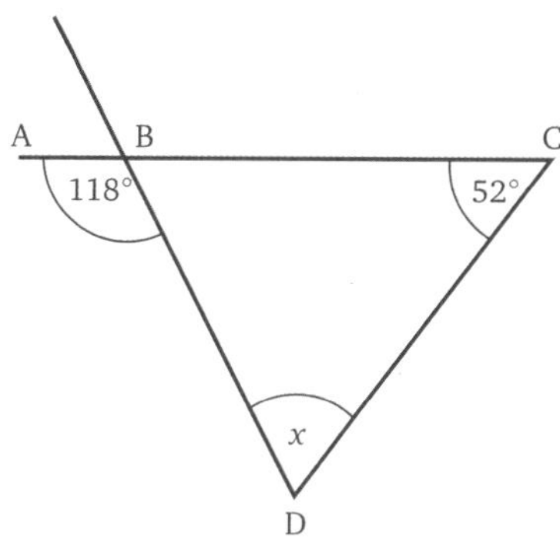

Prove that $A\hat{B}C = C\hat{D}E$

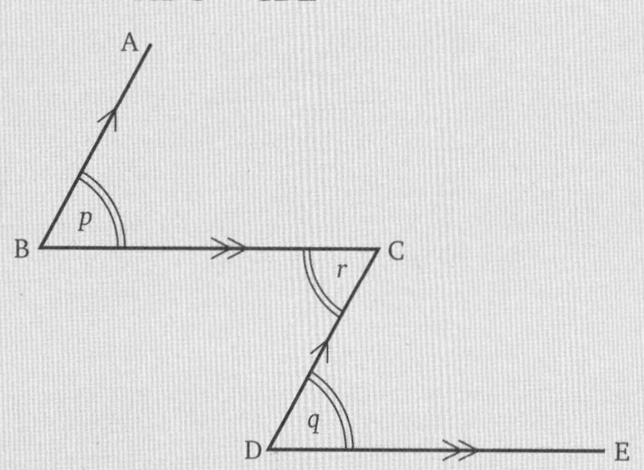

(Mark with a letter the angles you need to refer to. Use a symbol to show equal angles. We have used a double arc.)

From the diagram

$$p = r \text{ (alt. } \angle\text{s)}$$

$$r = q \text{ (alt. } \angle\text{s)}$$

$\therefore p = q$

i.e. $A\hat{B}C = C\hat{D}E$

7

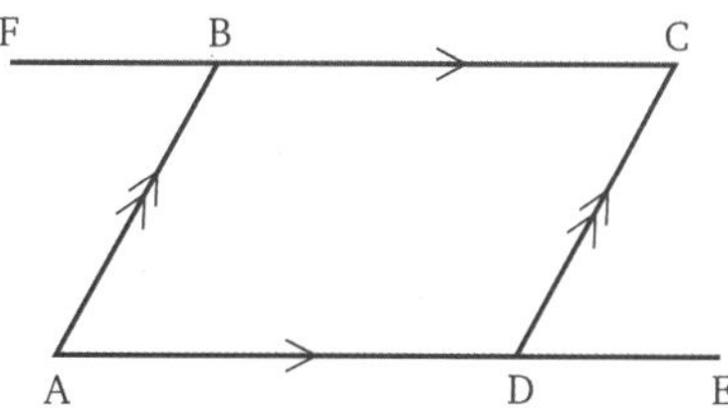

Prove that $A\hat{B}F = C\hat{D}E$

8

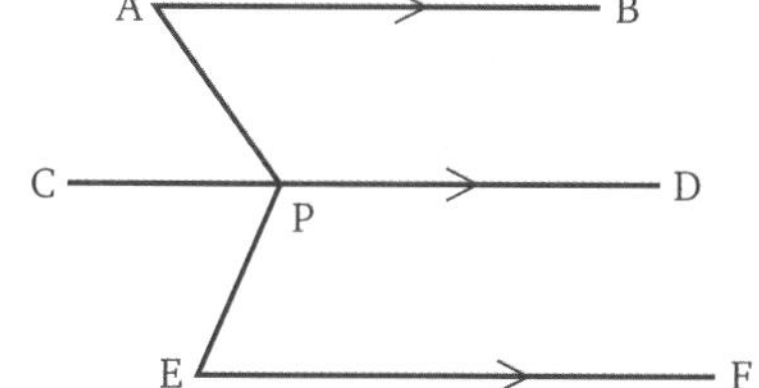

Prove that $A\hat{P}E = B\hat{A}P + F\hat{E}P$

9

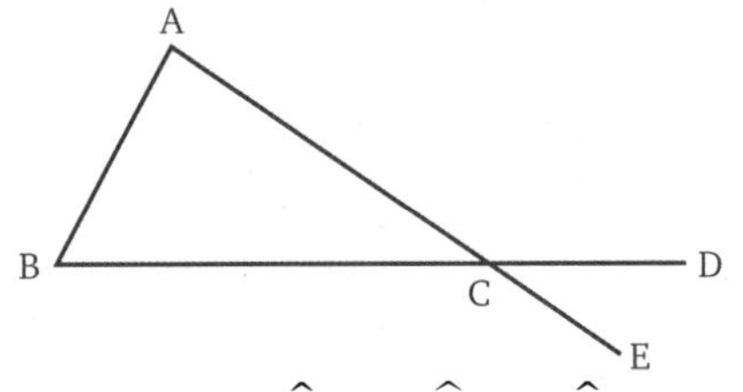

Prove that $D\hat{C}E + C\hat{A}B + C\hat{B}A = 180°$

10

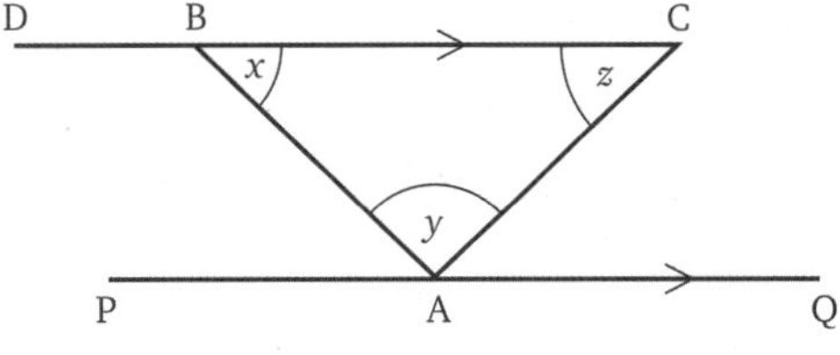

Prove that $x + y + z = 180°$

Congruent shapes

Two shapes are *congruent* if they are exactly the same shape and size, i.e. one shape is an exact copy of the other shape, although not necessarily drawn in the same position.

In each of these diagrams the two figures are congruent:

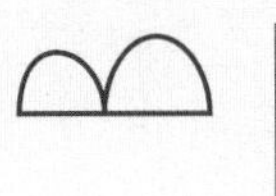
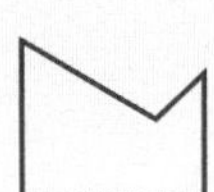

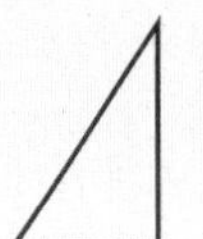

In each case the second shape is an exact copy of the first shape although it may be turned round or turned over.

In each of these diagrams the two figures are not congruent (they may be similar; i.e. have the same shape but different sizes):

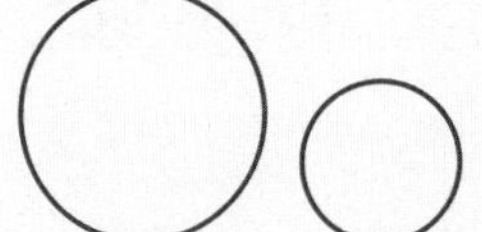

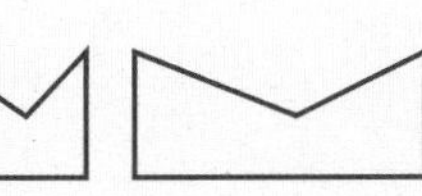

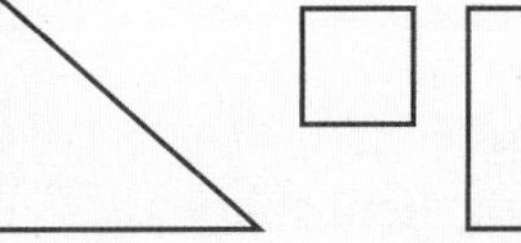

Exercise 7b

In the following questions state whether or not the two shapes are congruent.

If you are not sure, trace one shape and see if it fits exactly over the other shape: Remember 'congruent' means exactly the same shape and size.

1

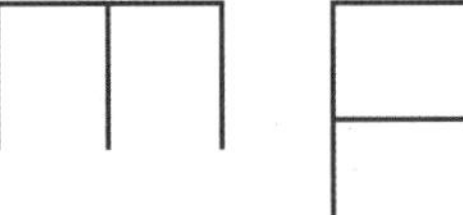

2

3

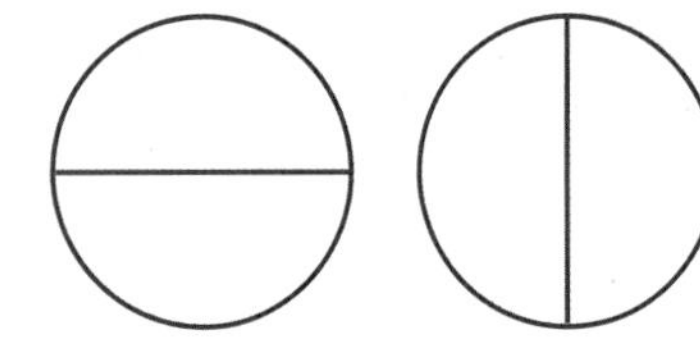

4

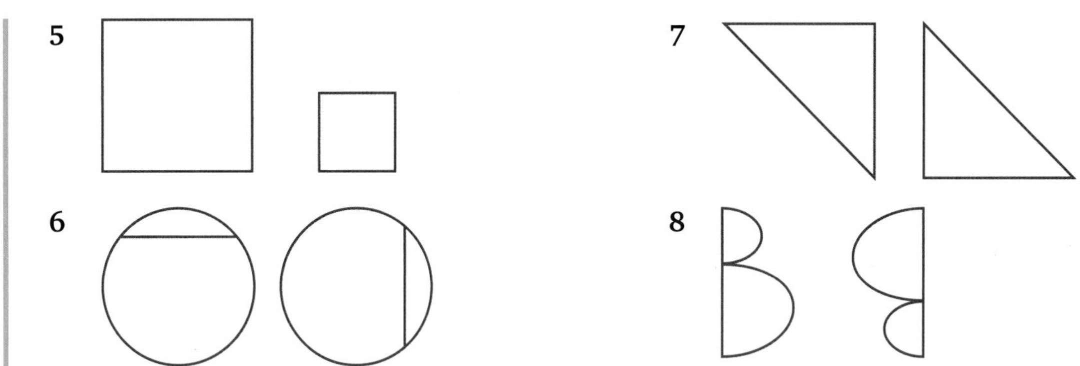

Transformations and congruent figures

The shape and size of a figure are not altered by certain transformations.

Reflection produces congruent shapes:

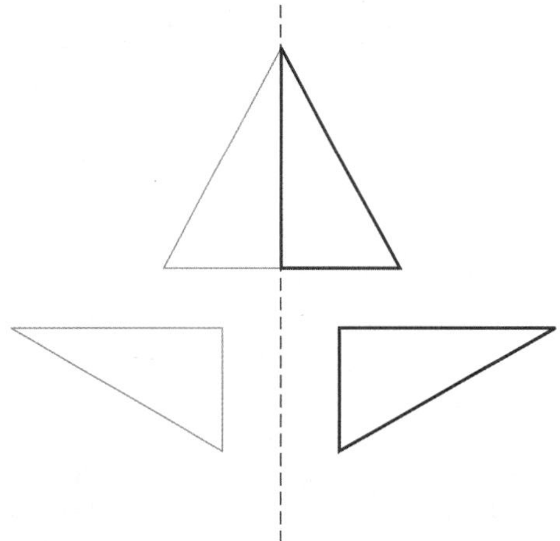

Rotation produces congruent shapes:

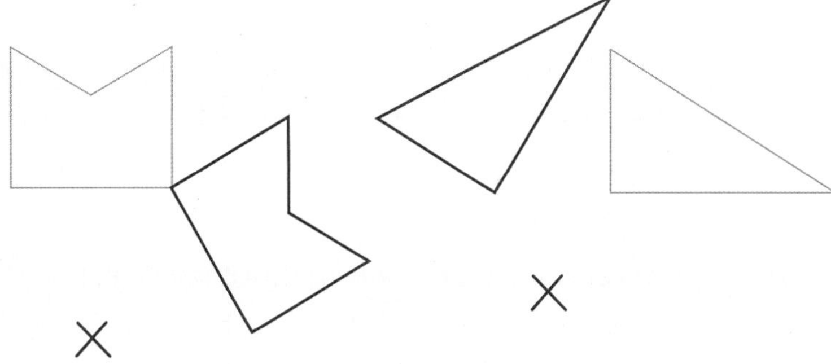

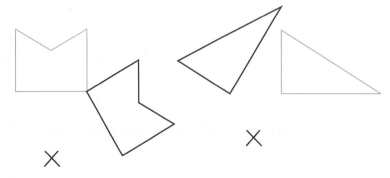

Translation produces congruent shapes:

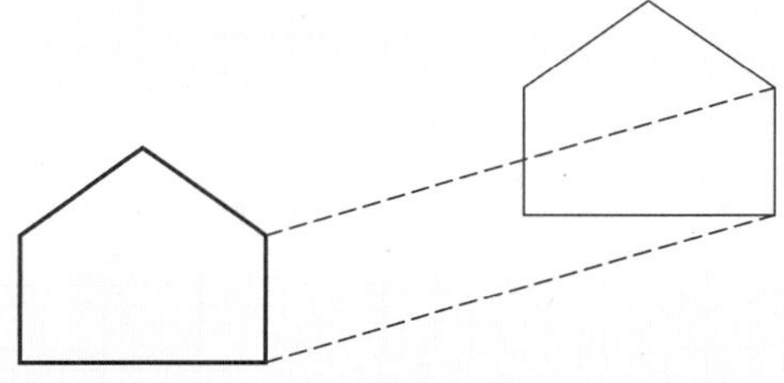

But enlargement does *not* produce congruent shapes, it produces shapes that are larger or smaller.

These are called *similar* shapes.

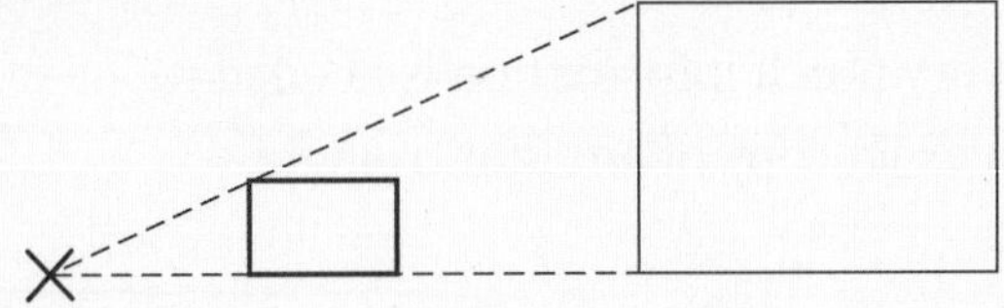

Exercise 7c

Describe the transformation in each of the following cases. The paler blue shape is the image. State whether the object and the image are congruent.

1

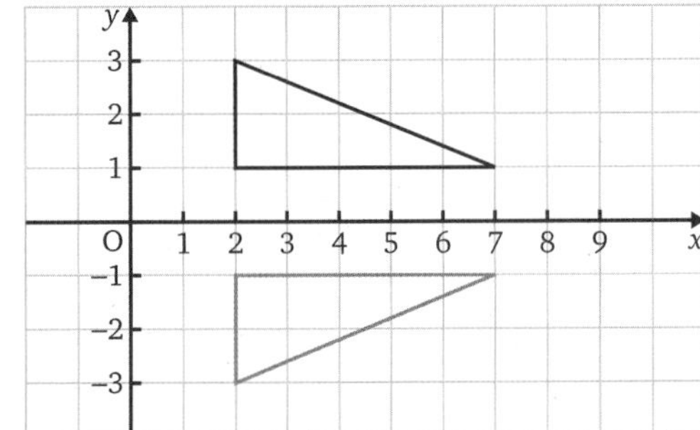

2

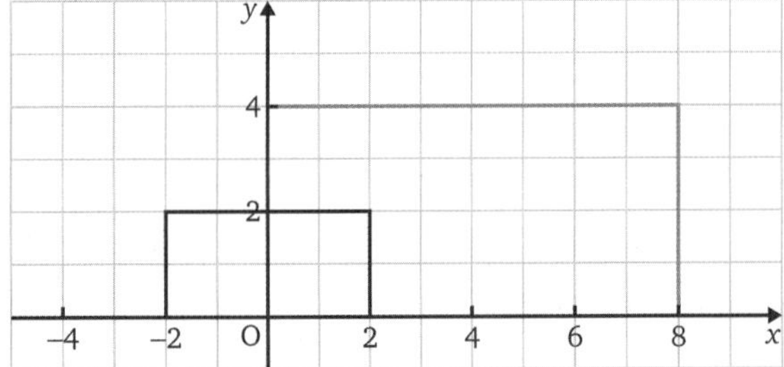

3

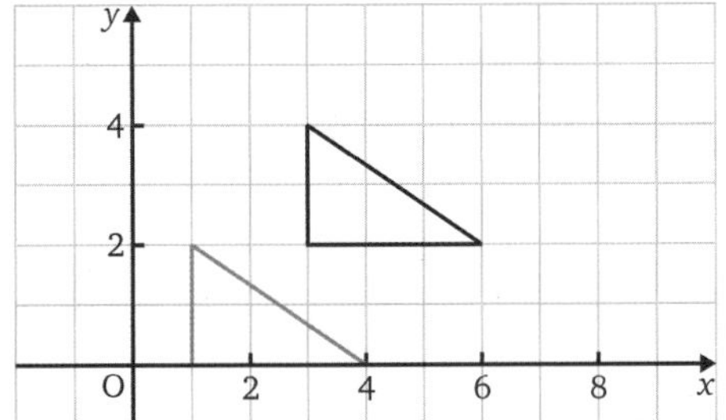

4

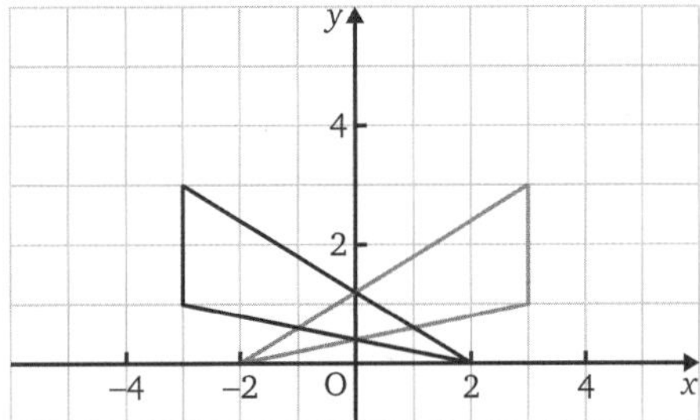

5

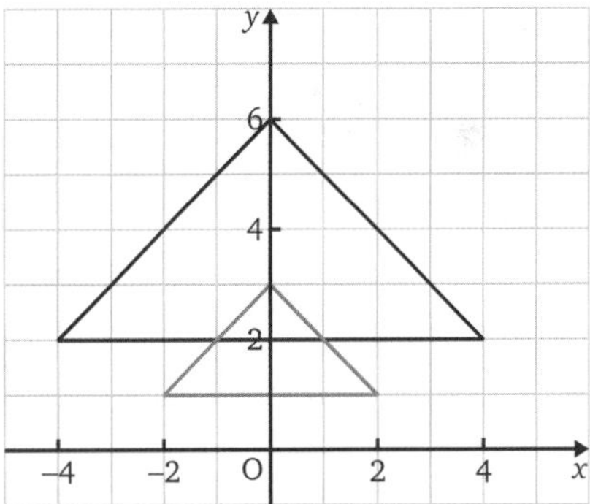

6

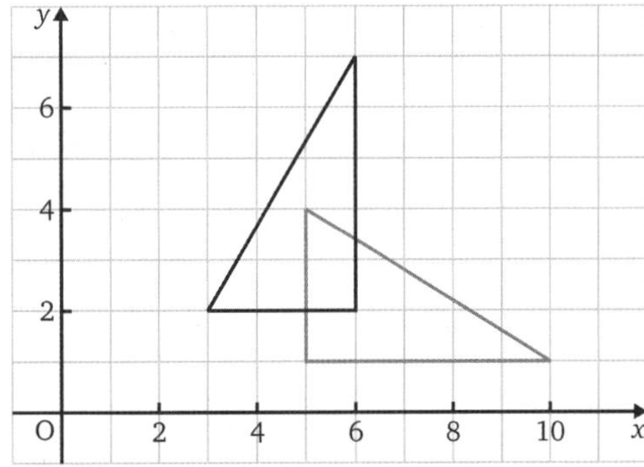

Congruent triangles

It is not always practical or possible to use tracing paper to determine whether two shapes are congruent.

Triangles are simple figures and not very much information is needed to determine whether one triangle is an exact copy of another triangle.

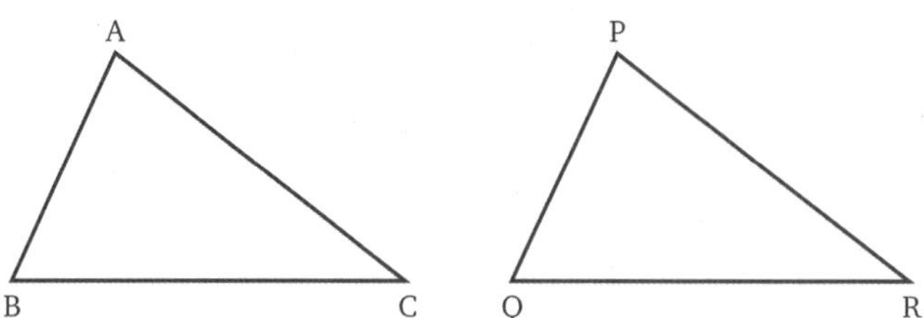

If $\triangle$s $\begin{matrix} ABC \\ PQR \end{matrix}$ are congruent it follows that $\left.\begin{matrix} AB = PQ \\ AC = PR \\ BC = QR \end{matrix}\right\}$ and $\left\{\begin{matrix} \hat{A} = \hat{P} \\ \hat{B} = \hat{Q} \\ \hat{C} = \hat{R} \end{matrix}\right.$

To make an exact copy of these triangles we do not need to know the lengths of all three sides and the sizes of all three angles: three measurements are usually enough and we now investigate which three measurements are suitable.

Exercise 7d

In each of the following questions make a rough sketch of $\triangle$ABC. Construct a triangle with the same measurements as those given for $\triangle$ABC. Can you construct a different triangle with the given measurements?

1 $\triangle$ABC, in which AB = 8 cm, BC = 5 cm, AC = 6 cm.

2 $\triangle$ABC, in which $\hat{A} = 40°$, $\hat{B} = 60°$, $\hat{C} = 80°$.

3 $\triangle$ABC, in which AB = 7 cm, BC = 12 cm, AC = 8 cm.

4 $\triangle$ABC, in which $\hat{A} = 20°$, $\hat{B} = 40°$, $\hat{C} = 120°$.

5 What extra information do you need about $\triangle$ABC in questions **2** and **4** in order to make an exact copy?

Three pairs of sides

From the last exercise you should be convinced that an exact copy of a triangle can be made if the lengths of the three sides are known. Therefore:

> Two triangles are congruent if the three sides of one triangle are equal to the three sides of the other triangle.

However if the three angles of one triangle are equal to the three angles of another triangle they may not be congruent. Similar triangles are also called equiangular triangles.

Exercise 7e

Decide whether the following pairs of triangles are congruent. Give brief reasons for your answers.

a

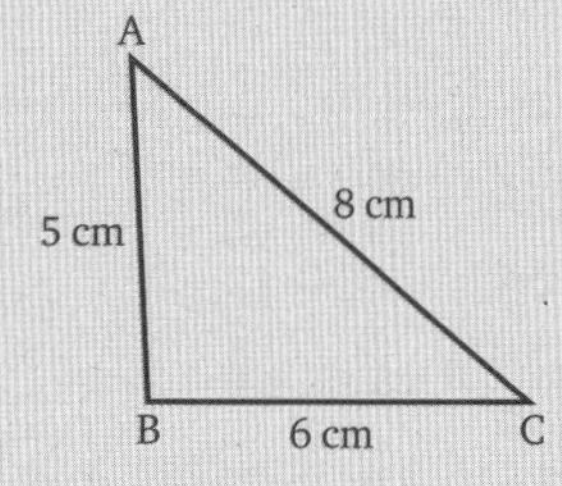

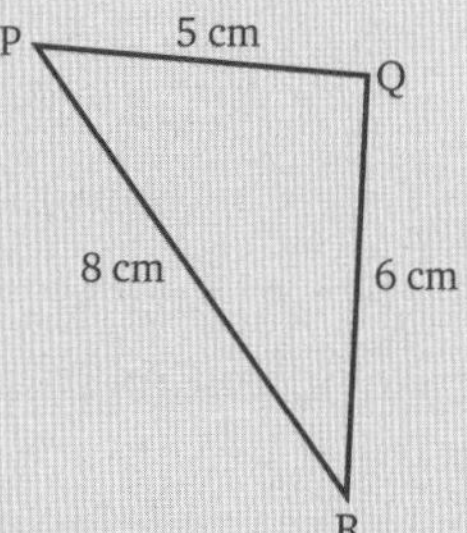

$$\left.\begin{array}{l} AB = PQ \\ BC = QR \\ AC = PR \end{array}\right\} \quad \therefore \quad \triangle s \; \begin{array}{c} ABC \\ PQR \end{array} \text{ are congruent (3 sides)}$$

(Notice that we write corresponding vertices one under the other.)

b

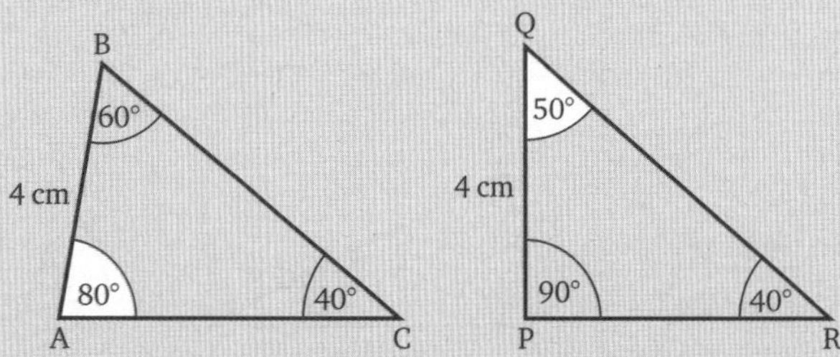

First we need to calculate the angles that are shaded white.

In $\triangle ABC$, $\hat{A} = 80°$ (angles of $\triangle$)

In $\triangle PQR$, $\hat{Q} = 50°$ (angles of $\triangle$)

The angles of the triangles are not equal.

$\therefore$ $\triangle ABC$ and $\triangle PQR$ are not congruent.

c

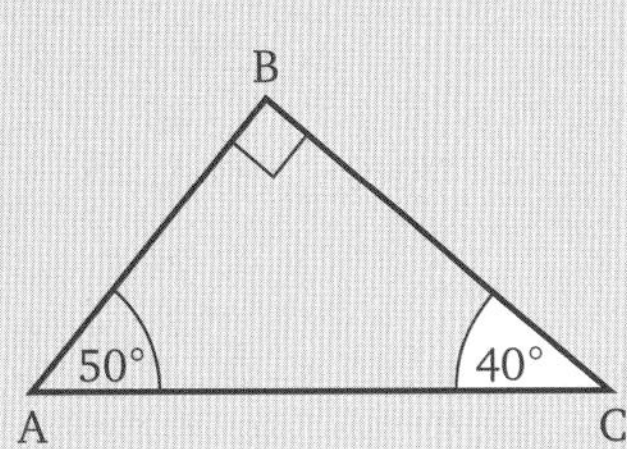

In $\triangle ABC$, $\hat{C} = 40°$ (angles of $\triangle$)

In $\triangle PQR$, $\hat{Q} = 90°$ (angles of $\triangle$)

$\therefore$ $\triangle$s $\begin{matrix} ABC \\ PQR \end{matrix}$ are similar, but probably not congruent because no dimensions are given.

In questions **1** to **4** state whether or not the two triangles are congruent. Give a brief reason for your answers. All lengths are in centimetres.

1

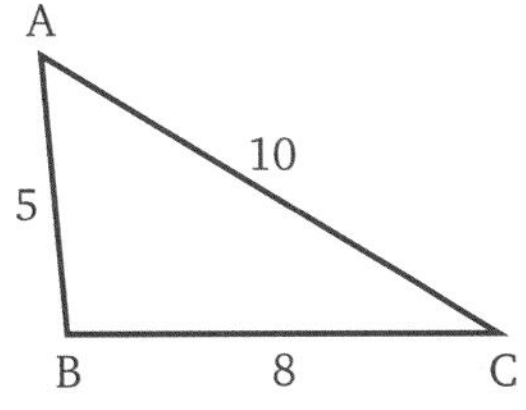

3

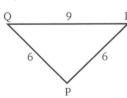

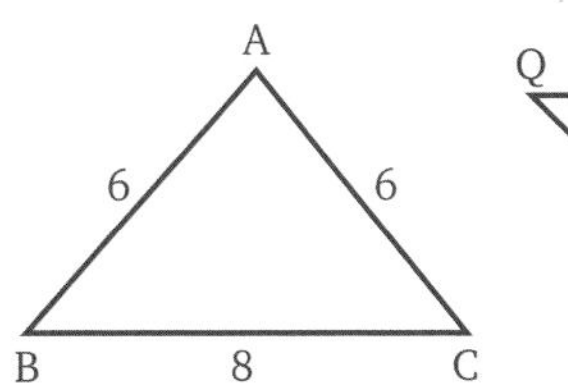

2

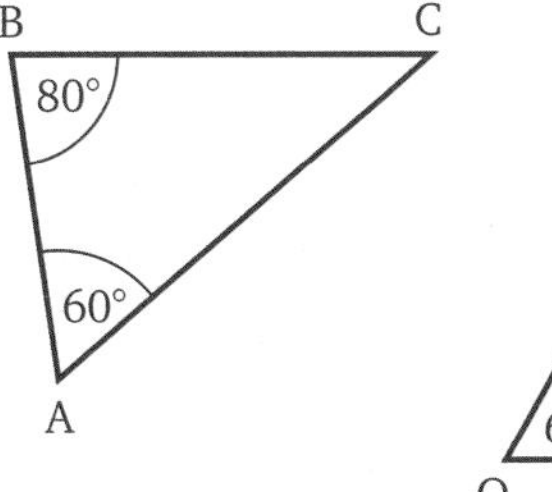

4

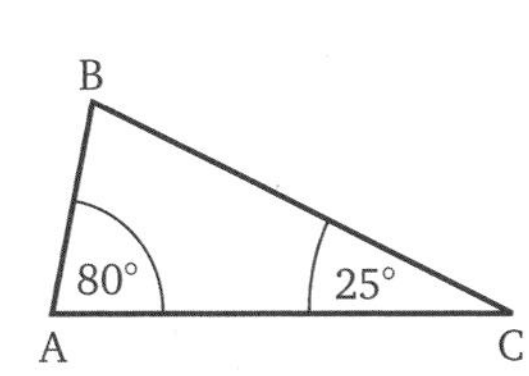

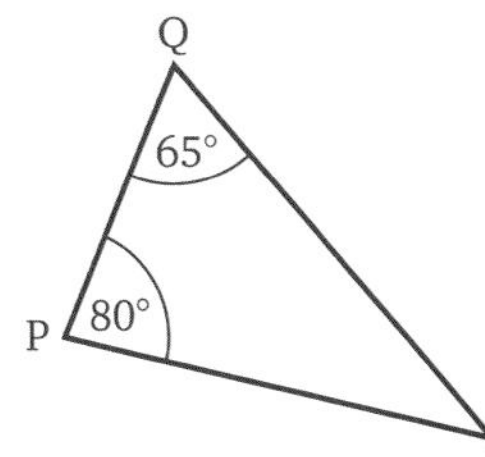

5

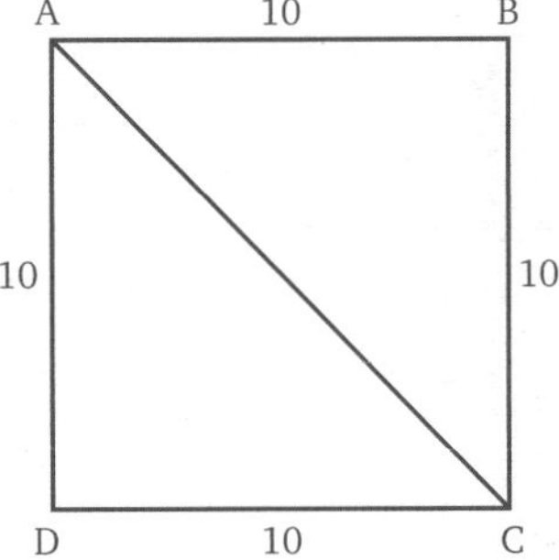

Are △ADC and △ABC congruent?

6

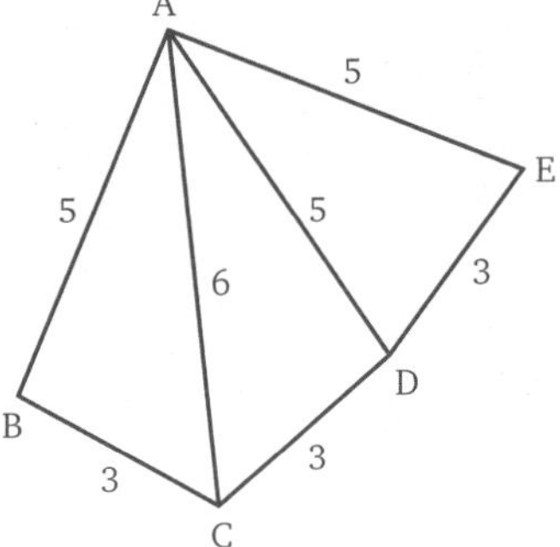

Which triangles are congruent?

7

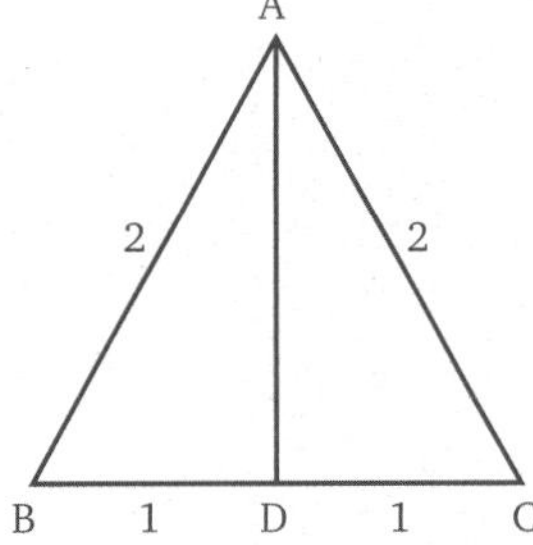

Are △ABD and △ACD congruent?

8

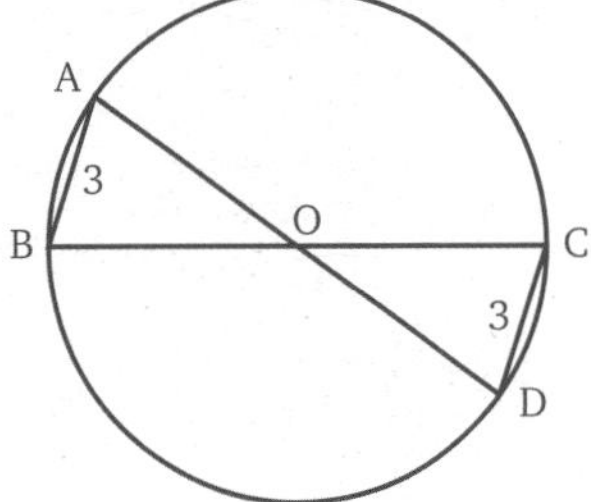

The point O is the centre of the circle and the radius is 5 cm. Are △ABO and △CDO congruent?

Two angles and a side

To make an exact copy of a triangle we need to know the length of at least one side.

Exercise 7f

You need a sharp pencil.

1. Construct △ABC, in which AB = 6 cm, $\hat{A} = 30°$, $\hat{B} = 60°$.
2. Construct △PQR, in which PR = 6 cm, $\hat{P} = 30°$, $\hat{Q} = 60°$.
3. Construct △LMN, in which LM = 6 cm, $\hat{L} = 30°$, $\widehat{M} = 60°$.
4. Construct △XYZ, in which YZ = 6 cm, $\hat{X} = 30°$, $\hat{Y} = 60°$.
5. How many of the triangles that you have constructed are congruent?
6. How many different triangles can you construct from the following information: one angle is 40°, another angle is 70° and the length of one side is 8 cm?

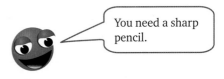

Now you can see that we are able to make an exact copy of a triangle if we know the sizes of two of its angles and the length of one side provided that we place the side in the same position relative to the angles in both triangles, i.e.

Two triangles are congruent if two angles and one side of one triangle are equal to two angles and the *corresponding side* of the other triangle.

Exercise 7g

Decide whether these triangles are congruent. Give a brief reason for your answer.

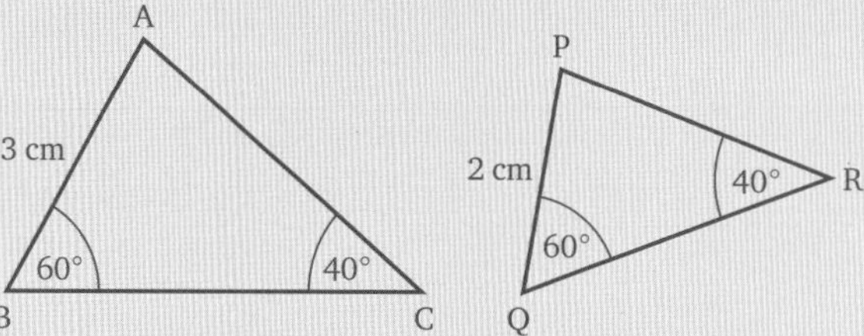

$\triangle$s $\begin{matrix}ABC\\PQR\end{matrix}$ are similar (angles equal)
but not congruent (AB and PQ are corr. sides and are *not* equal).

In questions **1** to **8** state whether or not the two triangles are congruent. Give brief reasons for your answers. All lengths are in centimetres.

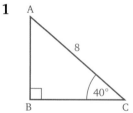

Remember, congruent triangles are identical in all respects.

1

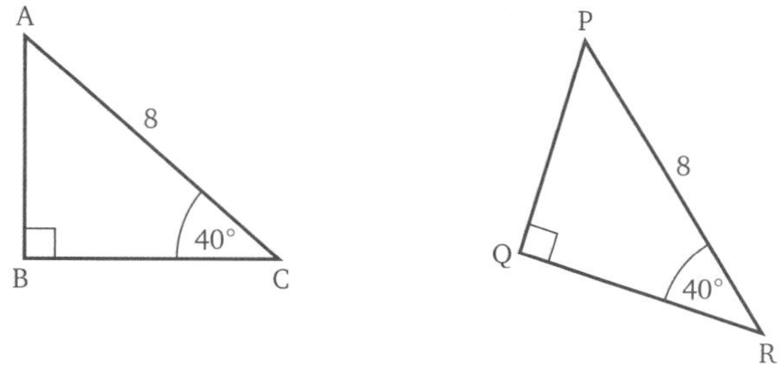

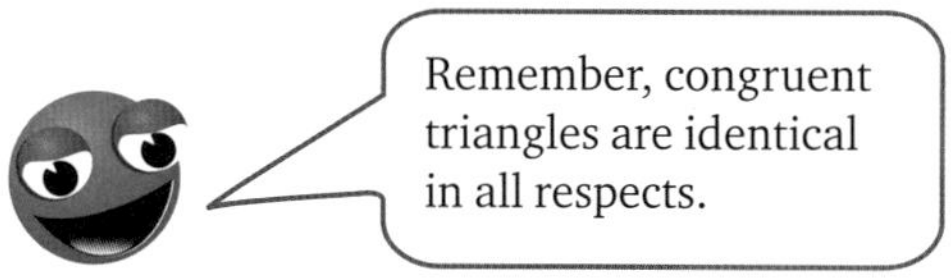

2

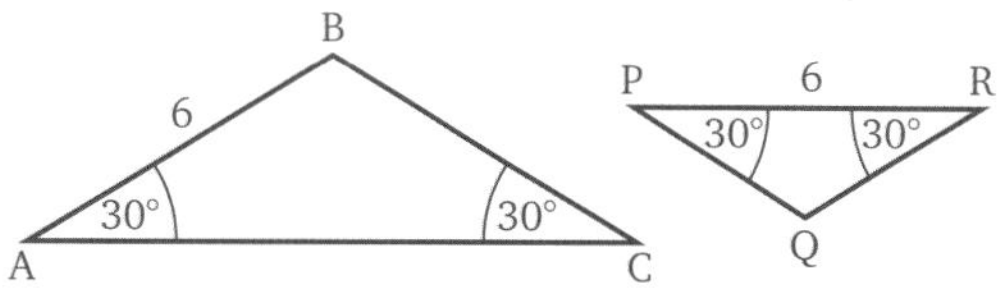

3

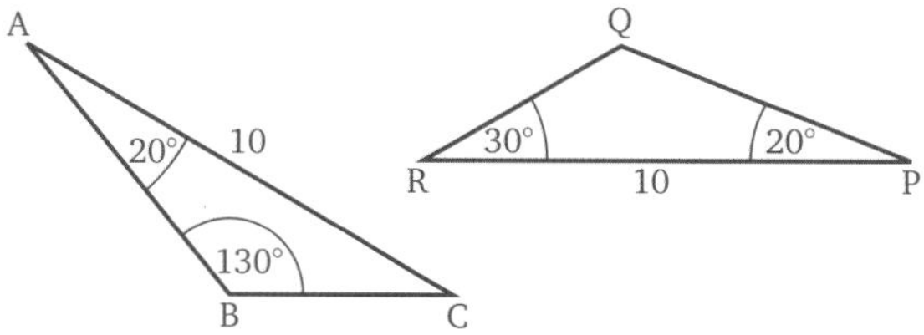

4

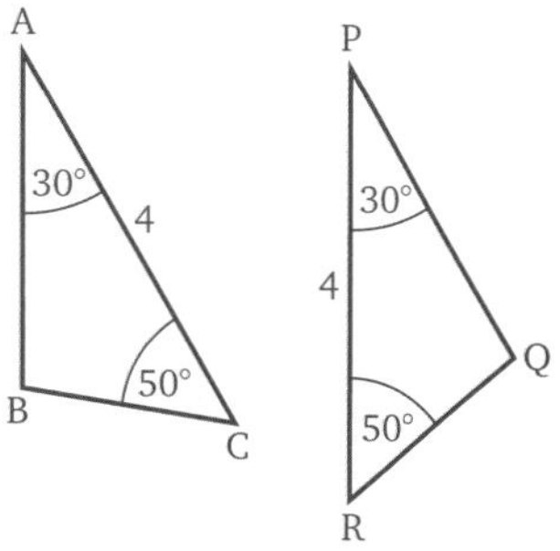

5

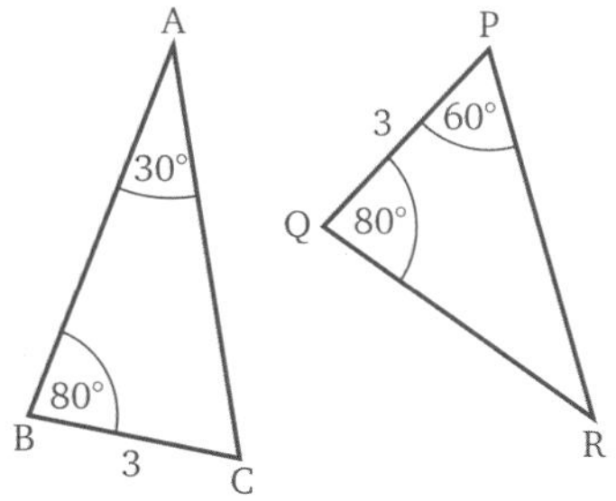

6

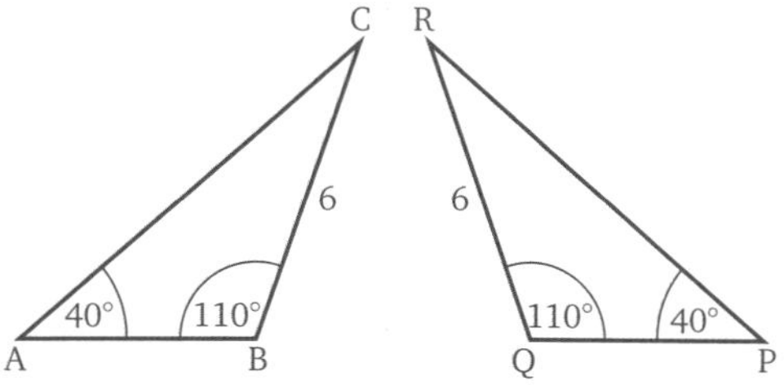

7

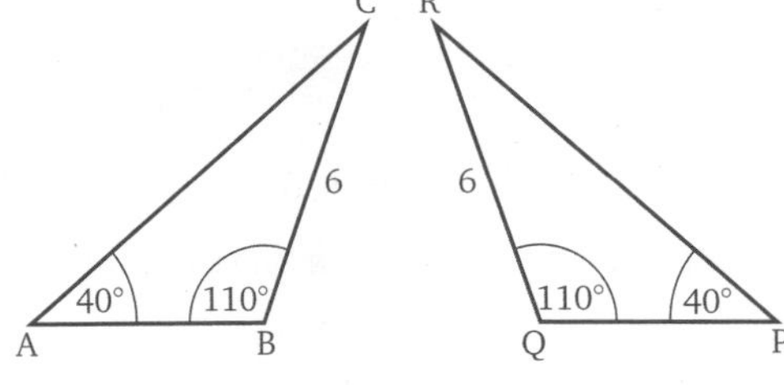

8

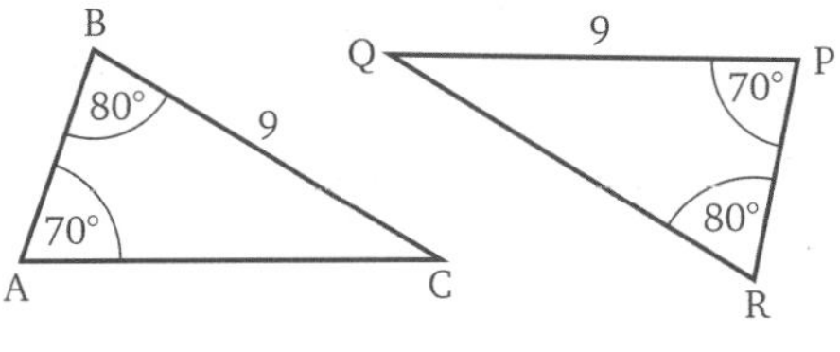

9 Are △ABC and △ADC congruent?

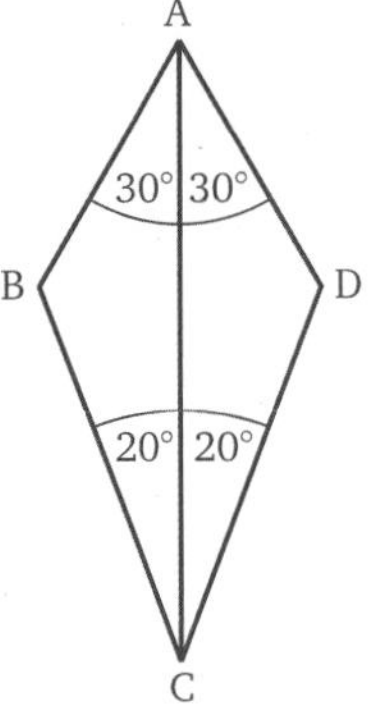

10 Are △ABC and △ADC congruent?

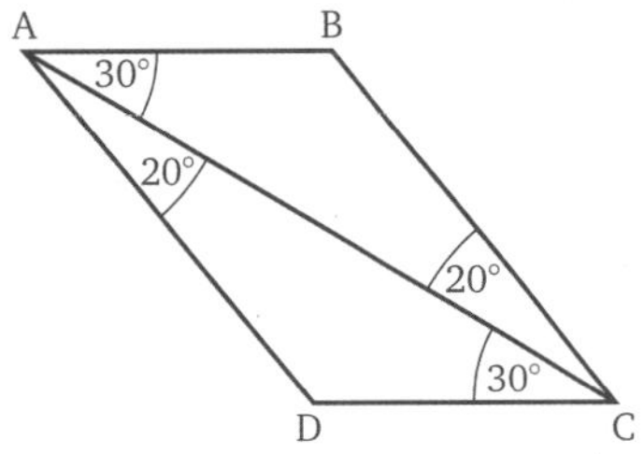

Two sides and an angle

We are now left with one more possible combination of three measurements: if we know the lengths of two sides and the size of one angle in a triangle, does this fix the size and shape of the triangle?

Exercise 7h

Can you make an exact copy of the following triangles from the information given about them? (Try to construct each triangle.)

1 △ABC, in which AB = 8 cm, BC = 5 cm, $\hat{B} = 30°$.

2 △XYZ, in which XY = 8 cm, XZ = 5 cm, $\hat{Y} = 30°$.

3 △PQR, in which $\hat{Q} = 60°$, PQ = 6 cm, QR = 8 cm.

4 △LMN, in which LM = 8 cm, $\hat{M} = 20°$, LN = 4 cm.

5 △DEF, in which DE = 5 cm, $\hat{E} = 90°$, EF = 6 cm.

Now it is possible to see that we can make an exact copy of a triangle if we know the lengths of two sides and the size of one angle, provided that the angle is between those two sides. Therefore:

> Two triangles are congruent if two sides and the *included angle* of one triangle are equal to two sides and the *included angle* of the other triangle.

If the angle is not between the two known sides, then we cannot always be sure that we can make an exact copy of the triangle. We will now investigate this case further.

Exercise 7i

Can you make an exact copy of each of the following triangles from the information given about them?

1 $\triangle$ABC, in which AB = 6 cm, $\hat{B} = 90°$, AC = 10 cm.

2 $\triangle$PQR, in which PQ = 8 cm, $\hat{Q} = 40°$, PR = 6.5 cm.

3 $\triangle$XYZ, in which XY = 5 cm, $\hat{Y} = 90°$, XZ = 13 cm.

4 $\triangle$LMN, in which LM = 5 cm, $\widehat{M} = 60°$, LN = 4.5 cm.

5 $\triangle$DEF, in which DE = 7 cm, $\hat{E} = 90°$, DF = 10 cm.

6 $\triangle$RST, in which RS = 5 cm, $\hat{S} = 120°$, RT = 8 cm.

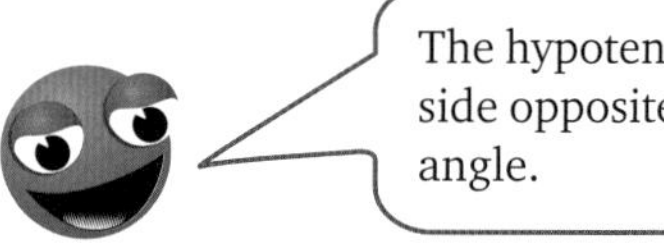

The hypotenuse is the side opposite the right angle.

Therefore, if we are told that one angle in a triangle is a right angle and we are also given the length of one side and the *hypotenuse*, then this information fixes the shape and size of the triangle since it is equivalent to knowing the lengths of the three sides.

> Two triangles are congruent if they both have a right angle, and the hypotenuse and a side of one triangle are equal to the hypotenuse and a side of the other triangle.

Exercise 7j

In questions **1** to **8** state whether or not the two triangles are congruent. Give brief reasons for your answers. All lengths are in centimetres.

1

A, C, B, 10, 8, 40°

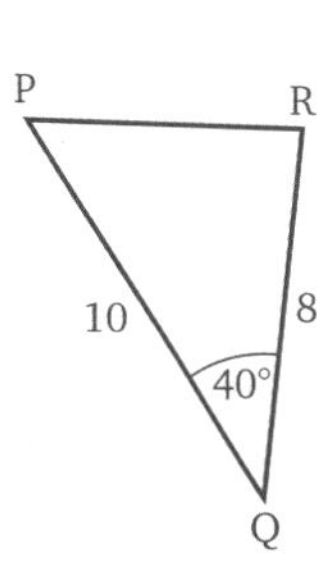

2

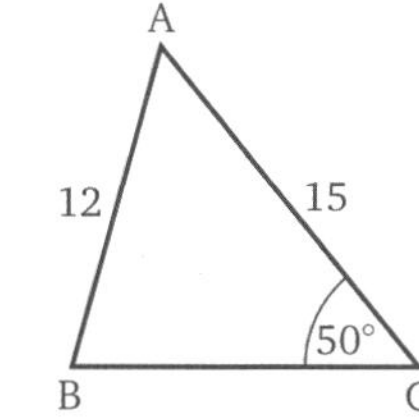

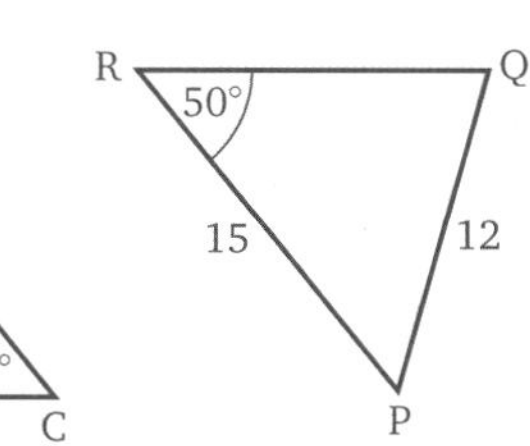

3

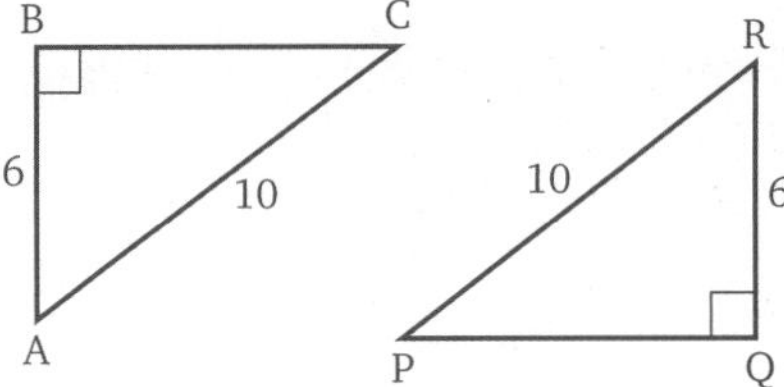

4

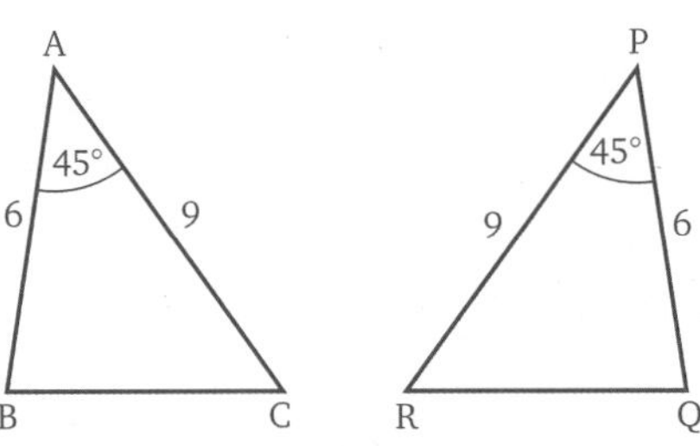

5

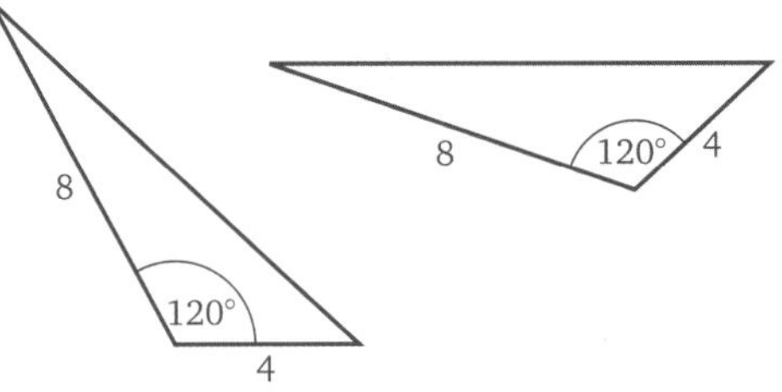

6

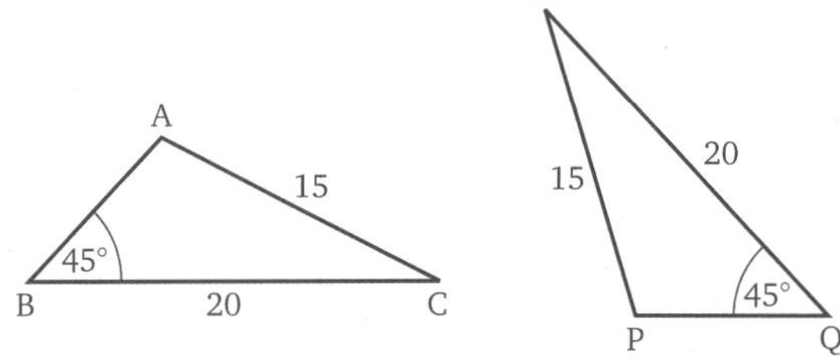

7

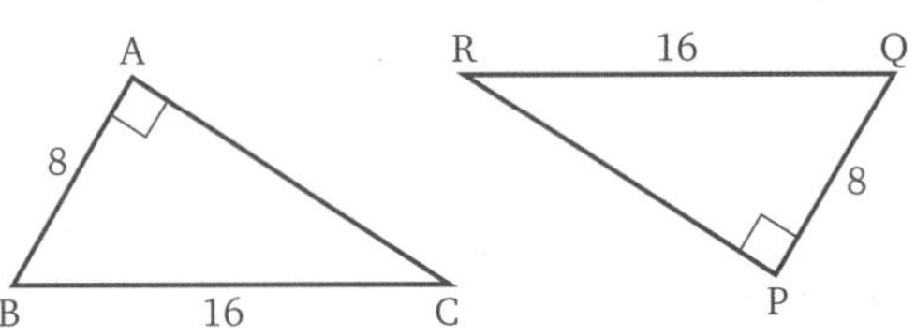

8

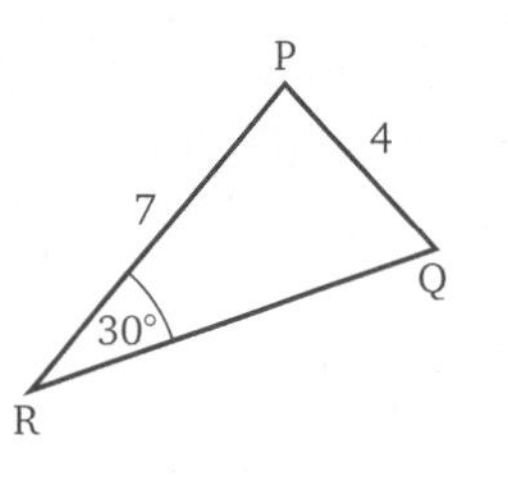

9

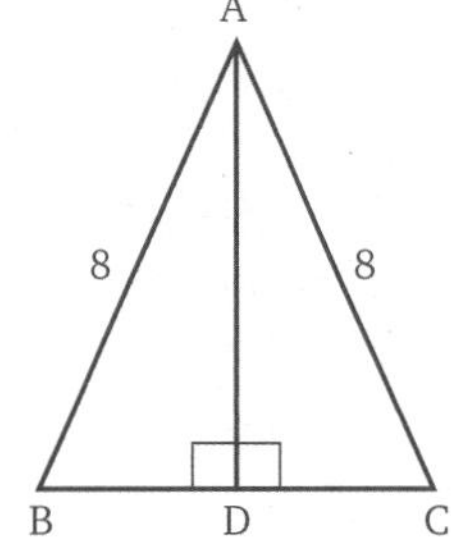

Are △ABD and △ACD congruent?

10

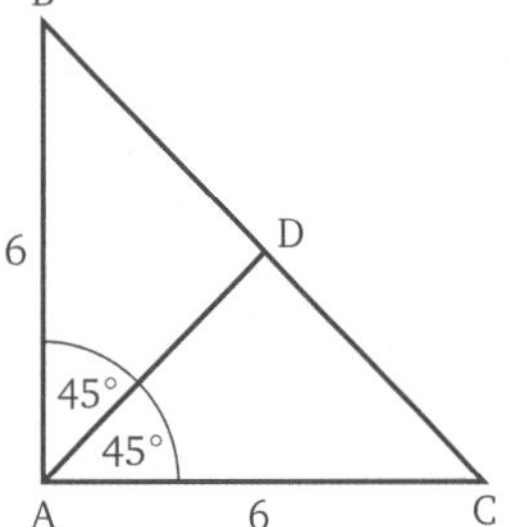

Are △ABD and △ACD congruent?

Summing up, two triangles are congruent if:

either the three sides of one triangle are equal to the three sides of the other triangle (SSS)

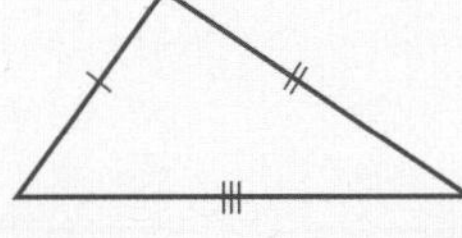

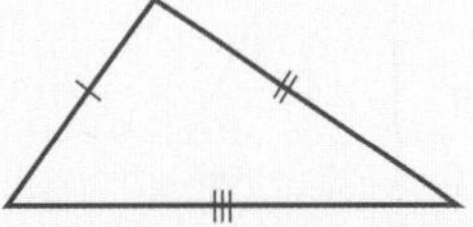

or two angles and a side of one triangle are equal to two angles and the corresponding side of the other triangle (AAS)

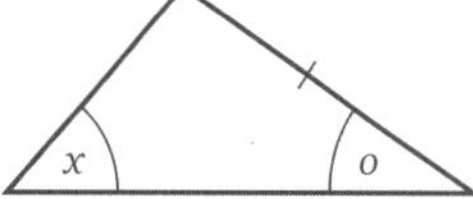

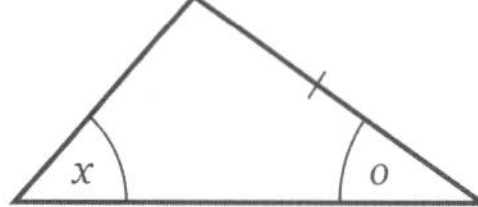

or two sides and the included angle of one triangle are equal to two sides and the included angle of the other triangle (SAS)

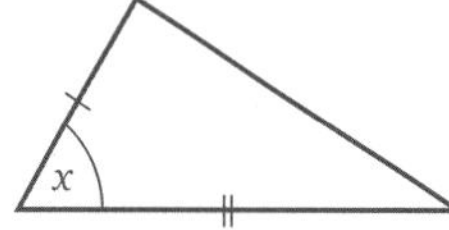

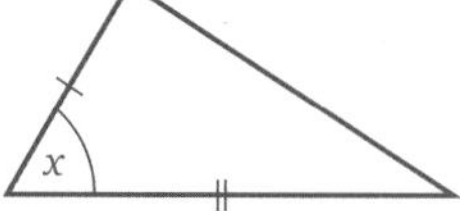

or two triangles each have a right angle, and the hypotenuse and a side of one triangle are equal to the hypotenuse and a side of the other triangle (RHS).

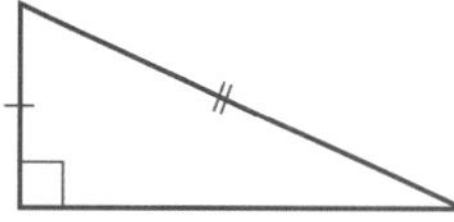
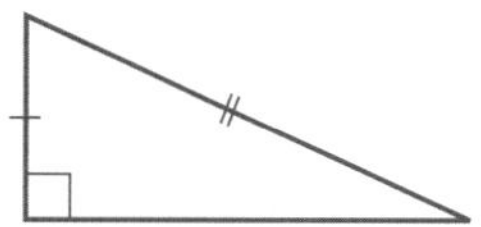

Exercise 7k

State whether or not each of the following pairs of triangles are congruent. Give brief reasons for your answers. All measurements are in centimetres.

1

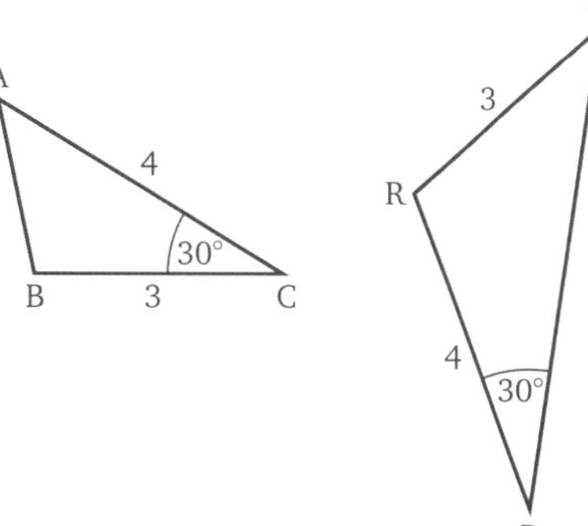

2

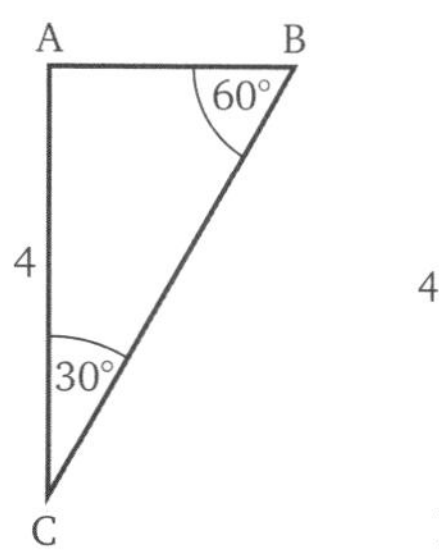

3

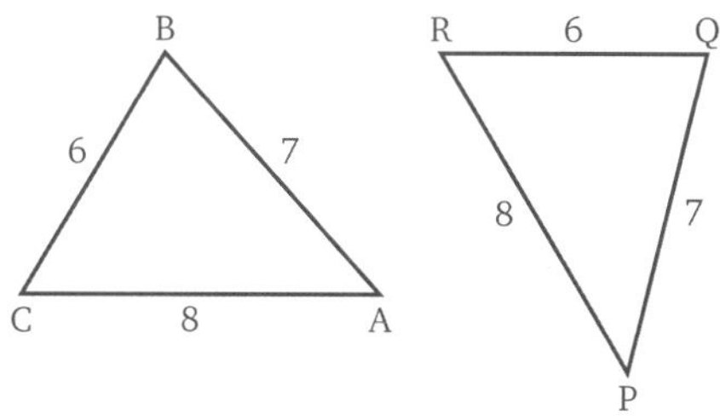

4

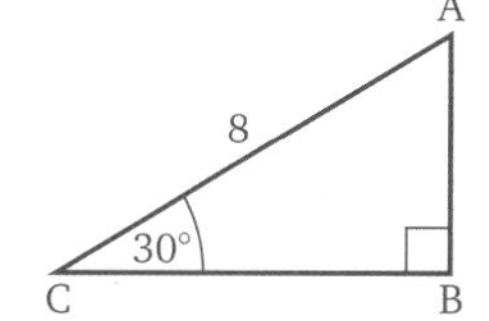

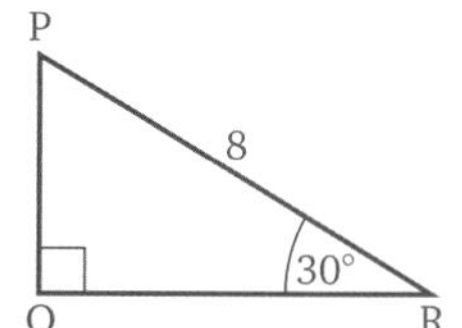

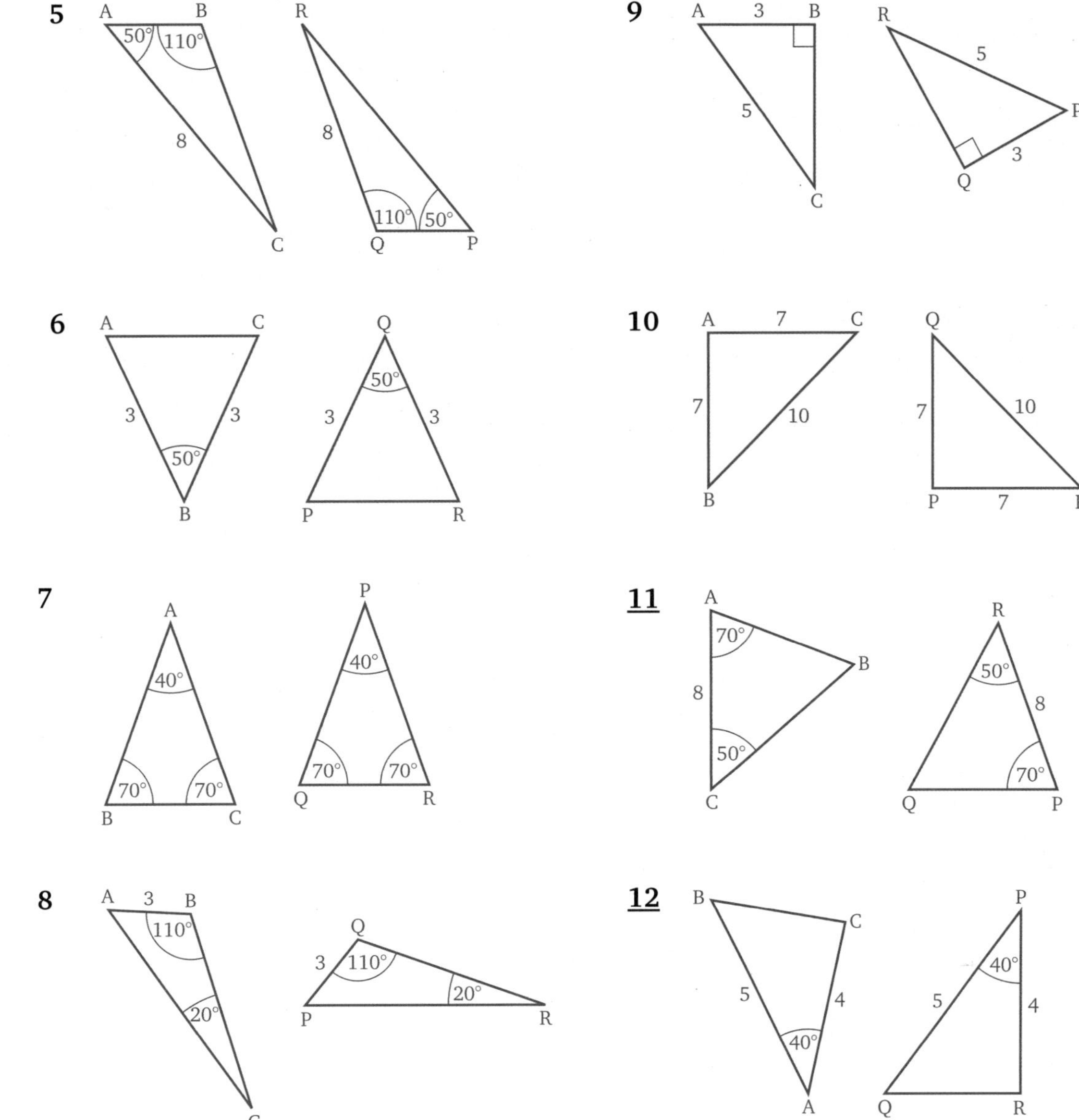

Problems

We do not need to know actual measurements to prove that triangles are congruent. If we can show that a correct combination of sides and angles are the same in both triangles, the triangles must be congruent.

Exercise 7I

In a quadrilateral ABCD, AB = DC and AD = BC. The diagonal BD is drawn. Prove that △ABD and △CDB are congruent.

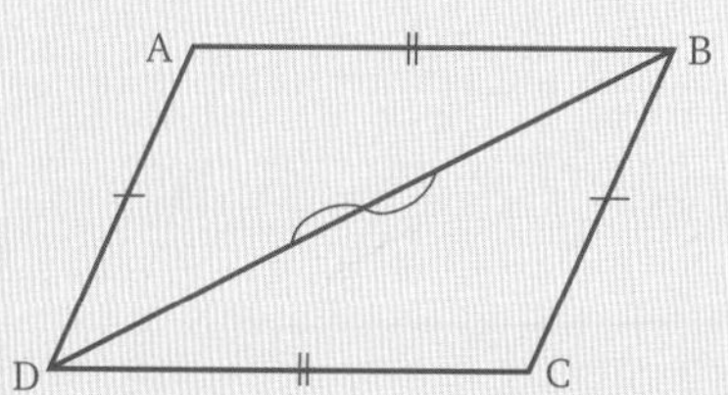

(Mark on your diagram all the information given and any further facts that you discover. The symbol ⁀ on BD indicates that it is common to both triangles.)

In △s ABD, CDB   AB = CD (given)

AD = CB (given)

DB is the same for both triangles

∴ △s ABD / CDB are congruent (SSS).

There are four possible ways of proving that two triangles are congruent. Go through these in turn for each pair of triangles to decide which set of conditions are met.

1

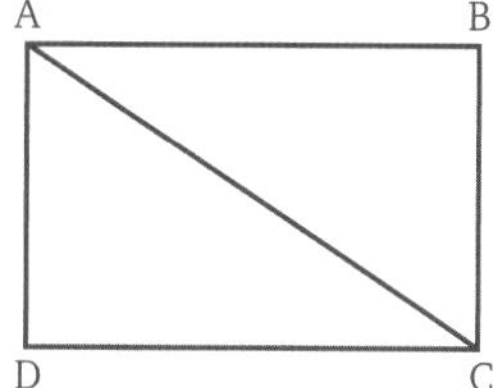

ABCD is a rectangle. Prove that △ABC and △CDA are congruent.

2

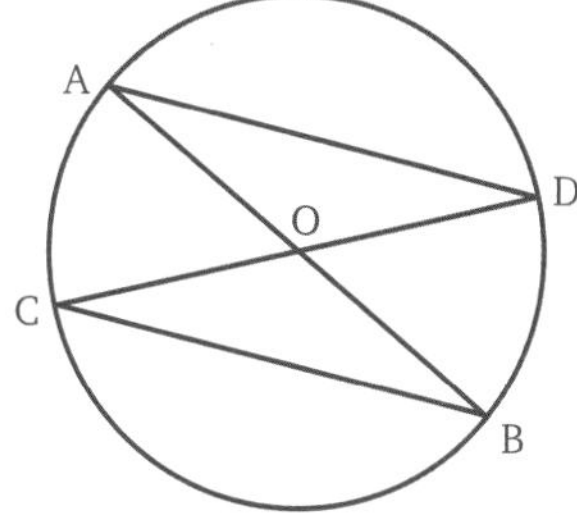

AB and CD are diameters of the circle and O is the centre. Prove that △AOD and △COB are congruent.

3

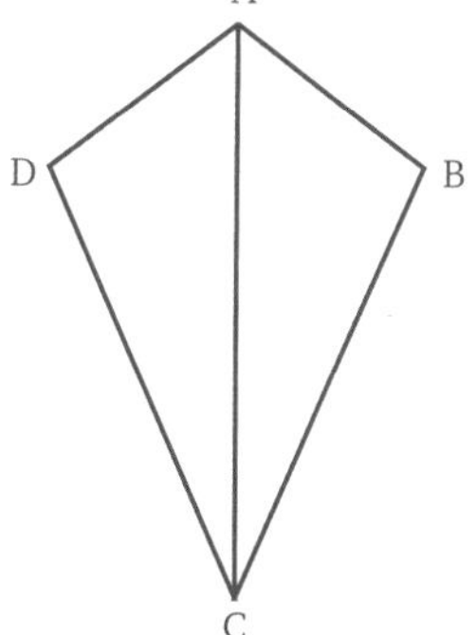

ABCD is a kite in which AD = AB and CD = BC. Prove that △ADC and △ABC are congruent.

4

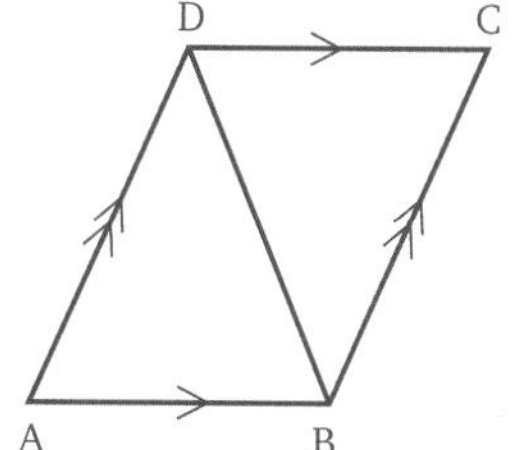

ABCD is a parallelogram. Prove that △ABD and △CDB are congruent.

5

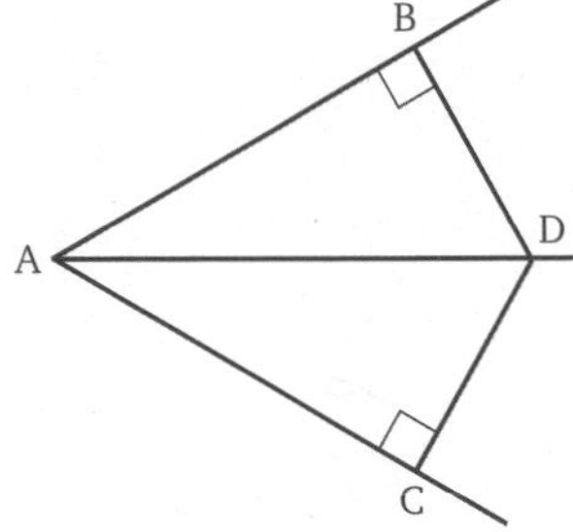

AD bisects $B\hat{A}C$, DB is perpendicular to AB and DC is perpendicular to AC. Prove that △ABD and △ACD are congruent.

6

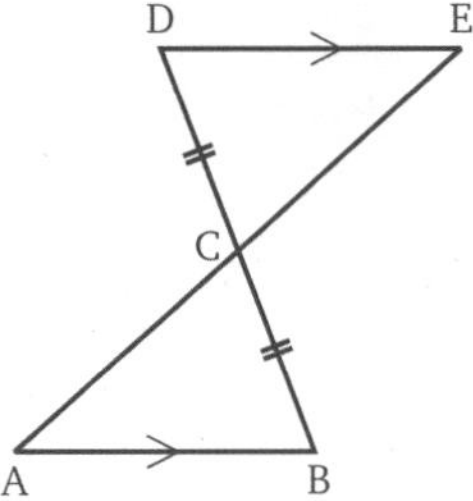

Prove that △ABC and △EDC are congruent.

7

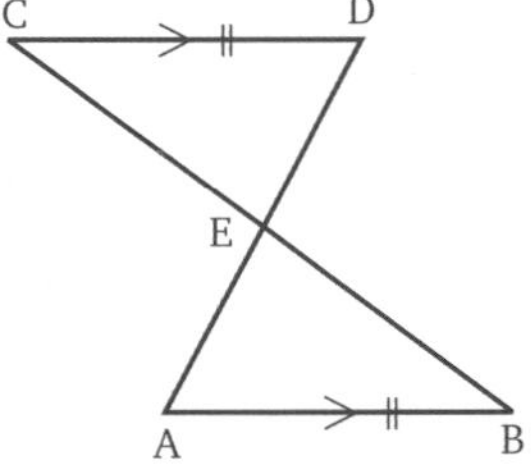

CD and AB are equal and parallel. Prove that △ABE and △DCE are congruent.

8

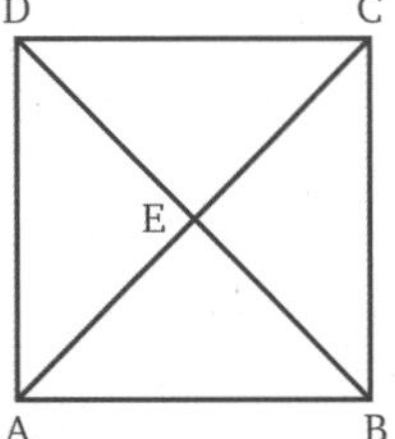

ABCD is a square. Show that △s ABE, BCE, CDE and DAE are all congruent.

9

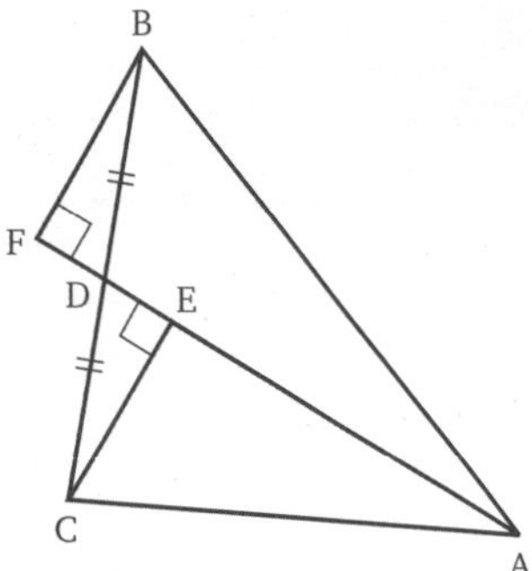

D is the midpoint of BC. CE and BF are perpendicular to AF. Find a pair of congruent triangles.

10

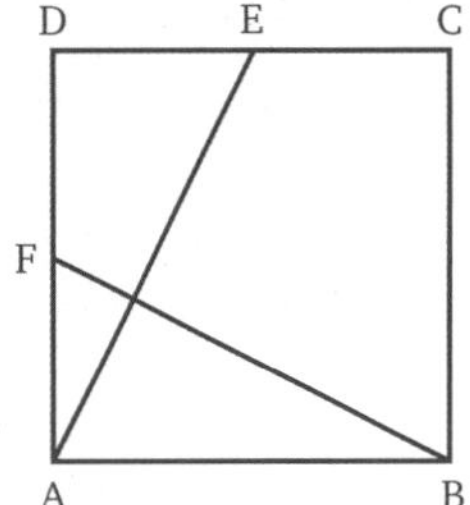

ABCD is a square. E is the midpoint of DC and F is the midpoint of AD. Show that △ADE and △BAF are congruent.

11 ABC is an isosceles triangle in which AB = AC. D is the midpoint of AB and E is the midpoint of AC. Prove that △BDC is congruent with △CEB.

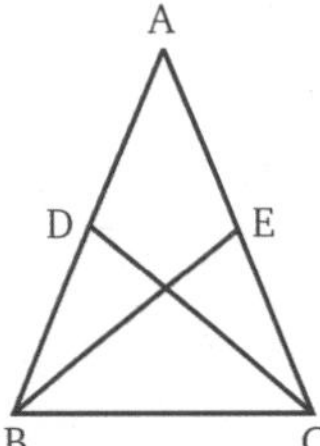

12 ABCD is a rectangle and E is the midpoint of AB. Join DE and CE and show that △ADE is congruent with △BCE.

13 ABCD is a rectangle. E is the midpoint of AB and F is the midpoint of DC. Join DE and BF and show that △ADE is congruent with △CBF.

Puzzle

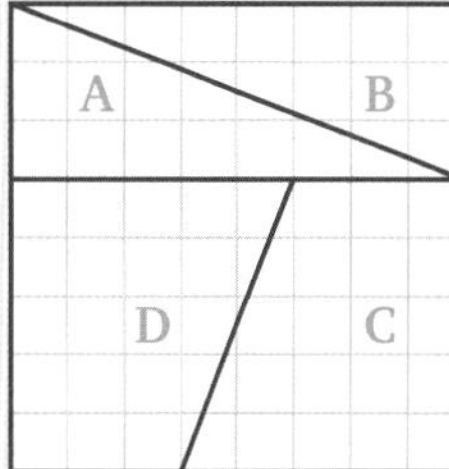

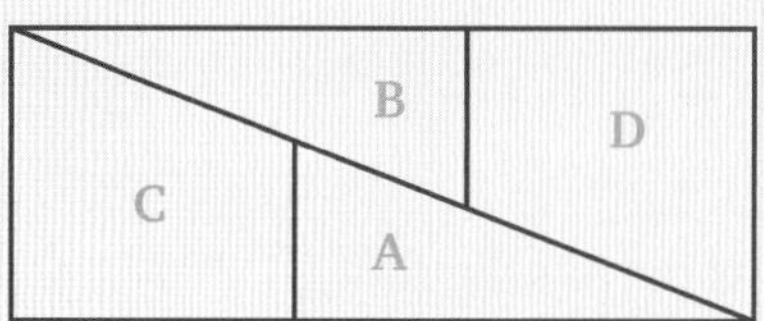

Draw a square of side 8 cm on centimetre squared paper. Divide the square into two congruent triangles and two congruent trapeziums as shown in the diagram on the left.

Rearrange the four shapes to form the rectangle on the right. This rectangle measures 13 cm by 5 cm so has an area of $13 \times 5\,\text{cm}^2 = 65\,\text{cm}^2$.

However, the area of the original square is $8 \times 8\,\text{cm}^2 = 64\,\text{cm}^2$.

How do you explain this apparent contradiction?

Using congruent triangles

Once two triangles have been shown to be congruent it follows that the other corresponding sides and angles are equal. This gives a good way of proving that certain angles are equal or that certain lines are the same length.

Exercise 7m

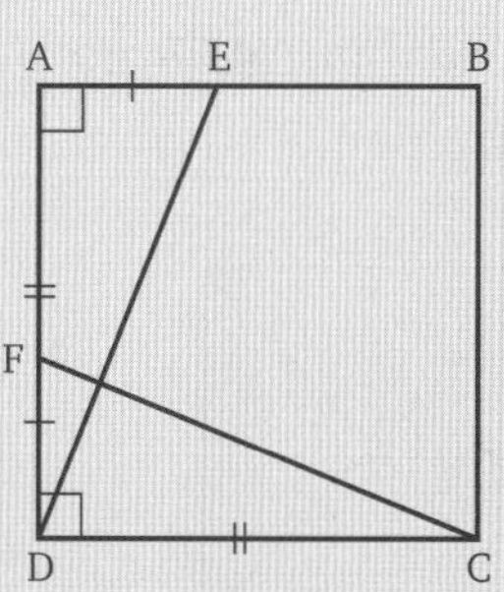

ABCD is a square and AE = DF.
Show that DE = CF.
In $\triangle$s DAE and CDF

AE = DF (given)

DA = CD (sides of a square)

$D\hat{A}E = C\hat{D}F$ (angles of a square are 90°)

$\therefore \triangle\text{s } \begin{matrix}\text{DAE} \\ \text{CDF}\end{matrix}$ are congruent (SAS)

(We have written the triangles so that corresponding vertices are lined up. We can then see the remaining corresponding sides and angles.)

$\therefore$ DE = CF

1 BD bisects $A\hat{B}C$. BE and BF are equal. Show that triangles BED and BFD are congruent and hence prove that ED = FD.

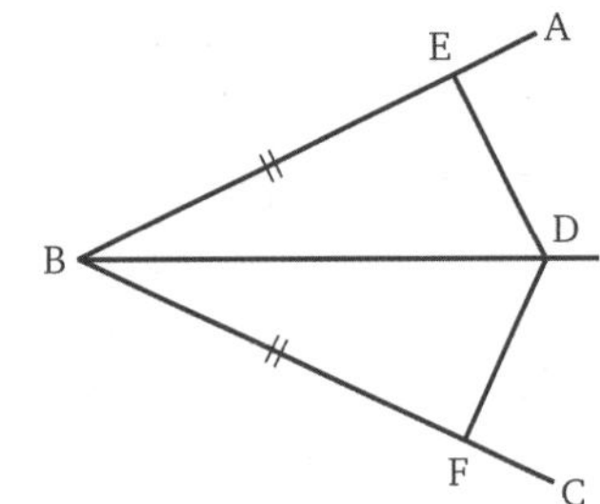

2 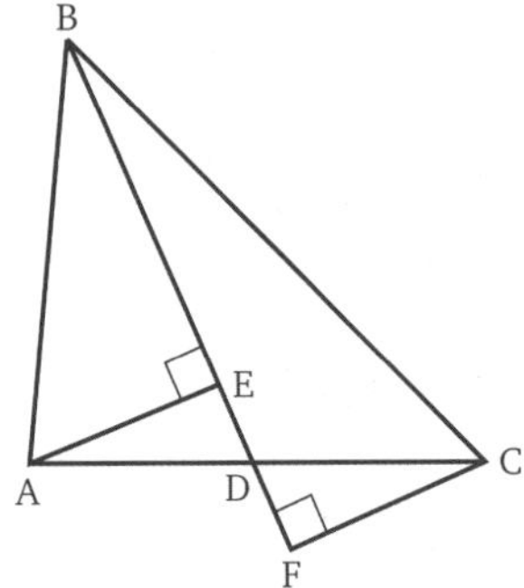

D is the midpoint of AC. AE and CF are both perpendicular to BF. Show that triangles AED and CFD are congruent and hence prove that AE = CF.

3 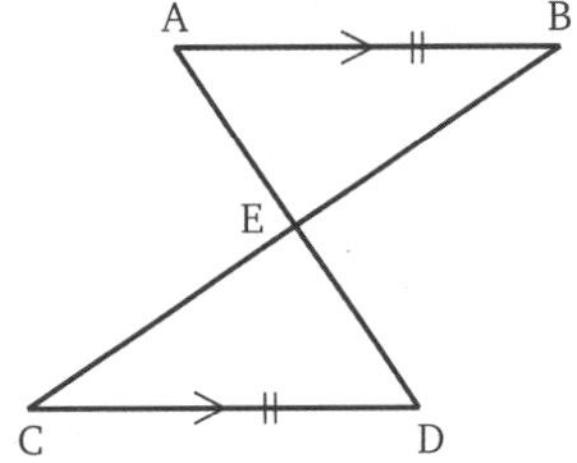

AB and CD are parallel and equal in length. Show that △AEB and △DEC are congruent and hence prove that E is the midpoint of both CB and AD.

ABCD is a square and P, Q and R are points on AB, BC and CD respectively such that AP = BQ = CR.

Show that $P\hat{Q}R = 90°$.

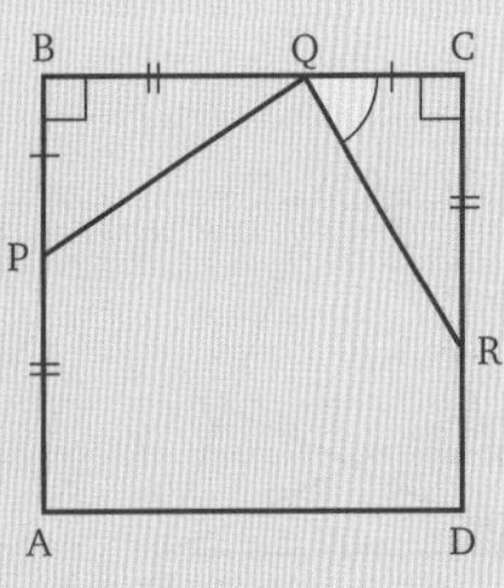

(We will first prove that △PBQ and △QCR are congruent.)

In △PBQ and △QCR

	BQ = CR	(given)
	$P\hat{B}Q = Q\hat{C}R = 90°$	(angles of a square)
also	PB = QC { AB = BC	(sides of a square)
	AP = BQ	(given)

∴ △s PBQ, QCR are congruent (SAS)

∴ $B\hat{Q}P = Q\hat{R}C$

In $\triangle QRC$	$Q\hat{R}C + C\hat{Q}R = 90°$	(angles of triangle)
$\therefore$	$B\hat{Q}P + C\hat{Q}R = 90°$	($B\hat{Q}P = Q\hat{R}C$, proved above)
But	$B\hat{Q}P + P\hat{Q}R + C\hat{Q}R = 180°$	(angles on a straight line)
$\therefore$	$P\hat{Q}R = 90°$	

4 ABCD is a square and E is the midpoint of the diagonal AC. First show that triangles ADE and CDE are congruent and hence prove that DE is perpendicular to AC.

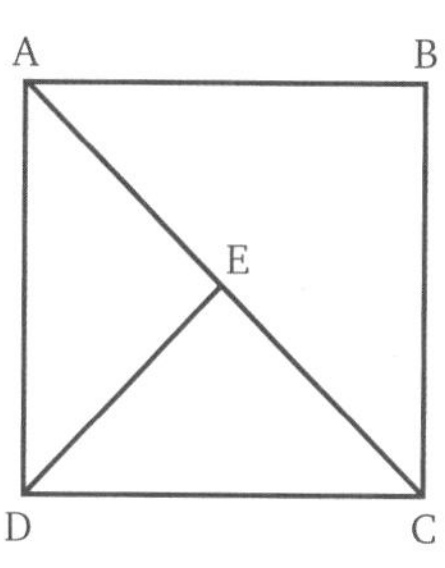

5 CD is parallel to BA and CD = CB = BA.

Show that $\triangle CDE$ is congruent with $\triangle BAE$ and hence that CA bisects BD.

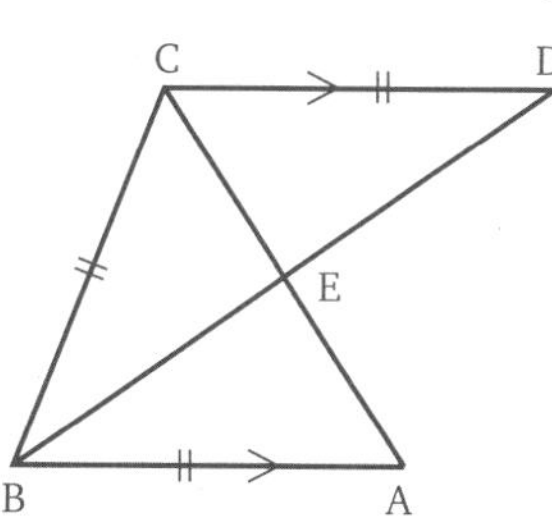

6 Using the same diagram and the result from question **5**, show that $\triangle BEC$ is congruent with $\triangle CED$. Hence prove that CA and BD cut at right angles.

7

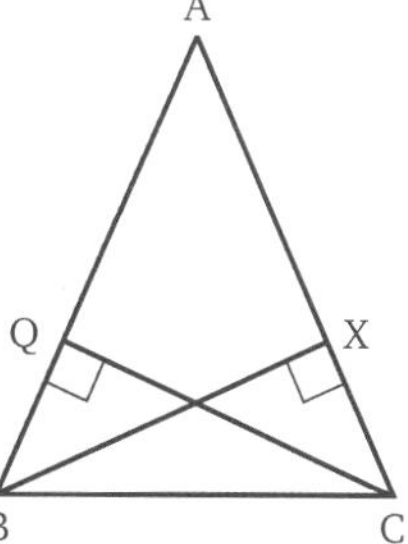

Triangle ABC is isosceles, with AB = AC. BX is perpendicular to AC and CQ is perpendicular to AB. Prove that BX = CQ.

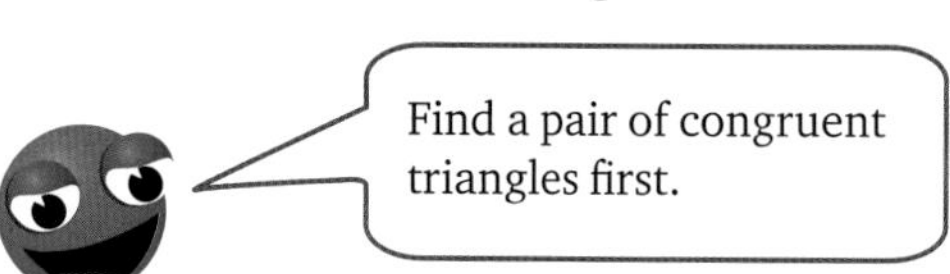

8

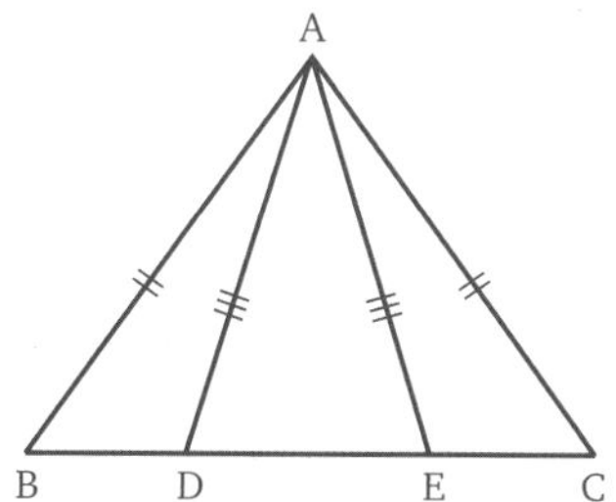

In the diagram, AB = AC and AD = AE. Prove that BD = EC.

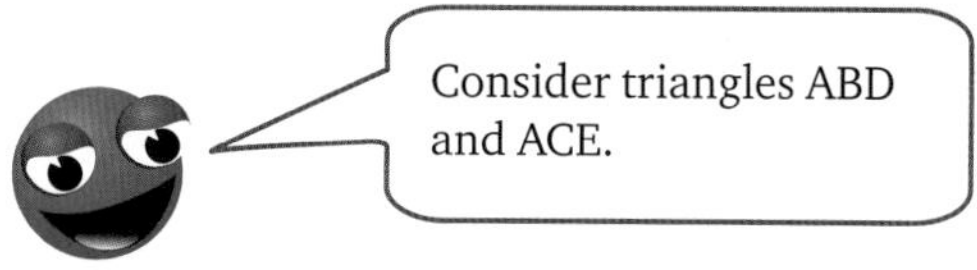

9 AB is a straight line. Draw a line AX perpendicular to AB. On the other side of AB, draw a line BY perpendicular to AB so that BY is equal to AX. Prove that $A\hat{X}Y = B\hat{Y}X$.

Properties of parallelograms

In Book 1 we briefly looked at parallelograms. Now we can use congruent triangles to prove that the properties we found are true for all parallelograms.

A parallelogram is formed when two pairs of parallel lines cross each other.

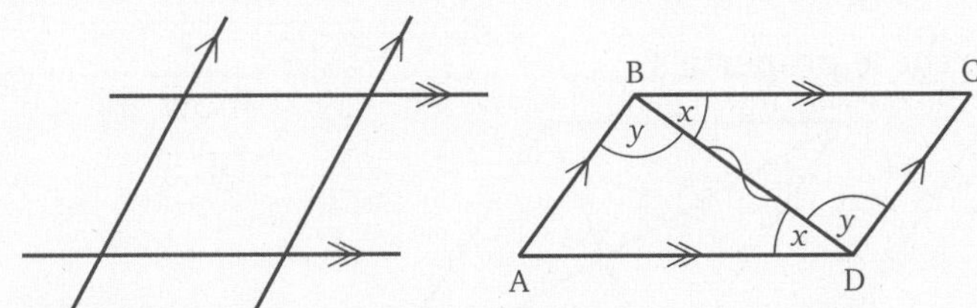

In the parallelogram ABCD, joining BD gives two triangles in which:

- the angles marked x are equal (they are alternate angles with respect to parallels AD and BC)
- the angles marked y are equal (they are alternate angles with respect to parallels AB and DC)
- and BD is the same for both triangles.

$\therefore$ $\triangle$s $\begin{matrix}\text{BCD} \\ \text{DAB}\end{matrix}$ are congruent (AAS)

$\therefore$ BC = AD and AB = DC

i.e. **The opposite sides of a parallelogram are the same length.**

Also from the congruent triangles

$$\hat{A} = \hat{C}$$

and $\quad A\hat{B}C = C\hat{D}A \ (x + y = y + x)$

i.e. **The opposite angles of a parallelogram are equal.**

Drawing both diagonals of the parallelogram gives four triangles.

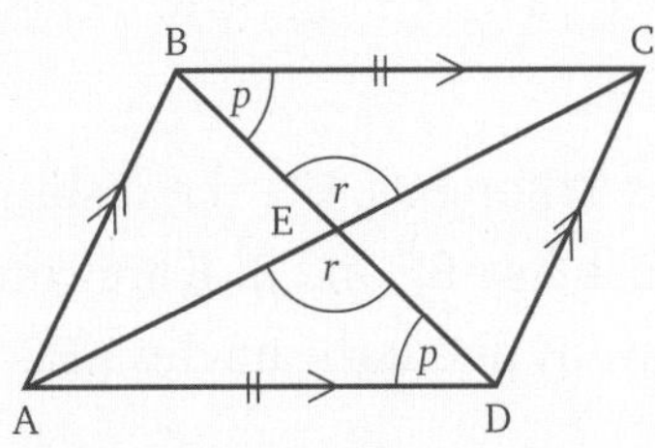

Considering the two triangles BEC, DEA

BC = AD (opp. sides of ||gram)

$E\hat{B}C = E\hat{D}A$ (alt. $\angle$s)

$B\hat{E}C = A\hat{E}D$ (vert. opp. $\angle$s)

$\therefore \triangle$s $\begin{matrix} \text{BEC} \\ \text{DEA} \end{matrix}$ are congruent (AAS)

$\therefore$ BE = ED and AE = EC

i.e. **The diagonals of a parallelogram bisect each other.**

The diagrams below summarise these properties.

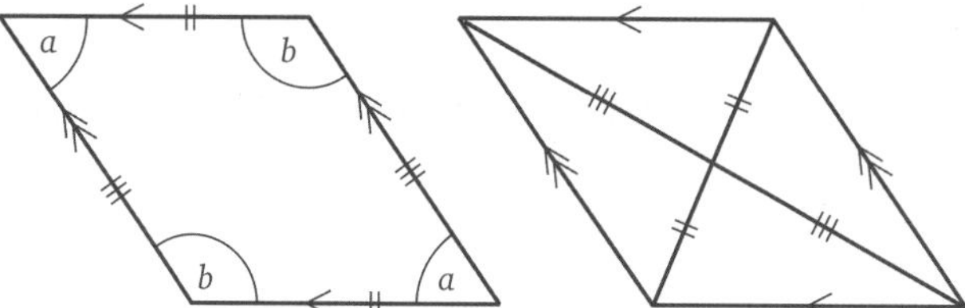

It is equally important to realise that, in general,

- the diagonals are *not* the same length
- the diagonals do *not* bisect the angles of a parallelogram, unless the sides are all of equal length.

In the exercise that follows, you are asked to investigate the properties of some of the other special quadrilaterals.

Exercise 7n

1 ABCD is a rhombus (a parallelogram in which all four sides are equal in length). Join AC and show that △ABC and △ADC are congruent. What does AC do to the angles of the rhombus at A and C? Does the diagonal BD do the same to the angles at B and D?

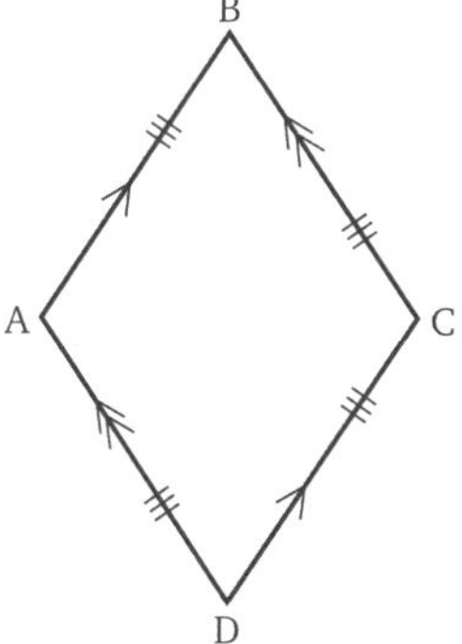

2 ABCD is a rhombus. Use the results from question **1** to show that △s ABE and BCE are congruent. What can you now say about the angles AEB and BEC?

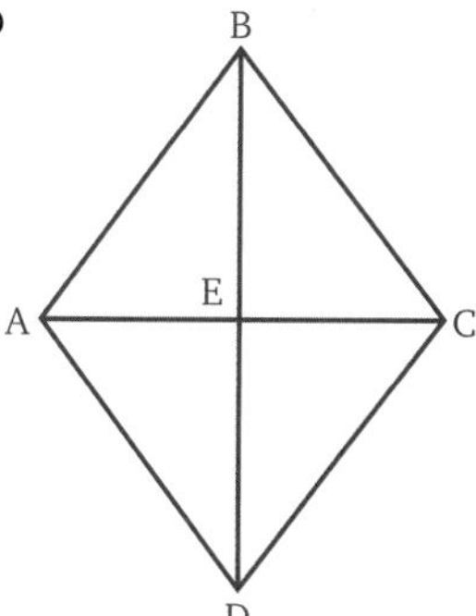

3 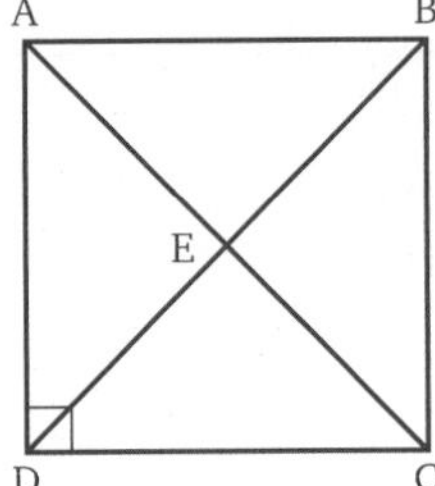

ABCD is a square (a rhombus with right-angled corners). Use the properties of the diagonals of a rhombus to show that △AEB is isosceles. Hence prove that the diagonals of a square are the same length.

Are the two diagonals of *every* rhombus the same length?

4 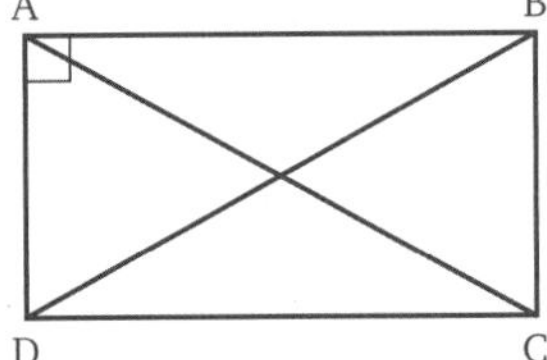

ABCD is a rectangle (a parallelogram with right-angled corners). Prove that △s ADB and DAC are congruent. What can you deduce about the lengths of AC and DB?

5 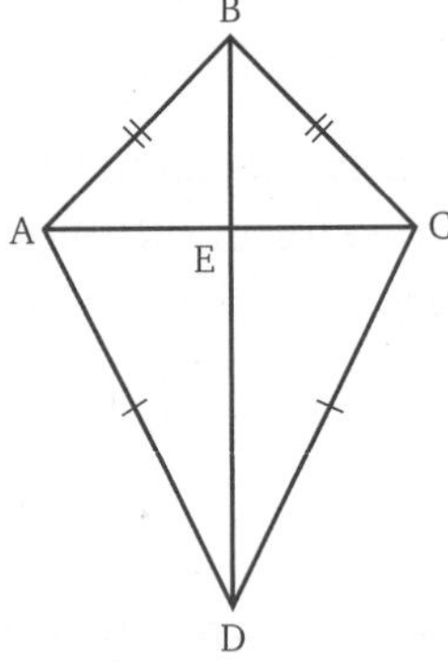

ABCD is a kite in which AB = BC and AD = DC.

Does the diagonal BD bisect the angles at B and D?

Does the diagonal AC bisect the angles at A and C?

Is E the midpoint of either diagonal?

What can you say about the angles at E?

6 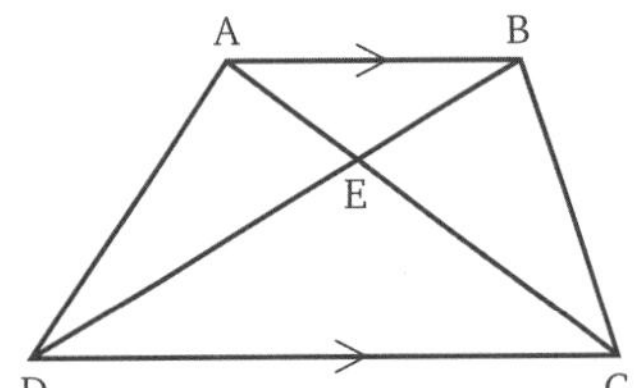

ABCD is a trapezium: it has just one pair of parallel sides. Are there any congruent triangles in this diagram?

7 In the diagram, ABCD and ABEF are parallelograms. Show that △s ADF and BCE are congruent.

By considering the shape ABCF and then removing each of the triangles AFD and BEC in turn, what can you say about the areas of the two parallelograms?

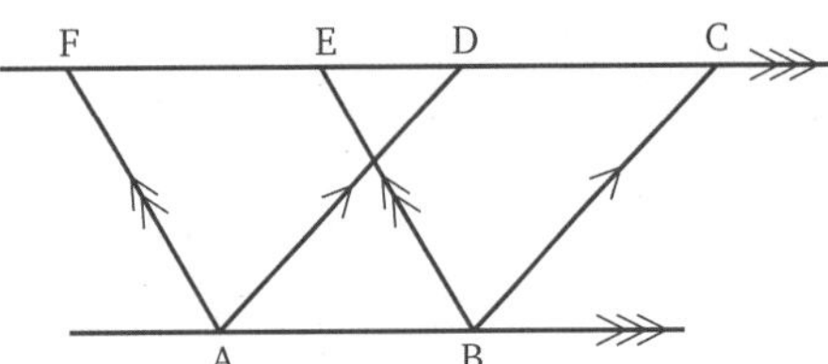

Puzzle

Penny pushed \$6 across the counter at the Post Office. 'Would you give me some 70 c stamps, two fewer 60 c stamps than 70 c stamps and seven 10 c stamps please'. How many stamps did she get?

Assume that there was no change.

Using properties of special quadrilaterals

In question **7** in Exercise 7n you proved a property of two parallelograms.

> Two parallelograms with the same base and drawn between the same pair of parallel lines are equal in area.

The diagrams below summarise the other results from Exercise 7n:

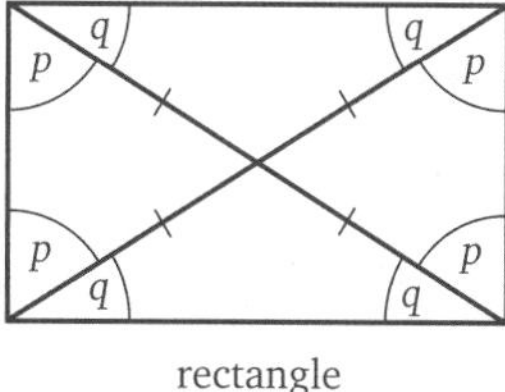

rectangle

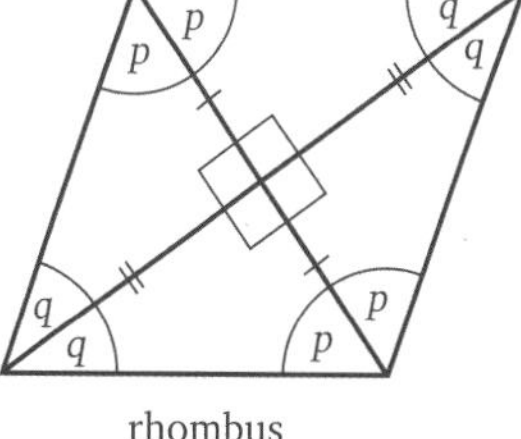

rhombus

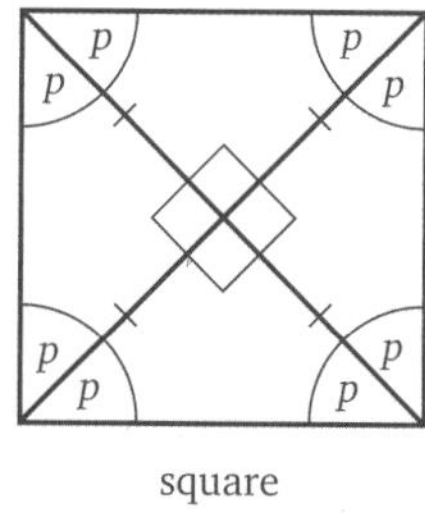

square

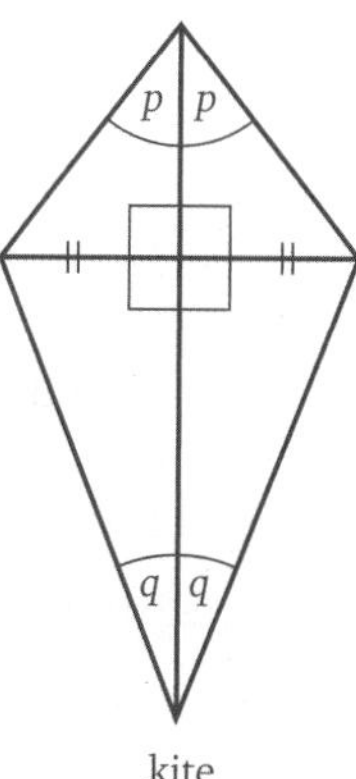

kite

You can now use any of these facts in the following exercise.

Exercise 7p

1 ABCD is a rectangle. The diagonals AC and DB cut at E. How far is E from BC?

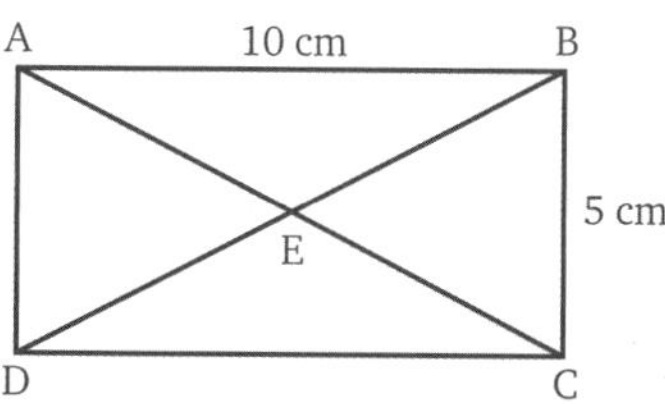

2

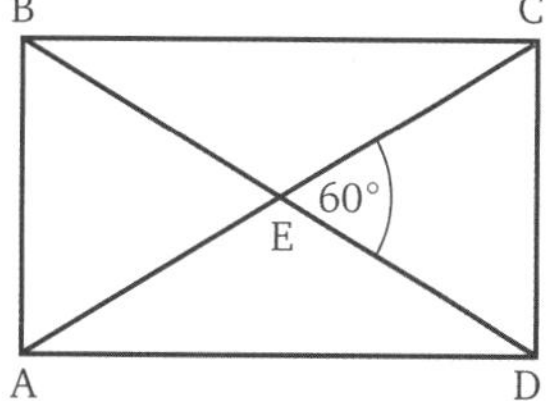

ABCD is a rectangle in which $\hat{CED} = 60°$. Find $\hat{ECD}$.

3 ABCD is a parallelogram in which $A\hat{B}C = 120°$ and $B\hat{C}A = 30°$. Show that ABCD is also a rhombus.

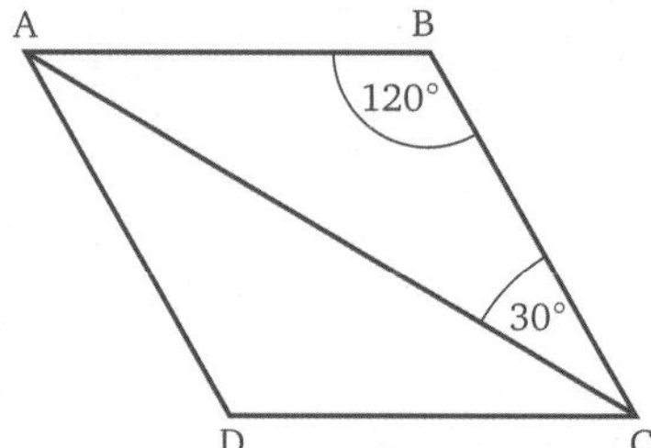

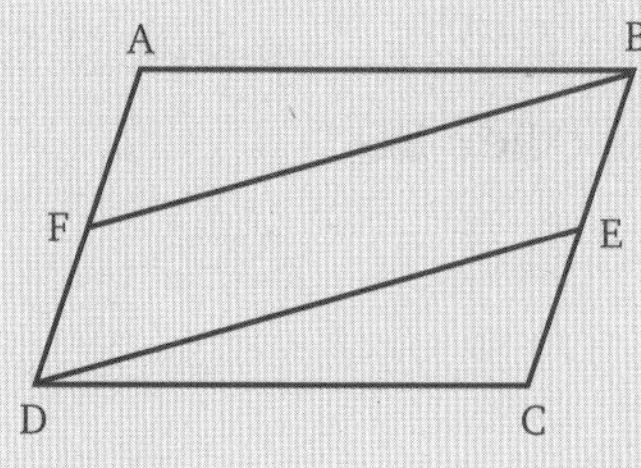

ABCD is a parallelogram. E is the midpoint of BC and F is the midpoint of AD.

Prove that BF = DE.

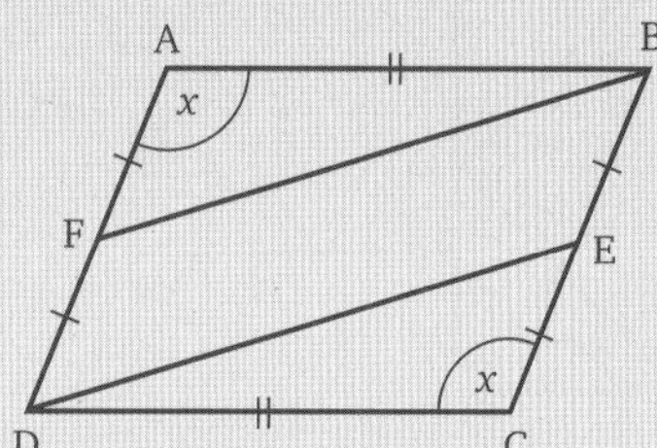

(Remember that in a parallelogram the opposite sides are equal and the opposite angles are equal.)

In △s ABF and CDE

AF = EC ($\frac{1}{2}$ opp. sides of parallelogram)

AB = DC (opp. sides of parallelogram)

$F\hat{A}B = E\hat{C}D$ (opp. angles of parallelogram)

∴ △s ABF/CDE are congruent (SAS)

∴ BF = DE

4

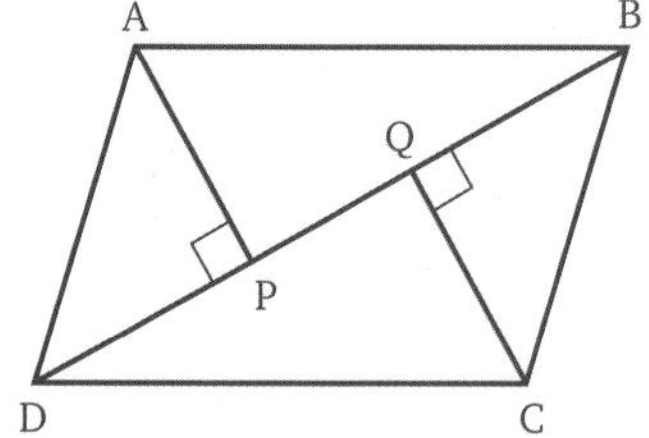

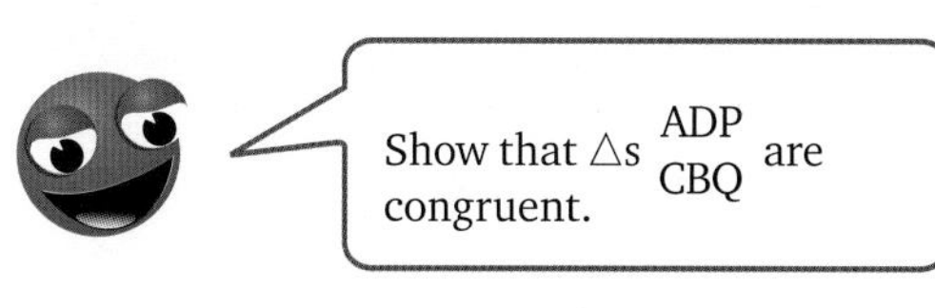

ABCD is a parallelogram. AP is perpendicular to BD and CQ is perpendicular to BD. Prove that AP = CQ.

5

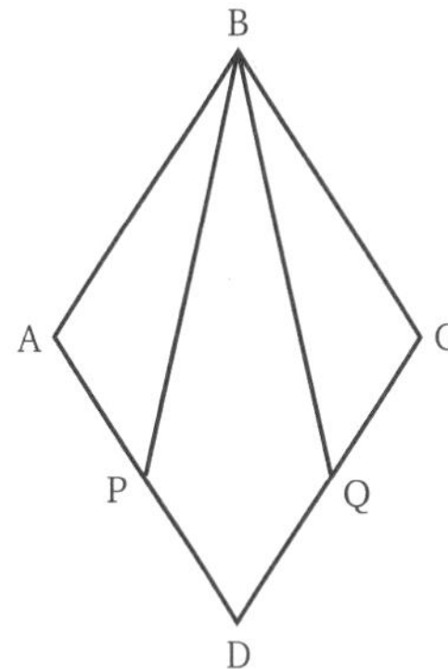

ABCD is a rhombus. P is the midpoint of AD and Q is the midpoint of CD. Prove that BP = BQ.

6

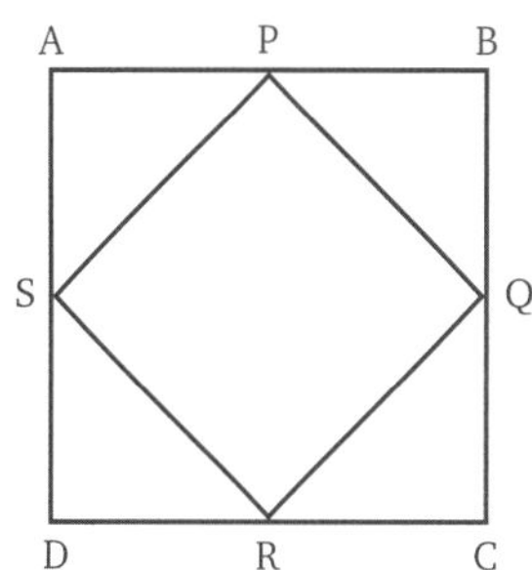

ABCD is a square and P, Q, R and S are the midpoints of AB, BC, CD and DA. Prove that PQRS is a square.

7

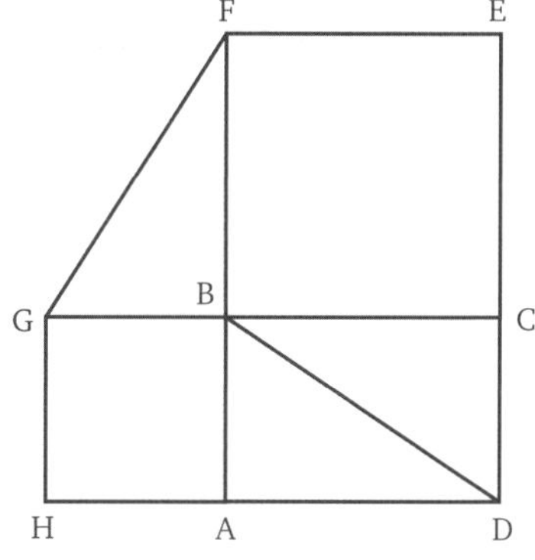

ABCD is a rectangle. ABGH and BCEF are squares. Show that GF = BD.

Exercise 7q

Select the letter that gives the correct answer.

Use this diagram for questions **1** to **3**.

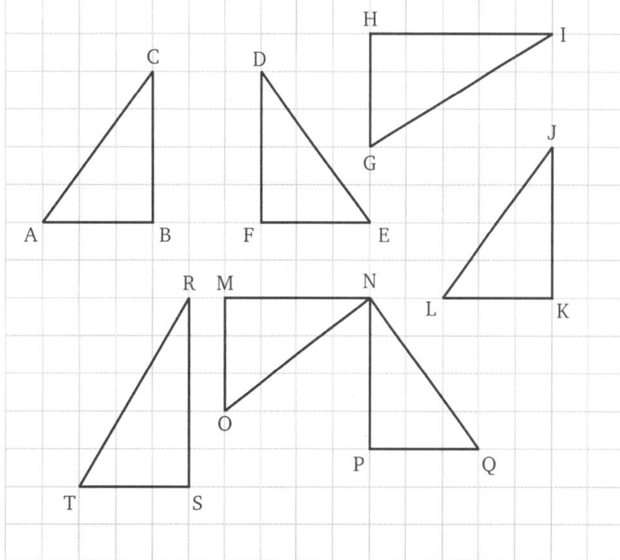

1 Triangle DEF is congruent to another triangle as a result of a reflection.

The other triangle is

A △ABC **B** △HIJ **C** △PQN **D** △JKL

2 Triangle RST is congruent to another triangle. The other triangle is

A △ABC **B** △HIJ **C** △PQN **D** △JKL

3 Triangle MNO is congruent to another triangle as a result of a rotation.

The other triangle is

A △HIJ **B** △JKL **C** △PQN **D** △RST

4 These two triangles are congruent.

Which set of conditions do they satisfy?

A AAS

B RHS

C SAS

D SSS

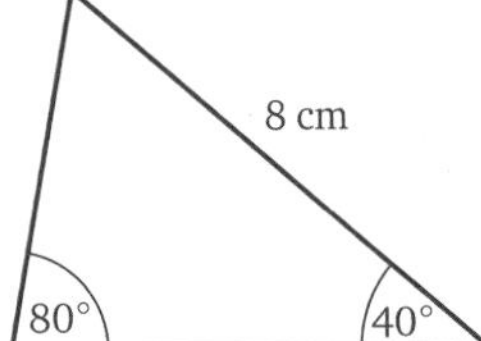

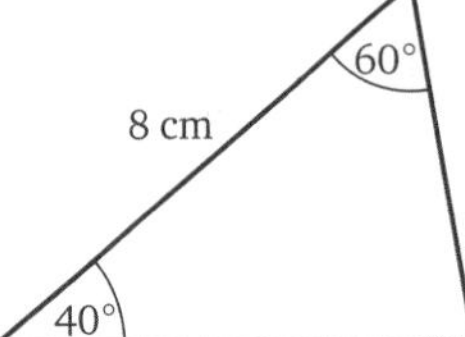

5 ABCD is a kite.

Are triangles ABC and ADC congruent?

If they are, which set of conditions do they satisfy?

A Yes, AAS

B Yes, SAS

C Yes, SSS

D No

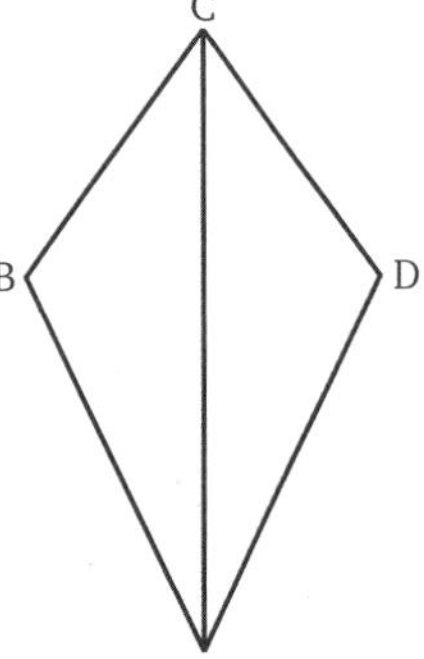

Did you know?

The Canadian mathematician Cathleen Morawetz was the first woman to head a mathematics institute – the Courant Institute of Mathematics in New York. Her father was the applied mathematician John Synge.

In this chapter you have seen that...

- ✔ congruent shapes are identical in every way
- ✔ similar shapes are the same shape, but different in size
- ✔ two triangles are congruent if

  the three sides of one triangle are equal to the three sides of the other triangle

  or two angles and one side of one triangle are equal to two angles and the *corresponding* side of the other triangle

  or two sides and the *included* angle of one triangle are equal to two sides and the *included* angle of the other triangle

  or both have a right angle, and the hypotenuse and a side of one triangle are equal to the hypotenuse and a side of the other triangle

  These conditions can be abbreviated as SSS, AAS, SAS and RHS
- ✔ congruent triangles can be used to prove the properties of the special quadrilaterals.

REVIEW TEST 1: CHAPTERS 1–7

In questions **1** to **11**, choose the letter for the correct answer.

1 In standard form or scientific form, 0.00732 =

A 0.0732×10^{-1} C 7.32×10^{-3}

B 0.732×10^{-2} D 73.2×10^{-4}

2 To two significant figures, 6.4783 =

A 6.5 B 6.74 C 6.75 D 6.8

3 $1101_2 + 101_2 =$

A 11110_2 B 11010_2 C 10110_2 D 10010_2

4 Which of the following is/are true for the diagonals of a rhombus?

i They bisect the angles.

ii They bisect each other.

iii They are perpendicular.

A **i** and **ii** only C **i** and **iii** only

B **ii** and **iii** only D **i, ii** and **iii**

5 When simplified $8 - 3(x - 2) =$

A $5x - 10$ B $14 - 3x$ C $6 - 3x$ D $5x - 2$

6 The value of $\left(\frac{2}{3}\right)^{-3}$ is

A $\frac{8}{27}$ B $\frac{4}{9}$ C $\frac{9}{4}$ D $\frac{27}{8}$

7 If the angle of elevation of a house on the top of a cliff from a boat out at sea is 34°, the angle of depression of the boat from the house is

A 34° B 66° C 114° D 146°

8 The circumference of a circle is 88 cm. What is its radius? (Take $\pi = \frac{22}{7}$)

A 11 cm B 14 cm C 22 cm D 44 cm

9 The value of $-9 + 3 - (-4)$ is

A −16 B −10 C −2 D 2

10 The side LM of a triangle measures 5 cm. The triangle is enlarged by a scale factor 2. What is the measure of the image of LM?

A 3 cm B 7 cm C 10 cm D 25 cm

11 What is the volume of a cylinder of radius $3\frac{1}{2}$ cm and length 4 cm? (Take $\pi = \frac{22}{7}$)

A 14 cm^3 B 44 cm^3 C 88 cm^3 D 154 cm^3

12 Give each number correct to: **i** 3 decimal places **ii** 3 significant figures

a 47.976 45 **b** 0.456 83 **c** 263.005 67

13 Find: **a** $\left(2\frac{1}{4} - 1\frac{1}{3}\right) \div \frac{11}{24}$ **b** $5\frac{3}{7} \times 7 - 12\frac{4}{5}$

14 ABCD is a parallelogram in which $A\hat{D}B = B\hat{D}C = 30°$ and $D\hat{A}C = 60°$.

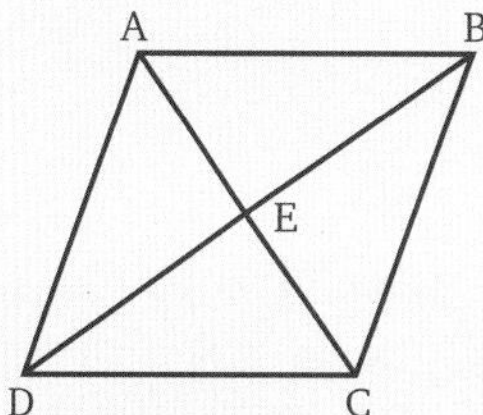

a Prove that triangles ADE and ABE are congruent.

b Prove that triangle ADC is isosceles.

15 State, with brief reasons, whether these two triangles are congruent.

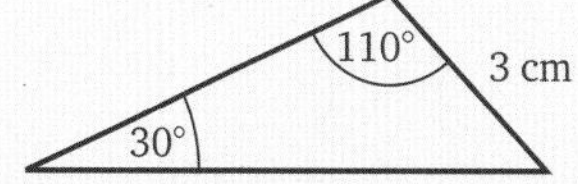

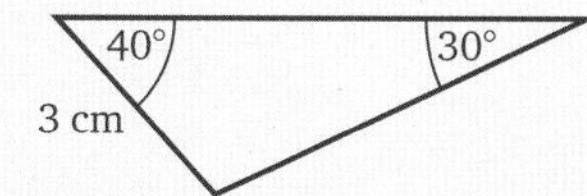

16 Find the size of each angle marked with a letter.

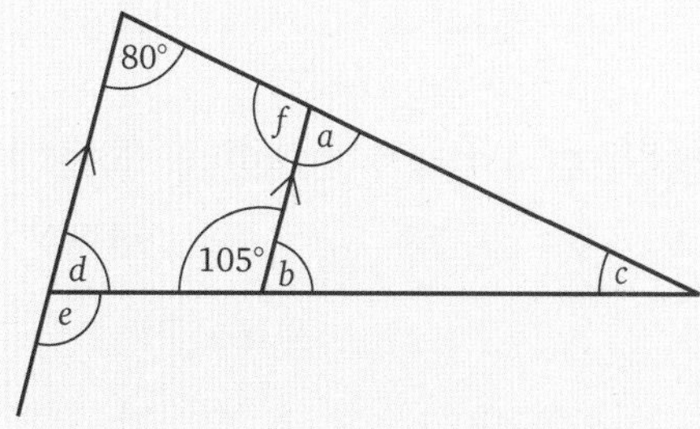

17 a Calculate the angle subtended at the centre of a circle of radius 5.8 cm by an arc of length 8.4 cm.

b Calculate the area of this sector.

18 **a** Find the volume of a pyramid that has a rectangular base measuring 4 cm by 2.5 cm given that the vertex is 6.3 cm vertically above the base.

b Find the curved surface area of a right circular cone that has a base radius of 6 cm and a slant height of 8.5 cm.

19 **a** The map ratio of a map is 1 : 20 000. What actual distance is represented by 3.5 cm on the map?

b On a map the area of a section of land is represented by 8.5 cm^2. The scale of the map is 1 : 10 000. What area, in hectares, does this represent?

20 $\triangle A'B'C'$ is the image of $\triangle ABC$. Give the centre of enlargement and the scale factor.

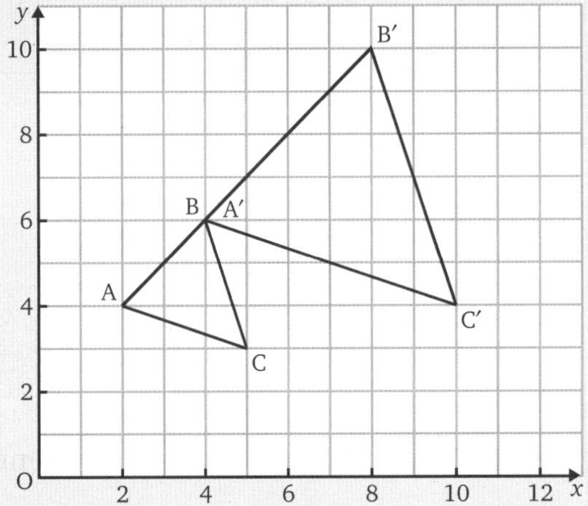

21 This shape consists of a semicircle on a rectangle. Calculate the area of the figure, correct to 2 decimal places.

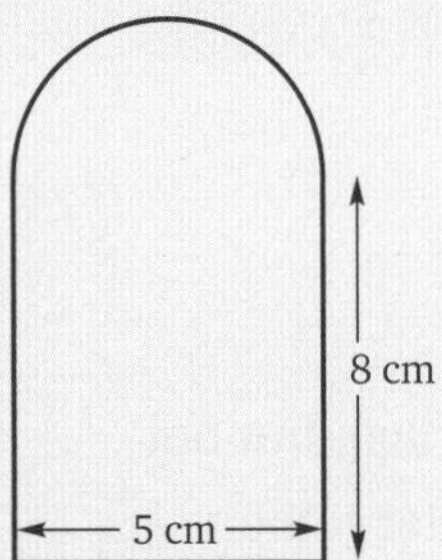

8 Similarity

At the end of this chapter you should be able to...

1 state whether or not given figures are similar
2 determine if two triangles are similar or not, by comparing the sizes of their angles or their sides
3 write equal ratios in two similar triangles
4 calculate the length of one side of a triangle from necessary data on a pair of similar triangles
5 use the scale factor for enlarging one triangle into another to find a missing length.

You need to know...

✔ the angle sum of a triangle
✔ how to find one quantity as a fraction of another
✔ how to solve equations involving fractions
✔ the meaning of ratio.

Key words

alternate angles, corresponding angles, corresponding sides, enlargement, ratio, scale factor, similar, vertically opposite angles

Similar figures

Two figures are *similar* if they are the same shape but not necessarily the same size. One figure is an enlargement of the other.

One may be turned round compared with the other.

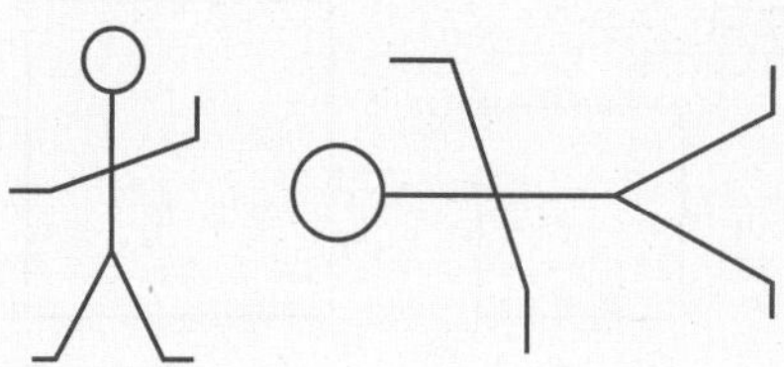

One figure may be turned over compared with the other.

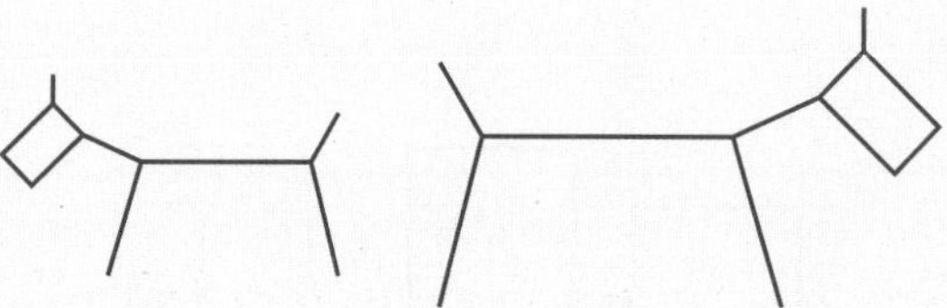

The following figures are not similar although their angles are equal.

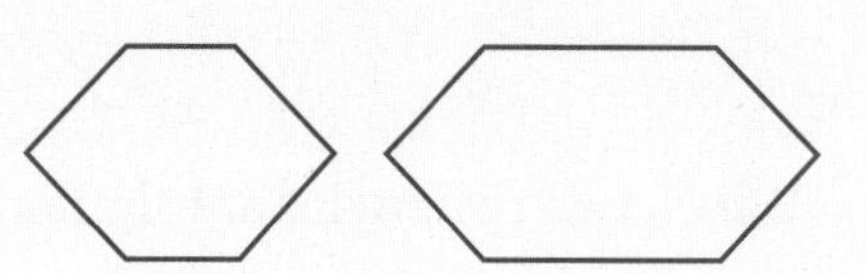

Exercise 8a

State whether or not the pairs of figures in questions **1** to **10** are similar.

1

2

3

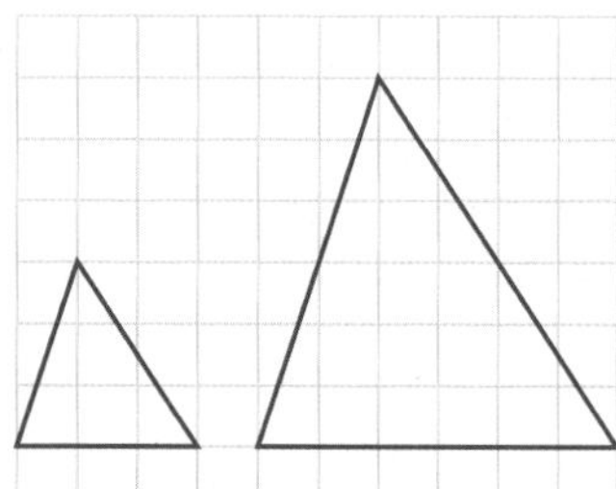

4

5

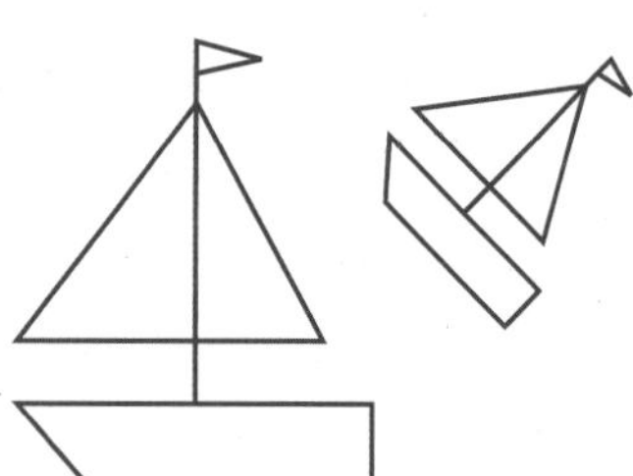

6

7

9

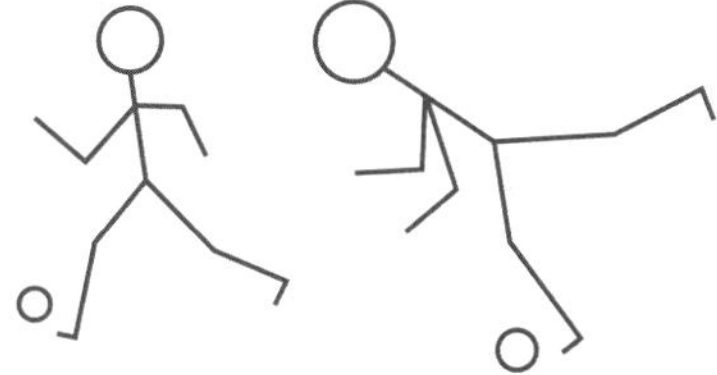

8

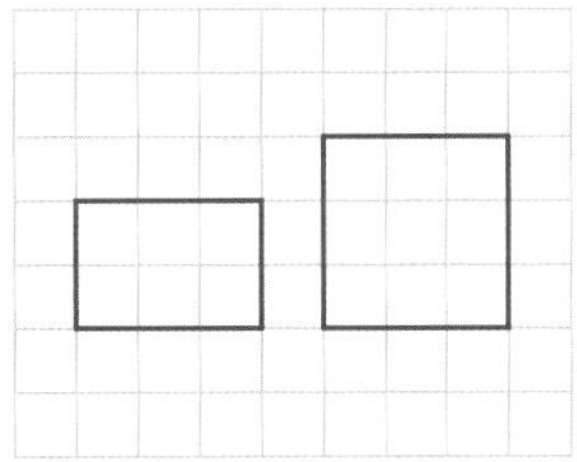

10

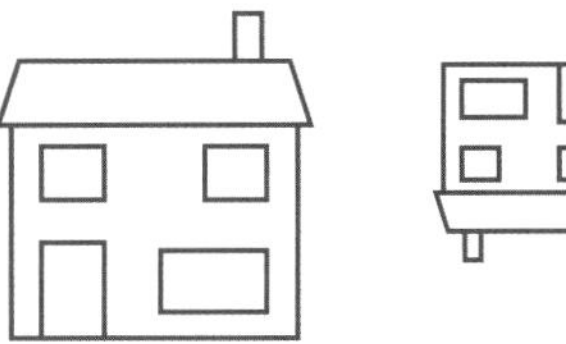

11 Which two rectangles are similar?

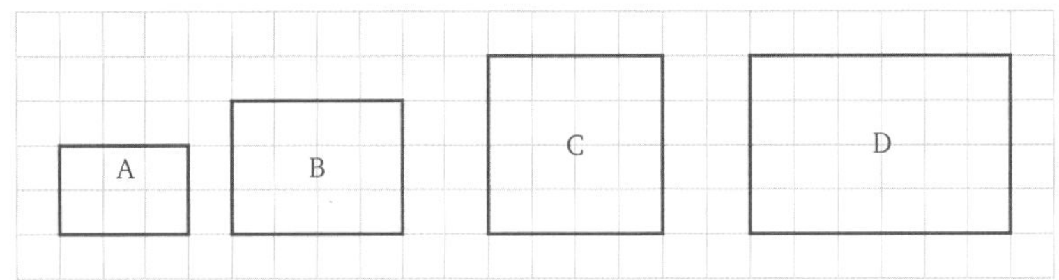

12 Draw your own pairs of figures and state whether or not they are similar. (The second figure may be turned round or over or both, compared with the first.)

Similar triangles

Some of the easiest similar figures to deal with are triangles. This is because only a small amount of information is needed to prove them to be similar.

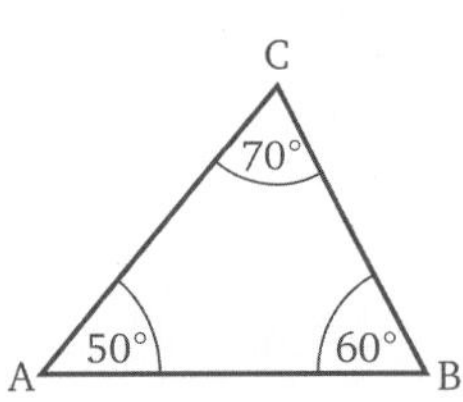

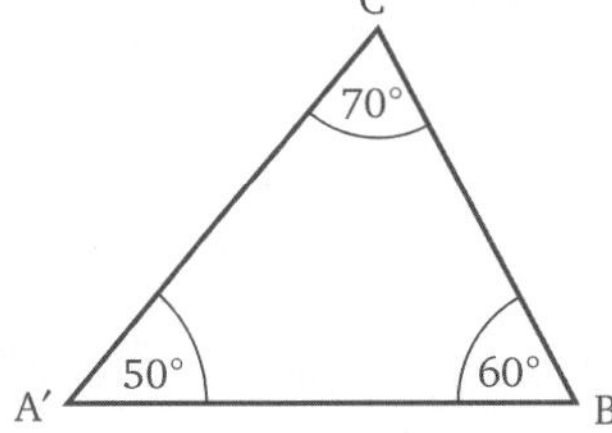

In these triangles the *corresponding angles* are equal and so the triangles are the same shape. One triangle is an *enlargement* of the other. These triangles are *similar*.

Exercise 8b

1 Draw the following triangles accurately:

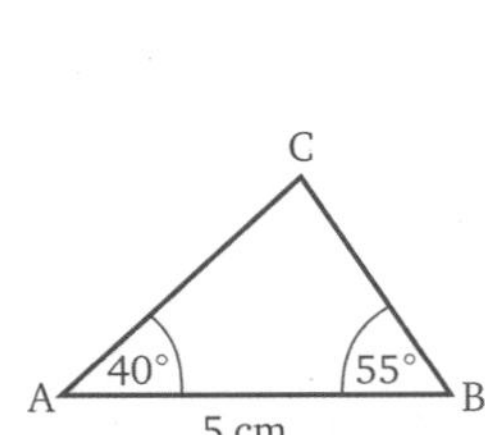

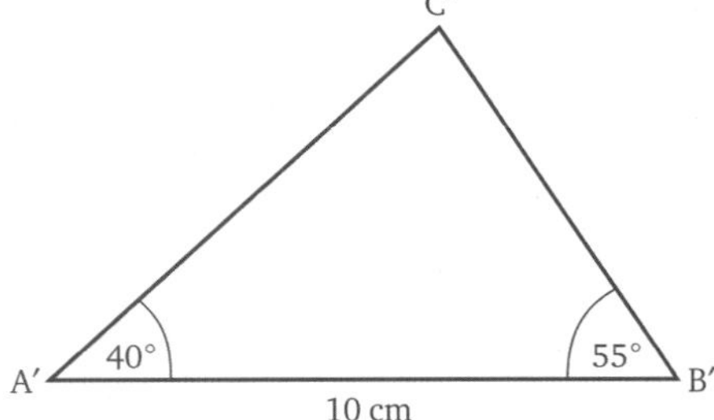

a Are the triangles similar?

b Measure the remaining sides.

c Find $\frac{A'B'}{AB}$, $\frac{B'C'}{BC}$ and $\frac{C'A'}{CA}$.

d What do you notice about the answers to part **c**?

Repeat question **1** for the pairs of triangles in questions **2** to **5**.

2

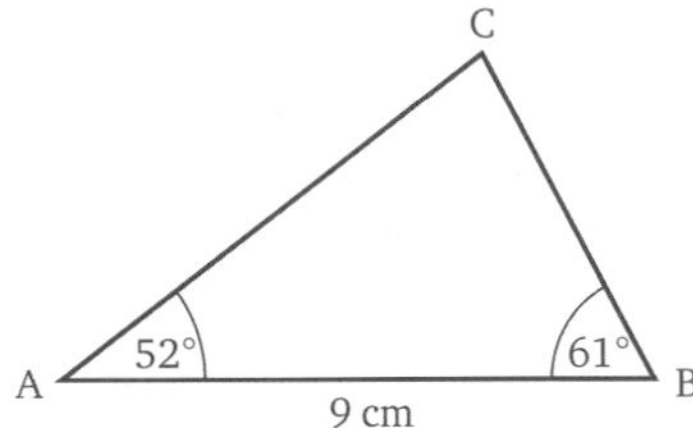

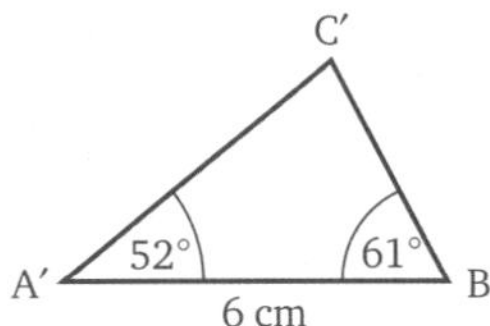

3

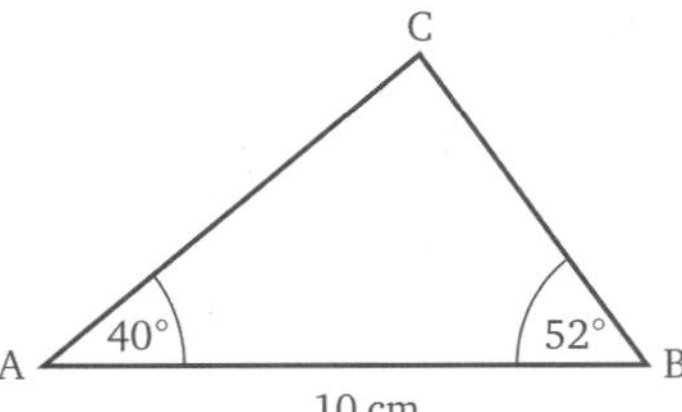

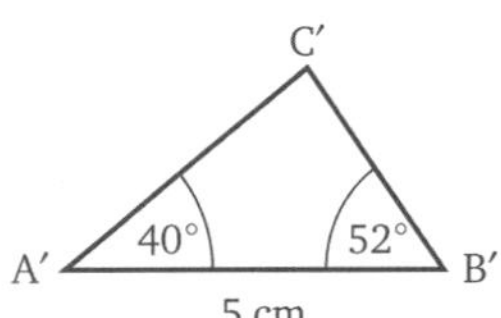

4

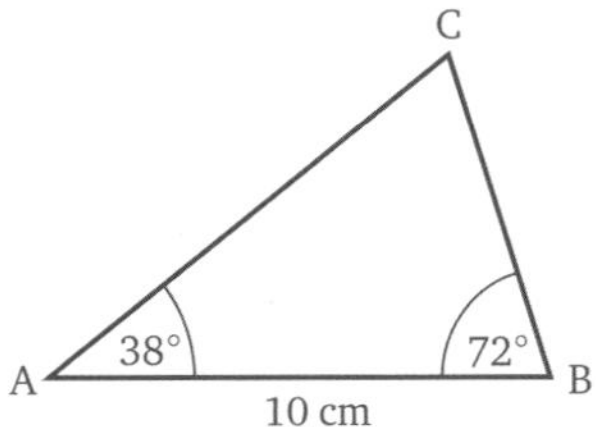

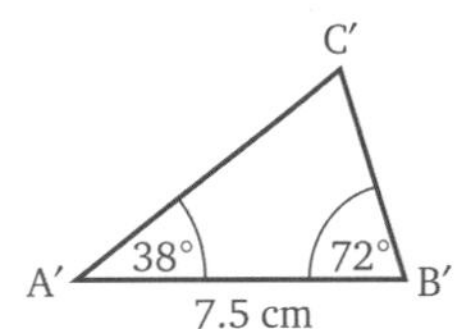

5

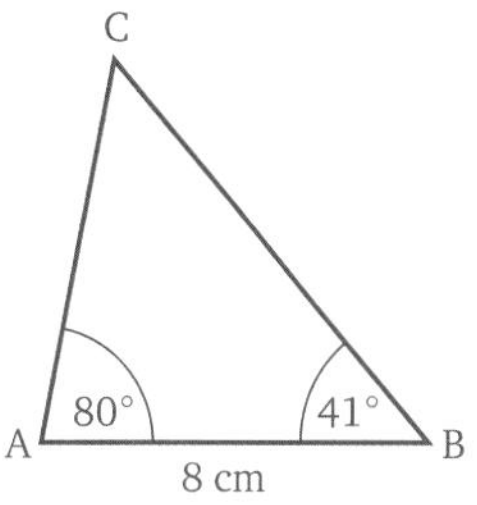

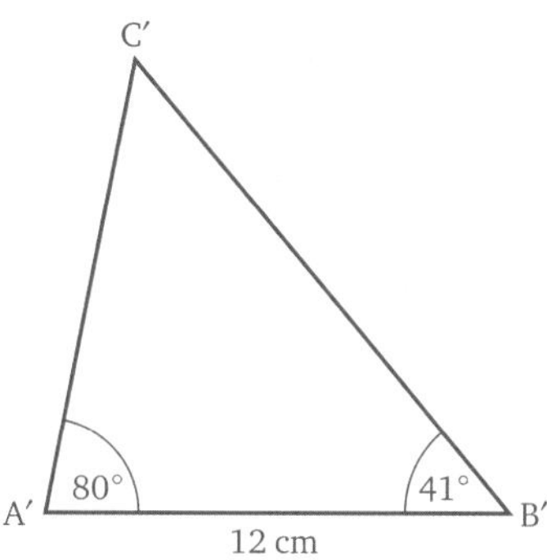

Sketch the following pairs of triangles and find the sizes of the missing angles. In each question state whether the two triangles are similar. (One triangle may be turned round or over compared with the other.)

6

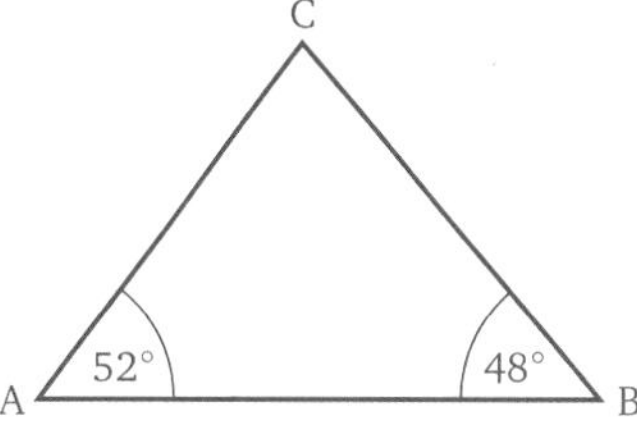

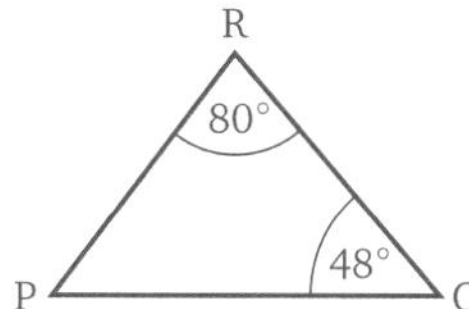

7

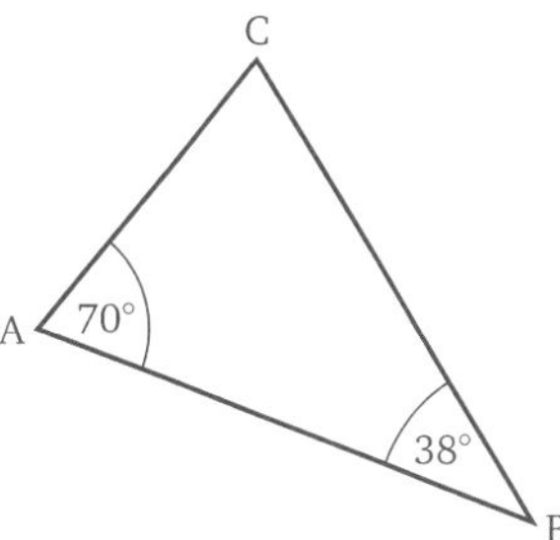

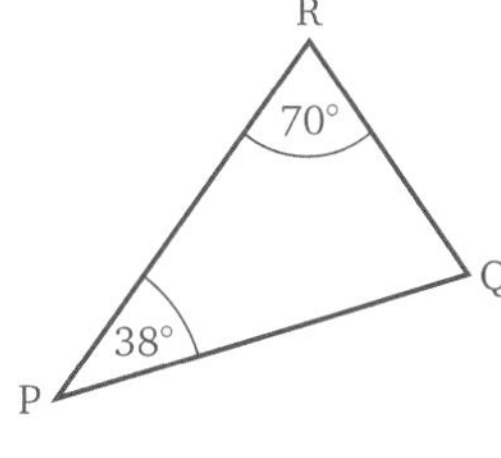

8

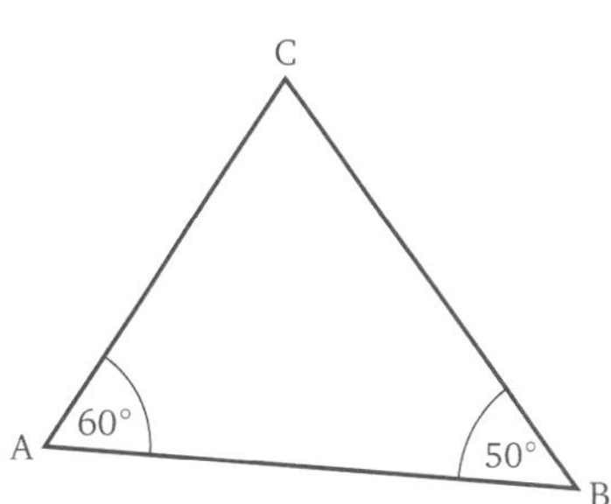

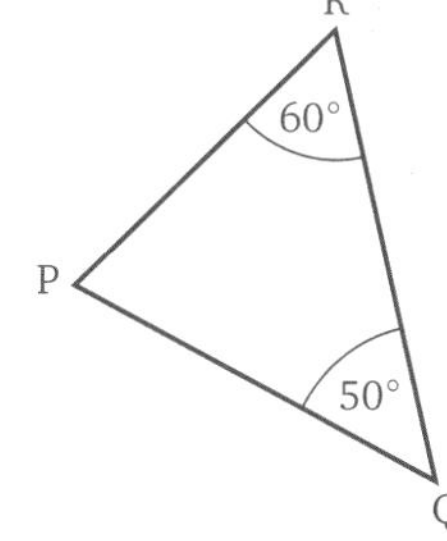

9

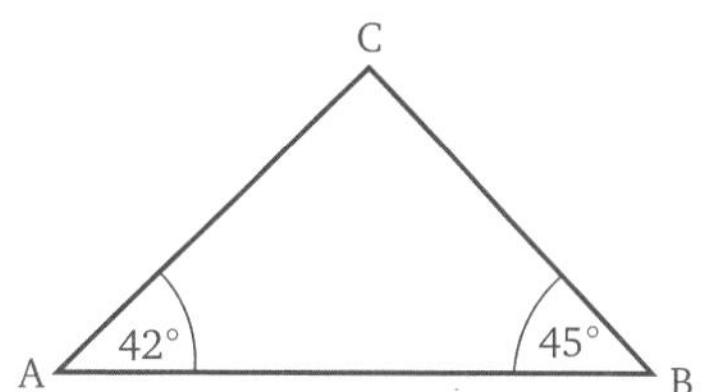

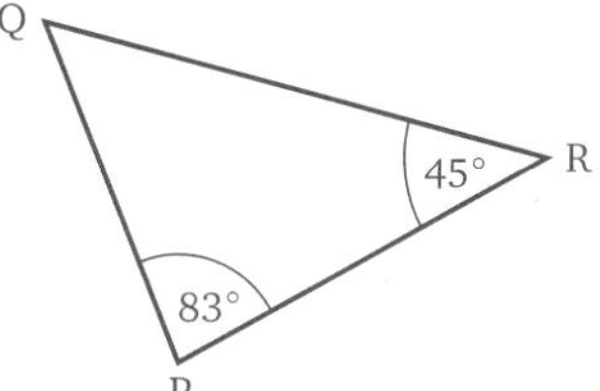

Corresponding vertices

These two triangles are similar and we can see that X corresponds to A, Y to B and Z to C.

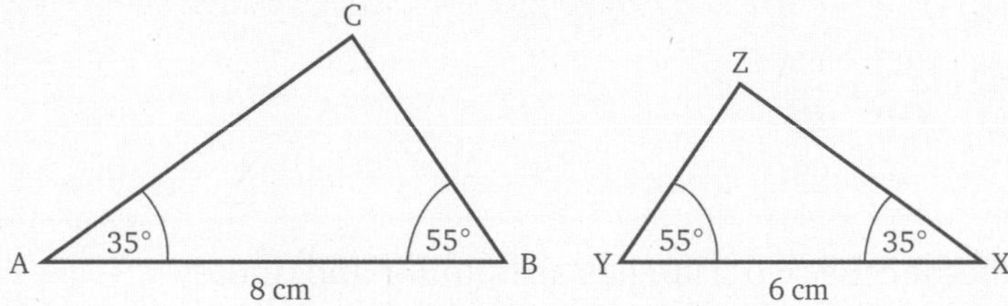

We can write $\triangle\text{s}\ \begin{matrix}\text{ABC}\\ \text{XYZ}\end{matrix}$ are similar

Make sure that X is written below A, Y below B and Z below C.

The pairs of *corresponding sides* are in the same ratio,

that is $$\frac{\text{AB}}{\text{XY}} = \frac{\text{BC}}{\text{YZ}} = \frac{\text{CA}}{\text{ZX}}$$

In this case, $\frac{\text{AB}}{\text{XY}} = \frac{8}{6} = \frac{4}{3}$. So the scale factor to get $\triangle$ABC from $\triangle$XYZ is $\frac{4}{3}$.

Exercise 8c

State whether triangles ABC and PQR are similar and, if they are, give the ratios of the sides.

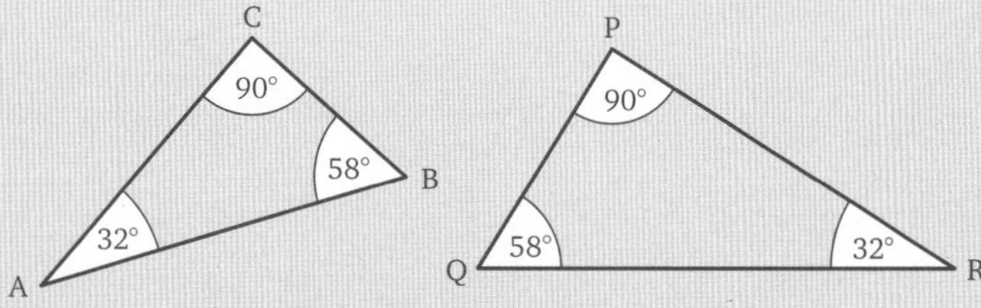

First find the third angle in each triangle

$\hat{\text{Q}} = 58°$ (angles of a triangle)

and $\hat{\text{C}} = 90°$

Now you can see that the triangles are similar and that A corresponds to R, and so on,

so $\quad \triangle s \begin{matrix} ABC \\ RQP \end{matrix}$ are similar

and $\quad \dfrac{AB}{RQ} = \dfrac{BC}{QP} = \dfrac{CA}{PR}$

In questions **1** to **4**, state whether the two triangles are similar and, if they are, give the ratios of the sides.

1

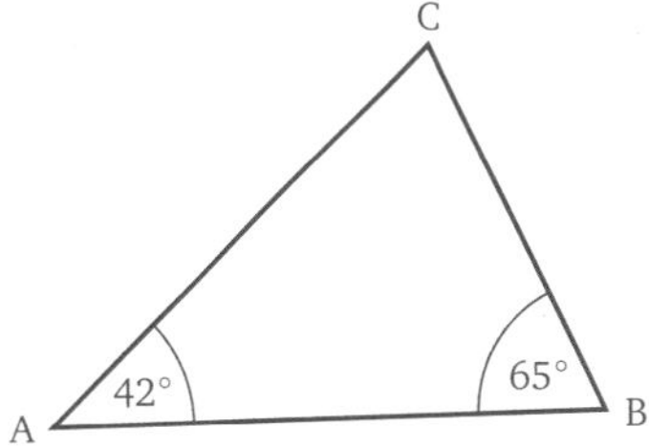

2

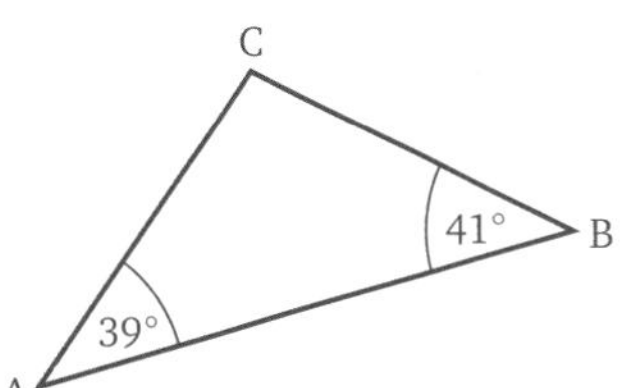

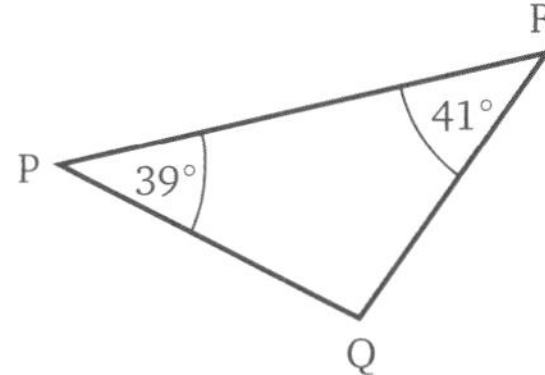

3

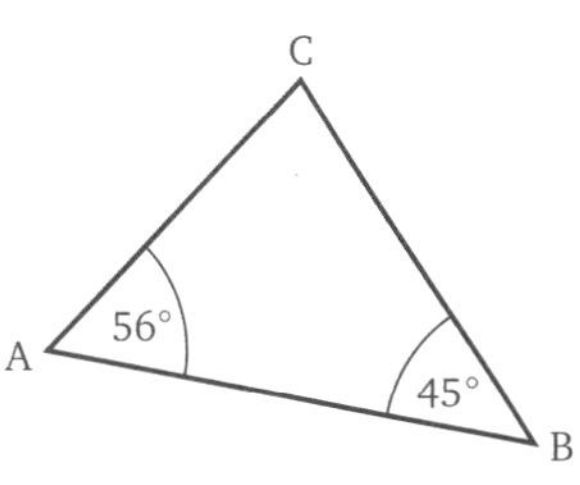

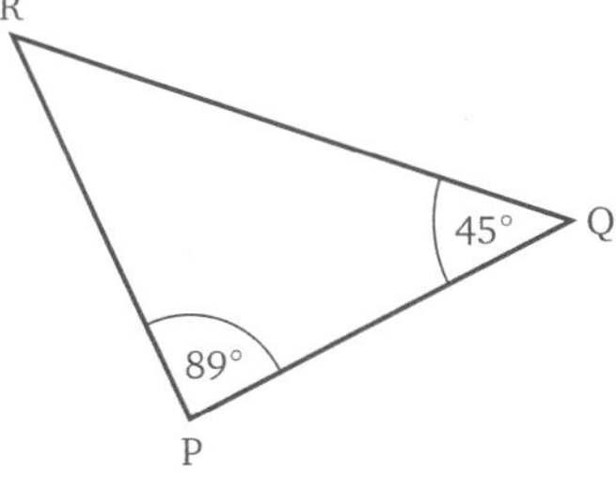

4

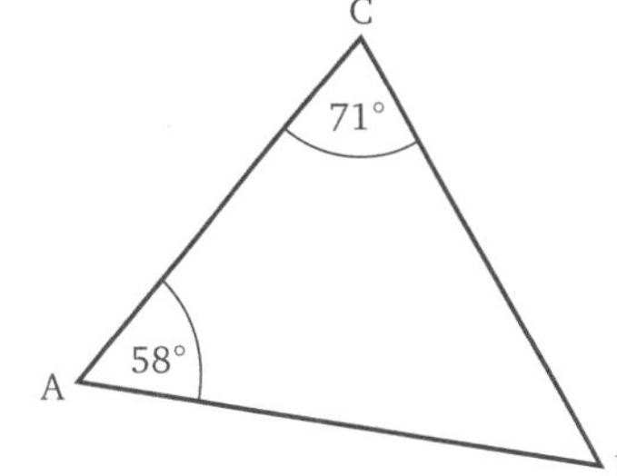

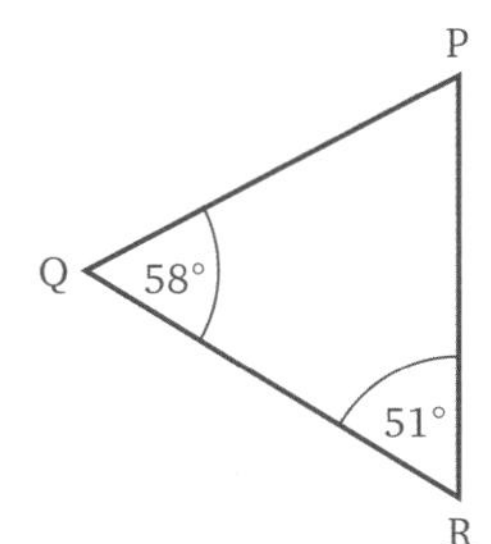

Puzzle

There are 13 stations on a railway line. All tickets are printed with the name of the station you board the train and the station you leave the train. How many different tickets are needed?

Using the scale factor to find a missing length

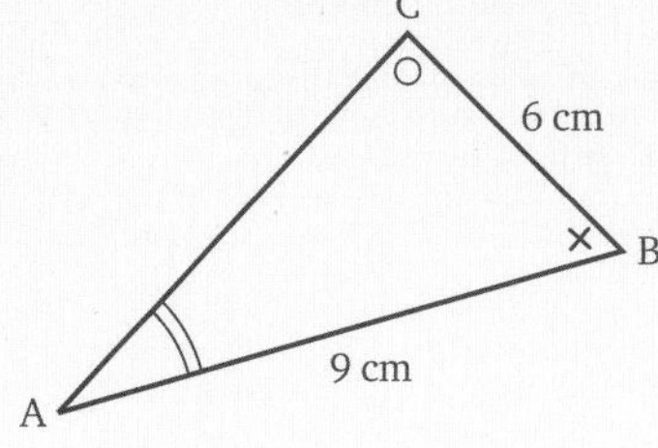

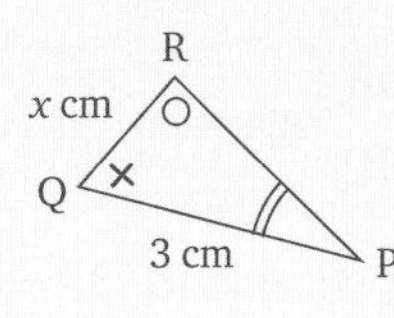

The two triangles above are similar.

PQ and AB are corresponding sides where $PQ = \frac{1}{3}AB$. So the scale factor is $\frac{1}{3}$.

QR and BC are corresponding sides so $QR = \frac{1}{3}BC = 2\,\text{cm}$.

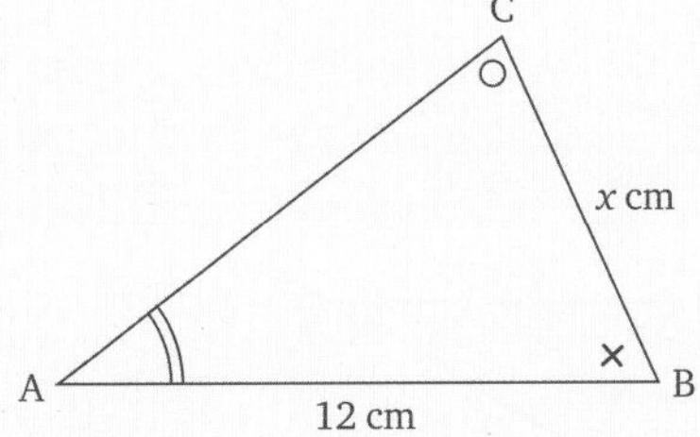

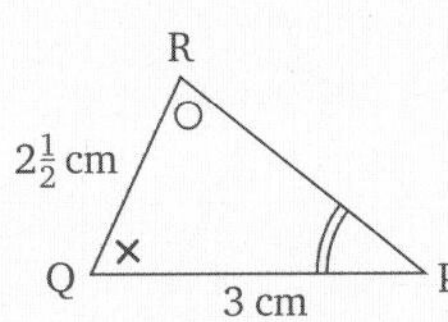

In these two similar triangles, AB and QP are corresponding sides where $AB = 4 \times QP$.

Therefore the scale factor is 4.

BC and QR are corresponding sides so $BC = 4 \times QR = 10\,\text{cm}$.

Exercise 8d

Find QR.

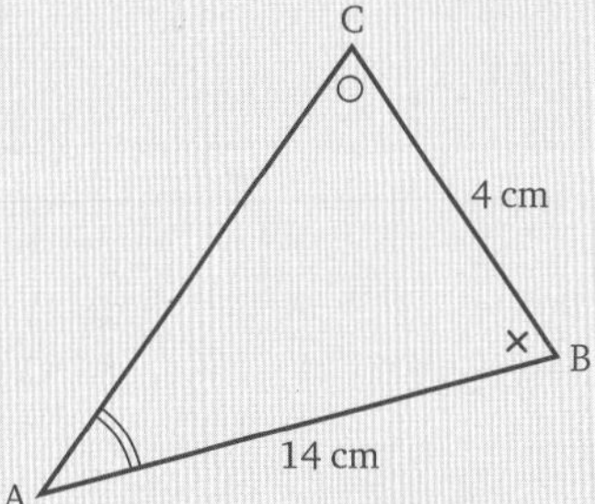

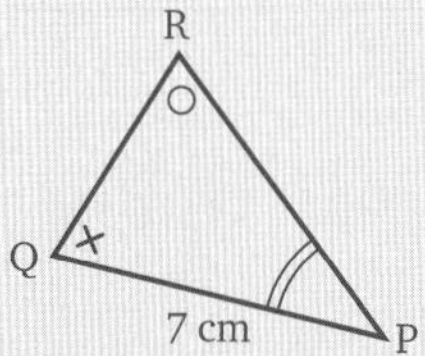

$\triangle$s $\begin{matrix} PQR \\ ABC \end{matrix}$ are similar (equiangular)

QP and BA are corresponding sides and $QP = \frac{1}{2}AB$.

So the scale factor is $\frac{1}{2}$.

QR and BC are corresponding sides so

$$QR = \frac{1}{2} \times 4\,\text{cm} = 2\,\text{cm}$$

Identify the corresponding sides and use them to find the scale factor.

1 Find BC.

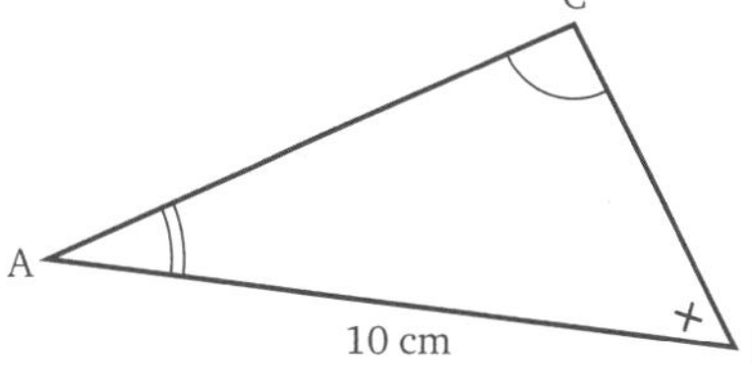

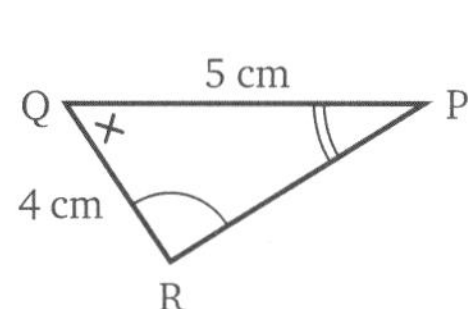

2 Find PR.

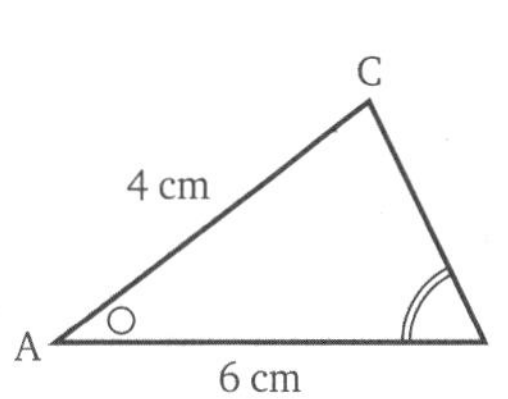

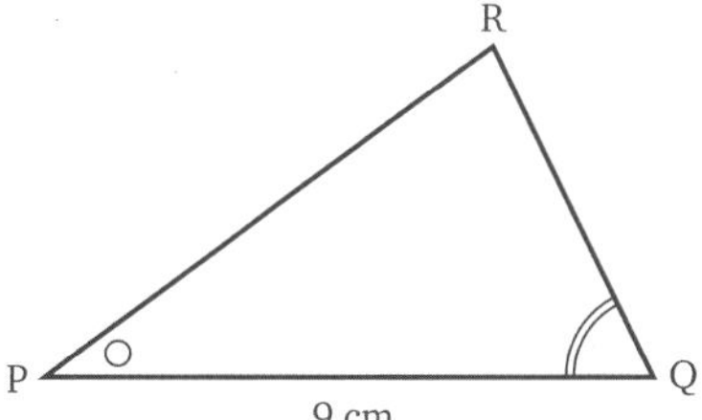

3 Find PR.

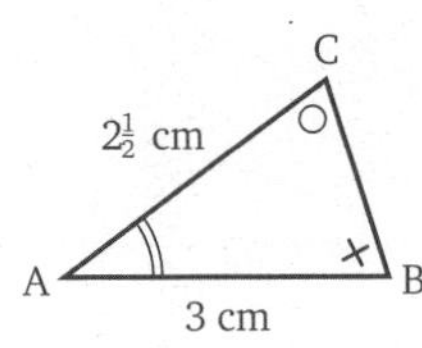

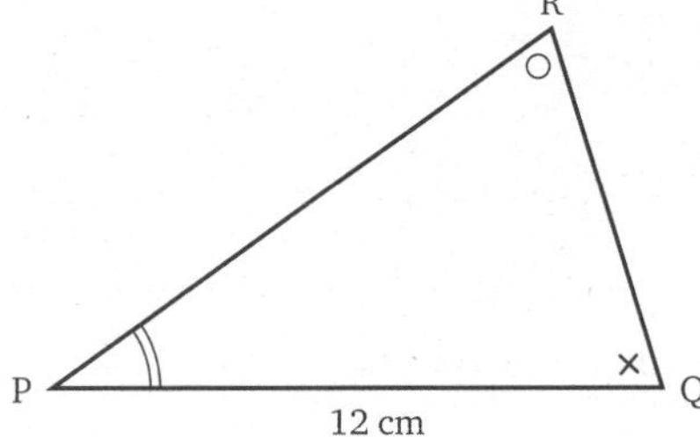

4 Find XY.

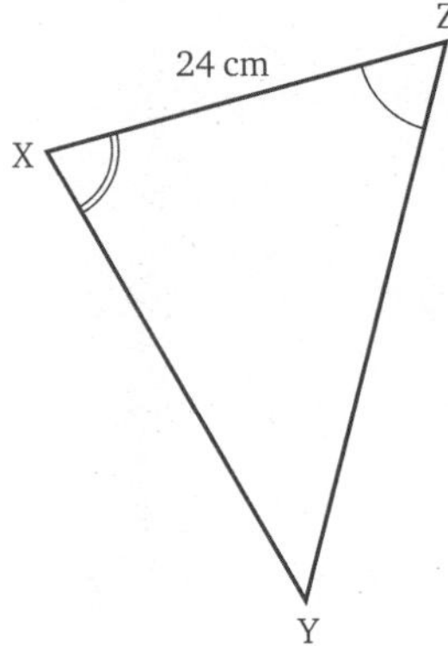

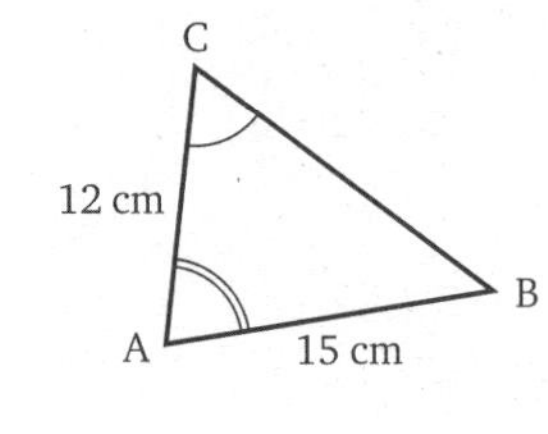

5 Find LN.

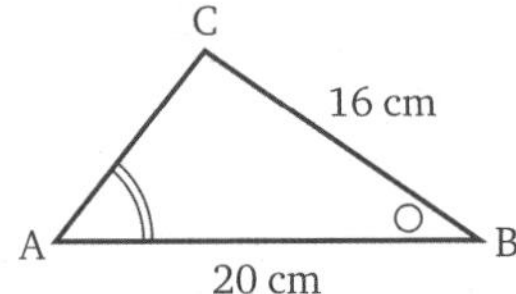

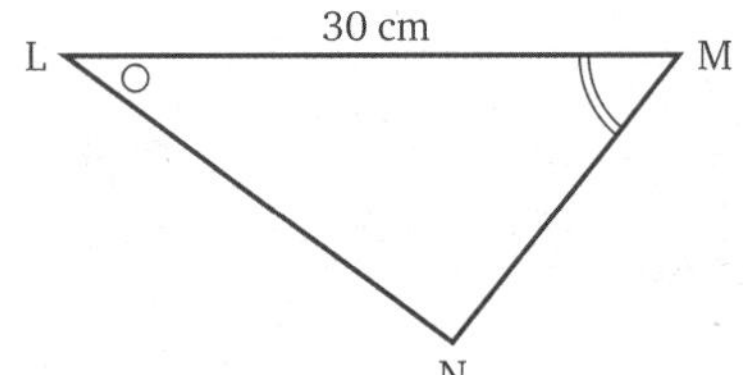

In questions **6** to **9** state whether the pairs of triangles are similar. If they are, find the required side.

6 Find PR.

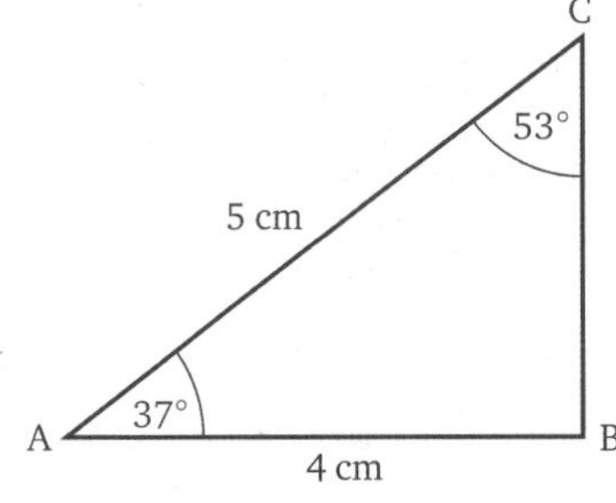

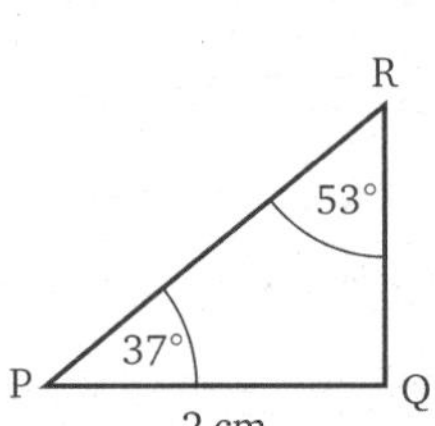

7 Find QR.

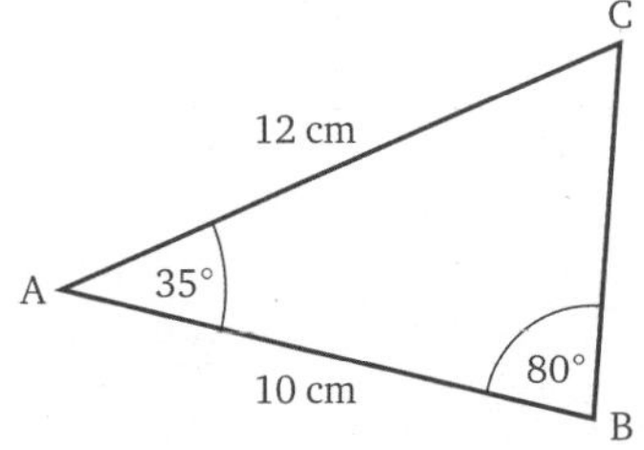

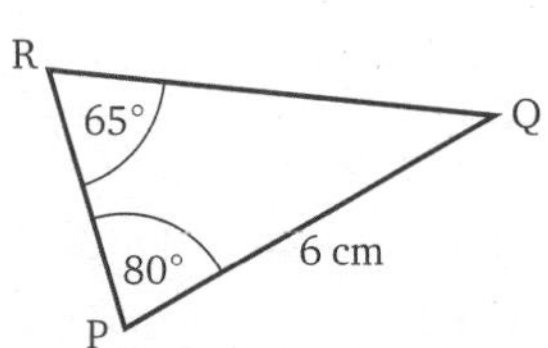

8 Find BC.

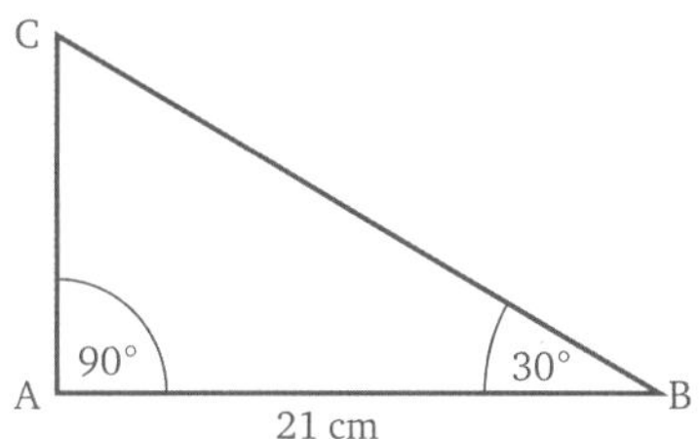

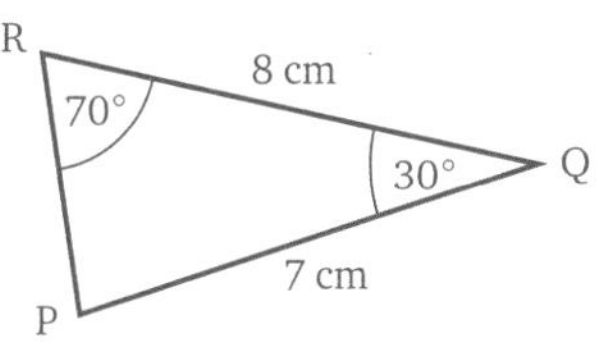

9 Find PR.

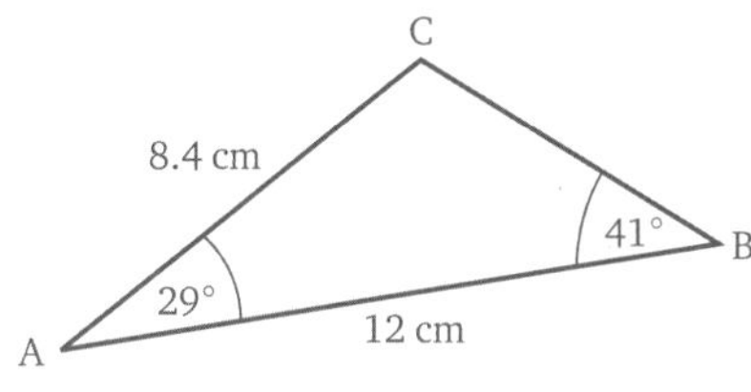

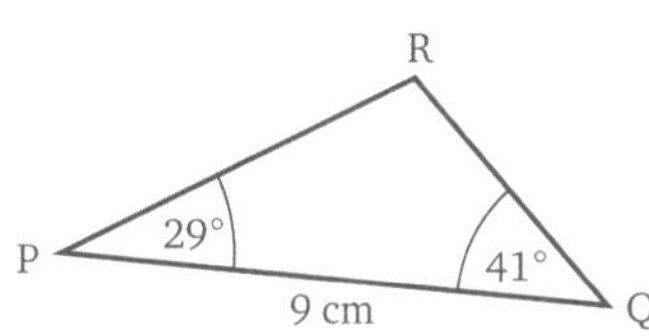

In $\triangle$s ABC and DEF, $\hat{A} = \hat{E}$ and $\hat{B} = \hat{D}$, AB = 4 cm, DE = 3 cm and AC = 6 cm.

Find EF.

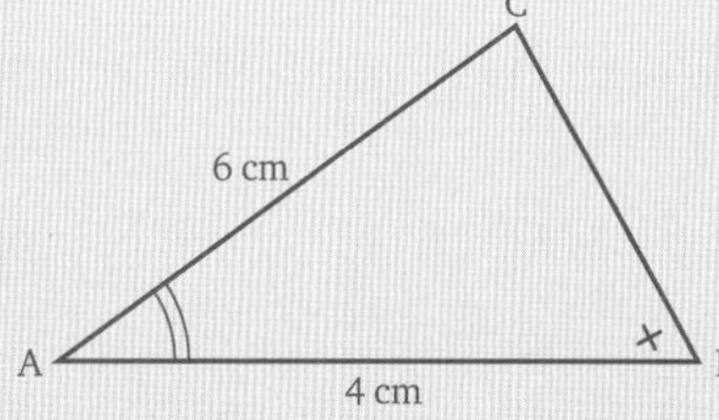

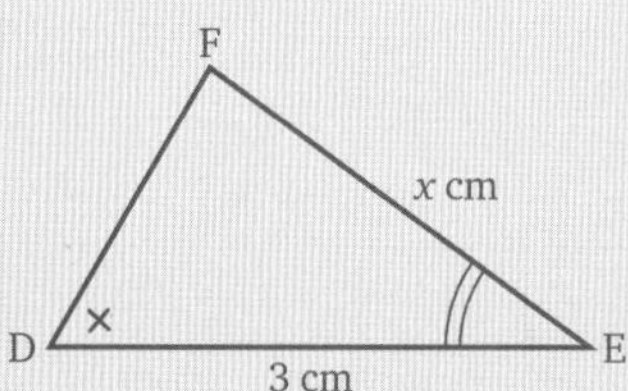

$\triangle$s $\begin{matrix}\text{EDF}\\\text{ABC}\end{matrix}$ are similar because they are equiangular.

AB and ED are corresponding sides and ED $= \frac{3}{4}$ AB

so the scale factor is $\frac{3}{4}$.

EF and AC are corresponding sides so EF $= \frac{3}{4}$ AC

$$= \frac{3}{4} \times 6\text{ cm}$$

$$= 4\tfrac{1}{2}\text{ cm}$$

10 In $\triangle$s ABC and XYZ, $\hat{A} = \hat{X}$ and $\hat{B} = \hat{Y}$.
AB = 6 cm, BC = 5 cm and XY = 9 cm. Find YZ.

Draw the triangles and mark the equal angles and the lengths of the sides that are given. Label the side you have to find x cm.

11 In $\triangle$s ABC and PQR, $\hat{A} = \hat{P}$ and $\hat{C} = \hat{R}$.
AB = 10 cm, PQ = 12 cm and QR = 9 cm. Find BC.

12 In $\triangle$s ABC and DEF, $\hat{A} = \hat{E}$ and $\hat{B} = \hat{F}$. AB= 3 cm, EF = 5 cm and AC = 5 cm. Find DE.

13 In $\triangle$s ABC and PQR, $\hat{A} = \hat{Q}$ and $\hat{C} = \hat{R}$. AC = 8 cm, BC = 4 cm and QR = 9 cm. Find PR.

a Show that triangles ABC and CDE are similar.

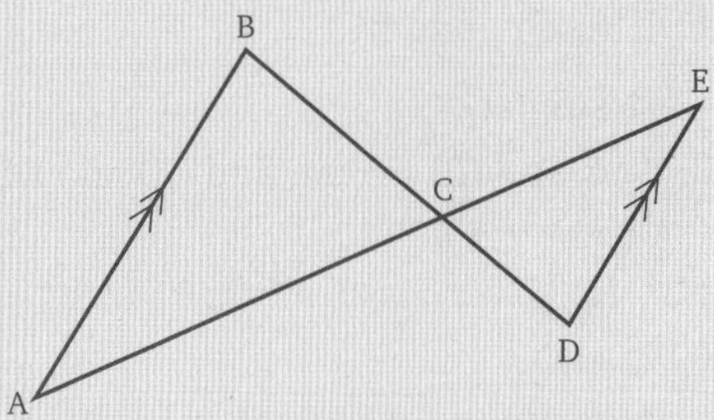

b Given that AC = 15 cm, CE = 9 cm and DE = 8 cm, find AB.

a $\hat{A} = \hat{E}$ (alternate angles, AB || DE)

$\hat{B} = \hat{D}$ (alternate angles, AB || DE)

(Or we could use $B\hat{C}A = E\hat{C}D$ as these are vertically opposite angles.)

so $\triangle$s $\begin{matrix} ABC \\ EDC \end{matrix}$ are similar.

b Sketch the diagram and mark the equal angles and the lengths of the sides that are given, and the side you need to find.

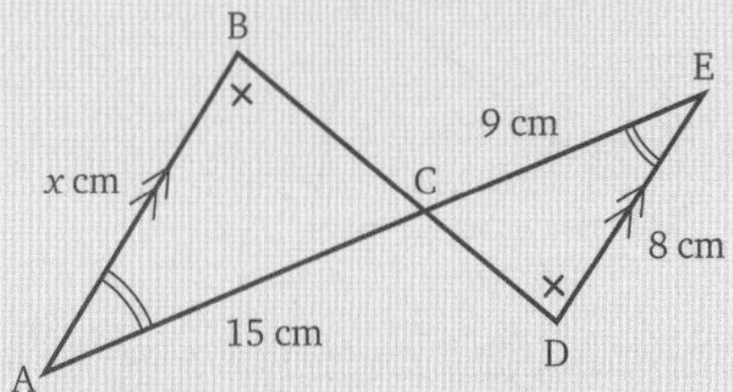

AC and EC are corresponding sides and AC $= \frac{15}{9}$ EC

AB and ED are corresponding sides so AB $= \frac{15}{9}$ ED

$= \frac{\cancel{15}^{5}}{\cancel{9}_{3}} \times 8 \text{ cm}$

$= \frac{40}{3} \text{ cm} = 13\frac{1}{3} \text{ cm}$

14

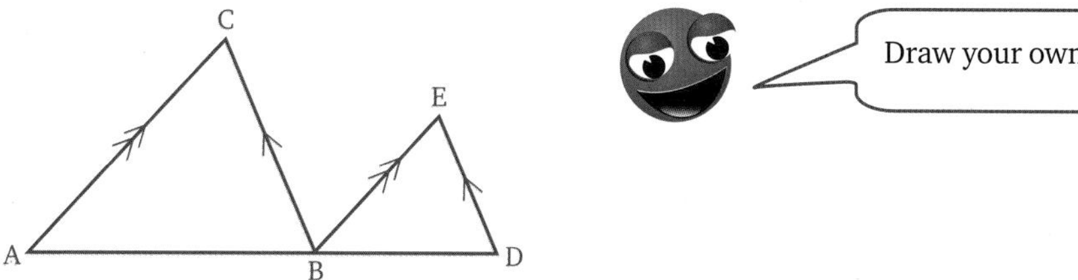

a Show that △s ABC and BDE are similar.

b If AB = 6 cm, BD = 3 cm and DE = 2 cm, find BC.

15 **a** Show that △s ABC and CDE are similar.

b If AB = 7 cm, BC = 6 cm, AC = 4 cm and CE = 6 cm, find CD and DE.

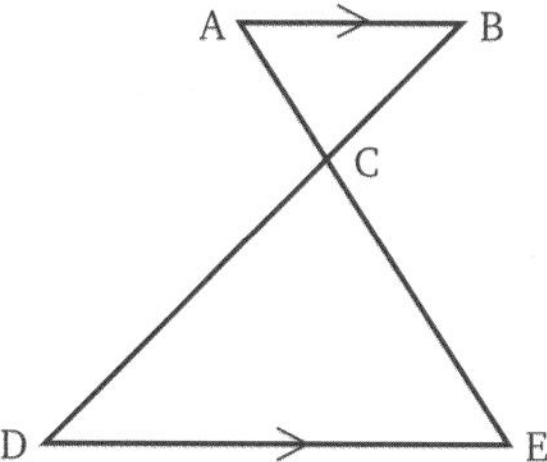

16 **a** ABCD is a square. EF is at right angles to BD.

Show that △s ABD and DEF are similar.

b If AB = 10 cm, DB = 14.2 cm and DF = 7.1 cm, find EF.

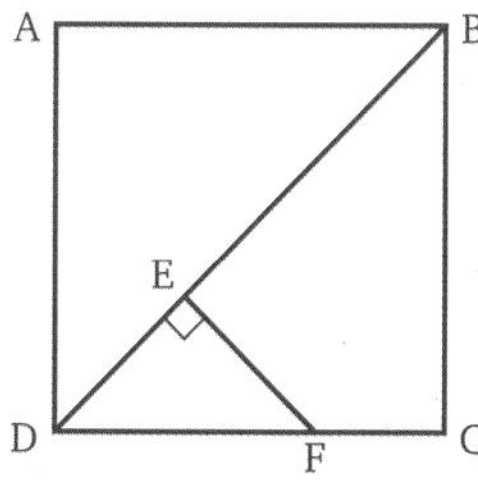

17

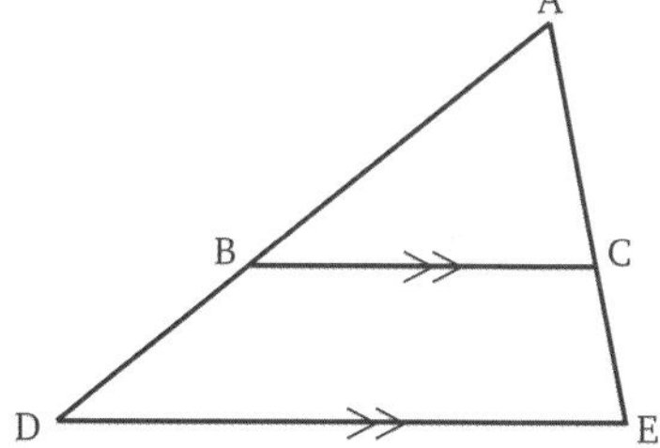

a Show that △s ABC and ADE are similar.

(Notice that $\hat{A}$ is *common* to both triangles.)

b If AB = 10 cm, AD = 15 cm, BC = 12 cm and AC = 9 cm, find DE, AE and CE.

? Puzzle

Arrange four 9s to make 100.

Corresponding sides

If the three pairs of sides of two triangles are in the same ratio, then the triangles are similar and their corresponding angles are equal.

When finding the ratio of three sides give the ratio as a whole number or as a fraction in its lowest terms.

Exercise 8e

State whether triangles ABC and PQR are similar. Say which angle, if any, is equal to $\hat{A}$.

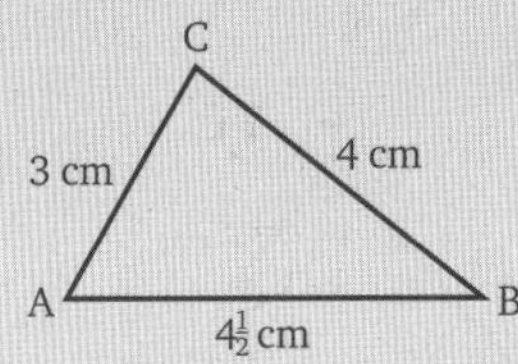

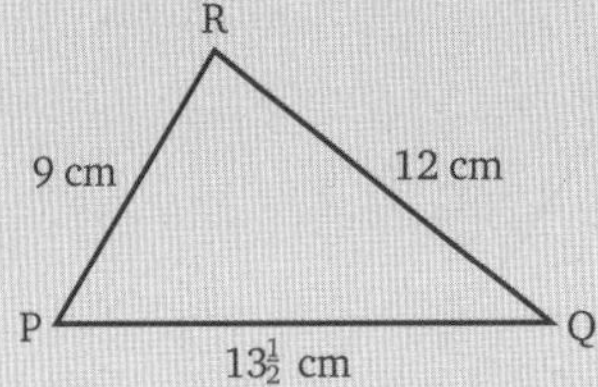

Start with the shortest side of each triangle: $\frac{PR}{AC} = \frac{9}{3} = 3$

Now the longest sides: $\frac{PQ}{AB} = \frac{13\frac{1}{2}}{4\frac{1}{2}} = \frac{27}{9} = 3$

Lastly the third sides: $\frac{QR}{BC} = \frac{12}{4} = 3$

so $\qquad \frac{PR}{AC} = \frac{PQ}{AB} = \frac{QR}{BC}$

$\therefore \qquad \triangle s \ \begin{matrix} PQR \\ ABC \end{matrix}$ are similar

and $\qquad \hat{P} = \hat{A}$

State whether the following pairs of triangles are similar. In each case say which angle, if any, is equal to $\hat{A}$.

1

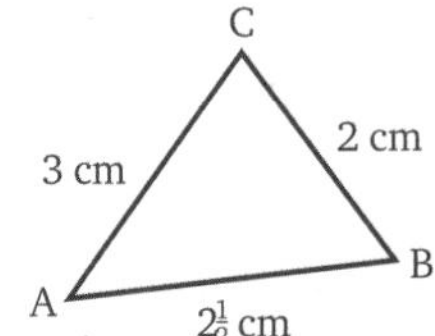

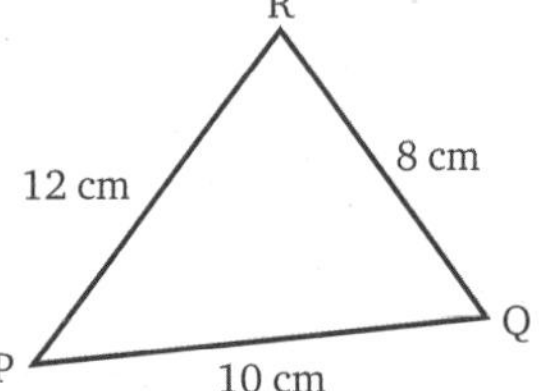

2

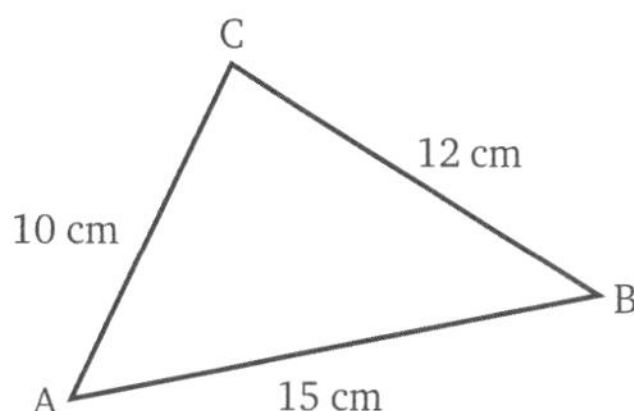

R
$9\frac{3}{5}$ cm
P
8 cm
12 cm
Q

3

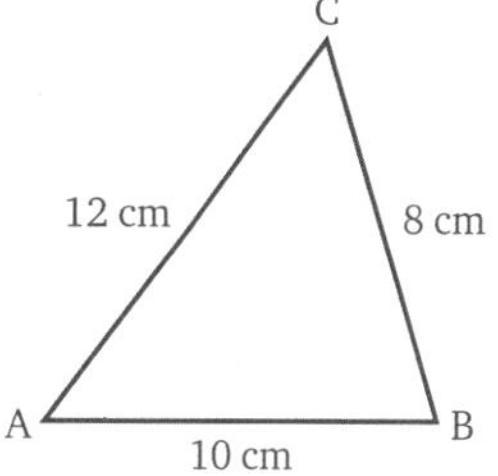

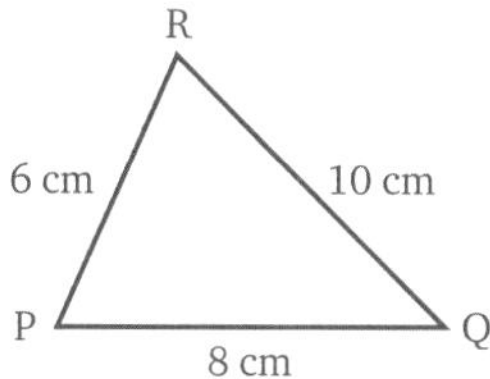

4

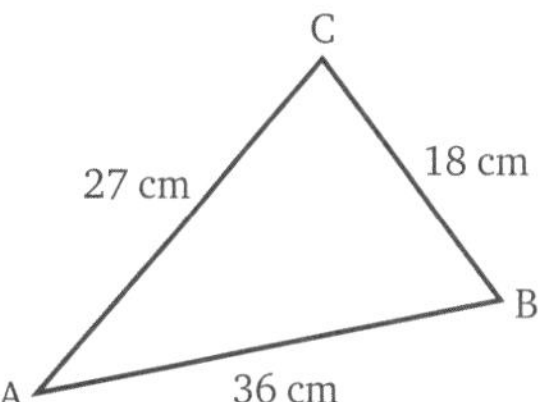

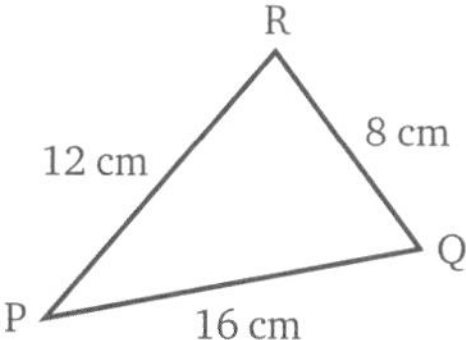

5

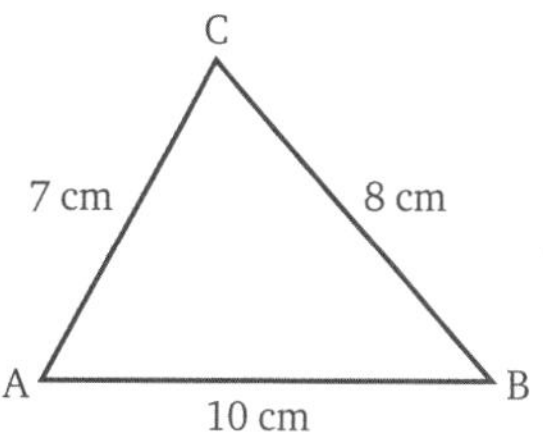

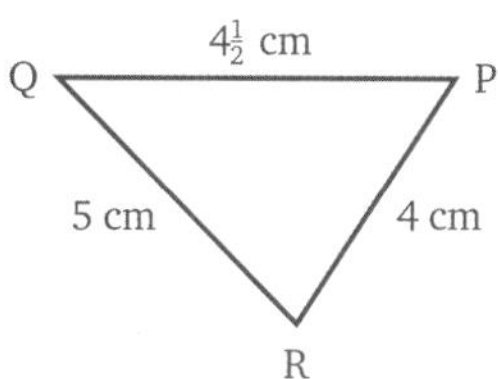

6

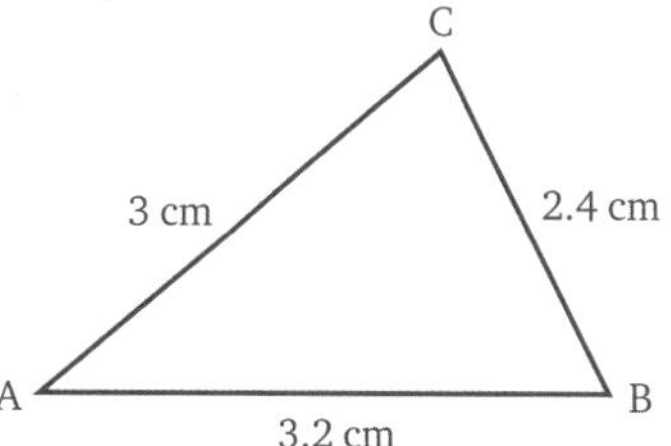

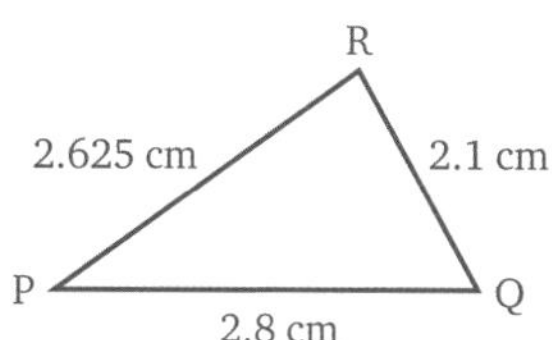

7 Are the triangles ABC and ADE similar?
Which angles are equal?
What can you say about lines BC and DE?

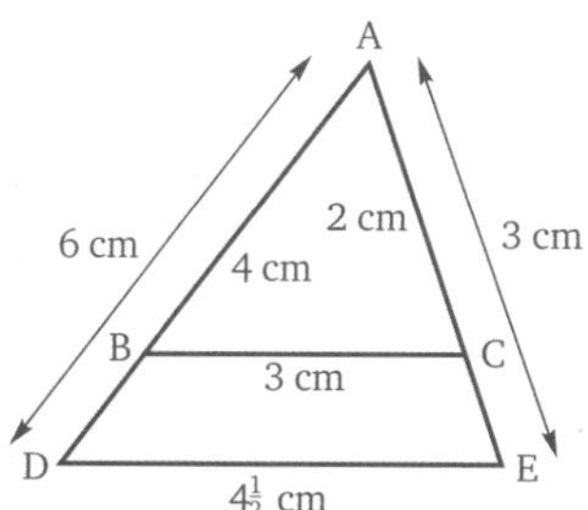

One pair of equal angles and two pairs of sides

The third possible set of information about similar triangles concerns a pair of angles and the sides containing them.

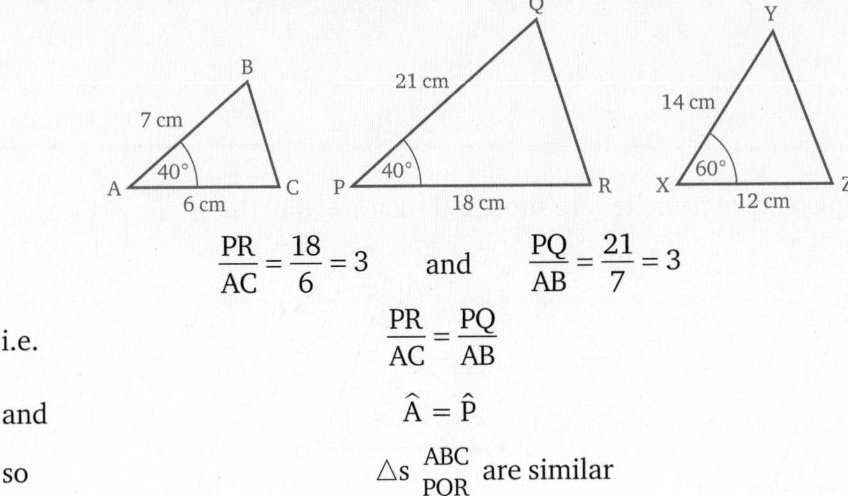

$$\frac{PR}{AC} = \frac{18}{6} = 3 \quad \text{and} \quad \frac{PQ}{AB} = \frac{21}{7} = 3$$

i.e. $\dfrac{PR}{AC} = \dfrac{PQ}{AB}$

and $\hat{A} = \hat{P}$

so $\triangle s \begin{matrix} ABC \\ PQR \end{matrix}$ are similar

We can see that $\triangle PQR$ is an enlargement of $\triangle ABC$ and that the scale factor is 3. (It is given by $\frac{PQ}{AB}$.)

On the other hand, $\triangle XYZ$ is a different shape from the other two triangles and is not similar to either of them. Although two pairs of sides are in the same ratio, the angles between the pairs of sides are not the same.

Exercise 8f

State whether triangles ABC and PQR are similar. If they are, find PQ.

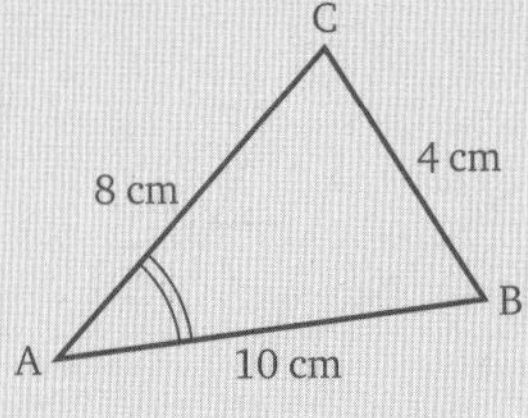

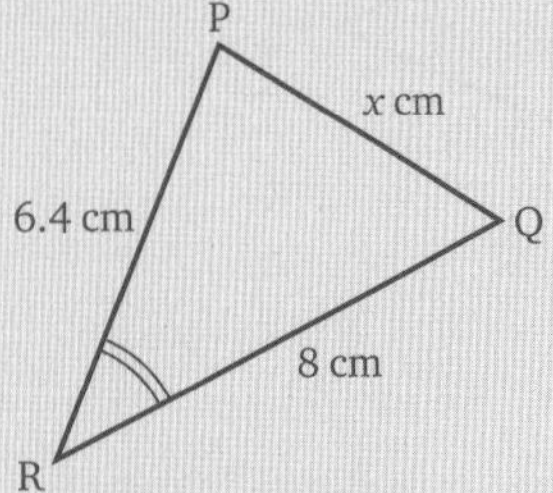

$\hat{A} = \hat{R}$ so compare the ratios of the arms containing these angles.

$\dfrac{RP}{AC} = \dfrac{6.4}{8} = 0.8$ (comparing the two shorter sides)

$\dfrac{RQ}{AB} = \dfrac{8}{10} = 0.8$ (comparing the other two arms)

$\therefore \quad \frac{RP}{AC} = \frac{RQ}{AB}$ and $\hat{A} = \hat{R}$

so $\quad \triangle s \begin{matrix} RQP \\ ABC \end{matrix}$ are similar

BC is half AC so PQ is half PR

PQ = 3.2 cm

State whether the following pairs of triangles are similar. If they are, find the missing lengths.

1

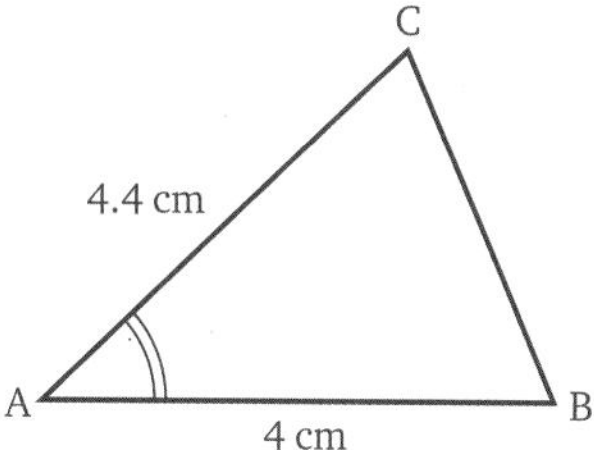

2

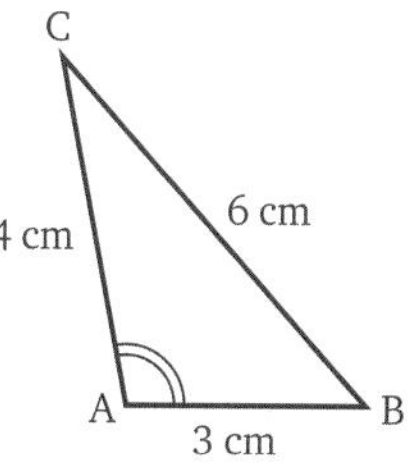

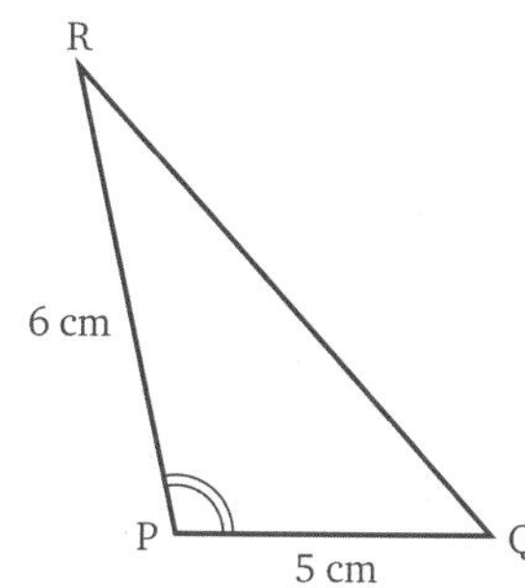

3

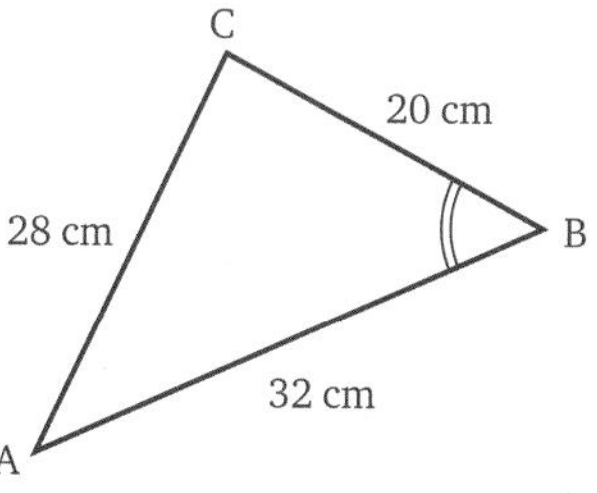

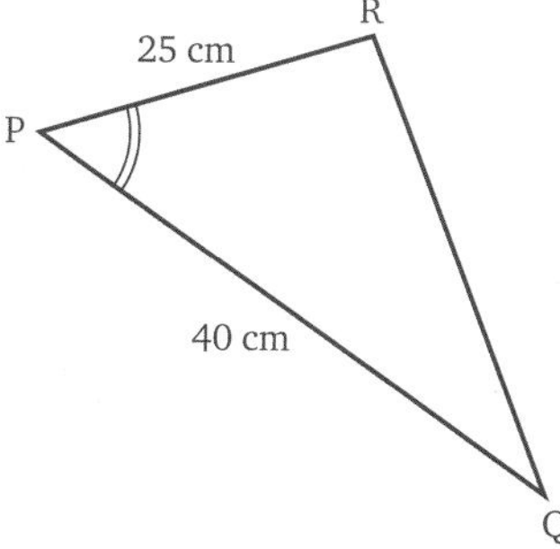

4

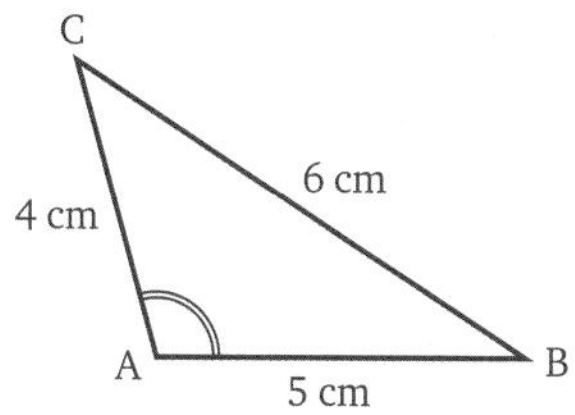

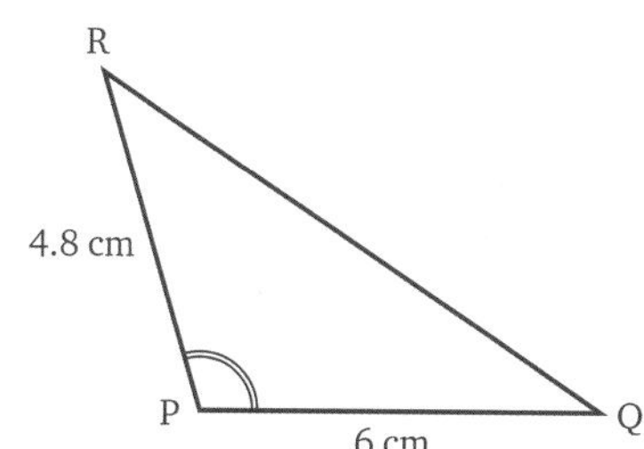

5

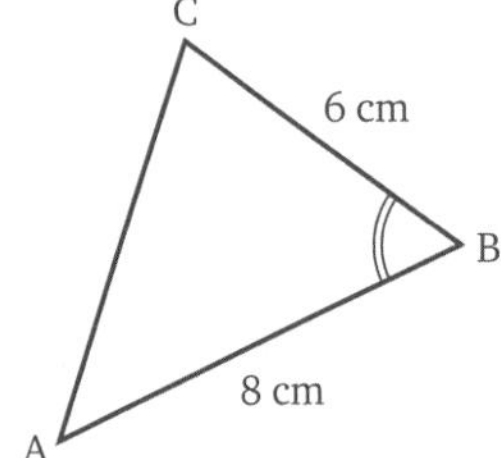

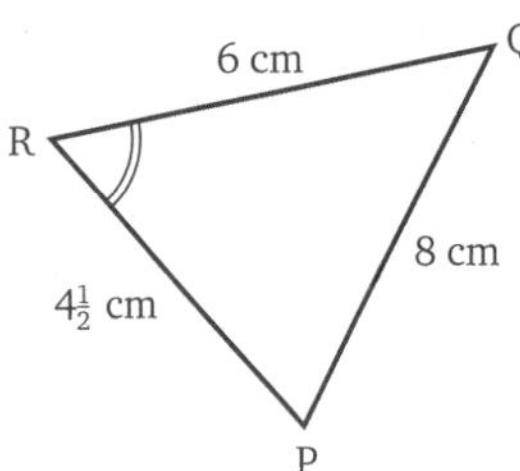

6. In △s ABC and PQR, $\hat{A} = \hat{P}$, AB = 8 cm, BC = 8.5 cm, CA = 6.5 cm, PQ = 4.8 cm and PR = 3.9 cm. Find QR.

7. In △s PQR and XYZ, $\hat{P} = \hat{X}$, PQ = 4 cm, PR = 3 cm, QR = $2\frac{1}{4}$ cm, XY = $5\frac{1}{3}$ cm and XZ = 4 cm. Find ZY.

Summary: similar triangles

If two triangles are the same shape (but not necessarily the same size) they are said to be *similar*. This word, when used in mathematics, means that the triangles are *exactly* the same shape and not vaguely alike, as two sisters may be.

One triangle may be turned over or round compared with the other.

Pairs of corresponding sides are in the same ratio. This ratio is the *scale factor* for the enlargement of one triangle into the other.

To check that two triangles are similar we need to show *one* of the three following sets of facts:

- the angles of one triangle are equal to the angles of the other

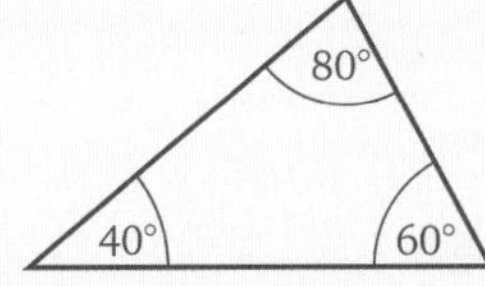

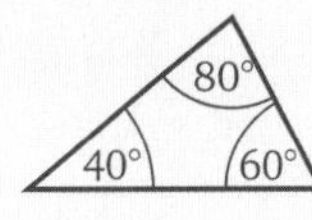

- the three pairs of corresponding sides are in the same ratio

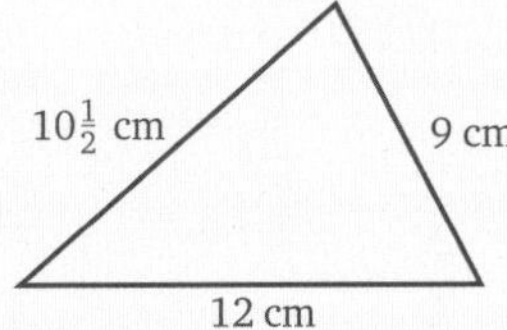

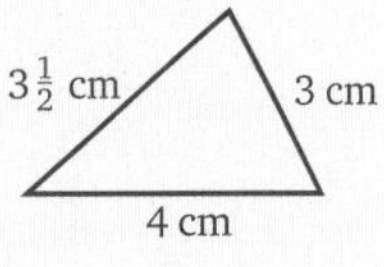

- there is one pair of equal angles and the sides containing the known angles are in the same ratio.

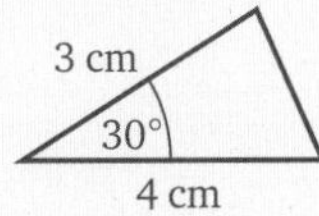

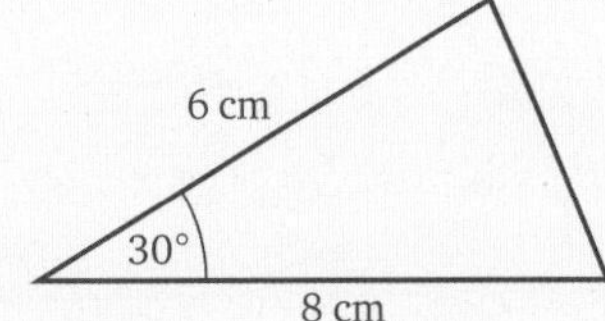

Mixed exercise

Exercise 8g

State whether or not the pairs of triangles in questions **1** to **10** are similar, giving your reasons. If they are similar, find the required side or angle.

1 Find BC.

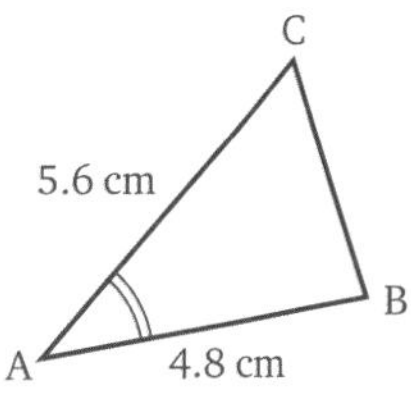

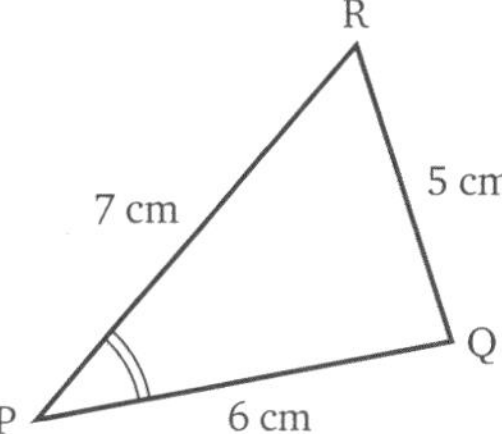

2 Find QR.

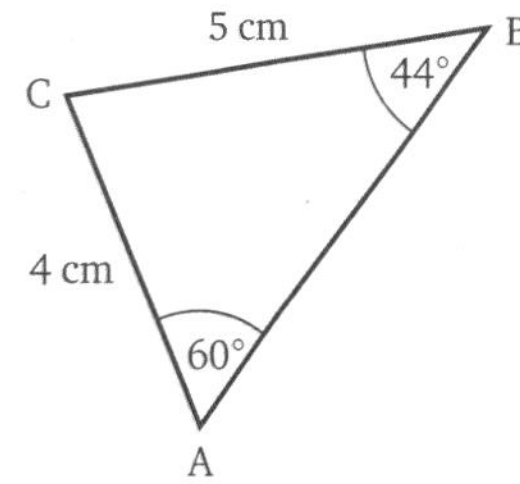

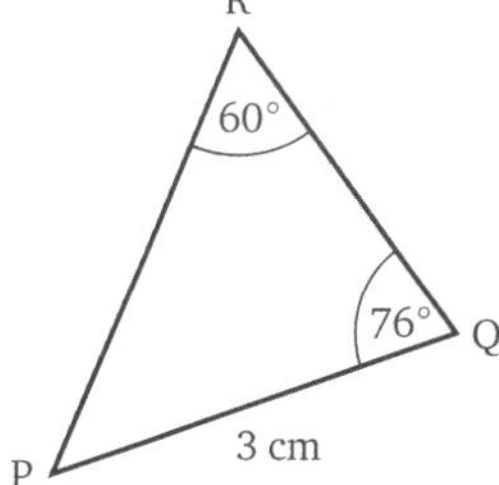

3 Find $\hat{Q}$.

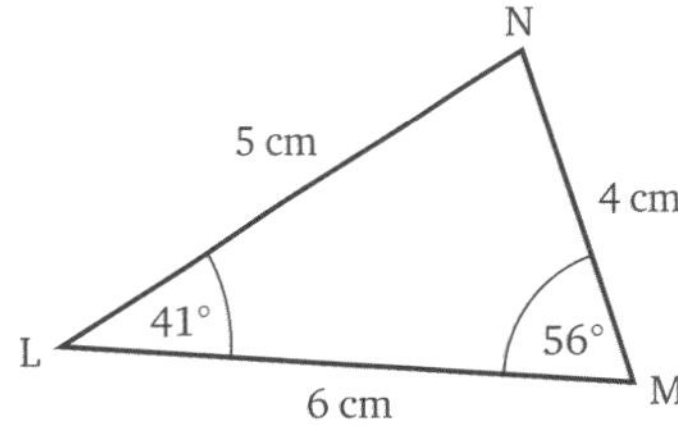

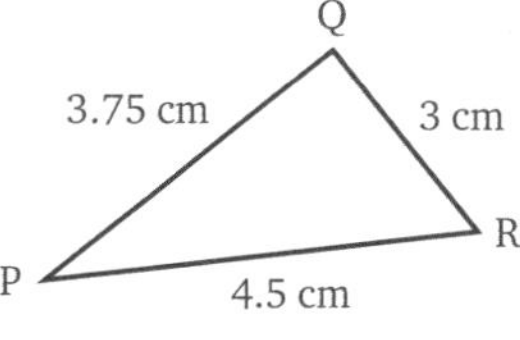

4 Find FE.

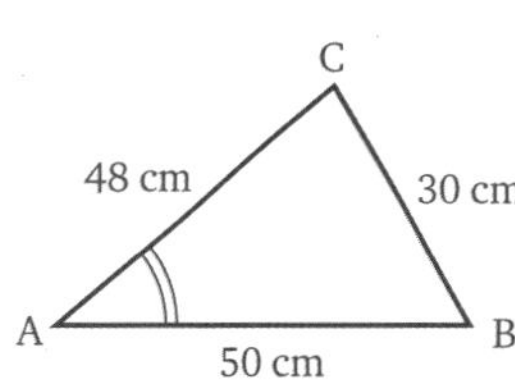

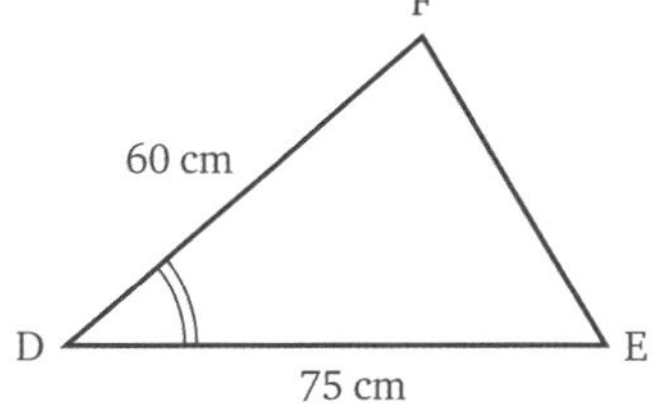

5 Find $\hat{P}$.

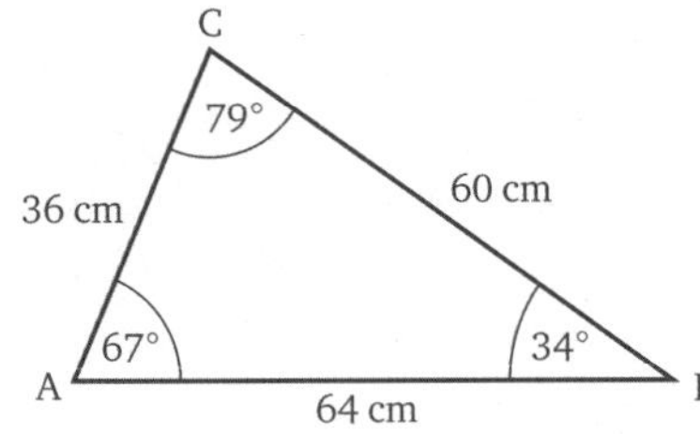

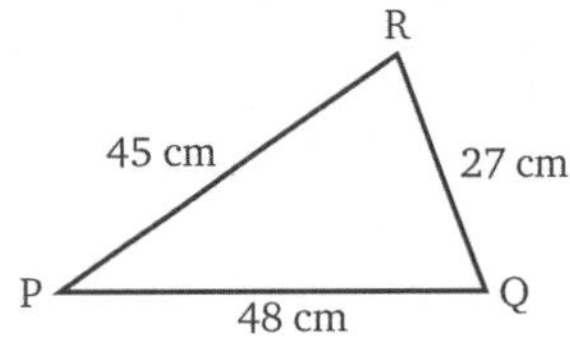

6 Find $\hat{Q}$.

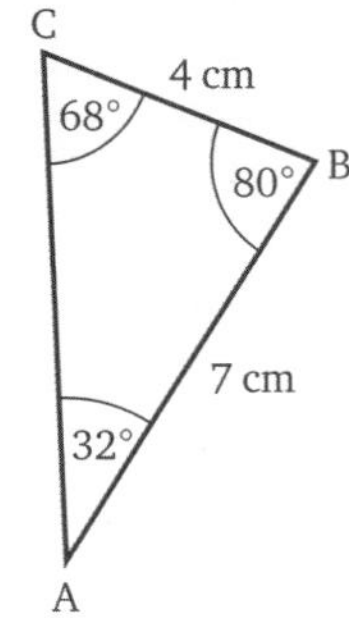

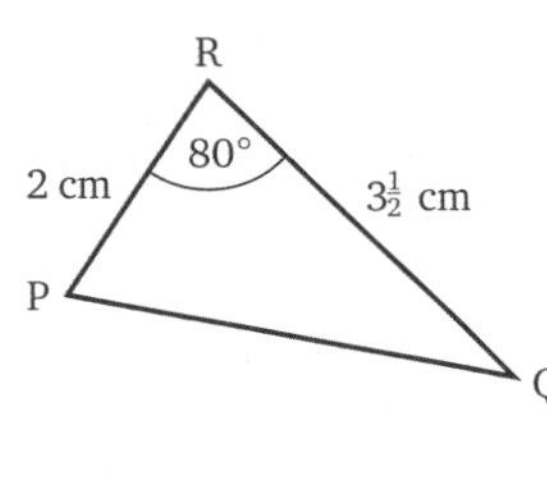

7 Find YZ.

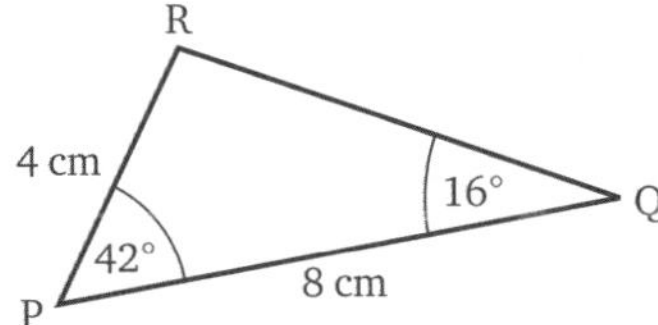

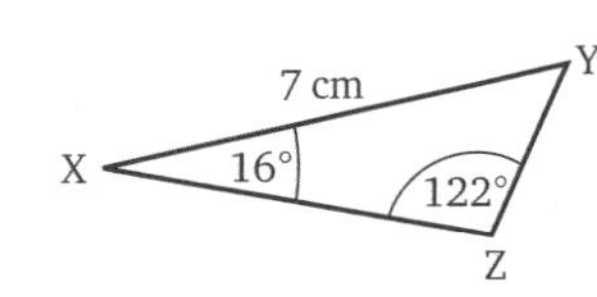

8 Find AC.

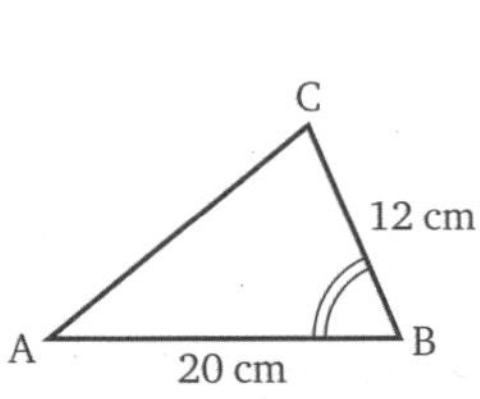

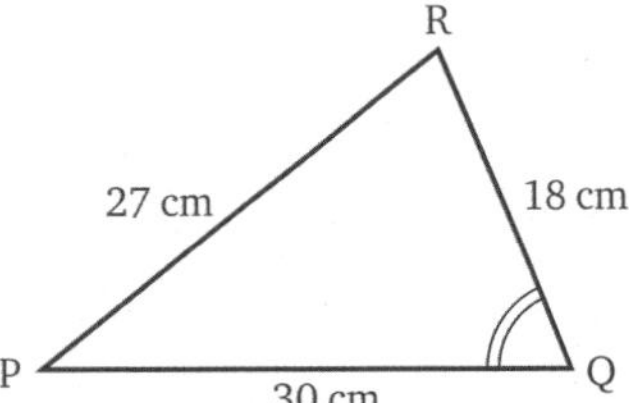

9 **a** Show that $\triangle$s ABC and ADE are similar.

b AB = 3.6 cm, AD = 4.8 cm and AE = 4.2 cm. Find AC and CE.

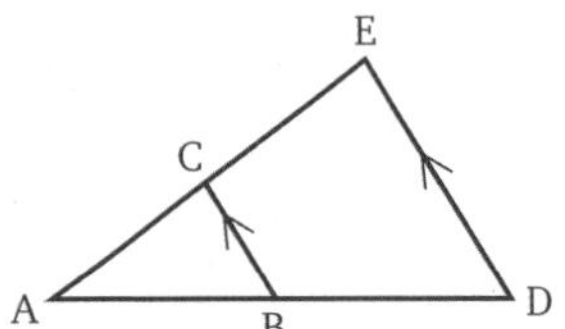

10 a Show that △s ABC and DEF are similar.

b AB = 40 cm, BC = 52cm and DE = 110 cm. Find EF.

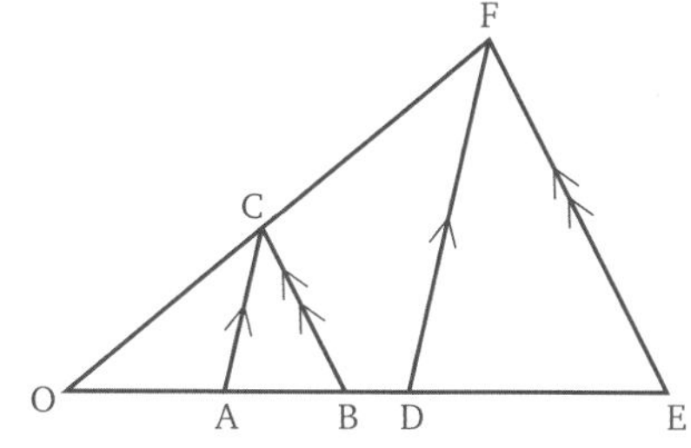

11 In the diagram there are three overlapping triangles.

a Show that △s ABC and ABD are similar.

b Show that △s ABC and BDC are similar.

c Are △s ABD and BDC similar?

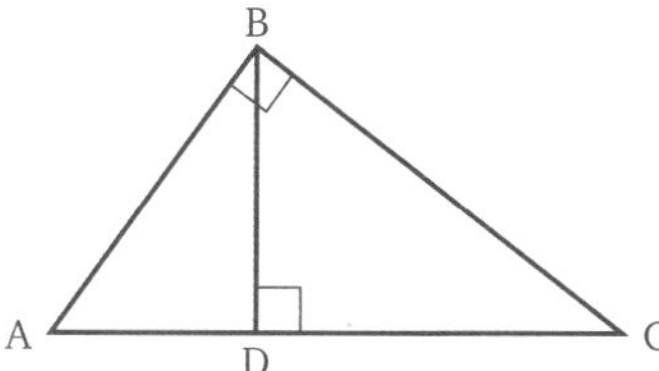

12 A pole, AB, 2 m high, casts a shadow, AC, that is 3 m long. Another pole, PQ, casts a shadow 15 m long. How high is the second pole?

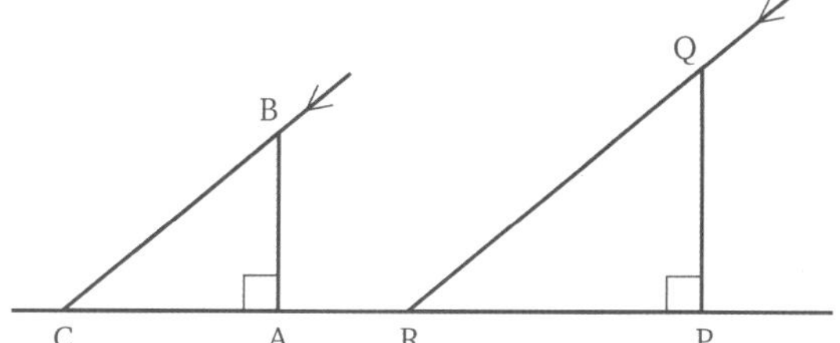

13 The shadow of a 1 m stick held upright on the ground is 2.4 m long. How long a shadow would be cast by an 8 m telegraph pole?

14 A photo on a tablet measures 1.8 cm by 2.4 cm. A picture 90 cm by 120 cm is projected on the screen. On the tablet, a house is 1.2 cm high. How high is the house in the picture on the screen?

Investigation

Draw a quadrilateral ABCD with four unequal sides. Mark the midpoints of the sides AB, BC, CD and DA with the letters P, Q, R and S in that order.

Join P, Q, R and S to give a new quadrilateral. Are the two quadrilaterals similar?

Investigate what happens if you repeat this with other quadrilaterals, including the square, rectangle, parallelogram, rhombus, kite and trapezium.

Did you know?

An engineer has to measure the height of a flag pole. He has a tape measure but can't keep the tape along the pole. A mathematician comes along and offers to solve the problem; he removes the pole from its hole and lays it on the ground and measures it easily. When he leaves, the engineer says, "Just like a mathematician! I need to know the height, and he gives me the length!".

In this chapter you have seen that...

✔ two shapes are similar if one is an enlargement of the other

✔ to prove that two triangle are similar you need to show that

- *either* the triangles have the same angles
- *or* all three sides of each triangle are in the same ratio
- *or* one pair of angles are equal and the sides round those angles are in the same ratio.

9 Pythagoras' theorem

At the end of this chapter you should be able to...

1 state the relationship between the hypotenuse and the other sides of a right-angled triangle
2 calculate the length of one side of a right-angled triangle, given the other two sides
3 identify Pythagorean triples
4 use Perigal's dissection
5 determine whether or not a triangle is right-angled given the lengths of the sides.

Did you know?

Did you know that the square root sign ($\sqrt{\ }$) comes from the first letter of the word *radix,* which was the Latin word for root?

You need to know...

✔ how to work with decimals
✔ the properties of the special quadrilaterals
✔ how to recognise right-angled triangles.

Key words

chord, converse, hypotenuse, Pythagoras' theorem, significant figures, symmetry

Squares and square roots

The following exercise covers the finding of squares and square roots. You should always find a rough estimate first.

Exercise 9a

Use a calculator to find the squares of:

a 2.3 **b** 23 **c** 2300 **d** 0.023

a $2.3^2 \approx 2 \times 2 = 4$

$2.3^2 = 5.29$

b $23^2 \approx 20 \times 20 = 400$

$23^2 = 529$

c $2300^2 \approx 2000 \times 2000 = 4\,000\,000$

$2300^2 = 5\,290\,000$

d $0.023^2 \approx 0.02 \times 0.02 = 0.0004$

$0.023^2 = 0.000\,529$

Always find a rough value of the square of a number because it is easy to press the wrong button on a calculator. Check that your calculator answer is sensible.

Find the squares of the following numbers, giving your answers correct to four significant figures where necessary:

1 6.2
2 13.7
3 242
4 2780
5 0.71
6 0.059
7 0.0017
8 312
9 3.12
10 0.0312
11 9.2
12 92
13 5210
14 52.1
15 0.521
16 0.0521

To estimate a square root, pair off the numbers each way from the decimal point. Then estimate the square root of the first pair of non-zero numbers.

Find the square root of 0.003 425 giving the answer correct to four significant figures.

$0.003\,425 = 0.\overset{\frown}{00}\overset{\frown}{34}\overset{\frown}{25}$

Therefore $\sqrt{0.003425} = \sqrt{0.\overset{\frown}{00}\overset{\frown}{34}\overset{\frown}{25}} \approx 0.05\ldots$ ($\sqrt{00} = 0$ and $\sqrt{34} \approx 5$)

Using a calculator $\sqrt{0.003425} = 0.058\,5234\ldots$

$= 0.058\,52$ correct to 4 s.f.

Find the square roots of the following numbers, giving your answers correct to four significant figures:

17 9.87
18 19.9
19 124
20 96 800
21 0.0482
22 0.004 82
23 96
24 321
25 2.62
26 0.062
27 0.000 78
28 0.5
29 0.461
30 4.61
31 461
32 0.000 461

Pythagoras' theorem

Pythagoras was a native of Samos who travelled frequently to Egypt for the purpose of education. The Egyptians are believed to have known this theorem many years before Pythagoras was born. It is very likely that the Egyptian priests explained this theorem to Pythagoras. Indeed, it is claimed that Pythagoras offered a sacrifice to the Muses when the Egyptian priests explained to him the properties of the right-angled triangle.

We can show that the properties involve a relationship between the lengths of the three sides.

Exercise 9b

First we will collect some evidence. Bear in mind that, however accurate your drawing, it is not perfect.

Construct the triangles in questions **1** to **6** and in each case measure the third side, the *hypotenuse*, which is the side opposite the right angle.

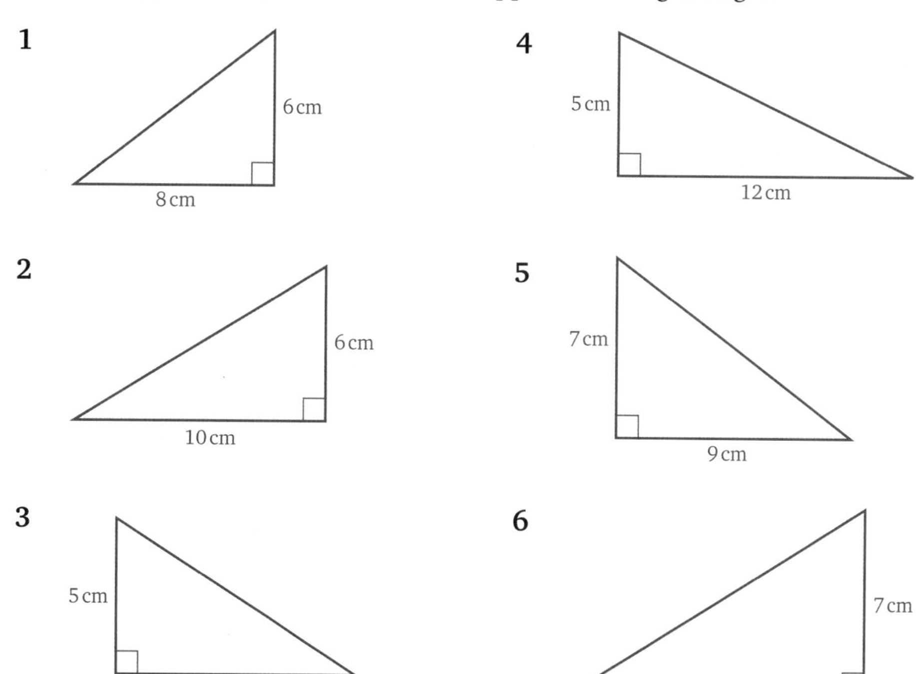

7 In each of the questions **1** to **6**, find the squares of the lengths of the three sides. Write the squares in ascending order (i.e. the smallest first). Can you see a relation between the first two squares and the third square?

If your drawings are reasonably accurate you will find that by adding the squares of the two shorter sides you get the square of the hypotenuse.

$AB^2 = 16$

$BC^2 = 9$

$AC^2 = 25$

$25 = 16 + 9$

so $AC^2 = AB^2 + BC^2$

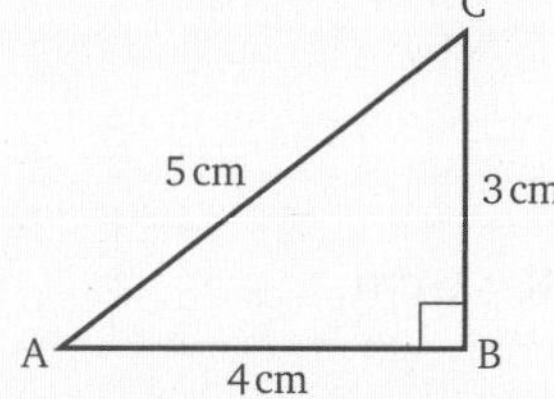

This result is called Pythagoras' theorem, which states that in a right-angled triangle the square of the hypotenuse is equal to the sum of the squares of the other two sides.

Activity

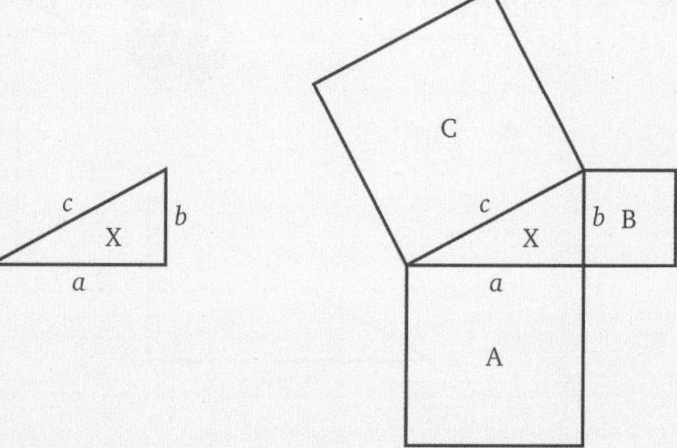

Draw any right-angled triangle and draw the square on each of the three sides. Mark the four areas A, B, C and X as shown in the diagram. Cut out one of each shape and make another three triangles identical to X. Arrange the shapes in two different ways as shown below. Sketch the two arrangements and mark in as many lengths as possible with a, b or c.

1 What can you say about the areas of these two diagrams? Justify your answer.

2 If the four triangles marked X are removed from each diagram, what can you say about the areas that remain? What relation does this give for

a areas A, B and C **b** lengths a, b and c?

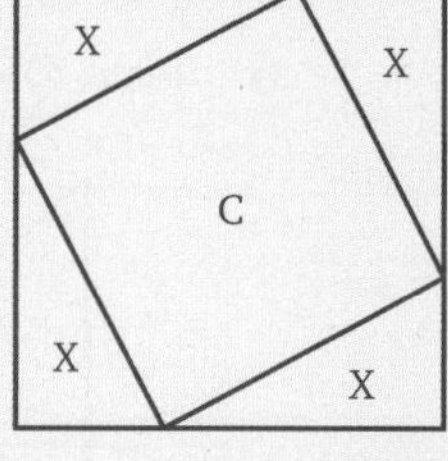

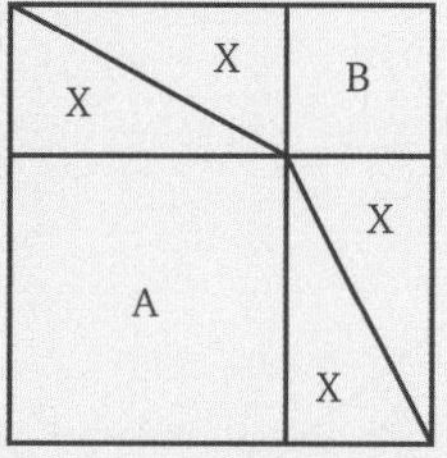

Finding the hypotenuse

Exercise 9c

Give your answers correct to 3 s.f.

In $\triangle PQR$, $\hat{R} = 90°$, $PR = 7\text{ cm}$ and $QR = 6\text{ cm}$.

Find PQ.

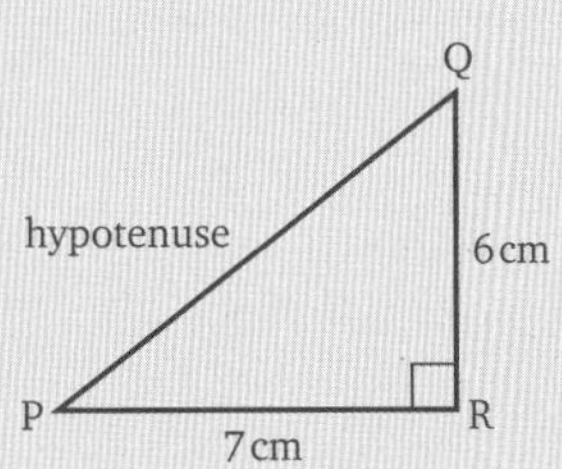

$$PQ^2 = PR^2 + QR^2 \quad \text{(Pythagoras' theorem)}$$
$$= 7^2 + 6^2$$
$$= 49 + 36 = 85$$
$$PQ = \sqrt{85} \quad (\simeq 9)$$
$$PQ = 9.22\text{ cm} \quad \text{correct to 3 s.f.}$$

In the following right-angled triangles find the required lengths.

Start each question by labelling the hypotenuse. Then write down Pythagoras' theorem in terms of the sides of this triangle.

1 Find AC.

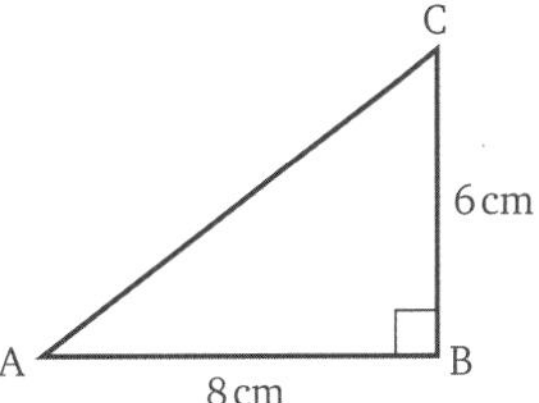

2 Find PR.

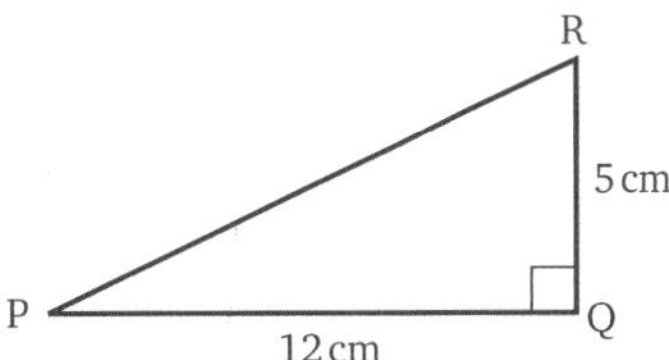

3 Find MN.

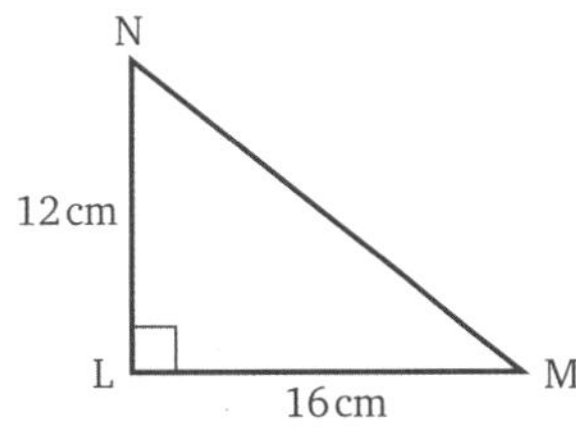

4 Find AC.

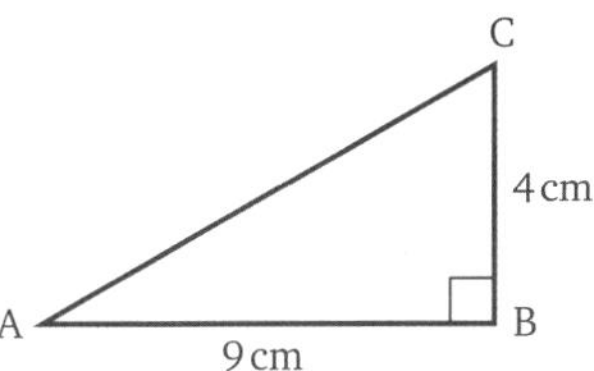

5 Find LN.

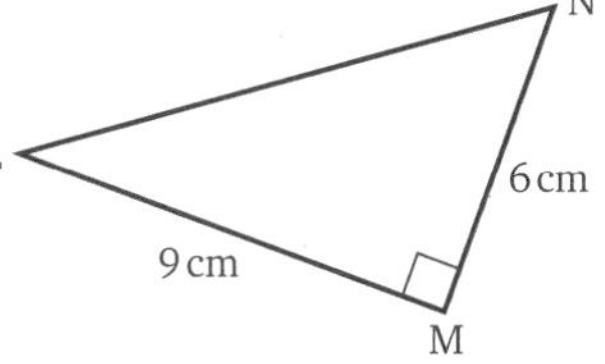

6 Find QR.

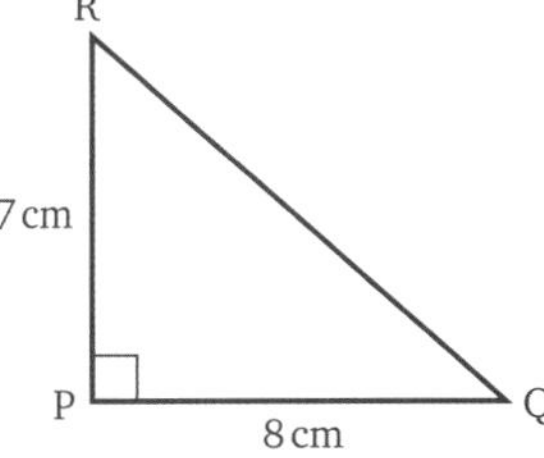

7 Find AC.

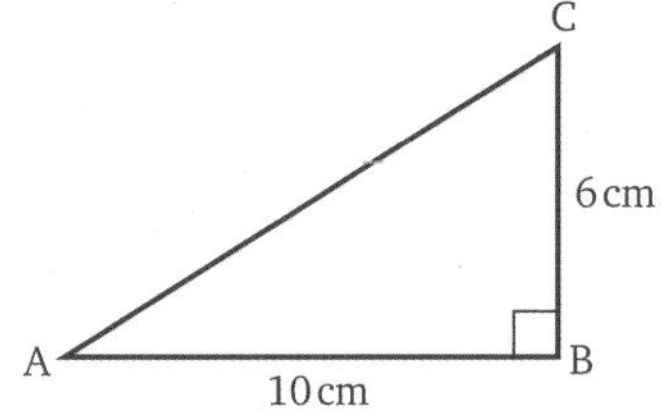

9 Find QR.

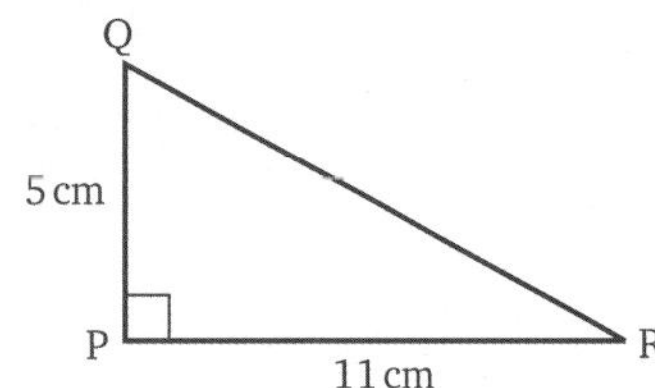

8 Find EF.

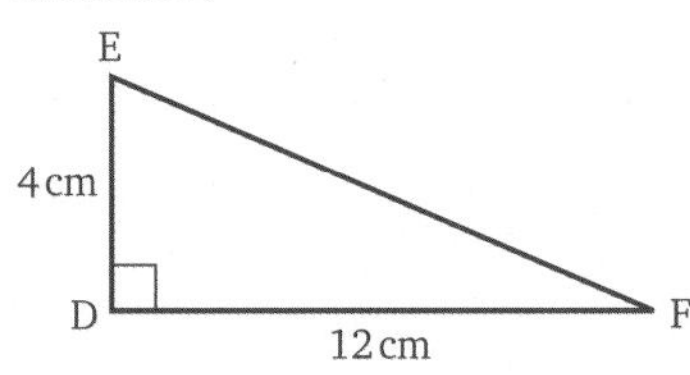

10 Find YZ.

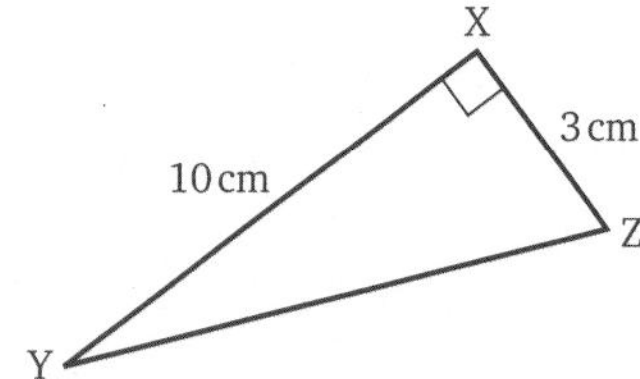

11 In $\triangle ABC$, $\hat{C} = 90°$, AC = 2 cm and BC = 3 cm. Find AB.

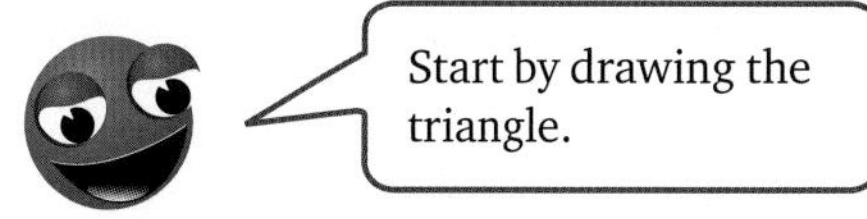

12 In $\triangle DEF$, $\hat{E} = 90°$, DE = 7 cm and EF = 9 cm. Find DF.

13 In $\triangle ABC$, $\hat{A} = 90°$, AB = 4 m and AC = 5 m. Find BC.

14 In $\triangle PQR$, $\hat{Q} = 90°$, PQ = 11 m and QR = 3 m. Find PR.

15 In $\triangle XYZ$, $\hat{X} = 90°$, YX = 12 cm and XZ = 2 cm. Find YZ.

In $\triangle XYZ$, $\hat{Z} = 90°$, XZ = 5.3 cm and YZ = 3.6 cm.
Find XY.

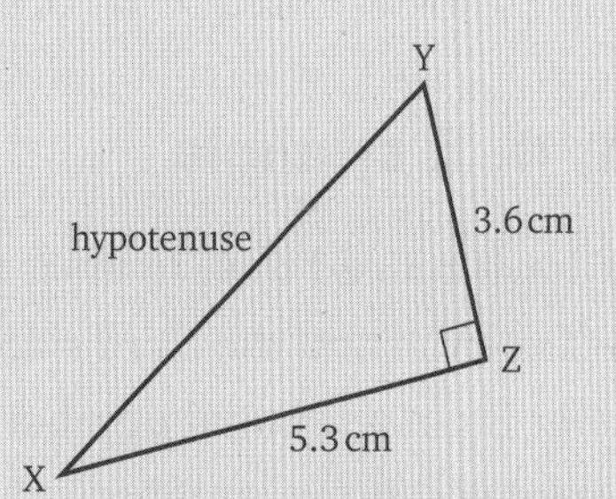

$XY^2 = XZ^2 + ZY^2$ (Pythagoras' theorem)

$= 5.3^2 + 3.6^2$ $\quad 5.3^2 \approx 5 \times 5 = 25$

$= 28.09 + 12.96$ $\quad 3.6^2 \approx 4 \times 4 = 16$

$= 41.05$

$XY = \sqrt{41.05} = 6.407...$ $\quad (\sqrt{41.05} \simeq 6)$

Length of XY = 6.41 cm correct to 3 s.f.

16 Find AC.

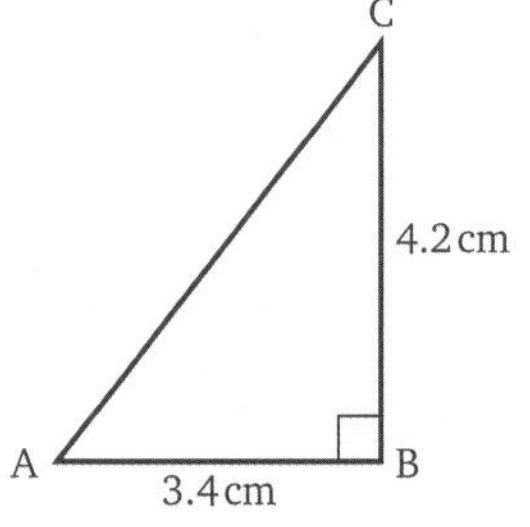

17 Find AC.

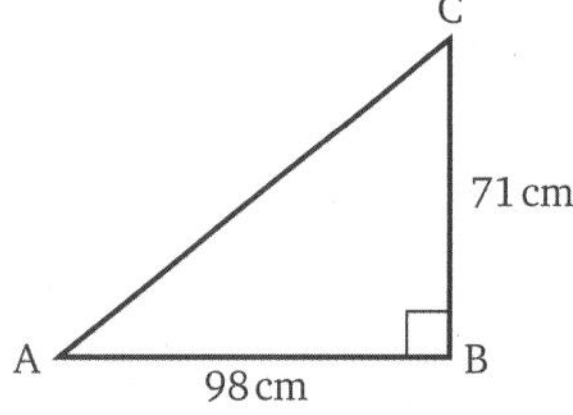

18 Find XY.

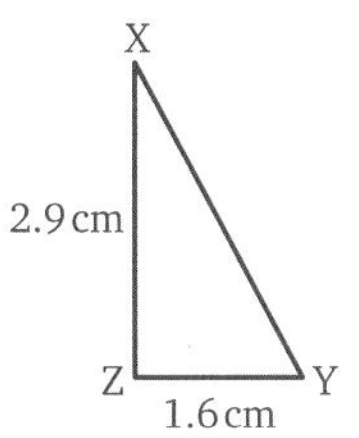

19 Find QR.

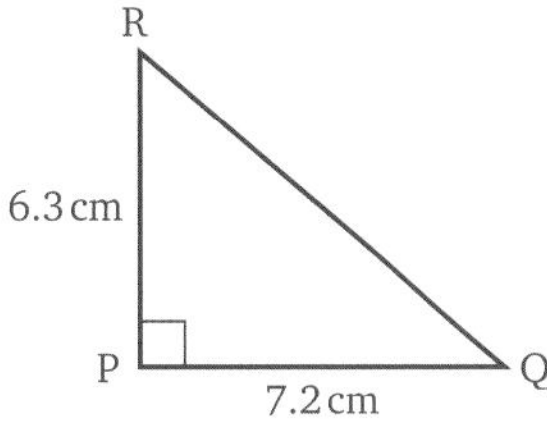

20 Find PR.

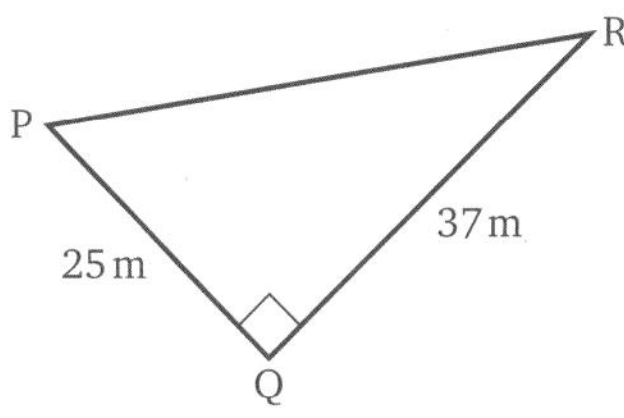

21 Find DF.

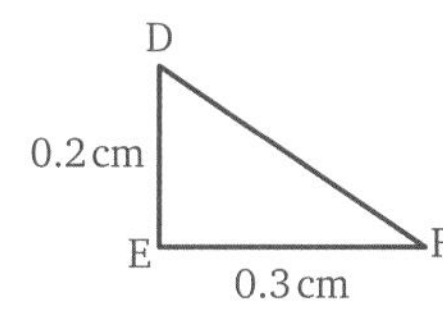

22 In $\triangle ABC$, $\hat{B} = 90°$, AB = 7.9 cm, BC = 3.5 cm. Find AC.

23 In $\triangle PQR$, $\hat{Q} = 90°$, PQ = 11.4 m, QR = 13.2 m. Find PR.

24 In $\triangle XYZ$, $\hat{Z} = 90°$, XZ = 1.23 cm, ZY = 2.3 cm. Find XY.

25 In $\triangle ABC$, $\hat{C} = 90°$, AC = 32 cm, BC = 14.2 cm. Find AB.

26 In $\triangle PQR$, $\hat{P} = 90°$, PQ = 9.6 m, PR = 8.8 m. Find QR.

27 In $\triangle DEF$, $\hat{F} = 90°$, DF = 10.1 cm, EF = 6.4 cm. Find DE.

The 3, 4, 5 triangle

You will have noticed that, in most cases when two sides of a right-angled triangle are given and the third side is calculated using Pythagoras' theorem, the answer is not a rational number. There are a few special cases where all three sides are rational numbers.

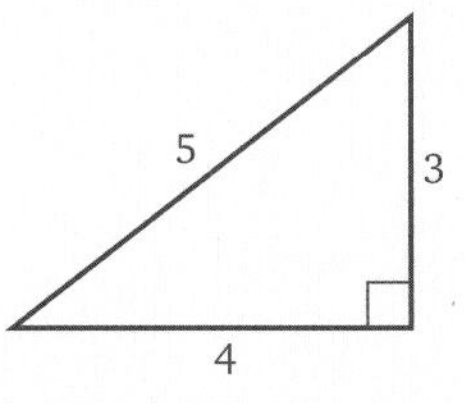

The simplest one is the 3, 4, 5 triangle. Any triangle similar to this has sides in the ratio 3 : 4 : 5, so whenever you spot this case you can find the missing side very easily.

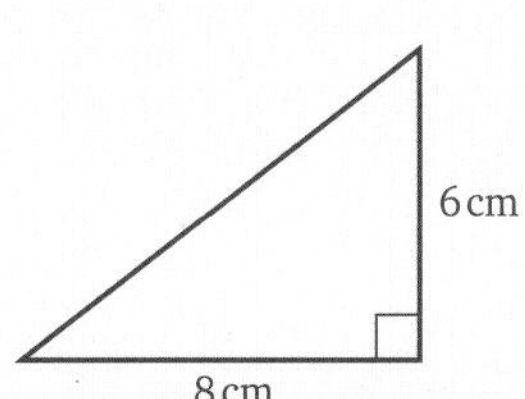

For instance, in this triangle, $6 = 2 \times 3$ and $8 = 2 \times 4$. The triangle is similar to the 3, 4, 5 triangle, so the hypotenuse is 2×5 cm, that is, 10 cm.

The other triangle with exact sides which might be useful is the 5, 12, 13 triangle. Sets of numbers like {3, 4, 5} and {5, 12, 13} are called *Pythagorean triples*.

Exercise 9d

In $\triangle ABC$, $\hat{B} = 90°$, AB = 20 cm and BC = 15 cm. Find AC.

Notice that BC = 3×5 cm and AB = 4×5 cm so the sides about the right angle are in the ratio 3 : 4.

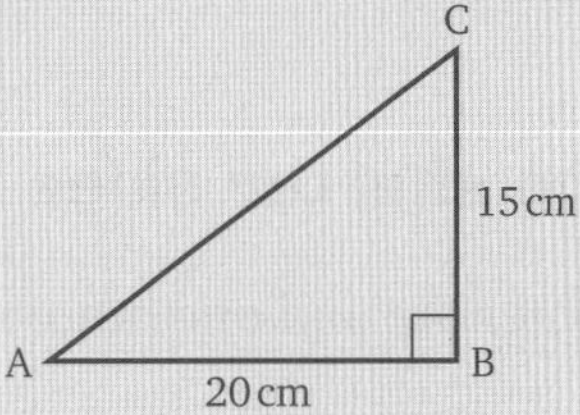

ABC is therefore a '3, 4, 5 triangle'.

So AC = 5×5 cm (3, 4, 5 $\triangle$)

= 25 cm

In each of the following questions, decide whether the triangle is similar to the 3, 4, 5 triangle or to the 5, 12, 13 triangle or to neither. Find the hypotenuse, using the method you think is easiest.

1

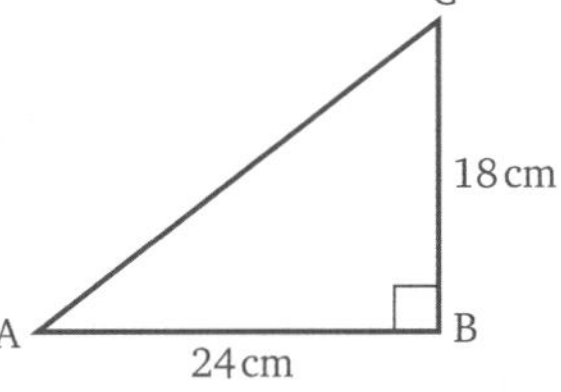

2

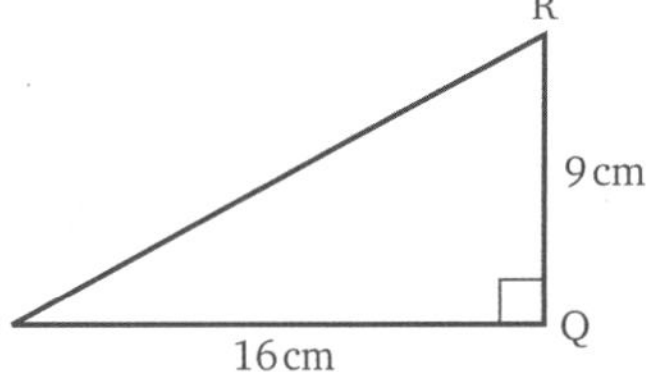

3

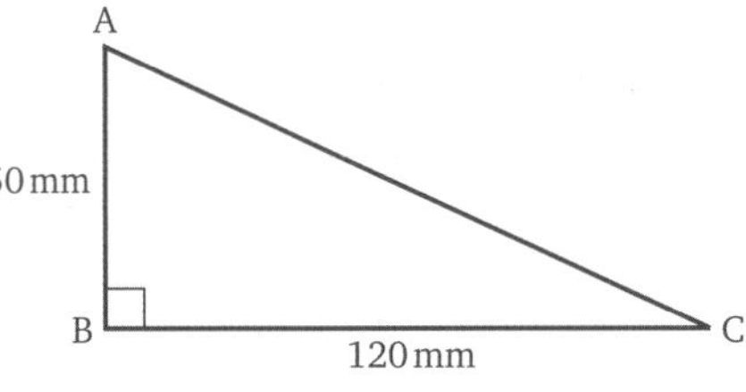

4

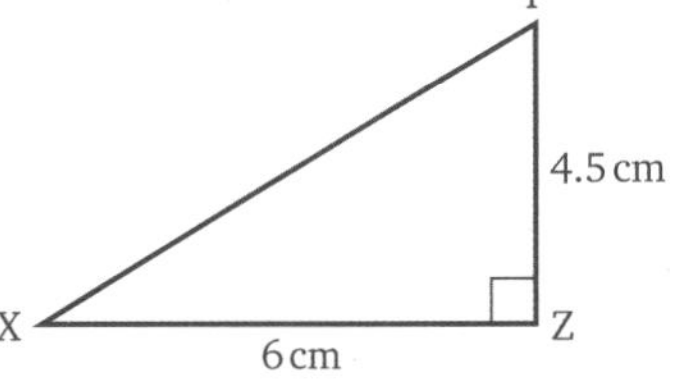

5

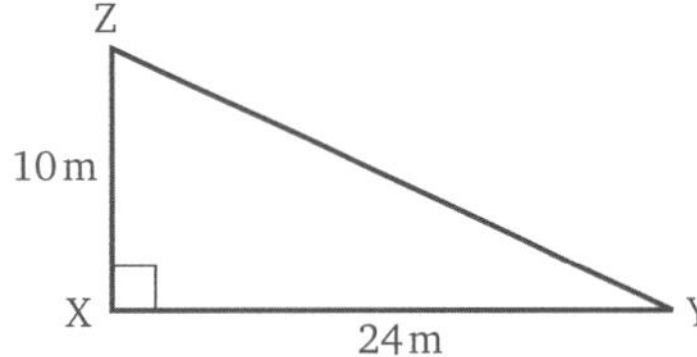

6

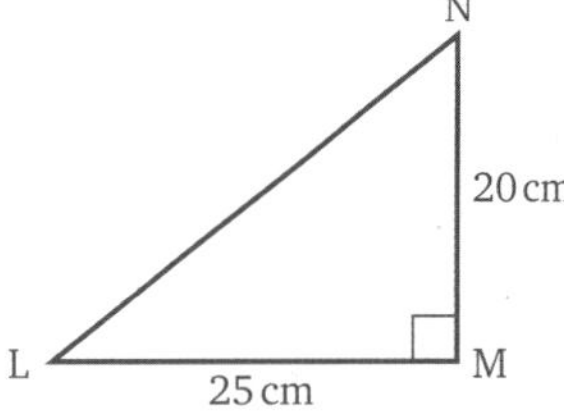

7

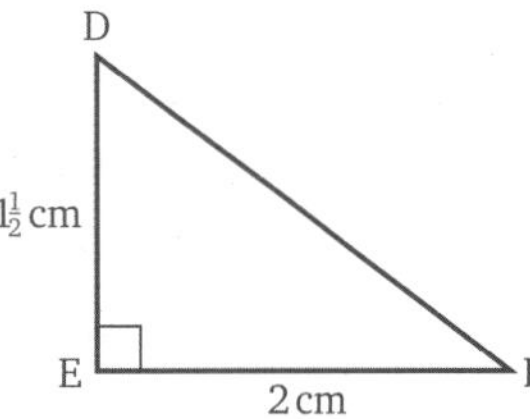

8

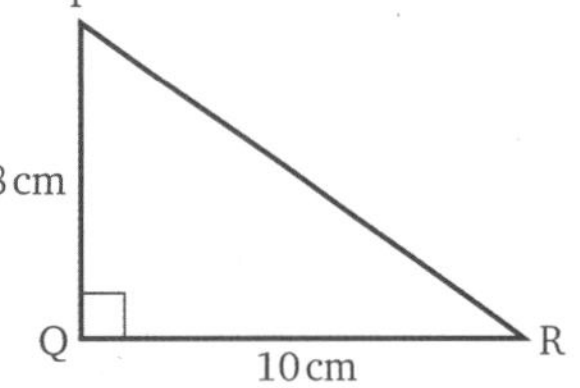

Investigation

Find more Pythagorean triples.

The two larger numbers are always consecutive whole numbers.

Finding one of the shorter sides

If we are given the hypotenuse and one other side we can find the third side.

Exercise 9e

In $\triangle ABC$, $\hat{B} = 90°$, AB = 7 cm and AC = 10 cm.
Find BC.

$AC^2 = BC^2 + AB^2$ (Pythagoras' theorem)

$10^2 = BC^2 + 7^2$

$100 = BC^2 + 49$

$51 = BC^2$ (taking 49 from both sides)

$BC = \sqrt{51} = 7.141...$

Length of BC = 7.14 cm correct to 3 s.f.

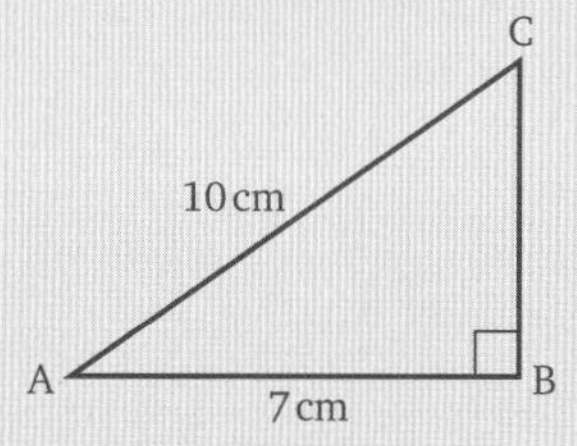

1 Find BC.

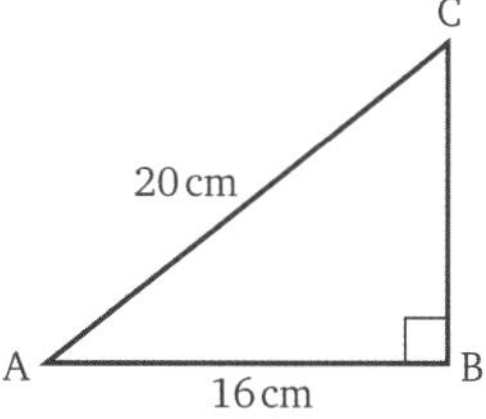

2 Find LM.

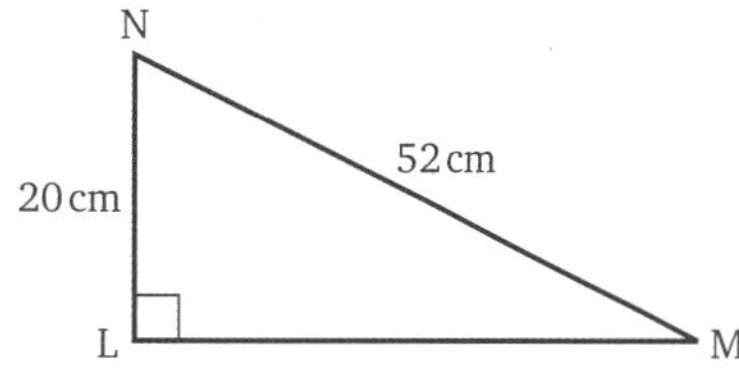

3 Find PQ.

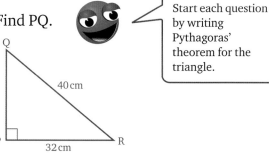

Start each question by writing Pythagoras' theorem for the triangle.

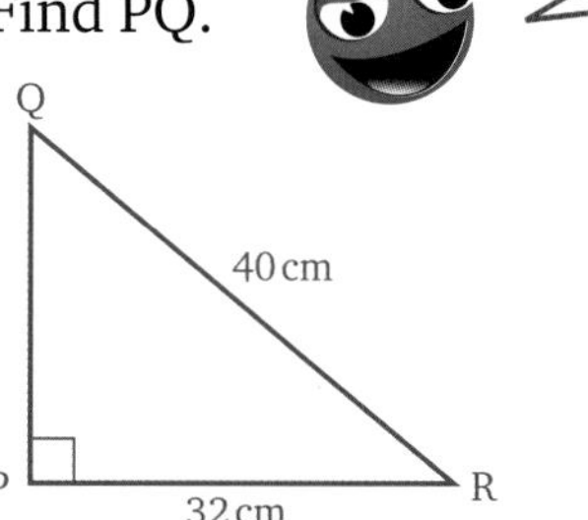

4 Find YZ.

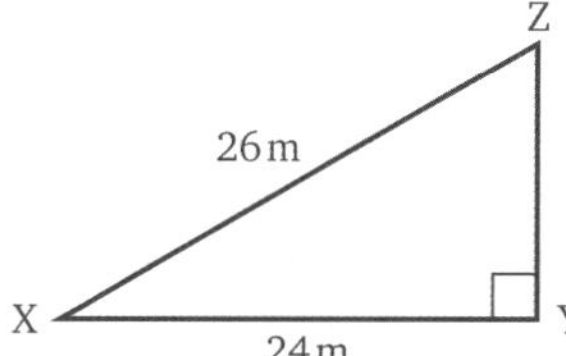

Give your answers to questions **5** to **14** correct to 3 s.f.

5 Find BC.

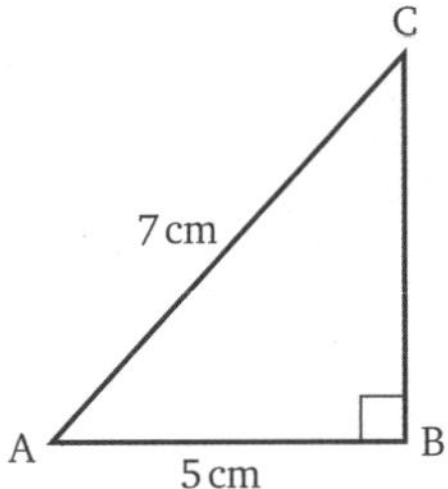

6 Find RQ.

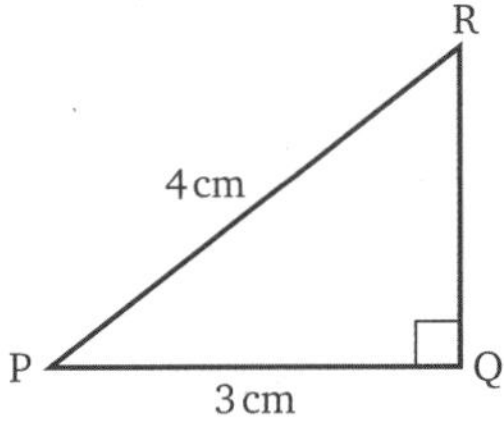

7 Find AB.

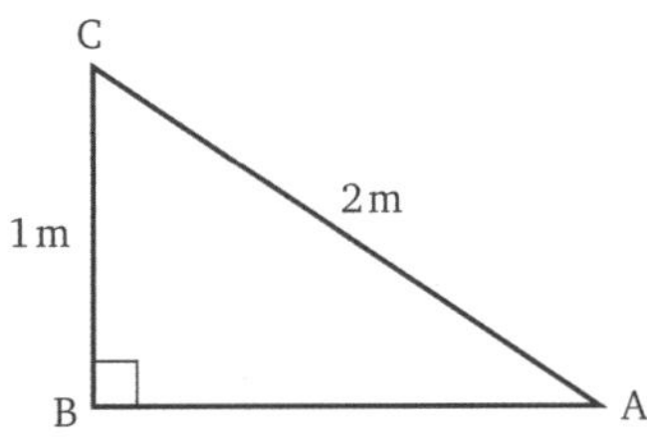

8 Find AB.

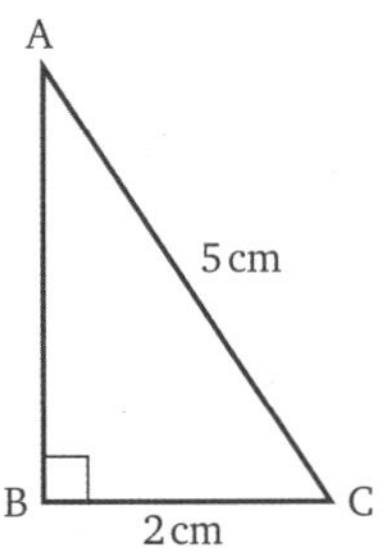

9 Find EF.

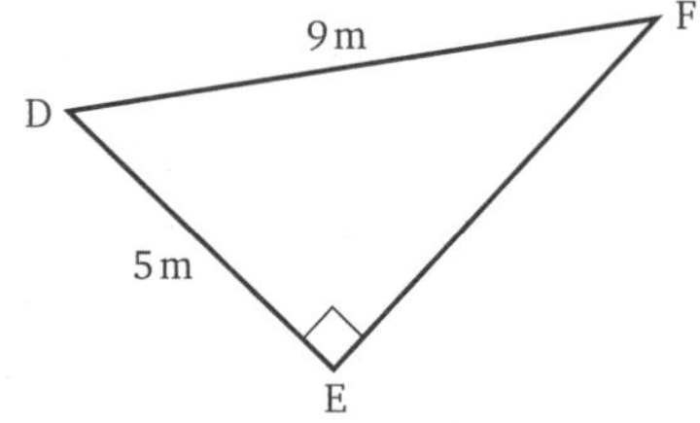

10 Find BC.

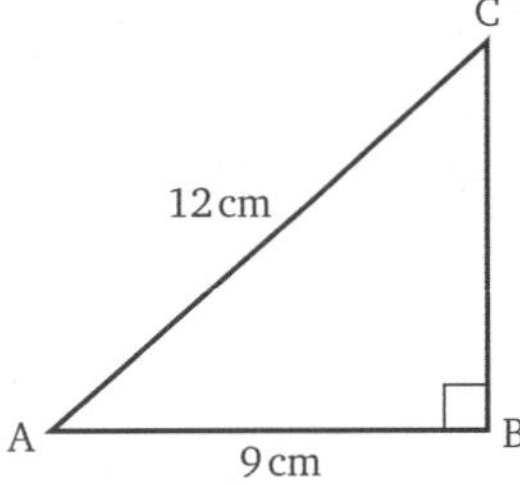

11 Find XY.

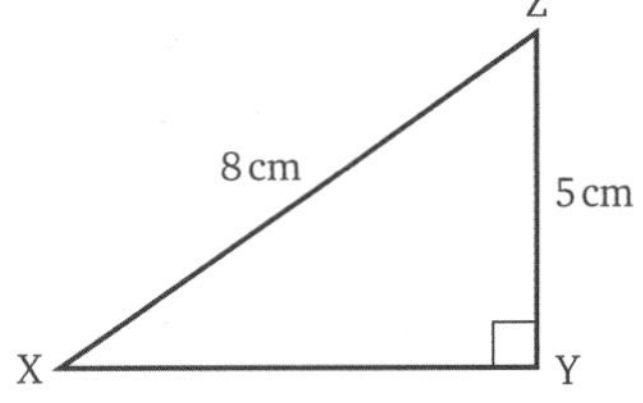

12 Find QR.

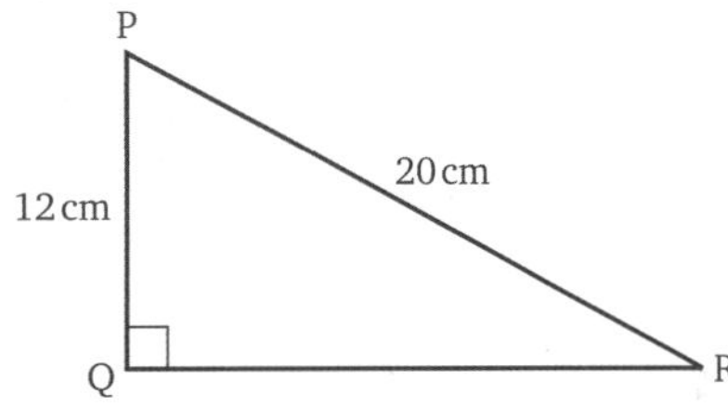

13 Find XY.

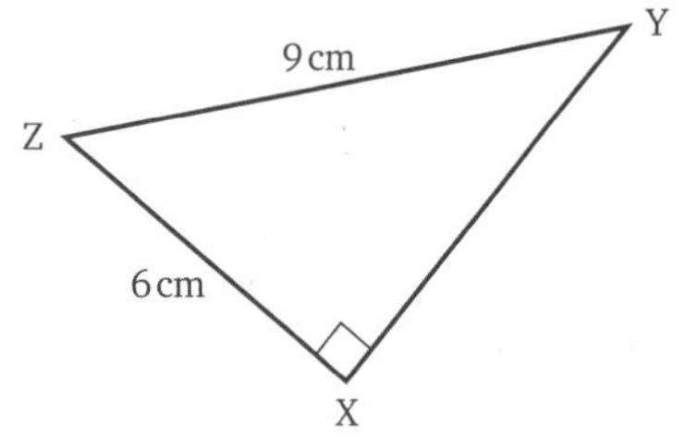

14 Find PQ.

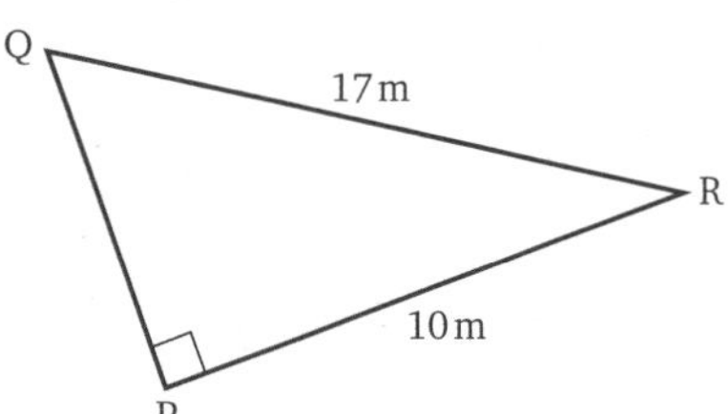

Mixed examples

Exercise 9f

In each case find the length of the missing side. If any answers are not exact give them correct to 3 s.f.

If you notice a 3, 4, 5 triangle or a 5, 12, 13 triangle, you can use it to get the answer quickly.

1 Find AC.

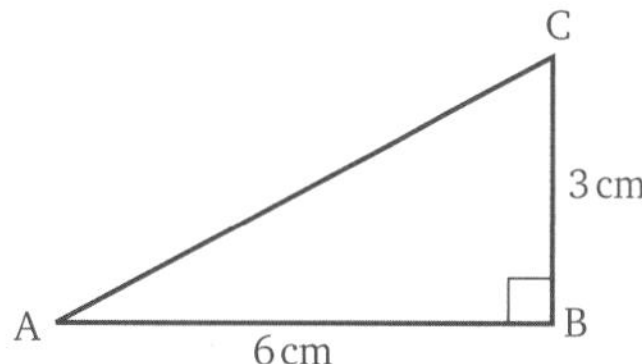

2 Find LM.

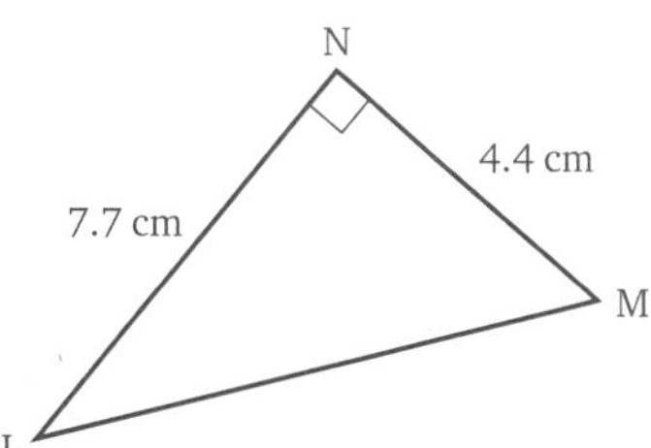

3 Find AB.

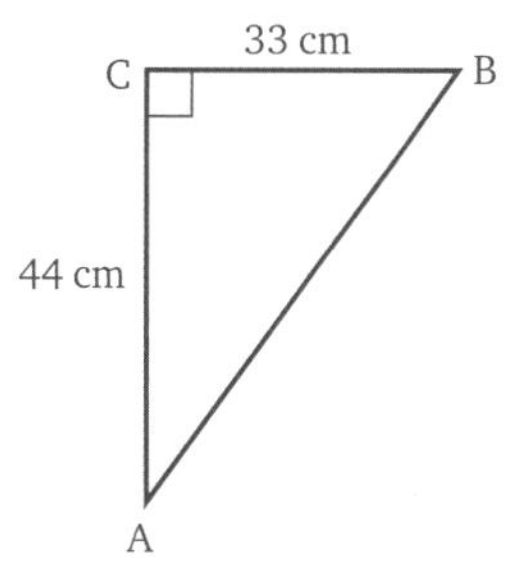

4 Find PR.

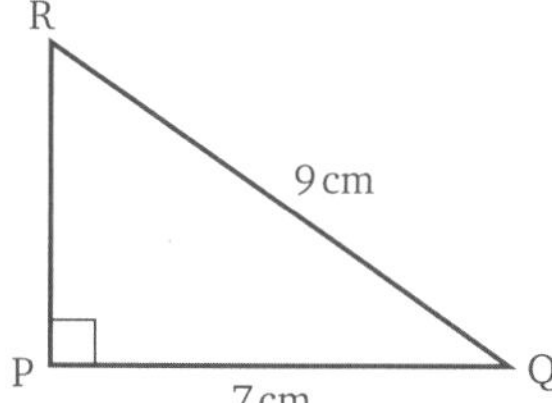

5 Find DF.

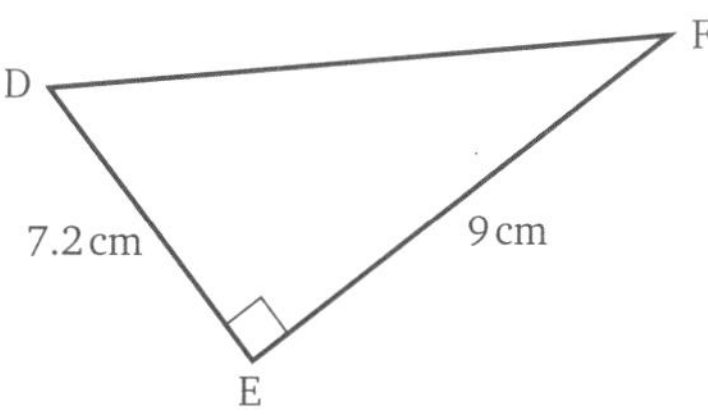

6 Find YZ.

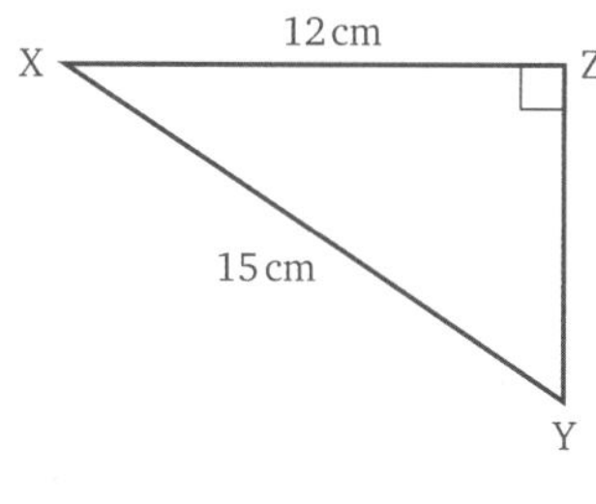

7 In $\triangle$ABC, $\hat{B} = 90°$, AB = 2 cm, AC = 4 cm. Find BC.

8 In $\triangle$ABC, $\hat{B} = 90°$, AB = 1.25 m, CA = 8.25 m. Find BC.

9 In $\triangle$PQR, $\hat{Q} = 90°$, PQ = 65 cm, QR = 60 cm. Find PR.

10 One number in a Pythagorean triple is 25. Find the other two.

11 In $\triangle$ABC, $\hat{C} = 90°$, AB = 17.5 cm, AC = 16.8 cm. Use the Pythagorean triple you found in question **10** to find BC.

12 In $\triangle$DEF, $\hat{D} = 90°$, DE = 124 cm, DF = 234 cm. Find EF.

13 In $\triangle$ABC, $\hat{C} = 90°$, AC = 3.2 cm, AB = 9.81 cm. Find BC.

14 In $\triangle$XYZ, $\hat{Y} = 90°$, XY = 1.5 cm, YZ = 2 cm. Find XZ.

15 In $\triangle PQR$, $\hat{P} = 90°$, $PQ = 5.1$ m, $QR = 8.5$ m. Find PR.

16 In $\triangle ABC$, $\hat{C} = 90°$, $AB = 92$ cm, $BC = 21$ cm. Find AC.

17 In $\triangle XYZ$, $\hat{X} = 90°$, $XY = 3.21$ m, $XZ = 1.43$ m. Find YZ.

Pythagoras' theorem using areas

The area of a square is found by squaring the length of its side, so we can represent the squares of numbers by areas of squares.

This gives us a version of Pythagoras' theorem, using areas:

In a right-angled triangle, the area of the square on the hypotenuse is equal to the sum of the areas of the squares on the other two sides.

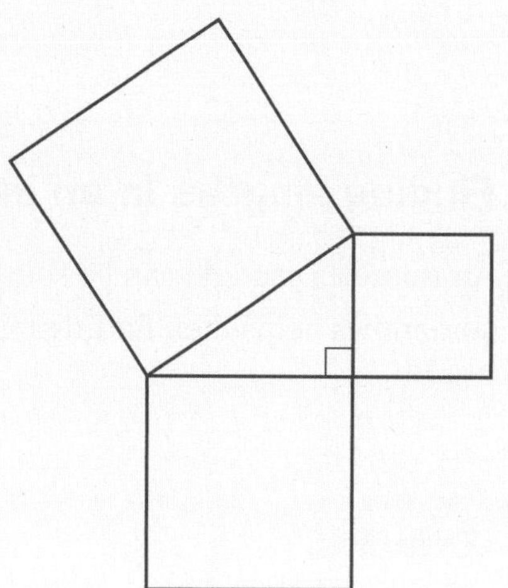

Activity

Perigal's dissection

On square grid paper, and using 1 cm to 1 unit, copy the left-hand diagram. Make sure that you draw an accurate square on the hypotenuse either by counting the squares or by using a protractor and a ruler. D is the centre of the square on AB. Draw a vector $\overrightarrow{DE}$ so that $\overrightarrow{DE} = \frac{1}{2}\overrightarrow{AC}$, i.e. DE must be parallel to AC.

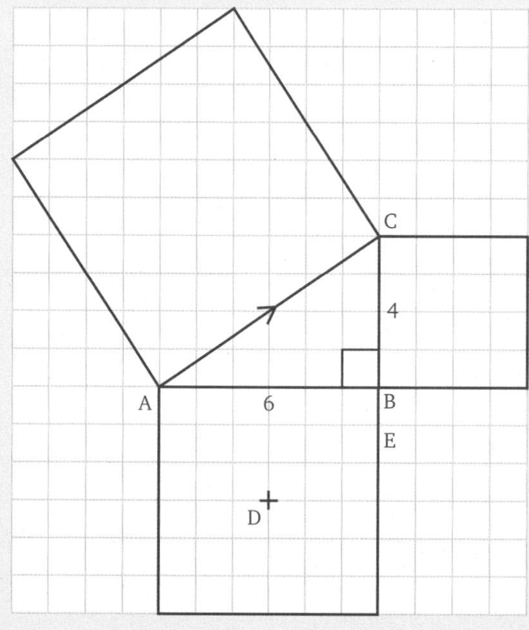

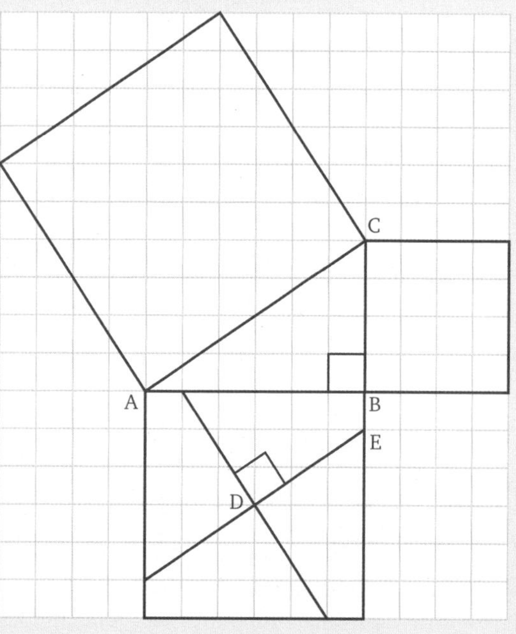

Now complete the drawing as in the right-hand diagram. Make sure that the angles at D are right angles.

Cut out the smallest square and the four pieces from the middle-sized square. These five pieces can be fitted exactly, like a jigsaw, into the outline of the biggest square.

Finding lengths in an isosceles triangle

An isosceles triangle can be split into two right-angled triangles. This can sometimes help when finding missing lengths.

Exercise 9g

In $\triangle ABC$, $AB = BC = 12$ cm and $AC = 8$ cm.
Find the height of the triangle.

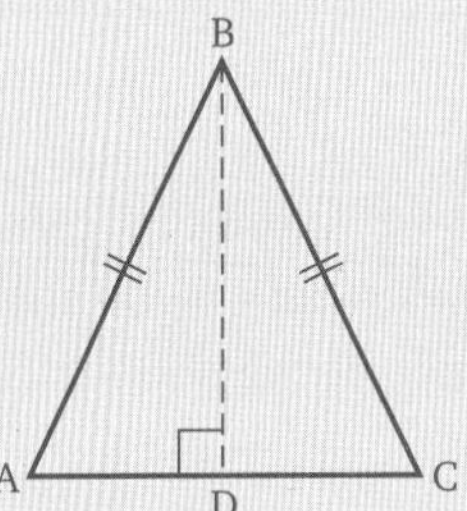

Join B to D, the midpoint of AC. Then we draw one of the right-angled triangles.

$$AB^2 = AD^2 + BD^2 \quad \text{(Pythagoras' theorem)}$$

$$12^2 = 4^2 + BD^2$$

$$144 = 16 + BD^2$$

$$128 = BD^2 \quad \text{(taking 16 from both sides)}$$

$$BD = \sqrt{128}$$

$$BD = 11.31... = 11.3 \quad \text{(correct to 3 s.f.)}$$

$\therefore$ length of BD is 11.3 cm

So the height of the triangle is 11.3 cm correct to 3 s.f.

Give your answers correct to 3 s.f.

1

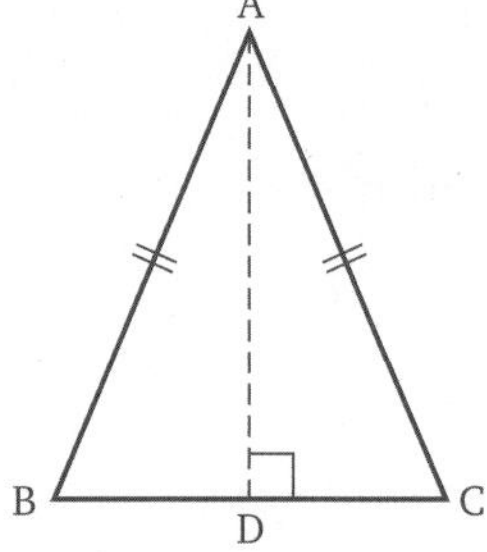

AB = AC = 16 cm. BC = 20 cm. Find the height of the triangle.

2

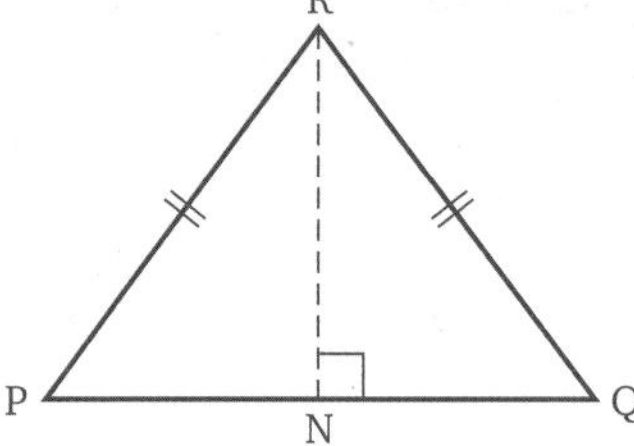

PQ = 12 cm, PR = RQ. The height of the triangle is 8 cm. Find PR.

3

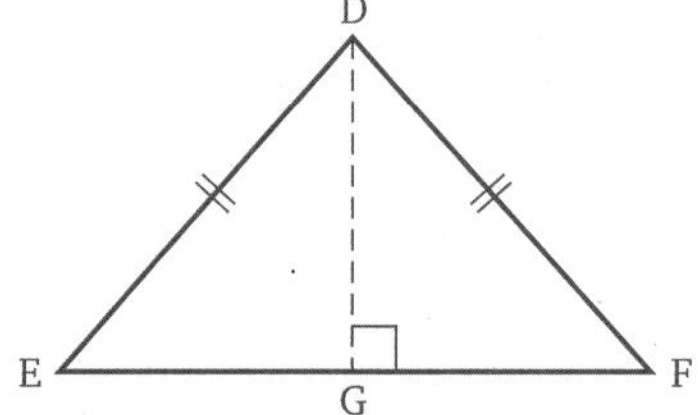

DE = DF = 20 cm. The height of the triangle is 13.2 cm. Find EG and hence EF.

4 In △ABC, AB = BC = 5.2 cm and AC = 6 cm. Find the height of the triangle.

5 In △PQR, PQ = QR = 9 cm and the height of the triangle is 7 cm. Find the length of PR.

Finding the distance of a chord from the centre of a circle

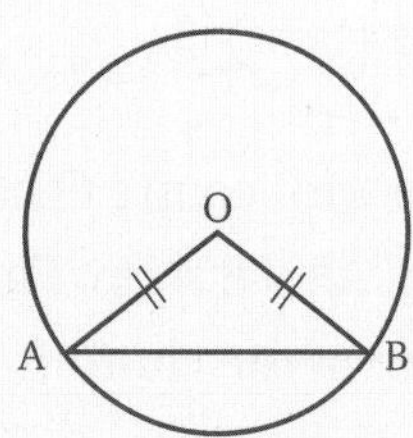

AB is a *chord* of a circle with centre O. OA and OB are radii and so are equal. Hence triangle OAB is isosceles and we can divide it through the middle into two right-angled triangles.

Exercise 9h

A chord AB of a circle with centre O is 10 cm long.
The chord is 4 cm from O. Find the radius of the circle.

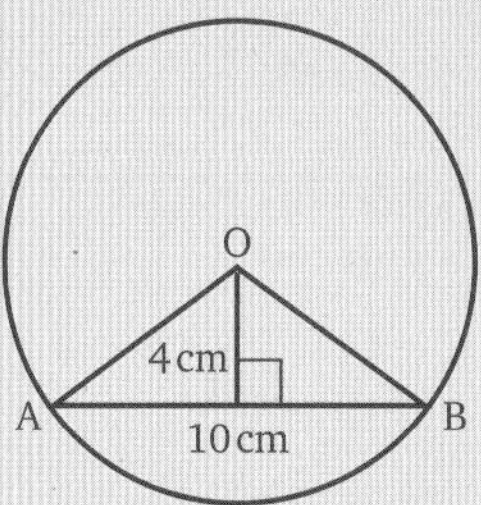

Draw one of the triangles, then use Pythagoras' theorem on this triangle. Label the third vertex C.

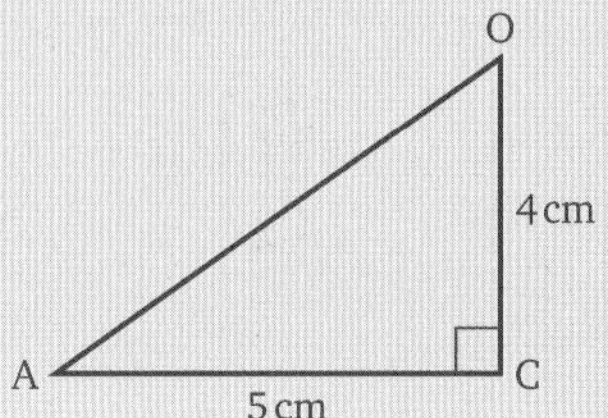

The distance from the centre is the perpendicular distance so OC = 4 cm. From symmetry AC = 5 cm.

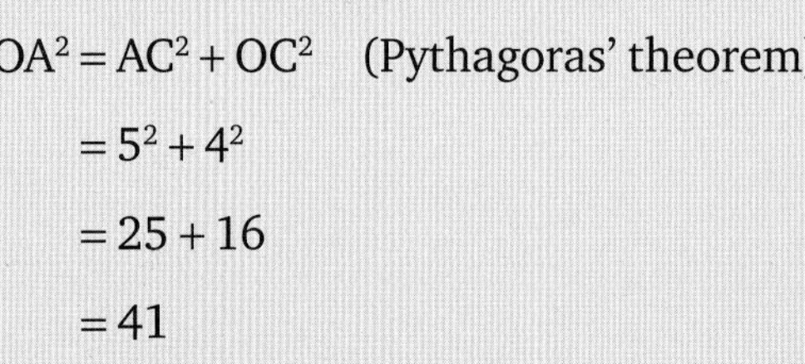

$$OA^2 = AC^2 + OC^2 \quad \text{(Pythagoras' theorem)}$$
$$= 5^2 + 4^2$$
$$= 25 + 16$$
$$= 41$$
$$OA = \sqrt{41} = 6.403\ldots$$
$$OA = 6.40 \text{ correct to 3 s.f.}$$

The radius of the circle is 6.40 cm correct to 3 s.f.

Give your answers correct to 3 s.f.

1

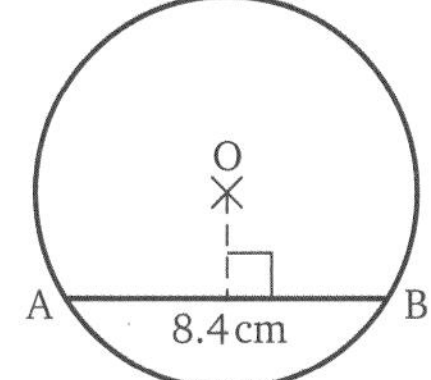

A circle with centre O has a radius of 5 cm. AB = 8.4 cm. Find the distance of the chord from the centre of the circle.

2

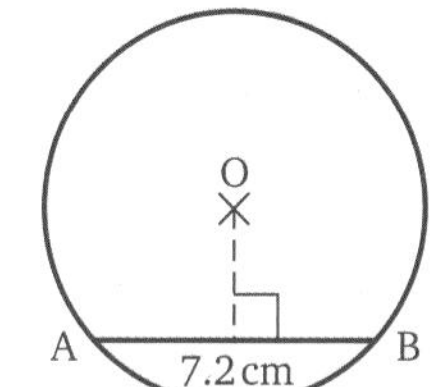

O is the centre of the circle and AB is a chord of length 7.2 cm. The distance of the chord from O is 3 cm. Find the radius of the circle.

3 In a circle with centre O, a chord AB is of length 7 cm. The radius of the circle is 11 cm. Find the distance of the chord from O.

4 In a circle with centre O and radius 17 cm, a chord AB is of length 10.4 cm. Find the distance of the chord from O.

5 In a circle with centre P and radius 7.6 cm, a chord QR is 4.2 cm from P. Find the length of the chord.

Puzzle

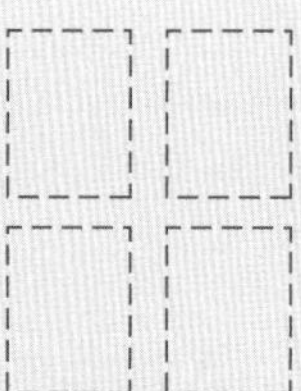

Molly has two 10 c stamps and two 5 c stamps.

She wants to stick then on an envelope as a block of four as shown.

How many different arrangements are possible?

Problems using Pythagoras' theorem

Exercise 9i

A man starts from A and walks 4 km due north to B, then 6 km due west to C. Find how far C is from A.

Draw the triangle and then use Pythagoras' theorem.

$AC^2 = BC^2 + AB^2$ (Pythagoras' theorem)

$= 6^2 + 4^2$

$= 36 + 16 = 52$

$AC = \sqrt{52} = 7.211...$

$AC = 7.21$ correct to 3 s.f.

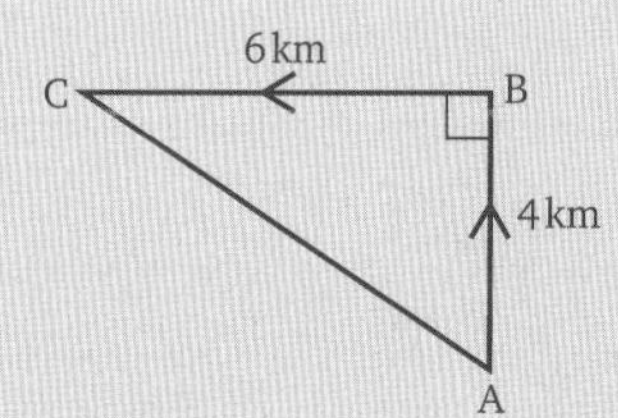

So the distance of C from A is 7.21 km, correct to 3 s.f.

Give your answers correct to 3 s.f.

1 A ladder 3 m long is leaning against a wall. Its foot is 1.5 m from the foot of the wall. How far up the wall does the ladder reach?

2 ABCD is a rhombus. AC = 10 cm and BD = 12 cm. Find the length of a side of the rhombus.

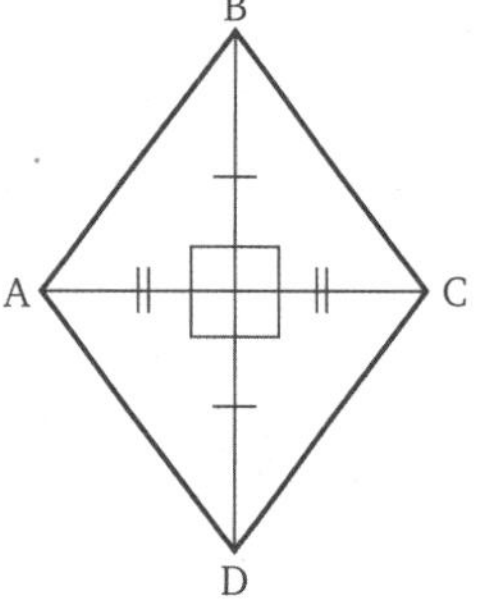

3 Find the length of a diagonal of a square of side 10 cm.

4 A hockey pitch measures 55 m by 90 m. Find the length of a diagonal of the pitch.

5 A wire stay 11 m long is attached to a telegraph pole at a point A, 8 m up from the ground. The other end of the stay is fixed to a point B, on the ground. How far is B from the foot of the telegraph pole?

6 In the kite ABCD, $\hat{A} = \hat{C} = 90°$. BC = 41 cm and DC = 62 cm. Find the length of the diagonal BD.

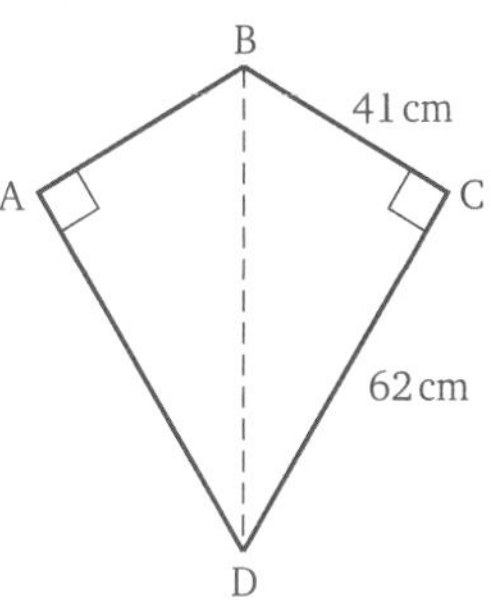

7 A diagonal of a football pitch is 130 m long and the long side measures 100 m. Find the length of the short side of the pitch.

8 The diagram shows the side view of a coal bunker. Find the length of the slant edge.

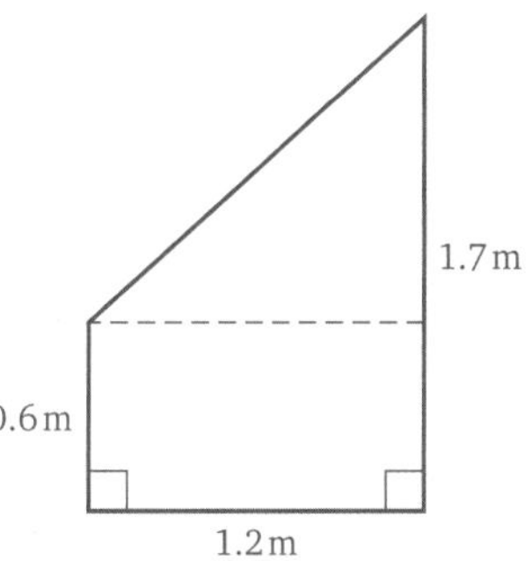

9 The slant height of a cone is 15 cm and the base radius is 5 cm. Find the height of the cone.

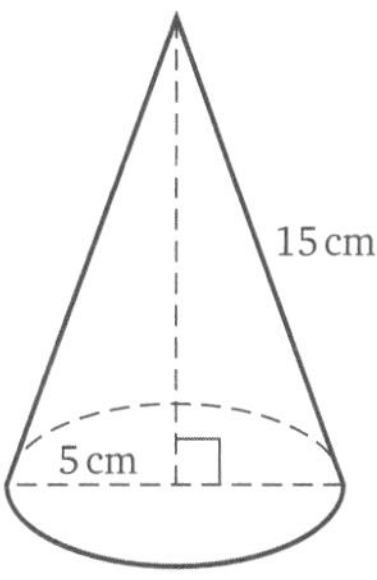

10 A man starts from A and walks 6.5 km due south to B; then he walks due east to C. He is then 9 km from A. How far is C from B?

11 A is the point (3, 1) and B is the point (7, 9). Find the length of AB.

First draw a diagram with AB the hypotenuse of a right-angled triangle. Mark the lengths of the other two sides.

12 A ship sails 32 nautical miles due north then 22 nautical miles due east. How far is it from its starting point?

13 A pole 4.5 m high stands on level ground. It is supported in a vertical position by two wires attached to its top and to points on opposite sides of the pole each 3.2 m from the foot of the pole. How long is each wire?

14 The diagonal AC of a rectangle ABCD is 0.67 m long and side AB is 0.32 m long. How long is side BC?

15 Find the length of the diagonal of a square of side 15 cm.

16 ABCD is a kite and AC is its line of symmetry. $\hat{B} = \hat{D} = 90°$, AB = 36 cm and BC = 16 cm. Find AC

17 In the diagram, $A\hat{D}B = 90°$
AB = 4 cm, AD = 3.2 cm and BC = 2.8 cm.

Find **a** BD **b** AC.

Is $A\hat{B}C$ a right angle?

Give a reason for your answer.

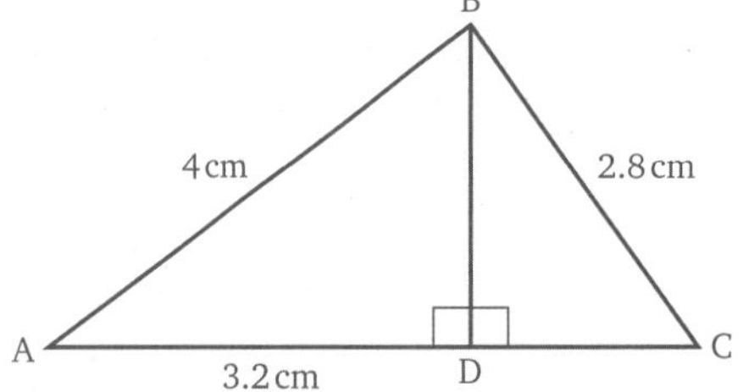

18 **a** *Construct* the figure in the diagram, starting with △ABC then adding △ADC and △ADE.

b Measure AC, AD and EA.

c *Calculate* AC, AD and AE and check the accuracy of your drawing.

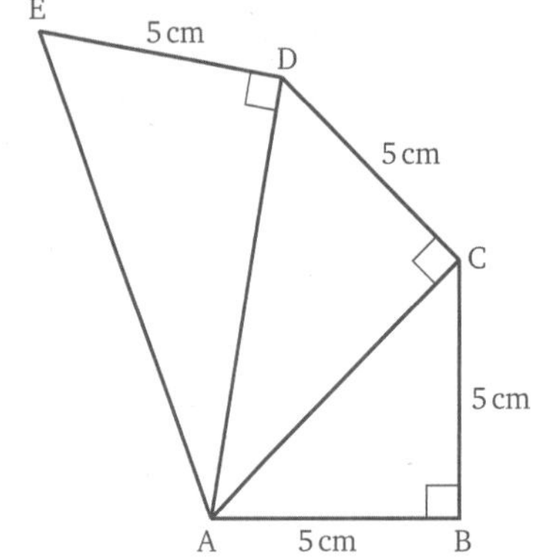

19 Construct a right-angled triangle, choosing whole numbers of centimetres for the lengths of the two shorter sides, such that the hypotenuse will be $\sqrt{65}$ cm long. Check the accuracy of your drawing by measuring the hypotenuse and by calculating $\sqrt{65}$.

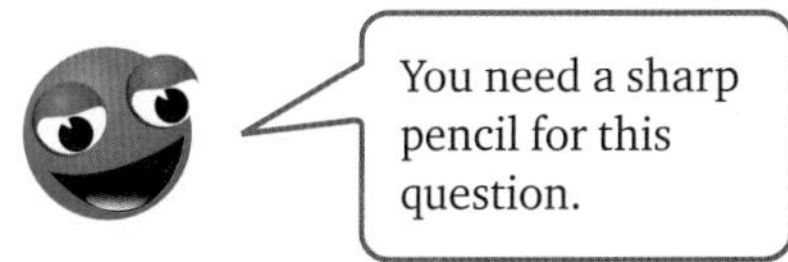

The converse of Pythagoras' theorem

If we are given three sides of a triangle, we can tell whether or not the triangle contains a right angle because if it does, the square on the longest side is equal to the sum of the squares on the other two sides. Bear in mind that, *if* there is a right angle, then the longest side will be the hypotenuse.

Exercise 9j

Are the following triangles right-angled?

a $\triangle$ABC: AB = 17 cm, BC = 8 cm, CA = 15 cm

b $\triangle$PQR: PQ = 15 cm, PR = 7 cm, RQ = 12 cm

a

$$AB^2 = 17^2 = 289$$

$$AC^2 + BC^2 = 15^2 + 8^2 = 225 + 64 = 289$$

$\therefore AC^2 + BC^2 = AB^2$

$\therefore$ by Pythagoras' theorem, $\hat{C} = 90°$.

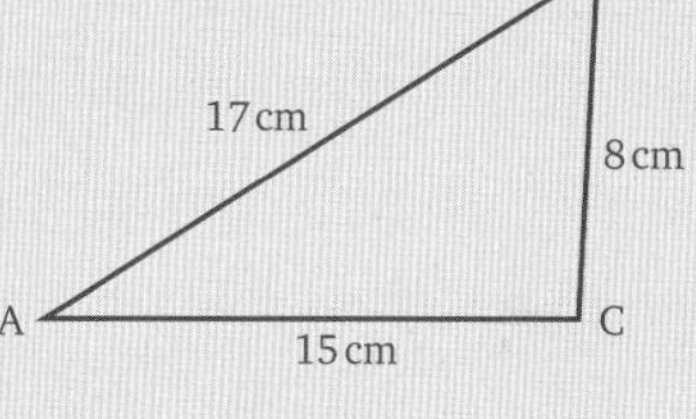

b

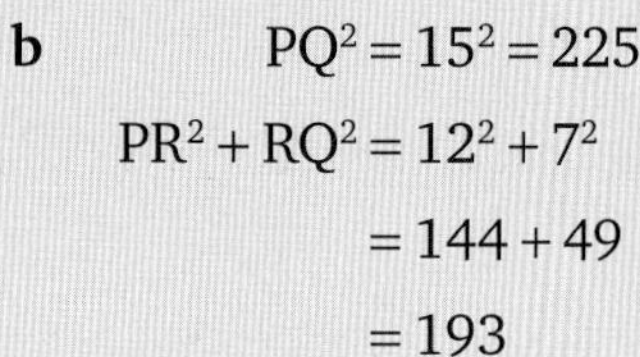

$$PQ^2 = 15^2 = 225$$

$$PR^2 + RQ^2 = 12^2 + 7^2 = 144 + 49 = 193$$

$\therefore PR^2 + RQ^2 \neq PQ^2$

$\therefore$ the triangle is not right-angled.

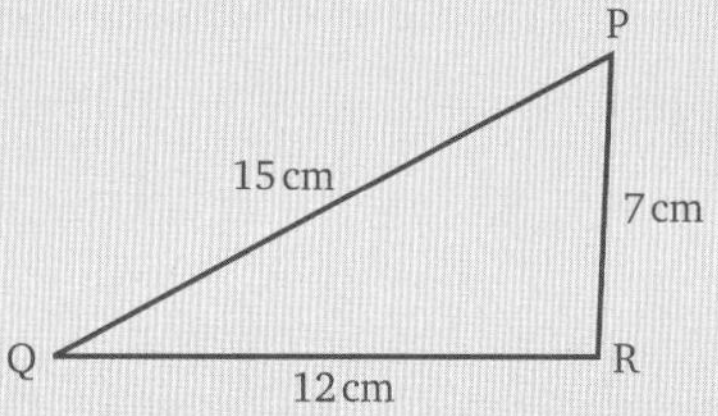

Are the following triangles right-angled?

Start by drawing a triangle and marking the sides. Then find the square of the longest side and compare this value with the sum of the squares of the other two sides.

1. Triangle ABC: AB = 48 cm, BC = 64 cm and CA = 80 cm.
2. Triangle PQR: PQ = 2.1 cm, QR = 2.8 cm and RP = 3.5 cm.
3. Triangle LMN: LM = 6 cm, MN = 7.2 cm and NL = 9 cm.
4. Triangle ABC: AB = 9.2 cm, BC = 6.3 cm and CA = 4.6 cm.
5. Triangle DEF: DE = 6.4 cm, EF = 12 cm and DF = 13.6 cm.
6. Triangle XYZ: XY = 32 cm, YZ = 40 cm and ZX = 48 cm.

Mixed exercises

Exercise 9k

Find the missing lengths in the following triangles:

1

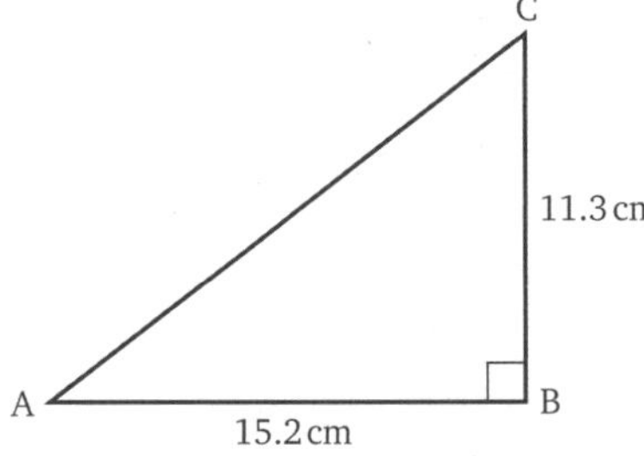

2

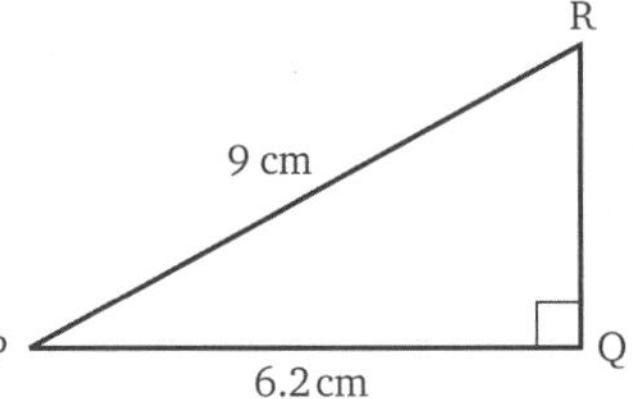

3

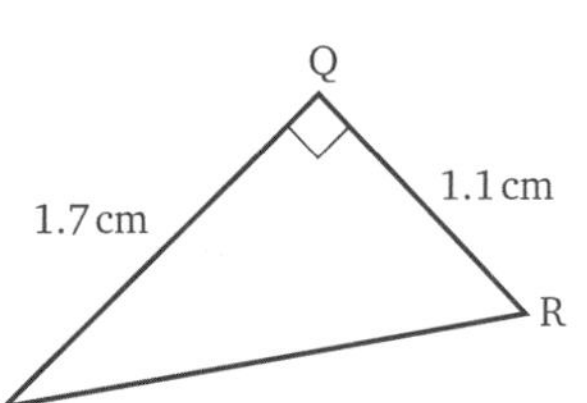

4

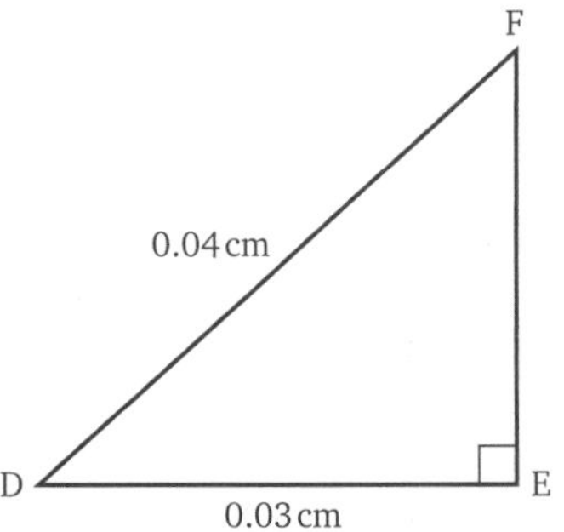

5

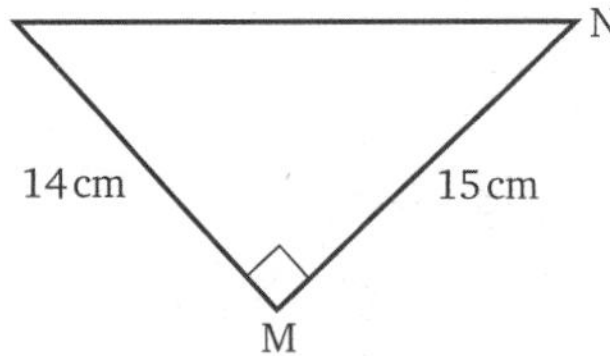

6

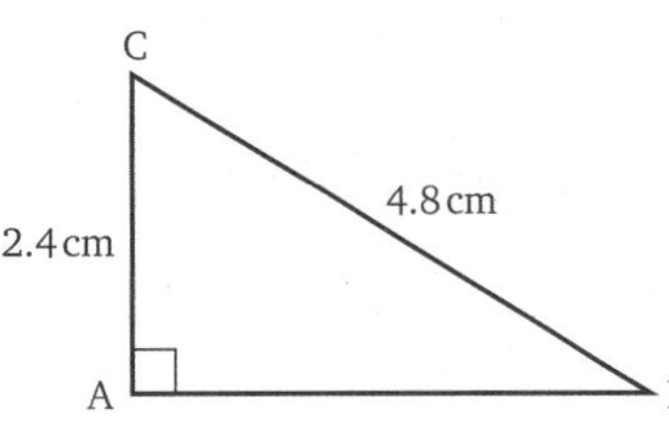

7

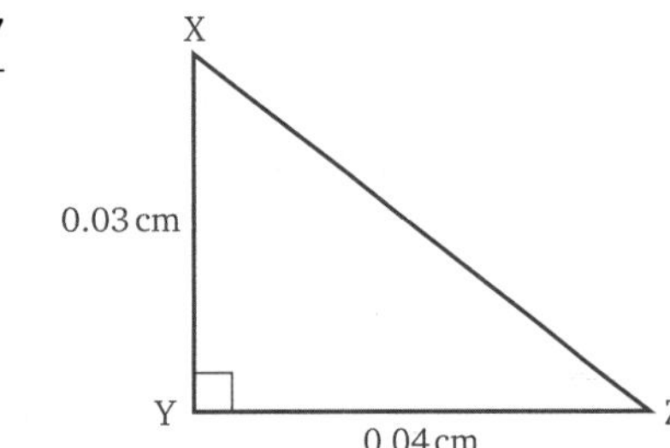

8

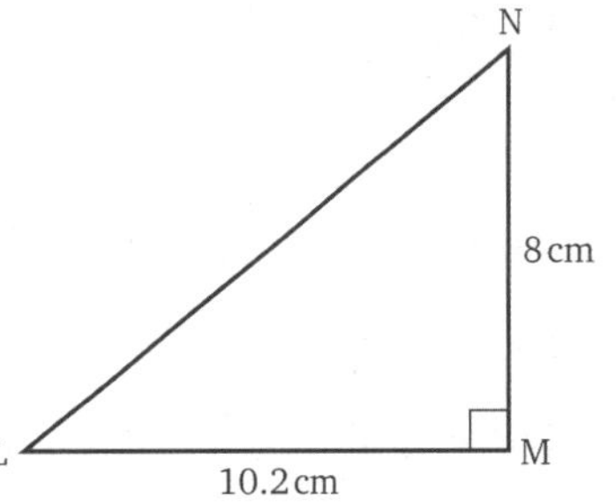

9 In triangle ABC, $\hat{A} = 90°$, AB = 3.2 cm and BC = 4.8 cm. Find AC.

Start by drawing a diagram and marking the sides.

10 In triangle PQR, $\hat{Q} = 90°$, PQ = 56 cm and QR = 32 cm. Find PR.

11 In triangle ABC, AB = 1 cm, BC = 2.4 cm and CA = 2.6 cm. Is $\hat{B}$ a right angle?

12 In triangle DEF, $\hat{F} = 90°$, DF = 2.8 cm and DE = 4.2 cm. Find EF.

13 In triangle XYZ, $\hat{Y} = 90°$, XY = 17 cm and YZ = 20 cm. Find XZ.

14 In triangle LMN, NL = 25 cm, LM = 24 cm and MN = 7 cm. Is the triangle right-angled? If it is, which angle is 90°?

Exercise 9I

Select the letter that gives the correct answer.

1 The square root of 200, correct to 3 s.f., is

A 12.1 **B** 13.1 **C** 14.1 **D** 15.1

2 AC is the hypotenuse of a right-angled triangle. The lengths of the other two sides are 5 cm and 12 cm. The length of AC is

A 13 cm **B** 14 cm **C** 15 cm **D** 16 cm

3 The two shorter sides of a right-angled triangle are of lengths 6 cm and 8 cm.

The length of the hypotenuse is

A 9 cm **B** 9.5 cm **C** 10 cm **D** 10.5 cm

4 The length of AC, correct to 3 s.f., is

A 10.0 cm

B 10.8 cm

C 11.0 cm

D 11.5 cm

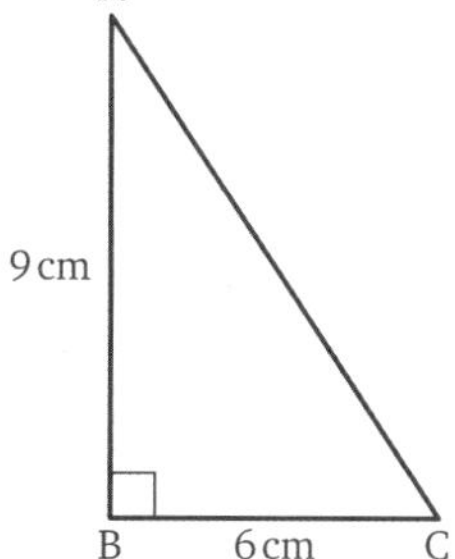

5 PQ is a chord of length 10 cm in a circle of radius 6 cm. The distance of the chord from the centre of the circle, correct to 2 d.p., is

A 3.30 cm **B** 3.31 cm **C** 3.32 cm **D** 3.33 cm

6 The diagonals of a rhombus are of lengths 20 cm and 16 cm.

The length of a side of this rhombus, correct to 3 s.f., is

A 12.6 cm **B** 12.7 cm **C** 12.8 cm **D** 12.9 cm

Did you know?

Do you think that a person could be his own worst enemy?

A great mathematician named Evariste Galois (1811–1832) was considered such a person. He had a short unhappy life filled with hate and conceit. He hated school, and his teachers, whom he considered to be very stupid. The teachers thought that he was bad, stupid and strange. He studied mathematics and found that he was a genius in the subject. At the age of seventeen he wrote some ideas and sent them to the French Academy. While awaiting the reply on his work from the academy his father killed himself. This caused him to hate even more. He was expelled from university for inciting a riot for the French Revolution. He fell in love but his girlfriend left him. This caused him to hate even more. He was killed in a duel at the age of twenty years. The ideas he wrote down the night before his death were finally understood around 1900, many years after his death.

In this chapter you have seen that...

✔ Pythagoras' theorem states that, in a right-angled triangle, the square of the hypotenuse is equal to the sum of the squares of the other two sides, i.e. in this triangle $AC^2 = AB^2 + BC^2$

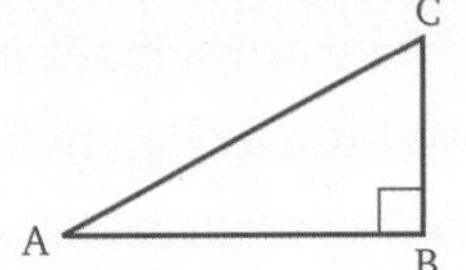

✔ some special triplets of numbers like 3, 4, 5 and 5, 12, 13, or multiples of these, give a right-angled triangle whatever unit of measurement is used

✔ if, in a triangle ABC, $AC^2 = AB^2 + BC^2$, then the triangle contains a right angle and AC is the hypotenuse, but if AC is the longest side and $AC^2 \neq AB^2 + BC^2$, then the triangle is not right-angled.

10 Trigonometry

At the end of this chapter you should be able to...

1. define sine, cosine and tangent of an angle in a right-angled triangle
2. use a calculator to find the sine, cosine or tangent of a given angle
3. use a calculator to find an angle given its sine, cosine or tangent
4. calculate the size of an angle in a right-angled triangle, given the lengths of the sides of the triangle
5. calculate the length of a side of a right-angled triangle, given one side and another angle
6. draw diagrams to show angles of elevation or depression
7. use trigonometric ratios to solve problems on angles of elevation and depression
8. use Pythagoras' theorem and trigonometry to solve problems in three dimensions.

Did you know?

The word 'trigonometry' first appears in the English translation in 1614 of a book written by Bartholomeo Pitiscus (1561–1613) and published in 1595. The full title in the English translation is *Trigonometry: or The Doctrine of Triangles*.

You need to know...

- ✔ how to work with decimals and fractions
- ✔ how to solve equations
- ✔ the properties of isosceles triangles
- ✔ the properties of similar triangles
- ✔ the meaning of angles of elevation and depression
- ✔ Pythagoras' theorem.

Key words

adjacent side, angle of depression, angle of elevation, cosine of an angle, hypotenuse, opposite side, right-angled triangle, sine of an angle, tangent of an angle

Tangent of an angle

This chapter deals with finding angles and lengths in *right-angled triangles*.

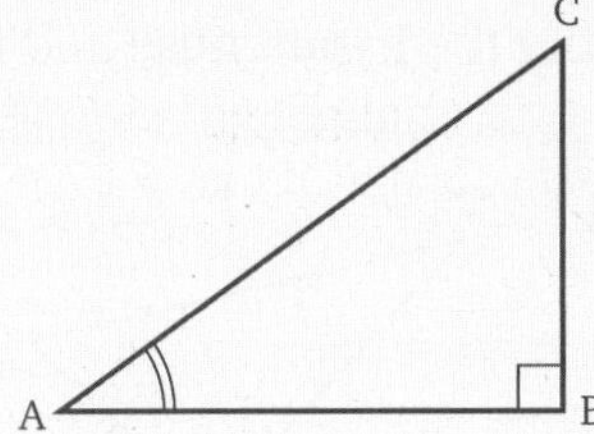

In triangle ABC, AC is the *hypotenuse*, opposite to the right angle.

BC is the *opposite side* to angle A.

AB is the *adjacent side* (or neighbouring side) to angle A.

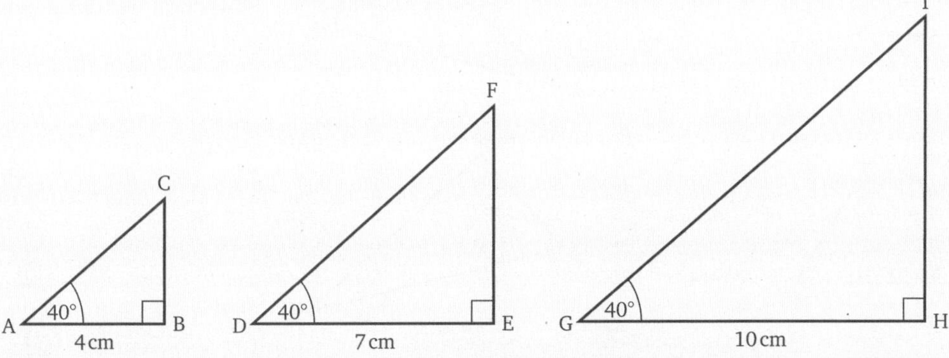

In the three triangles above, the opposite side and the adjacent side are in the same ratio, i.e. This is also true in any other right-angled triangle containing an angle of 40°.

$$\frac{BC}{AB} = \frac{EF}{DE} = \frac{HI}{GH}$$

This ratio is called the *tangent* of 40° or, in shortened form, tan 40°. Its size is stored, together with the tangents of other angles, in natural tangent tables and in scientific calculators.

$$\tan \hat{A} = \frac{\text{opposite side}}{\text{adjacent side}}$$

Exercise 10a

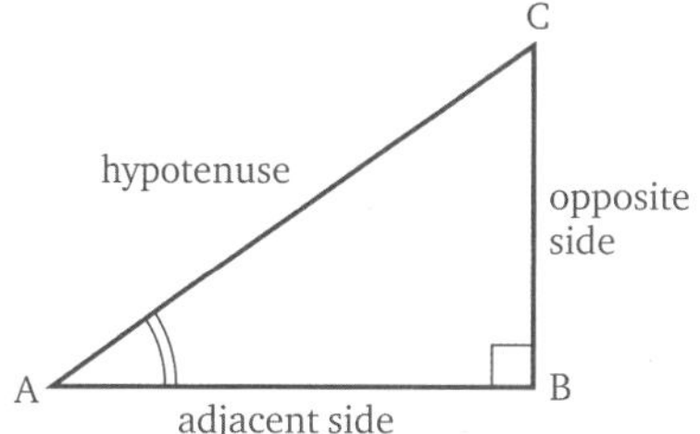

In questions **1** to **6**, copy the diagram. Identify the hypotenuse and the sides opposite and adjacent to the marked angle:

1

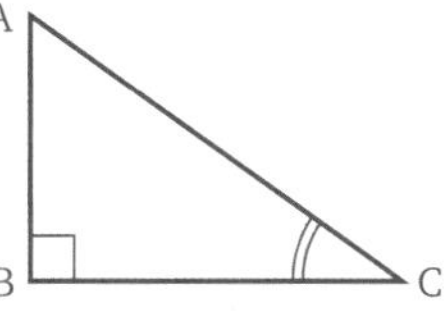

2

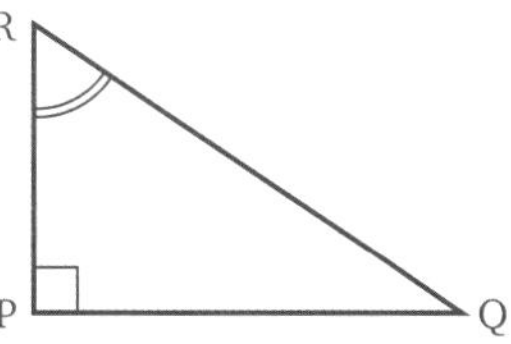

3

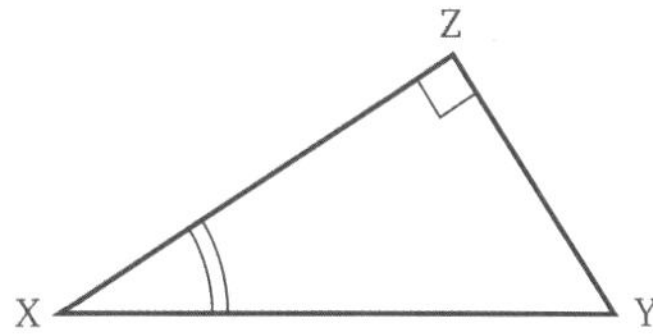

4

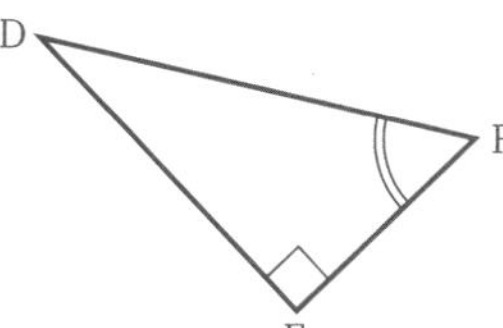

5

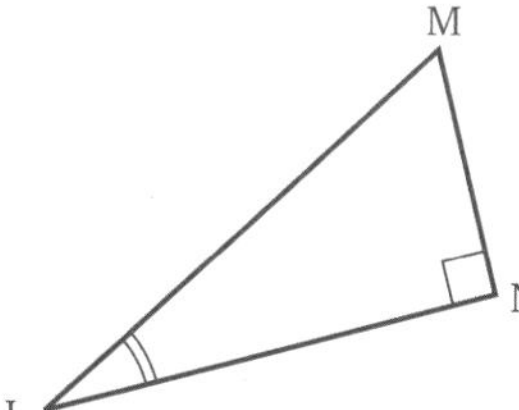

6

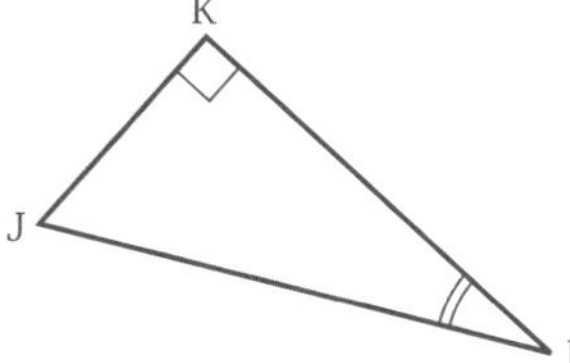

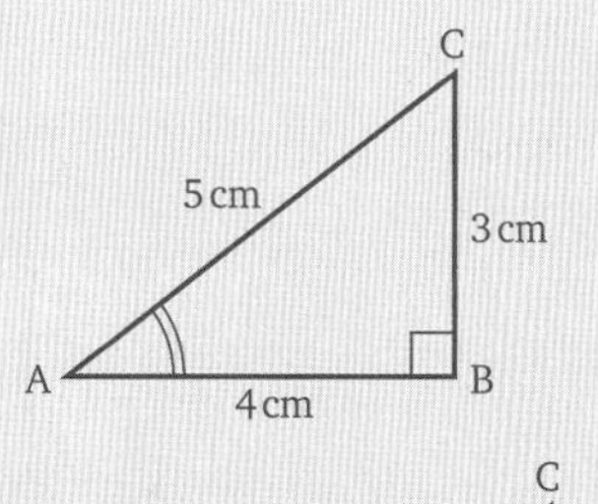

In $\triangle ABC$, $\hat{B} = 90°$, $AB = 4$ cm, $BC = 3$ cm and $AC = 5$ cm.

Write $\tan \hat{A}$ as a fraction and as a decimal.

C

hypotenuse 5 cm

opposite 3 cm

A

B

4 cm adjacent

(First identify the sides and mark them on the diagram.)

$$\tan \hat{A} = \frac{\text{opposite}}{\text{adjacent}}$$

$$= \frac{3}{4}$$

$$= 0.75$$

In each of the following questions write the tangent of the marked angle as a fraction and as a decimal (correct to four decimal places where necessary):

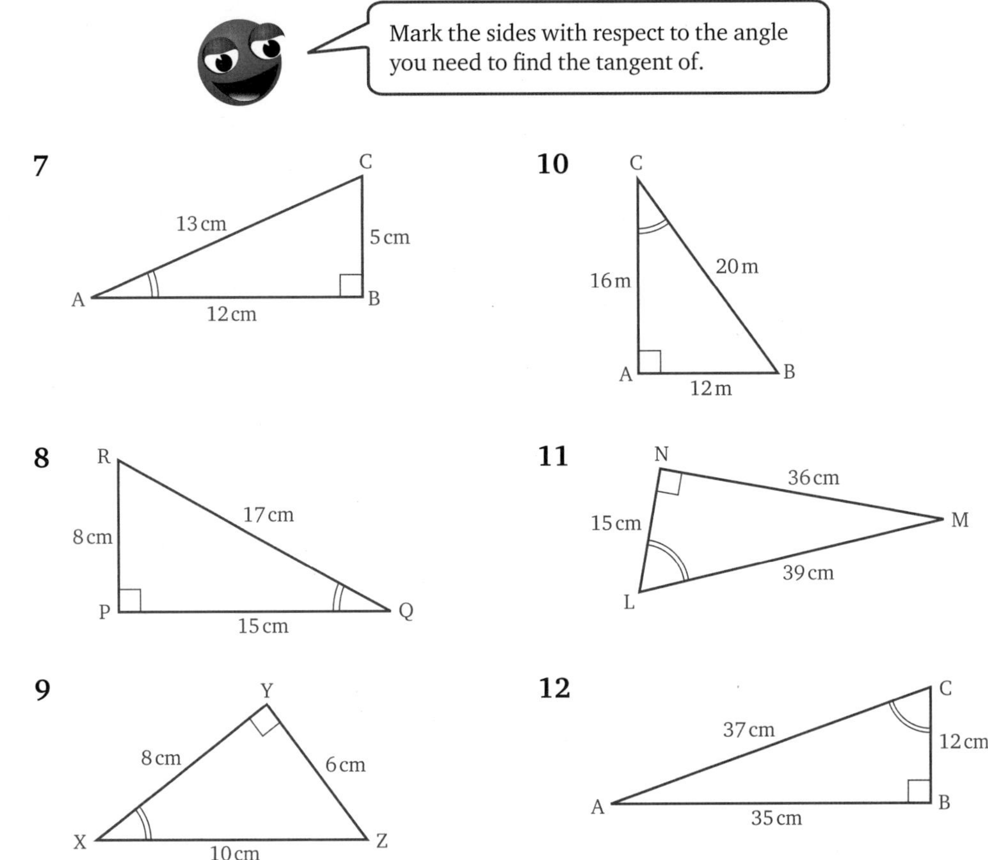

Using a calculator

To find the tangent of an angle, enter the size of the angle, then press the 'tan' button. Write the answer correct to four decimal places.

$$\tan 42.4° = 0.9131$$

To find an angle given its tangent, enter the value of the tangent and then press the inverse button followed by the tangent button. Write the size of the angle correct to one decimal place.

If these instructions do not work, consult the manual for your calculator.

Exercise 10b

Find the tangents of the following angles:

1 62°	4 16.8°	<u>7</u> 78.4°	<u>10</u> 48.2°
2 14°	5 4.6°	<u>8</u> 45°	<u>11</u> 3°
3 30.5°	6 72°	<u>9</u> 30°	<u>12</u> 29.4°

Find the angles whose tangents are given in questions **13** to **24**:

13 0.179	**16** 0.4326	<u>**19**</u> 0.9213	<u>**22**</u> 2.683
14 0.356	**17** 1.362	<u>**20**</u> 0.8	<u>**23**</u> 0.924
15 1.43	**18** 0.632	<u>**21**</u> 0.3214	<u>**24**</u> 0.0024

Finding an angle

Exercise 10c

In triangle ABC, $\hat{B} = 90°$, AB = 12 cm, BC = 9 cm and AC = 15 cm. Find $\hat{A}$.

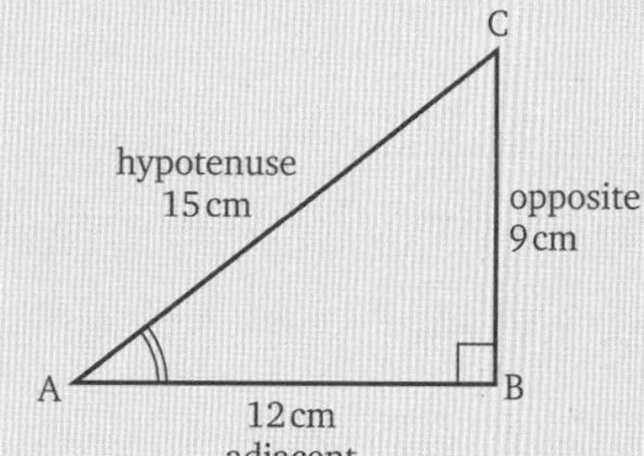

$$\tan \hat{A} = \frac{\text{opp}}{\text{adj}} = \frac{9}{12}$$
$$= 0.75$$
$$\hat{A} = 36.9° \text{ (to 1 d.p.)}$$

Use the information given on the diagrams to find $\hat{A}$ and give your answers correct to one decimal place.

Draw the triangle, mark the angle required, then label the sides with respect to this angle.

1

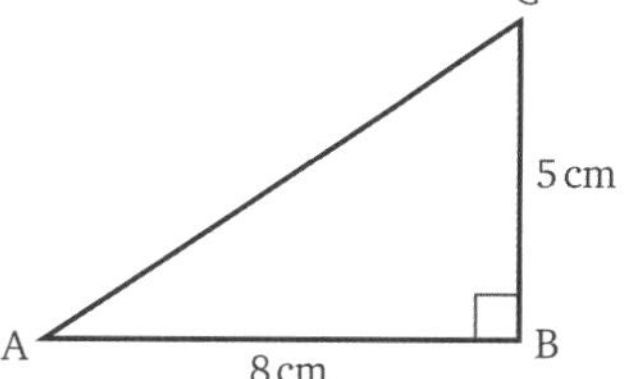

2

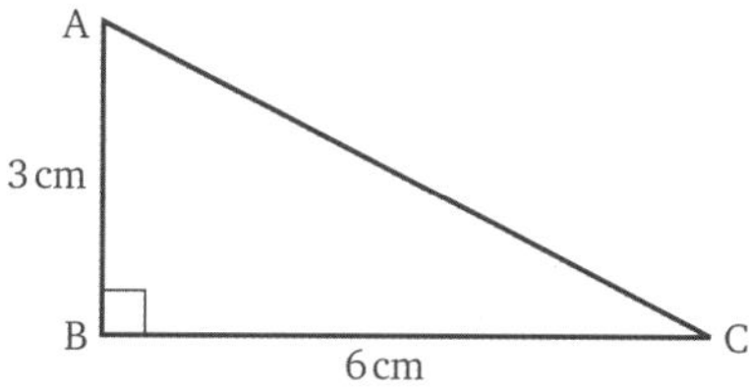

3

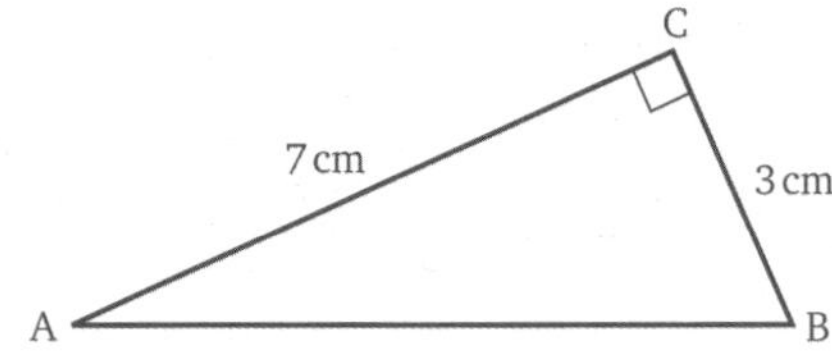

4

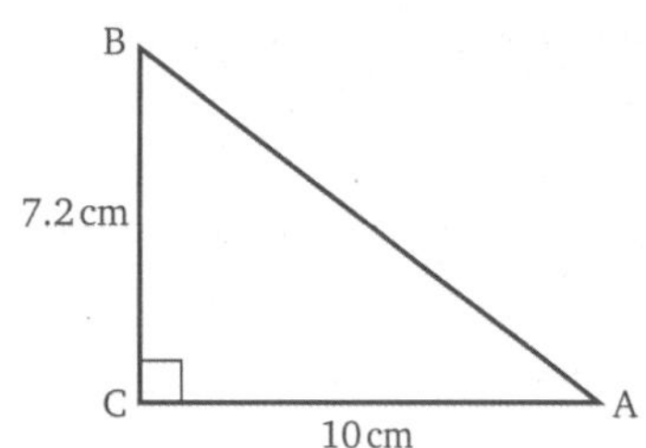

5 In triangle PQR, $\hat{P} = 90°$, QP = 6 cm and PR = 10 cm. Find $\hat{R}$.

6 In triangle XYZ, $\hat{Y} = 90°$, XY = 4 cm and YZ = 5 cm. Find $\hat{X}$.

7 In triangle LMN, $\hat{L} = 90°$, LM = 7.2 cm and LN = 6.4 cm. Find $\hat{N}$.

8 In triangle DEF, $\hat{D} = 90°$, DE = 210 cm and DF = 231 cm. Find $\hat{E}$.

9 In △ABC, $\hat{C} = 90°$, AC = 3.2 m and BC = 4.7 m. Find $\hat{B}$.

Finding a side

Exercise 10d

In triangle ABC, $\hat{B} = 90°$, AB = 4 cm and $\hat{A} = 32°$. Find BC.

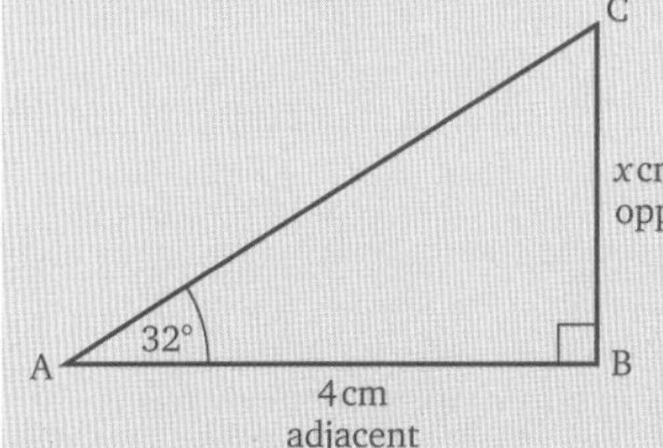

$$\frac{x}{4} = \frac{\text{opp}}{\text{adj}} = \tan 32°$$

$$\frac{x}{4} = 0.6248\ldots$$

$$4 \times \frac{x}{4} = 4 \times 0.6248\ldots$$

Multiply both sides of the equation by 4 to eliminate the denominator on the left-hand side.

Do not clear the display on your calculator.

Press [×] [4] [=]

$$x = 2.4994\ldots$$

∴ BC = 2.50 cm (to 3 s.f.)

Use the information given in the diagram to find the required side.

When you use a calculator write down the first four figures in the display for intermediate steps. Do not clear the display; use the entry for the next step in the calculation.

1 Find RQ.

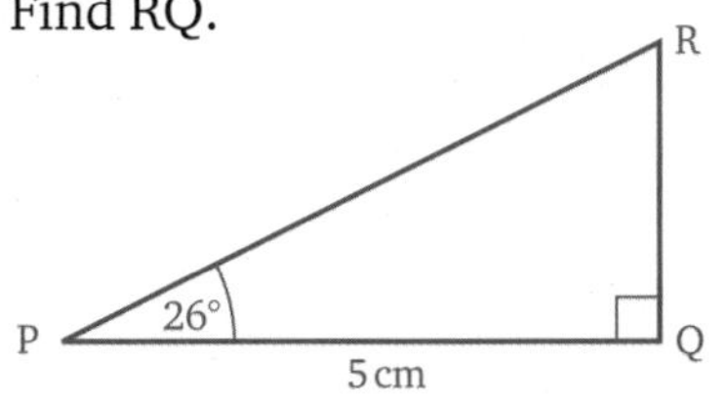

2 Find BC.

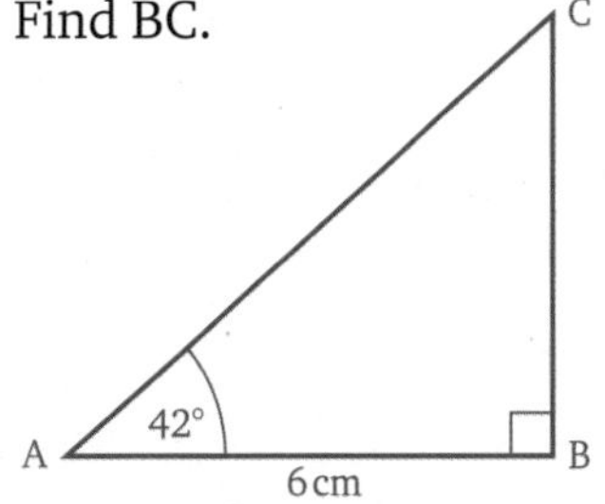

3 Find YZ.

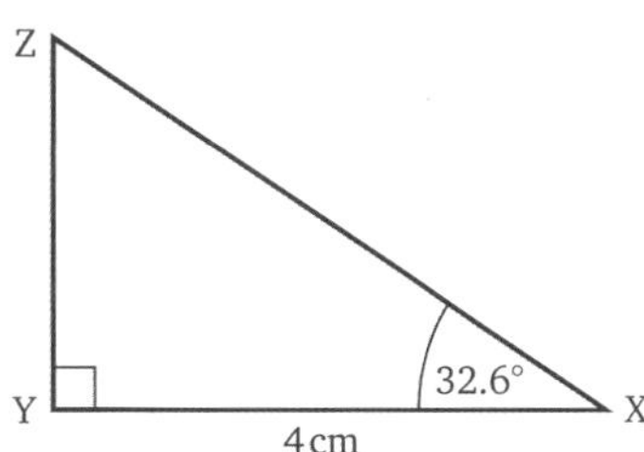

4 Find PR.

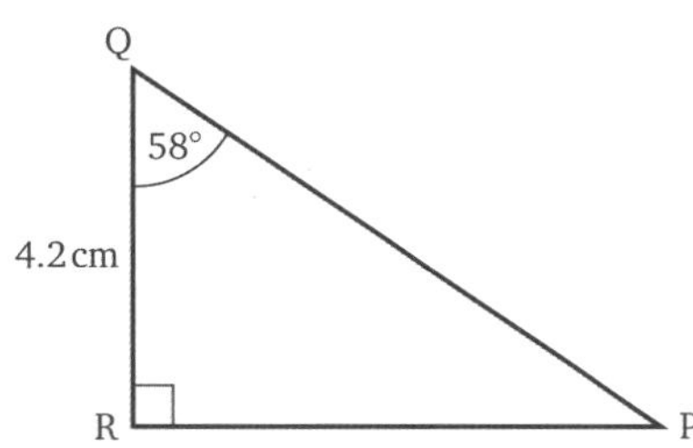

5 Find AB.

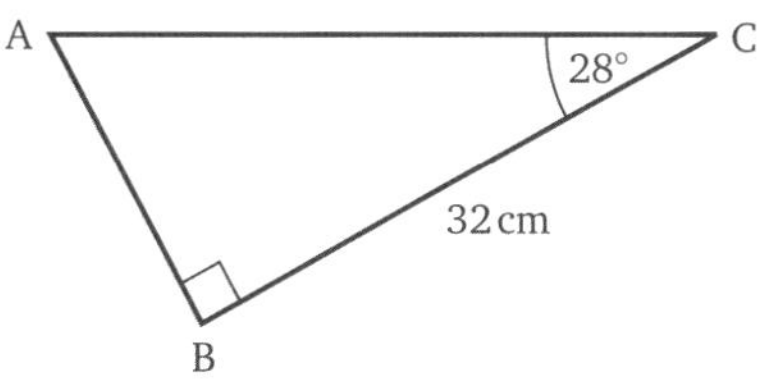

6 Find LN.

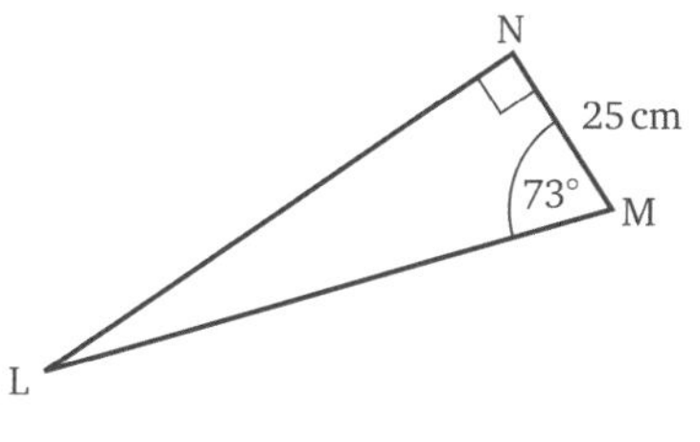

7 In triangle ABC, $\hat{B} = 90°$, $\hat{A} = 32°$ and AB = 9 cm. Find BC.

8 In triangle DEF, $\hat{D} = 90°$, $\hat{E} = 48°$ and DE = 20 cm. Find DF.

9 In triangle PQR, $\hat{R} = 90°$, $\hat{Q} = 10°$ and RQ = 16 cm. Find PR.

10 In triangle XYZ, $\hat{Z} = 90°$, $\hat{Y} = 67°$ and ZY = 3.2 cm. Find XZ.

In $\triangle$ABC, $\hat{B} = 90°$, $\hat{A} = 24°$ and BC = 6 cm. Find AB.

(It is easier to find AB if it is on top of the tangent ratio, i.e. if AB is the opposite side. AB is opposite to $\hat{C}$, so find $\hat{C}$ first.)

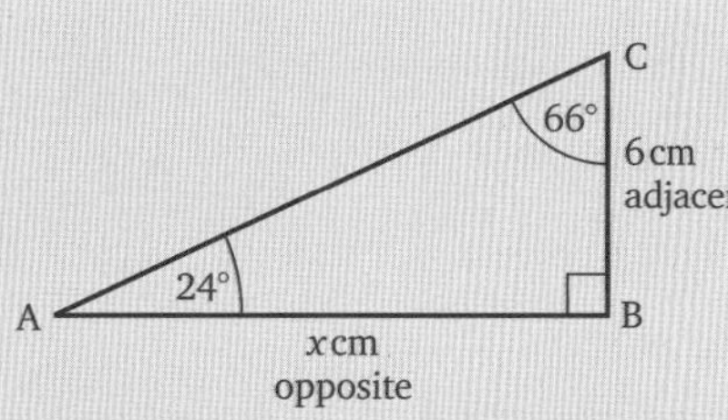

$\hat{C} = 66°$ ($\angle$s of a triangle)

$$\frac{x}{6} = \frac{\text{opp}}{\text{adj}} = \tan 66°$$

$$\frac{x}{6} = 2.246...$$

$$6 \times \frac{x}{6} = 6 \times 2.246...$$

$$x = 13.476...$$

$\therefore$ AB is 13.5 cm (to 3 s.f.)

Use the information given in the diagram to find the required side. It may be necessary to find the third angle of the triangle first.

11 Find AB.

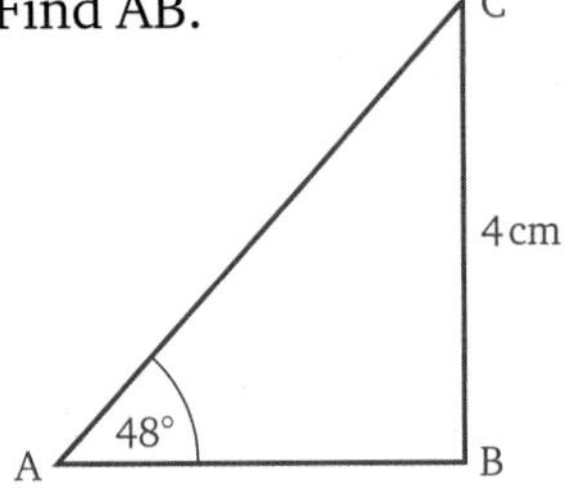

12 Find PQ.

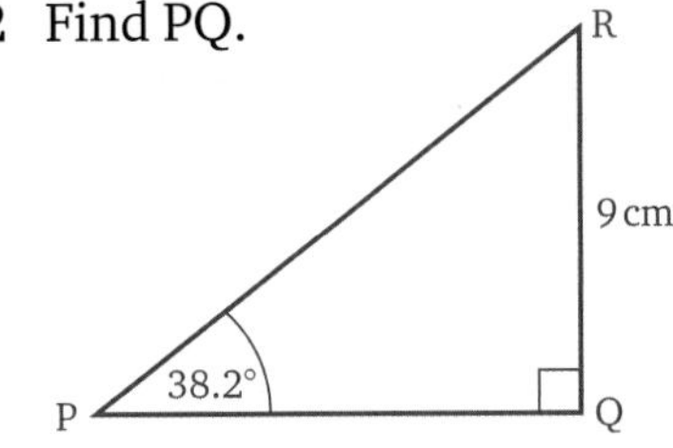

13 Find NL.

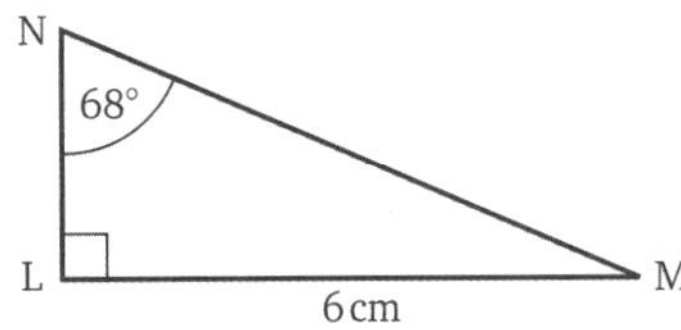

14 Find ZY.

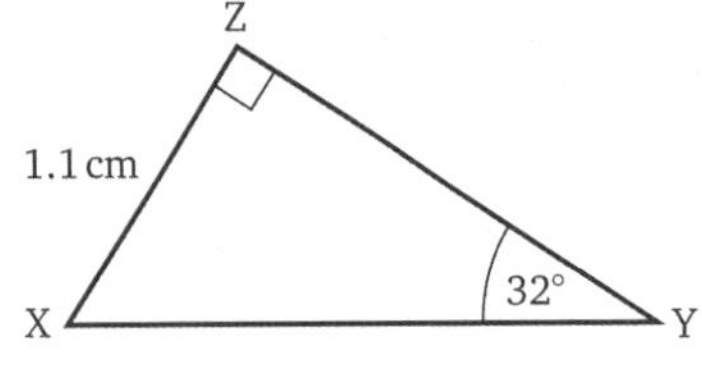

15 Find DE.

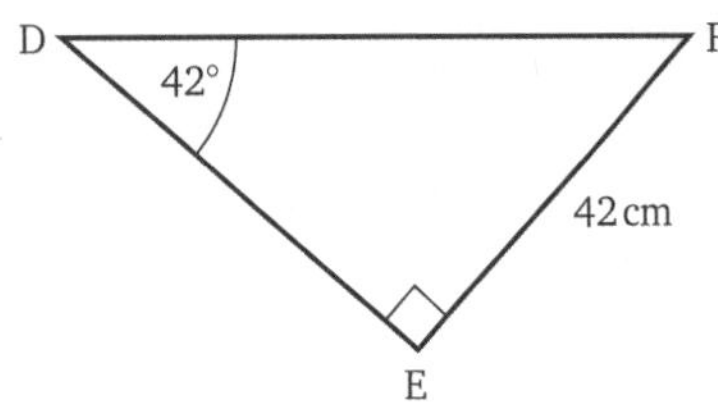

16 Find AC.

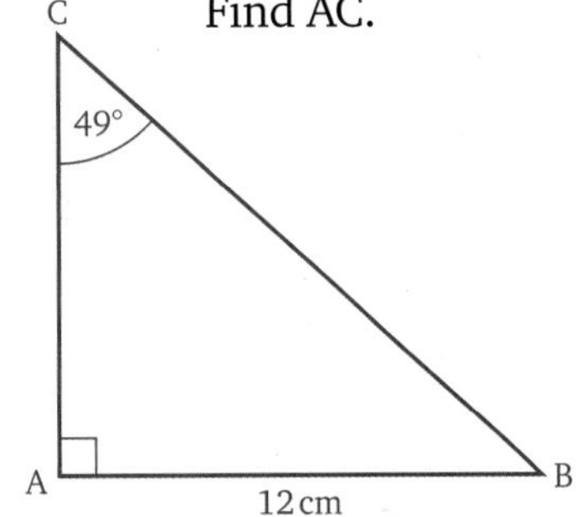

17 In triangle PQR, $\hat{P} = 90°$, $\hat{Q} = 52°$ and PR = 6 cm. Find QP.

18 In triangle ABC, $\hat{A} = 90°$, $\hat{B} = 31°$ and AC = 220 cm. Find AB.

19 In triangle XYZ, $\hat{Z} = 90°$, $\hat{X} = 67°$ and YZ = 2.3 cm. Find XZ.

20 In triangle LMN, $\hat{L} = 90°$, $\hat{M} = 9°$ and LN = 11 m. Find LM.

Using the hypotenuse

So far, we have used only the opposite and adjacent sides. If we wish to use the hypotenuse we need different ratios.

The sine of an angle

For an angle in a right-angled triangle, the name given to the ratio $\frac{\text{opposite side}}{\text{hypotenuse}}$ is the *sine* of the angle where sine is abbreviated to sin.

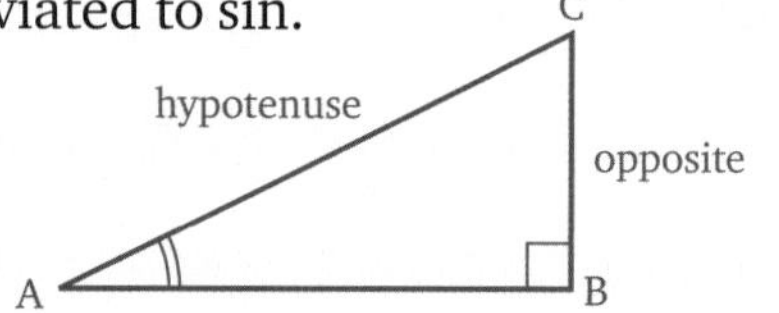

In triangle ABC $\qquad \frac{BC}{AC} = \sin\hat{A}$

The use of sines is similar to the use of tangents.

Exercise 10e

Find the sines of the following angles:

1 62.4°

2 70°

3 14.3°

4 9°

5 15.2°

6 37.5°

7 59.6°

8 30°

9 82°

10 27.8°

11 15.8°

12 87.2°

Press sin 62.4

Find the angles whose sines are given:

13 0.271

14 0.442

15 0.524

16 0.909

17 0.6664

18 0.3720

19 0.614

20 0.7283

21 0.1232

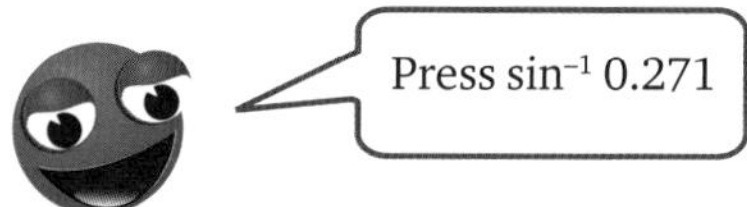

Exercise 10f

In triangle ABC, $\hat{B} = 90°$, BC = 3 cm and AC = 7 cm. Find $\hat{A}$.

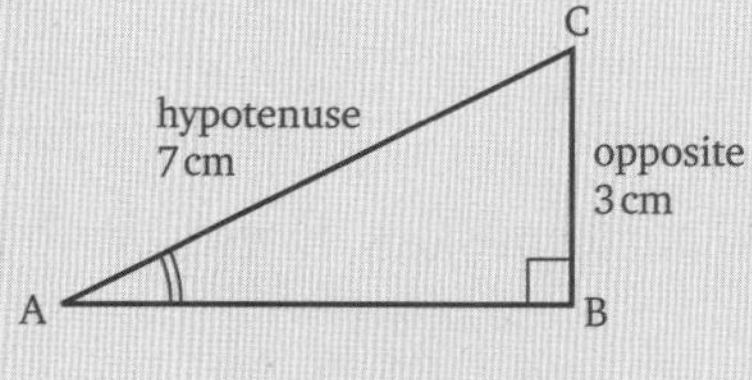

$$\sin\hat{A} = \frac{\text{opp}}{\text{hyp}} = \frac{3}{7}$$

$$= 0.4285\ldots$$

$$\hat{A} = 25.4° \text{ (to 1 d.p.)}$$

Use the information given in the diagram to find the marked angle:

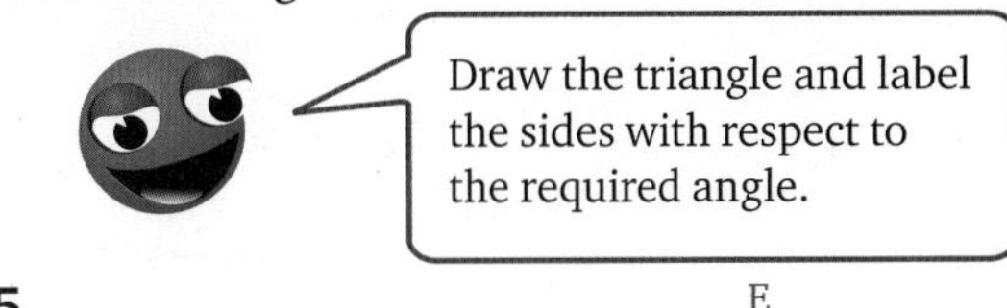

Draw the triangle and label the sides with respect to the required angle.

1

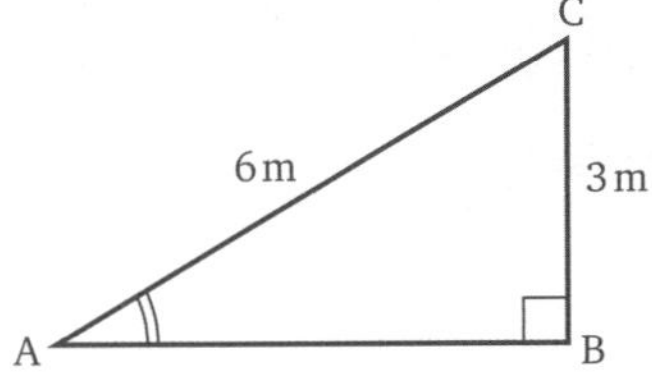

2

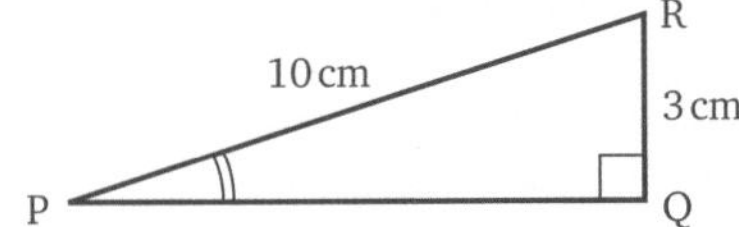

3

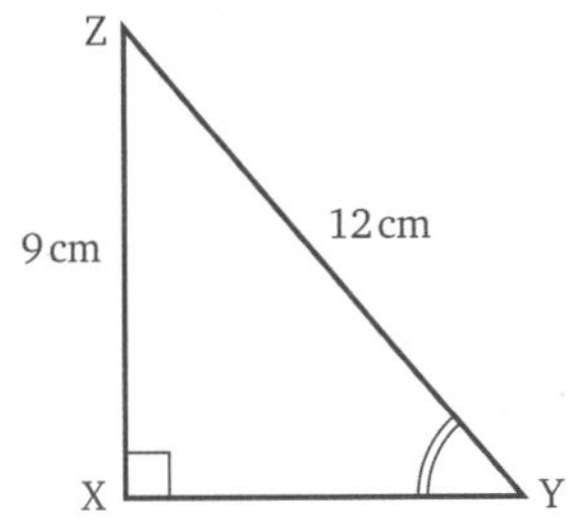

4

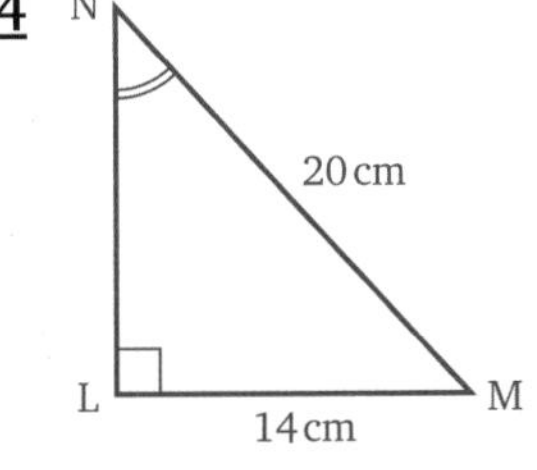

5

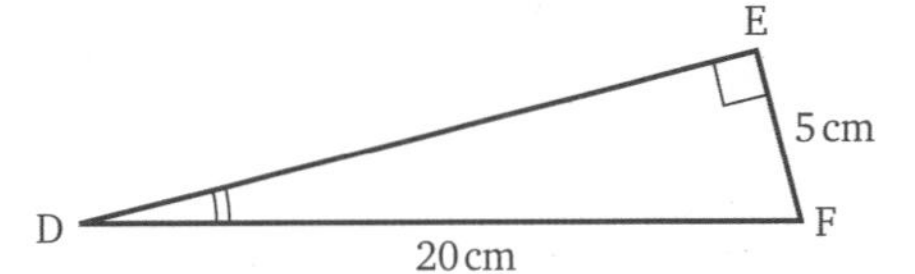

6

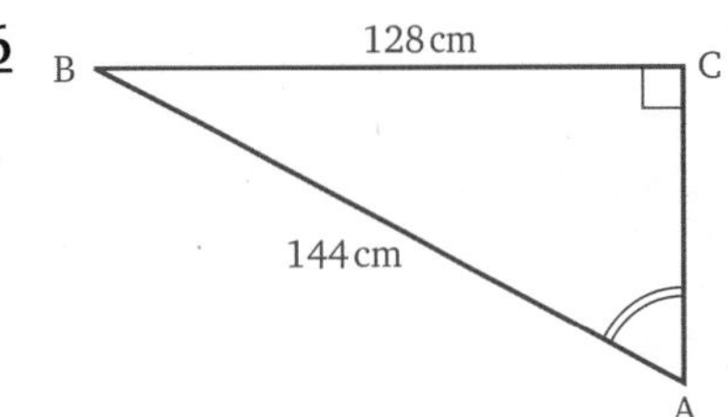

7 In triangle ABC, $\hat{C} = 90°$, BC = 7 cm and AB = 10 cm. Find $\hat{A}$.

8 In triangle PQR, $\hat{Q} = 90°$, PQ = 30 cm and PR = 45 cm. Find $\hat{R}$.

9 In triangle LMN, $\widehat{M} = 90°$, MN = 3.2 cm and LN = 8 cm. Find $\hat{L}$.

10 In triangle DEF, $\hat{E} = 90°$, EF = 36 cm and DF = 108 cm. Find $\hat{D}$.

In triangle PQR, $\hat{P} = 90°$, $\hat{Q} = 32.4°$ and RQ = 4 cm. Find PR.

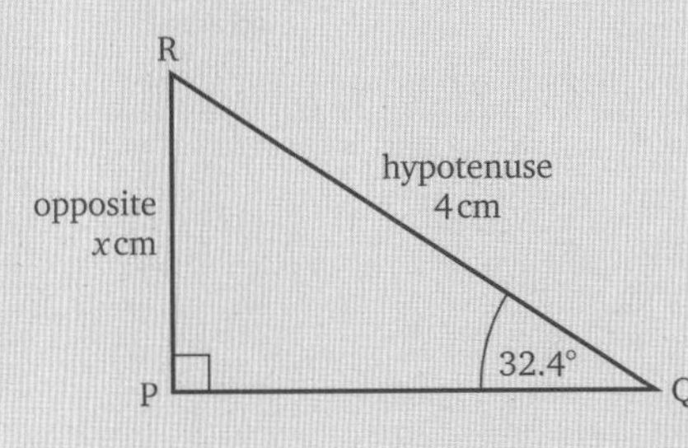

$$\frac{x}{4} = \frac{\text{opp}}{\text{hyp}} = \sin 32.4°$$

$$4 \times \frac{x}{4} = 4 \times 0.5358\ldots$$

$$x = 2.1433\ldots$$

$\therefore$ PR = 2.14 cm (to 3 s.f.)

Use the information given in the diagram to find the required length:

11 Find AC.

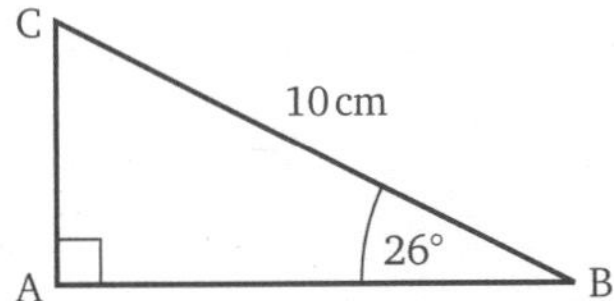

12 Find XY.

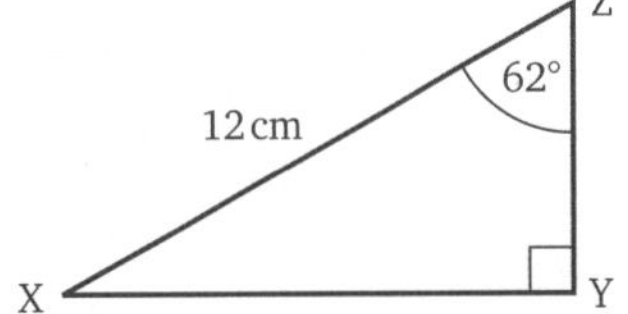

13 Find EF.

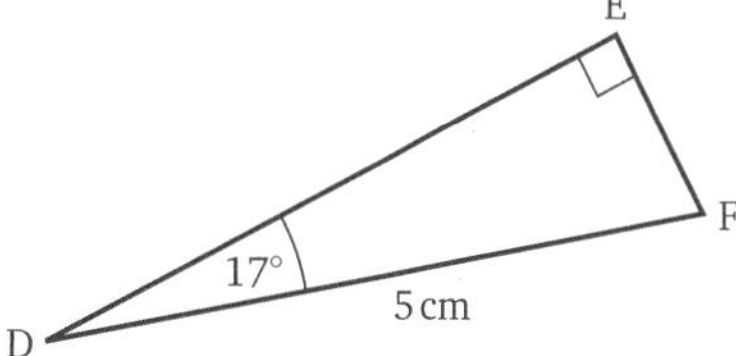

14 Find PR.

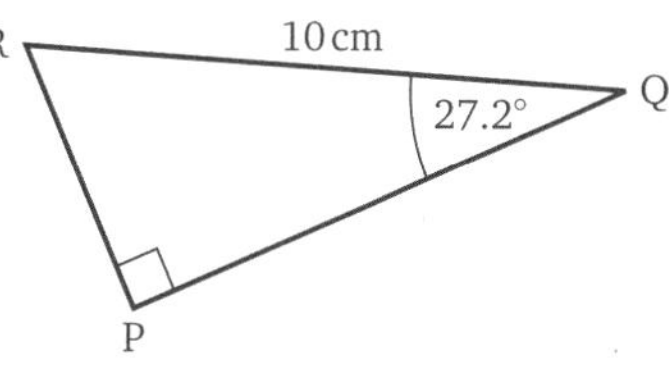

15 Find BC.

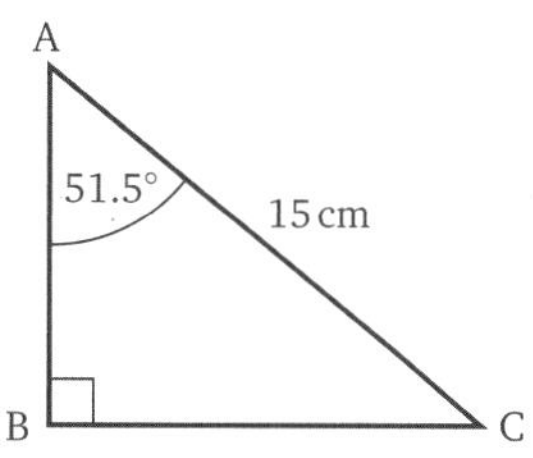

16 Find PR.

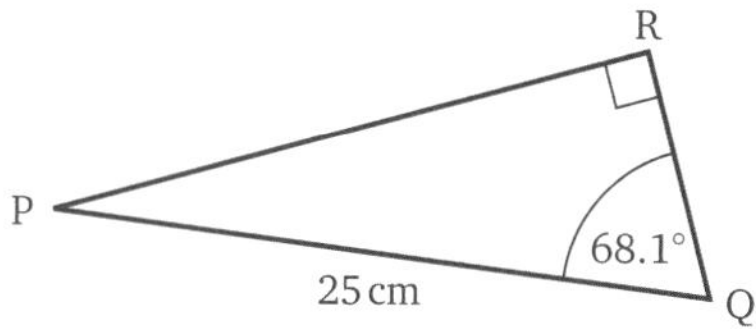

17 In triangle ABC, $\hat{A} = 90°$, BC = 11 cm and $\hat{C} = 35°$. Find AB.

18 In triangle PQR, $\hat{P} = 90°$, QR = 120 m and $\hat{Q} = 10.5°$. Find PR.

19 In triangle XYZ, $\hat{X} = 90°$, YZ = 3.6 cm and $\hat{Y} = 68°$. Find XZ.

20 In triangle DEF, $\hat{F} = 90°$, DE = 48 m and $\hat{D} = 72°$. Find EF.

The cosine of an angle

For an angle in a right-angled triangle, the name given to the ratio $\frac{\text{adjacent side}}{\text{hypotenuse}}$ is the *cosine* of the angle (cosine is abbreviated to cos).

In triangle ABC $\frac{AB}{AC} = \cos\hat{A}$

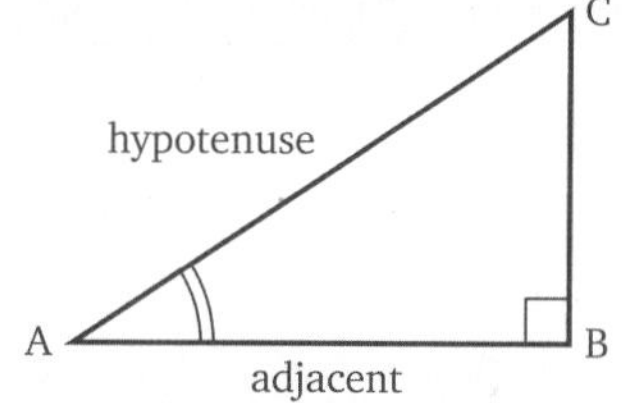

Exercise 10g

Find the cosines of the following angles:

1 32°	3 82°	5 60°	7 52.1°
2 41.8°	4 47.8°	6 15.6°	8 49°

Find the angles whose cosines are given:

9 0.347	11 0.719	13 0.6281	15 0.865
10 0.936	12 0.349	14 0.3149	16 0.014

Exercise 10h

In triangle ABC, $\hat{B} = 90°$, AC = 20 cm and AB = 15 cm. Find $\hat{A}$.

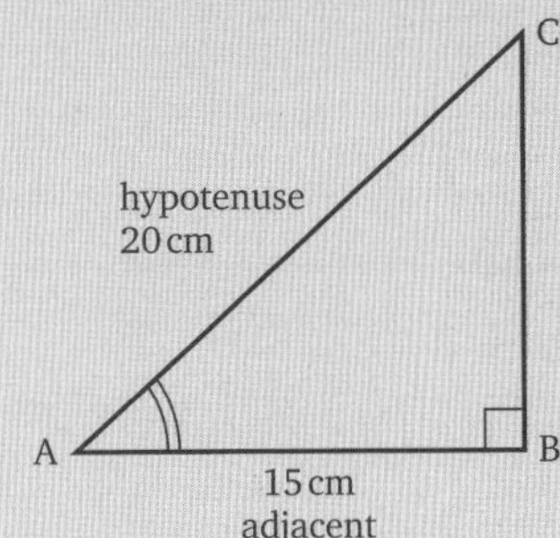

$$\cos\hat{A} = \frac{\text{adj}}{\text{hyp}} = \frac{15}{20}$$
$$= 0.75$$
$$\hat{A} = 41.40\ldots°$$
$$= 41.4° \text{ (to 1 d.p.)}$$

Find the marked angles in the following triangles:

1

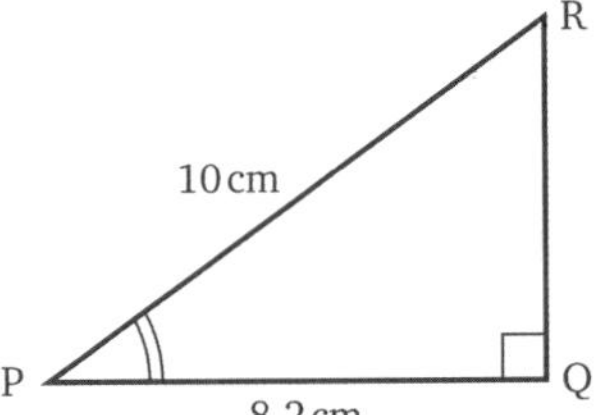

4

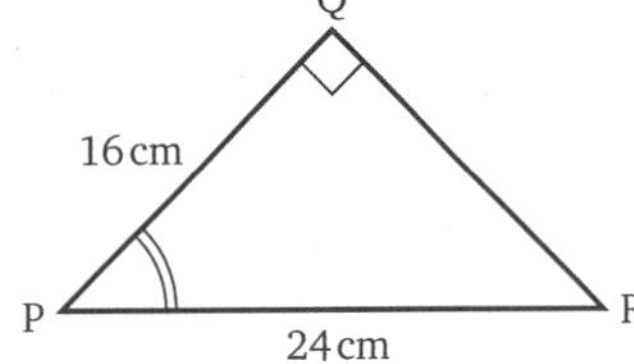

2

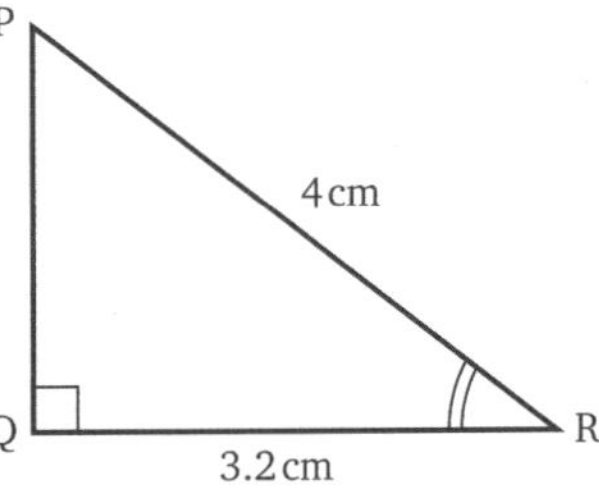

5

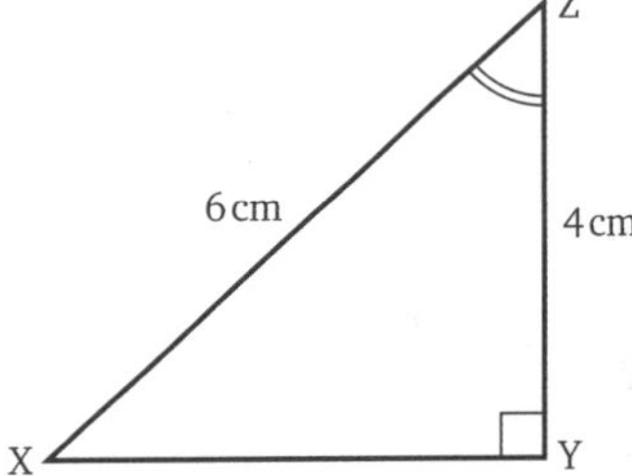

3

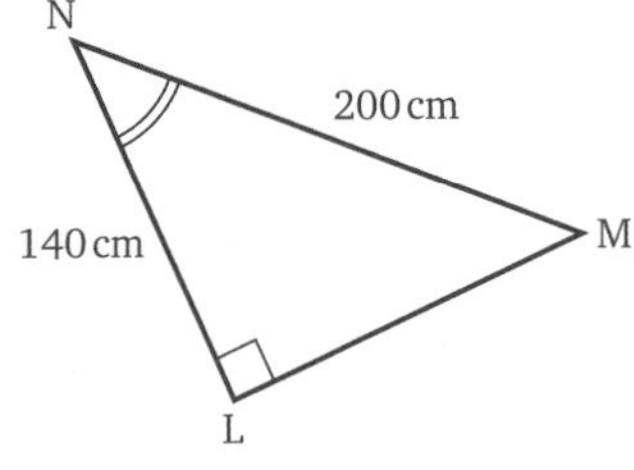

6

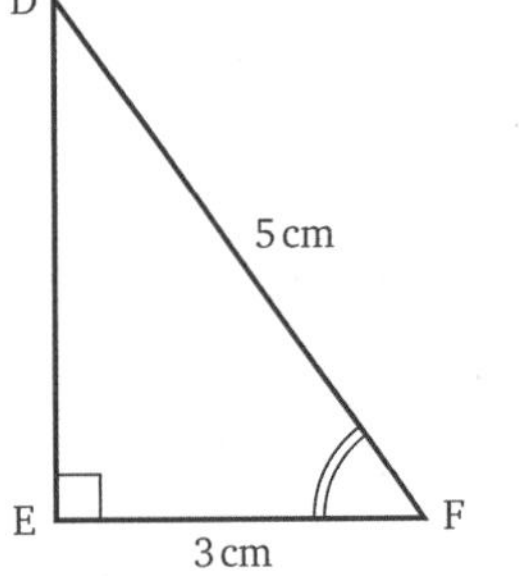

7 In triangle ABC, $\hat{B} = 90°$, AB = 3.2 cm and AC = 5 cm. Find $\hat{A}$.

8 In triangle PQR, $\hat{P} = 90°$, QR = 12 cm and PQ = 4.8 cm. Find $\hat{Q}$.

9 In triangle LMN, $\hat{L} = 90°$, MN = 20 cm and ML = 3 cm. Find $\hat{M}$.

10 In triangle DEF, $\hat{F} = 90°$, DE = 18 cm and DF = 16.2 cm. Find $\hat{D}$.

11 In triangle XYZ, $\hat{Z} = 90°$, XY = 14 m and YZ = 11.6 m. Find $\hat{Y}$.

In triangle XYZ, $\hat{X} = 90°$, $\hat{Y} = 27°$ and ZY = 3.2 cm. Find XY.

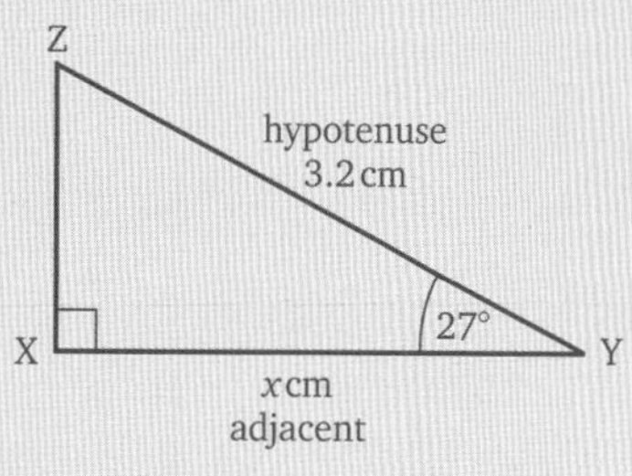

$$\frac{x}{3.2} = \frac{\text{adj}}{\text{hyp}} = \cos 27°$$

$$\frac{x}{3.2} = 0.8910...$$

$$3.2 \times \frac{x}{3.2} = 0.8910... \times 3.2$$

$$x = 2.8512...$$

$$\therefore \text{ XY} = 2.85 \text{ cm (to 3 s.f.)}$$

Use the information given in the diagrams to find the required lengths.

12 Find AB.

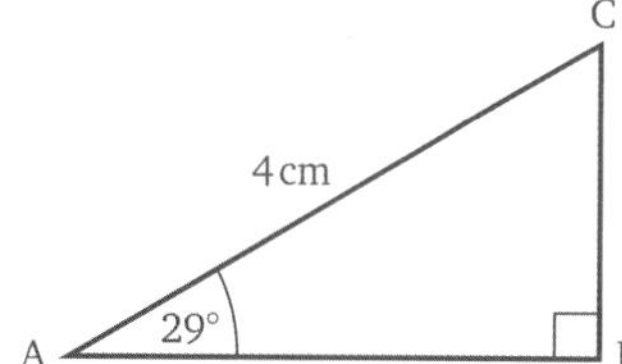

13 Find XY.

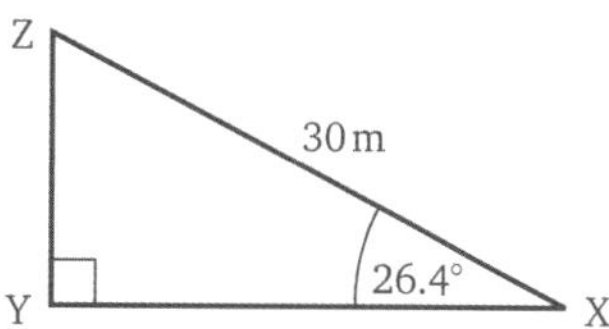

14 Find ED.

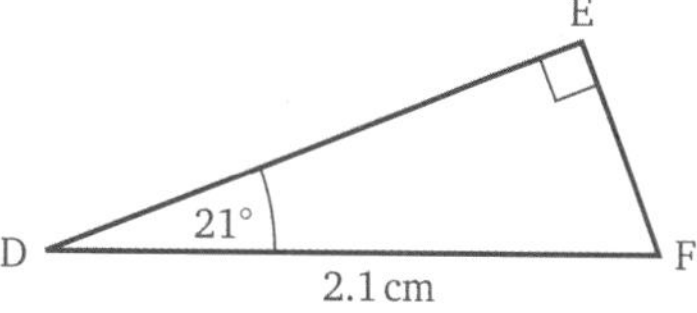

15 Find MN.

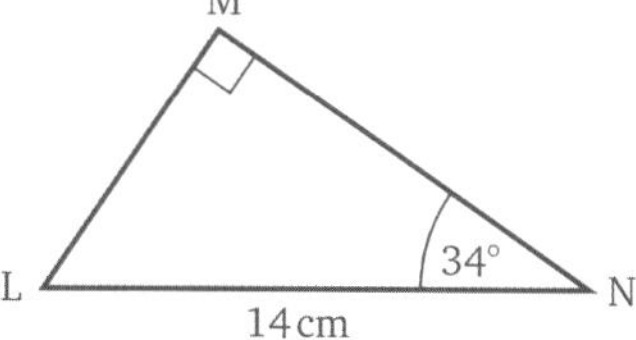

<u>16</u> Find PQ.

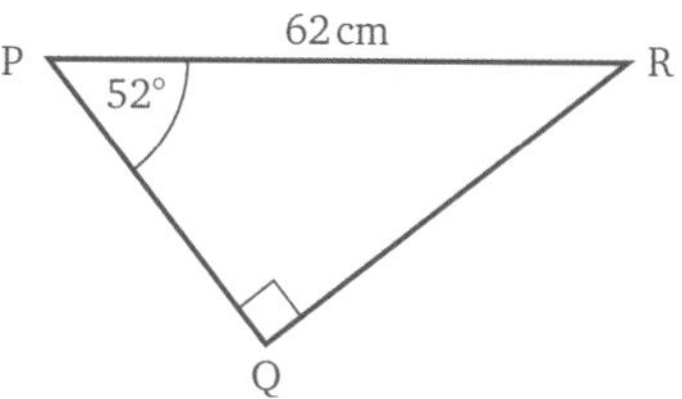

<u>17</u> Find YZ.

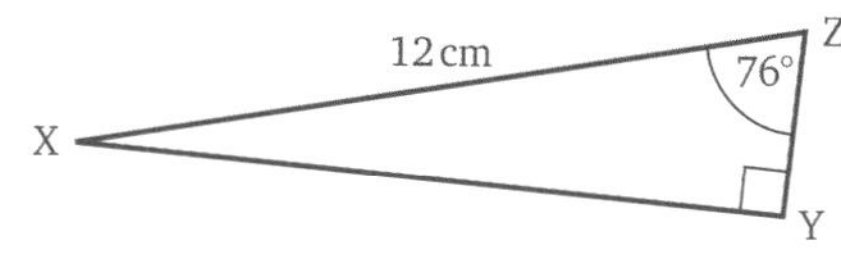

18 In triangle PQR, $\hat{Q} = 90°$, $\hat{P} = 31°$ and PR = 20 cm. Find PQ.

19 In triangle LMN, $\hat{N} = 90°$, $\hat{L} = 42°$ and LM = 3 cm. Find LN.

<u>20</u> In triangle DEF, $\hat{D} = 90°$, $\hat{E} = 68°$ and EF = 11 cm. Find DE.

<u>21</u> In triangle XYZ, $\hat{Z} = 90°$, $\hat{Y} = 15°$ and YX = 14 cm. Find ZY.

Summary

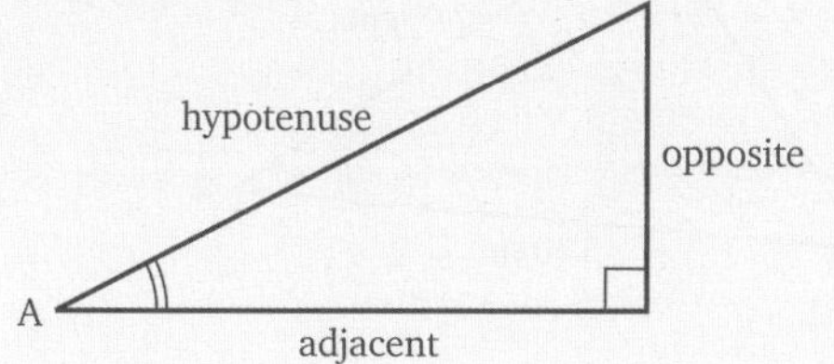

$$\text{Sin}\,\hat{A} = \frac{\text{Opposite}}{\text{Hypotenuse}} \quad \text{(SOH)}$$

$$\text{Cos}\,\hat{A} = \frac{\text{Adjacent}}{\text{Hypotenuse}} \quad \text{(CAH)}$$

$$\text{Tan}\,\hat{A} = \frac{\text{Opposite}}{\text{Adjacent}} \quad \text{(TOA)}$$

Some people remember these definitions by using the word 'SOHCAHTOA' or a sentence like 'Some Old Hangars Can Almost Hold Two Old Aeroplanes'.

Sines, cosines and tangents

Exercise 10i

In questions **1** to **8**, find the marked angles.

Remember to first label the given sides with respect to the angle required and then decide which ratio you will have to use.

1

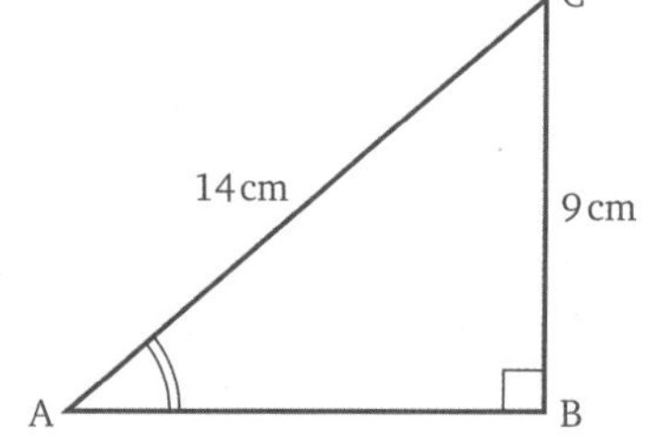

4

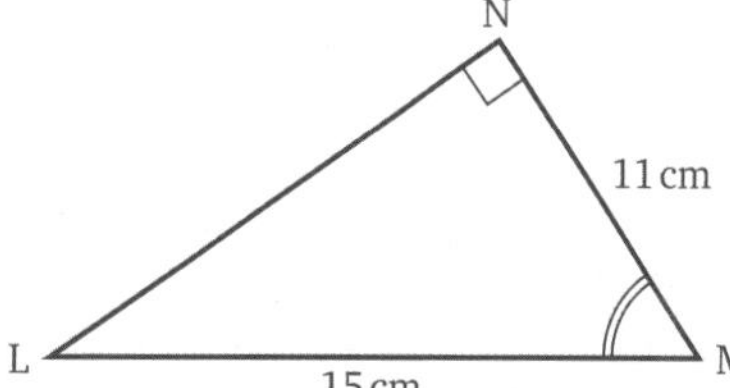

2

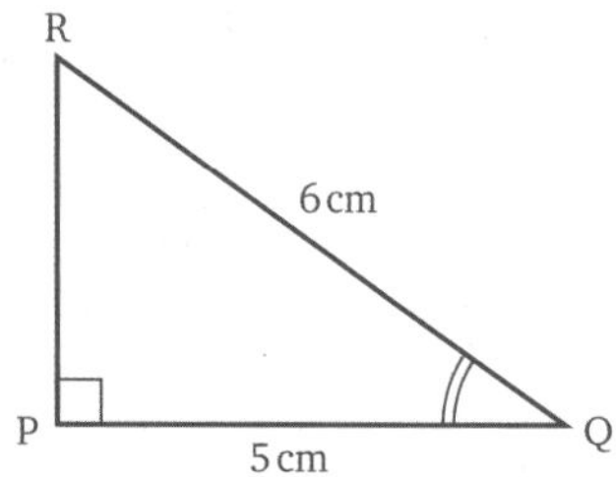

<u>5</u>

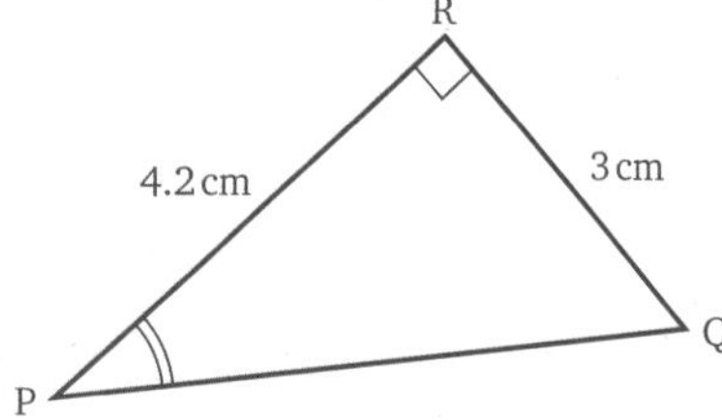

3

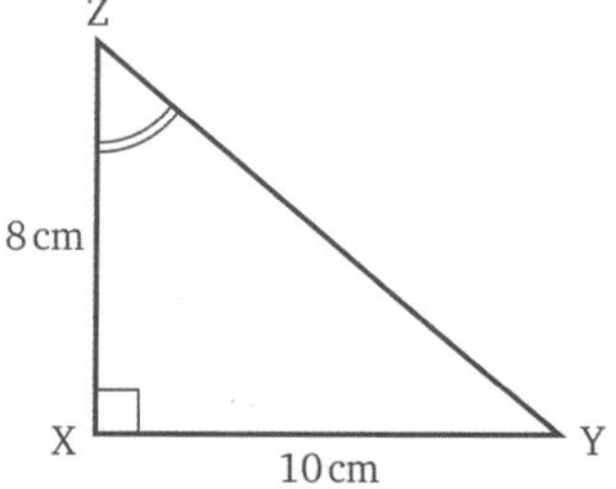

<u>6</u>

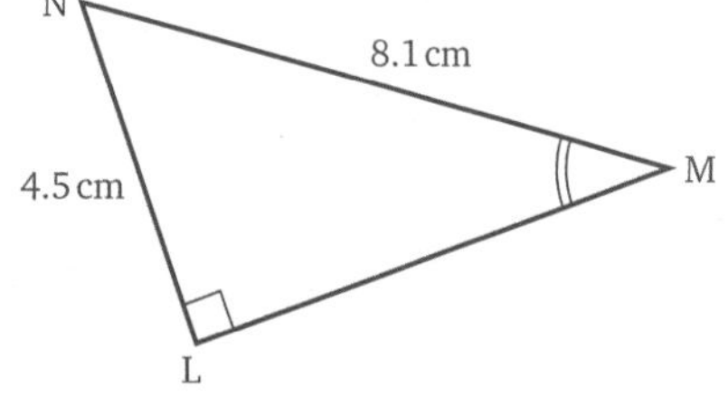

7
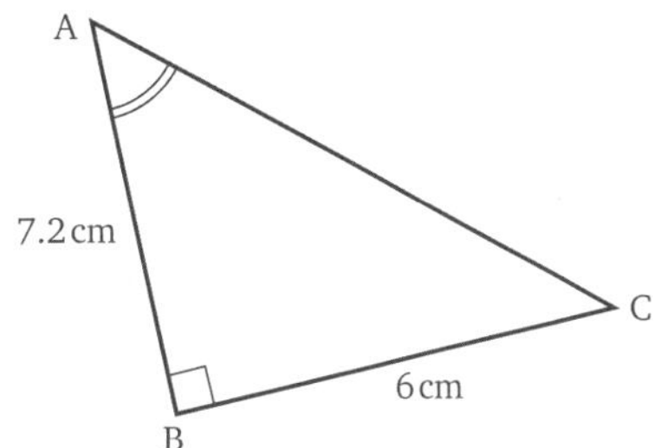

9
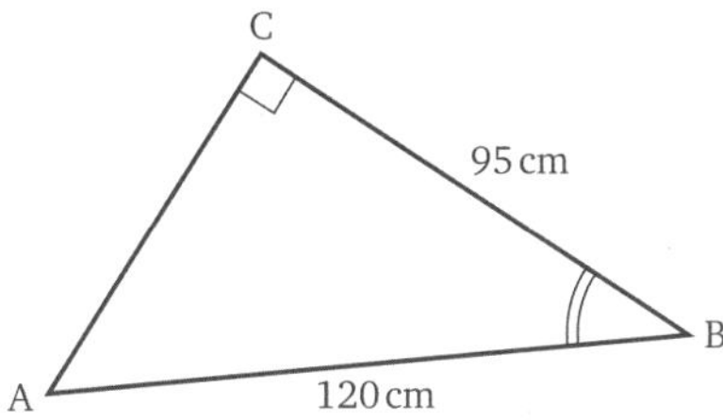

8
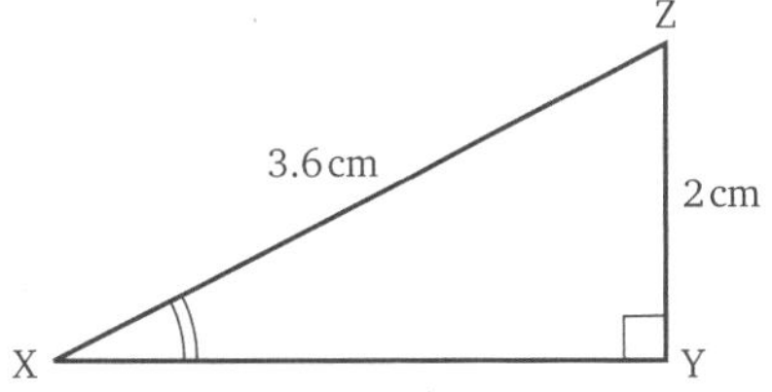

10
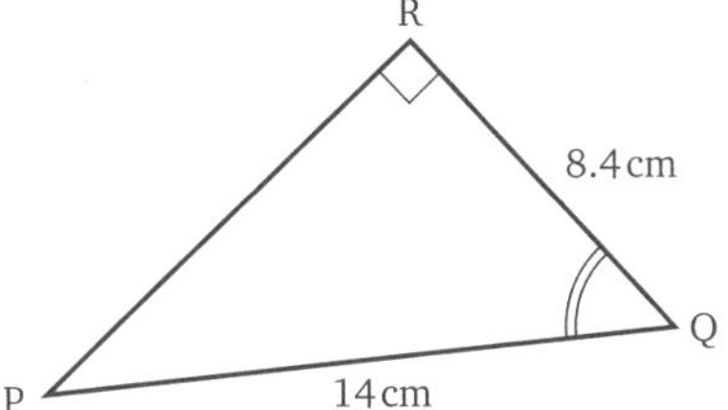

11 In triangle ABC, $\hat{B} = 90°$, AC = 60 cm and BC = 22 cm. Find $\hat{C}$.

12 In triangle PQR, $\hat{R} = 90°$, PQ = 24 cm and QR = 6 cm. Find $\hat{P}$.

13 In triangle ABC, $\hat{B} = 90°$, AC = 1.5 cm and BC = 0.82 cm. Find $\hat{C}$.

14 In triangle PQR, $\hat{R} = 90°$, RQ = 8 cm and RP = 6.2 cm. Find $\hat{Q}$.

15 In triangle DEF, $\hat{F} = 90°$, DF = 16.2 cm and EF = 19.8 cm. Find $\hat{E}$.

16 In triangle XYZ, $\hat{X} = 90°$, YZ = 1.6 m and XY = 1.32 m. Find $\hat{Z}$.

17 In triangle DEF, $\hat{E} = 90°$, DE = 1.9 m and EF = 2.1 m. Find $\hat{F}$.

18 In triangle GHI, $\hat{H} = 90°$, GI = 52 cm and IH = 21 cm. Find $\hat{I}$.

Use the information given in the diagram to find the required length.

19 Find BC.

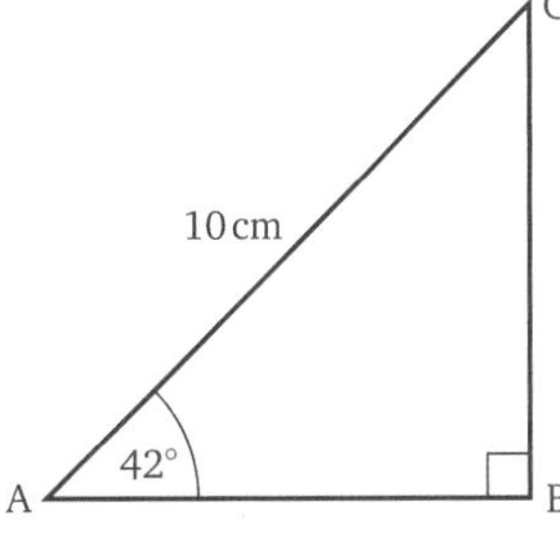

20 Find PQ.

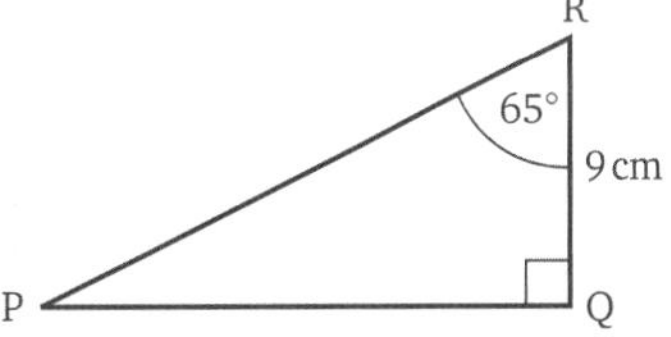

21 Find ZY.

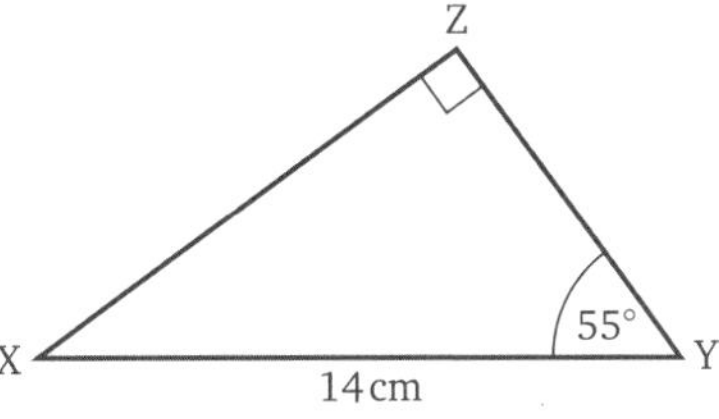

22 Find AB.

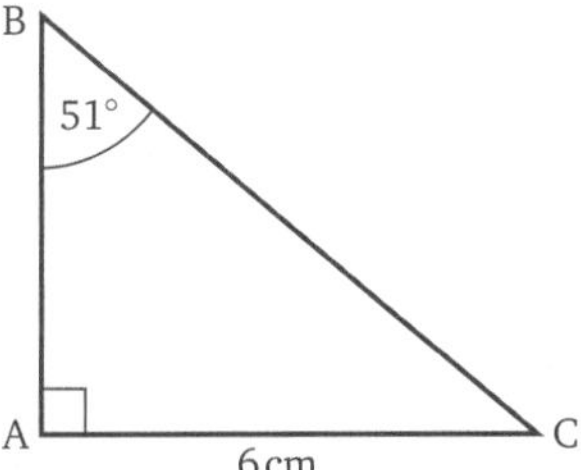

23 Find MN.

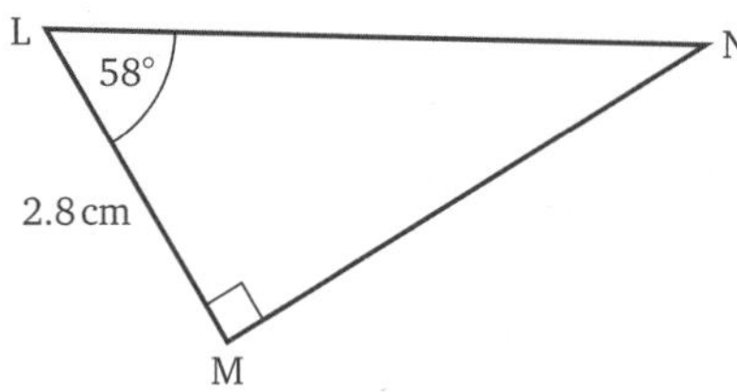

24 Find DE.

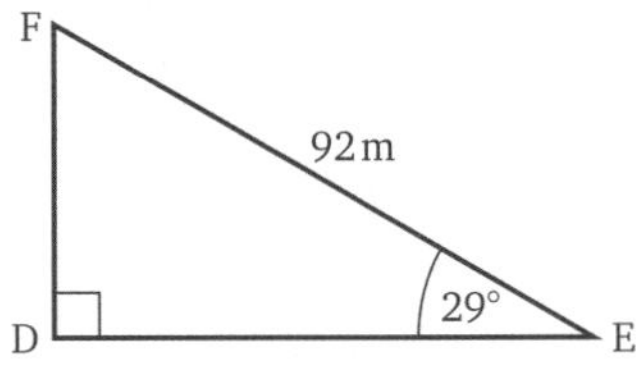

25 Find YZ.

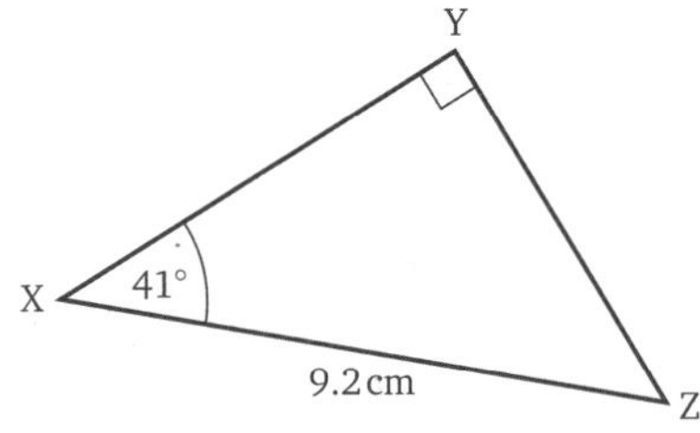

26 Find AB.

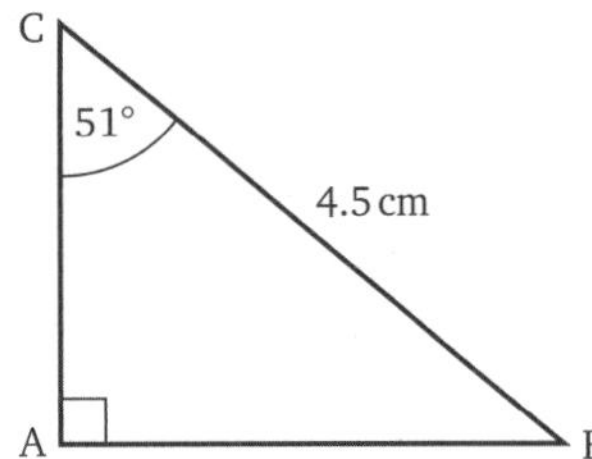

27 Find BC.

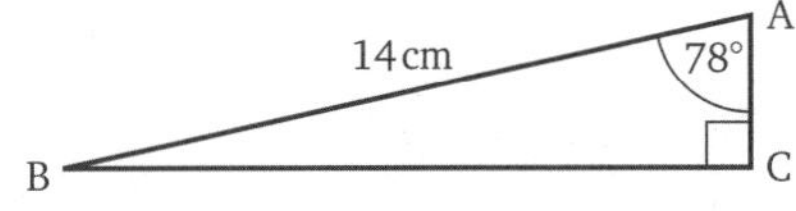

28 Find PQ.

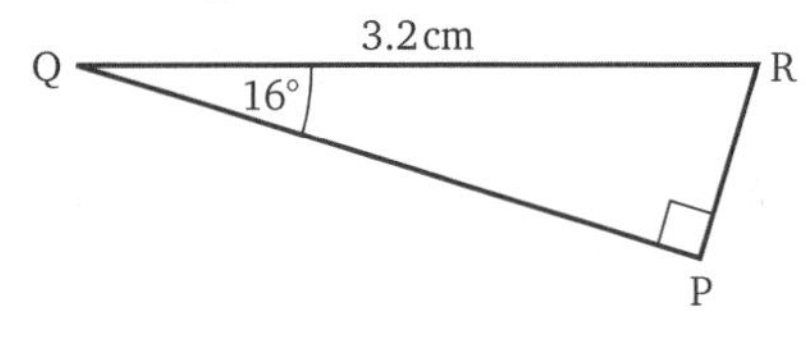

29 In triangle ABC, $\hat{C} = 90°$, $\hat{A} = 78°$ and AC = 24 cm. Find BC.

30 In triangle PQR, $\hat{P} = 90°$, $\hat{Q} = 36°$ and QR = 3.2 cm. Find PQ.

31 In triangle XYZ, $\hat{X} = 90°$, $\hat{Y} = 36°$ and YZ = 17 cm. Find XZ.

32 In triangle DEF, $\hat{F} = 90°$, $\hat{E} = 51°$ and DF = 9.2 cm. Find EF.

33 In triangle LMN, $\widehat{M} = 90°$, $\hat{N} = 25°$ and LN = 16 cm. Find MN.

34 In triangle LMN, $\hat{L} = 90°$, $\widehat{M} = 56.2°$ and LN = 32 cm. Find ML.

35 In triangle ABC, $\hat{C} = 90°$, $\hat{B} = 72.8°$ and AB = 78 cm. Find AC.

36 In triangle PQR, $\hat{R} = 90°$, $\hat{P} = 31.2°$ and PQ = 117 cm. Find QR.

? Puzzle

As part of an aerobatics display, six aeroplanes fly at the same speed away from each other in a fan of 60° to each other.

This is what it looks like from the ground.

What does it look like to the pilot of aircraft A when he looks back?

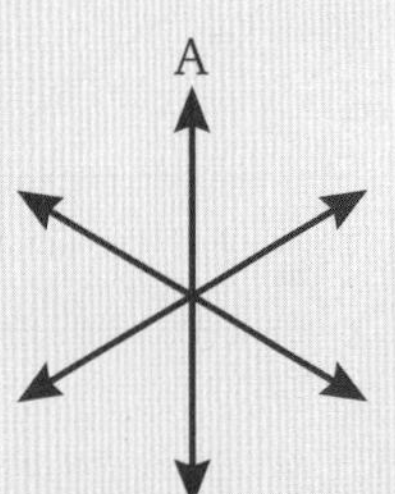

Finding the hypotenuse

Up to now, when finding the length of a side, we have been able to form an equation in which our unknown length is on the top of the fraction. If we wish to find the hypotenuse, this is not possible and the equation we form takes slightly longer to solve.

Exercise 10j

In triangle ABC, $\hat{B} = 90°$, AB = 8 cm and $\hat{C} = 62°$. Find AC.

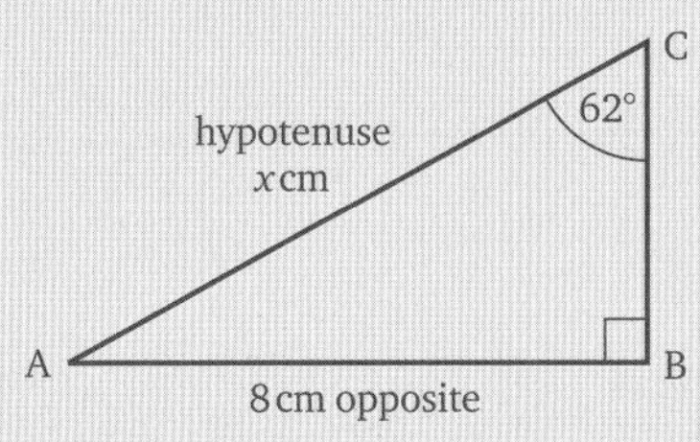

$$\frac{8}{x} = \frac{\text{opp}}{\text{hyp}} = \sin 62°$$

$$\frac{8}{x} = \sin 62°$$

$$x \times \frac{8}{x} = x \times \sin 62° \quad \text{Multiplying both sides by } x$$

$$\frac{8}{\sin 62°} = x \quad \text{Dividing both sides by } \sin 62°$$

$$x = 9.060\ldots$$

$$\therefore \quad AC = 9.06 \text{ cm (to 3 s.f.)}$$

Use the information given in the diagram to find the hypotenuse:

1

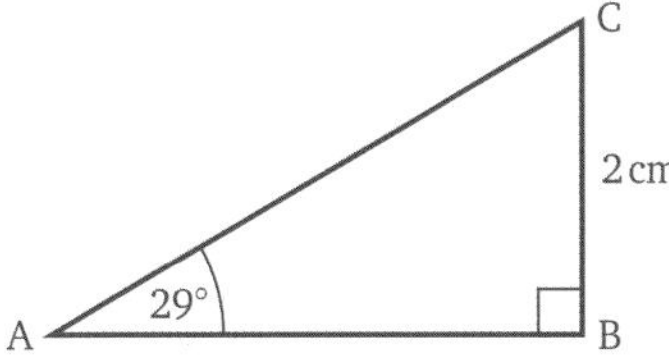

3

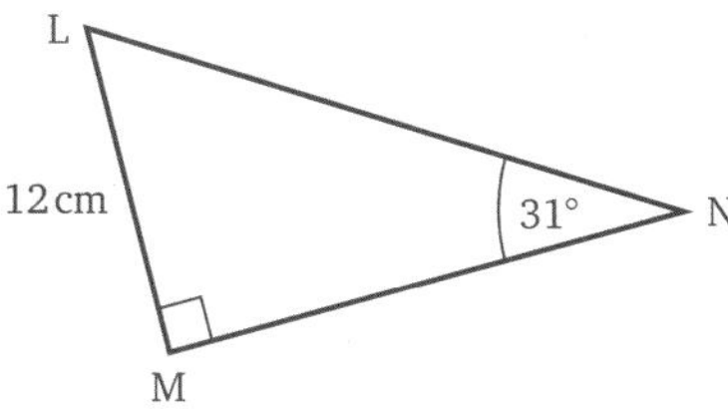

2

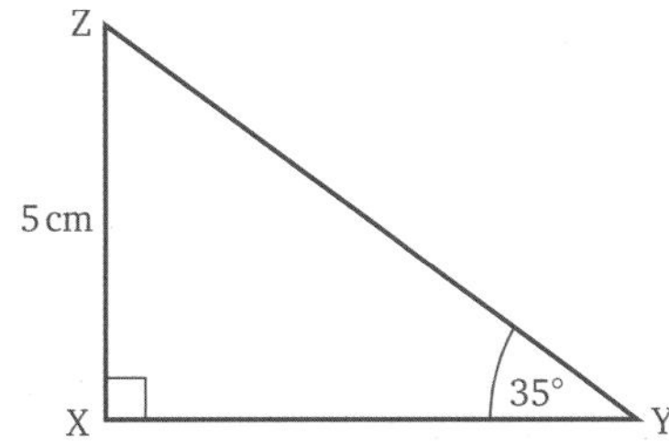

4

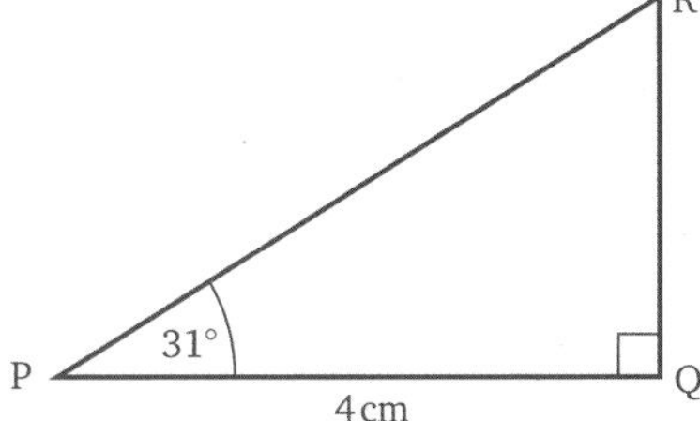

5

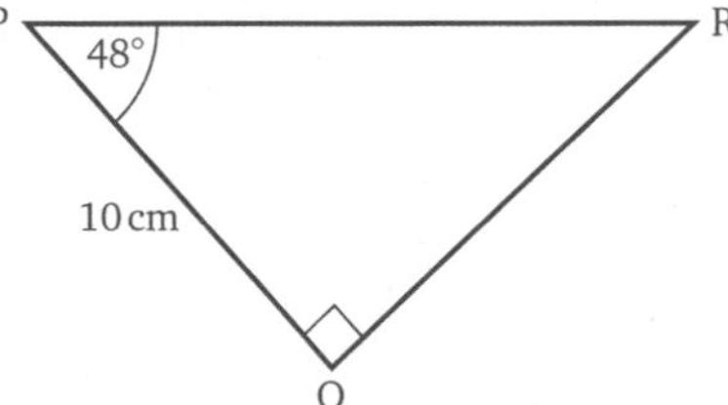

6

X Z

8 cm

62°

Y

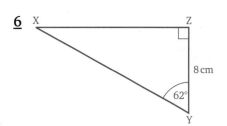

7 In triangle ABC, $\hat{B} = 90°$, $\hat{A} = 43°$ and BC = 3 cm. Find AC.

8 In triangle PQR, $\hat{P} = 90°$, $\hat{Q} = 28°$ and PR = 7 cm. Find QR.

9 In triangle LMN, $\hat{L} = 90°$, $\widehat{M} = 14°$ and LN = 8 cm. Find MN.

10 In triangle XYZ, $\hat{Z} = 90°$, $\hat{Y} = 62°$ and ZY = 20 cm. Find XY.

Angles of elevation and depression

You met angles of elevation and depression in Chapter 6. You can use trigonometry to solve problems involving angles of depression and elevation.

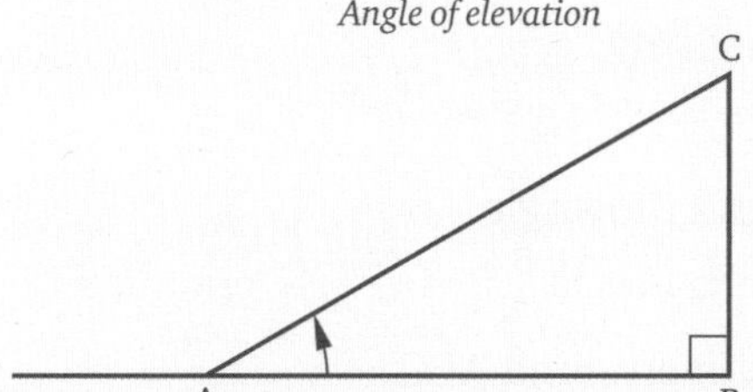

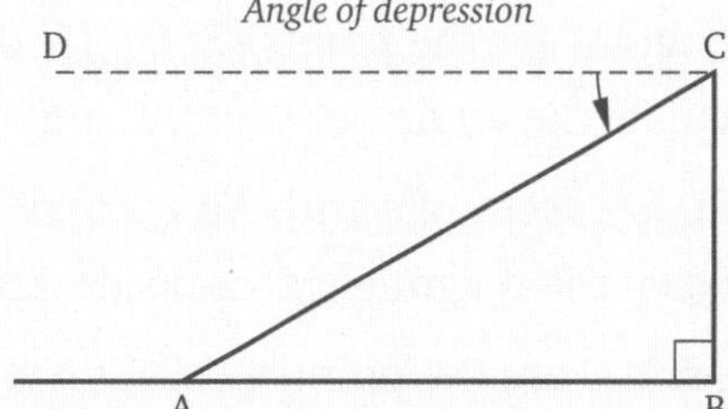

$B\hat{A}C$ is the *angle of elevation* of C from A.

$D\hat{C}A$ is the *angle of depression* of A from C.

Exercise 10k

A flagpole stands on level ground. From a point on the ground 30 m away from its foot, the angle of elevation of the top of the pole is 22°. Find the height of the pole.

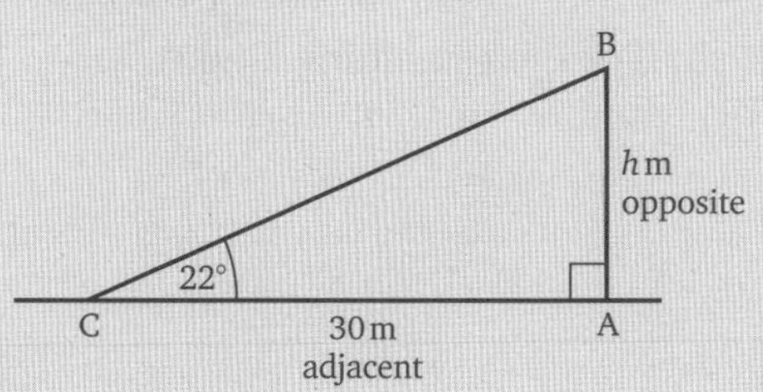

$$\frac{h}{30} = \frac{\text{opp}}{\text{adj}} = \tan 22°$$

$$\frac{h}{30} = 0.4040\ldots$$

$$30 \times \frac{h}{30} = 0.4040 \times 30$$

$$h = 12.12$$

The pole is 12.1 m high (to 3 s.f.)

Draw a diagram. Mark the sides and angles given and required. Label the sides with respect to the angles. Then you can see which ratio you need to use.

1 In triangle ABC, AC = CB = 10 m and $\hat{A} = 64°$.

Find the height of the triangle.

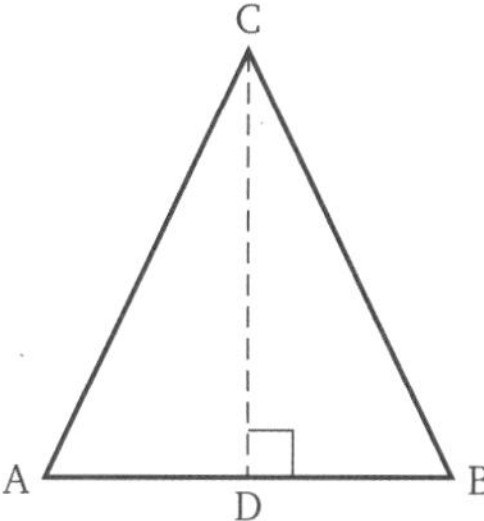

2 From a point on level ground 40 m from the base of a pine tree, the angle of elevation of the top of the tree is 50°. Find the height of the tree.

3 The angle of elevation of the top of a church tower, from a point on level ground 500 m away, is 16°. Find the height of the tower.

4 A , B and C are the points (2, 0), (8, 0) and (8, 5), respectively. Calculate the angle between AC and the x-axis.

5 ABCD is a rectangle with AB = 26 cm and BC = 48 cm. Find the angle between the diagonal AC and side AB.

6 A, B and C are the points (1, 2), (3, 2) and (1, 5), respectively. Find $A\hat{B}C$.

7 ABCD is a rhombus of side 15 cm. The diagonal AC is of length 20 cm. Find the angle between AC and the side CD.

8 A boat C is 200 m from the foot B of a vertical cliff, which is 40 m high. What is the angle of depression of the boat from the top of the cliff?

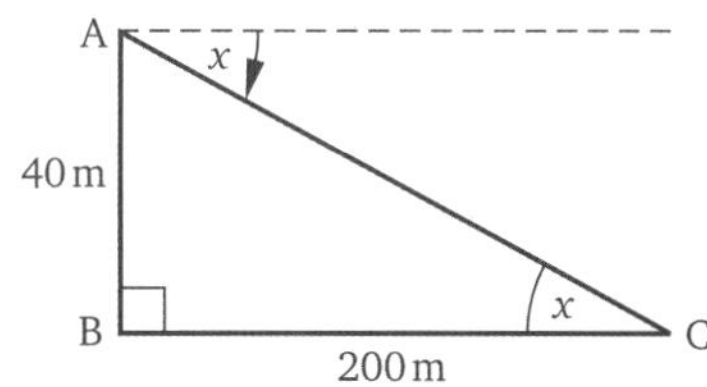

9

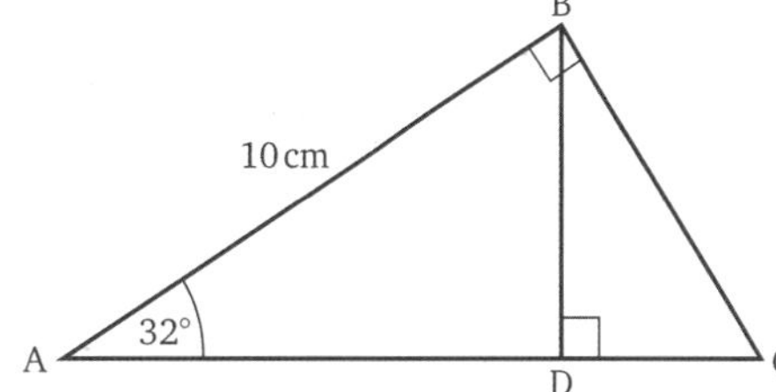

In the figure, AB = 10 cm, $\hat{A} = 32°$ and $A\hat{B}C = B\hat{D}C = 90°$. Copy the figure and then mark in the sizes of the remaining angles.

Find **a** BD **b** BC

10 Triangle ABC is an equilateral triangle of side 6 cm.

Find **a** its height **b** its area.

11 A lamp post stands on level ground. From a point which is 10 m from its foot, the angle of elevation of the top is 25°. How high is the lamp post?

Puzzle

There are three different routes from Ian's home to the nearest post box and two different routes from the post box to school. How many different ways are there for Ian to go to school if he must pass the post box on the way?

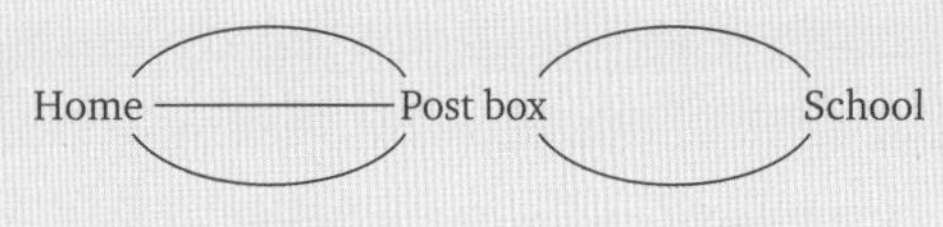

Mixed exercise

Exercise 10I

Select the letter that gives the correct answer.

1 The tangent of the angle 72.6°, correct to 4 s.f., is

A 3.078 **B** 3.190 **C** 3.191 **D** 3.271

2 The angle whose sine is 0.8829 is

A 28.0° **B** 41.4° **C** 48.6° **D** 62.0°

3 The angle whose cosine is 0.7071 is

A 41° **B** 43° **C** 45° **D** 47°

4 The angle whose tangent is 3.732 is

A 75.0° **B** 75.5° **C** 76.0° **D** 76.5°

5 In triangle PQR, $\angle P = 90°$, $\angle Q = 42°$ and PQ = 9.3 cm.
The length of PR, correct to 3 s.f., is

A 8.36 cm **B** 8.37 cm **C** 8.38 cm **D** 8.39 cm

6 The angle of elevation of the top of a church spire from a point 600 m away on level ground is 15°. The height of the top of the spire, correct to the nearest metre, is

A 151 m **B** 156 m **C** 161 m **D** 166 m

Puzzle

The integral triples (40, 42, 58), (24, 70, 74) and (15, 112, 113) are Pythagorean triples. Calculate the areas of triangles having these triples as the lengths of their sides.

In this chapter you have seen that...

✔ in a right-angled triangle ABC,

$$\tan C = \frac{\text{opp}}{\text{adj}}, \quad \sin C = \frac{\text{opp}}{\text{hyp}}, \quad \cos C = \frac{\text{adj}}{\text{hyp}}$$

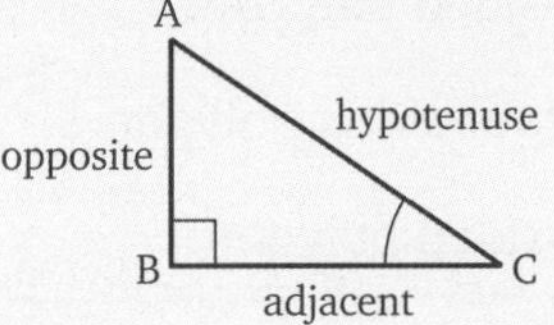

11 Polygons

At the end of this chapter you should be able to...

1 classify polygons in terms of their number of sides
2 identify regular polygons
3 state the sum of the exterior angles of a given polygon with n sides as 360°
4 state the sum of the interior angles of a polygon with n sides as $(n - 2)180°$
5 calculate the size of an exterior or interior angle of a regular polygon
6 use the formula for the sum of the exterior angles of a polygon and that for interior angles to solve problems
7 make patterns using regular polygons that tessellate.

You need to know...

✔ about triangles and their angle properties

✔ about quadrilaterals and their angle properties

✔ properties of the special quadrilaterals.

Key words

dodecahedron, equilateral, exterior angle, hexagon, interior angle, isosceles, octagon, parallelogram, pentagon, polygon, polyhedra, quadrilateral, rectangle, regular, rhombus, square, tessellate, triangle

Polygons

In Book 2 we saw that a *polygon* is a plane (flat) figure bounded by straight line segments.

- A triangle is a three-sided polygon.
- A quadrilateral is a four-sided polygon.
- A pentagon is a five-sided polygon.

- A six-sided polygon is called a hexagon.
- An eight-sided polygon is called an octagon.

In a *regular* polygon, all the sides are the same length and all the angles are the same size.

The exterior angle of a regular polygon

You know that the sum of the exterior angles of any polygon is 360°. If a polygon is regular, all its exterior angles are the same size. Since we know that the sum of the exterior angles is 360°, the size of one exterior angle is easily found; we just divide 360° by the number of sides of the polygon, i.e.

in a *regular* polygon with n sides, the size of an exterior angle is $\frac{360°}{n}$.

Exercise 11a

Find the size of each exterior angle of a 24-sided regular polygon.

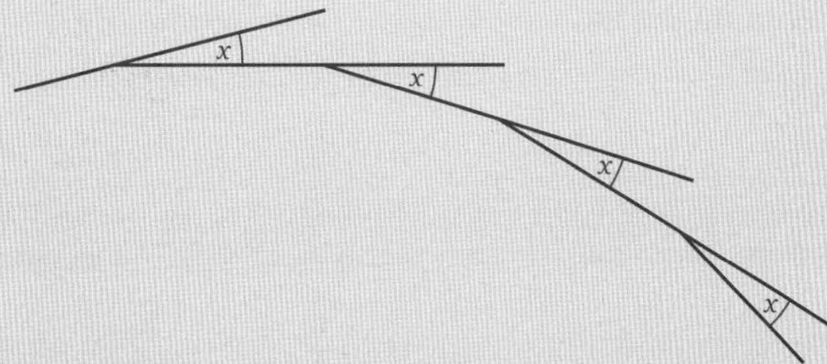

(There are 24 exterior angles, each of the same size. Their sum is 360°)

Each exterior angle $= \frac{360°}{24} = 15°$.

Find the size of each exterior angle of a regular polygon with:

1	10 sides	**4**	6 sides	<u>7</u>	9 sides
2	8 sides	**5**	15 sides	<u>8</u>	16 sides
3	12 sides	**6**	18 sides	<u>9</u>	20 sides

The sum of the interior angles of a polygon

Consider an octagon:

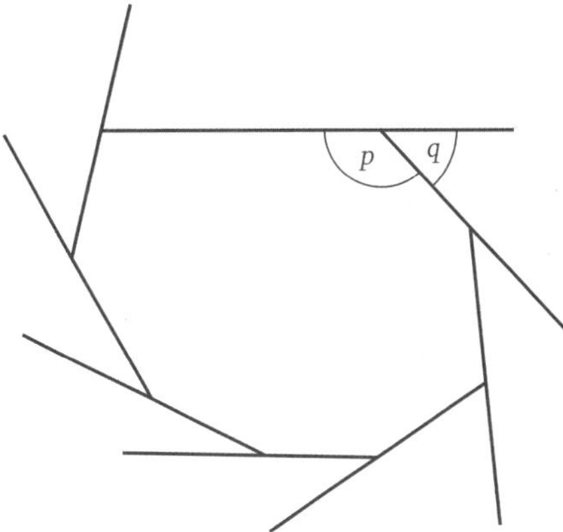

At each vertex there is an interior angle and an exterior angle and the sum of these two angles is 180° (angles on a straight line), i.e. $p + q = 180°$ at each one of the eight vertices.

Therefore, the sum of the interior angles and exterior angles together is

$$8 \times 180° = 1440°$$

The sum of the eight exterior angles is 360°.

Therefore, the sum of the interior angles is

$$1440° - 360° = 1080°$$

Exercise 11b

Find the sum of the interior angles of a 14-sided polygon.

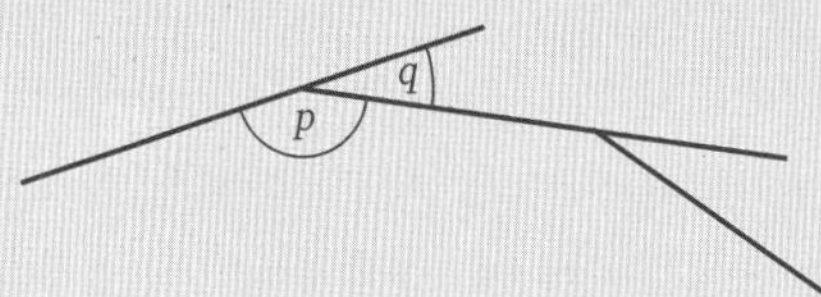

At each vertex $\quad p + q = 180°$

If there are 14 sides there are 14 pairs of exterior and interior angles.

$\therefore$ sum of interior angles and exterior angles is

$$14 \times 180° = 2520°$$

$\therefore$ sum of interior angles $= 2520° - 360°$

$= 2160°$

Find the sum of the interior angles of a polygon with:

1 6 sides

2 5 sides

3 10 sides

4 4 sides

5 7 sides

6 12 sides

<u>**7**</u> 18 sides

<u>**8**</u> 9 sides

<u>**9**</u> 15 sides

Formula for the sum of the interior angles

If a polygon has n sides, the sum of the interior and exterior angles together is $n \times 180° = 180n°$. Therefore the sum of the interior angles only is $180n° - 360°$. As $360° = 180° \times 2$, this can be written as $(n-2)180°$,

i.e.

> in a polygon with n sides, the sum of the interior angles is
> $(180n - 360)°$ or $(n-2)180°$

Exercise 11c

1 Find the sum of the interior angles of a polygon with

a 20 sides **b** 16 sides **c** 11 sides.

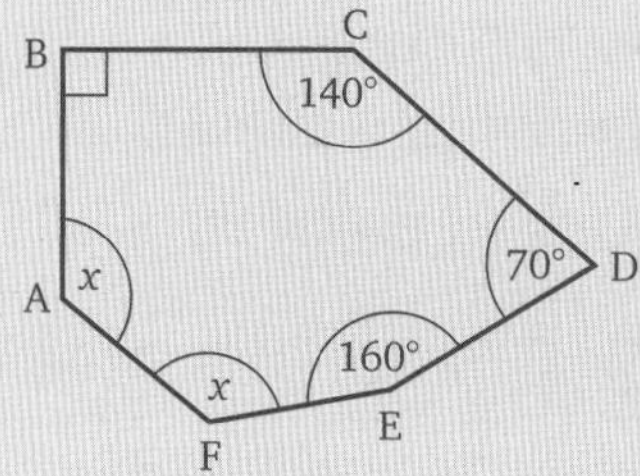

In the hexagon ABCDEF, the angles marked x are equal. Find the value of x.

The sum of the interior angles is $180° \times 6 - 360° = 1080° - 360° = 720°$

$$\therefore 90° + 140° + 70° + 160° + 2x = 720°$$

$$460° + 2x = 720°$$

$$2x = 260°$$

$$x = 130°$$

In each of the following questions find the size of the angle(s) marked x:

2

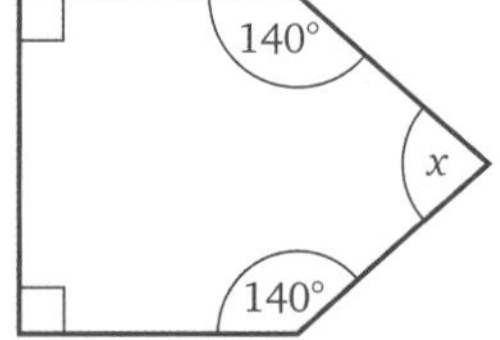

3

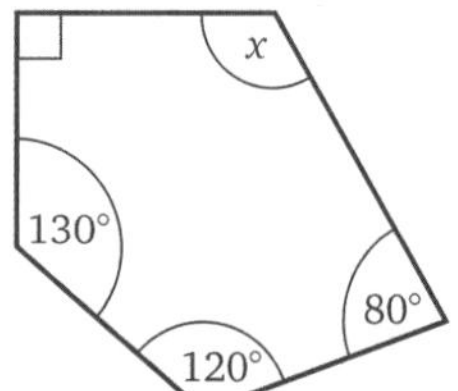

4

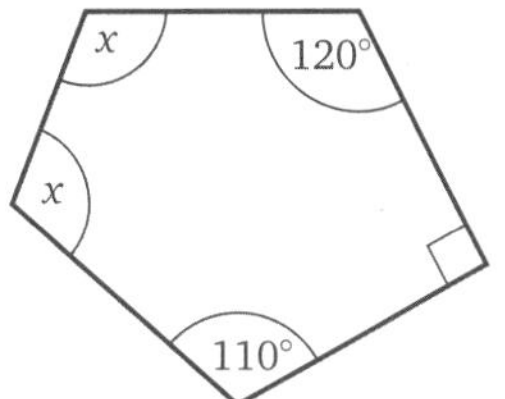

6

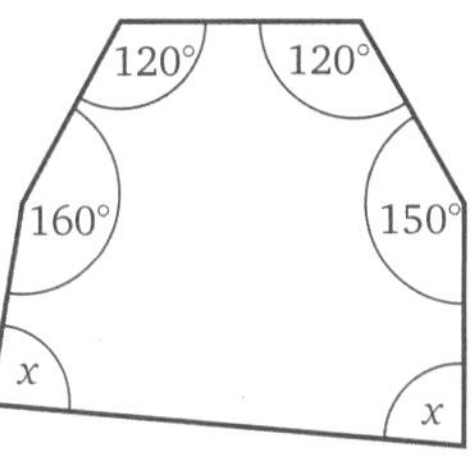

5

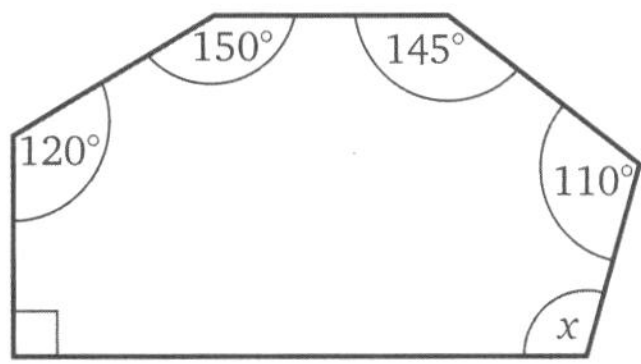

7

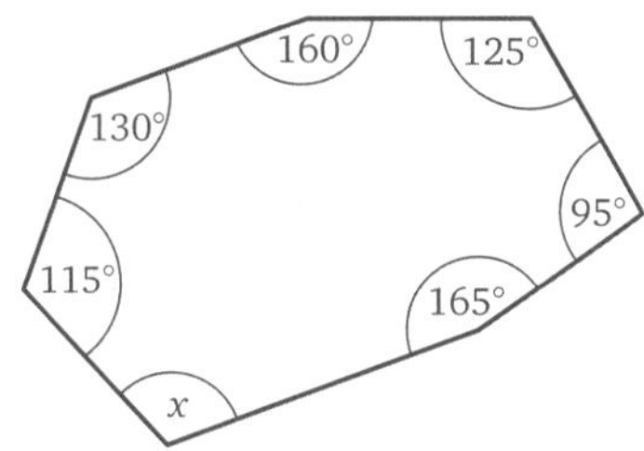

Find the size of each interior angle of a regular nine-sided polygon.

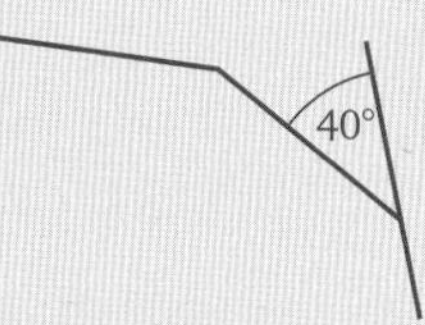

(As the polygon is regular, all the exterior angles are equal and all the interior angles are equal.)

Method 1 Sum of exterior angles = 360°

∴ each exterior angle = 360° ÷ 9 = 40°

∴ each interior angle = 180° − 40° = 140°

Method 2 Sum of interior angles = 180° × 9 − 360° = 1260°

∴ each interior angle = 1260° ÷ 9 = 140°

Find the size of each interior angle of each shape:

8 a regular pentagon

9 a regular hexagon

10 a regular octagon

11 a regular ten-sided polygon

12 a regular 12-sided polygon

13 a regular 20-sided polygon.

14 How many sides has a regular polygon if each exterior angle is

a 20° **b** 15°?

15 How many sides has a regular polygon if each interior angle is

a 150° **b** 162°

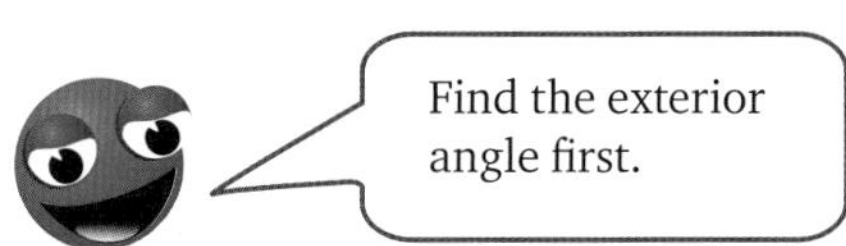

16 Is it possible for each exterior angle of a regular polygon to be

a 30° **c** 50° **e** 70°

b 40° **d** 60° **f** 90°?

In those cases where it is possible, give the number of sides.

17 Is it possible for each interior angle of a regular polygon to be

a 90° **c** 180° **e** 170°

b 120° **d** 175° **f** 135°?

In those cases where it is possible, give the number of sides.

18 Construct a regular pentagon with sides 5 cm long.

19 Construct a regular octagon of side 5 cm.

Find the size of each interior angle, then use your protractor.

Puzzle

Arrange ten counters in such a way as to form five rows with four counters only in each row.

Mixed problems

Exercise 11d

ABCDE is a pentagon, in which the interior angles at A and D are each $3x°$ and the interior angles at B, C and E are each $4x°$. AB and DC are produced until they meet at F.

Find $B\hat{F}C$.

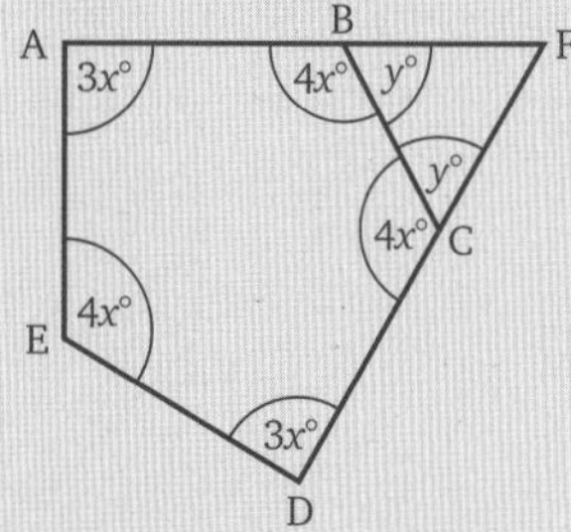

Sum of the interior angles of a pentagon $= 180° \times 5 - 360°$

$= 540°$

$\therefore \quad 3x + 4x + 3x + 4x + 4x = 540$

$18x = 540$

$x = 30$

$\therefore \quad A\hat{B}C = 120°$ and $B\hat{C}D = 120°$

so $\quad y = 60$ (angles on a straight line)

$\therefore \quad B\hat{F}C = 180° - 2 \times 60°$ (angle sum of $\triangle BFC$)

$= 60°$

In questions **1** to **10** find the value of x:

1

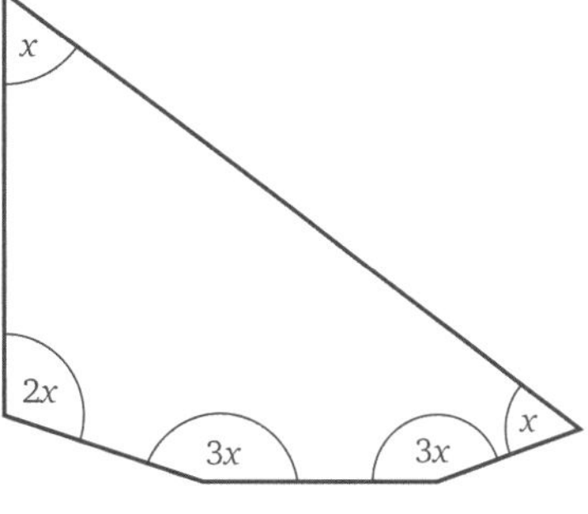

2

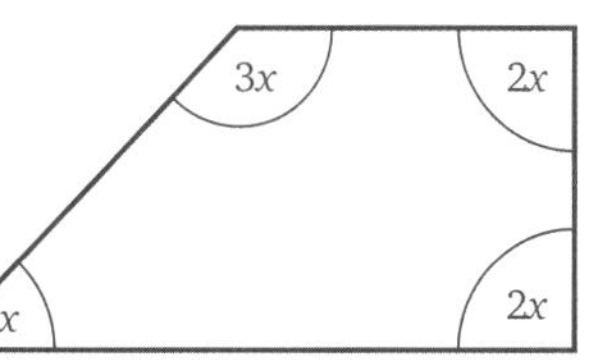

3

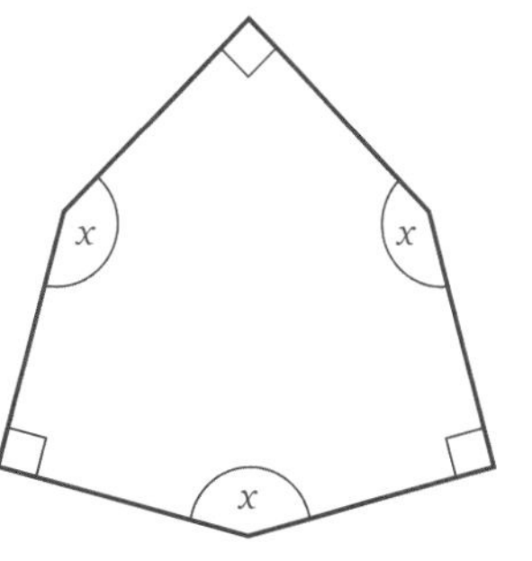

4

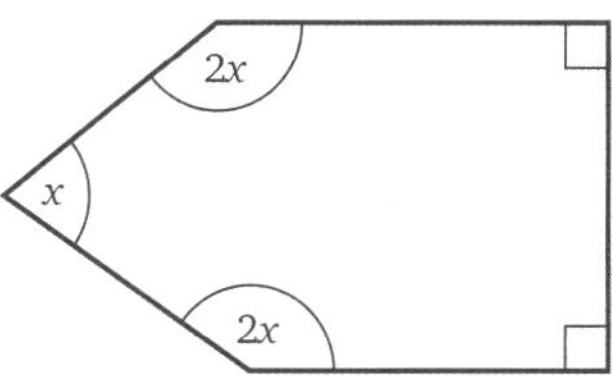

5

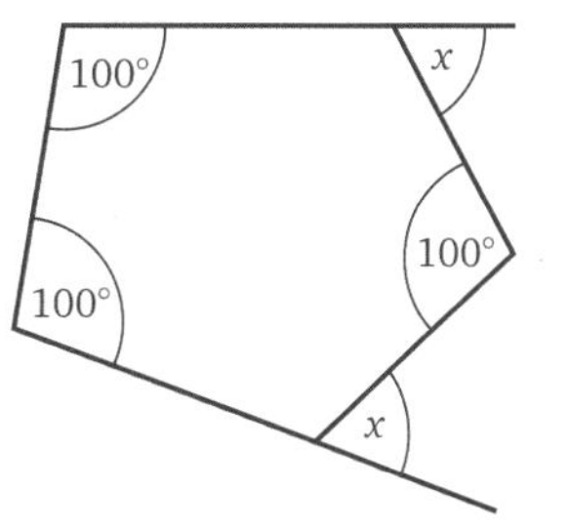

6

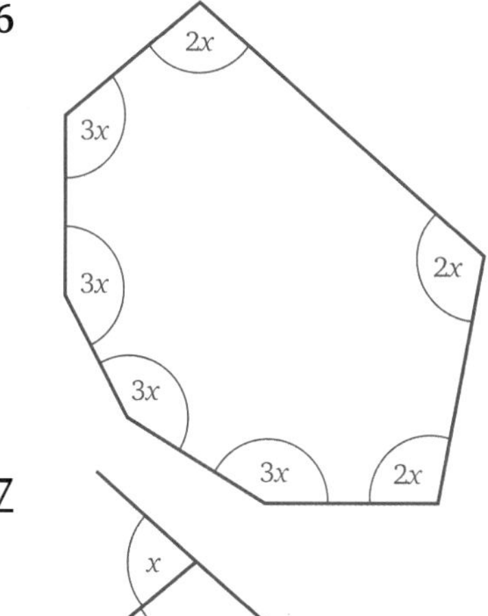

7

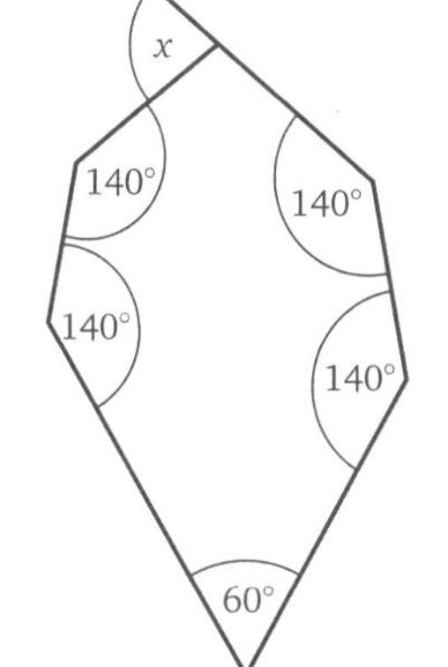

8

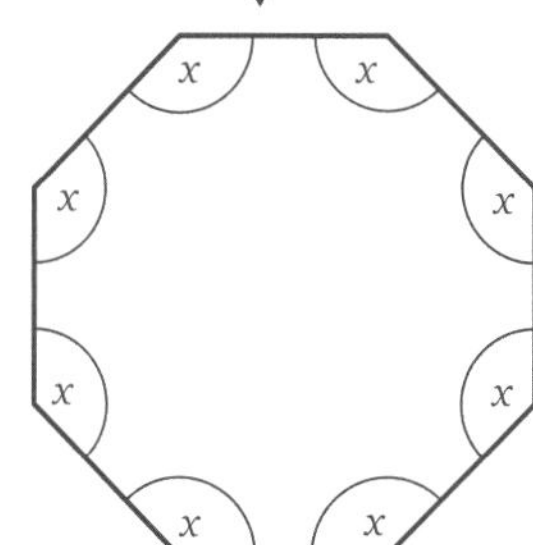

9

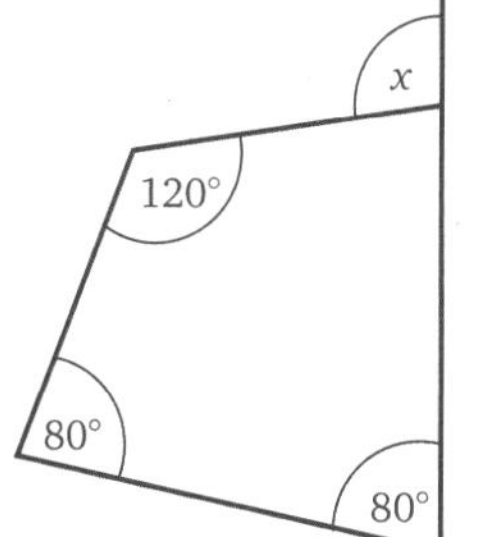

10

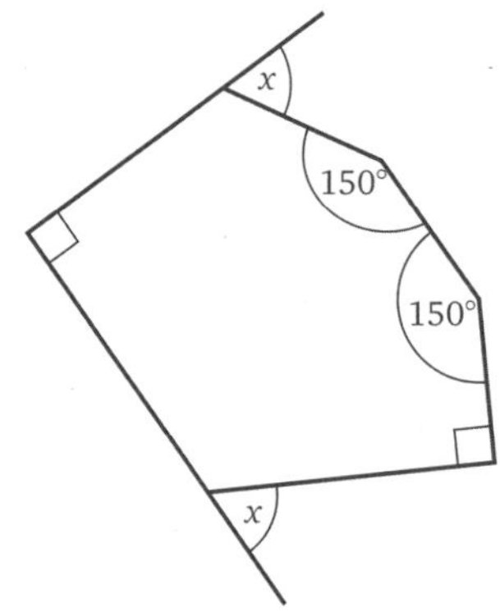

11 ABCDE is a regular pentagon.
OA = OB = OC = OD = OE.
Find the size of each angle at O.

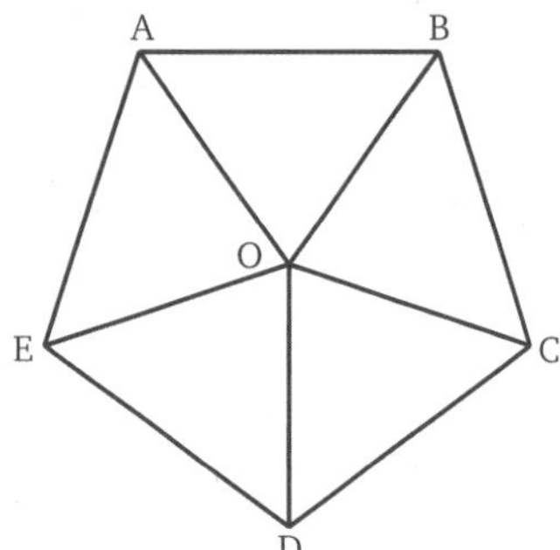

12 ABCDEFGH is a regular octagon. O is a point in the middle of the octagon such that O is the same distance from each vertex. Find $A\hat{O}B$.

13 ABCDEF is a regular hexagon. AB and DC are produced until they meet at G. Find $B\hat{G}C$.

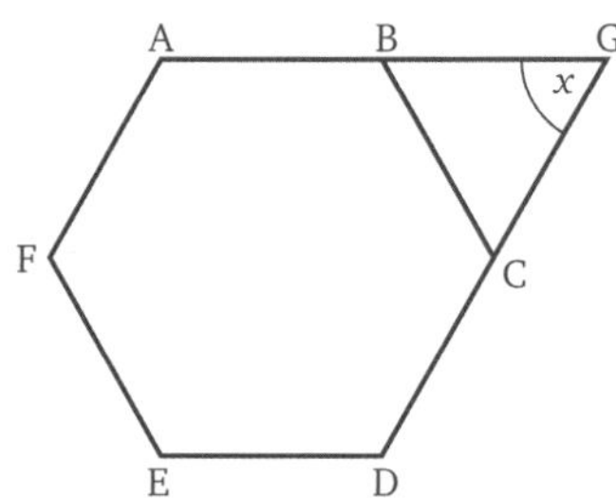

14 ABCDE is a regular pentagon. AB and DC are produced until they meet at F. Find $B\hat{F}C$.

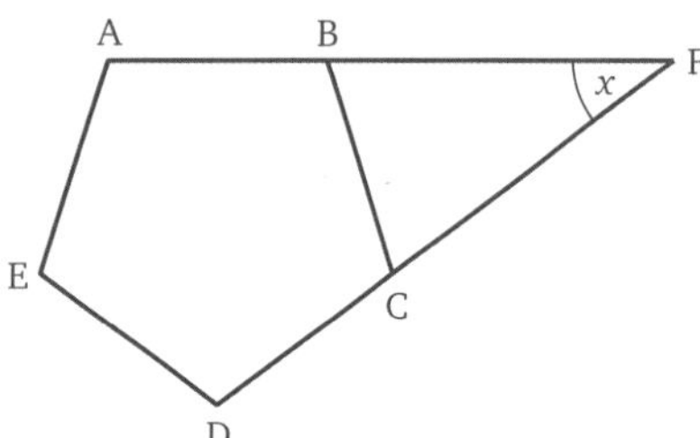

ABCDEF is a regular hexagon.
Find $A\hat{D}B$.

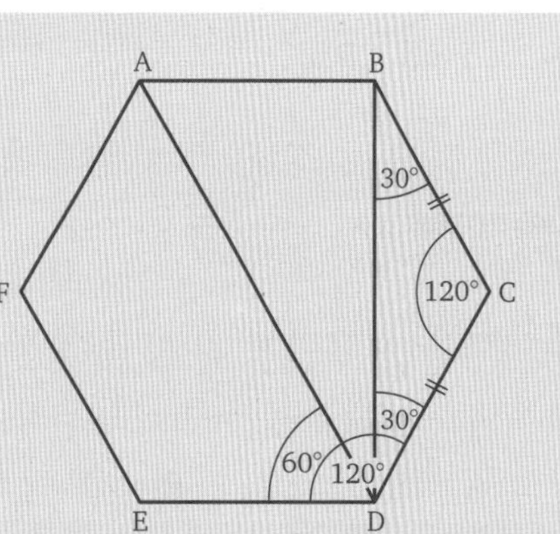

As ABCDEF is regular, the exterior angles are all equal.

Each exterior angle = 360° ÷ 6 = 60°

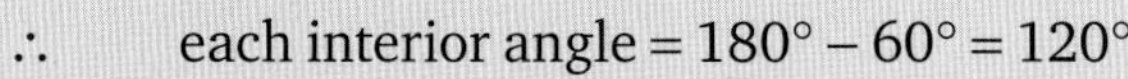

∴ each interior angle = 180° − 60° = 120°

△BCD is isosceles (BC = DC).

∴ $C\hat{B}D = B\hat{D}C = 30°$ (angle sum of △BCD)

AD is a line of symmetry for the hexagon.

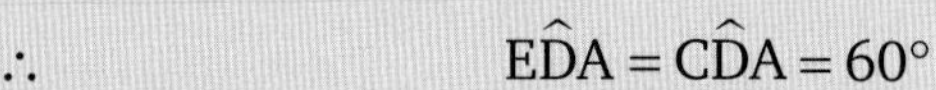

∴ $E\hat{D}A = C\hat{D}A = 60°$

∴ $A\hat{D}B = 60° - 30°$

$= 30°$

In questions **15** to **20**, each polygon is regular. Give answers correct to one decimal place where necessary.

15

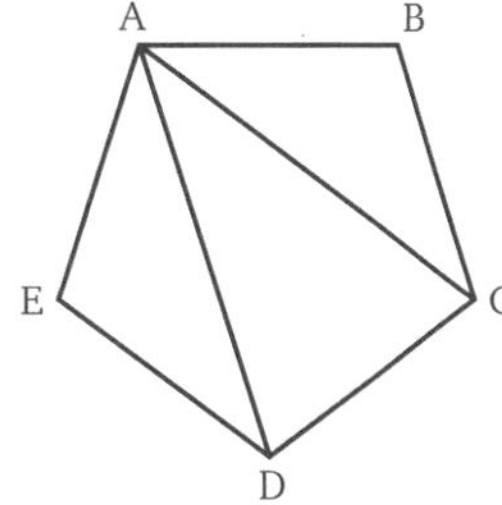

Find **a** $A\hat{C}B$ **b** $D\hat{A}C$.

16

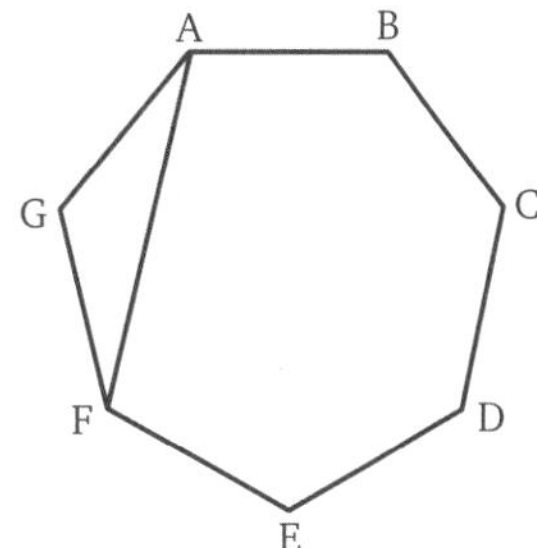

Find **a** $A\hat{G}F$ **b** $G\hat{A}F$.

17

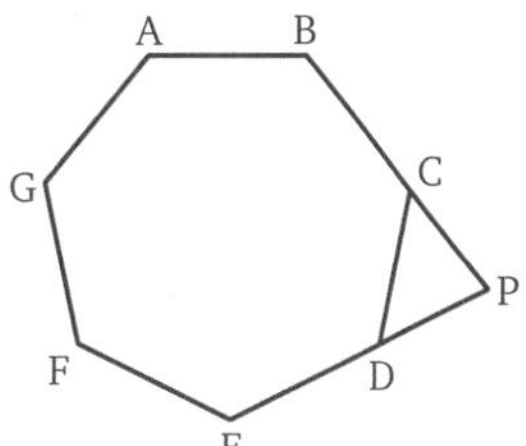

Find $C\hat{P}D$.

18

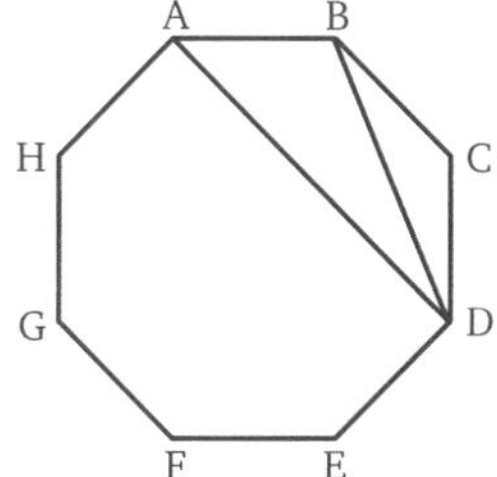

Find **a** $C\hat{B}D$ **b** $B\hat{D}A$.

19

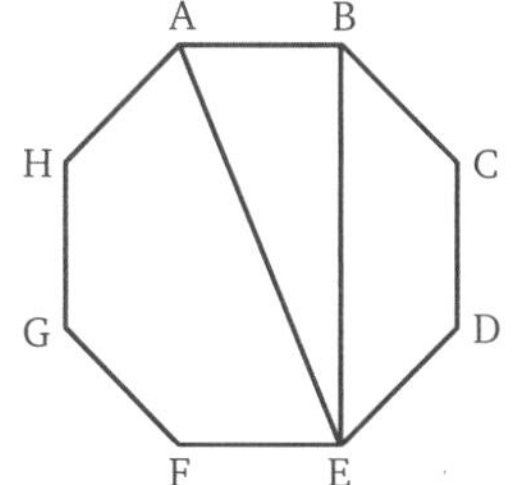

Find $A\hat{E}B$.

20

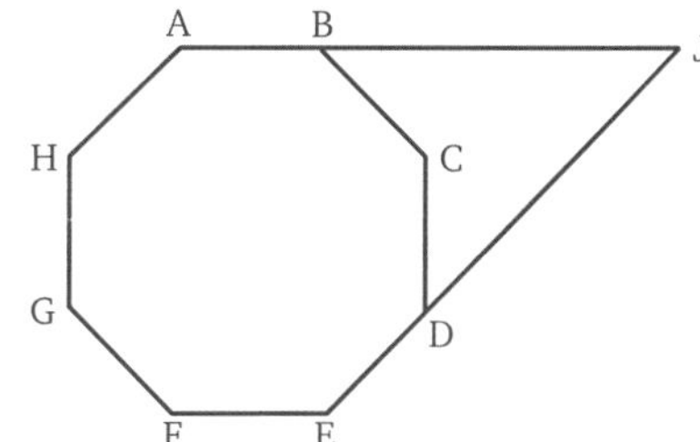

Find $B\hat{J}D$.

Exercise 11e

Select the letter that gives the correct answer.

1 A regular polygon has 18 sides. The size of one of its exterior angles is

A 18° **B** 20° **C** 22° **D** 24°

2 The exterior angle of a regular polygon is $22\frac{1}{2}°$. The number of sides this polygon has is

A 16 **B** 18 **C** 20 **D** 22

3 The sum of the interior angles of a polygon with 10 sides is

A 1080° **B** 1400° **C** 1800° **D** 2340°

4 Which two of these angles are possible exterior angles for a regular polygon?

A 40° and 45° B 40° and 50° C 40° and 55° D 50° and 55°

5 The value of x in this regular polygon is

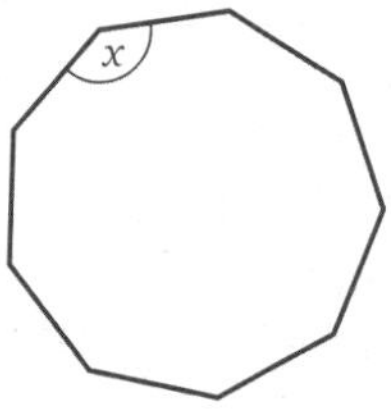

A 120°

B 140°

C 150°

D 160°

6 How many sides has a regular polygon if each interior angle is 160°?

A 12 B 15 C 18 D 20

Pattern-making with regular polygons

Regular hexagons fit together without leaving gaps, to form a flat surface. We say that they *tessellate*.

The hexagons tessellate because each interior angle of a regular hexagon is 120°, so three vertices fit together to make 360°.

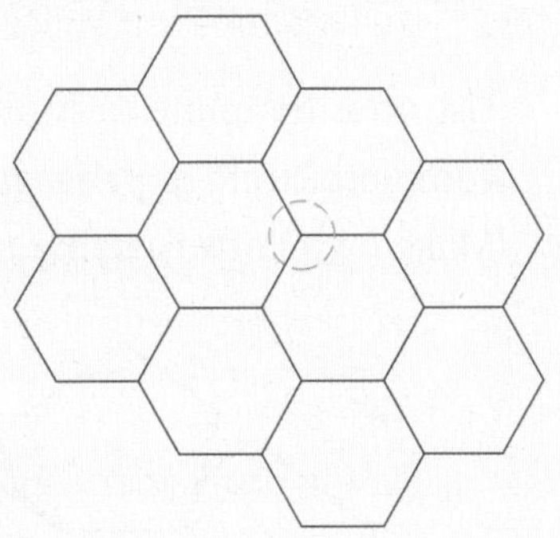

Exercise 11f

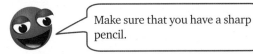

1 This is a pattern using regular octagons. They do not tessellate.

a Explain why they do not tessellate.

b What shape is left between the four octagons?

c Continue the pattern. (Trace one of the shapes above, cut it out and use it as a template.)

Make sure that you have a sharp pencil.

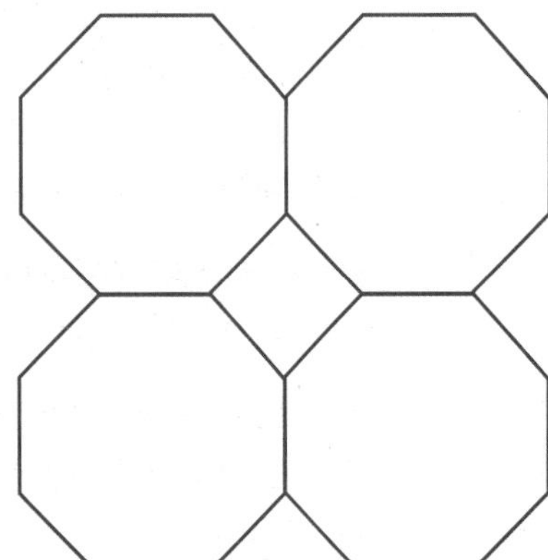

2 Trace this regular pentagon and use it to cut out a template.

a Will regular pentagons tessellate?

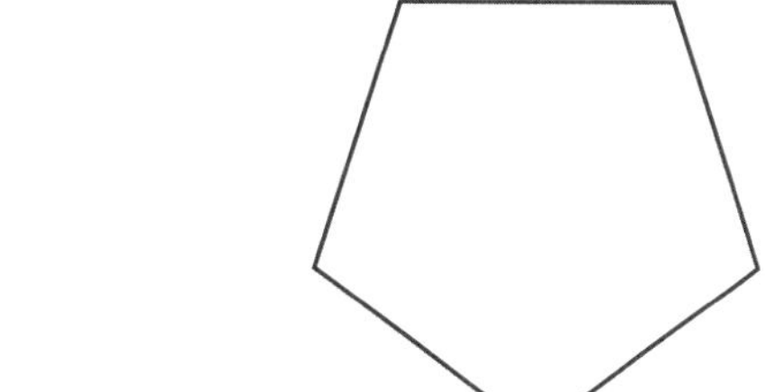

b

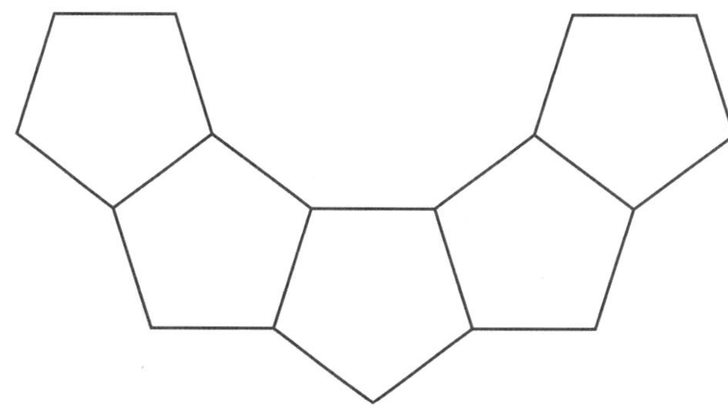

Use your template to copy and continue this pattern until you have a complete circle of pentagons. What shape is left in the middle?

c Make up a pattern using pentagons.

3

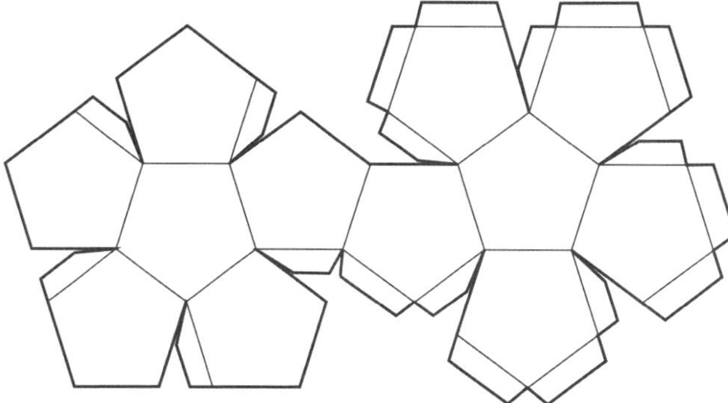

Use your template from question **2** to copy this net on to thick paper. Cut it out and fold along the lines. Stick the edges together using the flaps. You have made a regular dodecahedron.

4 Apart from the hexagon, there are two other regular polygons that tessellate. Which are they, and why?

5 Regular hexagons, squares and equilateral triangles can be combined to make interesting patterns. An example is given here:

Copy this pattern and extend it. (If you make templates to help you, make each shape of side 2 cm.)

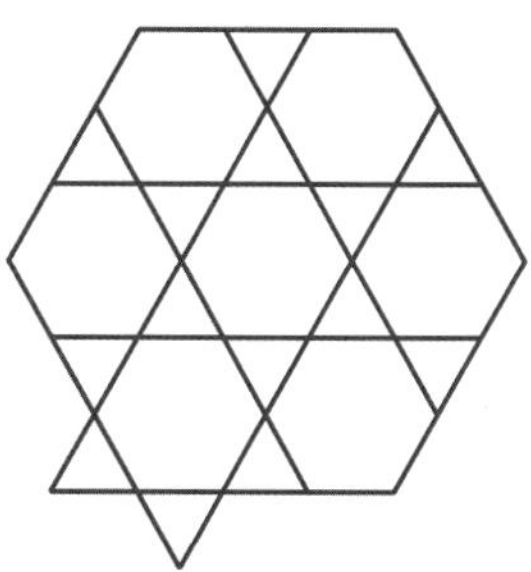

6 Make some patterns of your own using the shapes in question **5**.

Did you know?

A polyhedron is a solid whose faces are polygons. There are only five regular convex polyhedra that can be made from regular shapes.

They are:

- a tetrahedron, which uses 4 equilateral triangles
- an octahedron, which uses 8 equilateral triangles
- an icosahedron, which uses 20 equilateral triangles
- a cube, which uses 6 squares
- a dodecahedron, which uses 12 regular pentagons.

These five solids are called the Platonic solids.

In this chapter you have seen that...

✔ the sum of the exterior angles of any polygon is 360°

✔ if a polygon is regular (i.e. equal sides and angles) the exterior angles are equal and the size of each one is 360° ÷ the number of sides

✔ for a polygon with n sides the sum of the interior angles is $(180n - 360)°$ or, in a slightly more useful form, $(n - 2)180°$

✔ some regular polygons tessellate, i.e. they fit together without leaving gaps.

12 Constructions

At the end of this chapter you should be able to construct...

1 a line parallel to a given line through a given point
2 various triangles
3 various quadrilaterals
4 a rhombus
5 a regular polygon with up to six sides
6 the circumcircle of a given triangle.

Did you know?

The ratio of the circumference to the diameter of a circle which we know as π cannot be expressed as the ratio of two whole numbers. Mathematicians tried for centuries to do this but in modern times it was found impossible. Numbers such as π belong to a subset of the set of irrational numbers. They are called transcendental numbers.

You need to know...

✔ the angle properties of a triangle
✔ the angle sum of a quadrilateral
✔ the properties of angles formed by a pair of parallel lines and a transversal
✔ the properties of isosceles and equilateral triangles
✔ the properties of special quadrilaterals
✔ how to construct triangles and quadrilaterals using a ruler and a pair of compasses
✔ how to bisect an angle
✔ how to construct an angle equal to a given angle
✔ how to bisect a straight line
✔ how to drop the perpendicular from a point to a line.

Key words

alternate angles, arc, bisect, centre, chord, circumcircle, compasses, diagonal, diameter, equiangular, isosceles, parallel, perpendicular, perpendicular bisector, quadrilateral, radius, rectangle, rhombus, symmetry, trapezium

Basic constructions

In Book 2 you learnt how to construct and bisect angles, how to bisect a straight line, and how to drop a perpendicular from a point to a line. Exercise 12a revises these skills.

Exercise 12a

You may use a protractor to measure the angles in questions **1** to **3**.

1 Construct △ABC in which AB = 6 cm, ∠BAC = 70° and ∠ABC = 40°.

 a Measure and record the size of ∠ACB.

 b What special name do we give to this triangle?

2 Construct △DEF in which DE = 8 cm, ∠EDF = 35° and ∠DEF = 100°. Measure and record

 a the length of DF and EF **b** the size of ∠DFE.

3 Construct △GHI in which GH = 10 cm, GI = 8 cm and HI = 6 cm. Measure its angles. What special name do we give to this triangle?

In questions **4** to **12** construct the figures using only a ruler and a pair of compasses.

For an angle of 30° construct an angle of 60° and bisect it, and for an angle of 45° construct an angle of 90° and bisect it.

4

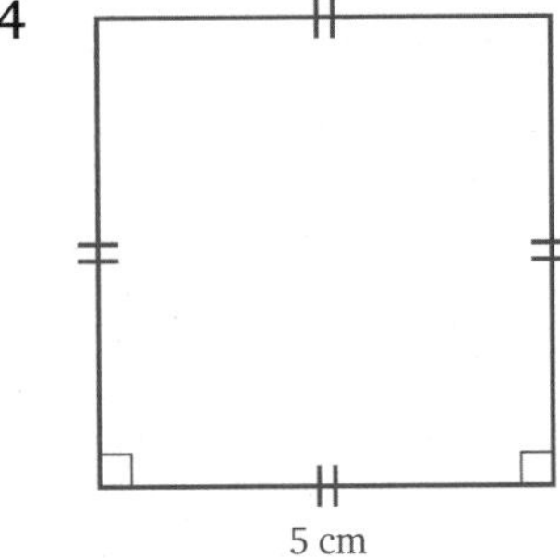

6

5

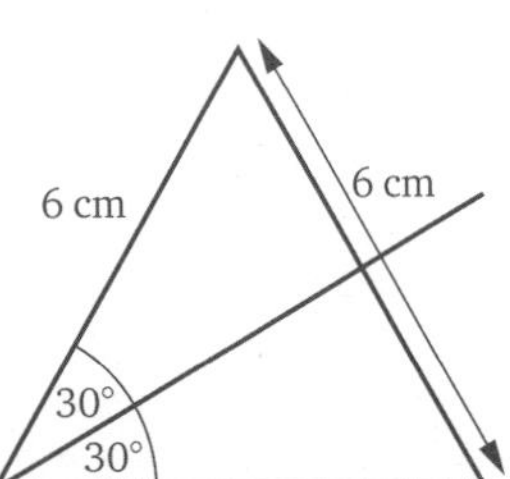

7

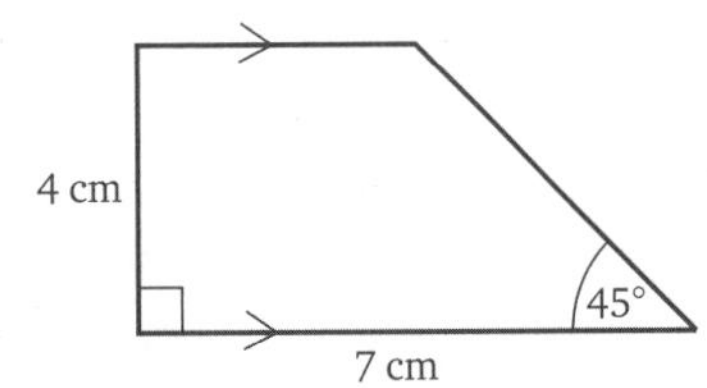

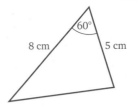

For questions **8** to **12**, draw a rough sketch before starting the construction.

8 Construct a quadrilateral, PQRS, in which PQ = 10 cm, $\hat{P} = 60°$, PS = 5 cm, $\hat{Q} = 60°$ and QR = 5 cm. What can you say about the lines PQ and SR?

9 Construct a triangle, ABC, in which AB = 12 cm, ∠ABC = 30° and ∠BAC = 45°. What size should ∠ACB be? How accurate is your construction?

10 Construct a triangle, ABC, in which AB = 6 cm, ∠ABC = 90° and ∠BAC = 45°.

What length do you expect BC to be?

What size do you expect ∠BCA to be?

How accurate is your construction?

11 Construct a triangle, DEF, in which DE = 9.5 cm, ∠EDF = 45° and ∠DEF = 60°. What size do you expect ∠DFE to be?
How accurate is your construction?

12 Construct a quadrilateral LMNO with LM = 8.4 cm, MN = 5.2 cm, the angle OLM = 60° and ON parallel to LM.

To construct a line parallel to a given line through a given point

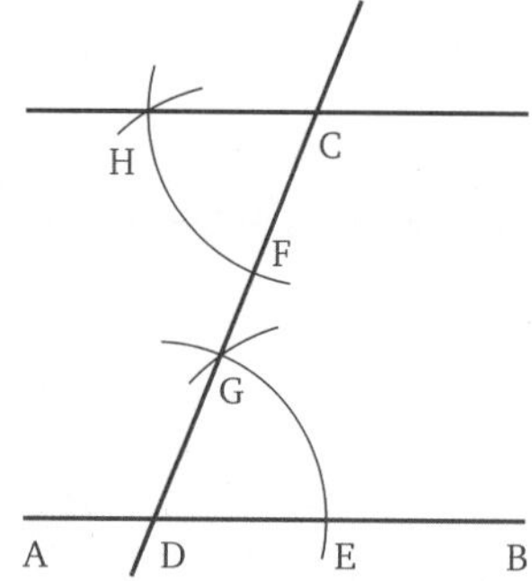

C is a point above the line AB.

To draw a line through C parallel to AB proceed as follows:

- Draw a line through C to cut AB at D.
- With centre D and any suitable radius (it must not be too small) draw an arc to cut AB at E and CD at G.
- With centre C and the same radius draw an arc to cut CD at F.
- With centre E open out your compasses to a radius that passes through G.
- With this radius place the point of you compasses at F and draw the first arc at H.
- Join CH.

CH is parallel to AB as you have constructed angles EDG and FCH as equal angles. You have constructed *alternate angles*.

Exercise 12b

1 Construct triangle ABC such that AB = 9.5 cm, angle A = 65° and AC = 6.4 cm. Construct the perpendicular bisector of AC to cut AC at E. Finally construct the line through E parallel to AB to intersect BC at F. Measure EF. How does the length of EF compare with the length of AB?

2 R is a point on a straight line PQ.

- **a** Construct an angle QRS such that $\angle QRS = 45°$ and RS = 4.4 cm.
- **b** Construct the line through S parallel to PQ. Mark a point on it T such that ST = RQ.
- **c** Construct the perpendicular from S to PQ to meet PQ at U.
- **d** Measure RU and SU. How do they compare? Is this what you expected? Justify your answer.
- **e** Measure QT. How does its length compare with RS?
- **f** What name do we give to the quadrilateral RSTQ?

3 Draw AB = 8.5 cm. Construct $\angle ABC = 60°$ and mark BC = 10 cm. Construct the perpendicular bisector of BC to intersect BC at D. Construct the line through D parallel to AB and mark the point E on it such that DE = 5 cm and E is on the same side of BC as A. Join AE. What name do we give to the quadrilateral ABDE?

The rhombus

This exercise investigates some properties of the *rhombus*.

Exercise 12c

1 Draw a line 12 cm long across your page. Label the ends A and C. Open your compasses to a radius of 9 cm. With the point on A, draw an arc above AC and another arc below AC. Keeping the same radius, move the point of your compasses to C. Draw arcs above and below AC to cut the first pair of arcs. Where the arcs intersect (i.e. cross), label the points B and D.

Join A to B, B to C, C to D and D to A. ABCD is called a rhombus.

Questions **2** to **9** refer to the figure that you have constructed in question **1**.

2 Without measuring them, what can you say about the lengths of AB, BC, CD and DA?

3 ABCD has two lines of symmetry. Name them.

4 If ABCD is folded along BD, where is A in relation to C?

5 If ABCD is folded along AC, where is D in relation to B?

6 Where AC and BD cut, label the point E. With ABCD unfolded, where is E in relation to A and C?

7 Where is E in relation to B and D?

8 If ABCD is folded first along BD and then folded again along AE, what is the size of the angle at E?

9 With ABCD unfolded, what are the sizes of the four angles at E?

10 In a rhombus ABCD, AB = 7 cm and the diagonal AC is 12 cm. Make a rough sketch of the rhombus and then construct ABCD. Measure BD.

11 In a rectangle ABCD, AB = 6 cm and the diagonal BD is 10 cm. Make a rough sketch of the rectangle and then construct ABCD. Measure AD.

12 In a rhombus ABCD, the diagonal AC is 8 cm and the diagonal BD is 6 cm. Construct the rhombus and measure AB. (Remember first to make a rough sketch.)

13 ABCD is a parallelogram in which the diagonal AC is 10 cm and the diagonal BD is 12 cm. AC and BD cut at E and $A\hat{E}B = 60°$. Make a rough sketch of the parallelogram and then construct ABCD. Measure BC.

14 Construct a rhombus ABCD in which the sides are 5 cm long and the diagonal AC is 8 cm long. Measure the diagonal BD.

15 Construct a square ABCD whose diagonal, AC, is 8 cm long. Measure the side AB.

Properties of the diagonals of a rhombus

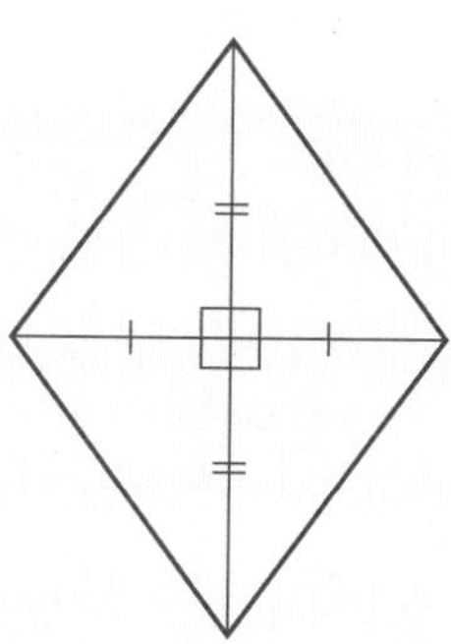

From the last exercise you should be convinced that

the diagonals of a rhombus bisect each other at right angles.

These properties form the basis of the next two constructions.

Circle constructions

Any point on the perpendicular bisector of the line joining two points A and B is equidistant from those two points.

LMN is the perpendicular bisector of the line joining AB. For any point P on this line PA = PB.

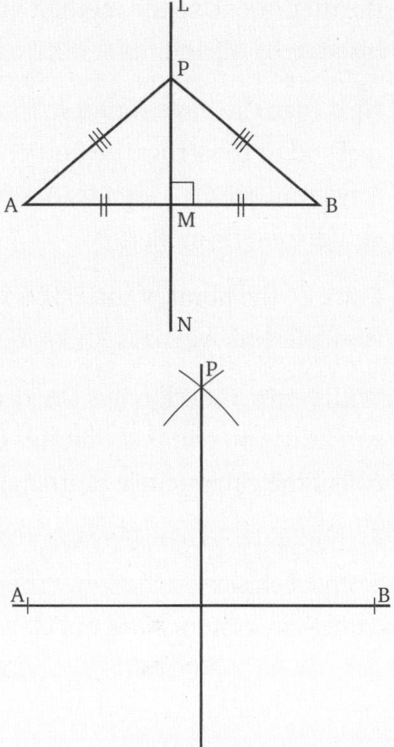

Use the following method to construct the perpendicular bisector of the line joining two points A and B.

- With centre A and radius more than half AB, draw arcs above and below AB.
- *Keeping the radius the same*, move the point of your compasses to B and draw arcs above and below AB so that they intersect the first two arcs at P and Q.
- Join P to Q.

PQ is the perpendicular bisector of AB. Any point on PQ is equidistant from A and B.

To construct the circumcircle to a given triangle

The *circumcircle* of a given triangle is the circle that passes through its vertices.

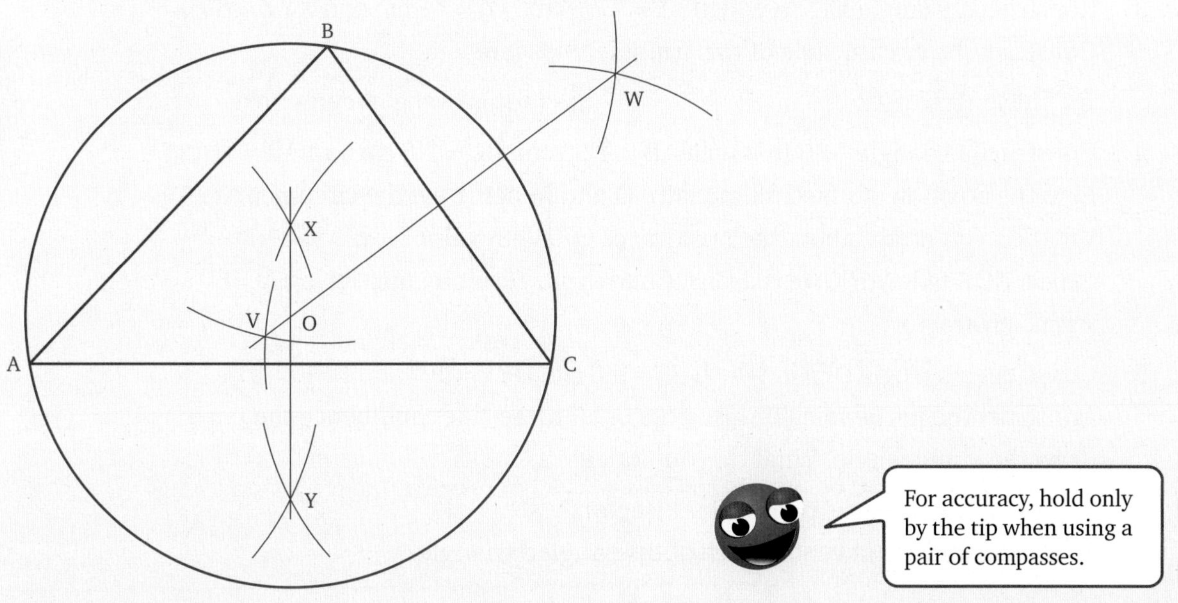

- Draw a triangle ABC similar in size and shape to the triangle shown in the diagram. Use the method given above to construct the perpendicular bisector of AC and mark it XY.
- Next turn the page round so that BC is at the bottom and use the same method to construct the perpendicular bisector of BC. Mark this line VW. Any point on XY is equidistant from A and C and any point on VW is equidistant from B and C.
- Mark O, the point of intersection of XY and VW. The point O is equidistant from all three vertices A, B and C.
- With centre O and radius OA, draw a circle. If you have done your constructions carefully, you will find that this circle passes through A, B and C. This circle is called the circumcircle of triangle ABC and its centre O is called the circumcentre.

Now that you know exactly what to do, draw another triangle of a similar size and repeat this construction. When you have finished, the triangle and the circumcircle should stand out clearly from all construction lines.

Exercise 12d

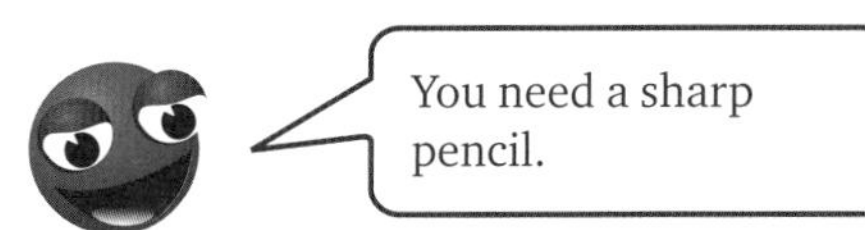

1 Draw a triangle of any size and construct its circumcircle.

2 Construct a triangle PQR in which PQ = 11 cm, PR = 10 cm and QR = 9 cm. Construct the circumcircle of this triangle. Measure its radius.

3 Construct a triangle XYZ in which XY = 12.5 cm, YZ = 7.5 cm and $X\hat{Y}Z = 60°$. Construct the circumcircle of this triangle. Measure

   a the length of XZ **b** the radius of the circumcircle.

4 Construct a triangle ABC in which AB = 12.5 cm, BC = 7.5 cm and AC = 10 cm. Find the position of the circumcentre O and hence draw the circumcircle. What do you notice about the position of O? What value would you now expect $A\hat{C}B$ to have? Give reasons. Check your result by measuring $A\hat{C}B$ with a protractor.

5 Construct a triangle DEF in which EF = 8.8 cm, $D\hat{E}F = 30°$ and $D\hat{F}E = 45°$. Construct the perpendicular bisectors of all three sides and hence the draw the circumcircle. What do you notice

   a about the three perpendicular bisectors

   b about the circumcentre of an obtuse angled triangle?

6 Construct a trapezium ABCD in which AB = 10.2 cm, BC = AD = 5.2 cm, $A\hat{B}C = 60°$, $D\hat{A}B = 60°$, $A\hat{D}C = 120°$ and $B\hat{C}D = 120°$. Construct the circumcircle to triangle ABC. Does this circle pass through any other particular point? Can you give a reason for what has happened? Will this happen for every trapezium?

7 Construct triangle XYZ in which XY = 9 cm, YZ = 7 cm and XZ = 5.5 cm. Construct the circumcircle to this triangle. Measure and record its radius.

8 Draw two lines AB and BC such that AB = 6 cm, ∠ABC = 120° and BC = 4 cm. Construct the circle that passes through A, B and C. Mark its centre O. Measure and record its radius.

9 Draw lines PQ and QR such that PQ = 5.5 cm, ∠PQR = 100° and QR = 5 cm. Construct the circle that passes through the points P, Q and R. If O is the centre of this circle measure OP, OQ and OR. What is the radius of this circle?

10 Draw a circle, centre O, radius 4 cm. Mark any point A on the circumference. With centre A and radius 6 cm draw an arc to cut the circle again at B.

Join AB and construct its perpendicular bisector.

Does this line pass through O?

With centre A, radius 3.5 cm intersect the circle at C such that ∠BAC is obtuse.

Construct the perpendicular bisector of AC.

At what special point do you expect these perpendicular bisectors to intersect?

How accurate is your construction?

Constructing regular polygons

A polygon is regular when all its sides are the same length and all its angles are the same size.

The best way to construct a regular polygon is to use the fact that all the vertices lie on a circle.

The diagram shows a regular polygon with 6 sides.

All the angles at the centre of the circle are equal.

Since the sum of all the angles at O is 360°

each angle is $\frac{360°}{6} = 60°$.

For a regular polygon with n sides the angle at the centre of the circle would be $\frac{360°}{n}$.

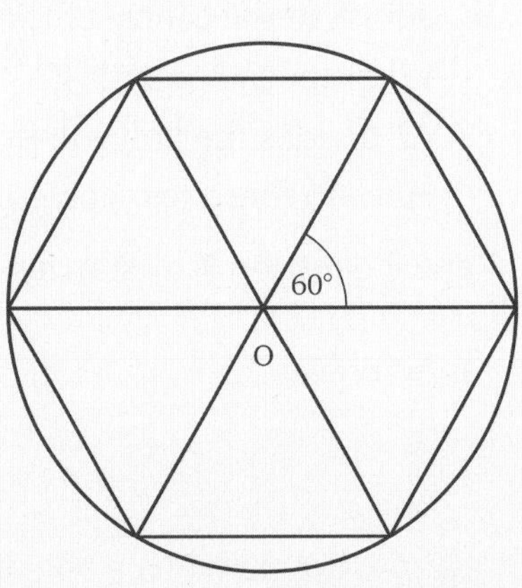

Exercise 12e

1 Find the angle at the centre of the circumscribing circle for a regular polygon with

a 5 sides **b** 8 sides **c** 10 sides **d** 15 sides.

2 Construct a regular polygon with four sides where each side is 6 cm long. Measure the length of each diagonal. Are they the same length? What name do we give to give to this regular polygon?

3 Using ruler and a pair of compasses only, construct a regular hexagon ABCDEF with sides of length 3 cm.

a Measure angles ABC and DEF. How do they compare?

b Measure the lengths of AE and DF. How do they compare?

c Measure the lengths of AD and BE. How do these lengths compare with the length of a side of the polygon?

4 Repeat question **3** by constructing a regular hexagon with sides of length 4 cm.

5 Construct a regular polygon with 8 sides (called a regular octagon). Start with a circle of radius 5 cm. What is the length of a side of the octagon?

6 Construct a regular polygon with 7 sides (called a regular heptagon). Start with a circle of radius 5 cm. What is the length of a side of the heptagon?

7 Draw a circle of radius 5 cm. Now construct a regular polygon ABCDE with five sides (known as a pentagon) such that the vertices of the polygon lie on this circle. (You will need to measure 5 angles of 72° at the centre of the circle.)

a What is the length of a side of this polygon?

b Join A to the centre of the circle and produce it to cut DC at F. What special point is F?

c AF divides the polygon into two polygons ABCFA and AEDFA. How do these two polygons compare?

8 Repeat question **7** by starting with a circle of radius 6 cm.

Mixed exercises

Exercise 12f

In this exercise angles of 30°, 45°, 60°, 90° and 120° should be constructed. Other angles may be measured with a protractor.

1 Construct a triangle ABC in which AB = 10 cm, BC = 6 cm and AC = 8 cm. Using a ruler and pair of compasses only, drop the perpendicular from C to AB. Measure its length.

2 Construct a triangle PQR in which PQ = 10 cm, PR = 8 cm and RQ = 7 cm. Construct the perpendicular from R to PQ. Measure and record its length.

3 Construct the isosceles triangle ABC in which AB = 6 cm, AC = BC = 7 cm. Construct the perpendicular bisector of AB to bisect AB at D. How do the triangles ADC and BDC compare?

4 Construct the isosceles triangle XYZ in which XY = 5 cm, XZ = YZ = 6 cm. Construct the perpendicular bisector of YZ. Is this a line of symmetry? If not, why not?

5 PQ is a chord of a circle, centre O. The figure has one line of symmetry that is not shown. Make a rough sketch and mark the line of symmetry. How is this line related to PQ?

O
P
Q

6 Construct a triangle ABC in which AB = 9 cm, AC = 8 cm and BC = 7 cm. Construct the perpendicular bisectors of AC and BC. Mark the point where they cross E. With the point of your compasses on E and a radius equal to the length of EA, draw a circle. Does this circle pass through all the points you expected? Explain your answer.

7 Construct a square ABCD with sides 6 cm long. Construct the perpendicular bisectors of AB and BC. Mark X the point where they intersect. With the point of your compasses on X and the radius equal to the distance XA, draw a circle. Should this circle pass through the four vertices of the square? Justify your answer.

8 Draw a diameter AB in a circle, centre O, radius 5 cm. Draw another diameter CD such that angle AOC = 60° and a third diameter EF such that angle EOB = 60°. Join A, C, E, B, D, F, A. This shape is a regular hexagon. Measure the lengths of its sides. How do the lengths of the sides compare with the radius of the circle? Justify your comments.

9 Draw a radius OA in a circle, centre O, radius 5 cm. Mark B on the circumference such that angle AOB = 72°. Repeat this instruction to mark the points C, D and E as the radii turn clockwise about O. Join A, B, C, D, A to give a figure.

  a What name do we give to this shape? Is it regular? Justify your answer.

  b Describe triangle AOB.

10 Construct a square PQRS of side 9 cm. Construct the perpendicular bisectors of PQ and PS. Mark X the point where they intersect, and Y the point where the bisector cuts PQ.
Centre X, radius XY, draw the circle.
Does the circle touch the four sides of the square?

11 Construct a rhombus ABCD in which AB = BC = 5 cm and ∠ABC = 60°. Join the diagonals AC and BD. Check the angles between the diagonals. Is this what you expected them to be?

12 Construct a rhombus PQRS with sides of length 6 cm and angle PQR = 120°.

13 Construct a parallelogram ABCD in which AB = 7 cm, AD = 5 cm and ∠BAD = 45°.

14 Construct a quadrilateral ABCD in which AB = 4.5 cm, BC = 3.5, AC = 6 cm, AD = DC = 3.5 cm. Join BD and record its length.

15 Construct a trapezium PQRS in which PQ = 9 cm, ∠QPS = 75°, ∠PQR = 65° and PS = 5 cm.

  a Which side is parallel to PQ?

  b Measure the four angles of the trapezium. Is the total what you expected?

  c Find ∠PQR + ∠SRQ. It this total what you expected?
  Justify your answer.

16 Construct a parallelogram ABCD with diagonals intersecting at X given that AC = 8 cm, BD = 10 cm and ∠AXD = 60°.
Measure and record the lengths of the sides of the parallelogram.

17 ABC is an equilateral triangle of side 6.5 cm. The line which bisects ∠B cuts AC at D and BD is produced to E so that DE = BD.

  a Sketch the quadrilateral ABCD.

  b What type of quadrilateral is ABCE? Give reasons.

18 Construct a rectangle with diagonals of length 12.6 cm containing an angle of 45°.
Measure and record the lengths of the sides of the rectangle.

19 a Draw a line AC that is 8 cm long.

b Draw the perpendicular bisector of AC.

c Hence construct the square for which AC is one diagonal.

20 Construct $\angle ABC = 120°$, AB = 4.8 cm and BC = 6.4 cm. Construct the perpendicular bisectors of AB and BC to intersect at O.

a Centre O, radius OA draw the arc of the circle.
Does this circle pass through B and C?

b Measure the angle at O between the perpendicular bisectors.
How is it related to the angle at B? Justify your answer.

Exercise 12g

1 Construct triangle ABC is which AB = 5 cm, BC = 7 cm and AC = 6 cm. Construct the perpendicular AD, from A to BC. Measure and record the length of AD.

2 Construct a rectangle with diagonals of length 12 cm containing an angle of 30°.
Measure and record the dimensions of the rectangle.

3 Construct triangle ABC is which AB = 6 cm, angle A = 70° and angle B = 40°. Measure angle C. What special triangle is this?

4 Construct triangle DEF in which DE = 8 cm, angle DEF = 100° and angle EDF = 35°.
Measure and record

a the length of **i** DF **ii** EF

b the size of angle DFE.

5 Construct triangle XYZ in which XY = 10 cm, XZ = 9 cm and YZ = 7 cm. Now construct the circumcircle to this triangle. Measure and record its radius.

6 Construct a trapezium PQRS in which PQ = 9.3 cm, angle P = 45°, angle Q = 60° and QR = 4.4 cm. Measure and record the length of PS and SR.

7 Construct a rhombus ABCD in which diagonal AC = 6 cm and diagonal BD = 6 cm. Measure and record the length of a side of the rhombus

8 Draw a circle of radius 6 cm. Now construct a regular polygon with five sides whose vertices lie on this circle. What is the length of a side of this polygon?

Did you know?

A grain, which is a unit of weight, refers to the weight of a grain of barley, which has remained constant for over 1000 years. The carat, which is used to measure the mass of gold and gemstones, has its origin in the carob seeds used originally by Arab jewellers to weigh precious metals and stones.

Puzzle

What's the largest number you can write using three 2s?

In this chapter you have seen that...

- ✔ you can construct triangles with given angles using a protractor
- ✔ you can construct a line parallel to a given line through a given point
- ✔ you can construct the circumcircle to a given triangle
- ✔ you can construct triangles and quadrilaterals, including a square, rectangle, rhombus, parallelogram, trapezium, regular pentagon and regular hexagon, from given information.

13 Consumer arithmetic

At the end of this chapter you should be able to...

1 calculate workers' wages and salaries

2 understand and work out taxes

3 work out the income from saving and the cost of borrowing money

4 calculate utility bills

5 calculate compound interest.

Did you know?

The Muslims brought together the mathematical knowledge of the earlier civilisations of Babylon, India and China by uniting the arithmetic and algebraic traditions of those countries with the geometric traditions of Greece. It was Muslim mathematicians who established modern algebra and discovered trigonometry.

You need to know...

✔ how to work with decimals and fractions

✔ how to use a calculator

✔ how to work with percentages.

Key words

amount, bonus, commission, compound interest, deductions, gross and net wages, income tax, kilowatt-hour, overtime, pension, salary, sales tax, simple interest, standing charge

Percentage change

If the cost of a television set is \$1200 but goes up by 5% the new cost of a set is

$$\$1200 \times \frac{(100+5)}{100} = \$1200 \times \frac{105}{100} = \$1260$$

If I bought a car for \$23 000 and in the first year it depreciated (i.e. went down in value) by 10%, its value at the end of the year would be

$$\$23\,000 \times \frac{(100-10)}{100} = \$23\,000 \times \frac{90}{100} = \$20\,700$$

Exercise 13a

1 If a number is increased by the given percentage, what percentage is the new number of the original number?

a 40% b 60% c 25% d 150% e $5\frac{1}{2}$%

2 If a number is decreased by the given percentage, what percentage is the new number of the original number?

a 30% b 60% c 5% d $33\frac{1}{3}$% e $3\frac{1}{2}$%

3 Increase

a 100 by 30% b 2400 by 62% c 545 by 14% d 838 by 155%

4 Decrease

a 100 by 70% b 3300 by 45% c 1465 by 25% d 224 by 35%

5 a Increase 144 by $33\frac{1}{3}$%. b Decrease 123 by $33\frac{1}{3}$%.

6 A piece of furniture is priced at $3400 plus value added tax at 12%. How much does it actually cost?

7 The number of workers employed at a factory is 5% fewer than last year. Last year there were 1200. How many workers are employed this year?

8 Phillip's weight has decreased by 12% since he decided to eat less sugar. Before he changed his sugar intake he weighed 95 kg. What does he weigh now?

9 Charles was promised a 12% increase in his weekly pay. At present he earns $250 a week.

a What will be his weekly pay after the rise?

b After the increase the amount taken off will be 15% of his new pay. Calculate his new take-home pay.

10 Tom Lewis went out for a meal. It cost him $45 plus a service charge of 15%. He paid the waiter with $55 in notes. How much change should he get?

Earnings

When we go to work we expect to get paid. It may be for an agreed hourly rate, a weekly rate or it may be for an annual salary. Whichever method is used there will be *deductions*. These may be for government taxes or pension contributions. There will probably also be ways of increasing your income by working 'overtime' or earning 'commission'. Our earnings before any deductions are called our *gross* earnings. After deductions they are referred to as our *net* earnings.

Exercise 13b

1 Calculate the gross weekly wage for each of the following employees.

Name	Number of hours worked	Hourly rate of pay
P H Singh	40	\$16
S T Edwards	38	\$15.20
B E Smith	42	\$18.50
D J Pierre	$38\frac{1}{2}$	\$16.40

2 Megan Jones starts work each day at 7 a.m. and finishes at 4 p.m. She has a 45-minute lunch break for which she is not paid. How many hours does she work in a normal 5-day week?
Find her gross weekly wage if she is paid \$14.80 per hour.

3 Mike Joseph works afternoons. He starts at 3 p.m. and finishes at 11 p.m. If he is entitled to an unpaid meal break from 7 p.m. to 7.45 p.m., how many hours does he work

a in a day **b** in a five-day week?

c Calculate his gross weekly wage if he is paid \$13.12 per hour.

4 John Alexander works a 5-day week. He starts work at 7.30 a.m. and finishes at 4.45 p.m. He gets unpaid breaks during the day that total 60 minutes.

a How many hours does he work each day?

b Find his gross weekly pay if he is paid \$18.80 an hour.

5 Lewis John's timesheet showed that he worked 8 hours overtime in addition to his basic 40-hour week. If his basic hourly rate is \$11.10 and overtime is paid at time-and-a-half, find his gross pay for the week.

6 During the week before Christmas, Pearl Rampersand worked 9 hours each day from Monday to Friday together with 4 hours on Saturday. Her normal working week was $7\frac{1}{2}$ hours each day from Monday to Friday.

a How many hours make up her normal working week?

b Calculate her basic weekly wage at \$11.00 an hour.

c How much overtime did she work?

d Calculate her gross wage if overtime was paid at time-and-a-half.

7 Phil Stroud works a basic week of $41\frac{1}{2}$ hours. Overtime is paid at time-and-three-quarters. How much does he earn in a week when he works $48\frac{3}{4}$ hours if his normal hourly rate is \$9.28?

8 In addition to a weekly wage of $560, Tom Francis is paid a bonus of $1 for every box of stationery he sells after the first 35. During one week last month he sold 45 on Monday, 32 on Tuesday, 47 on Wednesday, 24 on Thursday and 56 on Friday. Calculate Tom's gross earnings for the week.

9 Felix Khan is paid a basic weekly wage of $490 plus commission of 2% on all sales over $510. Find his gross income in a week when he sells goods to the value of $15 128.

10 Peter Roberts is paid a basic wage of $370 per week plus commission of $1\frac{1}{2}$% on all sales over $2000. Find his gross income in a week when he sells goods to the value of $29 200.

11 Enid Hosein receives an annual salary of $9768.

   a If she is paid once a calendar month, calculate her gross monthly salary.

   b Deductions from her monthly salary amount to 12% of her earnings. Calculate her net monthly salary.

12 Peter John receives his pension once every four weeks. Each payment is $3808. This amount is his net pension after 15% has been deducted from the gross amount due.

   a How many payments does Peter receive in a year?

   b Calculate his gross pension for each four-week period.

   c Hence calculate his gross annual pension.

Taxes

Most people who work pay tax on their income. This is known as *income tax,* and the amount varies depending on the amount earned. In general the more you earn the more you pay.

The government is forever looking for ways of extracting money from us to pay for its spending. One such way is to put a tax on almost everything that is sold. This *sales tax* is usually a fixed percentage of the selling price. It is also called value added tax (VAT) in some countries.

Exercise 13c

1 Jane Axe earns $20 000 a year. She pays tax on this at 15%.

   a How much tax must she pay?

   b Find her net income.

Net income is the income received after the tax is deducted.

2 Freddy Davis earns $35 000 a year. He pays tax at 18%.

   a How much tax does he pay?

   b Work out his net income   i a year   ii a week.

3 Complete the table:

Name	Gross weekly pay	Tax rate	Tax due	Net weekly pay
M Davis	\$1640	10%		
P Evans	\$2460	12%		
G Brown	\$3530	18%		
A Khan	\$4364	25%		

4 A CD costs \$76 plus sales tax at 12%. Find

a the sales tax to be added **b** the price I must pay for the CD.

In questions **5** to **7** find the total purchase price of the item. Take the rate of sales tax as 17.5%.

5 An electric cooker marked \$3200 + sales tax.

6 A calculator costing \$40 + sales tax.

7 A van marked \$42 000 + sales tax.

8 The price tag on a television gives \$1310 plus sales tax at 15%. What does the customer have to pay?

9 In March, Nicki looked at a camera costing \$640 plus sales tax. The sales tax rate at that time was $17\frac{1}{2}$%. How much would the camera have cost in March? Nicki decided to wait until June to buy the camera but by then the sales tax had been raised to 22%. How much did she have to pay?

10 An electric cooker was priced in a showroom at \$2200 plus sales tax at 15%.

a What was the price to the customer?

Later in the year sales tax was increased to 17.5%. The showroom manager placed a notice on the cooker that read:

Due to the increase in sales tax, this cooker will now cost you \$2593.25

b Was the manager correct?

c If your answer is 'Yes', state how the manager calculated the new price. If your answer is 'No', give your reason and find the correct price.

Property tax

The government needs to collect money to pay for the services they provide for the community. One method is to tax property. This tax varies considerably. It depends on such factors as the size of the property, where it is located and what it is used for.

One method of determining how much is to be paid on a particular property is to charge according to its rateable value.

Exercise 13d

The rateable value of a property is \$1850. How much is due in rates when the rate is 32 c in the \$?

32 c in the \$ means that 32 c is charged for each \$ of rateable value.

Sum due is $32\text{c} \times 1850$

$= 59\,200\text{c}$

$= \$592$

1. Fred Burrows lives in a property with a rateable value of \$2650. How much is due in rates when the rate is
   a \$0.24 in the \$ **b** 36c in the \$ **c** \$0.55 in the \$?
2. The rateable value of Mr Francis' property is \$1640. At present the property tax is 40 c in the \$. Next year it will increase by 10%. How much will Mr Francis have to pay
   a this year **b** next year?
3. The rateable value of a house in Princess Street is \$1500 whereas the rateable value of a house in Riverside Row is \$1800.
   a When the rate of tax is 44c in the \$ how much is the property tax for a house in
   i Princess Street **ii** Riverside Road?
   b There are 35 houses in Princess Street. Find the total collected from all the houses in this street.
   c If there are 44 houses in Riverside Row how much more is collected in total from Riverside Row than from Princess Street?
4. The total rateable value of the properties in a town is \$12 000 000.
   a How much income would be generated by a rate of
   i 4% **ii** 38 c in the \$?
   b What rate in the \$ is needed to collect
   i \$4 200 000 **ii** \$6 600 000?

Saving and borrowing

In Book 1 we saw that you could calculate the *simple interest*, \$*I*, on a sum of money using the formula $I = \frac{PRT}{100}$ where *P* is the principal, *R* the rate per cent each year, and *T* the time in years for which the principal is borrowed or invested. The formula can be arranged as $100I = PRT$, which can be used to find any one quantity if the other three are known.

Sometimes, when the interest is due, it is added to the sum invested.

Suppose \$2000 is invested for 1 year at 8%.

The interest earned is $\$2000 \times 0.08 = \$160$

so the amount at the end of the year is \$2160.

If this amount is invested for a year at 8% the interest due is $\$2160 \times 0.08 = \$172.80$

The amount now is $\$2160 + \$172.80 = \$2332.80$

If you invest money, do not spend the interest, and the annual rate stays the same, your money will increase by larger and larger amounts each year. The total amount by which it grows is called the *compound interest*.

Exercise 13e

1 Find the simple interest on

- a \$420 invested for 3 years at 10% p.a.
- b \$280 invested for 6 years at 12% p.a.
- c \$834 invested for 5 years at 9% p.a.
- d \$500 invested for 8 years at $12\frac{1}{2}\%$ p.a.
- e \$726 invested for 3 years at $7\frac{1}{2}\%$ p.a.

2 What sum of money invested for 5 years at 12% p.a. gives \$264 simple interest?

3 How long must \$370 be invested at 9% p.a. simple interest to give interest of \$233.10?

4 What annual rate of simple interest is necessary to give interest of \$416 on a principal of \$800 invested for 8 years?

5 What sum of money earns \$312 simple interest if invested for 8 years at 13%?

6 Find the annual rate per cent that earns \$234 simple interest when \$900 is invested for $6\frac{1}{2}$ years.

7 Find the amount if \$280 is invested for 5 years at 9% p.a. simple interest.

Find the compound interest on \$550 invested for 2 years at 6%.

Interest for first year at 6% is 6% of the original principal.

New principal at end of first year = 100% of original principal + 6% of original principal
= 106% of original principal
= $1.06 \times$ original principal

$\therefore$ principal at end of first year $= 1.06 \times \$550 = \$583$

Similarly, new principal at end of second year = 106% of principal at beginning of second year
= 1.06 × \$583 = \$617.98

Compound interest = principal at end of second year – original principal
= \$617.98 – \$550 = \$67.98

Find the compound interest on

8 \$200 for 2 years at 10% p.a.

9 \$300 for 2 years at 12% p.a.

10 \$400 for 3 years at 8% p.a.

11 \$650 for 3 years at 9% p.a.

12 \$520 for 2 years at 13% p.a.

13 \$624 for 3 years at 11% p.a.

14 \$40 000 is invested at compound interest of 10% each year. What will it be worth in 2 years' time?

15 Brian Barnes borrows \$5000 at 12% compound interest. He agrees to clear the debt at the end of 2 years. How much must he pay?

16 A postage stamp increases in value by 15% each year. If it is bought for \$50, what will it be worth in 3 years' time?

17 A motorcycle bought for \$1500 depreciates in value by 10% each year. Find its value after 3 years.

Find 10% of the purchase price and subtract this from the purchase price to give the value after 1 year. Now find 10% of the new value. Deduct this from the value at the end of the first year to give the value at the end of the second year, and so on.

18 A motor car bought for \$20 000 depreciates in any one year by 20% of its value at the beginning of that year. Find its value after 2 years.

19 An antique silver teapot bought for \$900 appreciates by 5% a year. Find its value after

a 3 years **b** 5 years.

20 A property bought for \$400 000 depreciated by 10% a year for the first 4 years after it had been purchased.

What was its estimated value

a after 2 years **b** after 4 years?

Telephone bills

Today, more and more people use a cell phone. Users can buy such a telephone outright and pay a monthly charge to their provider, or they can hire the phone and at the end of the contract period, the cell phone becomes theirs. From then on they can pay a much smaller charge or, as the service provider hopes, upgrade to a more up-to-date device.

Many people still use a landline. The cost of calls on a landline depends on the line rental charge, the distance between the caller and the person being called, the length of the call and the time of day at which the call is being made.

Exercise 13f

1 Sheila Persad buys a cell phone for $2600 and has to spend $70 a month for the SIM card.

  a How much does the phone cost her for the first two years?

  b If she had opted for a two-year contract the terms would have been $189 a month with no other charges.
  Would this have been a cheaper way of having a cell phone?
  Calculate the cost of each method of having a cell phone to justify your answer.

2 Mr Ramkissoon has a cell phone provided by his employer. It costs $105 a month but there are extra costs when he exceeds the agreed usage. Each extra call costs 20 c a minute, extra texts cost 15 c each and there is a charge of 55 c for each extra 10 megabyte of data downloaded.

  a Calculate Mr Ramkissoon's total bill for a month when he makes 25 extra calls totalling 205 minutes, sends 36 additional texts and uses 40 MB for downloading extra data.

  b The company could have agreed to a different arrangement costing $145 a month with no extra charges. Would this have been a cheaper way of providing Mr Ramkissoon with a cell phone? Justify your answer.

Questions **3** to **8** refer to landline telephones. For these there is a fixed charge for each metered unit used, plus a standing charge. Bills are normally paid quarterly.

Find the quarterly bill for each of the following households.

	Name	Number of units used	Cost per unit	Standing charge
3	Mr Ali	850	6 c	$35
4	Mrs Persad	1235	7 c	$44.50
5	Ms Roberts	997	9 c	$37.80
6	Mr Phillips	573	8.2 c	$52.10
7	Ms Maharaj	1690	11.5 c	$48.75
8	Mrs Charles	884	9.4 c	$55.34

Electricity bills

Electrical appliances are rated in kilowatts (kW) or watts (W), where 1 kW = 1000 W.

A *kilowatt-hour* is the unit of electrical power. Apart from a quarterly standing charge, the amount we pay for electricity depends on the number of units of electricity, or kilowatt-hours, we have consumed. The cost per unit often increases after a certain number of units have been used. Electrical appliances that provide heat cost far more to run than lights. A 2 kW electric fire costs much more to run per hour than a 40 W light bulb – actually fifty times as much.

Exercise 13g

1 How many kilowatt-hours (units of electricity) will each of the following appliances use in 1 hour?

a a 2 kW electric fire **b** a 40 W bulb **c** a 6 kW cooker

2 How many units of electricity would

a a 1 kW electric fire use in 4 hours

b a 40 W bulb use in a week if it was used for 6 hours every day

c a 150 W refrigerator use in 24 hours?

3 How long could the following appliances run on 1 unit of electricity?

a a 120 W television set

b a 350 W power tool

c a 5 W bulb

d a 2 kW electric fire

4 If 1 unit of electricity costs 8 c how much does it cost to run

a a 100 W bulb for 10 hours

b a 3 kW heater for 30 minutes

c a 5 W clock for a week?

Find the quarterly electricity bills for each of the following households:

	Name	Standing charge	Number of units used	Cost per unit
5	Mr Singh	\$25	400	5 c
6	Mrs Charles	\$35	760	8 c
7	Mrs Lewis	\$27.80	850	12 c
8	Mr Joseph	\$35.38	1447	7.66 c
9	Mrs Francis	\$40.22	1038	6.47 c
10	Mr Pierre	\$34.40	953	11.5 c

Find the quarterly electricity bills for each of the following households. Assume that there is standing charge of $30 and that off-peak units are bought at half price.

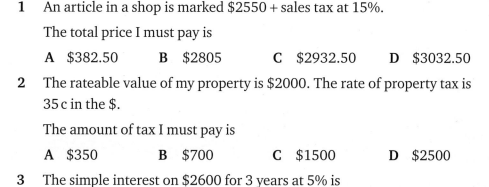

	Name	Number of units used at the basic price	Number of off-peak units used	Basic cost per unit
11	Mrs Roberts	1200	600	10 c
12	Mr Williams	1400	500	8 c
13	Mr Persad	850	750	9.5 c
14	Mrs Bennett	776	455	8.45 c

Mixed exercise

Exercise 13h

Select the letter that gives the correct answer.

1 An article in a shop is marked $2550 + sales tax at 15%.

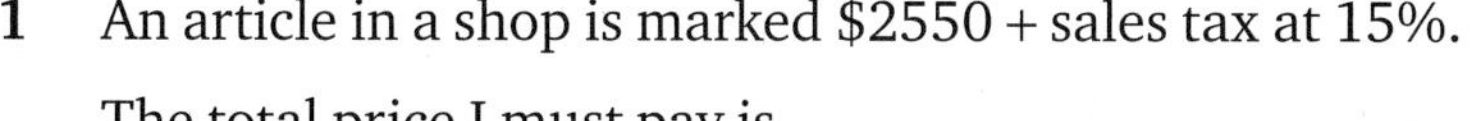

The total price I must pay is

A $382.50 **B** $2805 **C** $2932.50 **D** $3032.50

2 The rateable value of my property is $2000. The rate of property tax is 35 c in the $.

The amount of tax I must pay is

A $350 **B** $700 **C** $1500 **D** $2500

3 The simple interest on $2600 for 3 years at 5% is

A $285 **B** $295 **C** $325 **D** $390

4 Last quarter the standing charge for my landline telephone was $53.50. In addition I used 2140 units at 8.5 c per unit. The total quarterly bill was

A $181.90 **B** $231.90 **C** $235.40 **D** $243.50

5 How long would a 75 W bulb take to use 1 kW hour of electricity?

A 75 min **B** 6 h 20 min **C** 12 h **D** 13 h 20 min

6 If 1 unit of electricity costs 9 c, how much does it cost to run a 3 kW fire for 4 hours?

A 96 c **B** 98 c **C** $1.08 **D** $2.16

Investigation

Look up the meaning of 'inflation' in your dictionary, then discuss it with your teacher.

Now try the following problem.

1 If an item is bought for $1.00 now and inflation continues at 10% per year, how many years will it take for the price to double? Make up a table like the one below to help you.

Year	Cost
Now	$1.00
1	$1.00 + (0.10 × 1.00) = 1.1 × 1.00 = $1.10
2	$1.10 +(0.10 × 1.10) = 1.1 × 1.10 = $1.21

Compute the remaining costs.

2 Investigate inflation rates in your country.

3 If you invest $1000 in your country at 5% compound interest and the inflation rate is 10% per annum, are you better off or worse off?

Puzzle

Farmer Giles has a problem. He has 4 hens and they laid 4 eggs in 4 days. He buys another 8 hens and has an order for 36 eggs. How long will it take 12 hens to lay 36 eggs?

In this chapter you have seen that...

- ✔ wages can be checked when you have all the relevant details
- ✔ there are deductions made from earnings for tax and other things
- ✔ sales tax is added to the selling price of an article at a fixed rate by the government
- ✔ bills for domestic utilities usually include a fixed charge plus a charge for the number of units used
- ✔ you earn money, called interest, when you invest money
- ✔ simple interest is when the amount invested remains the same but the interest is added every year
- ✔ compound interest is when the interest is added to the amount so the sum on which the interest is paid increases every year
- ✔ you have to pay, often at very high cost, when you borrow money.

14 Simultaneous equations

At the end of this chapter you should be able to...

1 solve a pair of simultaneous equations by

  a the method of elimination

  b the substitution method

  c a graphical method.

2 solve problems using simultaneous equations

3 identify a pair of equations which have

  a no solution

  b an infinite number of solutions.

Did you know?

Equations containing several unknown quantities were known to the ancient Egyptians, Greeks and Indians. The Hindus used the names of colours to distinguish the unknown quantities.

You need to know...

✔ how to solve a linear equation in one unknown

✔ the rules for working with negative numbers

✔ how to draw the graph of a straight line from its equation.

Key words

elimination, equation, infinite, simultaneous, substitution

Equations with two unknown quantities

Up to now the equations we have solved have had only one unknown quantity, but there can be more.

Looking at the equation $2x+y=8$, we can see that there are many possible values which will fit, for instance $x=2$ and $y=4$, or $x=1$ and $y=6$. We could also have $x=-1$ and $y=10$ or even $x=1.681$ and $y=4.638$. Indeed, there is an *infinite* set of pairs of solutions.

If, however, we are *also* told that $x+y=5$, then we shall find that not every pair of numbers that satisfies the first equation also satisfies the second. While $x=2$, $y=4$ satisfies the first equation, it does not satisfy $x+y=5$. On the other hand $x=3,\ y=2$ satisfies both equations.

These two equations together form a pair of *simultaneous* equations. 'Simultaneous' means that the two equations are both satisfied by the same values of x and y; that is, when x has the same value in both equations then y has the same value in both.

There are several different methods for solving simultaneous equations. We start with the simplest.

Elimination method

Whenever we meet a new type of equation, we try to reorganise it so that it is similar to equations we have already met.

Previous equations have had only one unknown quantity, so we try to *eliminate* one of the two unknowns.

Consider the pair of equations

$$2x+y=8 \qquad [1]$$
$$x+y=5 \qquad [2]$$

In this case, if we try subtracting the second equation from the first we find that the y term disappears but the x term does not:

i.e. [1] – [2] gives $x=3$

Then, substituting 3 for x in equation [2], we see that $3+y=5$ so $y=2$

We can check that $x=3$ and $y=2$ also satisfy equation [1].

Notice that it is essential to number the equations and to say that you are subtracting them.

Sometimes it is easier to subtract the first equation from the second rather than the second equation from the first. (In this case we would write equation [1] again, underneath equation [2].)

Sometimes we can eliminate x rather than y.

Exercise 14a

Solve the equations $\begin{aligned} x+y&=5 \\ 3x+y&=7 \end{aligned}$

$$x+y=5 \qquad [1]$$
$$3x+y=7 \qquad [2]$$
$$x+y=5 \qquad [1]$$

[2] – [1] gives $2x=2$

$$x=1$$

(To find y choose the simpler equation, i.e. the first.)
Substituting 1 for x in [1] gives

$$1+y=5$$
$$y=4$$

(Check in the equation *not* used for finding y.)

Check in [2] left-hand side $= 3+4$
$= 7 =$ right-hand side

Therefore the solution is $x=1, y=4$

Solve the following pairs of equations:

1 $x+y=5$
$4x+y=14$

2 $5x+y=14$
$3x+y=10$

3 $2a+b=11$
$4a+b=17$

4 $2x+3y=23$
$x+3y=22$

<u>**5**</u> $5x+2y=14$
$7x+2y=22$

<u>**6**</u> $x+2y=12$
$x+y=7$

<u>**7**</u> $4p+3q=-5$
$7p+3q=-11$

<u>**8**</u> $12x+5y=65$
$9x+5y=50$

9 $3x+4y=15$
$3x+2y=12$

10 $9c+2d=54$
$c+2d=6$

<u>**11**</u> $2x+3y=-8$
$2x+y=-4$

<u>**12**</u> $9x+5y=45$
$4x+5y=45$

Not all pairs of simultaneous equations can be solved by subtracting one from the other.

Consider $4x+y=6$ [1]
$2x-y=0$ [2]

If we subtract we get $2x+2y=6$ which is no improvement.

On the other hand, if we add we get $6x=6$ which eliminates y.

If the signs in front of the letter to be eliminated are the same we should *subtract*;
if the signs are different we should *add*.

Exercise 14b

Solve the equations $x - 2y = 1$
$3x + 2y = 19$

$$x - 2y = 1 \quad [1]$$
$$3x + 2y = 19 \quad [2]$$

[1] + [2] gives $4x = 20$
$x = 5$

(It is easier to use the equation with the + sign to find y.)

Substitute 5 for x in [2] $15 + 2y = 19$

Subtract 15 from both sides $2y = 4$
$y = 2$

Check in [1] left-hand side = 5 – 4 = 1 = right-hand side

Therefore the solution is $x = 5, y = 2$

Solve the following pairs of equations:

1 $x - y = 2$
$3x + y = 10$

2 $2x - y = 6$
$3x + y = 14$

3 $p + 2q = 11$
$3p - 2q = 1$

4 $3a - b = 10$
$3a + b = 2$

5 $6x + 2y = 19$
$x - 2y = 2$

6 $4x + y = 37$
$2x - y = 17$

<u>7</u> $x + y = 2$
$2x - y = 10$

<u>8</u> $5p + 3q = 5$
$4p - 3q = 4$

<u>9</u> $3x - 4y = -24$
$5x + 4y = 24$

To solve the following equations, first decide whether to add or subtract:

10 $3x + 2y = 12$
$x + 2y = 8$

11 $x - 2y = 6$
$4x + 2y = 14$

12 $x + 3y = 12$
$x + y = 8$

13 $9x + 2y = 48$
$x - 2y = 2$

14 $4x + y = 19$
$3x + y = 15$

<u>15</u> $2x + 3y = 13$
$2x + 5y = 21$

<u>16</u> $5x - 2y = 24$
$x + 2y = 0$

<u>17</u> $x + 3y = 0$
$x - y = -4$

<u>18</u> $5p - 3q = 9$
$4p + 3q = 9$

Solve the equations $\begin{aligned} 4x - y &= 10 \\ x - y &= 1 \end{aligned}$

$$4x - y = 10 \quad [1]$$
$$x - y = 1 \quad [2]$$

(The signs in front of the y terms are the same so we subtract:
remember that $-y-(-y) = -y + y = 0$)

[1] – [2] gives $3x = 9$

$x = 3$

Substitute 3 for x in [2] $3 - y = 1$

Add y to both sides $3 = 1 + y$

Subtract 1 from both sides $2 = y$

Check in [1] left-hand side $= 12 - 2 = 10 =$ right-hand side

Therefore the solution is $x = 3, y = 2$

Solve the following pairs of equations:

19 $2x - y = 4$
$x - y = 1$

20 $2p - 3q = -7$
$4p - 3q = 1$

21 $x - y = 3$
$3x - y = 9$

<u>22</u> $6x - y = 7$
$2x - y = 1$

<u>23</u> $5x - 2y = -19$
$x - 2y = -7$

<u>24</u> $2x - 3y = 14$
$2x - y = 10$

25 $3x - 2y = 14$
$x + 2y = 10$

26 $3p - 5q = -3$
$4p - 5q = 1$

27 $3p + 5q = 17$
$4p + 5q = 16$

<u>28</u> $3p - 5q = 7$
$4p + 5q = -14$

<u>29</u> $3p + 5q = 35$
$4p - 5q = 0$

30 $3x - y = 10$
$x + y = -2$

Harder elimination

Equations are not always as simple as the ones we have had so far.

Consider $2x + 3y = 4$ [1]
$4x + y = -2$ [2]

Whether we add or subtract neither letter will disappear, so it is necessary to do something else first.

If we multiply the second equation by 3 to give $12x + 3y = -6$, we have the same number of y's in each equation. Then we can use the same method as before:

[2] × 3	$12x + 3y = -6$	[3]
	$2x + 3y = 4$	[1]
[3] – [1] gives	$10x = -10$	
	$x = -1$	
Substitute –1 for x in [2]	$-4 + y = -2$	
Add 4 to both sides	$y = 2$	

Therefore the solution is $x = -1, y = 2$

Exercise 14c

Solve the equations $\begin{aligned} 3x - 2y &= 1 \\ 4x + y &= 5 \end{aligned}$

	$3x - 2y = 1$	[1]
	$4x + y = 5$	[2]
[2] × 2 gives	$8x + 2y = 10$	[3]
	$3x - 2y = 1$	[1]
[1] + [3] gives	$11x = 11$	
	$x = 1$	
Substitute 1 for x in [2]	$4 + y = 5$	
Subtract 4 from both sides	$y = 1$	
Check in [1]	left-hand side $= 3 - 2$	
	$= 1 =$ right-hand side	

Therefore the solution is $x = 1, y = 1$

Solve the following pairs of equations:

1 $2x + y = 7$
$3x + 2y = 11$

2 $5x - 4y = -3$
$3x + y = 5$

3 $9x + 7y = 10$
$3x + y = 2$

4 $5x + 3y = 21$
$2x + y = 3$

5 $6x - 4y = -4$
$5x + 2y = 2$

6 $4x + 3y = 25$
$x + 5y = 19$

Solve the following pairs of equations:

7 $5x + 3y = 11$
$4x + 6y = 16$

8 $2x - 3y = 1$
$5x + 9y = 19$

9 $2x + 5y = 1$
$4x + 3y = 9$

10 $9x + 5y = 15$
$3x - 2y = -6$

11 $4x + 3y = 1$
$16x - 5y = 21$

12 $7p + 2q = 22$
$3p + 4q = 11$

Multiplying the top equation by 2 will give $6y$ in both equations.

Exercise 14d

Solve the equations $3x + 5y = 6$
$2x + 3y = 5$

$$3x + 5y = 6 \quad [1]$$
$$2x + 3y = 5 \quad [2]$$

We can choose to either get the same number of x's ([1] × 2 and [2] × 3 does this) or the same number of y's, which is what we will do.

[1] × 3 gives $9x + 15y = 18$ [3]
[2] × 5 gives $10x + 15y = 25$ [4]
$9x + 15y = 18$ [3]
[4] – [3] gives $x = 7$
Substitute 7 for x in [2] $14 + 3y = 5$
Subtract 14 from both sides $3y = -9$
Divide both sides by 3 $y = -3$
Check in [1] left-hand side $= 21 - 15$
$= 6 =$ right-hand side

Therefore the solution is $x = 7, y = -3$

Solve the following pairs of equations:

1 $2x + 3y = 12$
$5x + 4y = 23$

2 $3x - 2y = -7$
$4x + 3y = 19$

3 $2x - 5y = 1$
$5x + 3y = 18$

4 $6x + 5y = 9$
$4x + 3y = 6$

5 $14x - 3y = -18$
$6x + 2y = 12$

6 $6x - 7y = 25$
$7x + 6y = 15$

7 $5x + 4y = 21$
$3x + 6y = 27$

8 $9x + 8y = 17$
$2x - 6y = -4$

9 $9x-2y=14$, $7x+3y=20$

10 $5x+4y=11$, $2x+3y=3$

11 $4x+5y=26$, $5x+4y=28$

12 $2x-6y=-6$, $5x+4y=-15$

13 $5x-6y=6$, $2x+9y=10$

14 $3p+4q=5$, $2p+10q=18$

15 $6x+5y=8$, $3x+4y=1$

16 $7x-3y=20$, $2x+4y=-4$

17 $10x+3y=12$, $3x+5y=20$

18 $6x-5y=4$, $4x+2y=-8$

19 $5x+3y=8$, $3x+5y=8$

20 $7x+2y=23$, $3x-5y=4$

21 $6x-5y=17$, $5x+4y=6$

22 $3x+8y=56$, $5x-6y=16$

23 $7x+3y=-9$, $2x+5y=14$

24 $7x+6y=0$, $5x-8y=43$

25 $2x+6y=30$, $3x+10y=49$

26 $4x-3y=-7$, $3x+2y=16$

27 $17x-2y=47$, $5x-3y=9$

28 $8x+3y=-17$, $7x-4y=5$

Mixed questions

Exercise 14e

Solve the following pairs of equations:

1 $x+2y=9$, $2x-y=-2$

2 $x+y=4$, $x+2y=9$

3 $2x+3y=0$, $3x+2y=5$

4 $3x-y=-10$, $4x-y=-4$

5 $5x+2y=16$, $2x-3y=-5$

6 $3x+2y=-5$, $3x-4y=1$

7 $x+y=6$, $x-y=1$

8 $3x-5y=13$, $2x+5y=-8$

9 $7x+3y=35$, $2x-5y=10$

10 $9x+2y=8$, $7x+3y=12$

11 $2x-5y=1$, $3x+4y=13$

12 $3x-2y=-2$, $5x-y=-15$

Sometimes the equations are arranged in an awkward fashion and need to be rearranged before solving them.

Exercise 14f

Solve the equations $x=4-3y$
$2y-x=1$

$$x=4-3y \qquad [1]$$
$$2y-x=1 \qquad [2]$$

(We must first arrange the equations so that the letters are in the same corresponding positions in both equations.

By adding $3y$ to both sides, equation [1] can be written $3y+x=4$)

$$3y+x=4 \qquad [3]$$
$$2y-x=1 \qquad [2]$$

[3] + [2] gives $5y = 5$

$y = 1$

Substitute 1 for y in [1] $x = 4 - 3$

$x = 1$

Check in [2] left-hand side $= 2 - 1 = 1 =$ right-hand side

Therefore the solution is $x = 1, y = 1$

Solve the following pairs of equations:

1 $y = 6 - x$
$2x + y = 8$

2 $x - y = 2$
$2y = x + 1$

3 $3 = 2x + y$
$4x + 6 = 10y$

<u>**4**</u> $9 + x = y$
$x + 2y = 12$

<u>**5**</u> $2y = 16 - x$
$x - 2y = -8$

<u>**6**</u> $3x + 4y = 7$
$2x = 5 - 3y$

So far, we have rearranged the equations so the letter terms are in the same order on the left-hand side and the right-hand side is just the number term. However, as long as the x and y and number terms are in corresponding positions in the two equations, we can work with them without rearrangement.

Solve the equations $y = x + 5$
$y = 7 - x$

$y = x + 5$ [1]

$y = 7 - x$ [2]

Rewrite [1] as $y = 5 + x$ [3]

[2] + [3] gives $2y = 12$

$y = 6$

Substitute 6 for y in [1] $6 = x + 5$

$x = 1$

Check in [2] left-hand side $= 6$

right-hand side $= 7 - 1 = 6$

Therefore the solution is $x = 1, y = 6$

Solve the following pairs of equations:

7 $y = 9 + x$
$y = 11 - x$

8 $x = 3 + y$
$2x = 4 - y$

9 $y = 4 - x$
$y = x + 6$

<u>**10**</u> $2y = 4 + x$
$y = x + 8$

<u>**11**</u> $x + 4 = y$
$y = 10 - 2x$

<u>**12**</u> $x + y = 12$
$y = 3 + x$

Special cases

Some pairs of equations have no solution and some have an infinite number of solutions.

Exercise 14g

Try solving the following pairs of equations. Comment on why the method breaks down:

1 $x + 2y = 6$
$x + 2y = 7$

2 $3x + 4y = 1$
$6x + 8y = 2$

3 $y = 4 + 2x$
$y - 2x = 6$

4 $9x = 3 - 6y$
$3x + 2y = 1$

5 Make up other pairs of equations which either have no solution or have an infinite set of solutions.

Substitution method

This is a method for solving simultaneous equations that avoids adding or subtracting equations. We start with one of the equations and rearrange it to make one unknown on its own on one side of the equals sign.

For example, for the equations $2x - y = 9$ [1]
and $3y + x = 1$ [2]

we can choose [2] to 'solve' for x: $x = 1 - 3y$ (subtracting $3y$ from both sides)

The next step is to substitute $1 - 3y$ for x in equation [1].

This gives $2(1 - 3y) - y = 9$

Solving this equation gives

$$
\begin{aligned}
2 - 6y - y &= 9 && \text{(expanding the bracket)}\\
2 - 7y &= 9 && \text{(collecting like terms)}\\
2 &= 9 + 7y && \text{(adding } 7y \text{ to both sides)}\\
-7 &= 7y && \text{(subtracting 9 from both sides)}\\
-1 &= y \quad \text{or} \quad y = -1
\end{aligned}
$$

Then using $x = 1 - 3y$ and substituting -1 for y gives $x = 1 - 3(-1)$
$= 1 + 3 = 4$

So the solution is $x = 4$ and $y = -1$

Exercise 14h

Use the substitution method to solve the following pairs of equations.

1 $2x+y=4$
$5x-2y=1$

2 $3a-2b=1$
$2a=5-b$

3 $3x-y=8$
$y=2-2x$

4 $2x+3y=4$
$4x=1-y$

Start by choosing the equation with a single letter and 'solve' it for that letter, i.e. make that letter the subject of the 'formula'.

5 $3s-2t=1$
$3t=4s$

6 $2a=b-3$
$2a-5b=1$

Use the second equation to find t in terms of s. Be careful with the fractions.

Use the substitution method to solve questions **7** to **12** of Exercise 14f.

Puzzle

There are 12 identical coins. One of them is a forgery and its weight is different from the others. It is not known if the forged coin is heavier or lighter than the genuine coins. How can you find the forged coin by three weighings on a simple balance?

Problems

You can solve problems involving two unknowns by forming a pair of simultaneous equations. Then use either elimination or substitution to solve the equations.

Exercise 14i

I think of two numbers. If I add three times the smaller number to the bigger number I get 14. If I subtract the bigger number from twice the smaller number I get 1. Find the two numbers.

First allocate letters to the unknown numbers.

Let the smaller number be x and the bigger number be y.

Now interpret the information in terms of these letters.

Second sentence $\Rightarrow$	$3x+y=14$	[1]
Third sentence $\Rightarrow$	$2x-y=1$	[2]
[1] + [2] gives	$5x=15$	
	$x=3$	

Substitute 3 for x in [1] $\quad 9 + y = 14$

Subtract 9 from both sides $\quad y = 5$

Therefore, the two numbers are 3 and 5.

(Check by reading the original statements to see if the numbers fit.)

Solve the following problems by forming a pair of simultaneous equations:

1 The sum of two numbers is 20 and their difference is 4. Find the numbers.

2 The sum of two numbers is 16 and they differ by 6. What are the numbers?

3 I think of two numbers. If I double the first and add the second I get 18. If I double the first and subtract the second I get 14. What are the numbers?

4 Three times a number added to a second number is 33. The first number added to three times the second number is 19. Find the two numbers.

5 Find two numbers such that twice the first added to the second is 26 and the first added to three times the second is 28.

6 Find the two numbers such that twice the first added to the second gives 27 and twice the second added to the first gives 21.

A shop sells bread rolls. If five brown rolls and six white rolls cost 98 c while three brown rolls and four white rolls cost 62 c, find the cost of each type of roll.

First allocate letters to the unknown quantities.

Let one brown roll cost x c and one white roll cost y c.

Now interpret the information in terms of x and y.

	$5x + 6y = 98$	[1]
	$3x + 4y = 62$	[2]
[1] × 2 gives	$10x + 12y = 196$	[3]
[2] × 3 gives	$9x + 12y = 186$	[4]
[3] – [4] gives	$x = 10$	
Substitute 10 for x in [1]	$50 + 6y = 98$	
Subtract 50 from both sides	$6y = 48$	
	$y = 8$	

Therefore one brown roll costs 10 c and one white roll costs 8 c.

7 I buy x choc ices and y orange ices and spend \$2.30. I buy ten ices altogether. The choc ices cost 30 c each and the orange ices cost 20 c each. How many of each do I buy?

8 x is bigger than y.
The difference between x and y is 18.
Find x and y.

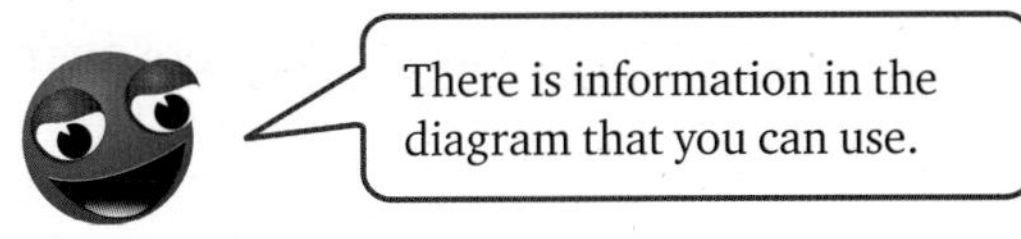

There is information in the diagram that you can use.

9 A cup and saucer cost \$3.15 together. A cup and two saucers cost \$4.50. Find the cost of a cup and of a saucer.

10 The cost of two roti is the same as the cost of three patties. One roti and one patty together cost \$3.50. What do they each cost?

11 In a test, the sum of Harry's marks and Adam's marks is 42. Sam has twice as many marks as Adam, and the sum of Harry's and Sam's marks is 52. What are the marks of each of the three boys?

12 The perimeter of triangle ABC is 14 cm. AB is 2 cm longer than AC. Find x and y.

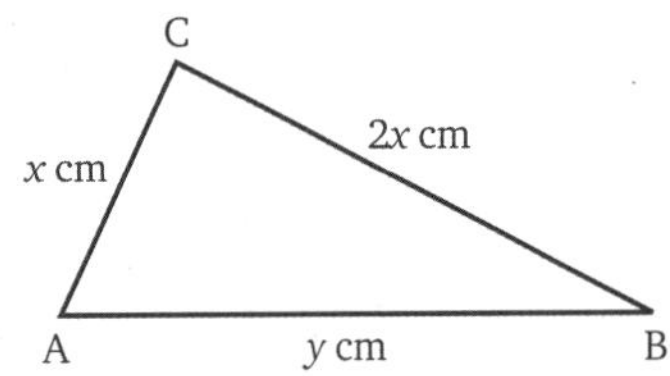

13 The perimeter of the rectangle is 31 cm. The difference between the lengths of AB and BC is $3\frac{1}{2}$ cm.

Find the lengths of AB and BC.

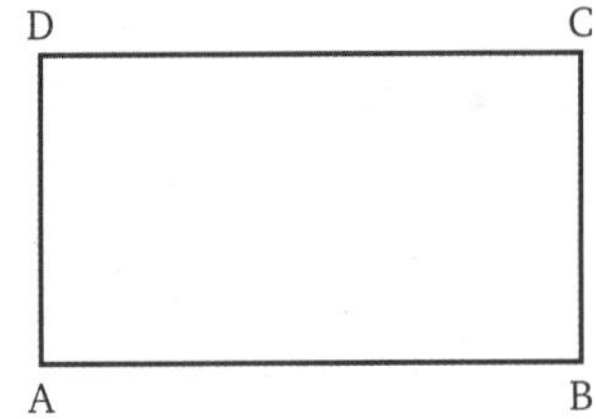

14 The equation of a straight line is $y = mx + c$. When $x = 1, y = 6$ and when $x = 3, y = 10$. Form two equations for m and c and hence find the equation of the line.

Puzzle

Andy wants to invest some money now that will give him enough to pay a deposit on a house in 5 years' time. He sees an advertisement offering a bond that states that after 5 years it would be worth an amount equivalent to earning simple interest paid at 5% per annum.

How much does he need to invest so that the bond will be worth \$60 000 when he withdraws it?

Graphical solutions of simultaneous equations

We saw in Book 2 that when we are given an equation we can draw a graph. Any of the equations which occur in this chapter give us a straight line. Two equations give us two straight lines which usually cross one another.

Consider the two equations $x + y = 4$, $y = 1 + x$

Suppose we know that the x-coordinate of the point of intersection is in the range $0 \leqslant x \leqslant 5$: this means that we can plot these lines in that range.

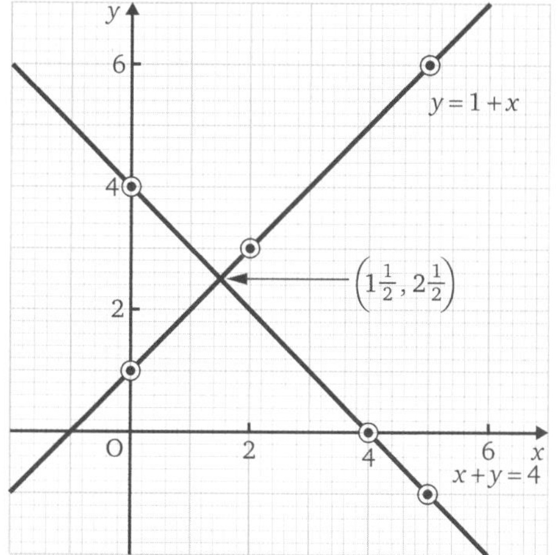

$x + y = 4$

x	0	4	5
y	4	0	−1

$y = 1 + x$

x	0	2	5
y	1	3	6

At the point where the two lines cross, the values of x and y are the same for both equations, so they are the solutions of the pair of equations.

From the graph we see that the solution is $x = 1\frac{1}{2}$, $y = 2\frac{1}{2}$.

Exercise 14j

Solve the following equations graphically. In each case draw axes for x and y and use values in the ranges indicated, taking 2 cm to 1 unit:

1 $x + y = 6$, $y = 3 + x$ $\quad 0 \leqslant x \leqslant 6, 0 \leqslant y \leqslant 6$

2 $x + y = 5$, $y = 2x + 1$ $\quad 0 \leqslant x \leqslant 6, 0 \leqslant y \leqslant 6$

3 $y = 4 + x$, $y = 1 + 3x$ $\quad 0 \leqslant x \leqslant 6, 0 \leqslant y \leqslant 6$

4 $x + y = 1$, $y = x + 2$ $\quad -3 \leqslant x \leqslant 2, -2 \leqslant y \leqslant 4$

5 $2x + y = 3$, $x + y = 2\frac{1}{2}$ $\quad 0 \leqslant x \leqslant 3, -3 \leqslant y \leqslant 3$

<u>**6**</u> $y = 5 - x$, $y = 2 + x$ $\quad 0 \leqslant x \leqslant 5, 0 \leqslant y \leqslant 7$

<u>**7**</u> $3x + 2y = 9$, $2x - 2y = 3$ $\quad 0 \leqslant x \leqslant 4, -2 \leqslant y \leqslant 5$

<u>**8**</u> $2x + 3y = 4$, $y = x + 2$ $\quad -2 \leqslant x \leqslant 2, 0 \leqslant y \leqslant 4$

<u>**9**</u> $x + 3y = 6$, $3x - y = 6$ $\quad 0 \leqslant x \leqslant 5, 0 \leqslant y \leqslant 5$

<u>**10**</u> $x = 2y - 3$, $y = 2x + 1$ $\quad -2 \leqslant x \leqslant 3, 0 \leqslant y \leqslant 4$

Mixed exercise

Exercise 14k

Select the letter that gives the correct answer.

1 If $2x + y = 7$ and $x - y = 2$, then

A $x = 2, y = -3$ B $x = 2, y = -1$ C $x = 2, y = 3$ D $x = 3, y = 1$

2 The values of x and y that satisfy the equations $5x + y = 13$ and $3x - y = 3$ are

A $x = 2, y = 3$ B $x = 2, y = 5$ C $x = 3, y = 2$ D $x = 15, y = 2$

3 The solutions of the equations $4x + 5y = 11$ and $3x + 2y = 3$ are

A $x = -1, y = 2$ B $x = -1, y = 3$ C $x = 1, y = 2$ D $x = 1, y = 3$

4 In a right-angled triangle the difference between the other two angles is 18°.

The other two angles are

A 33° and 57° B 34° and 56° C 37° and 47° D 37° and 57°

5 Two numbers are such that twice the first added to the second gives 17, whereas twice the second added to the first gives 19.

The two numbers that satisfy these statements are

A 3 and 11 B 4 and 9 C 5 and 7 D 5 and 7

Investigation

Try to solve the following equations graphically. Why do you think the method breaks down?

1 $x + y = 9$ $0 \leqslant x \leqslant 9$
$x + y = 4$ $0 \leqslant y \leqslant 9$

2 $y = 2x + 3$ $0 \leqslant x \leqslant 4$
$y = 2x - 1$ $-1 \leqslant y \leqslant 11$

In this chapter you have seen that...

- ✔ two linear equations in two unknowns usually have one solution, that is one value for each unknown
- ✔ you can solve two simultaneous equations by adding or subtracting the equations when they both have the same number of one of the unknowns: this eliminates that unknown
- ✔ you may have to multiply one or both equations by numbers in order to get the same number of one unknown
- ✔ you can also solve two simultaneous equations by using one equation to express one letter in terms of the other letter, then substituting that expression into the other equation; this gives one equation in one unknown
- ✔ you can solve two simultaneous equations graphically by drawing the lines that the equations represent; the point of intersection gives the solution.

REVIEW TEST 2: CHAPTERS 8–14

In questions **1** to **12**, choose the letter for the correct answer.

1 In the diagram LM =

A 14 cm

B 15 cm

C 16 cm

D 20 cm

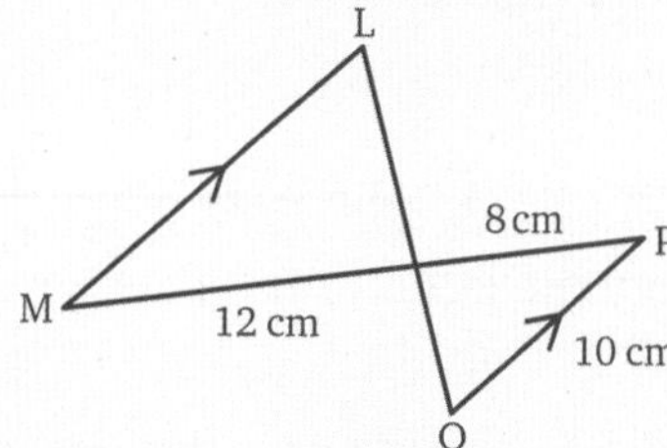

2 The square root of 0.004 325 correct to 3 significant figures is

A 0.067 B 0.0658 C 0.0657 D 0.006 58

3 If 240 is increased by 25% the result is

A 60 B 180 C 300 D 360

4 In triangle ABC, angle A = 90°, AB = 3 cm, AC = 5cm, BC =

A 4 cm B 5 cm C 5.83 cm D 6 cm

5 Correct to 3 significant figures, the hypotenuse of a right-angled triangle in which the other two sides are 5.2 cm and 6.4 cm is

A 8.45 cm B 8.246 cm C 8.25 cm D 8.24 cm

6 The sine of angle A is 0.8290. The value of the supplement of angle A is

A 56° B 124° C 140° D 146°

7 In a regular polygon with 8 sides an exterior angle is

A 60° B 36° C 45° D 30°

8 Which of these triangles have the same area?

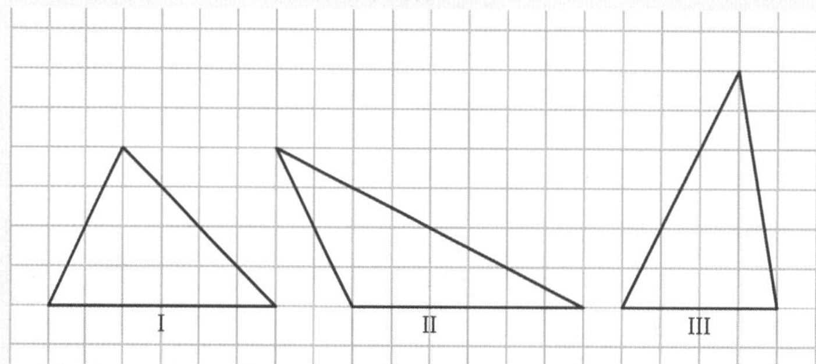

A I and II only B II and III only C I and III only D I, II and III

9 This is a net for a cube.
The corners that meet with B are

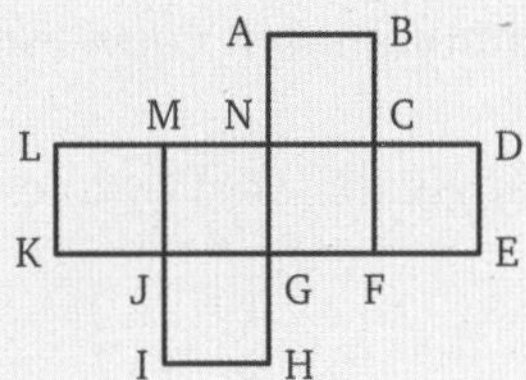

A K and D B D and F C F and H D L and D

10 The interior angle of a regular polygon is 144°. The number of sides this polygon has is

A 6 B 8 C 10 D 12

11 The cross-section of a prism is a regular hexagon. The number of faces it has is

A 6 B 7 C 8 D 9

12 The price of a cell phone is \$700 plus sales tax of 15%. The total cost is

A \$105 B \$715 C \$805 D \$905

13 State whether or not triangles ABC and PQR are similar. If they are, find the length of PR.

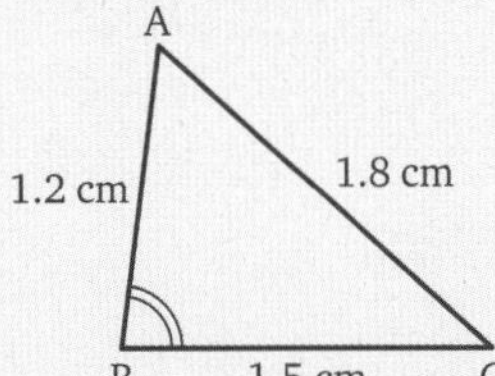

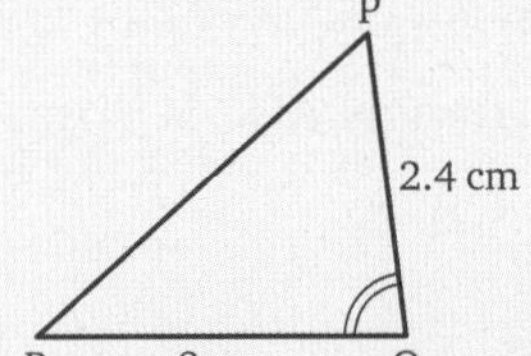

14 The lengths of the diagonals in a rhombus are 18 cm and 24 cm. Find the length of one of the sides of the rhombus.

15 The length of the hypotenuse in a right-angled triangle is 3.9 cm. One of the other sides is 3.6 cm. Find the length of the third side.

16 **a** A television set costs \$2400 plus sales tax at 17.5%. How much must I pay for it?

b A piece of furniture is marked \$1800. In a sale it is marked '20% off'. How much will it cost me?

17 **a** How long will a 40 W electric light bulb operate on 1 unit of electricity?

b If electricity is 10 c a unit, how much does it cost to run this bulb for 10 hours?

18 Solve the simultaneous equations $5x + 2y = 4$, $3x - 4y = 18$

19 Find each angle denoted by a letter.

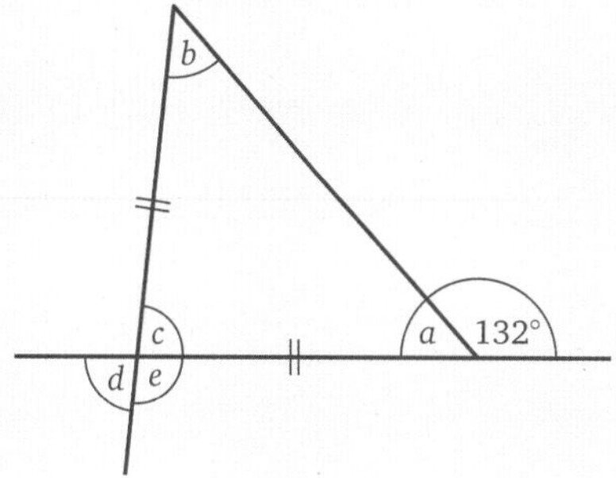

20 In degrees, the angles of a pentagon are x, $x + 37$, $x - 12$, $x + 26$ and $x + 14$.
Form an equation and solve it to find x.
Hence find the difference in the size of the largest and smallest angles.

21 In triangle XYZ, XZ = 30 cm, $\angle YXZ = 90°$ and $\angle XZY = 37°$.
Find **a** XY **b** YZ

22 ABCD is a parallelogram in which $\hat{ADB} = \hat{BDC} = 30°$ and $\hat{DAC} = 60°$.

a Prove that triangles ADE and ABE are congruent.

b Prove that triangle ADC is isosceles.

23 **a** Are triangles ABC and ADE similar?
Justify your answer.

b Which angles are equal?

c What can you say about the lines BC and DE?

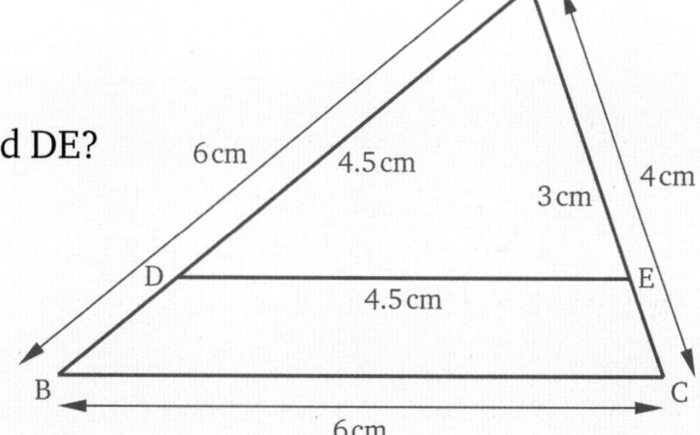

15 Sets

At the end of this chapter you should be able to...

1 remember all the facts relating to sets

2 solve harder problems using Venn diagrams.

Did you know?

One of the best selling mathematics books ever published was *Mathematics for the Million*.

It was written by Lancelot Hogben, an English zoologist and geneticist who held academic posts in the UK, Canada and South Africa. He applied mathematical principles to genetics and was concerned with the way statistical methods could be used in the biological and behavioural sciences. This book was published in 1933.

You need to know...

- ✔ the meaning of: equal sets, empty or null set, finite and infinite sets, intersection and union of two sets, subset, universal set
- ✔ the meaning of the complement of a set
- ✔ the meaning of the symbols $\in$, $\notin$, $\subset$, $\subseteq$, $\cup$, $\cap$, $\varnothing$ and U
- ✔ how to draw a Venn diagram
- ✔ the meaning of $\mathbb{N}$, $\mathbb{Z}$, $\mathbb{Q}$ and $\mathbb{R}$.

Key words

complement, element, empty set, equal set, finite set, infinite set, intersection of sets, member, null set, proper subset, set, subset, union of sets, universal set, Venn diagram, the symbols $\in$, $\notin$, $\subset$, $\subseteq$, $\cup$, $\cap$, $\varnothing$ and U

Reminders

In previous books we introduced set notation and used sets to solve simple problems. We saw that

- a *set* is a collection of things having something in common
- things that belong to a set are called *members* or *elements*
- the symbol $\in$ means 'is a member of' and $\notin$ means 'is not a member of'
- the members in an *infinite set* cannot be counted
- in a *finite set* all the members can be counted
- $n(A)$ means the number of members in set A
- two sets are equal if they contain exactly the same elements or members
- a set with no members is called an *empty set* or *null set*. It is denoted by { } or $\varnothing$
- a set that contains all the elements of the sets under consideration (and possibly some more) is called a *universal set*. It is denoted by U or &
- if all the members of a set B are also members of a set A, then B is a *subset* of A. If B does not contain all the members of A, B is called a *proper subset* of A. This is written $B \subset A$. If B contains all the members of A we write $B \subseteq A$
- $A \cup B$ means the *union* of A and B and is the set of members in A and/or in B
- $A \cap B$ means the *intersection* of A and B and is the set of members in both A and B
- A' means the complement of the set A and is the set of elements in the universal set that are not in A.

Notation

We can describe a set in words, e.g. the set of whole numbers that are less than 20.

We can also describe this set by listing the elements enclosed in curly brackets, e.g.

{1, 2, 3, 4, 5, 6, 7, 8, 9, 10, 11, 12, 13, 14, 15, 16, 17, 18, 19}.

A shorter way of describing this set is to write $\{x{:}1 \leqslant x < 20, x \in \mathbb{N}\}$, where the colon (:) means 'such that'. Remember that $\mathbb{N}$ means the set of natural numbers.

$\{x : 1 \leqslant x < 20, x \in \mathbb{N}\}$ reads 'the values of x such that x is greater than or equal to 1 and less than 20 and x is a member of the set of natural numbers.'

Exercise 15a

1 Are the following sets finite or infinite?

a {even numbers}

b {vowels}

c {number of students in Trinidad}

d {prime numbers less than 30}

2 a Find the number of elements in each set:

i A = {consonants}

ii B = {players in a cricket team}

b $C = \{\text{prime numbers between 10 and 20}\}$

i Find $n(C)$.

ii Write down the subset of C whose elements are odd numbers. Is this a proper subset of C?

iii Write down the subset of C whose elements are even numbers.

3 $U = \{\text{integers bigger than 10 but smaller than 30}\}$
$A = \{\text{prime numbers}\}$, $B = \{\text{integers exactly divisible by 2 and by 3}\}$,
$C = \{\text{factors of 18}\}$.

List the sets A, B and C.

4 List the members of the set $\{x : x \leqslant 10, x \in \mathbb{N}\}$

5 **a** List any ten members of the set $\{x : x = 2n, n \in \mathbb{N}\}$

b Is this set finite or infinite?

6 List the members of the set $\{x: -2 < x < 3, \} x \in \mathbb{Z}\}$

7 List the members of the set $A = \{(x, y) : y = 3x, -1 \leqslant x \leqslant 1, x \in \mathbb{Z}\}$

8 Find $n(A)$ where $A = \{x : x = \sqrt{m}, 0 < m < 20, x \in \mathbb{Z}\}$

9 $U = \{x : 1 \leqslant x < 15, x \in \mathbb{N}\}$
$P = \{\text{multiples of 3}\}$, $Q = \{\text{even numbers}\}$, $R = \{\text{multiples of 5}\}$.
List the sets P, Q and R.

10 $U = \{x : -6 \leqslant x < 6, x \in \mathbb{Z}\}$
$A = \{\text{even numbers}\}$, $B = \{\text{negative numbers}\}$, $C = \{\text{positive prime numbers}\}$.
List the sets A, B and C.

11 List the set A' where $A = \{2, 4, 6\}$ and $U = \{1, 2, 3, 4, 5, 6, 7, 8\}$.

12 **a** Copy the Venn diagram and shade the region representing A'.

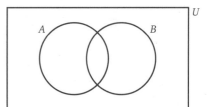

b Copy the Venn diagram and shade the region representing B'.

c Copy the Venn diagram and shade the region representing $(A \cup B)'$.

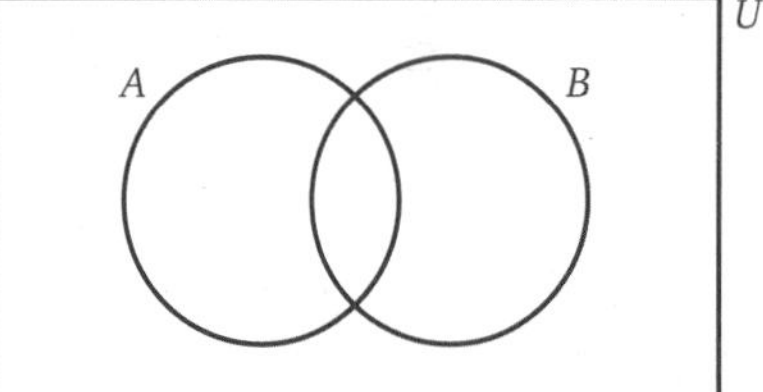

Problems

Exercise 15b

Given $U = \{1, 2, 3, 4, 5, 6, 7, 8, 9, 10\}$

$A = \{\text{odd numbers}\} = \{1, 3, 5, 7, 9\}$

$B = \{\text{multiples of 3}\} = \{3, 6, 9\}$

Show these sets on a Venn diagram.

Use your diagram to list the following sets:

a A' **b** B' **c** $A \cup B$ **d** the complement of $A \cup B$ **e** $A' \cap B'$.

(Each of the numbers in the given sets is placed in the correct position on the following Venn diagram.)

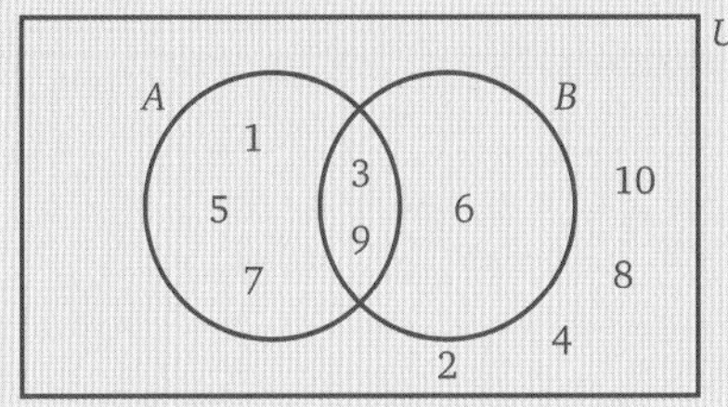

From the diagram

a $A' = \{2, 4, 6, 8, 10\}$ (A' is the set of all members not members of A.)

b $B' = \{1, 2, 4, 5, 7, 8, 10\}$

c $A \cup B = \{1, 3, 5, 6, 7, 9\}$
(the set of members in A or in B; don't count any member twice)

d $(A \cup B)' = \{2, 4, 8, 10\}$

e $A' \cap B' = \{2, 4, 8, 10\}$
(the set of members that are not in A and also not in B)

Notice that $(A \cup B)' = A' \cap B'$

1 $U = \{1, 2, 3, 4, 5\}, A = \{1, 2, 3, 5\}, B = \{2, 4\}$

Show the sets on a Venn diagram and use it to find

a A' **b** B' **c** $A \cup B$ **d** $(A \cup B)'$ **e** $A' \cap B'$

2 $U = \{\text{whole numbers less than } 17\}$
$P = \{\text{multiples of } 3\}$, $Q = \{\text{even numbers}\}$.
Show these on a Venn diagram and use it to find

a P' **b** Q' **c** $P \cup Q$ **d** $(P \cup Q)'$ **e** $P' \cap Q'$

3 $U = \{1, 2, 3, 4, 5, 6, 7, 8, 9, 10, 11, 12\}$

$A = \{\text{multiples of } 4\}$, $B = \{\text{even numbers}\}$.

Show these sets on a Venn diagram and use this diagram to list the sets

a A' **b** B' **c** $A \cup B$ **d** $(A \cup B)'$ **e** $A' \cap B'$

4 $U = \{\text{whole numbers from 10 to 25 inclusive}\}$

$P = \{\text{multiples of } 4\}$, $Q = \{\text{multiples of } 5\}$.

Show these sets on a Venn diagram and use this diagram to list the sets

a P' **b** Q' **c** $P \cup Q$ **d** $(P \cup Q)'$ **e** $P' \cap Q'$

5 $U = \{\text{different letters in the word GENERAL}\}$

$A = \{\text{different letters in the word ANGEL}\}$

$B = \{\text{different letters in the word LEAN}\}$

Show these sets on a Venn diagram and use this diagram to list the sets

a A' **c** $A \cap B$ **e** $(A \cap B)'$

b B' **d** $A \cup B$ **f** $A' \cap B'$

6 $U = \{p, q, r, s, t, u, v, w\}$

$X = \{r, s, t, w\}$, $Y = \{q, s, t, u, v\}$.

Show U, X and Y on a Venn diagram entering all the members.

Hence list the sets

a X' **b** Y' **c** $X' \cap Y'$ **d** $X \cup Y'$ **e** $(X \cup Y)'$

Which two sets are equal?

7 $U = \{1, 2, 3, 4, 5, 6, 7, 8, 9, 10, 11, 12\}$

$X = \{\text{factors of } 12\}$, $Y = \{\text{even numbers}\}$.

Show U, X and Y on a Venn diagram entering all the members.

Hence list the sets

a X' **c** $X' \cap Y'$ **e** $X \cup Y$

b Y' **d** $X' \cup Y'$ **f** $(X \cup Y)'$

Which two sets are equal?

8 Draw this diagram six times. Use shading to illustrate each of the following sets.

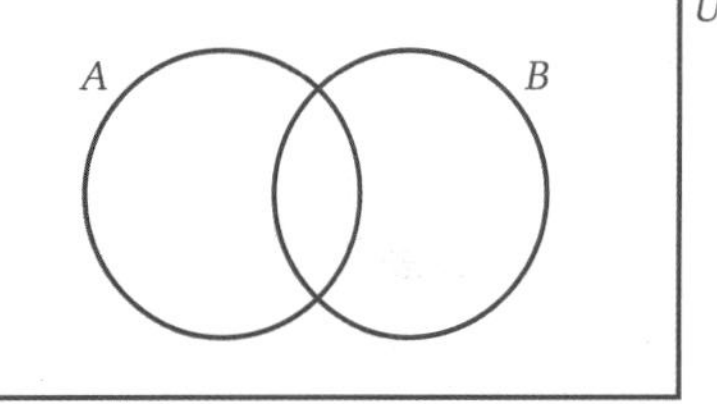

a A' **c** $A' \cap B'$ **e** $A \cup B$

b B' **d** $A' \cup B'$ **f** $(A' \cup B)'$

9 $U = \{\text{different letters in the word MATHEMATICS}\}$

$A = \{\text{different letters in the word ATTIC}\}$

$B = \{\text{different letters in the word TASTE}\}$

Show U, A and B on a Venn diagram entering all the elements.

Hence list the sets

a A' **c** $A \cup B$ **e** $A' \cup B'$

b B' **d** $(A \cup B)'$ **f** $A' \cap B'$

10 $U = \{\text{pupils in my class}\}$

$P = \{\text{those with compasses}\}$

$Q = \{\text{those with protractors}\}$

Describe

a P' **c** $P' \cap Q'$ **e** $P \cup Q$

b Q' **d** $(P \cup Q)'$

11 $U = \{x : 1 \leqslant x < 12, x \in \mathbb{N}\}$

$A = \{\text{multiples of } 3\}$, $B = \{\text{even numbers}\}$.

List the sets

a A' **b** B' **c** $A' \cap B'$ **d** $(A \cup B)'$

12 $U = \{x: -6 \leqslant x < 8, x \in \mathbb{Z}\}$

$P = \{\text{odd numbers}\}$, $Q = \{\text{prime numbers}\}$.

List the sets

a P' **c** $P' \cap Q'$ **e** $(P \cup Q)'$

b Q' **d** $P' \cup Q'$

13 $U = \{x : 10 \leqslant x < 25, x \in \mathbb{N}\}$

$A = \{\text{multiples of } 4\}$, $B = \{\text{multiples of } 3\}$.

List the sets

a A' **b** B' **c** $A' \cap B'$ **d** $(A \cup B)'$

Number of members

Exercise 15c

Illustrate on a Venn diagram the sets A and B if

$A = \{\text{Sunday, Monday, Tuesday, Wednesday}\}$
$B = \{\text{Wednesday, Thursday, Friday, Saturday, Sunday}\}$

Use your diagram to find

a $n(A)$ **b** $n(B)$ **c** $n(A \cup B)$ **d** $n(A \cap B)$

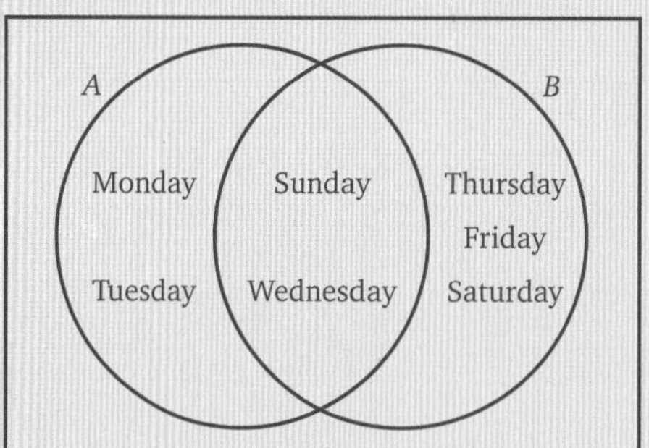

Counting the number of elements in the various regions gives

a $n(A) = 4$ **b** $n(B) = 5$

c $n(A \cup B) = 7$ **d** $n(A \cap B) = 2$

In questions **1** to **4** count the number of elements in the various regions to find

a $n(A)$ **b** $n(B)$ **c** $n(A \cup B)$ **d** $n(A \cap B)$

1

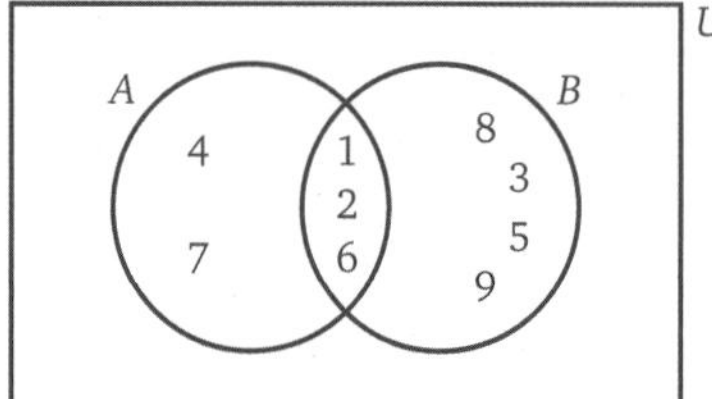

3

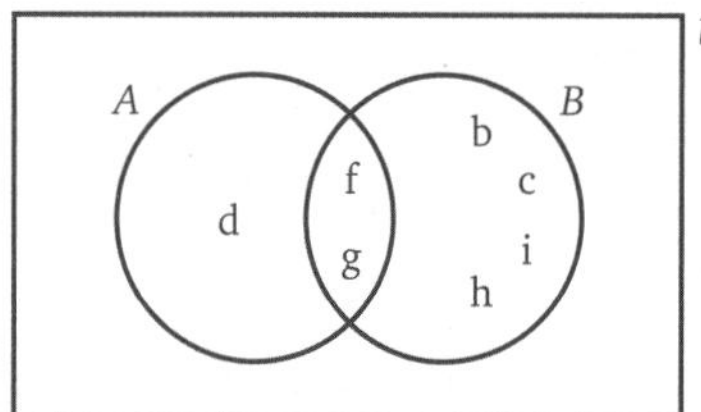

2

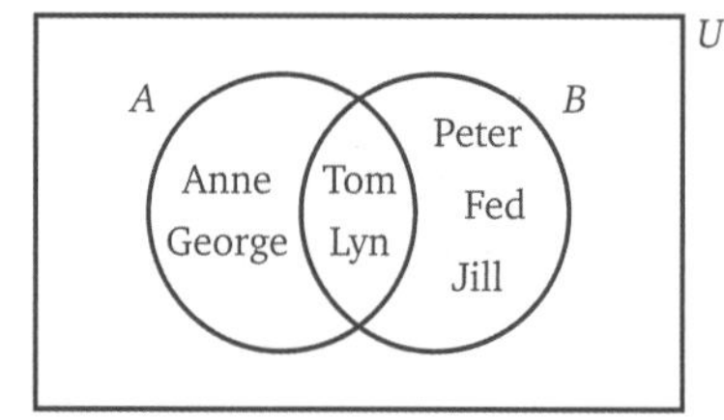

4

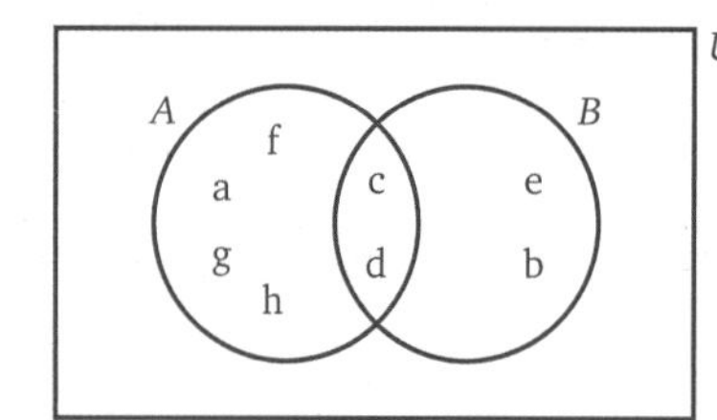

In the remaining questions in this exercise, the numbers in the various regions of the Venn diagrams show the *number of elements in*, or *members of, the set in that region*.

In questions **5** to **8** use the the information given in the Venn diagrams to find

a $n(X)$ **b** $n(Y)$ **c** $n(X \cup Y)$ **d** $n(X \cap Y)$

5

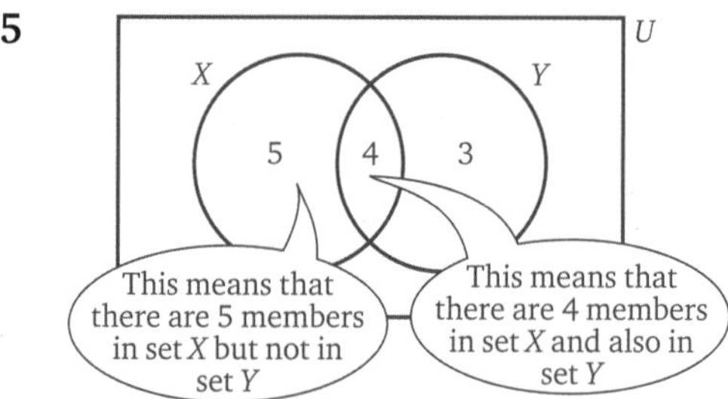

7

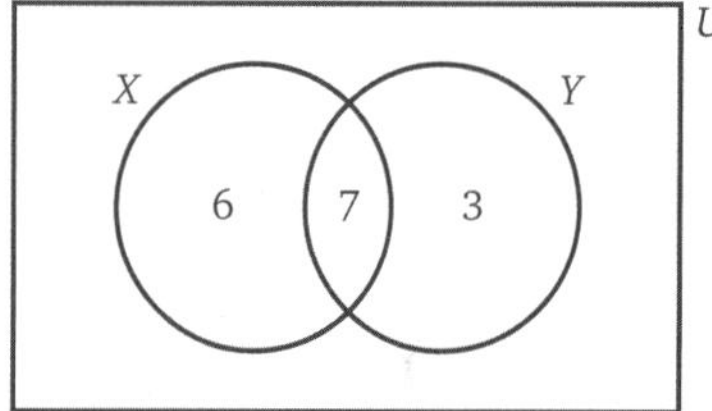

6

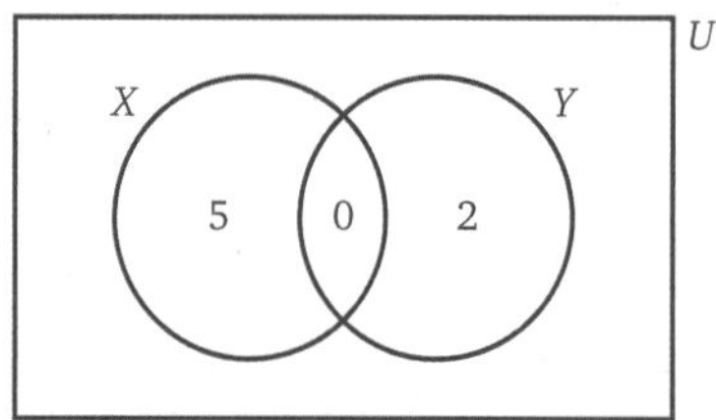

8

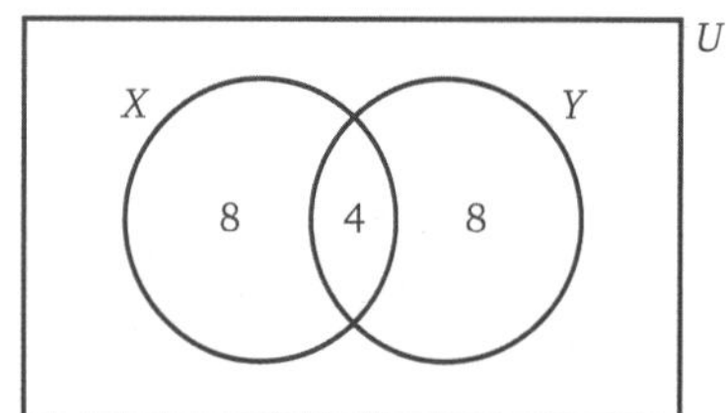

Use the information given in the Venn diagram to find

$n(A)$, $n(B)$, $n(A')$, $n(B')$, $n(A \cup B)$, $n(A \cap B)$,
$n(A' \cup B')$, $n[(A \cap B)']$ for the given sets.

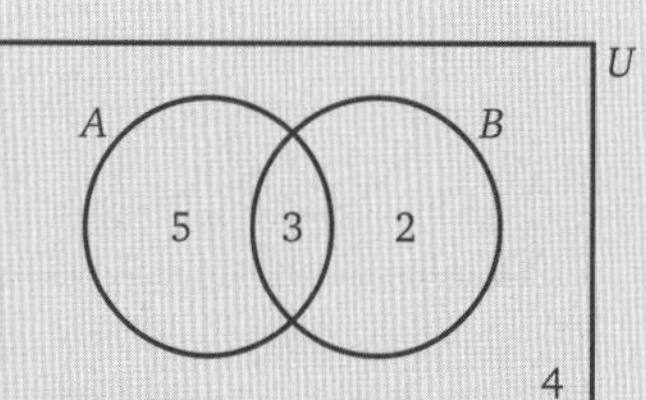

The numbers in the regions show the number of elements in that region.

$n(A) = 8$ (the number of elements in set A, i.e. $5 + 3$)

$n(B) = 5$ (the number of elements within the B circle, i.e. $3 + 2$)

$n(A') = 6$ (the number of elements not in set A)

$n(B') = 9$ (the number of elements not in set B)

$n(A \cup B) = 10$ (the sum of the numbers in either A or B, i.e. $5 + 3 + 2$)

$n(A \cap B) = 3$ (the number in both A and B)

$n(A' \cup B') = 11$ (the number not in set A $(2 + 4)$ plus the number not in set B and not already accounted for (5))

$n[(A \cap B)'] = 11$, (the number not in both A and B)

Use the information given in the following Venn diagrams to find $n(A)$, $n(B)$, $n(A')$, $n(B')$, $n(A \cup B)$, $n(A \cap B)$, $n(A' \cup B')$ and $n[(A \cap B)']$ for each of the given pairs of sets.

9

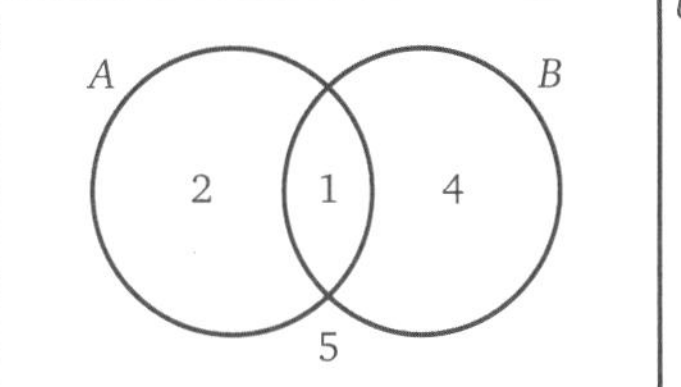

10

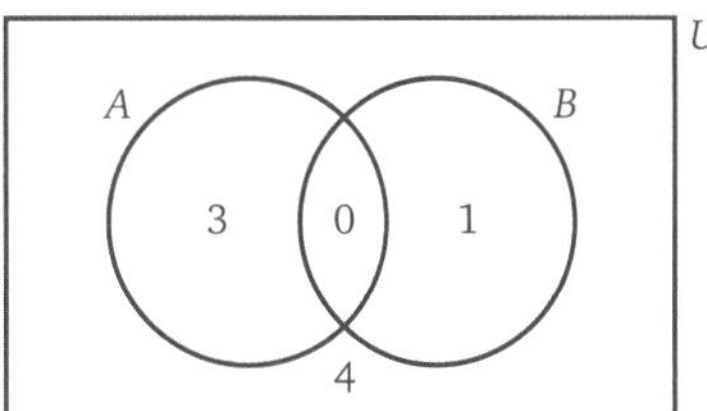

11

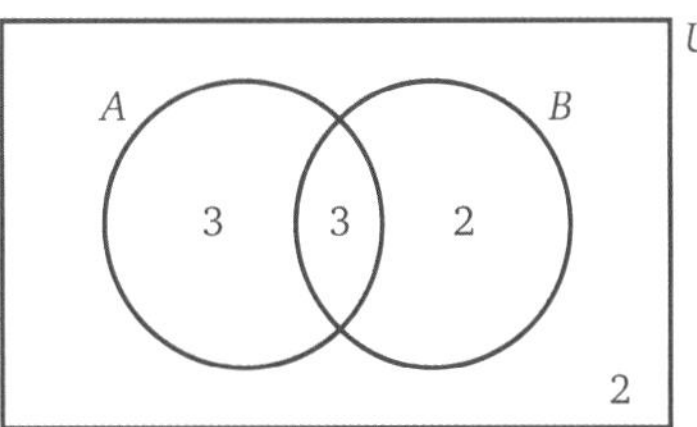

12

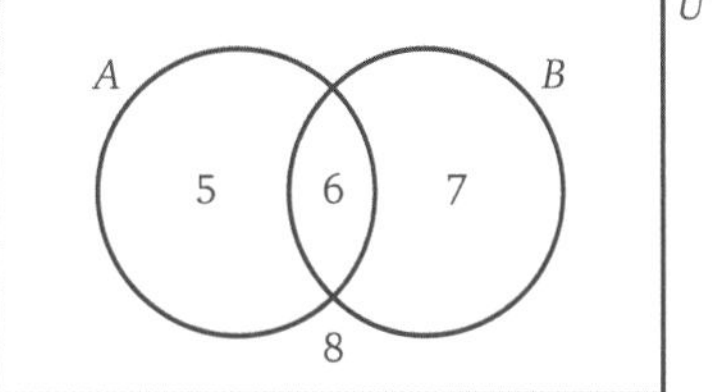

13

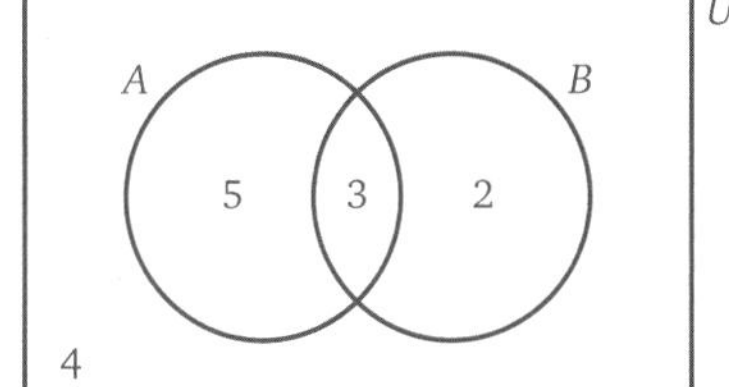

14

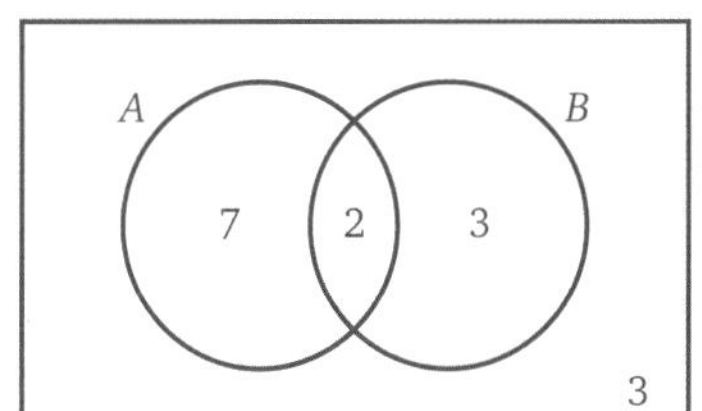

15

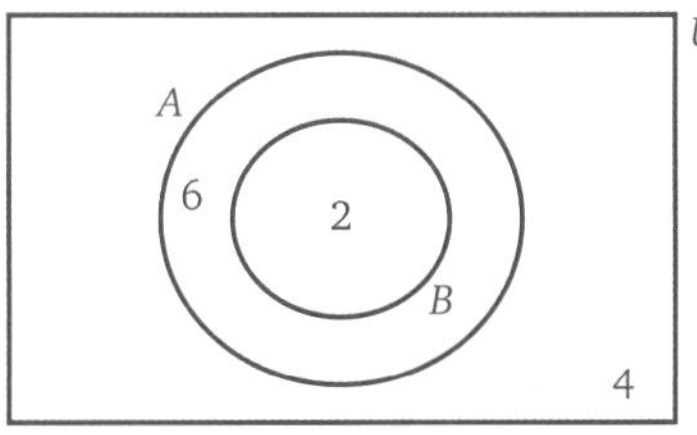

16

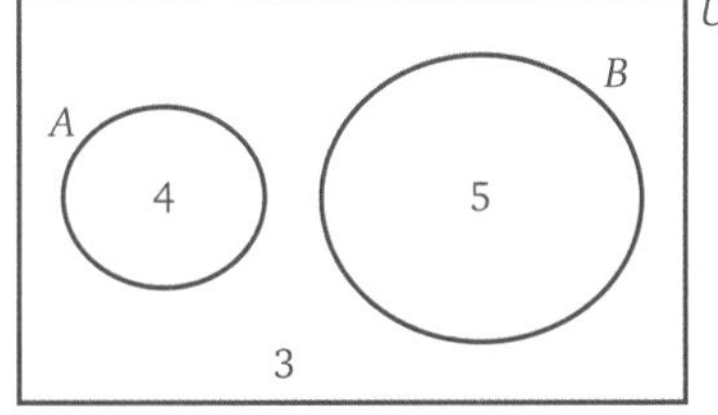

Further problems

Exercise 15d

The Venn diagram shows how many pupils in a class have cellphones (C) and tablets (T).

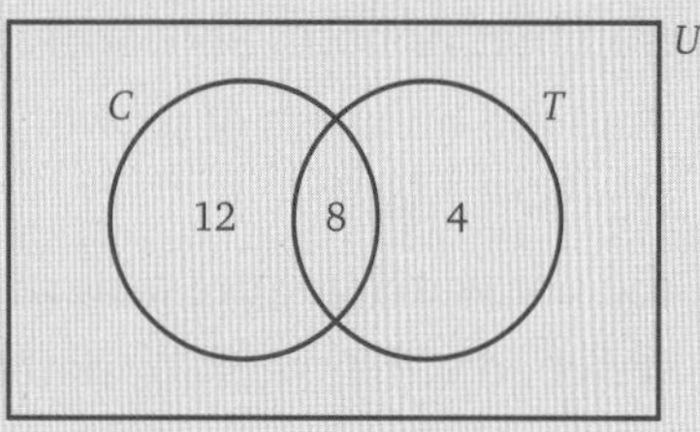

How many pupils have:

a both a cell phone and a tablet
b a cell phone
c a cell phone and/or a tablet
d a tablet but not a cell phone?

a The number of pupils with both is 8. (The number in both circles.)
b The number of pupils with a cell phone is $12 + 8$, i.e. 20. (The sum of the numbers in circle C.)
c The number of pupils with at least one of the two is $12 + 8 + 4$, i.e. 24. (The sum of the numbers in either circle.)
d 4 pupils have a tablet but not a cell phone. (The number in T but not in C.)

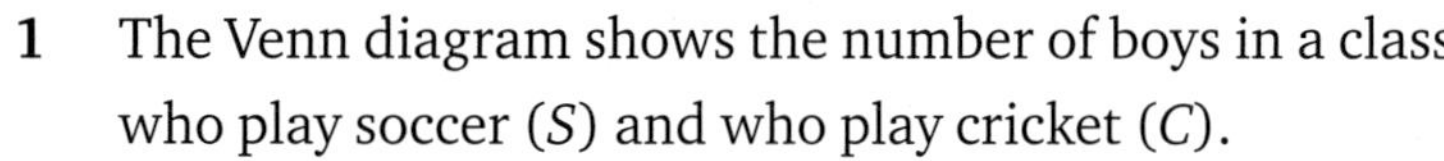

1 The Venn diagram shows the number of boys in a class who play soccer (S) and who play cricket (C).

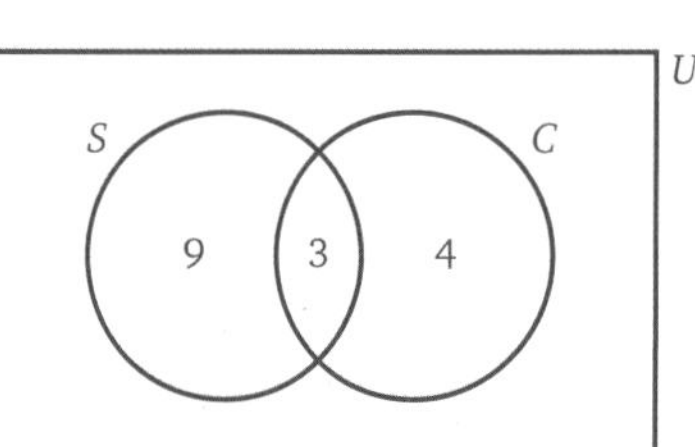

How many boys play

a both games
b only cricket
c soccer
d exactly one of these games?

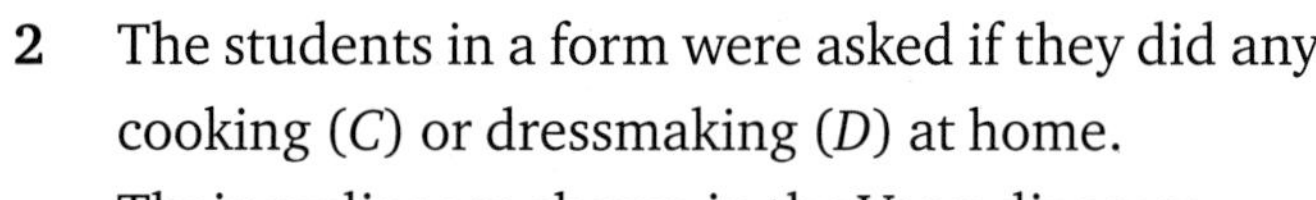

2 The students in a form were asked if they did any cooking (C) or dressmaking (D) at home. Their replies are shown in the Venn diagram.

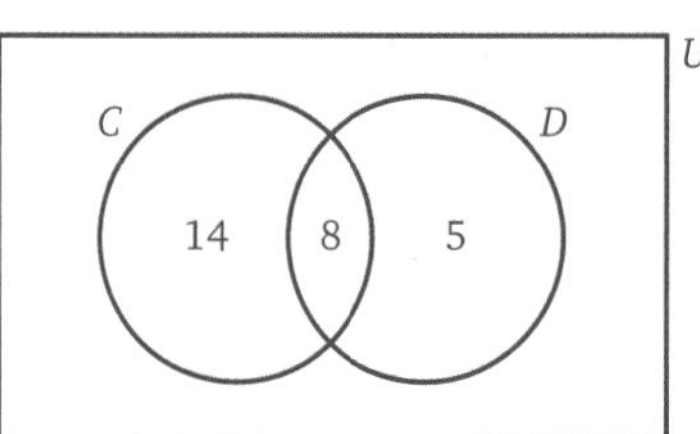

If all the students in the form took part in at least one of these activities, how many students

a are there in the form
b did only cooking
c did both
d did exactly one of these activities?

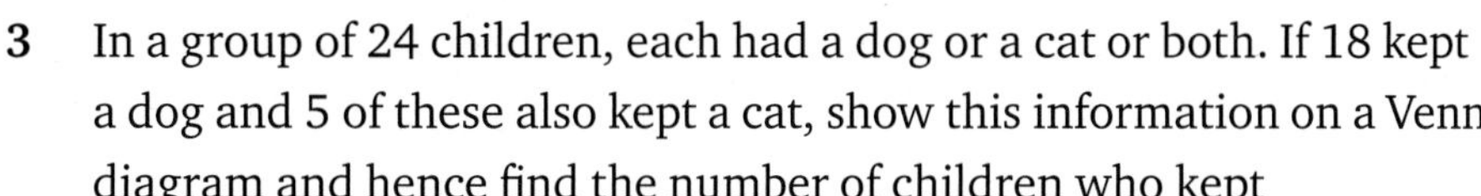

3 In a group of 24 children, each had a dog or a cat or both. If 18 kept a dog and 5 of these also kept a cat, show this information on a Venn diagram and hence find the number of children who kept

a a cat **b** only a dog **c** just one of these as a pet.

4 A group of 50 television addicts were asked if they watched sport programmes and nature programmes. The replies revealed that 21 watched both sport and nature programmes but 9 watched nature programmes only. All 50 people watched either sport or nature programmes or both. Show this information on a Venn diagram and use it to find the numbers of viewers who

a watched sport

b did not watch nature programmes

c watched either sport or nature programmes but not both.

5 In a youth club 35 teenagers said that they went to football matches, discos or both. Of the 22 who said they went to football matches, 12 said they also went to discos. Show this information on a Venn diagram. How many went to football matches or discos, but not to both?

6 There are 28 pupils in a form, all of whom take history or geography or both. If 14 take history, 5 of whom also take geography, show this information on a Venn diagram and hence find the number of pupils who take

a geography

b history but not geography

c just one of these subjects.

7 In a squad of 35 cricketers 20 said that they could bat and 8 said that they could bat and bowl. Show this information on a Venn diagram. How many more were willing to bowl than to bat?

The Venn diagram shows how many houses in a street have new windows (W) and how many have new front doors (D).

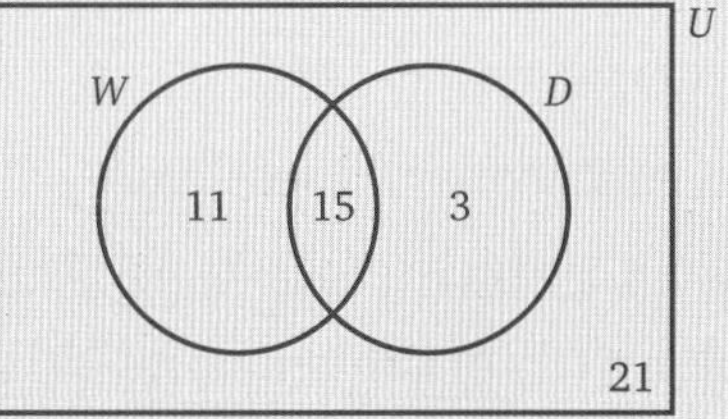

How many houses

a are there in the street

b do not have a new front door

c have either a new front door or new windows but not both?

a Number of houses in the street is $11 + 15 + 3 + 21$, i.e. 50 (The sum of all the numbers in U.)

b Number of houses without a new front door is $11 + 21$, i.e. 32 (The sum of the numbers outside D.)

c The numbers with either a new front door or new windows but not both is $11 + 3$, i.e. 14.

(The number in either W or D but not in both.)

8 The Venn diagram shows how many pupils in a class passed the English examination (E) and how many passed the mathematics examination (M).

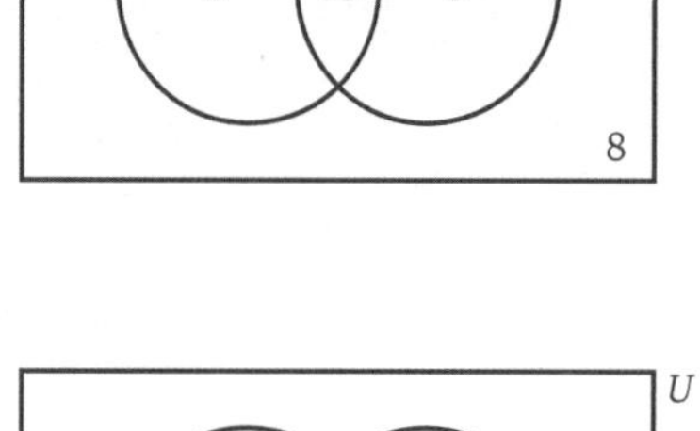

How many pupils

a passed in only one examination

b did not pass in English

c passed in at least one examination?

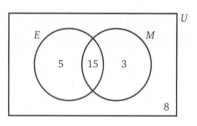

9 The Venn diagram shows how many pupils in a class kept goldfish (G), budgerigars (B) or both. How many pupils

a were there in the class

b did not have a budgerigar

c had at least one of these pets?

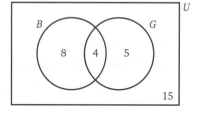

10 The passengers on a coach were questioned about the newspapers and weekly magazines they bought, 3 bought both a daily newspaper and a weekly magazine. 15 bought a daily newspaper, 8 bought a weekly magazine, 8 did not buy either a daily paper or a weekly magazine. Show this information on a Venn diagram.

a How many passengers were there on the coach?

b How many passengers bought a daily newspaper, a weekly magazine or both?

11 One evening all 78 members of a Youth Club were asked whether they liked swimming (S) and/or dancing (D). It was found that 34 liked swimming, 41 liked dancing and 19 liked both. Show this information on a Venn diagram. How many members were

a swimmers but not dancers

b dancers or swimmers but not both

c neither dancers nor swimmers?

12 During April, 36 cars were taken to a Motor Vehicle Testing Station for their annual inspection. The results showed that 8 had defective brakes and lights, 10 had defective brakes, and 13 had defective lights. How many cars

a failed the inspection

b passed the inspection

c had exactly one defect?

13 The 32 pupils in a class were asked whether they studied French or art or both. It was found that 8 studied both, 13 studied French and 6 did not study either subject. How many pupils studied

a art but not French

b French or art but not both?

Puzzle

Every map or shape divided into regions can be coloured so that no two touching edges of any regions are the same colour using not more than four different colours. Make a copy of the diagram given below and colour it so that no two touching edges of any regions are the same colour.

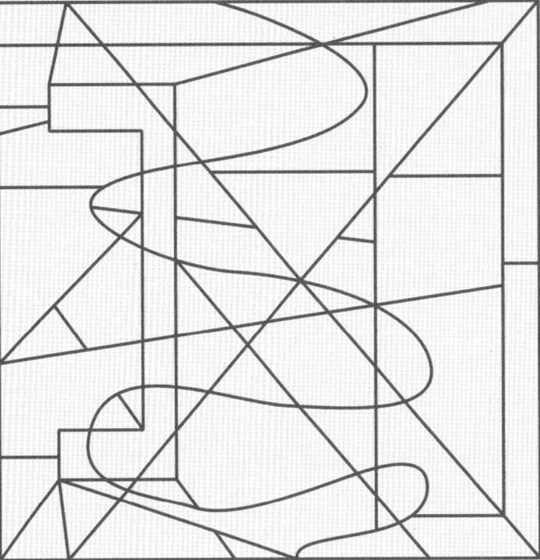

If you are successful, try using three different colours. Is it possible?

The following exercise extends the ideas that we have used so far, to three intersecting sets.

Exercise 15e

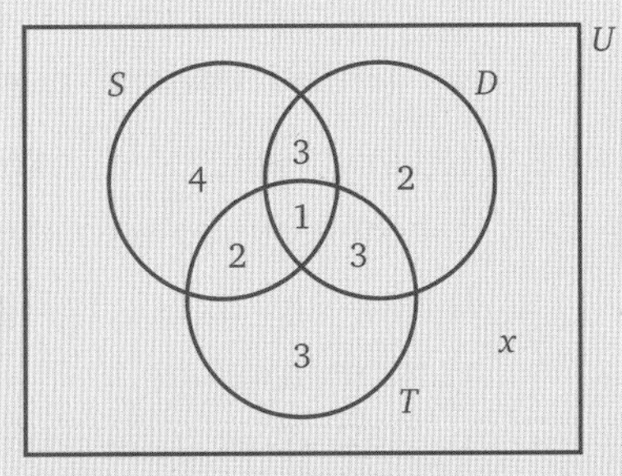

In a certain group of pupils, some are in one or more of the school swimming, debating and trampolining teams. The Venn diagram shows these numbers where

$S = \{$those in the swimming team$\}$

$D = \{$those in the debating team$\}$

and $T = \{$those in the trampolining team$\}$

How many pupils belong to

a the debating team only **b** at least one team **c** exactly two teams?

If there are 24 pupils in the group, find

d the value of x

e the number of pupils who do not belong to the debating team.

a 2 pupils belong to the debating team and nothing else. (The number in D but in no other set.)

b The number belonging to at least one team is $4+2+3+3+2+3+1$, i.e. 18 pupils. (The sum of the numbers in all the circles.)

c The number belonging to exactly two teams is $3+3+2$, i.e. 8 pupils. (The sum of the numbers in the overlaps of two circles. This does not include the number where the three circles overlap.)

d Since $18+x=24$, 6 pupils do not belong to any team, i.e. $x=6$.

e The number who do not belong to the debating team is $24-(3+2+3+1)$, i.e. 15 pupils.

1 The Venn diagram shows the number of students taking geography (G), history (H) and accounts (A) in a class of 43. Every student takes at least one of these subjects

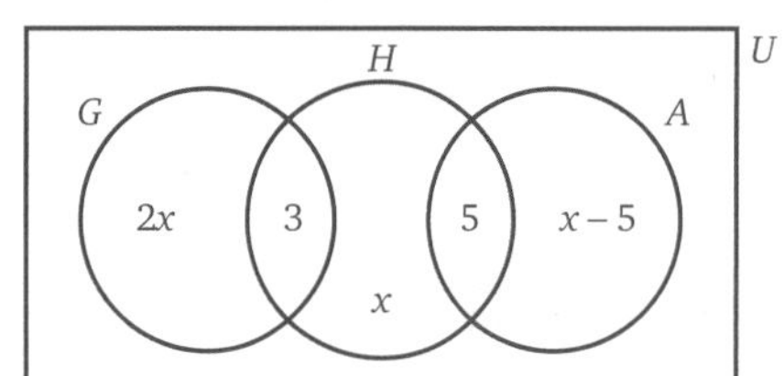

a Write down an expression, in terms of x, for the number of students who take history.

b Write down an expression, in terms of x, which shows the information given in the Venn diagram.

c Work out the number of students who take geography only.

d Work out the number of students who take accounts.

2 Given that $U=\{p, q, r, s, t, u, v\}$,
$A=\{p, q, s, t\}$, $B=\{q, r, s, u, v\}$ and $C=\{s, t, u\}$.

a Draw a Venn diagram showing the sets A, B, C and U.

b List the members of the set represented by $A \cup (B \cap C)$.

c Write down the value of $n(A \cup (B \cap C)')$.

3 The universal set U contains the sets A, B and C such that

$$B \subset A, C \subset A, B \cap C = \varnothing$$

Draw a Venn diagram to show the relation between the sets A, B and C.

4 The universal set U contains the sets P, Q and R such that $P \cap Q = \varnothing$, $P \cap R \neq \varnothing$, $Q \cap R \neq \varnothing$.

Draw a Venn diagram to show the relation between the sets P, Q and R.

5 The universal set U contains the sets P, Q and R such that
$P \not\subset Q$, $P \cap Q \neq \varnothing$, $R \subset Q'$, $R \subset P$.

Draw a Venn diagram to show the relation between the sets P, Q and R.

6 The universal set U contains the sets A, B and C such that

$B \subset A, A \cap C \neq \varnothing, B \cap C = \varnothing$.

Draw a Venn diagram to show the relation between the sets A, B and C.

7 $U = \{1, 2, 3, 4, 5, \ldots, 10\}, A = \{1, 2, 3, 4\}, B = \{1, 2, 5, 6\}$ and $C = \{2, 4, 6, 8, 10\}$.

a List the members of $A \cup B$ and $B \cup C$.
Hence show that $(A \cup B) \cup C = A \cup (B \cup C)$.

b List the members of $A \cap B$ and $B \cap C$.
Hence show that $(A \cap B) \cap C = A \cap (B \cap C)$.

c Draw a Venn diagram to show the relation between sets A, B and C.

8 The Venn diagram shows the relation between those who run (set R), those who hurdle (set H) and those who throw the javelin (set J).

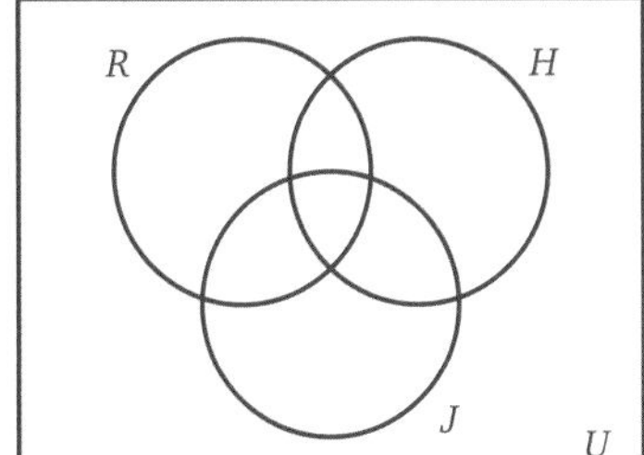

Copy the diagram and shade in different colours $J \cup H$ and $R \cap (J \cup H)$. Copy the diagram again and shade the area representing the union of $(R \cap H)$ and $(R \cap J)$.
On comparing the diagrams you should find that
$R \cap (H \cup J) = (R \cap H) \cup (R \cap J)$.

9 The universal set is U where U = {positive integers from 1 to 24 inclusive}. X, Y and Z are subsets of U and are defined as follows: X = {multiples of 4}, Y = {multiples of 5}, and Z = {prime numbers}. Draw a Venn diagram to illustrate this information and use it to list the elements of the sets.

a $X \cup Y$

b $X' \cap Z$

c $X' \cap Y' \cap Z'$

d $(X \cup Y) \cap (Y \cup Z)$

10 Given U = {letters of the alphabet}, A = {letters used to make the word ALGEBRA}, B = {letters used to make the word ARITHMETIC} and C = {letters used to make the word GEOMETRY}, write

a the elements in the set $(A \cup B) \cap C$ **b** $n(B \cup C)$

11 If U = {quadrilaterals}, A = {parallelograms}, B = {rectangles} and C = {squares}, draw a Venn diagram to illustrate the connection between the sets.

12 If U = {triangles}, X = {right-angled triangles}, Y = {equilateral triangles} and Z = {isosceles triangles}, draw a Venn diagram to show the relationship between the sets.

Describe the elements of

a $X \cap Z$ **b** $X' \cap Y$ **c** $X \cup Y$

13 Draw a Venn diagram to show three sets A, B and C in a universal set U. Enter numbers in the correct parts of your diagram using the following information:

$n(A \cap B \cap C) = 2$, $n(A \cap B) = 7$, $n(B \cap C) = 6$, $n(A \cap C) = 8$, $n(A) = 16$, $n(B) = 20$, $n(C) = 19$ and $n(U) = 50$.

Use your diagram to find

a $n(A' \cap C')$ **b** $n(A \cup B')$ **c** $n(A' \cap B' \cap C')$

14

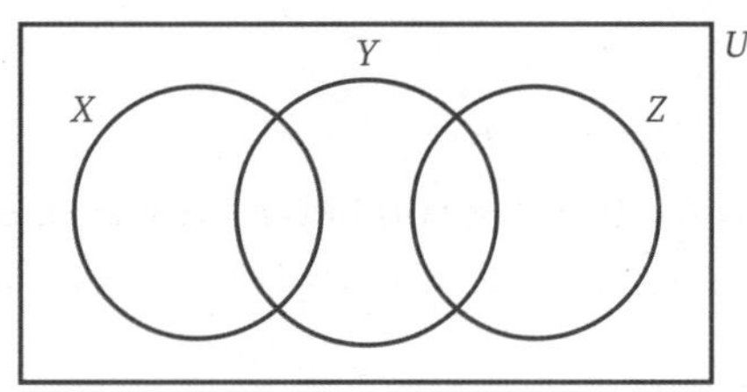

The Venn diagram shows three sets X, Y and Z contained within a universal set U. Enter numbers in the correct regions of your diagram using the following information:

$n(X \cap Y) = 3$, $n(Y \cap Z) = 4$, $n(X) = 8$, $n(Y) = 18$, $n(Z) = 10$, and $n(U) = 35$.

Use your diagram to find

a $n(X \cap Y \cap Z)$ **b** $n(X' \cup Y)$ **c** $n(X' \cap Z')$

15 Forty travellers were questioned about the various methods of transport they had used the previous day. Every one of them had used at least one of the methods shown in the Venn diagram.

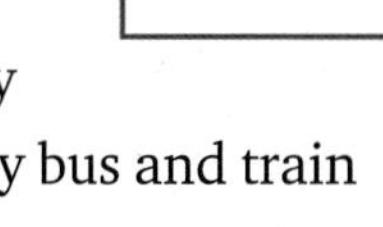

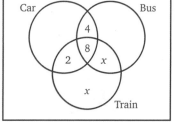

Of those questioned 8 had used all three methods of transport, 4 had travelled by bus and car only, and 2 by car and train only. The number (x) who had travelled by train only was equal to the number who had travelled by bus and train only.

If 20 travellers had used a train and 33 had used a bus find

a the value of x

b the number who travelled by bus only

c the number who used exactly two methods of transport

d the number who travelled by car only.

Mixed exercise

Exercise 15f

Select the letter that gives the correct answer.

Use this diagram for questions **1** to **3**.

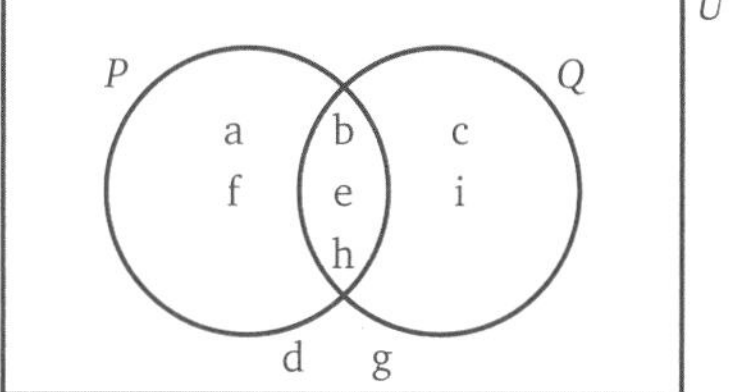

1 The members of the set $P \cap Q$ are

A {b, e, h} **B** {a, b, c, e, f, h} **C** {a, b, c, e, h, i} **D** {a, b, c, d, e, f, g, h, i}

2 The members of the set $P' \cap Q'$ are

A {d, g} **B** {b, e, h} **C** {a, d, f, g} **D** {c, i, f, g}

3 The members of the set $P' \cup Q$ are

A {d, g} **B** {c, d, g, i} **C** {a, b, d, e, f, g, h} **D** {b, c, d, e, g, h, i}

Use this diagram for questions **4** to **6**.

The Venn diagram shows the number of students taking physics, chemistry and biology in a class of 34. Every student takes at least one of these subjects.

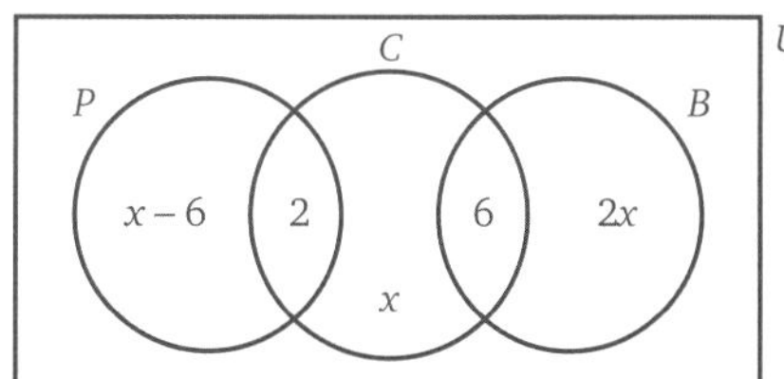

4 The value of x is

A 4 **B** 6 **C** 8 **D** 10

5 The number of students who take chemistry is

A 8 **B** 10 **C** 12 **D** 14

6 The number of students who do not take biology is

A 8 **B** 10 **C** 12 **D** 14

Did you know?

The famous French mathematician René Descartes (1596–1650) believed that the whole of human knowledge should be founded on the belief *cogito ergo sum* – I think, therefore I am. He also believed that the entire material universe could be explained in terms of mathematical physics. You will come across his name again in the branch called Cartesian or coordinate geometry.

In this chapter you have seen that...

✔ many problems involving details about two or three sets of data can be solved using Venn diagrams.

16 Straight-line graphs

At the end of this chapter you should be able to...

1 state the equations of lines drawn parallel to the coordinate axes

2 draw lines of the form $y = k$ and $x = h$ where h and k are constants

3 draw a line with equation $y = mx + c$, by finding points on the line

4 use the equation of a line to calculate the value of y for a given x

5 determine if a given point lies on a line whose equation is given

6 calculate the gradient of a line, given the coordinates of two points on the line

7 state the gradient of a line whose equation is given

8 determine if two lines whose equations are given are parallel

9 write the equation of a line given its gradient and intercept on the y-axis

10 write the equation of a line through two given points.

Did you know?

Although we always tend to think that the shortest distance between two points is a straight line, this is not always the case. The shortest distance between two points on a globe or curved surface is a geodesic.

You need to know...

✔ how to draw and scale a set of axes and plot points on the resulting grid

✔ how to read the coordinates of a point on a line

✔ how to solve a linear equation

✔ how to work with fractions and decimals

✔ how to work with directed numbers.

Key words

coefficient, intercept, parallel lines, positive or negative gradient of a line, slope of a line

Straight lines

Straight lines can lie anywhere and at any angle to the x-axis.

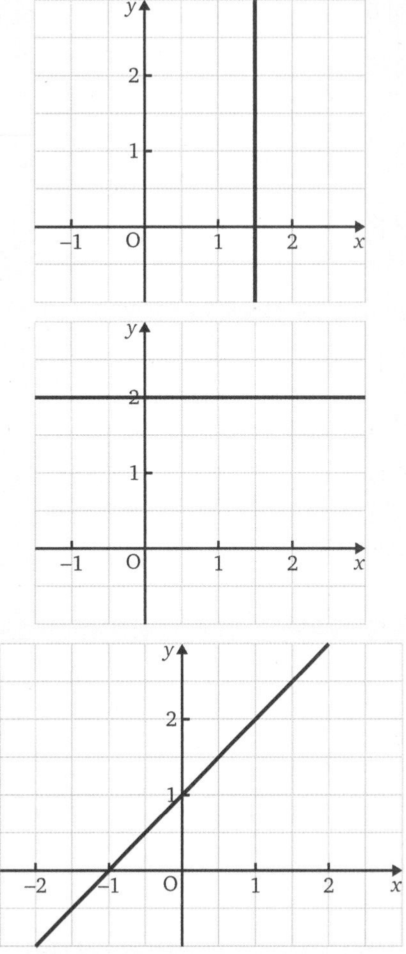

The lines go on for ever in both directions. We draw just part of the line.

Lines parallel to the axes

If we consider any point on the line given in the diagram we find that, no matter what the y-coordinate is, the x-coordinate is always 2.

We say that the equation of this line is $x = 2$.

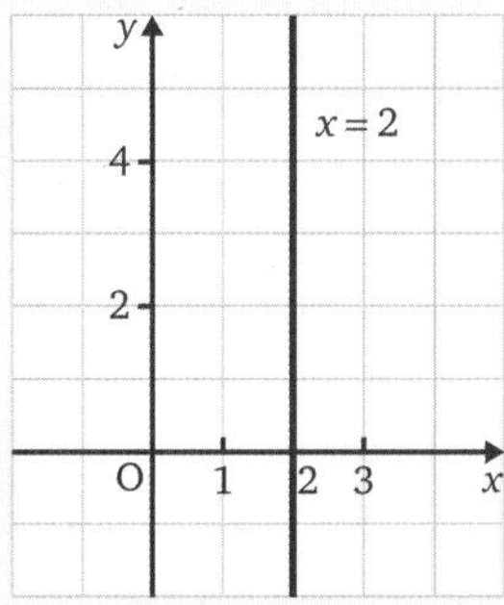

Notice that y is not mentioned because there is no restriction on the value it can take.

In the same way, any point on the line given in this diagram has a y-coordinate of 3, while the x-coordinate can take any value. The equation of this line is $y = 3$.

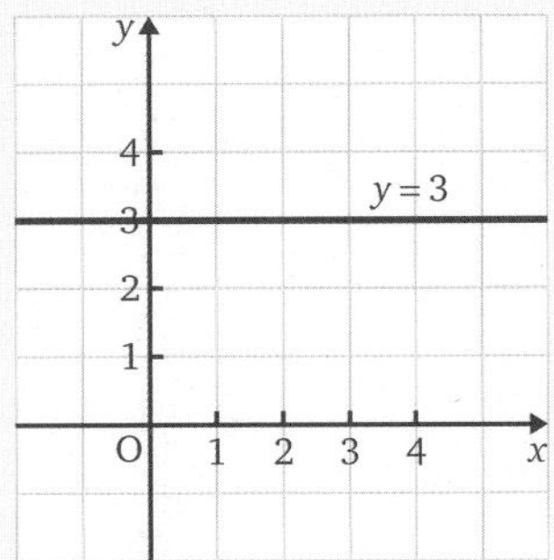

Exercise 16a

Give the equations of the lines in questions **1** to **4**:

1

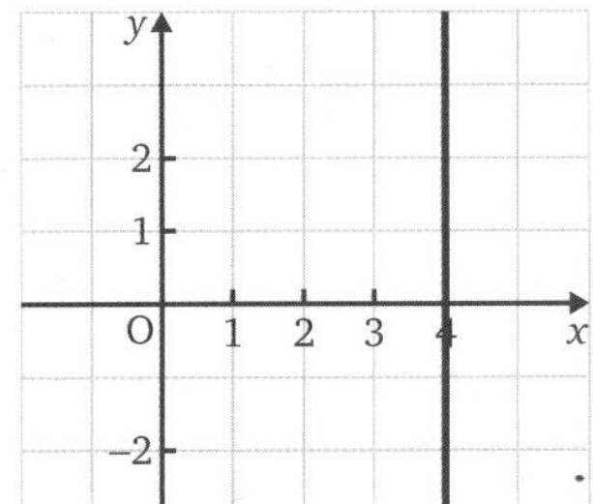

3

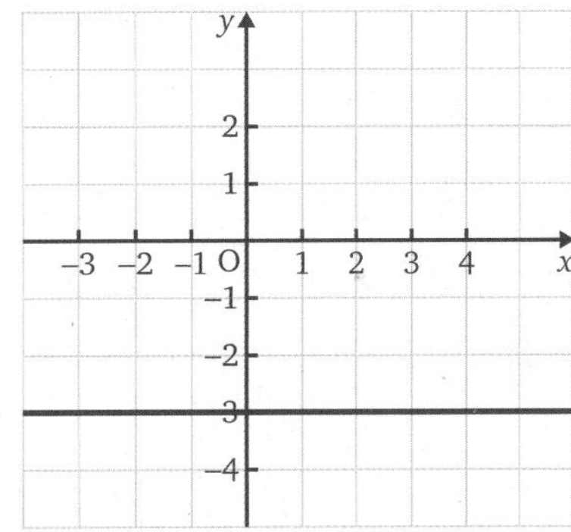

2

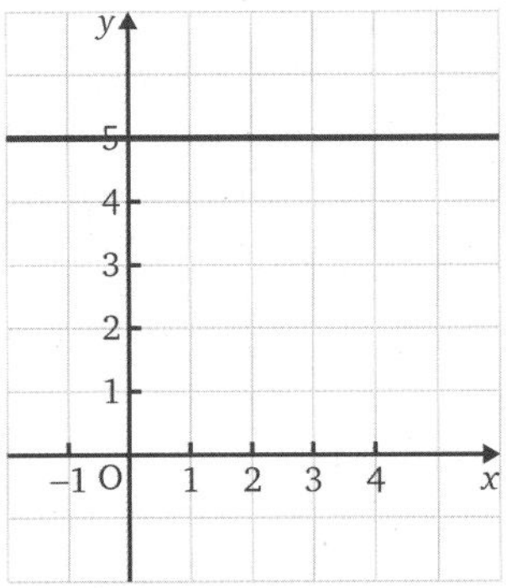

4

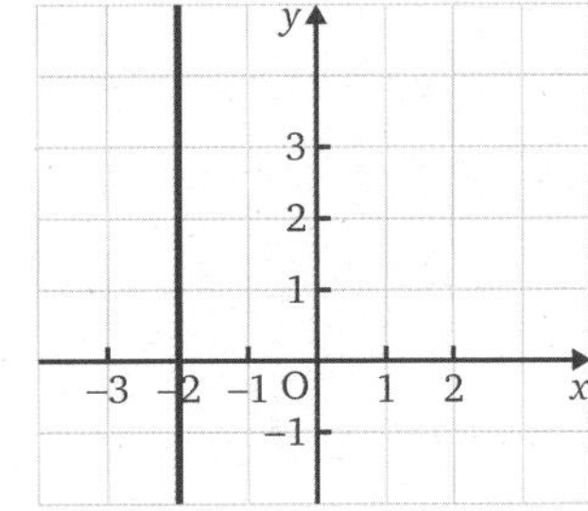

Draw similar diagrams to show the lines with the following equations:

5 $x = 1$ **6** $x = -4$ **7** $y = 4$ **8** $y = -3$

Slant lines

If we take any point on the line shown, say (2, 4) or $(3\frac{1}{2}, 5\frac{1}{2})$ or (–1, 1) or (0, 2), we find that the y-coordinate is always 2 units more than the x-coordinate.

The equation of the line is therefore $y = x + 2$.

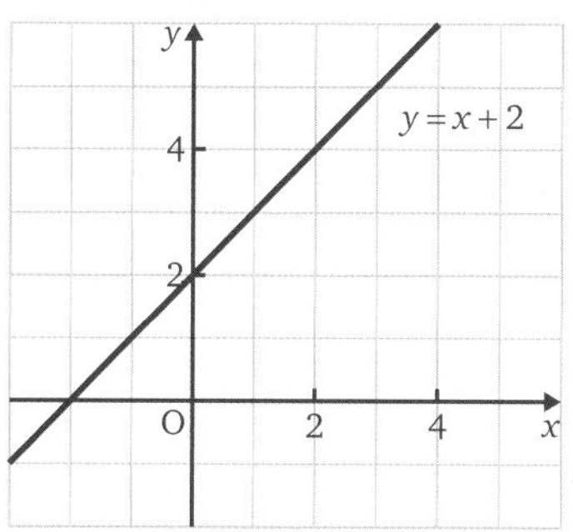

Conversely, if we are given the equation of a line we can draw the line by finding points on it. Two points are enough to draw a straight line but a third is useful as a check. If the three points do not lie in a straight line, at least one point is incorrect. Check all three points.

Suppose that we want to draw the line whose equation is $y = 2x + 1$. Think of this as an instruction for finding the y-coordinate to go with a chosen x-coordinate.

If $x = 1$, $y = 2 + 1 = 3$ so (1, 3) is a point on the line.

If $x = 3$, $y = 2 \times 3 + 1 = 7$ so (3, 7) is on the line.

If $x = -3$, $y = 2 \times (-3) + 1 = -5$ so (–3, –5) is on the line.

It is simpler to list this information in a table.

x	–3	1	3
y	–5	3	7

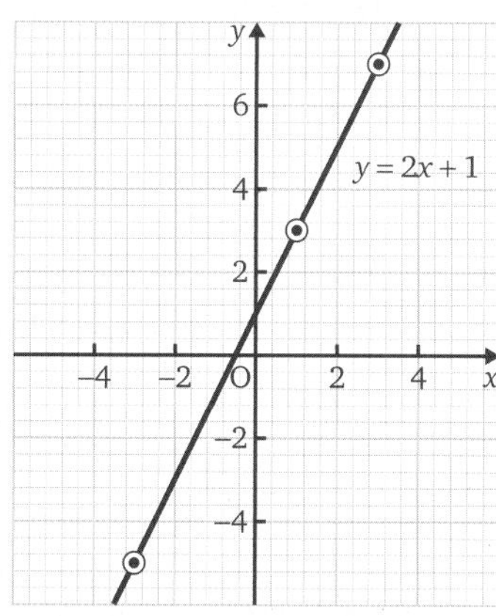

Exercise 16b

In all questions in this exercise use 1 cm to 1 unit.

In each of questions **1** to **4**, copy and complete the table. On graph paper, draw x and y axes for the ranges indicated in the brackets. Mark the points and, if they are in a straight line, draw that line.

1 $y = x + 4 \quad (-2 \leqslant x \leqslant 4, 0 \leqslant y \leqslant 8)$

x	−2	0	4
y			

2 $y = 2x + 1 \quad (-2 \leqslant x \leqslant 3, -4 \leqslant y \leqslant 8)$

x	−2	0	3
y			

3 $y = 4 - x \quad (-3 \leqslant x \leqslant 3, 0 \leqslant y \leqslant 8)$

x	−3	0	3
y			

4 $y = 2 - 3x \quad (-2 \leqslant x \leqslant 4, -10 \leqslant y \leqslant 8)$

x	−2	0	4
y			

In each of questions **5** to **8**, make a table, choosing your own values of x within the given range. (Choose one low value, one high value and one in between, such as zero.) Draw x and y axes for the ranges of values indicated. Draw the line.

5 $y = x - 3 \quad (-2 \leqslant x \leqslant 5, -5 \leqslant y \leqslant 2)$

6 $y = \frac{1}{2}x + 4 \quad (-2 \leqslant x \leqslant 4, 0 \leqslant y \leqslant 6)$

7 $y = 3 - 2x \quad (-2 \leqslant x \leqslant 4, -5 \leqslant y \leqslant 7)$

8 $y = 3x - 4 \quad (0 \leqslant x \leqslant 6, -5 \leqslant y \leqslant 14)$

Make a table which can be used for drawing the graph of $y = 6 + 2x$, taking values of x in the range $-3 \leqslant x \leqslant 3$. Decide from the table what range of values of y is suitable.

Choose values at each end of the range and one in the middle.

$y = 6 + 2x$

x	−3	0	3
y	0	6	12

The range for y must be $0 \leqslant y \leqslant 12$.

For each of questions **9** to **12**, make a table, choosing your own values of x within the given range. Decide on a suitable range of values of y after completing the table.

Draw x and y axes using the given range for the x-axis and the range you have chosen for the y-axis. Draw the line.

9 $y = 3 - x \quad (-3 \leqslant x \leqslant 3)$

10 $y = \frac{1}{2}x - 1 \quad (-3 \leqslant x \leqslant 3)$

11 $y = 2x + 2 \quad (-2 \leqslant x \leqslant 4)$

12 $y = 5 - 3x \quad (-1 \leqslant x \leqslant 3)$

You are given the graph of the line with equation $y = 1 - \frac{1}{2}x$.
From the graph, find

a the value of y, if x is 0.8

b the value of x, if y is 2.4

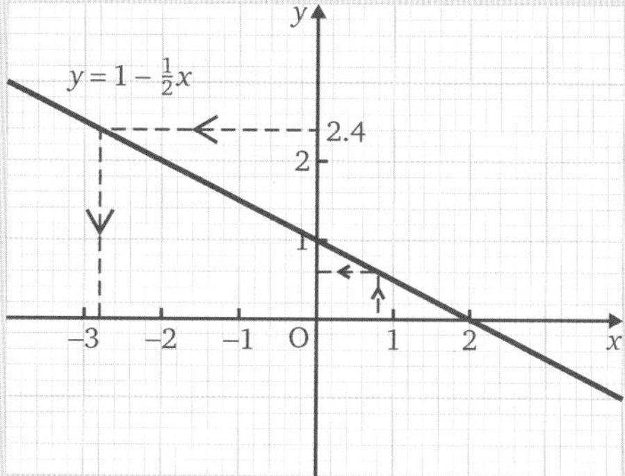

a Find 0.8 on the x-axis (4 small squares from the origin). Go up to the line then across to the y-axis. Read off the value (3 small squares, which corresponds to 0.6).

From the graph, if $x = 0.8$, $y = 0.6$

b From the graph, if $y = 2.4$, $x = -2.8$

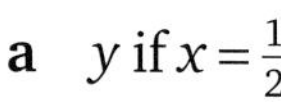

13 You are given the graph of the line with equation $y = x + 1$.

Make sure you know what numbers are represented by the intermediate graduations on the axes.

From the graph, find

a y if $x = \frac{1}{2}$

b x if $y = 1.4$

c x if $y = -0.6$

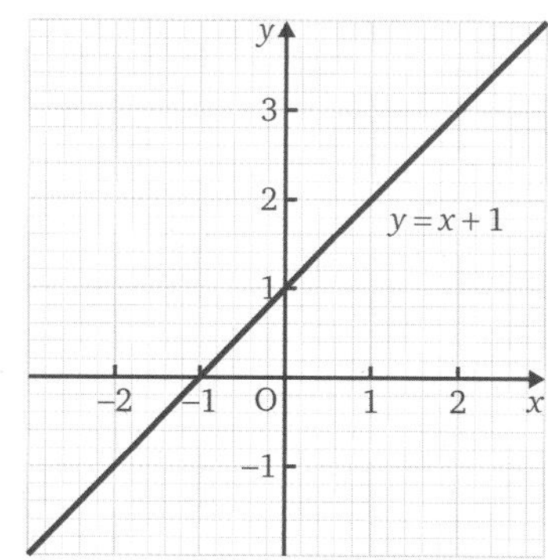

14 You are given the graph of the line with equation $y = 2x - 1$.

From the graph, find

a y if $x = \frac{1}{2}$

b x if $y = -2.6$

c y if $x = -1.2$

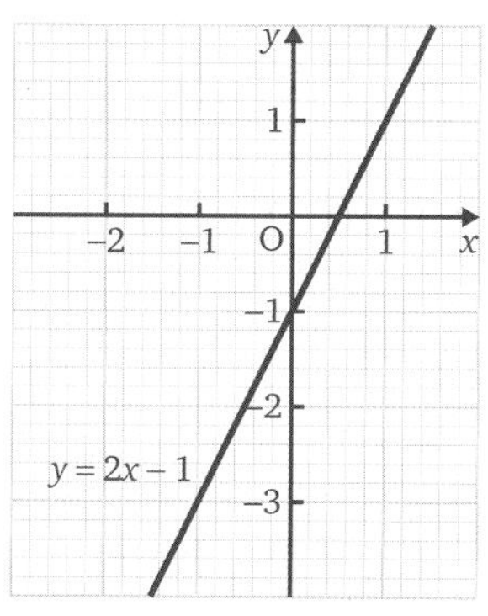

15 You are given the graph of the line with equation $y = -x - 1$.

From the graph, find

a y if $x = 1.6$

b x if $y = 0.8$

c x if $y = -2.2$

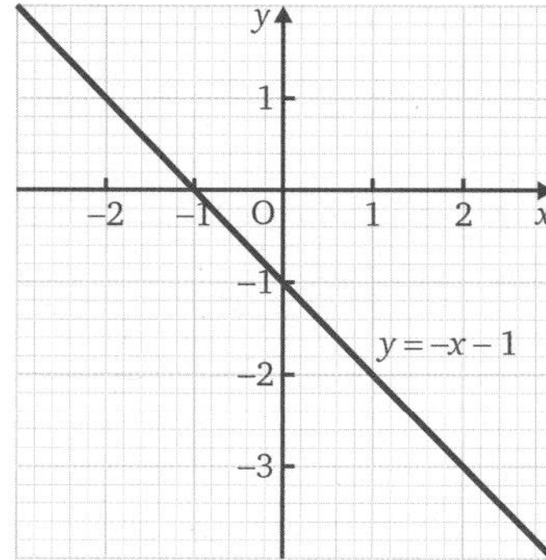

16 You are given the graph of the line with equation $y = 3 - 3x$.

From the graph, find

a y if $x = -0.2$

b x if $y = 1.2$

c x if $y = -0.6$

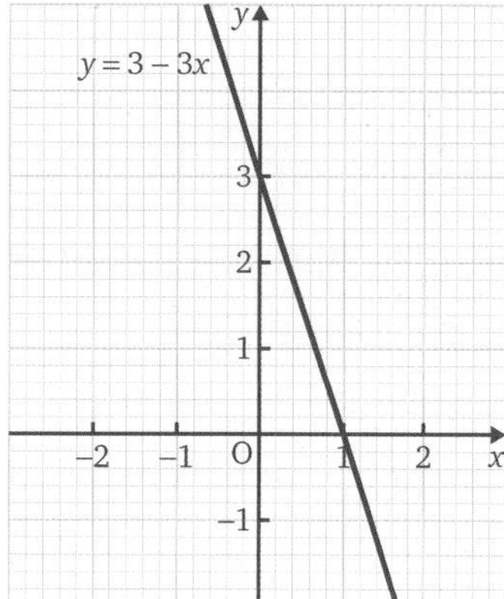

17 Using the graph you drew for question **5**, find

a y if $x = \frac{1}{2}$ **b** x if $y = 1.4$ **c** x if $y = -0.6$

18 Using the graph you drew for question **6**, find

a y if $x = 1.6$ **b** x if $y = 4.6$ **c** x if $y = -1.6$

19 Using the graph you drew for question **7**, find

a y if $x = 2.2$ **b** x if $y = 0.2$ **c** x if $y = -4$

20 Using the graph you drew for question **8**, find

a y if $x = 4.2$ **b** x if $y = 4.4$ **c** x if $y = 5$

Points on a line

Exercise 16c

Do the points (3, 6) and (−2, −10) lie on the line whose equation is $y = 3x - 4$?

$$y = 3x - 4$$

When $x = 3$, the value of y on the line is given by $y = 3 \times 3 - 4 = 5$. But for the point (3, 6), $y = 6$ so the point does not lie on the line.

When $x = -2$, the value of y on the line is given by $y = 3 \times (-2) - 4 = -10$. For the point (−2, −10), $y = -10$ so the point lies on the line.

Find whether the given points lie on the line whose equation is given:

1 $y = 2x - 1$; (5, 9), (1, 2)

2 $y = 3 + 3x$; (2, 9), (−4, −9)

3 $y = 6 - 2x$; (3, 1), (4, −1)

4 $y = \frac{1}{2}x + 4$; (4, 5), $(3, 5\frac{1}{2})$

5 $y = 5 + 4x$; $(\frac{1}{2}, 7)$, (−2, −3)

6 $y = 6 - \frac{1}{2}x$; (−2, 5), (−2, 7)

Comparing slopes

Exercise 16d

1 Draw, on the same pair of axes, the graphs of the lines

a $y = 2x - 3$ b $y = 2x$ c $y = 2x - 2$

for $-3 \leqslant x \leqslant 3$ and $-7 \leqslant y \leqslant 9$ using 1 cm to 1 unit.
Label each line with its equation.
What can you say about the lines?
What do the equations have in common?

2 Draw a pair of axes using $-2 \leqslant x \leqslant 2$ and $-7 \leqslant y \leqslant 9$. On these axes draw the three lines with the following equations:

a $y = -3x - 1$ b $y = -3x$ c $y = -3x + 3$

What can you say about the lines?
What do the equations have in common?

3 Draw a pair of axes using $-4 \leqslant x \leqslant 4$, $-7 \leqslant y \leqslant 6$. On these axes draw the three lines with the following equations:

a $y = \frac{1}{2}x - 4$ b $y = \frac{1}{2}x + 1$ c $y = \frac{1}{2}x + 3$

Comment on the three lines and their equations.

4 Draw x and y axes, marking values from −5 to 5 on each axis. Draw the three lines with the following equations:

a $y = x$ b $y = x - 3$ c $y = x + 2$

What do you notice?

5 Draw x and y axes, using $-3 \leqslant x \leqslant 3$, $-3 \leqslant y \leqslant 5$. Draw the three lines with the following equations:

a $y = 2x + 2$ b $y = -2x + 1$ c $y = 2x$

Which two lines are parallel?

6 Draw x and y axes, marking values from −5 to 5 on each axis. Draw the lines with the following equations:

a $y = 4 - x$ b $y = -x$ c $y = -3 - x$

What do you notice?

Gradients

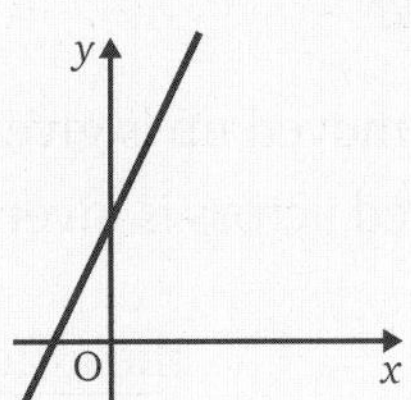

Different lines have different *gradients* or *slopes*. Some lines point steeply up to the right; they have large *positive* gradients.

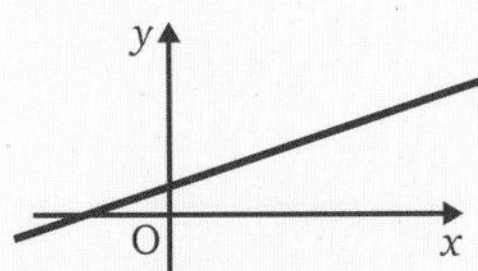

Some have a shallow slope up to the right; they have small *positive* gradients.

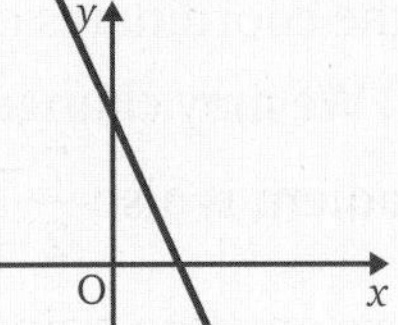

Some lines slope upwards to the left; they have *negative* gradients.

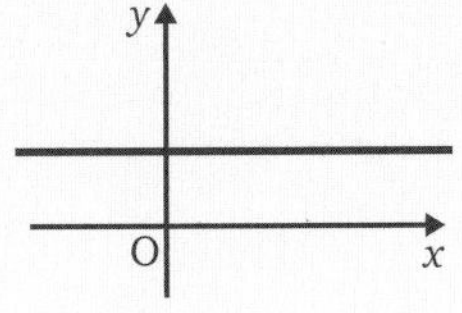

Some lines have zero gradient and are parallel to the x-axis.

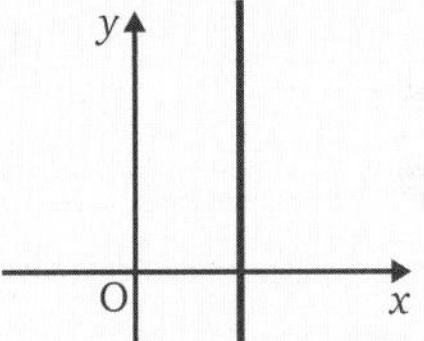

Some lines are parallel to the y-axis.

We can see from the questions in the last exercise that the *coefficient* of x (2 in question **1**, -3 in question **2** and $\frac{1}{2}$ in question **3**) has something to do with gradient.

Calculating the gradient of a line

First method

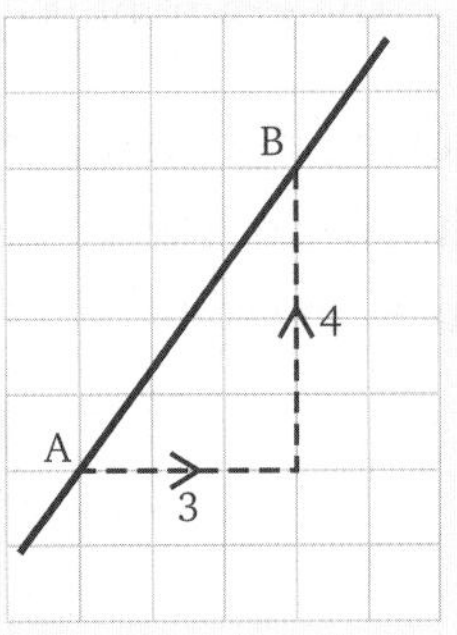

The gradient is found by comparing the amount you move up as you go from A to B, with the amount you move across.

In this case the gradient is $\frac{4}{3}$.

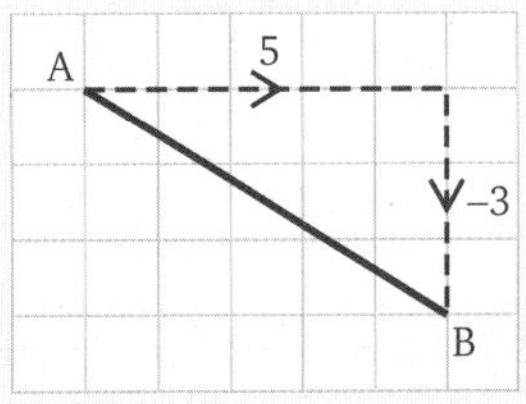

In the second case the distance moved is downwards so we take this distance as negative.

The gradient is $\frac{-3}{5}$, i.e. $-\frac{3}{5}$.

Second method

The distance moved up is given by the difference in the y-coordinates and the distance moved across is given by the difference in the x-coordinates, so the gradient is

$$\frac{\text{the difference in the } y\text{-coordinates}}{\text{the difference in the } x\text{-coordinates}}$$

If A is the point (3, 5) and B is (2, 7) then the gradient is $\frac{5-7}{3-2} = \frac{-2}{1} = -2$

Notice that the coordinates of B are taken away from the coordinates of A for both x and y. We may change the order as long as we change it for both x and y, i.e. the gradient is also $\frac{7-5}{2-3} = -2$

We can choose any two points on a line to calculate the gradient.

If these two points are (x_1, y_1) and (x_2, y_2) then

> the gradient of the line is given by $\frac{y_1 - y_2}{x_1 - x_2}$

Exercise 16e

Find the gradients of the lines joining the points

a (4, 2) and (6, 7) **b** (2, 3) and (4, –3)

a *Either* from the diagram the gradient is $\frac{5}{2}$

(In moving from left to right you go up 5 units (i.e. +5) and go across 2 units to the right, i.e. +2.)

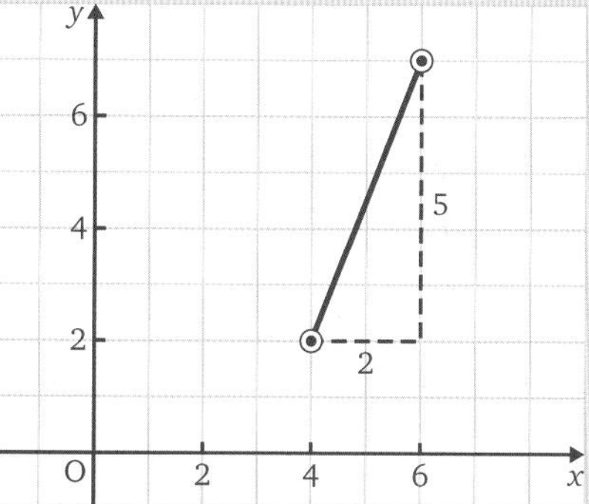

Or using $\frac{y_1 - y_2}{x_1 - x_2}$ with $(x_1, y_1) = (4, 2)$ and $(x_2, y_2) = (6, 7)$ gives

$$\text{gradient} = \frac{2-7}{4-6} = \frac{-5}{-2} = \frac{5}{2}$$

(We could also use $\frac{y_1 - y_2}{x_1 - x_2}$ in the form $\frac{y_2 - y_1}{x_2 - x_1}$ to avoid minus signs.)

b *Either* from the diagram

the gradient is $\frac{-6}{2} = -3$

(In moving from left to right you go down 6 units (–6) and across to the right 2 units, i.e. +2.)

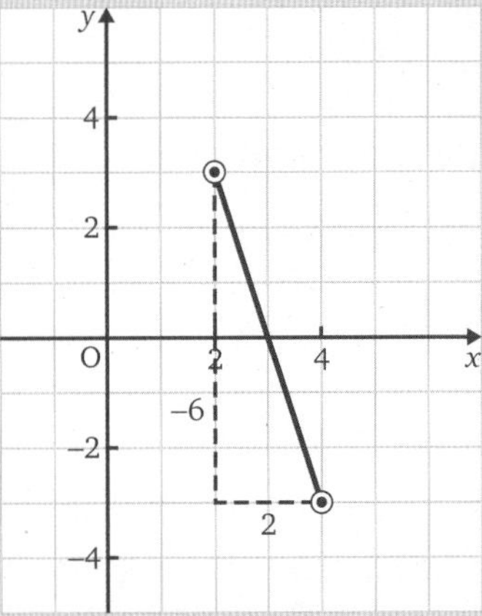

Or using $\frac{y_1 - y_2}{x_1 - x_2}$ with $(x_1, y_1) = (2, 3)$ and $(x_2, y_2) = (4, -3)$ gives

$$\text{gradient} = \frac{3-(-3)}{2-4} = \frac{6}{-2} = -3$$

Find the gradients of the lines joining the following pairs of points:

If you understand what is going on and can find the gradient without plotting the points on a grid, do so.

1 (5, 1) and (7, 9)

2 (3, 6) and (5, 2)

3 (3, 4) and (6, 7)

4 (–2, 4) and (2, 1)

5 (1, 2) and (6, –7)

6 (–3, 4) and (–6, 2)

7 Find the gradient of the line joining the points (4, 3) and (7, 3).

8 Which axis is parallel to the line joining the points (4, 3) and (4, 6)? What happens when you try to work out the gradient?

9 If lines are drawn joining the following pairs of points, state which lines have zero gradient and which are parallel to the *y*-axis:

a (0, 4) and (0, –2) **c** (–6, 0) and (–2, 0)

b (3, 0) and (–10, 0) **d** (0, 6) and (0, 12)

10 If (2, 1) is a point on a line and its gradient is 3, draw the line and find the coordinates of two other points on it.

Exercise 16f

Find the gradient of the line $y = -2x + 3$

Choose any two points on the line, e.g. $(-2, 7)$ and $(2, -1)$.

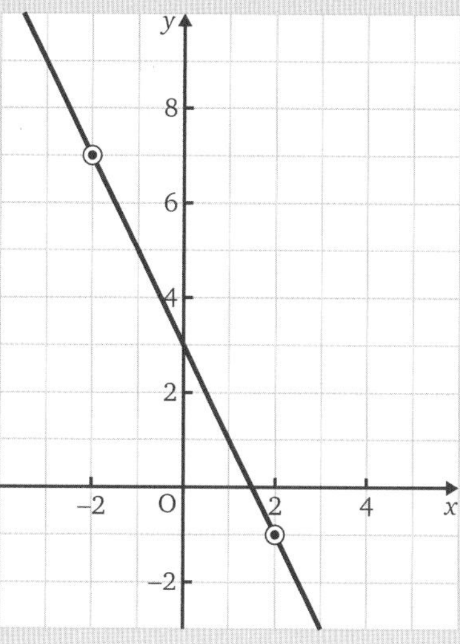

$$\text{Gradient} = \frac{-1-7}{2-(-2)} = \frac{-8}{4} = -2$$

(This is the same as the coefficient of x in the equation of the line.)

Choose two points on each line and hence find the gradient of the line. In each case compare your answer with the coefficient of x:

1 $y = 2x + 3$

2 $y = x + 4$

3 $y = 2x - 1$

4 $y = 3 - 2x$

You may find that drawing a diagram helps.

5 State the gradient of the line $y = 4x + 1$, without calculation if possible.

6 Give the gradients of the lines with equations

a $y = 4x + 4$ b $y = 2 - 3x$ c $y = x - 3$ d $y = \frac{1}{2}x + 1$

7 Sketch a line with a gradient of

a 3 b -1

<u>8</u> Sketch a line with a gradient of

a 4 b $\frac{1}{2}$

<u>9</u> Sketch a line with a gradient of

a -2 b 1

In Exercise 16f you saw that when the equation of a line is in the form $y = mx + c$, the value of m (i.e. the coefficient of x) gives the gradient of the line.

The intercept on the *y*-axis

Consider the line with equation $y = x + 3$.

When $x = 0$, $y = 3$, so the line crosses the y-axis where $y = 3$.

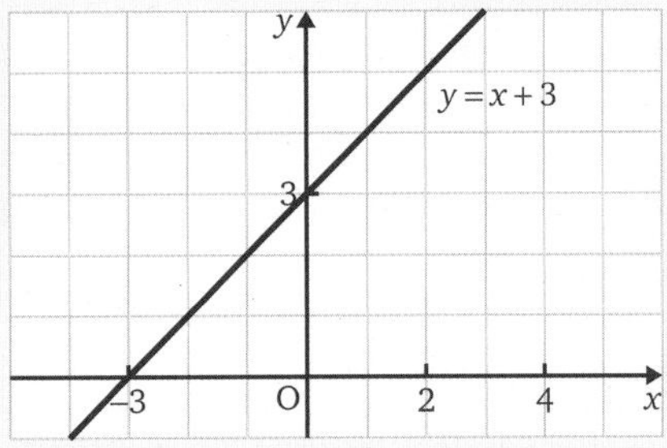

If the equation is $y = 2x - 3$ then, when $x = 0$, $y = -3$, i.e. the line cuts the y-axis where $y = -3$.

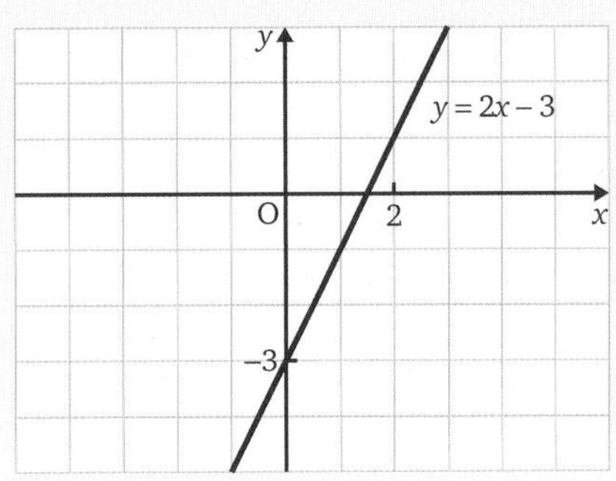

As long as the equation is of the form $y = mx + c$, i.e. like $y = 2x + 3$ or $y = -5x + 1$, then

> the number term c tells us where the line cuts the y-axis and m, the coefficient of x, tells us the gradient.

The equation $y = mx + c$ is the standard form of the equation of a straight line.

If the equation is $y = 3x$ then the number term is 0, i.e. the y-intercept is 0. Therefore, the line goes through the origin.

Exercise 16g

Give the gradient and the intercept on the y-axis of the line with equation $y = x + 5$. Sketch the line.

The gradient is the coefficient of x when the equation is written in the form $y = mx + c$, i.e. 1.

The intercept on the y-axis is 5.

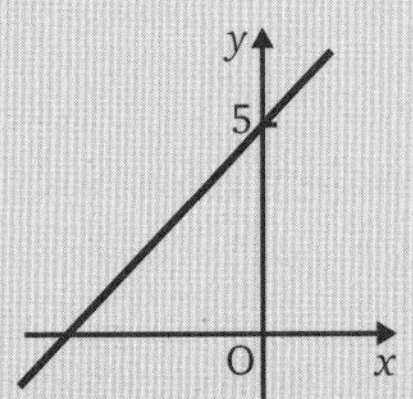

Give the gradients and the intercepts on the y-axis of the lines with the following equations. *Sketch* each line:

1 $y = 2x + 4$ **2** $y = 5x + 3$ **3** $y = 3x - 4$ **4** $y = x - 6$

Give the gradient and the intercept on the y-axis of the line with equation $y = 4 - 2x$. Sketch the line.

Rewrite the equation in the form $y = mx + c$, i.e. as $y = -2x + 4$

The gradient is -2 so the lines slope back to the left.

The intercept on the y-axis is 4.

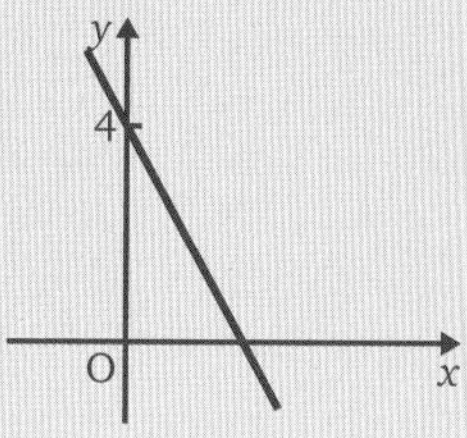

Give the gradients and the intercepts on the y-axis of the lines with the following equations. Sketch each line:

5 $y = 3 - 2x$

6 $y = -4x + 2$

7 $y = 2 + 5x$

8 $y = \frac{1}{2}x - 1$

9 $y = -\frac{1}{3}x + 4$

<u>10</u> $y = 3x - 7$

<u>11</u> $y = 7 - 3x$

<u>12</u> $y = \frac{1}{3}x + 7$

<u>13</u> $y = 9 - 0.4x$

<u>14</u> $y = 4 + 5x$

Give the gradient and the intercept on the y-axis of the line with equation $2y = 3x - 1$. Sketch the line.

$2y = 3x - 1$ (Write this equation in the form $y = mx + c$)

Divide both sides by 2 $y = \frac{3}{2}x - \frac{1}{2}$

The gradient is $\frac{3}{2}$ so the line slopes up to the right.

The intercept on the y-axis is $-\frac{1}{2}$.

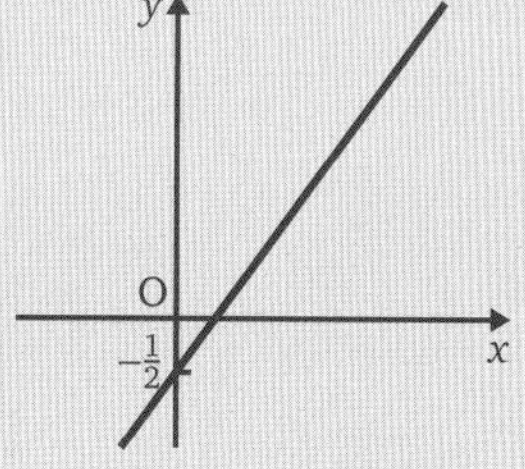

Give the gradients and the intercepts on the y-axis of the lines with the following equations. Sketch each line:

15 $2y = 4x + 5$ **16** $3y = x - 6$ **17** $5y = 5 + 2x$ **18** $4y = 8 - 3x$

A line has a gradient of -2 and the intercept on the y-axis is 4. Find the equation of the line.

Comparing with the equation $y = mx + c$, $m = -2$ and $c = 4$.

The equation is $y = -2x + 4$

Write down the equations of the lines with the given gradients and intercepts on the y-axis (y-intercepts):

	Gradient	y-intercept
19	2	7
20	3	1
21	1	3
22	2	−5

	Gradient	y-intercept
23	$\frac{1}{2}$	6
24	−2	1
25	1	−2
26	$-\frac{1}{2}$	4

Puzzle

A farmer grows cabbages on a square plot. He says he has 151 more cabbages this year than last year, when he also had a square plot. How many cabbages did he raise last year?

Parallel lines

Exercise 16h

Which of the lines with the following equations are parallel:

$y = 2x + 3,\quad y = 4 - 2x,\quad y = 4 + 2x,\quad 2y = x + 1,\quad y = x + 3$?

Written in the form $y = mx + c$ the equations of these lines are
$y = 2x + 3,\quad y = -2x + 4,\quad y = 2x + 4,\quad y = \frac{1}{2}x + \frac{1}{2}$ and $y = x + 3$.

The gradients of the lines are 2, −2, 2, $\frac{1}{2}$ and 1, so the first and third lines are parallel.

In questions **1** to **4**, state which of the lines with the given equations are parallel.

1 $y = 3x + 1,\quad y = \frac{1}{3}x - 4,\quad y = x + 1,$
$y = 4 - 3x,\quad y = 5 + 3x,\quad y = 3x - 4$

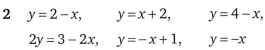

Write each equation in the form $y = mx + c$ first.

2 $y = 2 - x,\quad y = x + 2,\quad y = 4 - x,$
$2y = 3 - 2x,\quad y = -x + 1,\quad y = -x$

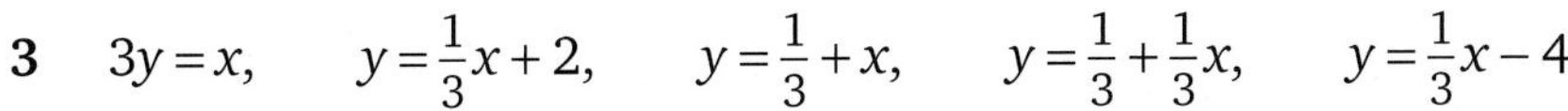

3 $3y = x,\quad y = \frac{1}{3}x + 2,\quad y = \frac{1}{3} + x,\quad y = \frac{1}{3} + \frac{1}{3}x,\quad y = \frac{1}{3}x - 4$

4 $y = \frac{1}{2}x + 2,\quad y = 2 - \frac{1}{2}x,\quad y = -x - 4,\quad y = \frac{1}{2}x - 1,\quad 2y = 3 - x$

5 What is the gradient of the line with equation $y = 2x + 1$? Give the equation of the line that is parallel to the first line and which cuts the y-axis at the point (0, 3).

6 What is the gradient of the line with equation $y = 6 - 3x$?

If a parallel line goes through the point (0, 1), what is its equation?

7 Give the equation of the line through the origin that is parallel to the line with equation $y = 4x + 2$.

8 Give the equations of any three lines that are parallel to the line with equation $y = 4 - x$.

9 Give the equations of the lines through the point (0, 4) that are parallel to the lines with equations

a $y = 4x + 1$ b $y = 6 - 3x$ c $y = \frac{1}{2}x + 1$

10 Give the equations of the lines, parallel to the line with equation $y = \frac{1}{3}x + 1$, that pass through the points

a (0, 6) b (0, 0) c (0, –3)

11 Give the equations of the lines with gradient 2 which pass through the points

a (0, 2) b (0, 10) c (0, –4)

12 Which two of the lines with the following equations are parallel?

$y = 3 + 2x$, $y = 3 - 2x$, $y = 2x - 3$

13 Find the gradients and the intercepts on the y-axis of the lines with equations $y = 4 - 3x$ and $y = 4x - 3$. Give the equation of the line that is parallel to the first line and cuts the y-axis at the same point as the second line.

14 A line of gradient –4 passes through the origin.

a Give its equation.

b Give the equation of the line that is parallel to the first line and that passes through the point (0, –7).

Different forms of the equation of a straight line

The terms in the equation of a straight line can only be x terms, y terms or number terms.

An equation containing terms like x^2, y^2, $\frac{1}{x}$, $\frac{1}{x^2}$ is not the equation of a straight line.

Sometimes the equation of a straight line is not given exactly in the form $y = mx + c$.

It could be $2x + y = 6$ or $\frac{x}{4} + \frac{y}{2} = 1$.

An easy way to draw a line when its equation is in one of these forms is to start by finding the points where it cuts each axis.

Exercise 16i

Draw on graph paper the line with equation

$$3x - 4y = 12 \text{ (use } 0 \leqslant x \leqslant 5)$$

Find the gradient of the line.

$$3x - 4y = 12$$

When $x = 0$, $-4y = 12$, i.e. $y = -3$

When $y = 0$, $3x = 12$, i.e. $x = 4$

So the points $(0, -3)$ and $(4, 0)$ lie on the line.

(Draw the line using these two points only.

Choose a point on the line, e.g. $(2, -1\frac{1}{2})$, to check.)

Check: when $x = 2$, $y = -1\frac{1}{2}$

$3x - 4y = 6 - 4 \times (-1\frac{1}{2}) = 6 + 6 = 12$, which is correct.

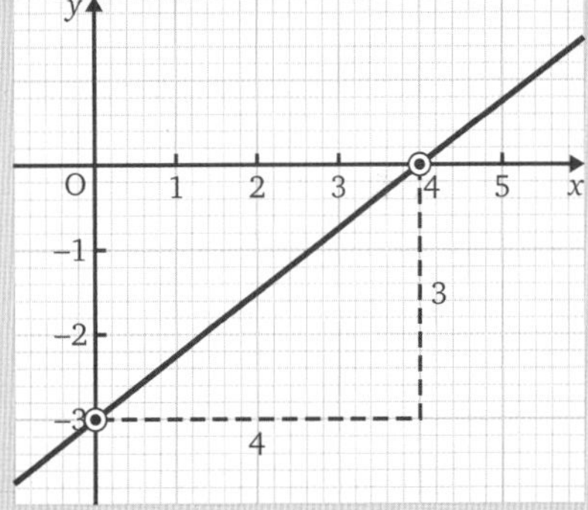

From the graph, the gradient $= \frac{3}{4}$ (lines that slope up to the right have a positive gradient).

Draw on graph paper the lines with the following equations. Use 1 cm to 1 unit.

Find the gradient of each line:

1 $3x + 5y = 15$ $\quad 0 \leqslant x \leqslant 6$

2 $2x + 6y = 12$ $\quad 0 \leqslant x \leqslant 6$

3 $x - 4y = 8$ $\quad 0 \leqslant x \leqslant 8$

4 $x + y = 6$ $\quad 0 \leqslant x \leqslant 7$

5 $2x + y = 5$ $\quad -2 \leqslant x \leqslant 4$

6 $x + 3y = 5$ $\quad 0 \leqslant x \leqslant 5$

7 $x - 3y = 6$ $\quad 0 \leqslant x \leqslant 6$

8 $2x - y = 3$ $\quad -2 \leqslant x \leqslant 2$

9 On the same axes ($-6 \leqslant x \leqslant 6$ and $-6 \leqslant y \leqslant 6$) draw the lines with equations $x + y = 1$, $x + y = 4$, $x + y = 6$, $x + y = -4$. Find their gradients.

Exercise 16j

Draw on graph paper the line with equation

$$\frac{x}{3}+\frac{y}{2}=1 \quad (-1 \leqslant x \leqslant 4)$$

Find its gradient.

When $x=0$, $\frac{y}{2}=1$, so $y=2$

When $y=0$, $\frac{x}{3}=1$, so $x=3$

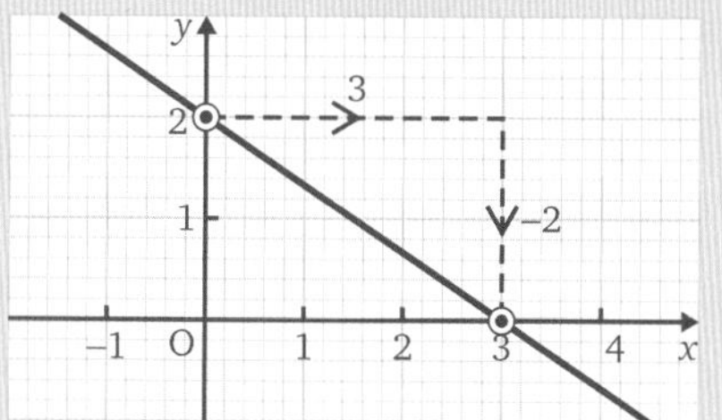

Check: from the graph, when $x=1\frac{1}{2}$, $y=1$

Therefore $\frac{x}{3}+\frac{y}{2}=\frac{1\frac{1}{2}}{3}+\frac{1}{2}=\frac{1}{2}+\frac{1}{2}=1$ which is correct.

The gradient is $-\frac{2}{3}$ (lines that slope up to the left have a negative gradient).

Draw on graph paper the lines whose equations are given below. Find the gradient of each line:

1 $\frac{x}{4}+\frac{y}{3}=1$

2 $\frac{x}{5}+\frac{y}{3}=1$

3 $\frac{x}{4}-\frac{y}{2}=1$

<u>4</u> $\frac{x}{3}+\frac{y}{6}=1$

<u>5</u> $\frac{x}{1}-\frac{y}{2}=1$

<u>6</u> $\frac{y}{3}-\frac{x}{4}=1$

7 Without drawing a diagram, state where the lines with the following equations cut the axes:

a $\frac{x}{2}+\frac{y}{4}=1$ **b** $\frac{x}{12}-\frac{y}{9}=1$

8 Form the equations of the lines which cut the axes at

a (0, 5) and (6, 0) **b** (0, −3) and (4, 0).

<u>9</u> Sketch the line with equation $\frac{x}{6}+\frac{y}{2}=1$ and find its gradient.

Getting information from the equation of a line

From the last exercise, we can see that if the equation of a line is in the form

$$\frac{x}{a}+\frac{y}{b}=1 \quad \text{(i.e. like questions } \mathbf{1} \text{ to } \mathbf{6}\text{)},$$

then the line cuts the x-axis at $x=a$

and the y-axis at $y=b$.

Then if we sketch the line we can work out the gradient.

If the equation is in the form $ax+by=c$, like those in Exercise 16i, we need to rearrange the equation so that it is in the form $y=mx+c$. Then the gradient and the intercept on the y-axis can be seen.

Exercise 16k

Find the gradient and the intercept on the y-axis of the line with equation $2x+3y=6$.

Change the equation to the form $y=mx+c$.

Subtract $2x$ from both sides $\quad 3y=6-2x$

Divide both sides by 3 $\quad y=2-\frac{2}{3}x$

i.e. $\quad y=-\frac{2}{3}x+2$

The gradient is $-\frac{2}{3}$ and the intercept on the y-axis is 2.

Find the gradient and the intercept on the y-axis of each of the following lines:

1 $3x+5y=15$

2 $2x+6y=12$

3 $x-4y=8$

4 $x-3y=6$

5 $y-3x=6$

6 $x+3y=6$

Find the gradient and the intercept on the y-axis of the line with equation $\frac{x}{2}+\frac{y}{5}=1$.

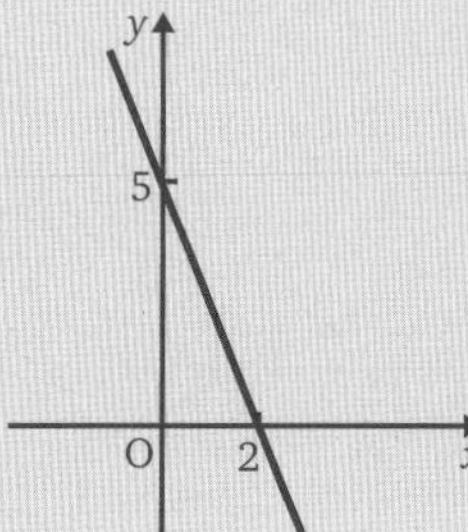

Either

If $y=0$ then $x=2$ and if $x=0$ then $y=5$ so this line cuts the axes at (2, 0) and (0, 5).

Hence the gradient is $-\frac{5}{2}$ and the intercept on the y-axis is 5.

Or $\quad \frac{x}{2}+\frac{y}{5}=1$

Multiply both sides by 5 $\quad \frac{5x}{2}+y=5$

Subtract $\frac{5x}{2}$ from both sides $\quad y=5-\frac{5x}{2}$

i.e. $\quad y=-\frac{5}{2}x+5$

Then the gradient is $-\frac{5}{2}$ and the intercept is 5.

Find the gradient and the intercept on the y-axis of each of the following lines:

7 $\frac{x}{4}+\frac{y}{3}=1$

8 $\frac{x}{5}+\frac{y}{3}=1$

9 $\frac{x}{4}-\frac{y}{2}=1$

10 $\frac{x}{2}+\frac{y}{6}=1$

11 $\frac{x}{3}+\frac{y}{4}=1$

12 $\frac{x}{3}-\frac{y}{4}=1$

13 $y=4x+2$

14 $x+y=4$

15 $\frac{x}{2}+\frac{y}{4}=1$

16 $2x+5y=15$

17 $y=5-\frac{1}{2}x$

18 $2y=4x+5$

19 $\frac{x}{2}-\frac{y}{4}=1$

20 $x+y=-3$

21 $3x+4y=12$

The equation of a line through two given points

Exercise 16I

Find the gradient and the intercept on the y-axis of the line which passes through the points (4, 2) and (0, 4). Hence give the equation of the line.

(A sketch only is needed.)

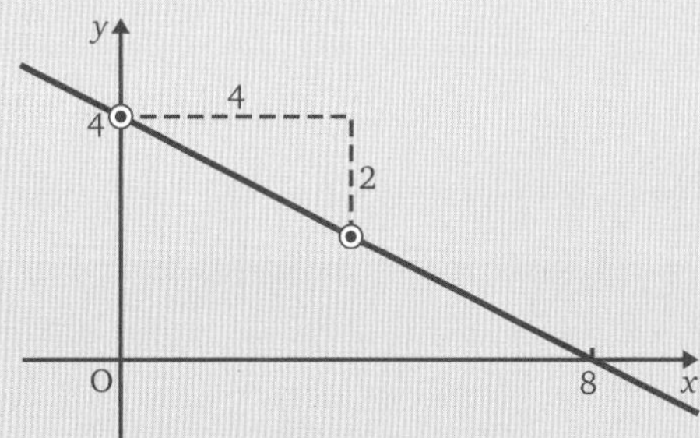

The equation of any line is $y=mx+c$, so to find the equation of this line we need to find the value m, i.e. the gradient, and c, i.e. where it cuts the y-axis.

$$\text{Gradient}=\frac{2-4}{4-0}=\frac{-2}{4}=-\frac{1}{2}$$

When $x=0, y=4$ so the y-intercept $=4$

$\therefore$ the equation is $y=-\frac{1}{2}x+4$

(Multiplying by 2 and rearranging, allows this equation to be written in the form $2y=8-x$ or $2y+x=8$.)

Find the gradient and the intercept on the y-axis of the line through the given points. Hence give the equation of the line:

1 (0, 4) and (3, 0)

2 (0, 7) and (2, 3)

3 (5, 4) and (0, 1)

4 (0, 2) and (3, –2)

5 (0, –4) and (2, 3)

6 (–6, –3) and (0, –1)

7 (6, 2) and (0, 1)

8 (5, 1) and (0, –3)

9 (0, –4) and (3, 1)

10 (–5, 0) and (0, –5)

11 (0, 12) and (–6, 0)

12 (–6, 1) and (0, 6)

13 A, B and C are the points (0, 4), (5, 6) and (3, –1). Find the equations of the lines AB and AC.

Find the gradient and the equation of the line through (6, 2) and (4, 8).

The gradient is $\frac{2-8}{6-4} = \frac{-6}{2} = -3$

(We do not know the intercept on the y-axis.)

Let the equation be $y = -3x + c$,

i.e. $m = -3$ in the equation $y = mx + c$.

When $x = 6, y = 2$ so $2 = -18 + c$

$\therefore$ $c = 20$

$\therefore$ the equation is $y = -3x + 20$

(*Check*: when $x = 4$, the equation gives $y = -12 + 20$, i.e. $y = 8$, which is correct.)

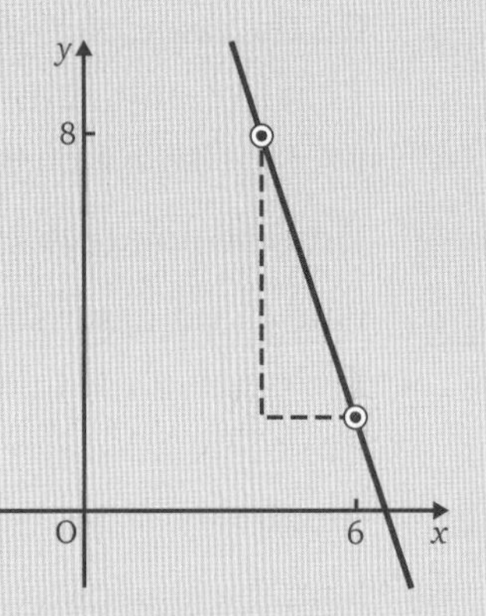

In questions **14** to **34**, find the gradient and the equation of the line through the given pair of points:

14 (4, 1) and (7, 10)

15 (1, 4) and (2, 1)

16 (3, 7) and (5, 12)

17 (–2, 3) and (–1, 5)

18 (4, –1) and (3, –6)

19 (5, –2) and (–4, 7)

20 (–6, 7) and (1, 0)

21 (4, –3) and (2, –7)

22 (–9, –3) and (6, 0)

23 (4, 0) and (0, 5)

24 (3, 0) and (0, 2)

25 (3, 0) and (0, –2)

26 (2, 0) and (0, 6)

27 (4, 2) and (6, 8)

28 (0, 4) and (3, 1)

29 (2, 1) and (0, –6)

30 (–1, 4) and (5, –2)

31 (0, 5) and (–2, 0)

32 (–6, 3) and (5, 5)

33 (–1, –2) and (–5, –6)

34 (3, 2) and (7, 1)

Problems

Exercise 16m

1 Find the equation of the line through the point (6, 2) which is parallel to the line $y = 3x - 1$.

Remember that parallel lines have the same gradient.

2 On the same pair of axes, for $-8 \leqslant x \leqslant 8$ and $-12 \leqslant y \leqslant 4$, using 1 cm to 1 unit, draw the four lines $y = 2x - 4$, $y = 2x + 6$, $x + 2y + 10 = 0$ and $2y + x = 0$. What type of quadrilateral is formed by the four lines?

3 On the same pair of axes, for $-4 \leqslant x \leqslant 10$ and $-6 \leqslant y \leqslant 10$ using 1 cm to 1 unit, draw the four lines $y = 3x + 4$, $y = 3x - 6$, $y = -3x$ and $y = 10 - 3x$. Name the type of quadrilateral formed by the lines.

4 Find the point where the lines $y = 2x + 2$ and $y = 4 - 2x$ meet.

5 Find the equation of the line with gradient -2 that passes through the midpoint of the line joining the points (3, 2) and (7, 4). (The midpoint can be found either from a drawing on square grid paper or from a rough sketch.)

6 Find the equation of the line that is parallel to the line joining $(-1, 4)$ and (3, 2) and which passes through the point (4, 0).

7 On the same pair of axes, for $-2 \leqslant x \leqslant 5$ and $-5 \leqslant y \leqslant 2$, using 1 cm to 1 unit, draw the four lines $4y = x + 1$, $4y = x - 16$, $4x + y - 13 = 0$ and $4x + y + 4 = 0$. Name the type of quadrilateral formed by the lines.

Mixed exercises

Exercise 16n

1 What is the gradient of the line with equation $y = 2x + 1$?

2 At what point does the line with equation $y = 4 - 2x$ cut the y-axis?

3 At what point does the line with equation $\frac{x}{4} - \frac{y}{3} = 1$ cut the x-axis?

4 On the line with equation $y = 6 - 2x$, if $x = -3$, what is y?

5 What is the equation of the line whose gradient is 5 and which passes through the origin?

6 At what point does the line with equation $2x + 3y = 24$ cut the x-axis?

7 Does the point (2, 4) lie on the line with equation $y = 6x - 8$?

8 Find the gradient of the line joining the points (6, 4) and (1, 1).

Exercise 16p

1 What is the gradient of the line with equation $y = 4 - 3x$?

2 Does the point (6, –1) lie on the line $3x + 11y = 8$?

3 What is the equation of the line that passes through the origin and has a gradient of –4?

4 At what point does the line with equation $y = 4 - x$ cut the y-axis?

5 At what points does the line with equation $x + y = 6$ cut the two axes?

6 Find the gradient of the line through the points (3, 1) and (5, –2).

7 Give the equation of the line that is parallel to the line with equation $y = 4 + \frac{1}{2}x$ and which passes through the origin.

8 At what points does the line $\frac{x}{2} + \frac{y}{3} = 1$ cut the two axes?

? Puzzle

A hunter met two shepherds. One shepherd had three small loaves while the other shepherd had five similar loaves. All the loaves were the same size. They decided to divide the eight loaves equally between the three of them. The hunter thanked the shepherds and paid them eight dinars.

How should the shepherds divide the money?

Did you know?

There is something special about the integers 1, 2 and 3. Their sum is equal to their product. There is only one other set of three integers that have this property. Can you find them?

In this chapter you have seen that...

- ✔ the equation $x = h$ gives a straight line parallel to the y-axis
- ✔ the equation $y = k$ gives a straight line parallel to the x-axis
- ✔ if you know one coordinate of a point on a line you can use the equation of the line to find the other coordinate
- ✔ the gradient of the straight line joining two points is

$$\frac{\text{the difference in the } y\text{-coordinates}}{\text{the difference in the } x\text{-coordinates}} = \frac{y_1 - y_2}{x_1 - x_2}$$

- ✔ a line that slopes up to the right has a positive gradient while a line that slopes the other way has a negative gradient; the bigger the gradient the steeper the slope
- ✔ any equation that can be arranged in the form $y = mx + c$ represents a straight line, with gradient m, that crosses the y-axis at the point $(0, c)$; c is called the y-intercept. For example, the equation $2x + 3y = 8$ can be rewritten as $y = -\frac{2}{3}x + \frac{8}{3}$ and so represents a straight line with gradient $\frac{-2}{3}$ and y-intercept $\frac{8}{3}$
- ✔ lines that have the same gradient are parallel.

17 Linear equations and inequalities

At the end of this chapter you should be able to...

1 solve simple linear equations involving fractions

2 solve inequalities algebraically

3 represent inequalities on a diagram

4 write down inequalities to describe a region.

Did you know?

Some numbers have special names. For example, 6 is known as a *perfect number* because the sum of the whole numbers that will divide into it exactly, i.e. its factors, is equal to the number.

The factors of 6 are 1, 2 and 3 and $1 + 2 + 3 = 6$

Another number that does this is 28 – check it.

The next such number is 496.

Show that the sum of the numbers that will divide into 496 exactly is 496.

Perfect numbers are also known as *aliquot* numbers.

You need to know...

✔ how to simplify expressions containing brackets

✔ how to collect terms

✔ how the multiply and divide one fraction by another

✔ the order in which to do multiplication, division, addition and subtraction

✔ how to multiply directed numbers

✔ the meaning of a formula

✔ what the lowest common multiple means

✔ the equations of lines parallel to the axes

✔ the meaning of the symbols $<$, $\leqslant$, $>$ and $\geqslant$

✔ how to draw a number line

✔ how to work with positive and negative numbers.

Key words

boundary line, brackets, common factor, coordinates, denominator, division, eliminate, equation, equilateral triangle, equivalent, formula (plural formulae), fraction, inequality, linear, lowest common multiple, multiplication, negative number, number line, numerator, one-dimensional, perimeter, range, rectangle, region, similar, symbols $<$, $\leqslant$, $>$ and $\geqslant$, two-dimensional space, x and y coordinates, xy plane

Linear equations

In Book 2 we learnt how to solve simple linear equations and equations involving *brackets*. The next exercise revises that work.

Exercise 17a

Solve the following equations:

1 $3x = 12$

2 $5 + 4x = 17$

3 $5x - 1 = 14$

4 $7 + 8x = 55$

5 $11 - 2x = 7$

6 $12 - 5x = 2$

7 $17 - 3x = 5$

8 $33 - 8x = 9$

Simplify:

9 $3(x + 5) + 2(x + 1)$

10 $4(x - 1) + 2(x + 5)$

11 $2(3x + 7) + 5(2 + 5x)$

12 $3(4 - 2x) + 7(2 + x)$

13 $5(x + 2) + 3(x + 3)$

14 $4(2x + 3) + 5(6 - x)$

15 $3(3x + 1) + 2(5x - 4)$

16 $6(4x - 3) + 3(3x + 1)$

Solve the following equations:

17 $3x + 5 = x + 13$

18 $4x - 2 = 3x + 5$

19 $1 - 3x = 7 - 5x$

20 $7 - 2x = 15 + x$

21 $3(x + 1) = 12$

22 $8(2x - 3) = 56$

23 $3(4 - 3x) = 9$

24 $5(3x - 2) = 7(2x + 1)$

25 $4(2x + 1) = 2(3x + 4)$

26 $2(x + 1) = 3(x - 2)$

27 $5(x + 2) = 3(4 + x)$

28 $2(1 - 5x) = 13$

29 $3(2x + 5) = 2(x + 9)$

30 $5(3 - 4x) = 3(4 - 3x)$

Multiplication and division of fractions

Remember that, to multiply fractions, the numerators are multiplied together and the denominators are multiplied together:

i.e. $\frac{3}{4} \times \frac{5}{7} = \frac{3 \times 5}{4 \times 7} = \frac{15}{28}$

Also $\frac{1}{6}$ of x means $\frac{1}{6} \times x = \frac{1}{6} \times \frac{x}{1} = \frac{x}{6}$ (1)

Remember that, to divide by a fraction, that fraction is turned upside down and multiplied:

i.e. $\frac{2}{3} \div \frac{5}{7} = \frac{2}{3} \times \frac{7}{5} = \frac{14}{15}$

and $x \div 6 = \frac{x}{1} \div \frac{6}{1} = \frac{x}{1} \times \frac{1}{6} = \frac{x}{6}$ (2)

Comparing (1) and (2) we see that

> $\frac{1}{6}$ of x, $\frac{1}{6}x$, $x \div 6$ and $\frac{x}{6}$ are all equivalent

Exercise 17b

Simplify $12 \times \frac{x}{3}$

$$12 \times \frac{x}{3} = \frac{\cancel{12}^{4}}{1} \times \frac{x}{\cancel{3}_{1}}$$
$$= 4x$$

Simplify $\frac{2x}{3} \div 8$

$$\frac{2x}{3} \div 8 = \frac{2x}{3} \div \frac{8}{1}$$
$$= \frac{{}^{1}\cancel{2}x}{3} \times \frac{1}{\cancel{8}_{4}}$$ (Now cancel common factors: remember that $2x = 2 \times x$)
$$= \frac{x}{12}$$

Simplify:

1 $4 \times \frac{x}{8}$

2 $\frac{1}{2} \times \frac{x}{3}$

3 $9 \times \frac{x}{6}$

4 $\frac{1}{3}$ of $2x$

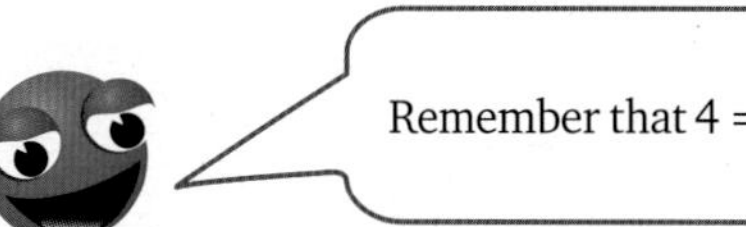

5 $\frac{2x}{3} \times \frac{6}{5}$

6 $\frac{1}{5}$ of $10x$

7 $\frac{2}{5} \times \frac{3x}{4}$

8 $\frac{3}{4} \times 2x$

9 $\frac{2}{3}$ of $9x$

10 $\frac{x}{2} \times \frac{x}{3}$

11 $\frac{5x}{2} \div 4$

12 $\frac{4x}{9} \div 8$

13 $\frac{x}{3} \div \frac{1}{6}$

14 $\frac{x}{4} \div \frac{1}{2}$

15 $\frac{2x}{3} \div \frac{5}{6}$

16 $\frac{3}{4} \times \frac{2x}{5}$

17 $\frac{4x}{9} \div \frac{2}{3}$

18 $\frac{3}{5}$ of $15x$

19 $\frac{3x}{2} \div \frac{1}{6}$

20 $\frac{5x}{3} \times \frac{6x}{15}$

Fractional equations

Exercise 17c

Solve the equation $\frac{x}{3} = 2$

(As $\frac{x}{3}$ means $\frac{1}{3}$ of x, to find x we need to make $\frac{x}{3}$ three times larger.)

$$\frac{x}{3} = 2$$

Multiply each side by 3 $\quad \frac{x}{3_1} \times \frac{3^1}{1} = 2 \times 3$

$$x = 6$$

Solve the following equations:

1 $\frac{x}{5} = 3$

2 $\frac{x}{2} = 4$

3 $\frac{x}{6} = 8$

4 $\frac{2x}{3} = 8$

5 $16 = \frac{9x}{2}$

<u>6</u> $\frac{2x}{5} = 9$

<u>7</u> $\frac{4x}{7} = 8$

<u>8</u> $\frac{6x}{5} = 10$

Solve the equation $\frac{2x}{5} = \frac{1}{3}$

$$\frac{2x}{5} = \frac{1}{3}$$

Multiply each side by 5 to get rid of the fraction on the left-hand side $\quad \frac{2x}{5_1} \times \frac{5^1}{1} = \frac{1}{3} \times \frac{5}{1}$

$$2x = \frac{5}{3}$$

Divide each side by 2 $\quad x = \frac{5}{3} \div 2$

$$x = \frac{5}{3} \times \frac{1}{2}$$

$$x = \frac{5}{6}$$

Solve the following equations:

9 $\frac{3x}{2}=\frac{1}{4}$ **11** $\frac{2x}{9}=\frac{1}{3}$ **<u>13</u>** $\frac{3x}{8}=\frac{1}{2}$ **15** $\frac{3x}{5}=\frac{1}{4}$

10 $\frac{4x}{3}=\frac{1}{5}$ **<u>12</u>** $\frac{6x}{5}=\frac{2}{3}$ **<u>14</u>** $\frac{5x}{7}=\frac{3}{4}$ **16** $\frac{4x}{7}=\frac{2}{5}$

Solve the equation $\frac{x}{5}+\frac{1}{2}=1$.

(Both 5 and 2 divide into 10, so by multiplying each side by 10 we can eliminate all fractions from this equation before we start to solve for x.)

$$\frac{x}{5}+\frac{1}{2}=1$$

Multiply both sides by 10 $$10\left(\frac{x}{5}+\frac{1}{2}\right)=10\times 1$$

$$\frac{\cancel{10}^{2}}{1}\times\frac{x}{\cancel{5}_{1}}+\frac{\cancel{10}^{5}}{1}\times\frac{1}{\cancel{2}_{1}}=10$$

$$2x+5=10$$

Subtract 5 from each side $$2x=5$$

Divide each side by 2 $$x=2\tfrac{1}{2}$$

Solve the following equations:

17 $\frac{x}{3}+\frac{1}{4}=1$ **19** $\frac{x}{5}+\frac{2x}{3}=3$ **21** $\frac{2x}{3}-\frac{1}{2}=4$ **<u>23</u>** $\frac{x}{3}-\frac{2}{9}=4$ **<u>25</u>** $\frac{3}{4}-\frac{x}{5}=1$

18 $\frac{x}{5}-\frac{3}{4}=2$ **20** $\frac{5x}{7}+\frac{x}{2}=2$ **<u>22</u>** $\frac{x}{3}+\frac{5}{6}=2$ **<u>24</u>** $\frac{3x}{4}-\frac{x}{2}=5$ **<u>26</u>** $\frac{5}{7}+\frac{3x}{4}=2$

Solve the following equations:

27 $\frac{x}{3}+\frac{1}{4}=\frac{1}{2}$

28 $\frac{x}{5}+\frac{2}{3}=\frac{14}{15}$

Multiply both sides by the lowest common multiple of the denominators.

29 $\frac{x}{4}-\frac{1}{2}=\frac{9}{4}$ **<u>33</u>** $\frac{5x}{6}+\frac{x}{8}=\frac{3}{4}$ **<u>37</u>** $\frac{3x}{4}+\frac{1}{3}=\frac{x}{2}+\frac{5}{8}$

30 $\frac{2x}{3}+\frac{2}{7}=\frac{1}{3}$ **<u>34</u>** $\frac{3x}{4}+\frac{1}{8}=\frac{1}{2}$ **<u>38</u>** $\frac{2x}{7}-\frac{3}{4}=\frac{x}{14}+\frac{1}{2}$

31 $\frac{x}{2}-\frac{3}{7}=\frac{1}{2}$ **<u>35</u>** $\frac{5x}{12}-\frac{1}{3}=\frac{x}{8}$ **<u>39</u>** $\frac{5x}{7}-\frac{2}{3}=\frac{3}{7}-\frac{x}{3}$

<u>32</u> $\frac{3x}{5}+\frac{2}{9}=\frac{11}{15}$ **<u>36</u>** $\frac{2x}{5}-\frac{x}{15}=\frac{5}{9}$ **<u>40</u>** $\frac{2x}{9}-\frac{3}{4}=\frac{7}{18}-\frac{5x}{12}$

41 $\frac{3}{11} - \frac{x}{2} = \frac{2x}{11} + \frac{1}{4}$

42 $\frac{3}{5} - \frac{x}{9} = \frac{2}{15} - \frac{2x}{45}$

43 $\frac{4}{7} + \frac{2x}{9} = \frac{15}{9} - \frac{4x}{21}$

44 $\frac{x}{3} + \frac{1}{4} - \frac{x}{6} = \frac{7}{12}$

45 $\frac{5}{8} - \frac{x}{6} + \frac{1}{12} = \frac{3}{4}$

46 $\frac{5}{9} - \frac{7x}{12} = \frac{1}{6} - \frac{x}{8}$

Problems

Exercise 17d

Form an equation for each of the following problems and then solve the equation.

A bag of sweets was divided into three equal shares. David had one share and he got 8 sweets. How many sweets were there in the bag?

Let x stand for the number of sweets in the bag.

One share is $\frac{1}{3}$ of x $\quad\therefore\quad \frac{1}{3}$ of $x = 8$

$$\frac{x}{3} = 8$$

Multiply each side by 3 $\quad x = 24$

Therefore there were 24 sweets in the bag.

1 Tracy Brown came first in the St James, Barbados Golf Tournament and won \$100. This was $\frac{2}{3}$ of the total prize money paid out. Find the total prize money.

2 Peter lost 8 marbles in a game. This number was one-fifth of the number that he started with. Find how many he started with.

Start by letting x or some other letter stand for the number you need to find.

3 The width of a rectangle is 12 cm. This is two-fifths of its length. Find the length of the rectangle.

4 I think of a number, halve it and the result is 6. Find the number that I first thought of.

5 The length of a rectangle is 8 cm and this is $\frac{1}{3}$ of its perimeter. Find its perimeter.

6 In an equilateral triangle, the perimeter is 15 cm. Find the length of one side of the triangle.

7 I think of a number, take $\frac{1}{3}$ of it and then add 4. The result is 7. Find the number I first thought of.

8 I think of a number and divide it by 3. The result is 2 less than the number I first thought of. Find the number I first thought of.

9 I think of a number and add $\frac{1}{3}$ of it to $\frac{1}{2}$ of it. The result is 10. Find the number I first thought of.

10 John Smith won the singles competition of a local tennis tournament, for which he got $\frac{1}{5}$ of the total prize money. He also won the doubles competition, for which he got $\frac{1}{20}$ of the prize money. He got \$250 altogether. How much was the total prize money?

Substituting numerical values into formulae involving fractions

Exercise 17e

Given that $s = \frac{1}{2}(a + b + c)$ find

a s when $a = 4$, $b = 5$ and $c = 6$ **b** b when $s = 13$, $a = 8$ and $c = 7$.

a When $a = 4$, $b = 5$ and $c = 6$

$s = \frac{1}{2}(4 + 5 + 6) = \frac{1}{2} \times 15 = 7\frac{1}{2}$

b When $s = 13$, $a = 8$ and $c = 7$

$13 = \frac{1}{2}(8 + b + 7)$

i.e. $26 = 15 + b$

$26 - 15 = b$

$b = 11$

1 Given that $s = \frac{1}{3}(a - b)$, find b when $s = 15$ and $a = 24$.

2 If $d = \frac{1}{2}(a + b + c)$, find a when $d = 16$, $b = 4$ and $c = -3$.

3 If $A = P + QT$, find the value of

a A when $P = 50$, $Q = \frac{1}{2}$ and $T = 4$

b A when $P = 70$, $Q = 5$ and $T = -10$

c P when $A = 100$, $Q = \frac{1}{4}$ and $T = 16$

d T when $A = 25$, $P = -15$ and $Q = -10$.

4 Given that $s = \frac{1}{2}(a - b)$, find the value of

a s when $a = 16$ and $b = 6$

b s when $a = -4$ and $b = -10$

c a when $s = 15$ and $b = 8$

d b when $s = 10$ and $a = -4$.

5 Given that $z = x - 3y$, find the value of

a z when $x = 3\frac{1}{2}$ and $y = \frac{3}{4}$

b z when $x = \frac{3}{8}$ and $y = -1\frac{1}{2}$

c x when $z = 5\frac{1}{3}$ and $y = 2\frac{1}{2}$

d y when $z = \frac{1}{4}$ and $x = \frac{7}{8}$.

6 If $P = \frac{2}{3}(2q + 3r + s)$ find

a P when $q = 2, r = 3, s = 2$

b s when $P = 6, q = 5$ and $r = 1\frac{1}{2}$.

7 If $A = B + \frac{1}{10}C$ find

a A when $B = 1\frac{1}{2}$ and $C = 5$

b C when $A = 2$ and $B = 1\frac{1}{2}$.

Solving inequalities

Reminder:

- an inequality remains true when the same number is added to, or subtracted from, both sides
- an inequality remains true when both sides are multiplied or divided by the same *positive* number. Do not multiply or divide an inequality by a negative number. It destroys the inequality.

Exercise 17f

Solve the following inequalities and illustrate the solutions on a number line:

1 $6 + \frac{x}{2} < 9$

2 $\frac{3x}{2} - 2 > 7$

3 $8 \geqslant 3 - \frac{5x}{3}$

4 $\frac{x}{5} \leqslant 1$

5 $\frac{x}{3} - 2 < \frac{1}{3}$

6 $\frac{2x}{3} + 1 \leqslant 5$

7 $2 + \frac{x}{5} < 3$

8 $\frac{7x}{3} + 8 \geqslant 1$

9 $\frac{x}{3} - 2 > \frac{x}{4} + 1$

10 $\frac{3x}{5} - 2 \geqslant 3 - \frac{2x}{5}$

11 Find, where possible, the range of values of x for which the two inequalities are both true:

a $\frac{x}{2} > 4$ and $\frac{x}{3} > 7$

b $\frac{3x}{2} \leqslant 5$ and $\frac{2x}{5} > 1$

Solve each of the following pairs of inequalities and then find the range of values of x which satisfy both of them

12 $\frac{x}{2} - 4 \leqslant 5$ and $\frac{x}{3} + 2 \geqslant 1$

13 $2 - 3x < 0$ and $\frac{x}{2} + 1 \leqslant 4$

Find the range of values of x for which the following inequalities are true:

14 $\frac{x}{2} - 3 < x - 1 < 2$

15 $\frac{x}{2} + 2 < \frac{3x}{2} + 1 < 3$

16 $\frac{2x}{3} - 4 < \frac{3x}{2} + 1 < 4$

17 $\frac{x}{2} - 1 < \frac{2x}{3} - 2 \leqslant 3$

Using two-dimensional space

In the above exercise we have considered inequalities in a purely algebraic way. Next we look at them in a more visual way, using graphs.

In Book 2 we saw how we could represent inequalities on a number line. We used one for values of x and one for values of y. It is sometimes more useful to use two-dimensional space with x and y axes, rather than a one-dimensional line.

Remember that a solid line is used when the boundary line is included in the range. A broken line is used when the boundary line is excluded from the range. Remember also that we shade the **unwanted** region.

These two diagrams show how we represented inequalities using a two-dimensional space in Book 2.

a $x \leqslant 2$

The *boundary line* is $x = 2$ (included).

The unshaded region represents $x \leqslant 2$

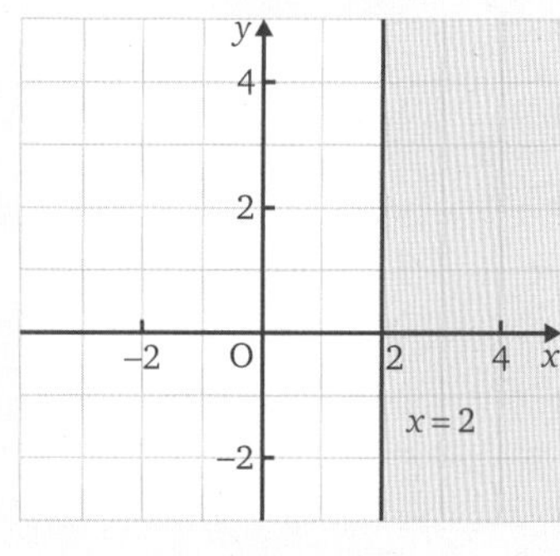

b $y > -1$

The boundary line is $y = -1$ (not included).

The unshaded region represents $y > -1$

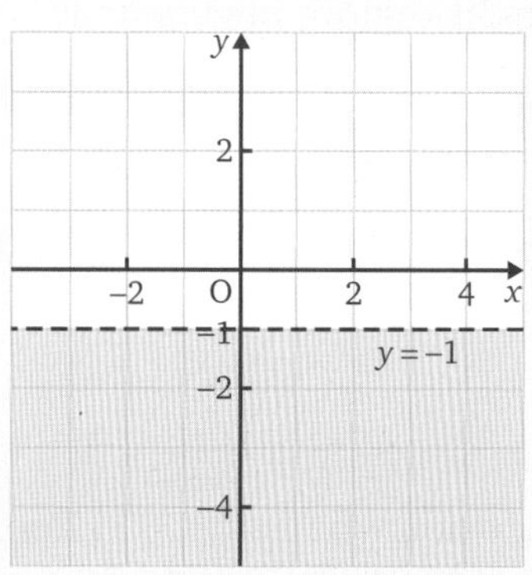

When we have fractions the principle is exactly the same.

We represent $x \geqslant \frac{3}{2}$ by the set of points whose x-coordinates are greater than or equal to $\frac{3}{2}$.

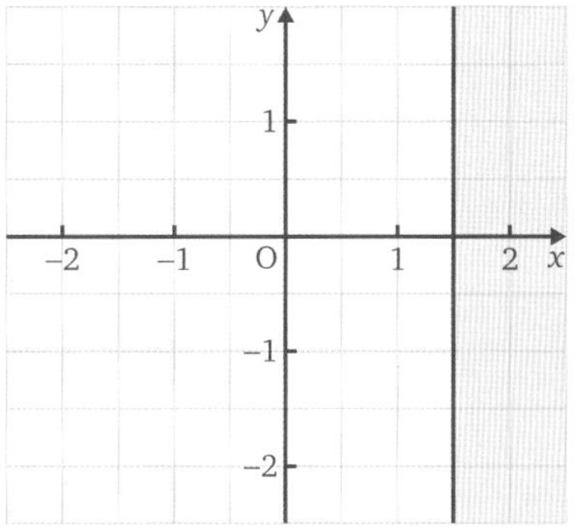

In like manner we can draw a similar diagram for $y < -\frac{5}{2}$

(The broken line shows that $y = -\frac{5}{2}$ is not included.)

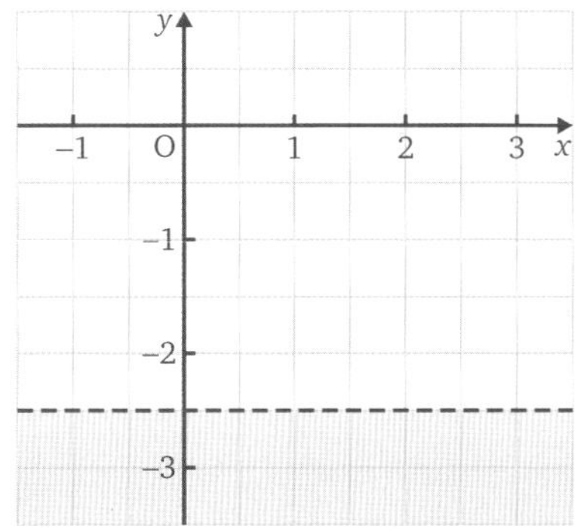

Exercise 17g

Draw diagrams to represent the following inequalities:

1 $x \geqslant 4$ **2** $x < 3$ **3** $x \leqslant 2$ **4** $x > -\frac{3}{2}$

Draw a diagram to represent $-2 < x < 4$ and state whether or not the points $(2, -5)$ and $(-3, 3)$ lie in the given region.

$-2 < x < 4$ represents two inequalities $-2 < x$ and $x < 4$. Shade the regions not wanted.

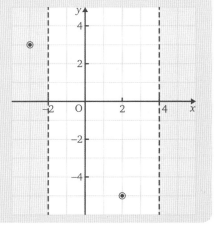

The unshaded region represents $-2 < x < 4$

Plot the points. You can see that $(2, -5)$ lies within the given region whereas $(-3, 3)$ does not.

Draw diagrams to represent the following pairs of inequalities

5 $3 < x < 6$ **6** $-\frac{5}{2} \leqslant x < 3$ **7** $-2 \leqslant y \leqslant 3$ **8** $2\frac{1}{2} \leqslant y < 4$

In each of the questions **5** to **8**, state whether or not the point (2, −3) lies in the unshaded region.

Give the inequalities that define the unshaded region

9

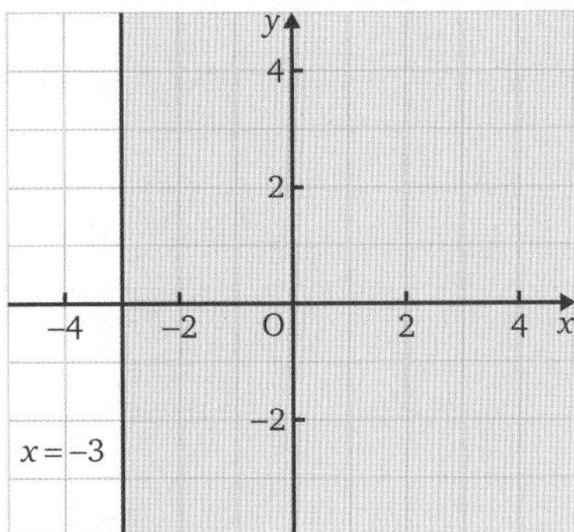

10

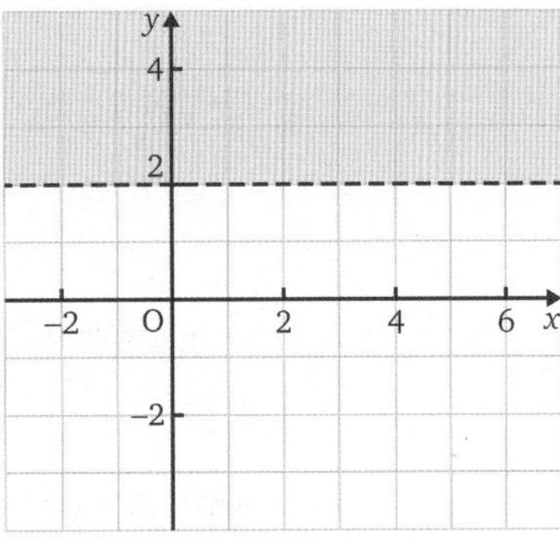

11

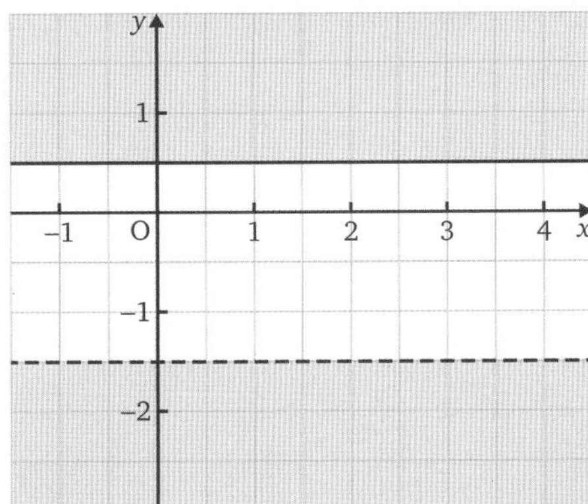

12

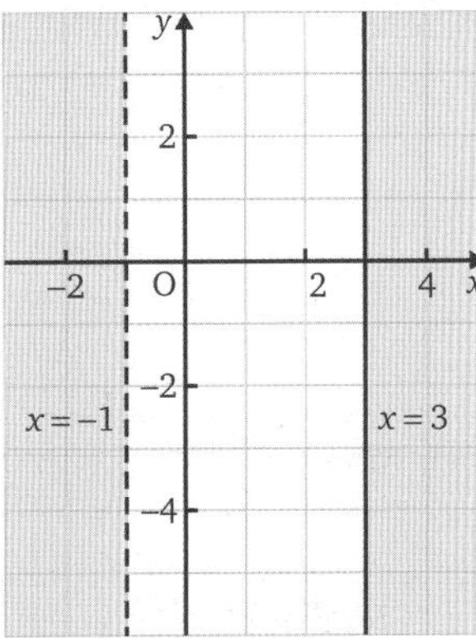

13

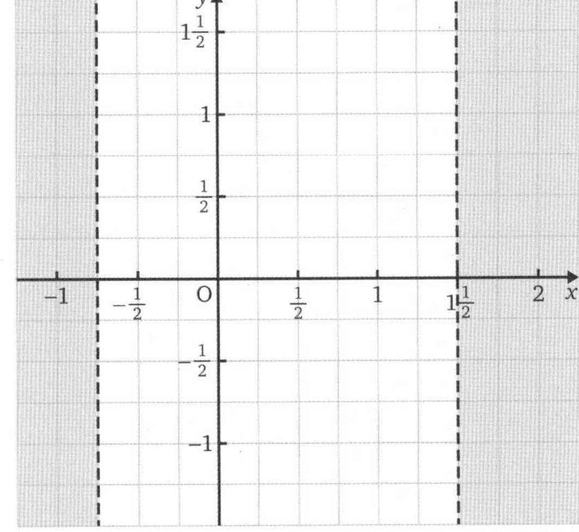

14 In each of the questions **9** to **13** state whether or not the point (4, 2) is in the unshaded region.
Give the inequalities that define the *shaded* regions.

Exercise 17h

Draw a diagram to represent the region defined by the set of inequalities $-2 \leqslant x \leqslant 5$ and $-4 \leqslant y < 1$.

There are four boundary lines here: $x = -2$, $x = 5$, $y = -4$ and $y = 1$.

$x = -2$: for $-2 \leqslant x$, shade the region on the left of the line.

$x = 5$: for $x \leqslant 5$, shade the region on the right of the line.

$y = -4$: for $-4 \leqslant y$, shade the region below the line.

$y = 1$: for $y < 1$, shade the region above the line.

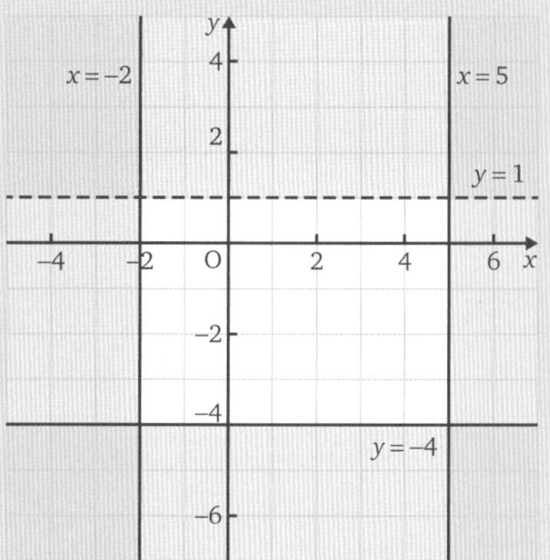

Draw diagrams to represent the regions described by the following sets of inequalities. In each case draw axes for values of x and y from -4 to 5.

1 $1 \leqslant x \leqslant 4, -1 \leqslant y \leqslant 4$

2 $-3\frac{1}{2} \leqslant x < 2, \ -1 \leqslant y$

3 $-2 < x < 0, -3 < y \leqslant 3$

4 $x \geqslant 1\frac{1}{4}, -1 < y \leqslant 3$

In questions **5** and **6** give the sets of inequalities that describe the unshaded regions.

5

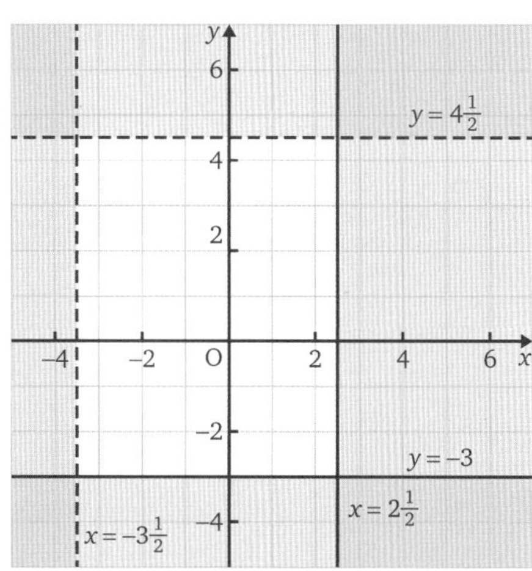

6

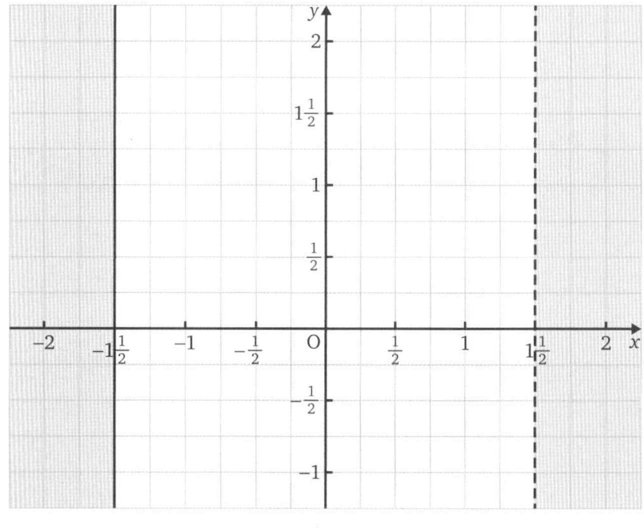

Exercise 17i

Select the letter that gives the correct answer.

1 $\frac{3x}{2} \div \frac{6}{5} =$

A $\frac{5}{9x}$ **B** $\frac{4}{5x}$ **C** $\frac{5x}{4}$ **D** $\frac{9x}{5}$

2 If $\frac{3}{5} - \frac{x}{4} = 1$, then $x =$

A $-1\frac{3}{5}$ **B** $-\frac{2}{5}$ **C** $\frac{2}{5}$ **D** $1\frac{3}{5}$

3 The solution of the inequality $5 + \frac{x}{3} < 9$ is

A $x < 3$ **B** $x < 4$ **C** $x < 5$ **D** $x < 12$

4 The solution of the inequality $\frac{x}{3} - 3 \geqslant \frac{x}{5} + 1$ is

A $x \geqslant 15$ **B** $x > 15$ **C** $x \geqslant 30$ **D** $x > 30$

5 The range of values of x that satisfy both the inequalities $\frac{x}{3} - 3 < 4$ and $\frac{x}{4} + 2 \geqslant 1$ is

A $-4 \leqslant x < 21$ **B** $-4 \leqslant x \leqslant 21$ **C** $4 < x < 21$ **D** $4 \leqslant x \leqslant 21$

Puzzle

What number goes in the empty square in the third arrangement if the four numbers in the surrounding squares are combined in the same way in all three arrangements?

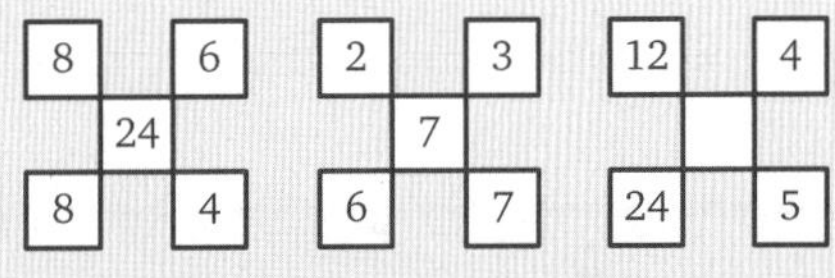

In this chapter you have seen...

- ✔ how to multiply and divide algebraic fractions in the same way as numerical fractions
- ✔ how to solve equations involving algebraic fractions by removing the fractions
- ✔ how to solve problems and use formulae involving fractions
- ✔ that an inequality remains true when the same number is added to, or subtracted from, both sides
- ✔ that an inequality remains true when both sides are multiplied or divided by the same *positive* number. Do not multiply or divide an inequality by a negative number. It destroys the inequality.
- ✔ that inequalities can be represented by a region in the *xy* plane.

18 Algebraic products

At the end of this chapter you should be able to...

1 calculate the product of expressions in two brackets, each of which contains two terms

2 square an expression of the form $(ax + b)$.

Did you know?

The branch of mathematics called algebra gets its name from the Arabic word *al-jebr*, which means 'the pulling together of broken parts'. In the seventeenth century it was used to describe the surgical treatment of fractures!

You need to know...

✔ how to work with directed numbers

✔ how to multiply out expressions such as $3(5x - 2)$ and $3a(3b + 2c)$.

Key words

collecting like terms, product

Brackets

Remember that $5(x+1)=5x+5$

and that $4x(y+z)=4xy+4xz$

Exercise 18a

Expand:

1 $2(x+1)$

2 $3(x-1)$

3 $4(x+3)$

4 $5(a+4)$

5 $3(b+7)$

6 $3(1-a)$

<u>7</u> $5(1-b)$

<u>8</u> $2(3a-1)$

9 $4(2+3b)$

10 $5a(b-c)$

11 $4a(b-2c)$

12 $3a(2a+b)$

13 $5x(3y+z)$

14 $4y(4x+3z)$

15 $2n(3p-5q)$

<u>16</u> $8r(2t-s)$

<u>17</u> $3a(b-5c)$

<u>18</u> $4x(3y+2z)$

The product of two brackets

Frequently, we wish to find the *product* of two brackets, each of which contains two terms, e.g. $(a+b)(c+d)$. The meaning of this product is that each term in the first bracket has to be multiplied by each term in the second bracket.

Always multiply the brackets together in the following order:

1 the first terms in the brackets

2 the outside terms

3 the inside terms

4 the second terms in the brackets.

Thus

$$(a+b)(c+d)=ac+ad+bc+bd$$

(1) (4) (3) (2)

Exercise 18b

Expand $(x+2y)(2y-z)$

$$(x+2y)(2y-z) = 2xy - xz + 4y^2 - 2yz$$

Multiply the first term in the first bracket by each term in the second, then the second term in the first bracket by each term in the second. Try to keep the same order when you multiply two brackets. You are less likely to leave a term out.

Expand:

1 $(a+b)(c+d)$

2 $(p+q)(s+t)$

3 $(2a+b)(c+2d)$

4 $(5x+2y)(z+3)$

5 $(x+y)(z-4)$

6 $(a-b)(c+d)$

7 $(x+y)(y+z)$

8 $(2a+b)(3c+d)$

9 $(5x+4y)(z+2)$

10 $(3x-2y)(5-z)$

11 $(p+q)(2s-3t)$

12 $(a-2b)(c-d)$

13 $(6u-5v)(w-5r)$

14 $(3a+4b)(2c-3d)$

15 $(3x+2y)(3z+2)$

16 $(3p-q)(4r-3s)$

17 $(3a-4b)(3c+4d)$

18 $(7x-2y)(3-2z)$

We get a slightly simpler form when we find the product of two brackets such as $(x+2)$ and $(x+3)$,

i.e. using the order we chose earlier

$$(x+2)(x+3) = x^2 + 3x + 2x + 6$$

$= x^2 + 5x + 6$ (since $2x$ and $3x$ are like terms)

i.e. $(x+2)(x+3) = x^2 + 5x + 6$

Exercise 18c

Expand:

1 $(x+3)(x+4)$

2 $(x+2)(x+4)$

3 $(x+1)(x+6)$

4 $(x+5)(x+2)$

5 $(x+8)(x+3)$

6 $(a+4)(a+5)$

7 $(b+2)(b+7)$

8 $(c+4)(c+6)$

9 $(p+3)(p+12)$

Expand $(x-4)(x-6)$

$$(x-4)(x-6) = x^2 - 6x - 4x + 24$$

Collect the like terms: $= x^2 - 10x + 24$

Expand:

10 $(x-2)(x-3)$

11 $(x-5)(x-7)$

12 $(a-2)(a-8)$

13 $(x-10)(x-3)$

14 $(b-5)(b-5)$

15 $(x-3)(x-4)$

16 $(x-4)(x-8)$

17 $(b-4)(b-2)$

Remember to keep to the same order when you multiply out the brackets.

18 $(a-4)(a-4)$

Expand $(x+3)(x-6)$

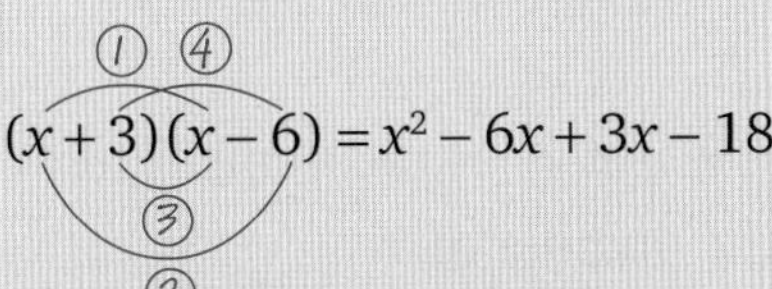

$$(x+3)(x-6) = x^2 - 6x + 3x - 18$$

Collect the like terms: $= x^2 - 3x - 18$

Expand:

19 $(x+3)(x-2)$

20 $(x-4)(x+5)$

21 $(x-7)(x+4)$

22 $(a+3)(a-10)$

23 $(p+5)(p-5)$

24 $(x+7)(x-2)$

25 $(x-5)(x+6)$

26 $(x+10)(x-1)$

27 $(b-8)(b-7)$

Investigation

Four 5s can be written as $5 \times 5 \div (5 \div 5)$. The answer is 25.

Investigate other ways of writing four 5s, together with any of the signs $+$, $-$, $\times$ or $\div$ to give an answer of 25.

Finding the pattern

You may have noticed in the previous exercise, that when you expanded the brackets and simplified the answers, there was a definite pattern,

e.g. $(x+5)(x+9) = x^2 + 9x + 5x + 45$

$= x^2 + 14x + 45$

We could have written it

$(x+5)(x+9) = x^2 + (9+5)\,x + (5) \times (9)$

$= x^2 + 14x + 45$

Similarly $(x+4)(x-7) = x^2 + (-7+4)\,x + (4) \times (-7)$

$= x^2 - 3x - 28$

and $(x-3)(x-8) = x^2 + (-8-3)\,x + (-3) \times (-8)$

$= x^2 - 11x + 24$

In each case there is a pattern:

the *product* of the two numbers in the brackets gives the number term in the expansion, while *collecting* them gives the number of x's.

Exercise 18d

Use the pattern given above to expand the following products:

1 $(x+4)(x+5)$

2 $(a+2)(a+5)$

3 $(x-4)(x-5)$

4 $(a-2)(a-5)$

5 $(x+8)(x+6)$

6 $(a+10)(a+7)$

7 $(x-8)(x-6)$

8 $(a-10)(a-7)$

9 $(a+2)(a-5)$

10 $(y-6)(y+3)$

11 $(z+4)(z-10)$

12 $(p+5)(p-8)$

13 $(a-10)(a+7)$

14 $(y+10)(y-2)$

15 $(z-12)(z+1)$

16 $(p+2)(p-13)$

17 $(x-5)(x-1)$

18 $(b+9)(b+7)$

19 $(a+4)(a-4)$

20 $(r-14)(r+2)$

21 $(p+12)(p+2)$

22 $(t+5)(t-12)$

23 $(c-5)(c+8)$

24 $(x+5)(x-5)$

The pattern is similar when the brackets are slightly more complicated.

Exercise 18e

Expand the product $(2x + 3)(x + 2)$

$$(2x + 3)(x + 2) = 2x^2 + 4x + 3x + 6$$

Collect like terms: $= 2x^2 + 7x + 6$

Expand the following products:

1 $(2x + 1)(x + 1)$

2 $(x + 2)(5x + 2)$

3 $(5x + 2)(x + 3)$

4 $(3x + 4)(x + 5)$

5 $(3x + 2)(x + 1)$

6 $(x + 3)(3x + 2)$

7 $(4x + 3)(x + 1)$

8 $(7x + 2)(x + 3)$

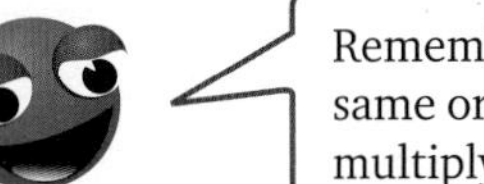

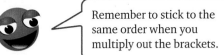

Remember to stick to the same order when you multiply out the brackets.

Expand the product $(3x - 2)(2x + 5)$

$$(3x - 2)(2x + 5) = 6x^2 + 15x - 4x - 10$$

$$= 6x^2 + 11x - 10$$

Expand:

9 $(3x + 2)(2x + 3)$

10 $(4x - 3)(3x - 4)$

11 $(5x + 6)(2x - 3)$

12 $(7a - 3)(3a - 7)$

13 $(5x + 3)(2x + 5)$

14 $(7x - 2)(3x - 2)$

15 $(3x - 2)(4x + 1)$

16 $(3b + 5)(2b - 5)$

17 $(2a + 3)(2a - 3)$

18 $(3b - 7)(3b + 7)$

19 $(7y - 5)(7y + 5)$

20 $(5a + 4)(4a - 3)$

21 $(4x + 3)(4x - 3)$

22 $(5y - 2)(5y + 2)$

23 $(3x - 1)(3x + 1)$

24 $(4x - 7)(4x + 5)$

Expand $(3x - 2)(5 - 2x)$

$$(3x - 2)(5 - 2x) = 15x - 6x^2 - 10 + 4x \qquad ((-2x) \times (-2) = +4x)$$

$$= 19x - 6x^2 - 10$$

$$= -6x^2 + 19x - 10$$

Expand:

25	$(2x+1)(1+3x)$	**29**	$(3x+2)(4-x)$	**<u>33</u>**	$(4x-3)(3-5x)$
26	$(5x+2)(2-x)$	**30**	$(4x-5)(3+x)$	**<u>34</u>**	$(3-p)(4+p)$
27	$(6x-1)(3-x)$	**<u>31</u>**	$(5x+2)(4+3x)$	**<u>35</u>**	$(x-5)(2+x)$
28	$(5a-2)(3-7a)$	**<u>32</u>**	$(7x+4)(3-2x)$	**<u>36</u>**	$(4x-3)(3+x)$

Important products

Three very important products are:

- $$\begin{aligned}(x+a)^2 &= (x+a)(x+a)\\ &= x^2+xa+ax+a^2\\ &= x^2+2ax+a^2 \text{ (since } xa \text{ is the same as } ax)\end{aligned}$$

  i.e. $(x+a)^2 = x^2+2ax+a^2$

  so $(x+3)^2 = x^2+6x+9$

- $$\begin{aligned}(x-a)^2 &= (x-a)(x-a)\\ &= x^2-xa-ax+a^2\end{aligned}$$

  i.e. $(x-a)^2 = x^2-2ax+a^2$

  so $(x-4)^2 = x^2-8x+16$

- $$\begin{aligned}(x+a)(x-\text{a}) &= x^2-xa+ax-a^2\\ &= x^2-a^2\end{aligned}$$

  i.e. $(x+a)(x-a) = x^2-a^2$

  and $(x-a)(x+a) = x^2-a^2$

  so $(x+5)(x-5) = x^2-25$

  and $(x-3)(x+3) = x^2-9$

You should learn these three results thoroughly, for they will appear time and time again. Given the left-hand side you should know the right-hand side, and vice versa.

Did you know?

Euclid of Alexandria – a mathematician more closely associated with geometry than algebra – was the first person to expand $(a+b)^2$ as $a^2+2ab+b^2$.

Exercise 18f

Expand $(x+5)^2$

Comparing with $(x+a)^2 = x^2 + 2ax + a^2$, $a = 5$

$$(x+5)^2 = x^2 + 10x + 25$$

Expand:

1 $(x+1)^2$
2 $(x+2)^2$
3 $(a+3)^2$
4 $(b+4)^2$
5 $(t+10)^2$
6 $(x+12)^2$
7 $(x+8)^2$
8 $(p+7)^2$
9 $(x+y)^2$
10 $(y+z)^2$
11 $(c+d)^2$
12 $(m+n)^2$
13 $(p+q)^2$
14 $(a+b)^2$
15 $(e+f)^2$
16 $(u+v)^2$

Expand $(2x+3)^2$

$$(2x+3)^2 = (2x)^2 + 2(2x)(3) + (3)^2$$

i.e. $(2x+3)^2 = 4x^2 + 12x + 9$

Expand:

17 $(2x+1)^2$
18 $(4b+1)^2$
19 $(5x+2)^2$
20 $(6c+1)^2$
21 $(3a+1)^2$
22 $(2x+5)^2$
23 $(3a+4)^2$
24 $(4y+3)^2$

Expand $(2x+3y)^2$

$$(2x+3y)^2 = (2x)^2 + 2(2x)(3y) + (3y)^2$$

i.e. $(2x+3y)^2 = 4x^2 + 12xy + 9y^2$

Expand:

25 $(x+2y)^2$
26 $(3x+y)^2$
27 $(2x+5y)^2$
28 $(3a+2b)^2$
29 $(3a+b)^2$
30 $(p+4q)^2$
31 $(7x+2y)^2$
32 $(3s+4t)^2$

Expand $(x-5)^2$

$$(x-5)^2 = x^2 - 10x + 25$$

Expand:

33 $(x-2)^2$
34 $(x-6)^2$
35 $(a-10)^2$
36 $(x-y)^2$
37 $(x-3)^2$
38 $(x-7)^2$
39 $(a-b)^2$
40 $(u-v)^2$

Expand $(2x-7)^2$

$$(2x-7)^2 = (2x)^2 + 2(2x)(-7) + (-7)^2$$

i.e. $$(2x-7)^2 = 4x^2 - 28x + 49$$

Expand:

41	$(3x-1)^2$	**43**	$(10a-9)^2$	**<u>45</u>**	$(2a-1)^2$	**<u>47</u>**	$(7b-2)^2$
42	$(5z-1)^2$	**44**	$(4x-3)^2$	**<u>46</u>**	$(4y-1)^2$	**<u>48</u>**	$(5x-3)^2$

Expand $(7a-4b)^2$

$$(7a-4b)^2 = (7a)^2 + 2(7a)(-4b) + (-4b)^2$$

i.e. $$(7a-4b)^2 = 49a^2 - 56ab + 16b^2$$

Expand:

49	$(2y-x)^2$	**51**	$(3m-2n)^2$	**<u>53</u>**	$(a-3b)^2$	**<u>55</u>**	$(5a-2b)^2$
50	$(5x-y)^2$	**52**	$(7x-3y)^2$	**<u>54</u>**	$(m-8n)^2$	**<u>56</u>**	$(3p-5q)^2$

The difference between two squares

Exercise 18g

Expand **a** $(a+2)(a-2)$ **b** $(2x+3)(2x-3)$

a $(a+2)(a-2) = a^2 - 4$

b $(2x+3)(2x-3) = 4x^2 - 9$

Expand:

1	$(x+4)(x-4)$	**<u>6</u>**	$(a-7)(a+7)$	**11**	$(7a+2)(7a-2)$
2	$(b+6)(b-6)$	**<u>7</u>**	$(q+10)(q-10)$	**12**	$(5a-4)(5a+4)$
3	$(c-3)(c+3)$	**<u>8</u>**	$(x-8)(x+8)$	**<u>13</u>**	$(5x+1)(5x-1)$
4	$(x+12)(x-12)$	**9**	$(2x-1)(2x+1)$	**<u>14</u>**	$(2a-3)(2a+3)$
<u>5</u>	$(x+5)(x-5)$	**10**	$(3x+1)(3x-1)$	**<u>15</u>**	$(10m-1)(10m+1)$

Expand $(3x+2y)(3x-2y)$

$$(3x+2y)(3x-2y) = (3x)^2 - (2y)^2$$
$$= 9x^2 - 4y^2$$

Expand:

16 $(3x+4y)(3x-4y)$

17 $(2a-5b)(2a+5b)$

18 $(1-2a)(1+2a)$

19 $(7y+3z)(7y-3z)$

20 $(10a-9b)(10a+9b)$

<u>21</u> $(5a-4b)(5a+4b)$

<u>22</u> $(1+3x)(1-3x)$

<u>23</u> $(3-5x)(3+5x)$

<u>24</u> $(5m+8n)(5m-8n)$

The results from Exercise 18g are very important when written the other way around,

i.e. $a^2 - b^2 = (a+b)(a-b)$

We refer to this as 'factorising the difference between two squares' and we will deal with it in detail in the next chapter.

Harder expansions

Exercise 18h

Simplify $(x+2)(x+5)+2x(x+7)$

Work out the brackets first:

$$(x+2)(x+5)+2x(x+7) = x^2+5x+2x+10+2x^2+14x$$

Collect like terms: $= 3x^2+21x+10$

Simplify:

1 $(x+3)(x+4)+x(x+2)$

2 $x(x+6)+(x+1)(x+2)$

3 $(x+4)(x+5)+6(x+2)$

4 $(a-6)(a-5)+2(a+3)$

5 $(a-5)(2a+3)-3(a-4)$

<u>6</u> $(x+3)(x+5)+5(x+2)$

<u>7</u> $(x-3)(x+4)-3(x+3)$

Expand the brackets first then collect like terms.

<u>8</u> $(x+7)(x-5)-4(x-3)$

<u>9</u> $(2x+1)(3x-4)+(2x+3)(5x-2)$

<u>10</u> $(5x-2)(3x+5)-(3x+5)(x+2)$

Expand $(xy-z)^2$

$$(xy-z)^2 = (xy)^2 - 2(xy)(z) + z^2$$

i.e. $(xy-z)^2 = x^2y^2 - 2xyz + z^2$

Expand:

11 $(xy-3)^2$

12 $(5-yz)^2$

13 $(xy+4)^2$

14 $(3pq+8)^2$

15 $(a-bc)^2$

16 $(ab-2)^2$

<u>17</u> $(6-pq)^2$

<u>18</u> $(mn+3)^2$

<u>19</u> $(uv-2w)^2$

Summary

The following is a summary of the most important types of examples considered in this chapter that will be required in future work.

1 $2(3x+4)=6x+8$

2 $(x+2)(x+3)=x^2+5x+6$

3 $(x-2)(x-3)=x^2-5x+6$

4 $(x-2)(x+3)=x^2+x-6$

5 $(2x+1)(3x+2)=6x^2+7x+2$

6 $(2x-1)(3x-2)=6x^2-7x+2$

7 $(2x+1)(3x-2)=6x^2-x-2$

Note that **a** if the signs in the brackets are the same, i.e. both + or both –, then the number term is +
(numbers **2**, **3**, **5** and **6**)

whereas **b** if the signs in the brackets are different, i.e. one + and one –, then the number term is –
(numbers **4** and **7**)

c the middle term is given by collecting the product of the outside terms in the brackets and the product of the inside terms in the brackets, i.e.

in **2** the middle term is $3x+2x$ or $5x$

in **3** the middle term is $-3x-2x$ or $-5x$

in **4** the middle term is $3x-2x$ or x

in **5** the middle term is $4x+3x$ or $7x$

in **6** the middle term is $-4x-3x$ or $-7x$

in **7** the middle term is $-4x+3x$ or $-x$.

Most important of all we must remember the general expansions:

$$(x+a)^2=x^2+2ax+a^2$$

$$(x-a)^2=x^2-2ax+a^2$$

$$(x+a)(x-a)=x^2-a^2$$

Mixed exercises

Exercise 18i

Expand:

1 $5(x+2)$

2 $8p\ (3q-2r)$

3 $(3a+b)(2a-5b)$

4 $(4x+1)(3x-5)$

5 $(x+6)(x+10)$

6 $(x-8)(x-12)$

7 $(4y+3)(4y-7)$

8 $(4y-9)(4y+9)$

9 $(5x+2)^2$

10 $(2a-7b)^2$

Exercise 18j

Expand:

1 $4(2-5x)$

2 $8a\ (2-3a)$

3 $(4a+3)(3a-11)$

4 $(x+11)(x-9)$

5 $(2x+5)(1-10x)$

6 $(y+2z)^2$

7 $(6y-z)(6y+5z)$

8 $(4a+1)^2$

9 $(5a-7)^2$

10 $(6z-13y)^2$

Exercise 18k

Select the letter that gives the correct answer.

1 $7(x-3) =$

A $x-21$ **B** $7x-21$ **C** $7x-3$ **D** $7x+21$

2 $(x+4)(x+6) =$

A $x^2+2x+24$ **B** $x^2+4x+10$ **C** $x^2+6x+10$ **D** $x^2+10x+24$

3 $(x-5)(x+2) =$

A $x^2-7x-10$ **B** $x^2-3x-10$ **C** $x^2+3x-10$ **D** $x^2-3x+10$

4 $(2x+3)(1-4x) =$

A $3-10x-8x^2$ **B** $3-10x+8x^2$ **C** $3+10x-8x^2$ **D** $8x^2+10x-3$

5 $(x+2y)^2 =$

A $x^2+4xy+y^2$ **B** $x^2+2xy+4y^2$ **C** x^2+4y+y^2 **D** $x^2+4xy+4y^2$

6 $(4x-3y)(4x+3y) =$

A $16x^2-24xy-9y^2$ **B** $16x^2-9y^2$ **C** $16x^2+9y^2$ **D** $16x^2+24xy+9y^2$

Did you know?

Do you know the meaning of TRISKAIDEKAPHOBIA? If the number 13 did not cause you any fear, then you do not suffer from triskaidekaphobia, which means 'the fear of the number 13'.

'Thirteen' is usually associated with awkwardness and bad luck. For this reason many buildings do not have a 13th floor.

In this chapter you have seen that...

- ✔ two brackets are multiplied together by multiplying each term in one bracket by every term in the other bracket, e.g.

  $(3a + 2b)(2c - 3d) = 6ac - 9ad + 4bc - 6bd$

  (Always try to do the multiplying in the same order.)

- ✔ three important products which you should commit to memory are:

  $(x + a)^2 = x^2 + 2ax + a^2$

  $(x - a)^2 = x^2 - 2ax + a^2$

  $(x + a)(x - a) = x^2 - a^2$ and $(x - a)(x + a) = x^2 - a^2$

- ✔ multiplying brackets of the form

  $(x + a)(x + b)$ gives $x^2 + (a + b)x + ab$.

19 Algebraic factors

At the end of this chapter you should be able to...

factorise expressions of the form

1 $ax + ab$

2 $ax^2 - bx$

3 $ax^2 + bx + c$

4 $a^2x^2 - b^2y^2$

5 $ax + ay + bx + by$.

Did you know?

Did you know that the way of writing decimals is not the same throughout the world? In most English-speaking countries, one point five is written as 1.5, but in much of mainland Europe it is written 1,5.

You need to know...

✔ how to expand algebraic expressions containing brackets

✔ how to collect like terms

✔ how to work with negative numbers.

Key words

coefficient, common factor, difference between two squares, expression, factor, factorising, perfect squares, product, quadratic

Finding factors

In a previous chapter we removed brackets and expanded expressions. Frequently we need to be able to do the reverse, i.e. to find the factors of an expression. This is called *factorising*.

Common factors

In the expression $7a + 14b$ we could write the first term as $7 \times a$ and the second term as $7 \times 2b$,

i.e. $$7a + 14b = 7 \times a + 7 \times 2b$$

The 7 is a *common factor*.

However, we already know that $7(a + 2b) = 7 \times a + 7 \times 2b$

$$\therefore \quad 7a + 14b = 7 \times a + 7 \times 2b = 7(a + 2b)$$

Exercise 19a

Factorise $3x - 12$

3 is a factor of $3x$ and of 12,

so $$3x - 12 = (3 \times x) - (3 \times 4)$$
$$= 3(x - 4)$$

Factorise:

1 $4x + 4$

2 $12x - 3$

3 $6a + 2$

4 $5a - 10b$

5 $3t - 9$

6 $10a - 5$

7 $12a + 4$

8 $2a + 4b$

9 $14x - 7$

Factorise $x^2 - 7x$

$$x^2 - 7x = x \times x - 7 \times x \quad \text{so } x \text{ is a common factor.}$$
$$= x(x - 7)$$

Factorise:

10 $x^2 + 2x$

11 $x^2 - 7x$

12 $a^2 + 6a$

13 $2x^2 + x$

14 $4t - 2t^2$

15 $x^2 + 5x$

16 $x^2 - 4x$

17 $b^2 + 4b$

18 $4a^2 - a$

Factorise $9ab + 12bc$

$$9ab + 12bc = 3b \times 3a + 3b \times 4c$$
$$= 3b(3a + 4c)$$

You may not at first see that both 3 and b are common factors. If you spot only 3 you would have $9ab + 12bc = 3(3ab + 4bc)$, then a check inside the bracket shows that b is also a common factor.

Factorise:

19 $2x^2 - 6x$

20 $2z^3 + 4z$

21 $25a^2 - 5a$

22 $12x^2 + 16x$

23 $5ab - 10bc$

24 $3y^2 + 27y$

25 $2a^2 - 12a$

26 $6p^2 + 2p$

27 $9y^2 - 6y$

Always check the terms inside the bracket to make sure that you have not missed any common factors.

Factorise $ab + 2bc + bd$

$$ab + 2bc + bd = b(a + 2c + d)$$

Factorise:

28 $2x^2 + 4x + 6$

29 $10a^2 - 5a + 20$

30 $ab + 4bc - 3bd$

31 $8x - 4y + 12z$

32 $9ab - 6ac - 3ad$

33 $3x^2 - 6x + 9$

34 $4a^2 + 8a - 4$

35 $5xy + 4xz + 3x$

36 $5ab + 10bc + 5bd$

37 $2xy - 4yz + 8yw$

Check all three terms.

Factorise $8x^3 - 4x^2$

$$8x^3 - 4x^2 = 4x^2(2x - 1)$$

You may do this in stages:

$$\begin{aligned} 8x^3 - 4x^2 &= 4(2x^3 - x^2) && \text{(take out 4)} \\ &= 4x(2x^2 - x) && \text{(take out } x\text{)} \\ &= 4x^2(2x - 1) && \text{(take out another } x\text{)} \end{aligned}$$

Factorise:

38 $x^3 + x^2$

39 $x^2 - x^3$

40 $20a^2 - 5a^3$

41 $12x^3 - 16x^2$

42 $4x^4 + 12x^2$

43 $a^2 + a^3$

44 $b^3 - b^2$

45 $4x^3 - 2x^2$

46 $27a^2 - 18a^3$

47 $10x^2 - 15x^4$

Factorise:

48 $12x + 8$

49 $8x^2 + 12x$

50 $9x^2 - 6x + 12$

51 $5x^3 - 10x$

52 $8pq + 4qr$

53 $x^2 - 8x$

54 $12 + 9y^2$

55 $12xy + 16xz + 8x$

56 $4x^3 + 6x$

Check inside the bracket for any missed common factors.

57 $\frac{1}{2}ah + \frac{1}{2}bh$

58 $mg - ma$

59 $\frac{1}{2}mv^2 + \frac{1}{2}mu^2$

60 $P + \frac{PRT}{100}$

61 $2\pi r^2 + \pi rh$

62 $\pi R^2 + \pi r^2$

63 $2gh_1 - 2gh_2$

64 $\frac{1}{2}mv^2 - mgh$

65 $\frac{4}{3}\pi r^3 - \frac{1}{3}\pi r^2 h$

66 $3\pi r^2 + 2\pi rh$

67 $\frac{1}{2}mu^2 + \frac{1}{2}mu$

68 $\frac{1}{2}bc - \frac{1}{4}ca$

Factorising by grouping

The expression $ax + ay + bx + by$ can be factorised by grouping the terms in pairs. If we group the first two terms followed by the remaining two terms, i.e. $(ax + ay)$ followed by $(bx + by)$, and factorise each group, we have $a(x + y)$ and $b(x + y)$

Therefore $\quad \overparen{ax + ay} + \overparen{bx + by} = a(x + y) + b(x + y)$

We can think of this as $aB + bB$, where B stands for $(x + y)$.

We have reduced the original four terms to two terms and these two terms now have the bracket B as a common factor.

Therefore

$$\begin{aligned} \overparen{ax + ay} + \overparen{bx + by} &= a(x + y) + b(x + y) \\ &= aB + bB \\ &= B(a + b) \\ &= (x + y)(a + b) \end{aligned}$$

If, on the other hand, we pair the first and third terms followed by the remaining terms, we have

$$\begin{aligned} ax + ay + bx + by &= x(a + b) + y(a + b) \\ &= (a + b)(x + y) \end{aligned}$$

This shows that, while it is often possible to pair the terms with a common factor in more than one way, the result is the same. Always check your factors by multiplying out.

Exercise 19b

Factorise $xy + 2x + 3y + 6$

$$\begin{aligned} \overparen{xy + 2x} + \overparen{3y + 6} &= xy + 2x && \text{(common factor } x) \\ &\quad + 3y + 6 && \text{(common factor 3)} \\ &= x(y + 2) + 3(y + 2) \\ & && \text{(common factor } y + 2) \\ &= (y + 2)(x + 3) \end{aligned}$$

Alternatively

$$\begin{aligned} xy + 2x + 3y + 6 &= y(x + 3) + 2(x + 3) \\ &= (x + 3)(y + 2) \end{aligned}$$

Check your answer by expanding the brackets.

Factorise the following expressions by grouping:

1 $xy+3x+3y+9$

2 $a+ab+2b+2b^2$

3 $a^2+ab+ac+bc$

4 $xy-3y+2x-6$

5 $xz+z+xy+y$

6 $xy+4x+2y+8$

7 $ac+4a+bc+4b$

8 $xy-2x+4y-8$

9 $pr+ps+qr+qs$

10 $xy-3y+4x-12$

11 $xy-5x+2y-10$

12 $pr-ps+qr-qs$

13 $ab-3a+2b-6$

14 $pr-qr+ps-qs$

15 $2p+pq+4q+8$

16 $6+2b+3a+ab$

Factorise $2x-2xy-y+y^2$

$$\overbrace{2x-2xy}-\overbrace{y+y^2}=2x(1-y)-y(1-y)$$

Check: $2x(1-y)=2x-2xy$ and $-y(1-y)=-y+y^2$

$\therefore$ $$2x-2xy-y+y^2=(1-y)(2x-y)$$

Check: $(1-y)(2x-y)=2x-y-2xy+y^2$

Factorise:

17 $pr-ps-qr+qs$

18 $9a-3b-3ab+b^2$

19 $2a-b-2ab+b^2$

20 $a^2+2ab-2a-4b$

21 $6-3x-2y+xy$

22 $4a^2-ab-8a+2b$

23 $6a^2-9a-2ab+3b$

24 $2m-3n-2mn+3n^2$

25 $t^2+tr+st+sr$

26 $x^2-x+xy-y$

27 $4a-4a^2+2b-2ab$

28 $x-xy+y-y^2$

29 $4a+6b-6a^2-9ab$

30 $2a^2+2ab+bc+ac$

31 $4x-4xy+2y-2y^2$

32 $xy+xz+y^2+yz$

Be careful with the signs. Check at each stage by mentally expanding the brackets.

Factorise $ac-ad+bd-bc$

$$\overbrace{ac-ad}+\overbrace{bd-bc}=a(c-d)+b(d-c)$$

$d-c=-1(c-d)$ so $b(d-c)=-b(c-d)$

$\therefore$ $$ac-ad+bd-bc=a(c-d)-b(c-d)$$

$$=(c-d)(a-b)$$

Factorise:

33 $5x-xy+2y-10$

34 $ab-3a-12+4b$

35 $xy-xz-3z+3y$

36 $2p-pq+4q-8$

37 $6-2b+ab-3a$

38 $3a-ab+4b-12$

Factorise $a^2 - ab + a - b$

$$a^2 - ab + a - b = a(a-b) + 1(a-b)$$
$$= (a-b)(a+1)$$

Alternatively $a^2 - ab + a - b = a^2 + a - ab - b = a(a+1) - b(a+1) = (a-b)(a+1)$

Factorise:

39 $m^2 + mn + m + n$

40 $a^2 - ab + a - b$

41 $2p^2 - 4pq + p - 2q$

42 $x - xy + 1 - y$

43 $a^2 + ab + a + b$

44 $a^2 - ab + a - b$

45 $x^2 + xy - x - y$

46 $2a^2 + ab - 2a - b$

47 $5x^2 + 10xy - x - 2y$

48 $mn - m - n + 1$

49 $3x^2 + xy - 3x - y$

50 $2p^2 + 4pq - p - 2q$

51 $3a + b - 3a^2 - ab$

52 $2x + y - 2xz - yz$

Factorising quadratic expressions

The type of expression we are most likely to want to factorise is one of the form $ax^2 + bx + c$, where a, b and c are numbers. $ax^2 + bx + c$ is called a *quadratic* expression.

To factorise such an expression we look for two brackets whose product is the original expression.

When we expanded $(x+2)(x+4)$ we had

$$(x+2)(x+4) = x^2 + 6x + 8$$

If we write $x^2 + 6x + 8 = (x+2)(x+4)$ we say we have factorised $x^2 + 6x + 8$,
i.e. just as 10 is 2×5 so $x^2 + 6x + 8$ is $(x+2) \times (x+4)$.

To factorise an expression of the form $x^2 + 7x + 10$, i.e. where all the terms are positive, we remind ourselves of the patterns we observed in the previous chapter.

We found when expanding brackets that:

- if the sign in each bracket is + then the number term in the expansion is +
- the x^2 term comes from $x \times x$
- the number term in the expansion comes from multiplying the numbers in the brackets together
- the middle term, or x term in the expansion, comes from collecting the product of the outside terms in the brackets and the product of the inside terms in the brackets.

Using these ideas in reverse order:

$$x^2 + 7x + 10 = (x+\ \ )(x+\ \ )$$
$$= (x+2)(x+5)$$

(choosing two numbers whose product is 10 and whose sum is 7).

Exercise 19c

Factorise $x^2 + 8x + 15$

$$x^2 + 8x + 15 = (x+3)(x+5) \quad \text{or} \quad (x+5)(x+3)$$

(The product of 3 and 5 is 15, and their sum is 8.)

Factorise and check your answer by expanding the brackets:

1 $x^2 + 3x + 2$	**6** $x^2 + 8x + 7$	**11** $x^2 + 8x + 16$	**16** $x^2 + 6x + 9$
2 $x^2 + 6x + 5$	**7** $x^2 + 8x + 12$	**12** $x^2 + 15x + 36$	**17** $x^2 + 20x + 36$
3 $x^2 + 7x + 12$	**8** $x^2 + 13x + 12$	**13** $x^2 + 19x + 18$	**18** $x^2 + 9x + 18$
4 $x^2 + 8x + 15$	**9** $x^2 + 16x + 15$	**14** $x^2 + 22x + 40$	**19** $x^2 + 11x + 30$
5 $x^2 + 21x + 20$	**10** $x^2 + 12x + 20$	**15** $x^2 + 9x + 8$	**20** $x^2 + 14x + 40$

To factorise an expression of the form $x^2 - 6x + 8$ remember the pattern:

- the numbers in the brackets must multiply to give $+8$, i.e. they must have the same sign. Since the middle term in the expression is negative they must both be negative
- the x^2 term comes from $x \times x$
- the middle term, or x term, comes from collecting the product of the outside terms and the product of the inside terms.

Thus $\quad x^2 - 6x + 8 = (x-2)(x-4)$

Since $\quad (-2) \times (-4) = +8$

and $\quad x \times (-4) + (-2) \times x = -4x - 2x = -6x$

Exercise 19d

Factorise $x^2 - 7x + 12$

$$x^2 - 7x + 12 = (x-3)(x-4)$$

(The product of -3 and -4 is $+12$.

The outside product is $-4x$ and the inside product is $-3x$.

Collecting these gives $-7x$.)

Factorise and check your answer by expanding the brackets:

1 $x^2 - 9x + 8$	**4** $x^2 - 11x + 28$	**7** $x^2 - 16x + 15$
2 $x^2 - 7x + 12$	**5** $x^2 - 13x + 42$	**8** $x^2 - 6x + 9$
3 $x^2 - 17x + 30$	**6** $x^2 - 5x + 6$	**9** $x^2 - 18x + 32$

Similarly $x^2 + x - 12 = (x+4)(x-3)$

If the number term in the expansion is negative the signs in the brackets are different.

Thus $(+4) \times (-3) = -12$

Working as before, the product of the outside terms is $-3x$

and the product of the inside terms is $+4x$

Therefore the total is $+x$.

Similarly $x^2 + 2x - 15 = (x+5)(x-3)$

or $x^2 + 2x - 15 = (x-3)(x+5)$

Exercise 19e

Factorise and check your answer by expanding the brackets:

1 $x^2 - x - 6$

2 $x^2 + x - 20$

3 $x^2 - x - 12$

4 $x^2 + 3x - 28$

5 $x^2 + 2x - 15$

6 $x^2 - 2x - 24$

7 $x^2 + 6x - 27$

8 $x^2 - 9x - 22$

9 $x^2 - 2x - 35$

Most of the values in the previous three exercises have been easy to spot. Should you have difficulty, set out all possible pairs of numbers, as shown below, until you find the pair that gives the original expression when you multiply back.

Factorise

a $x^2 - 11x + 24$

Possible numbers		Sum
−1	−24	−25
−2	−12	−14
−3	−8	−11

(Because the number term is + the two numbers in the brackets must have the same sign.)

$\therefore$ $x^2 - 11x + 24 = (x-3)(x-8)$

b $x^2 + 5x - 24$

Possible numbers		Sum
−1	+24	+23
−2	+12	+10
−3	+8	+5

(Because the number term is – the two numbers in the brackets have different signs.)

$\therefore$ $x^2 + 5x - 24 = (x-3)(x+8)$

Remember that a + before the number term means that the signs in the brackets are the same, whereas a – before the number term means that they are different.

Exercise 19f

Factorise:

1 $x^2+9x+14$
2 $x^2-10x+21$
3 $x^2+5x-14$
4 x^2+x-30
<u>5</u> x^2+9x+8
<u>6</u> $x^2-10x+25$
<u>7</u> x^2+8x-9
<u>8</u> $x^2-15x+26$
9 x^2+x-56
10 $x^2+32x+60$
11 $x^2-6x-27$
12 $x^2+16x-80$
<u>13</u> $x^2+14x+13$
<u>14</u> $x^2+12x-28$
<u>15</u> $x^2+2x-80$
<u>16</u> $x^2-11x+30$
17 $x^2+8x-48$
18 $x^2+18x+72$
19 $x^2+17x+52$
20 $x^2-12x-28$
<u>21</u> $x^2+11x+24$
<u>22</u> $x^2-11x-42$
<u>23</u> $x^2-18x+32$
<u>24</u> $x^2+7x-60$

Sometimes the terms need rearranging before we try to factorise.

Exercise 19g

Factorise:

1 $8+x^2+9x$
2 $9+x^2-6x$
3 $11x+28+x^2$
4 $-20+x^2-x$
<u>5</u> $9+x^2+6x$
<u>6</u> $8+x^2-9x$
<u>7</u> $17x+30+x^2$
8 $27-12x+x^2$
9 $x^2+22+13x$
10 $x^2-11x-26$
11 $7+x^2-8x$
12 $x+x^2-42$
<u>13</u> $x^2-5x-24$
<u>14</u> $14+x^2-9x$
<u>15</u> $28x+27+x^2$
<u>16</u> $2x-63+x^2$

Rearrange so that these expressions are in the form (x^2 term) then (x term) and lastly (constant).

Factorise:

17 $x^2+10x+25$
18 $x^2-10x+25$
19 x^2+4x+4
20 $x^2-14x+49$
<u>21</u> $x^2+12x+36$
<u>22</u> $x^2-12x+36$
<u>23</u> x^2-4x+4
<u>24</u> $x^2+16x+64$

These expressions are *perfect squares*.

Exercise 19h

Factorise $6-5x-x^2$

When the x^2 term is negative do not rearrange. Treat it as the last term.

$6-5x-x^2=(6+x)(1-x)$

Factorise:

1 $2 - x - x^2$
2 $6 + x - x^2$
3 $4 - 3x - x^2$
4 $8 + 2x - x^2$
<u>5</u> $6 - x - x^2$
<u>6</u> $2 + x - x^2$
<u>7</u> $8 - 2x - x^2$
<u>8</u> $5 - 4x - x^2$
9 $10 - 3x - x^2$
10 $12 + 4x - x^2$
11 $5 + 4x - x^2$
12 $14 - 5x - x^2$
<u>13</u> $6 + 5x - x^2$
<u>14</u> $20 - x - x^2$
<u>15</u> $15 - 2x - x^2$
<u>16</u> $12 + x - x^2$

The difference between two squares

In the last chapter, one of the expansions we listed was

$$(x+a)(x-a) = x^2 - a^2$$

If we reverse this we have

$$x^2 - a^2 = (x+a)(x-a)$$

or $$x^2 - a^2 = (x-a)(x+a)$$

(the order of multiplication of two brackets makes no difference to the result).

This result is known as *factorising the difference between two squares* and is *very important*.

When factorising do not confuse $x^2 - 4$ with $x^2 - 4x$.

$$x^2 - 4 = (x+2)(x-2)$$

whereas $x^2 - 4x = x(x-4)$ ($4x$ is *not* a perfect square)

Exercise 19i

Factorise $x^2 - 9$

$$x^2 - 9 = x^2 - 3^2$$

$$= (x+3)(x-3) \quad \text{or} \quad (x-3)(x+3)$$

Factorise:

1 $x^2 - 25$
2 $x^2 - 4$
3 $x^2 - 100$
4 $x^2 - 1$
5 $x^2 - 64$
6 $x^2 - 16$
<u>7</u> $x^2 - 36$
<u>8</u> $x^2 - 81$

Factorise $4 - x^2$

$$4 - x^2 = 2^2 - x^2$$

$$= (2+x)(2-x) \quad \text{or} \quad (2-x)(2+x)$$

Factorise:

9 $9-x^2$	**12** a^2-b^2	<u>**15**</u> $25-x^2$
10 $36-x^2$	**13** $9y^2-z^2$	<u>**16**</u> $81-x^2$
11 $100-x^2$	**14** $16-x^2$	<u>**17**</u> x^2-y^2

Calculations using factorising

Exercise 19j

Find $1.7^2+0.3\times1.7$

$$1.7^2+0.3\times1.7=1.7(1.7+0.3)$$
$$=1.7\times2$$
$$=3.4$$

Find, without using a calculator:

1 $2.5^2+0.5\times2.5$	**4** $8.76^2-4.76\times8.76$	<u>**7**</u> $4.3^2-1.3\times4.3$
2 $1.3\times3.7+3.7^2$	<u>**5**</u> $5.2^2+0.8\times5.2$	
3 $5.9^2-2.9\times5.9$	<u>**6**</u> $2.6\times3.4+3.4^2$	

Find 100^2-98^2

$$100^2-98^2=(100+98)(100-98)$$
$$=198\times2=396$$

8 55^2-45^2	**10** $7.82^2-2.82^2$	<u>**12**</u> $10.2^2-9.8^2$	<u>**14**</u> $8.79^2-1.21^2$
9 $20.6^2-9.4^2$	**11** $2.667^2-1.333^2$	<u>**13**</u> $13.5^2-6.5^2$	<u>**15**</u> $0.763^2-0.237^2$

Investigation

Using the digits 3 and 6 it is possible to make two 2-digit numbers, namely 36 and 63.

The difference between the squares of these two numbers is

$$63^2-36^2=2673$$
$$=99\times27$$
$$=99\times9\times3$$
$$=99\times(\text{the sum of the original digits})$$
$$\times(\text{the difference between the original digits})$$

Investigate whether or not this is true for other pairs of digits.

If you cannot find a pair of digits for which the above result is not true, then start again letting the two digits be x and y. Write the two numbers in terms of x and y. (They are not xy and yx.)

Mixed questions

Some quadratic expressions such as $x^2 + 9$ and $x^2 + 3x + 1$ will not factorise.

Exercise 19k includes some expressions that will not factorise.

Exercise 19k

Factorise where possible:

1 $x^2 + 13x + 40$
2 $x^2 - 36$
3 $x^2 + 4$
4 $x^2 - 8x + 12$
5 $x^2 + 6x - 7$
6 $x^2 - 11x + 24$
7 $x^2 + 14x - 15$
8 $x^2 + 8x + 12$
9 $x^2 - 49$
10 $x^2 - 7x + 2$
11 $x^2 + 13x + 42$
12 $4x^2 - 9y^2$
13 $x^2 + 11x - 26$
14 $x^2 + 11x + 18$
15 $x^2 - 10x + 24$
16 $4x^2 - 16y^2$
17 $x^2 - 11x - 10$
18 $x^2 + 13x - 30$
19 $a^2 - 16a + 63$
20 $1 + 2x + 4x^2 + 8x^3$
21 $x^2 + 13x - 68$
22 $p^3 + p^2 + p + 1$
23 $a^2 + 23a + 112$

Mixed exercises

Exercise 19l

1 Expand : **a** $7(a + 3)$ **b** $3(x - 2y)$
2 Expand: **a** $(x + 4)(x + 10)$ **b** $(2x - 3)(3x - 5)$
3 Expand: **a** $(5 + x)^2$ **b** $(5 - x)^2$ **c** $(5 + x)(5 - x)$
4 Factorise: **a** $10a + 20$ **b** $15p^2 - 10p$
5 Factorise: **a** $a^3 + a^2 + a + 1$ **b** $2km - kn + 2lm - ln$
6 Factorise: **a** $x^2 + 6x - 27$ **b** $a^2 - \frac{b^2}{4}$

Exercise 19m

1 Expand: **a** $4(a + 7)$ **b** $3x(2x - 3y)$
2 Expand: **a** $(x + 3)(x + 9)$ **b** $(5x - 2)(3x + 1)$
3 Expand: **a** $(5x + 2)^2$ **b** $(5x - 2)^2$ **c** $(5x + 2)(5x - 2)$
4 Factorise: **a** $12z^2 - 6z$ **b** $8xy - 12yz$

5 Factorise: **a** $z^3 + 2z^2 + z + 2$ **b** $3ac + bc + 6a + 2b$

6 Factorise: **a** $x^2 - 2x - 24$ **b** $9m^2 - \frac{n^2}{9}$

7 If n is a 3-digit number whose hundreds digit is a, tens digit is b and units digit is c, then $n = 100a + 10b + c$.

a Prove that if $a + b = 7$ and $b + c = 7$ then n is divisible by 7.

b Prove that if $a + b = 13$ and $b + c = 13$ then n is divisible by 13.

Exercise 19n

Select the letter that gives the correct answer.

1 $7x + 14 =$

A $7(x - 4)$ **B** $7(x - 2)$ **C** $7(x + 2)$ **D** $7(x + 4)$

2 $2x^2 - 4x =$

A $x(x - 4)$ **B** $x(2x + 4)$ **C** $2x(x - 2)$ **D** $2x(x + 2)$

3 $a^2 - a + ab - b =$

A $(a - 1)(a - b)$ **B** $(a - 1)(a + b)$ **C** $(a - 1)(b - 1)$ **D** $(a + 1)(b + 1)$

4 $x^2 + 8x + 15 =$

A $(x - 3)(x - 5)$ **B** $(x - 3)(x + 5)$ **C** $(x + 3)(x + 5)$ **D** $(x + 3)(x + 5)$

5 $21 - 10x + x^2 =$

A $(3 - x)(7 - x)$ **B** $(3 - x)(7 + x)$ **C** $(3 + x)(7 - x)$ **D** $(3 + x)(7 + x)$

Did you know?

Descartes used the symbol ∞ to mean 'is equal to'.

Find out what other symbols for 'is equal to' have been used in the past.

In this chapter you have seen that...

- ✔ when two or more terms in an algebraic expression have a common factor, you can write that expression as a product of the common factor and a bracket containing the terms without that factor
- ✔ an expression of the form $ax^2 + bx + c$ is called quadratic
- ✔ some, but not all, quadratic expressions can be written as the product of two brackets
- ✔ the difference of two squares can be factorised, for example

$$x^2 - y^2 = (x - y)(x + y) \quad \text{or} \quad (x + y)(x - y)$$

- ✔ some quadratic expressions have a common factor; this should be taken out before trying to factorise the quadratic
- ✔ sometimes an expression with four terms can be factorised by grouping the terms in pairs and and taking out a common factor of each pair.

20 Algebraic fractions

At the end of this chapter you should be able to...

1 reduce a given algebraic fraction to its lowest form
2 multiply or divide two algebraic expressions
3 find the LCM of a set of algebraic expressions
4 add or subtract two algebraic fractions
5 solve simple equations containing algebraic fractions.

You need to know...

✔ how to cancel fractions

✔ index notation

✔ how to find the LCM of a set of numbers

✔ how to remove brackets

✔ how to factorise a quadratic expression.

Key words

common denominator, denominator, equivalent fraction, factorise, lowest common multiple (LCM), numerator, product, reciprocal, simplify

Simplifying fractions

We simplify a fraction such as $\frac{10}{50}$ by recognising that 10 is a common factor of the numerator and denominator and then cancelling that common factor,

i.e. $$\frac{10}{50} = \frac{\cancel{10}^{1}}{5 \times \cancel{10}_{1}} = \frac{1}{5}$$

To simplify an algebraic fraction, we do exactly the same: we find and then cancel the common factors of the numerator and denominator.

Note that we do not have to write the number 50 as 5×10 but that when the factors are letters it helps at this stage to put in the multiplication sign.

For example xy can be written as $x \times y$

and $2(a+b)$ can be written as $2 \times (a+b)$

Exercise 20a

Simplify: **a** $\frac{2xy}{6y}$ **b** $\frac{2a}{a^2b}$

a $\frac{2xy}{6y} = \frac{\cancel{2}^1 \times x \times \cancel{y}^1}{{}_3\cancel{6} \times \cancel{y}_1} = \frac{x}{3}$

b $\frac{2a}{a^2b} = \frac{2 \times \cancel{a}^1}{{}_1\cancel{a} \times a \times b} = \frac{2}{ab}$

Simplify:

1	$\frac{2x}{8}$	4	$\frac{a^2}{ab}$	7	$\frac{2ab}{4bc}$	10	$\frac{a^2b}{abc}$	<u>13</u>	$\frac{b^2}{bd}$	<u>16</u>	$\frac{10x}{15xy}$
2	$\frac{ab}{2b}$	5	$\frac{xy}{y^2}$	8	$\frac{6p}{3pq}$	<u>11</u>	$\frac{7a}{14}$	<u>14</u>	$\frac{4}{12x}$	<u>17</u>	$\frac{m^2n}{kmn}$
3	$\frac{p^2}{pq}$	6	$\frac{3}{6a}$	9	$\frac{5p^2q}{10p}$	<u>12</u>	$\frac{yz}{2y}$	<u>15</u>	$\frac{3pq}{6p}$	<u>18</u>	$\frac{5s^2}{20st}$

Factors

We know that $3 \times 2 = 6$ but neither $3 + 2$ nor $3 - 2$ is equal to 6.

We can write a number as the product of its factors but, in general, we cannot write a number as the sum or difference of its factors.

Thus $\begin{cases} p \text{ and } q \text{ are factors of } pq \\ a \text{ and } (a-b) \text{ are factors of } a(a-b) \end{cases}$

but in general $\begin{cases} p \text{ is } \textit{not} \text{ a factor of } p+q \\ b \text{ is } \textit{not} \text{ a factor of } a-b \end{cases}$

This means that in the fraction $\frac{p+q}{pq}$ we *cannot* cancel q because q is not a factor of the numerator.

Sometimes the common factors in a fraction are not very obvious.

Consider $\frac{x-2}{y(x-2)}$

Placing the numerator in brackets and using the multiplication sign gives $\frac{(x-2)}{y \times (x-2)}$

Now we can see clearly that $(x - 2)$ is a common factor, so

$$\frac{\cancel{(x-2)}^1}{y \times \cancel{(x-2)}_1} = \frac{1}{y}$$

Exercise 20b

Simplify where possible: **a** $\frac{2a(a-b)}{a-b}$ **b** $\frac{pq}{p-q}$

a $\frac{2a(a-b)}{a-b} = \frac{2 \times a \times (a-b)^1}{(a-b)_1}$ (place the denominator in brackets)

$= 2a$

b $\frac{pq}{p-q} = \frac{p \times q}{(p-q)}$ which cannot be simplified.

Simplify where possible:

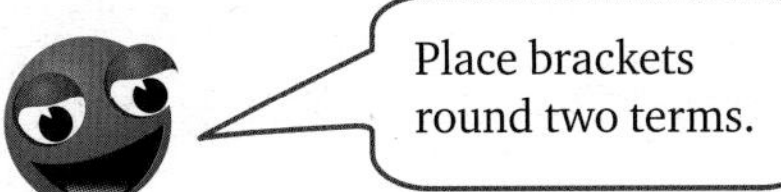
Place brackets
round two terms.

1 $\frac{x-y}{x(x-y)}$

2 $\frac{st}{s(s-t)}$

3 $\frac{2a}{a-b}$

4 $\frac{p+q}{2p}$

5 $\frac{4x}{8(x-y)}$

6 $\frac{3(a+b)}{6ab}$

7 $\frac{(p-q)(p+q)}{p+q}$

8 $\frac{(4+a)}{(4+a)(4-a)}$

9 $\frac{(a-b)}{3(a+b)}$

<u>10</u> $\frac{u-v}{v(u-v)}$

<u>11</u> $\frac{xy}{x(x+y)}$

<u>12</u> $\frac{s-t}{2(s-t)}$

<u>13</u> $\frac{10a}{15(a-b)}$

<u>14</u> $\frac{8(x-y)}{12xy}$

<u>15</u> $\frac{s-t}{3s}$

<u>16</u> $\frac{(u+v)(u-v)}{u+v}$

<u>17</u> $\frac{x+y}{2(x-y)}$

<u>18</u> $\frac{s+6}{(s+6)(s-6)}$

Sometimes we have to factorise the numerator and/or the denominator before we look for common factors.

Consider for example $\frac{12a-4b}{3a-b}$

In the numerator there is a common factor of 4, so

$$12a - 4b = 4(3a-b)$$

The fraction becomes $\frac{4(3a-b)}{(3a-b)}$

It is now clear that 4 and $(3a-b)$ are factors of $12a-4b$ so we can cancel

$(3a-b)$, i.e. $\frac{4(3a-b)^1}{(3a-b)_1} = 4$

We have been writing expressions such as $4(3a-b)$ in the form $4 \times (3a-b)$, but the multiplication sign is not necessary and we will no longer put it in. If, however, you find that the multiplication sign makes it easier to see individual factors, then continue to use it.

Exercise 20c

Simplify $\dfrac{xy - y^2}{3y}$

Start by looking for a common factor in the numerator.

$$\frac{xy - y^2}{3y} = \frac{{}^{1}\cancel{y}(x - y)}{3\cancel{y}_{1}}$$

$$= \frac{x - y}{3}$$

Simplify:

Look for a common factor in the denominator.

1 $\dfrac{4a}{8a - 2b}$

2 $\dfrac{2pq}{p^2 - pq}$

3 $\dfrac{a - b}{a^2 - ab}$

4 $\dfrac{3a - 6b}{5a - 10b}$

5 $\dfrac{2x - x^2}{3xy}$

6 $\dfrac{a^2}{3a - ab}$

7 $\dfrac{2a - 3b}{6a^2 - 9ab}$

8 $\dfrac{2s^2 - st}{2s - t}$

9 $\dfrac{3a - 6b}{a^2 - 2ab}$

10 $\dfrac{6x}{9x - 3y}$

11 $\dfrac{3ab}{ab + b^2}$

12 $\dfrac{p^2 + pq}{5p}$

13 $\dfrac{2p - 4q}{6p - 12q}$

14 $\dfrac{3a + a^2}{4ab}$

15 $\dfrac{2x - xy}{x^2}$

16 $\dfrac{2x + y}{6xy + 3y^2}$

17 $\dfrac{a^2b - ac}{ab - c}$

18 $\dfrac{p^2 + 2pq}{2p + 4q}$

Simplify $\dfrac{pq - 3q}{p^2 - 6p + 9}$

(The quadratic expression in the denominator factorises.)

$$\frac{pq - 3q}{p^2 - 6p + 9} = \frac{q\cancel{(p - 3)}^{1}}{(p - 3)\cancel{(p - 3)}_{1}}$$

$$= \frac{q}{p - 3}$$

Simplify:

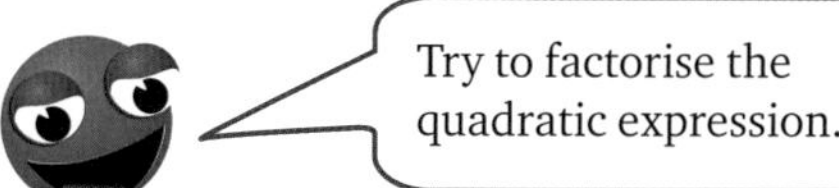
Try to factorise the
quadratic expression.

19 $\dfrac{a - 4}{a^2 - 6a + 8}$

20 $\dfrac{x - 2}{x^2 - 6x + 8}$

21 $\dfrac{y + 3}{y^2 + 5y + 6}$

22 $\dfrac{2a - 8}{a^2 - a - 12}$

23 $\dfrac{3x+12}{x^2+7x+12}$

24 $\dfrac{9y-36}{y^2-2y-8}$

25 $\dfrac{xy-2y}{x^2-4x+4}$

26 $\dfrac{pq+5q}{p^2+7p+10}$

27 $\dfrac{st-t}{s^2-8s+7}$

28 $\dfrac{p+3}{p^2+6p+9}$

29 $\dfrac{x-5}{x^2+x-30}$

30 $\dfrac{2x+6}{x^2-x-12}$

31 $\dfrac{3x-15}{x^2-9x+20}$

32 $\dfrac{uv+6v}{u^2+12u+36}$

33 $\dfrac{xy-7y}{x^2-9x+14}$

Further simplifying

The next exercise contains slightly more complicated factorising.

Remember that $a^2 - b^2 = (a-b)(a+b)$

It sometimes happens that the numerator has a factor $(a-b)$

and the denominator has a factor $(b-a)$

Now $(a-b) = (-1)(b-a)$

therefore a fraction such as $\dfrac{a-b}{b-a}$ can be simplified,

i.e. $\dfrac{a-b}{b-a} = \dfrac{(-1)(b-a)}{(b-a)} = -1$

Exercise 20d

Simplify: $\dfrac{a^2-2ab+b^2}{b^2-ab}$

$$\frac{a^2-2ab+b^2}{b^2-ab} = \frac{(a-b)(a-b)}{b(b-a)}$$

$$= \frac{(-1)(b-a)(a-b)}{b(b-a)}$$

$$= \frac{(-1)(a-b)}{b}$$

$$= \frac{b-a}{b}$$

Simplify:

1 $\dfrac{4x-8}{x^2-4}$

2 $\dfrac{2-x}{x^2-4x+4}$

3 $\dfrac{a^2-b^2}{b^2-2ab+a^2}$

4 $\dfrac{x^2-5x+6}{3y-xy}$

5 $\dfrac{a-a^2}{a-1}$

6 $\dfrac{x^2-6xy+9y^2}{x^2-3xy}$

7 $\dfrac{a-1}{1-a^2}$

8 $\dfrac{ac+bc-ad-bd}{c-d}$

9 $\dfrac{x^2-xy-2y^2}{y^2+xy}$

10 $\dfrac{y+x+xy+y^2}{x^2+2xy+y^2}$

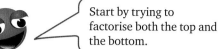

Start by trying to factorise both the top and the bottom.

Remember that $2-x=(-1)(x-2)$.

Multiplying and dividing fractions

Reminder: The product of two fractions is found by multiplying the numerators and multiplying the denominators,

e.g. $\dfrac{2}{3}\times\dfrac{4}{5}=\dfrac{2\times 4}{3\times 5}=\dfrac{8}{15}$

and $\dfrac{p}{q}\times\dfrac{(a-b)}{(a+b)}=\dfrac{p(a-b)}{q(a+b)}$

To divide by a fraction, we multiply by its reciprocal,

e.g. $\dfrac{2}{3}\div\dfrac{3}{4}=\dfrac{2}{3}\times\dfrac{4}{3}=\dfrac{8}{9}$, $\dfrac{p}{q}\div r=\dfrac{p}{q}\times\dfrac{1}{r}=\dfrac{p}{qr}$

and $\dfrac{p}{q}\div\dfrac{a}{(a-b)}=\dfrac{p}{q}\times\dfrac{(a-b)}{a}=\dfrac{p(a-b)}{qa}$

Exercise 20e

Find:

1 $\dfrac{a}{b}\times\dfrac{c}{d}$

2 $\dfrac{a}{b}\div\dfrac{c}{d}$

3 $\dfrac{x-y}{2}\times\dfrac{5}{x}$

4 $\dfrac{x-y}{2}\div\dfrac{5}{x}$

5 $\dfrac{a}{b}\div c$

6 $\dfrac{a}{b}\times c$

7 $\dfrac{(a-b)}{4}\div\dfrac{(a+b)}{3}$

8 $\dfrac{(x-2)}{3}\times(x+3)$

9 $\dfrac{(x-2)}{3}\div(x+3)$

10 $\dfrac{p}{q}\div\dfrac{1}{r}$

Remember that to divide by a fraction you multiply by its reciprocal.

Simplify $\frac{ab}{4}\times\frac{8}{a^2}$

As is the case in number fractions, it is sometimes possible to simplify before multiplying.

$$\frac{ab}{4}\times\frac{8}{a^2}=\frac{\not{a}b}{\not{4}_1}\times\frac{\not{8}^2}{\not{a}^2_a}$$

$$=\frac{2b}{a}$$

Simplify:

11 $\frac{2a}{b}\div\frac{a^2}{3b^2}$

12 $\frac{pq}{6}\times\frac{3}{p^2}$

13 $\frac{4xy}{3}\times\frac{9}{x^2}$

14 $\frac{2ab}{5}\div\frac{a}{b}$

15 $\frac{2p^2}{3}\times\frac{q}{4p}$

<u>16</u> $\frac{x^2}{4}\div\frac{xy}{2}$

<u>17</u> $\frac{1}{b^2}\div\frac{2}{b}$

<u>18</u> $\frac{7p}{5q}\times\frac{10q}{21p^2}$

<u>19</u> $\frac{a^2}{2b}\div 2a$

<u>20</u> $\frac{a}{b}\times\frac{2a}{3b}\div\frac{2b}{3a}$

Simplify $\frac{(a^2-b^2)}{a}\times\frac{b}{(a+b)}$

$$\frac{(a^2-b^2)}{a}\times\frac{b}{(a+b)}=\frac{(a-b)\cancel{(a+b)}\,b}{a\cancel{(a+b)}}$$

$$=\frac{b(a-b)}{a}$$

(Notice that we leave the answer in factor form.)

Simplify $(x^2-3x-4)\div(x-4)$

(Remember that $7\div4$ can be written $\frac{7}{4}$; similarly $(x^2-3x-4)\div(x-4)$ can be written $\frac{x^2-3x-4}{x-4}$.)

$$(x^2-3x-4)\div(x-4)=\frac{x^2-3x-4}{x-4}$$

$$=\frac{\cancel{(x-4)}(x+1)}{\cancel{(x-4)}}$$

$$=x+1$$

Simplify:

Remember to try to factorise quadratic expressions and that division by a fraction is the same as multiplying by its reciprocal.

21 $\frac{(b-2)}{4} \times \frac{1}{(b^2-4b+4)}$

22 $\frac{(x^2-4)}{3} \times \frac{6}{(x+2)}$

23 $\frac{(a^2-9)}{2} \div \frac{(a-3)}{4}$

24 $\frac{(3b-6)}{5} \div \frac{(b-2)}{10}$

25 $(x^2-6x+9) \div (x-3)$

26 $\frac{1}{(x-2)} \times (x^2-5x+6)$

27 $(x-4) \div (x^2-6x+8)$

28 $(2x-4) \times \frac{1}{(x^2+2x-8)}$

29 $\frac{(x^2-4)}{5} \times \frac{3}{(x^2+8x+12)}$

30 $\frac{(4x^2-9)}{3} \div \frac{(6x+9)}{2}$

31 $\frac{(ab+a^2)}{b} \times \frac{b}{a+b}$

32 $\frac{a^2-b^2}{c} \div \frac{b^2-ab}{c^2}$

33 $\frac{(x^2-5x+4)}{(x+2)} \times \frac{(x^2-4)}{(x-1)}$

Investigation

Multiply 32 547 891 by 6. Compare your answer with the original number.

What do you notice?

Investigate similar relationships. For example, is there an 8-digit number using every digit from 1 to 9 except 7 which, when multiplied by 7, gives a 9-digit answer which uses every digit from 1 to 9 once?

Lowest common multiple

Before we can simplify $\frac{2}{3}+\frac{1}{5}$ we must change both $\frac{2}{3}$ and $\frac{1}{5}$ into equivalent fractions with the same denominator. This *common denominator* must contain both 3 and 5 as factors; there are many numbers we could choose but 15 is the lowest such number, i.e. 15 is the *lowest common multiple* (LCM) of 3 and 5.

To simplify $\frac{3}{x}+\frac{2}{y}$ we follow the same pattern. We need a common denominator with both x and y as factors. Again there are many we could use, but the simplest is xy; this is the LCM of x and y.

Exercise 20f

Find the LCM of ab and c

The LCM is abc

Find the LCM of:

1 p, q

2 r, st

3 2, 3, 5

4 a, b, c

5 x, y, wz

6 a, d

<u>7</u> v, uw

<u>8</u> 3, 7, 8

Find the LCM of: **a** 4, 10 **b** ab, a^2 **c** $2x, 6x$

a $4 = 2 \times 2$ and $10 = 2 \times 5$

(The LCM is the *lowest* number that 4 and 10 divide into exactly, so the factors it must include are

2×2 from 4 and 5 from 10

The factor of 2 from 10 is not needed as 2 is already included.)

$\therefore$ the LCM of 4 and 10 is $2 \times 2 \times 5 = 20$

b $ab = a \times b$ and $a^2 = a \times a$

$\therefore$ the LCM is $a \times b \times a = a^2b$

c $2x = 2 \times x$ and $6x = 2 \times 3 \times x$

$\therefore$ the LCM is $2 \times 3 \times x = 6x$

Find the LCM of:

9 x, xy

10 $x^2, 2x$

11 $pq, 3p$

12 $x^2, 2xy$

13 ab, bc

14 s, st

<u>15</u> $3p, p^2$

<u>16</u> $5a, ab$

<u>17</u> $3pq, q^2$

18 $2x, 3x$

19 $4x, 8x$

20 $6a, 9a$

21 6, 4, 10

22 a, ab, a^2

23 $10x, 15x$

<u>24</u> $4x, 6x$

<u>25</u> $3y, 5y$

<u>26</u> $2x, 3x, 4x$

Addition and subtraction of fractions

To add or subtract fractions we first have to change them into equivalent fractions with a common denominator.

Thus to find $\frac{2}{3} + \frac{1}{5}$, we choose a common denominator of 15 which is the LCM of 3 and 5.

Now $\frac{2}{3} = \frac{2 \times 5}{3 \times 5} = \frac{10}{15}$ and $\frac{1}{5} = \frac{1 \times 3}{5 \times 3} = \frac{3}{15}$

Therefore $\frac{2}{3}+\frac{1}{5}=\frac{10+3}{15}=\frac{13}{15}$

To simplify $\frac{3}{x}+\frac{2}{y}$ we follow the same pattern:

xy is the LCM of x and y.

$$\frac{3}{x}=\frac{3\times y}{x\times y}=\frac{3y}{xy} \text{ and } \frac{2}{y}=\frac{2\times x}{y\times x}=\frac{2x}{xy}$$

$$\therefore \quad \frac{3}{x}+\frac{2}{y}=\frac{3y+2x}{xy}$$

Exercise 20g

Simplify $\frac{1}{2a}+\frac{1}{b}$

($2ab$ is the LCM of $2a$ and b)

$$\frac{1}{2a}+\frac{1}{b}=\frac{(1)\times(b)+(1)\times(2a)}{2ab}=\frac{b+2a}{2ab}$$

Simplify $\frac{3}{4x}-\frac{1}{6x}$

($12x$ is the LCM of $4x$ and $6x$)

$$\frac{3}{4x}-\frac{1}{6x}=\frac{(3)\times(3)-(1)\times(2)}{12x}=\frac{7}{12x}$$

Simplify:

1 $\frac{1}{x}+\frac{1}{y}$

2 $\frac{3}{p}+\frac{2}{q}$

3 $\frac{2}{s}-\frac{1}{t}$

4 $\frac{3}{a}+\frac{1}{2b}$

5 $\frac{1}{3x}-\frac{2}{5y}$

6 $\frac{1}{a}+\frac{5}{2b}$

7 $\frac{2}{x}-\frac{3}{y}$

8 $\frac{4}{3p}+\frac{2}{q}$

9 $\frac{3}{x}-\frac{2}{y}$

10 $\frac{5}{7a}+\frac{3}{4b}$

11 $\frac{1}{2x}+\frac{1}{3x}$

12 $\frac{2}{5x}-\frac{3}{7x}$

To simplify the sum or difference of two fractions you must put them over a common denominator.

13 $\frac{2}{y}-\frac{3}{4y}$

14 $\frac{3}{8p}-\frac{1}{4p}$

15 $\frac{1}{a}+\frac{5}{8a}$

16 $\frac{1}{3x}-\frac{1}{7x}$

17 $\frac{4}{7x}-\frac{2}{5x}$

18 $\frac{1}{y}-\frac{2}{3y}$

Simplify $\frac{4a}{3b} - \frac{b}{6a}$

($3b = 3 \times b$ and $6a = 2 \times 3 \times a$, $\therefore$ LCM $= 6ab$)

$$\frac{4a}{3b} - \frac{b}{6a} = \frac{(4a) \times (2a) - (b) \times (b)}{6ab}$$

$$= \frac{8a^2 - b^2}{6ab}$$

Simplify:

19 $\frac{1}{2a} + \frac{3}{4b}$

20 $\frac{a}{2b} - \frac{a^2}{b^2}$

21 $\frac{3}{x} - \frac{4}{xy}$

22 $\frac{2}{p^2} - \frac{3}{2p}$

23 $\frac{3a}{4b} + \frac{b}{6a}$

24 $\frac{5}{2p} - \frac{3}{4q}$

25 $\frac{s}{t^2} + \frac{s^2}{2t}$

26 $\frac{5}{2a} + \frac{2}{3ab}$

27 $\frac{1}{x^2} + \frac{2}{3x}$

28 $\frac{2y}{3x} - \frac{3x}{2y}$

29 $\frac{5}{8x} + \frac{2}{4y}$

30 $\frac{p}{3q} + \frac{p^2}{q^2}$

Always begin by finding the LCM of the denominator.

31 $\frac{5}{7x} - \frac{3}{14xy}$

32 $\frac{9}{a^2} - \frac{3}{2ab}$

33 $\frac{3x}{2y} - \frac{3y}{2x}$

34 $\frac{7}{9p} - \frac{5}{6q}$

35 $\frac{a^2}{b^2} + \frac{4a}{5b}$

36 $\frac{7}{5pq} + \frac{8}{15q}$

Exercise 20h

Simplify $\frac{x-2}{3} - \frac{x-4}{2}$

$$\frac{(x-2)}{3} - \frac{(x-4)}{2} = \frac{2(x-2) - 3(x-4)}{6}$$

$$= \frac{2x - 4 - 3x + 12}{6}$$

$$= \frac{-x + 8}{6}$$

$$= \frac{8 - x}{6}$$

(Notice that we placed brackets round the numerators *before* putting the fractions over a common denominator. This ensured that each numerator was kept together and that the signs were not confused.)

Simplify:

1 $\frac{x+2}{5}+\frac{x-1}{4}$

2 $\frac{x+3}{4}-\frac{x+1}{3}$

3 $\frac{2x-1}{3}+\frac{x+2}{5}$

4 $\frac{2x+3}{4}-\frac{x-2}{6}$

5 $\frac{x+3}{7}-\frac{x+2}{5}$

6 $\frac{x+4}{5}+\frac{x-1}{2}$

7 $\frac{2x-1}{7}-\frac{x-2}{5}$

8 $\frac{3x+1}{14}-\frac{2x+3}{21}$

Simplify:

9 $\frac{1}{7}(2x-3)-\frac{1}{3}(4x-2)$

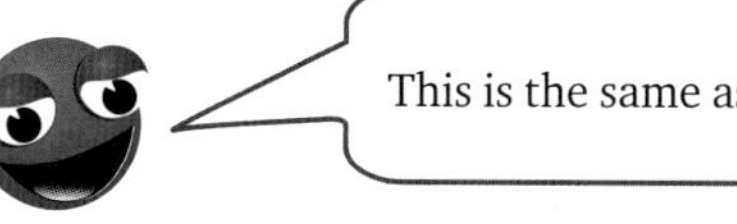

This is the same as $\frac{2x-3}{7}-\frac{4x-2}{3}$

10 $\frac{1}{4}(5x-1)-\frac{1}{3}(2x-3)$

11 $\frac{5-2x}{3}+\frac{4-3x}{2}$

12 $\frac{1}{4}(3-x)+\frac{1}{6}(1-2x)$

13 $\frac{1}{8}(5x+4)-\frac{1}{3}(4x-1)$

14 $\frac{2x+3}{5}-\frac{3x-2}{4}$

15 $\frac{3-x}{2}+\frac{1-2x}{6}$

16 $\frac{2+5x}{8}-\frac{3-4x}{6}$

17 $\frac{1}{5}(4-3x)+\frac{1}{10}(3-x)$

18 $\frac{1}{9}(4-x)-\frac{1}{6}(2+3x)$

Simplify $\frac{2(x+1)}{3}-\frac{3(x-2)}{5}$

$$\frac{2(x+1)}{3}-\frac{3(x-2)}{5}=\frac{5\times 2(x+1)-3\times 3(x-2)}{15}$$

$$=\frac{10(x+1)-9(x-2)}{15}$$

(Now multiply out the brackets.)

$$=\frac{10x+10-9x+18}{15}$$

$$=\frac{x+28}{15}$$

Simplify:

19 $\frac{4(x+2)}{3}+\frac{2(x-1)}{5}$

20 $\frac{3(x-1)}{4}+\frac{2(x+1)}{3}$

21 $\frac{2(x-2)}{3}-\frac{3(x-1)}{7}$

22 $\frac{5(2x-1)}{2}-\frac{4(x+3)}{5}$

23 $\frac{3(x-1)}{2}+\frac{3(x+4)}{7}$

24 $\frac{7(x-3)}{3}-\frac{2(x+5)}{9}$

25 $\frac{2(3x-1)}{5}+\frac{4(2x-3)}{15}$

26 $\frac{3(x-2)}{5}-\frac{7(x-4)}{6}$

Simplify $\frac{2}{x} - \frac{1}{x+2}$

$$\frac{2}{x} - \frac{1}{(x+2)} = \frac{(2)(x+2) - (1)(x)}{x(x+2)}$$

$$= \frac{2x+4-x}{x(x+2)}$$ (Multiplying out the brackets in the numerator.)

$$= \frac{x+4}{x(x+2)}$$

(Notice that we placed the two-term denominator in brackets. Notice also that we left the common denominator in factorised form.)

Simplify:

27 $\frac{2}{a} + \frac{1}{a+3}$

28 $\frac{4}{x+2} + \frac{2}{x}$

29 $\frac{3}{x-4} + \frac{1}{2x}$

30 $\frac{2}{2x+1} - \frac{3}{4x}$

31 $\frac{3}{a} + \frac{2}{a+4}$

32 $\frac{3}{x-1} + \frac{4}{x}$

33 $\frac{3}{2x+1} + \frac{1}{3x}$

34 $\frac{5}{2x+3} - \frac{2}{5x}$

Investigation

You now know how to express the sum of two fractions such as

$\frac{1}{x+1} + \frac{1}{x-1}$ as a single fraction,

i.e. $\frac{1}{x+1} + \frac{1}{x-1} = \frac{(x-1)+(x+1)}{(x-1)(x+1)} = \frac{2x}{(x-1)(x+1)}$

Therefore starting with a single fraction such as $\frac{2x}{(x-1)(x+1)}$ it must be possible to reverse the process and express it as the sum (or difference) of two fractions.

Investigate how $\frac{2}{(x+1)(x-1)}$ can be expressed as the sum or difference of two fractions.

If you think you have found a method that will work with any such fraction, try it by expressing $\frac{4}{(x+2)(2x-1)}$ as the sum or difference of two fractions.

Mixed questions

Exercise 20i

Simplify:

1 $\frac{2}{a}-\frac{b}{c}$

2 $\frac{pq}{r}\times\frac{r^3}{p^2}$

3 $\frac{x+2}{4}+\frac{x-5}{3}$

4 $\frac{a^2+ab}{a^2-b^2}$

5 $\frac{3}{4x}-\frac{2}{3x}$

6 $\frac{x+3}{x^2+5x+6}$

7 $\frac{p^2-pq}{q^2-p^2}$

8 $\frac{4}{x^2}-\frac{2}{3x}$

9 $\frac{1}{x}-\frac{3}{x+1}$

10 $\frac{a^2}{bc}\div\frac{a}{b^2}$

11 $\frac{2}{5x}\div\frac{3}{4x}$

12 $\frac{2}{5x}+\frac{3}{4x}$

13 $\frac{2}{5x}\times\frac{3}{4x}$

14 $\frac{x+4}{5}+\frac{2x-1}{10}$

15 $\frac{x+4}{5}\times\frac{2x-1}{10}$

16 $\frac{5}{4x}+\frac{5}{6x}$

17 $\frac{5}{4x}\times\frac{5}{6x}$

18 $\frac{5}{4x}\div\frac{5}{6x}$

19 $\frac{1}{3x}+\frac{6}{x-1}$

20 $\frac{1}{3x}\times\frac{6}{x-1}$

21 $\frac{3}{2a}-\frac{2}{a-1}$

22 $\frac{3}{2a}\times\frac{2}{a-1}$

23 $\frac{3}{4y-3}\div\frac{y}{4y-3}$

24 $\frac{3}{4y-3}-\frac{4y}{4y-3}$

Solving equations with fractions

Remember that when solving an equation we *must* keep the equality true. This means that if we alter the size of one side of the equation then we must alter the other side in the same way.

Consider the equation $\frac{1}{x}+\frac{1}{2x}=\frac{5}{6}$

If we choose to multiply each side by the LCM of the denominators, we can remove all fractions from the equation.

The LCM of x, $2x$ and 6 is $6x$.

Multiplying each side by $6x$ gives

$$6x\left(\frac{1}{x}+\frac{1}{2x}\right)=6x\times\frac{5}{6}$$

$$\therefore \quad \frac{\overset{1}{\cancel{6x}}}{1}\times\frac{1}{\underset{1}{\cancel{x}}}+\frac{\overset{3}{\cancel{6x}}}{1}\times\frac{1}{\underset{1}{\cancel{2x}}}=\frac{\overset{1}{\cancel{6}}x}{1}\times\frac{5}{\underset{1}{\cancel{6}}}$$

$$\therefore \quad 6+3=5x$$

$$9=5x$$

$$\frac{9}{5}=x \quad \text{i.e.} \quad x=1\tfrac{4}{5}$$

Exercise 20j

Solve the following equations:

1 $\frac{1}{2}+\frac{4}{x}=1$

2 $\frac{2}{3}-\frac{1}{x}=\frac{13}{15}$

3 $\frac{3}{4}-\frac{2}{x}=\frac{5}{12}$

4 $\frac{1}{x}-\frac{1}{3x}=\frac{1}{2}$

5 $\frac{1}{2x}+\frac{2}{x}=\frac{1}{4}$

6 $\frac{3}{x}+\frac{3}{10}=\frac{9}{10}$

7 $\frac{3}{8}-\frac{2}{x}=\frac{1}{6}$

8 $\frac{3}{2x}+\frac{1}{4x}=\frac{1}{3}$

9 $\frac{1}{x}-\frac{1}{2}=\frac{3}{2x}$

10 $\frac{3}{2x}+\frac{2}{5}=\frac{5}{x}$

The LCM is 15x.

The LCM is 6x.

Solve the equation $\frac{x-2}{4}-\frac{x-3}{6}=2$

$$\frac{(x-2)}{4}-\frac{(x-3)}{6}=2$$

Multiply each side by 12:

$$12\left[\frac{(x-2)}{4}-\frac{(x-3)}{6}\right]=12\times 2$$

$$\therefore \quad \frac{\overset{3}{\cancel{12}}}{1}\times\frac{(x-2)}{\cancel{4}_1}-\overset{2}{\cancel{12}}\times\frac{(x-3)}{\cancel{6}_1}=24$$

$$\therefore \quad 3(x-2)-2(x-3)=24$$

$$3x-6-2x+6=24$$

$$x=24$$

Solve the following equations:

11 $\frac{x+2}{4}+\frac{x-3}{2}=\frac{1}{2}$

12 $\frac{x}{4}-\frac{x+3}{3}=\frac{1}{2}$

13 $\frac{x}{5}+\frac{x+1}{4}=\frac{8}{5}$

14 $\frac{2x}{5}-\frac{x-3}{8}=\frac{1}{10}$

15 $\frac{x-4}{3}-\frac{x+1}{4}=\frac{1}{6}$

16 $\frac{x+3}{5}+\frac{x-2}{4}=\frac{3}{10}$

17 $\frac{2}{3}-\frac{x+1}{9}=\frac{5}{6}$

18 $\frac{x+3}{4}-\frac{x}{2}=5$

19 $\frac{3x}{20}+\frac{x-2}{8}=\frac{3}{10}$

20 $\frac{x+3}{7}-\frac{x-4}{3}=1$

21 $\frac{2x-1}{7}+\frac{3x-3}{4}=\frac{1}{7}$

22 $\frac{2x}{9}-\frac{3x+2}{4}=\frac{7}{12}$

Put brackets around the numerators before you multiply each side by the LCM.

Mixed exercises

Exercise 20k

1 Simplify:

a $\dfrac{ab^2}{2ab}$ b $\dfrac{a(a+b)}{a+b}$ c $\dfrac{a^2-b^2}{a+b}$

2 Simplify:

a $\dfrac{1}{x}+\dfrac{1}{3x}$ b $\dfrac{1}{x}\times\dfrac{1}{3x}$ c $\dfrac{1}{x}\div\dfrac{1}{3x}$

3 Solve the equation $\dfrac{x+1}{3}-\dfrac{x-1}{2}=3$

4 a Simplify $\dfrac{1}{2}(x-1)+\dfrac{1}{3}(x-2)$

b Solve the equation $\dfrac{1}{2}(x-1)+\dfrac{1}{3}(x-2)=\dfrac{1}{4}$

Exercise 20l

1 Simplify:

a $\dfrac{uv^2}{wu^2v}$ b $\dfrac{a-b}{(b-a)(b-2a)}$ c $\dfrac{x^2}{3x-x^2}$

2 Simplify:

a $\dfrac{3s}{t}\div\dfrac{1}{6st}$ b $\dfrac{x^2-4}{3}\times\dfrac{6}{x+2}$ c $\dfrac{3}{4x-1}-\dfrac{2}{x}$

3 Solve the equation $\dfrac{x-2}{4}-\dfrac{x-3}{5}=\dfrac{3}{10}$

4 a Simplify $\dfrac{1}{2}(x-2)-\dfrac{1}{3}(x-3)$

b Solve the equation $\dfrac{1}{2}(x-2)-\dfrac{1}{3}(x-3)=5$

5 Solve the equations:

a $\dfrac{x}{5}-\dfrac{x}{8}=3$ b $\dfrac{x}{3}-\dfrac{x}{7}=4$ c $\dfrac{x}{6}-\dfrac{x}{11}=5$

What pattern do you notice in the above?

6 Solve for x:

$\dfrac{x}{a}-\dfrac{x}{b}=b-a$

Exercise 20m

Select the letter that gives the correct answer.

1 $\frac{9xy}{6x^2} =$

A $\frac{y}{x}$ B $\frac{3y}{2}$ C $\frac{3y}{2x}$ D $\frac{3y}{x^2}$

2 $\frac{2}{x} \div \frac{4}{x^2} =$

A $\frac{x}{4}$ B $\frac{x^2}{4}$ C $\frac{x}{2}$ D $\frac{8}{x}$

3 $\frac{1}{3a} - \frac{1}{4a} =$

A $\frac{1}{12a}$ B $\frac{1}{4a}$ C $\frac{1}{3a}$ D $\frac{1}{7a}$

4 $\frac{2}{3}(x+1) + \frac{1}{2}(x-2) =$

A $\frac{x}{2}$ B $\frac{x}{3}$ C $\frac{7x-2}{6}$ D $\frac{7x+2}{6}$

5 $\frac{x-2}{x^2+x-6} =$

A $\frac{1}{x-3}$ B $\frac{2}{x-2}$ C $\frac{2}{x+2}$ D $\frac{1}{x+3}$

6 The solution of the equation $\frac{3}{2x} - \frac{1}{x} = \frac{3}{5}$ is

A $\frac{3}{5}$ B $\frac{5}{6}$ C $1\frac{1}{6}$ D $1\frac{1}{5}$

Did you know?

On what day of the week were you born? Can you answer this question? There is a formula which you may use to help you.

If d = day of the month, y = year and m = month, then

$$w = d + 2m + [3(m+1)/5] + y + [y/4] - [y/100] + [y/400] + 2$$

January is taken as the 13th month of the previous year, and February as the 14th month. All other months are given their regular number.

The numbers in the 'square' brackets denote 'the greatest whole number less than the number'

e.g. $[7.6] = 7$ and $[18.39] = 18$.

When you have a value for w, divide it by 7. Your remainder is the day of the week. Sunday is the first day and Saturday is day 0.

On what day of the week did New Year's Day fall in 1982?

$d = 1$, $m = 13$, $y = 1981$ (using the previous year for January) we have,

$$\begin{aligned} w &= 1 + 2(13) + [3(14)/5] + 1981 + [1981/4] - [1981/100] + [1981/400] + 2 \\ &= 1 + 26 + [8.4] + 1981 + [495.25] - [19.81] + [4.9525] + 2 \\ &= 1 + 26 + 8 + 1981 + 495 - 19 + 4 + 2 = 2498 \end{aligned}$$

$2498/7 = 356$ remainder 6. The day of the week is therefore Friday.

Try the following exercises:

1 Find the day of the week on which you were born.

2 On what day of the week will your birthday fall in the year 2030?

In this chapter you have seen that...

- ✔ algebraic expressions can often be simplified by cancelling factors that are common to the numerator and denominator
- ✔ some expressions need factorising before a common factor becomes apparent
- ✔ two fractions can be multiplied together by multiplying their numerators and multiplying their denominators
- ✔ to divide by a fraction, turn it upside down and multiply
- ✔ to add or subtract algebraic fractions, express each fraction as an equivalent fraction with the LCM of all the denominators as the denominator
- ✔ to solve equations with fractions, multiply every term by the LCM of the denominators. The resulting equation should be of a type you are familiar with.

21 Quadratic equations

At the end of this chapter you should be able to...

1 solve quadratic equations of the form $(ax+b)(cx+d)=0$

2 solve quadratic equations by factorisation

3 solve equations of the form $x^3+bx^2+cx=0$

4 form quadratic equations to solve given problems.

Did you know?

The Babylonians found an approximate value for the square root of a number using the formula $\sqrt{a^2+b} \approx a+\frac{b}{2a}$.

For example $\sqrt{53}=\sqrt{49+4} \approx 7+\frac{4}{14}=7.285\ldots$

Using a calculator $\sqrt{53}=7.280\ldots$ so the estimate is quite good.
Use the formula to find the square root of 20, 42, 93 and 131. Check the accuracy of your result using a calculator.

You need to know...

✔ how to work with fractions

✔ how to work with directed numbers

✔ that if a number is multiplied by zero the answer is zero.

Key words

factorisation, linear equation, perfect square, quadratic equation, root

Multiplication by zero

Exercise 21a

Find the value of $(x-3)(x-7)$ if

a $x=8$ **b** $x=7$ **c** $x=3$

a If $x=8$, $(x-3)(x-7)=(8-3)(8-7)$

$=(5)(1)$

$=5$

b If $x=7$, $(x-3)(x-7)=(4)(0)$
$=0$

(If any quantity is multiplied by 0 the answer is 0.)

c If $x=3$, $(x-3)(x-7)=(0)(-4)$
$=0$

1 Find the value of $(x-4)(x-2)$ if

a $x=6$ **b** $x=4$ **c** $x=2$

2 Find the value of $(x-5)(x-9)$ if

a $x=5$ **b** $x=10$ **c** $x=9$

3 Find the value of $(x-7)(x-1)$ if

a $x=1$ **b** $x=8$ **c** $x=7$

<u>4</u> Find the value of $(x-4)(x-6)$ if

a $x=4$ **b** $x=6$ **c** $x=3$

Find the value of $(x-2)(x+4)$ if

a $x=2$ **b** $x=4$ **c** $x=-4$

a If $x=2$ $(x-2)(x+4)=(0)(6)$
$=0$

b If $x=4$ $(x-2)(x+4)=(2)(8)$
$=16$

c If $x=-4$ $(x-2)(x+4)=(-6)(0)$
$=0$

5 Find the value of $(x-3)(x+5)$ if

a $x=6$ **b** $x=3$ **c** $x=-5$

6 Find the value of $(x-4)(x+6)$ if

a $x=0$ **b** $x=-6$ **c** $x=4$

7 Find the value of $(x-7)(x+2)$ if

a $x=-7$ **b** $x=-2$ **c** $x=7$

The results of this exercise show that if the product of two factors is 0, then either one or both of these factors must be 0.

In general we can say

if $A \times B=0$

then either $A=0$ or/and $B=0$

Exercise 21b

In questions **1** to **12** find, if possible, the value or values of A. Note that if $A \times 0 = 0$ then A can have any value.

1 $A \times 6 = 0$

2 $A \times 7 = 0$

3 $A \times 4 = 0$

4 $A \times 0 = 0$

5 $3 \times A = 12$

6 $8 \times A = 8$

7 $A \times 10 = 0$

8 $A \times 9 = 18$

9 $A \times 20 = 0$

10 $A \times 3 = 21$

11 $0 \times A = 0$

12 $4 \times A = 0$

13 If $AB = 0$ find **a** A if $B = 2$ **b** B if $A = 10$

14 If $AB = 0$ find **a** A if $B = 5$ **b** B if $A = 5$

15 If $AB = 0$ find **a** A if $B = 10$ **b** B if $A = 3$

16 If $AB = 0$ find **a** B if $A = 6$ **b** A if $B = 0$

Find a and b if $a(b - 3) = 0$

Either $\quad a = 0$ or/and $b - 3 = 0$

i.e. either $\quad a = 0$ or/and $b = 3$

Find a and b if:

17 $a(b - 1) = 0$

18 $a(b - 5) = 0$

19 $a(b - 2) = 0$

20 $(a - 3)b = 0$

21 $(a - 9)b = 0$

22 $a(b - 4) = 0$

23 $a(b - 10) = 0$

24 $(a - 1)b = 0$

25 $(a - 7)b = 0$

Quadratic equations

Previously we have considered equations such as $x - 1 = 0$ and $3x + 2 = 0$. These are examples of *linear equations*. The first equation is true only for $x = 1$ and the second only for $x = -\frac{2}{3}$.

If, however, we consider the equation

$$(x - 1)(x - 2) = 0$$

we find that it is true either when $x - 1 = 0$ or when $x - 2 = 0$,
i.e. either when $x = 1$ or when $x = 2$.

There are, therefore, two values of x that satisfy the equation $(x - 1)(x - 2) = 0$

Expanding the left-hand side gives

$$x^2 - 3x + 2 = 0$$

Equations like this, which contain an x^2 term, are called *quadratic equations*.

When we are given a quadratic equation we can often factorise the left-hand side into two linear factors,

e.g. $x^2 - 5x + 4 = 0$

gives $(x-4)(x-1) = 0$

It is this technique that concerns us in the present chapter.

Exercise 21c

What values of x satisfy the equation $x(x-9) = 0$?

$$x(x-9) = 0$$

Either $x = 0$ or $x - 9 = 0$

i.e. either $x = 0$ or $x = 9$

What values of x satisfy the following equations?

1 $x(x-3) = 0$

2 $x(x-5) = 0$

3 $(x-3)x = 0$

4 $x(x+4) = 0$

5 $(x+5)x = 0$

<u>6</u> $x(x-6) = 0$

<u>7</u> $x(x-10) = 0$

<u>8</u> $(x-7)x = 0$

<u>9</u> $x(x+7) = 0$

What values of x satisfy the equation $(x-3)(x+5) = 0$?

$$(x-3)(x+5) = 0$$

Either $x - 3 = 0$ or $x + 5 = 0$

i.e. either $x = 3$ or $x = -5$

What values of x satisfy the following equations?

10 $(x-1)(x-2) = 0$

11 $(x-5)(x-9) = 0$

12 $(x-10)(x-7) = 0$

13 $(x-4)(x-7) = 0$

14 $(x-6)(x-1) = 0$

<u>15</u> $(x-8)(x+11) = 0$

<u>16</u> $(x-3)(x+5) = 0$

<u>17</u> $(x+7)(x-2) = 0$

<u>18</u> $(x+2)(x+3) = 0$

<u>19</u> $(x+4)(x+9) = 0$

20 $(x+1)(x+8) = 0$

21 $(x-p)(x-q) = 0$

22 $(x+a)(x+b) = 0$

23 $(x-4)(x+1) = 0$

24 $(x+9)(x-8) = 0$

<u>25</u> $(x+6)(x+7) = 0$

<u>26</u> $(x+10)(x+11) = 0$

<u>27</u> $(x-a)(x-b) = 0$

Exercise 21d

Solve the following equations:

1 $(2x-5)(x-1)=0$

2 $(x-4)(3x-2)=0$

3 $(5x-4)(4x-3)=0$

4 $x(4x-5)=0$

5 $x(10x-3)=0$

6 $(5x+2)(x-7)=0$

7 $(6x+5)(3x-2)=0$

8 $(8x-3)(2x+5)=0$

9 $(7x-8)(4x+15)=0$

10 $(4x+3)(2x+3)=0$

<u>11</u> $(3x-7)(x-2)=0$

<u>12</u> $(3x-5)(2x-1)=0$

<u>13</u> $x(3x-1)=0$

<u>14</u> $x(7x-3)=0$

<u>15</u> $(2x+3)(x-3)=0$

<u>16</u> $(4x+3)(2x-5)=0$

<u>17</u> $(10x+9)(5x-4)=0$

<u>18</u> $(3x-2)(4x+9)=0$

<u>19</u> $(5x-12)(2x+7)=0$

<u>20</u> $(5x+8)(4x+3)=0$

Either $x-1=0$ (so $x=1$) or $2x-5=0$, which can be solved to find x.

Solution by factorisation

The previous two exercises suggest that if the left-hand side of a quadratic equation can be expressed as two factors of the form $ax+b$, we can use these factors to solve the equation.

Exercise 21e

Solve the equation $x^2-10x+9=0$

If $\quad x^2-10x+9=0$

then $\quad (x-1)(x-9)=0$

$\therefore$ either $\quad x-1=0 \quad$ or $\quad x-9=0$

i.e. $\quad x=1 \quad$ or $\quad x=9$

Solve the equations:

1 $x^2-3x+2=0$

2 $x^2-8x+7=0$

3 $x^2-5x+6=0$

4 $x^2-7x+10=0$

5 $x^2-7x+12=0$

<u>6</u> $x^2-6x+5=0$

<u>7</u> $x^2-12x+11=0$

<u>8</u> $x^2-6x+8=0$

<u>9</u> $x^2-8x+12=0$

<u>10</u> $x^2-13x+12=0$

Start by factorising the left-hand side.

Solve the equations:

11 $x^2 + 6x - 7 = 0$

12 $x^2 - 2x - 8 = 0$

13 $x^2 + x - 12 = 0$

14 $x^2 - 2x - 15 = 0$

15 $x^2 + 7x - 18 = 0$

16 $x^2 - 12x - 13 = 0$

17 $x^2 + x - 6 = 0$

18 $x^2 - 4x - 12 = 0$

19 $x^2 + x - 20 = 0$

20 $x^2 - 5x - 24 = 0$

These equations have one negative solution.

Solve the equations:

21 $x^2 + 3x + 2 = 0$

22 $x^2 + 8x + 7 = 0$

23 $x^2 + 8x + 15 = 0$

24 $x^2 + 8x + 12 = 0$

25 $x^2 + 11x + 18 = 0$

26 $x^2 + 7x + 6 = 0$

27 $x^2 + 7x + 10 = 0$

28 $x^2 + 14x + 13 = 0$

29 $x^2 + 16x + 15 = 0$

30 $x^2 + 9x + 18 = 0$

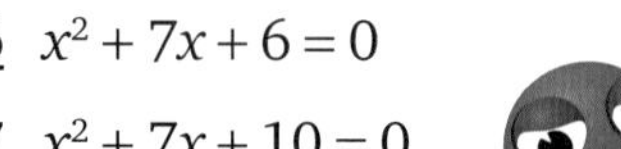

These equations have two negative solutions.

Solve the equation $x^2 - 49 = 0$

$$x^2 - 49 = 0$$

$$(x + 7)(x - 7) = 0$$

Either $x + 7 = 0$ or $x - 7 = 0$

i.e. $x = -7$ or $x = 7$

Solve the equations:

31 $x^2 - 1 = 0$

32 $x^2 - 9 = 0$

33 $x^2 - 16 = 0$

34 $x^2 - 81 = 0$

35 $x^2 - 169 = 0$

36 $x^2 - 4 = 0$

37 $x^2 - 25 = 0$

38 $x^2 - 100 = 0$

39 $x^2 - 144 = 0$

40 $x^2 - 36 = 0$

The difference between two squares can always be factorised.

The equations we have solved by factorising have all been examples of the equation $ax^2 + bx + c = 0$ when $a = 1$. We consider next the case when $c = 0$, e.g. solve the equation $3x^2 + 2x = 0$

Since x is common to both terms on the left-hand side we can rewrite this equation

$$x(3x + 2) = 0$$

Then, either $x = 0$ or $3x + 2 = 0$

i.e. $x = 0$ or $3x = -2$

i.e. $x = 0$ or $x = -\frac{2}{3}$

Exercise 21f

Solve the equations:

Start by looking for a common factor, then factorise the left-hand side.

1 $x^2 - 2x = 0$

2 $x^2 - 10x = 0$

3 $x^2 + 8x = 0$

4 $2x^2 - x = 0$

5 $4x^2 - 5x = 0$

6 $x^2 - 5x = 0$

7 $x^2 + 3x = 0$

8 $x^2 + x = 0$

9 $3x^2 - 5x = 0$

10 $5x^2 - 7x = 0$

11 $2x^2 + 3x = 0$

12 $8x^2 + 5x = 0$

13 $x^2 - 7x = 0$

14 $3x^2 + 5x = 0$

15 $7x^2 - 12x = 0$

16 $6x^2 + 7x = 0$

17 $12x^2 + 7x = 0$

18 $x^2 + 4x = 0$

19 $7x^2 - 2x = 0$

20 $14x^2 + 3x = 0$

Sometimes a quadratic equation has two answers, or *roots*, that are exactly the same.

Consider $x^2 - 4x + 4 = 0$

then $(x-2)(x-2) = 0$

i.e. either $x - 2 = 0$ or $x - 2 = 0$

i.e. $x = 2$ or $x = 2$

i.e. $x = 2$ (twice)

Such an equation involves a *perfect square*. As with any quadratic equation, it has two answers, or roots, but they are equal. We say that such an equation has a repeated root.

Exercise 21g

Solve the equation $x^2 + 14x + 49 = 0$

$$x^2 + 14x + 49 = 0$$

$$(x+7)(x+7) = 0$$

Either $x + 7 = 0$ or $x + 7 = 0$

i.e. $x = -7$ (twice)

Solve the equations:

1 $x^2 - 2x + 1 = 0$

2 $x^2 - 10x + 25 = 0$

3 $x^2 - 20x + 100 = 0$

4 $x^2 + 8x + 16 = 0$

5 $x^2 + 6x + 9 = 0$

6 $x^2 - 6x + 9 = 0$

7 $x^2 - 8x + 16 = 0$

8 $x^2 - 18x + 81 = 0$

9 $x^2 + 2x + 1 = 0$

10 $x^2 + 20x + 100 = 0$

Always begin by trying to factorise.

11 $x^2+18x+81=0$

12 $x^2-14x+49=0$

13 $x^2-22x+121=0$

14 $x^2+12x+36=0$

15 $x^2-x+\frac{1}{4}=0$

16 $x^2+10x+25=0$

17 $x^2-12x+36=0$

18 $x^2-40x+400=0$

19 $x^2-16x+64=0$

20 $x^2+\frac{4}{3}x+\frac{4}{9}=0$

Exercise 21h

Solve the equation $x^2-x=12$

$$x^2-x=12$$

First arrange the equations so that the left-hand side = 0, then try to factorise.

Subtracting 12 from each side gives

$$x^2-x-12=0$$

$$(x-4)(x+3)=0$$

Either $x-4=0$ or $x+3=0$

i.e. $x=4$ or $x=-3$

Solve the equations:

1 $x^2-x=30$

2 $x^2-6x=16$

3 $x^2+9x=36$

4 $x^2-x=6$

5 $x^2+6x=7$

6 $x^2=2x+3$

7 $x^2=2x+24$

8 $x^2=12x-35$

9 $x^2=3x+10$

10 $x^2=6x-8$

11 $10=7x-x^2$

12 $7=8x-x^2$

13 $8=6x-x^2$

14 $21=10x-x^2$

Subtract $2x$ and 3 from each side.

15 $12=8x-x^2$

16 $20=9x-x^2$

17 $35=12x-x^2$

18 $15=8x-x^2$

Summary

To solve a quadratic equation by factorising:

- collect all terms on one side of the equation, i.e. arrange it in the form $ax^2+bx+c=0$
- take out any common factors (these may or may not include x)
- factorise.

Exercise 21i

Solve the equations:

1 $x^2 - x - 20 = 0$

2 $x^2 = 4x - 4$

3 $9x^2 - 1 = 0$

4 $2x^2 + 7x = 0$

5 $x^2 + 13x + 12 = 0$

6 $1 - 16x^2 = 0$

7 $x^2 - 6x = 0$

8 $x^2 = 2x + 35$

9 $x^2 = 7 - 6x$

10 $4 = 25x^2$

11 $4x^2 = 25$

12 $x^2 + 11x + 18 = 0$

13 $5x - 2x^2 = 0$

14 $7x = 4x^2$

Solve the equations:

15 $x(x+1) = 12$

16 $x(x-1) = x + 3$

17 $x(x-5) = 24$

In questions **15** to **26** multiply out the brackets and arrange each equation in the form $ax^2 + bx + c = 0$. Then try to factorise.

18 $x(x+3) = 5(3x-7)$

19 $(x+2)(x+3) = 56$

20 $(x+9)(x-6) = 34$

21 $(x-2)(x+6) = 33$

22 $(x+3)(x-8) + 10 = 0$

23 $(x-5)(x+2) = 18$

24 $(x+8)(x-2) = 39$

25 $(x+1)(x+8) + 12 = 0$

26 $(x-1)(x+10) + 30 = 0$

Solve the equations:

27 $\frac{x+5}{2} + \frac{1}{x} = 1$

28 $\frac{2}{x} + \frac{x+1}{3} = 2$

29 $\frac{x+2}{2} + \frac{2}{x} + 1 = 0$

30 $\frac{x+12}{3} + \frac{3}{x} = 2$

31 $\frac{x+9}{2} - \frac{2}{x} = 3$

32 $x + 8 + \frac{9}{x} = 2$

33 $\frac{1}{x} - \frac{2}{x-2} = 3$

34 $\frac{2}{x+3} + x = 0$

Start by multiplying both sides by the LCM of the denominators.

Investigation

The earliest record of a pair of simultaneous equations that needed to be solved, where one was a quadratic equation and the other linear, is in Babylon *c.* 2000 BCE.

The equations were $x^2 + y^2 = 1000$ and $y = \frac{2x}{3} - 10$. Can you solve them?

Will your method work for other simultaneous equations where one is quadratic and the other is linear?

Problems

Exercise 21j

I think of a positive number x, square it and then add three times the number I first thought of. If the answer is 54, form an equation in x and solve it to find the number I first thought of.

If the given number is x, its square is x^2 and three times the number is $3x$, adding gives $x^2 + 3x$, which we know is 54,

i.e. $$x^2 + 3x = 54$$

$$x^2 + 3x - 54 = 0$$

$$(x - 6)(x + 9) = 0$$

Either $x - 6 = 0$ or $x + 9 = 0$

i.e. $x = 6$ or $x = -9$

The positive number I first thought of was therefore 6.

Read each question carefully; several times if necessary.

1 The square of a number x is 16 more than six times the number. Form an equation in x and solve it.

When $6x$ is subtracted from x^2 the answer is 16.

2 When five times a number x is subtracted from the square of the same number, the answer is 14. Form an equation in x and solve it.

3 I think of a number x. If I square it and add it to the number I first thought of the total is 42. Find the number I first thought of.

4 Peter had x marbles. The number of marbles Fred had was six fewer than the square of the number Peter had. Together they had 66 marbles. Form an equation in x and solve it. How many marbles did Fred have?

5 Ahmed is x years old and his father is x^2 years old. If the sum of their ages is 56 years, form an equation in x and solve it to find the age of each.

6 Kathryn is x years old. If her mother's age is two years more than the square of Kathryn's age, and the sum of their ages is 44 years, form an equation in x and solve it to find the ages of Kathryn and her mother.

7 Peter is x years old and his sister is 5 years older. If the product of their ages is 84, form an equation in x and solve it to find Peter's age.

8 Sally is x years old and her sister Ann is 4 years younger. If the product of their ages is 140, form an equation in x and solve it to find Ann's age.

A rectangle is 4 cm longer than it is wide. If it is x cm wide and has an area of 77 cm^2, form an equation in x and solve it to find the dimensions of the rectangle.

$(x+4)$ cm

x cm

The area of a rectangle is length × breadth.

$$\text{Area} = (x+4) \times x \text{ cm}^2$$

But the area is 77 cm^2,

$$\therefore \qquad (x+4)x = 77$$

$$\text{i.e.} \qquad x^2 + 4x = 77$$

$$x^2 + 4x - 77 = 0$$

$$(x-7)(x+11) = 0$$

$$\text{Either} \qquad x-7=0 \quad \text{or} \quad x+11=0$$

$$\text{i.e.} \qquad x=7 \quad \text{or} \quad x=-11$$

The breadth of a rectangle cannot be negative, so we use $x = 7$.

Therefore, the rectangle measures $(7+4)$ cm by 7 cm, i.e. 11 cm by 7 cm.

9 A rectangle is x cm long and is 3 cm longer than it is wide. If its area is 28 cm^2, form an equation in x and solve it to find the dimensions of the rectangle.

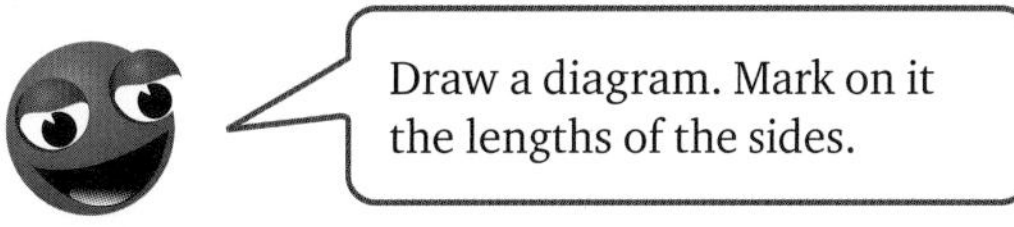

Draw a diagram. Mark on it the lengths of the sides.

10 A rectangle is 5 cm longer than it is wide. If its width is x cm and its area is 66 cm^2, form an equation in x and solve it. Hence find the dimensions of the rectangle.

11 The base of a triangle is x cm long and its perpendicular height is half the length of its base. If the triangle has an area of 25 cm^2, form an equation in x and solve it. What is the height of the triangle?

12 A rectangular lawn measuring 30 m by 20 m is bordered on two adjacent sides by a uniform path of width x m as shown in the diagram.

a Express in terms of x each of the areas denoted by the letters A, B and C.

b If the area of the path is 104 m^2, form an equation in x and solve it to find the width of the path.

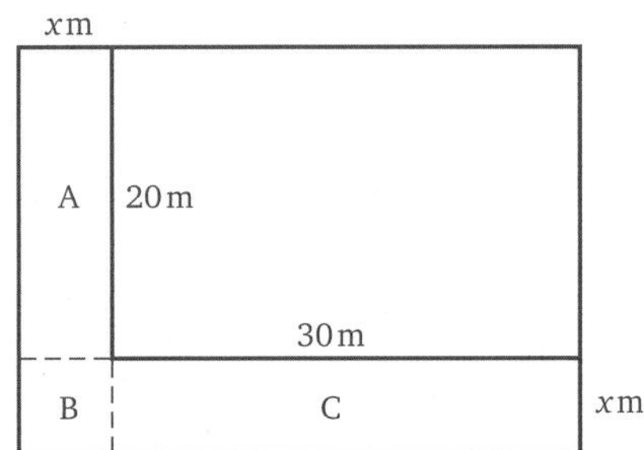

Mixed exercises

Exercise 21k

1 Find the value of $(x+4)(x-3)$ if **a** $x=1$ **b** $x=3$ **c** $x=4$

2 Find the value of $(2x-1)(x+2)$ if

a $x=0$ **b** $x=\frac{1}{2}$ **c** $x=2$ **d** $x=-2$

3 Find the value of $(5x+1)(x-3)$ if

a $x=2$ **b** $x=3$ **c** $x=-\frac{1}{5}$

4 Solve: **a** $x(x+7)=0$ **b** $4x(2x-1)=0$

5 Solve: **a** $3x(x-2)=0$ **b** $x(7x+3)=0$

6 Solve: **a** $5x(x+7)=0$ **b** $3x(4x-3)=0$

7 Solve: **a** $(x-3)(x-8)=0$ **b** $(x-2)(5x+3)=0$

8 Solve:

a $(x-2)(x+5)=0$ **b** $(3x-4)(x+2)=0$ **c** $(2x+3)(2x-3)=0$

9 Solve:

a $(x+4)(x-5)=0$ **b** $(4x-7)(x+3)=0$ **c** $(5x-3)(5x+3)=0$

10 Solve: **a** $x^2-2x-35=0$ **b** $x^2-13x+40=0$

11 Solve: **a** $x^2+x-6=0$ **b** $x^2+11x+30=0$

12 Solve: **a** $x^2-2x-15=0$ **b** $x^2+12x+32=0$

13 Solve: **a** $x(x+4)=45$ **b** $x(x+2)=x+30$

14 Solve: **a** $x(x+6)=3x+10$ **b** $x(x+8)=x+30$

Exercise 21l

Select the letter that gives the correct answer.

1 $x(x-12)=0$ The values of x are

A 0, −12 **B** 0, 12 **C** 1, −12 **D** 1, 12

2 $(x-4)(x-7)=0$ The values of x are

A −4, −7 **B** −4, 7 **C** 4, −7 **D** 4, 7

3 $(x+3)(x-5)=0$ The values of x are

A −3, −5 **B** −3, 5 **C** 3, −5 **D** 3, 5

4 $(x+6)(x+8)=0$ The values of x are

A −6, −8 **B** −6, 8 **C** 6, −8 **D** 6, 8

5 $5x^2-10x=0$ The values of x are

A 0, −2 **B** 0, 2 **C** 0, 5 **D** 0, 10

6 $x^2-4x+3=0$ The values of x are

A −1, −3 **B** −1, 3 **C** 1, 3 **D** 3, 4

 **Puzzle**

A bird table is 3 m from one corner, 4 m from another corner and 5 m from a third corner of a square patio. Find the length of an edge of the patio.

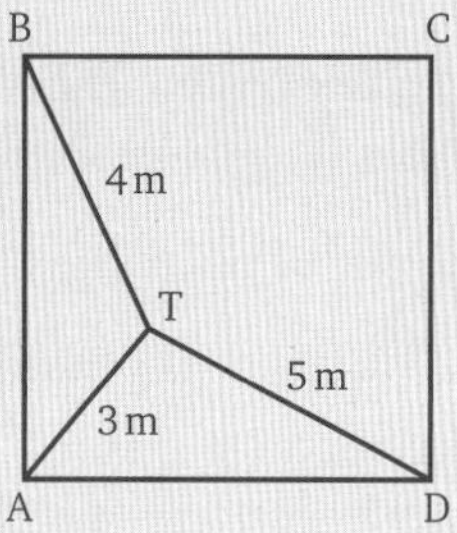

Did you know?

Emmy Noether (1882–1935) was an outstanding mathematician. Her father, Max Noether, was also a distinguished mathematician. Emmy was the only woman in a class of over 900 at the University of Erlangen, in Germany, where her father was a lecturer. She was a mentor for several female mathematicians including Olga Taussky-Todd, Ruth Stauffer McKee, Marie Weiss and Grace Shover-Quinn.

In this chapter you have seen that...

- ✔ if $A \times B = 0$ then either $A = 0$ and/or $B = 0$
- ✔ the two values of x that satisfy the equation $(x - a)(x - b) = 0$ are $x = a$ and $x = b$
- ✔ many quadratic equations can be solved by factorising, e.g. $x^2 - 7x + 12 = 0$ can be rewritten as $(x - 3)(x - 4) = 0$, from which $x = 3$ or $x = 4$, and $4x^2 - 7x = 0$ becomes $x(4x - 7) = 0$, from which $x = 0$ or $x = \frac{7}{4}$.

22 Probability

At the end of this chapter you should be able to...

1 write the set of outcomes of an experiment

2 state the number of possible outcomes of an experiment

3 calculate the probability of an event A happening as

$$\frac{\text{the number of ways in which A can occur}}{\text{the total number of equally likely outcomes}}$$

4 calculate the probability that event A does not happen as

$1 - P(\text{A does happen})$

5 estimate the number of times an event might occur

6 perform experiments, collect data and hence calculate required probabilities.

Did you know?

Do you know how to play Tic-Tac-Toe in such a way that you never lose? If you do, you are using a topic in mathematics called Game Theory. We told you that maths was fun!

X	X	O
O	O	X
X	O	X

A game is won either by chance or by using a strategy.

Probability and statistics as mathematical sciences arose because game players wanted to use game odds to best advantage.

After studying mathematics carefully, mathematicians defined numbers called *probabilities* which helped them to explain how likely some 'outcome' or 'event' was to happen or fail to happen.

You need to know...

✔ how to simplify a fraction

✔ how to add and subtract fractions

✔ the cards in an ordinary pack of playing cards.

Key words

approximation, biased, certainty, chance, equally likely events, equally likely outcomes, event, experiment, fair, impossibility, integer, odds, outcome, prime numbers, probability, random, unbiased

Outcomes of experiments

If you throw an ordinary die there are six possible scores that you can get. These are 1, 2, 3, 4, 5 or 6.
The act of throwing the die is called an *experiment*.
The score that you get is called an *outcome* or an *event*.
The set {1, 2, 3, 4, 5, 6} is called the *set of all possible outcomes*.

Exercise 22a

How many possible outcomes are there for the following experiments? Write down the set of all possible outcomes in each case.

1. Tossing a 10 c coin. (Assume that it lands flat.)
2. Taking one disc from a bag containing 1 red, 1 blue and 1 yellow disc.
3. Choosing one number from the first ten positive integers. (An integer is a whole number.)
4. Taking one crayon from a box containing 1 red, 1 yellow, 1 blue, 1 brown, 1 black and 1 green crayon.
5. Taking one item from a bag containing 1 packet of chewing gum, 1 packet of boiled sweets and 1 bar of chocolate.
6. Taking one coin from a bag containing one 1 c coin, one 10 c coin, one 25 c coin and one 50 c coin.
7. Choosing one card from part of a pack of ordinary playing cards containing just the suit of clubs.
8. Choosing one letter from the vowels of the alphabet.
9. Choosing one number from the first 5 prime numbers.
10. Choosing an even number from the first 20 whole numbers.

Probability

If you throw an ordinary die, what are the chances of getting a four? If you throw it fairly, it is reasonable to assume that you are as likely to throw any one score as any other, i.e. all outcomes are equally likely. As throwing a four is only 1 of the 6 equally likely outcomes you have a 1 in 6 *chance* of throwing a four.

Odds is another word in everyday language that is used to describe chances.

In mathematical language we use the word 'probability' to describe chances. We say that the probability of throwing a four is $\frac{1}{6}$.

This can be written more briefly as

$$P(\text{throwing a four}) = \frac{1}{6}$$

Probabilities can be given in various ways, either as a fraction or as a percentage, or even as a 1 in n chance as above.

We will now define exactly what we mean by 'the probability that something happens'.

If A stands for a particular event, the probability of A happening is written $P(\text{A})$ where

$$P(\text{A}) = \frac{\text{the number of ways in which A can occur}}{\text{the } \textit{total} \text{ number of equally likely outcomes}}$$

We can use this definition to work out, for example, the probability that if one card is drawn *at random* from a full pack of ordinary playing cards, it is the ace of spades.

(The phrase 'at random' means that any one card is as likely to be picked as any other.)

There are 52 cards in a full pack, so there are 52 equally likely outcomes.

There is only one ace of spades, so there is only one way of drawing that card,

i.e. $$P(\text{ace of spades}) = \frac{1}{52}$$

Exercise 22b

In the following questions, assume that all possible outcomes are equally likely.

1 One letter is chosen at random from the letters in the word SALE. What is the probability that it is A?

2 What is the probability that a red pencil is chosen from a box containing 10 different coloured pencils, one of which is red?

3 What is the probability of choosing a prime number from the numbers 6, 7, 8, 9, 10?

4 What is the probability of choosing the most expensive car from a range of six different new cars in a showroom?

5 What is the probability of choosing an integer that is exactly divisible by 5 from the set {6, 7, 8, 9, 10, 11, 12}?

6 In a raffle 200 tickets are sold. If you have bought one ticket, what is the probability that you will win first prize?

7 One card is chosen at random from a pack of 52 ordinary playing cards. What is the probability that it is the ace of hearts?

8 What is the probability of choosing the colour blue from the colours of the rainbow?

9 A whole number is chosen from the first 15 whole numbers. What is the probability that it is exactly divisible both by 3 and by 4?

? Puzzle

Charlie keeps his socks in a drawer. They are all either brown or grey. One night, in the dark, due to an electricity cut, he pulls out some socks to put on. What is the smallest number of socks he must pull out to be certain of having a pair of the same colour?

Experiments where an event can happen more than once

If a card is picked at random from an ordinary pack of 52 playing cards, what is the probability that it is a five?

There are 4 fives in the pack: the five of spades, the five of hearts, the five of diamonds and the five of clubs.

That is, there are 4 ways in which a five can be chosen.

Altogether there are 52 cards that are equally likely to be chosen,

therefore $P(\text{choosing a five}) = \frac{4}{52} = \frac{1}{13}$

Now consider a bag containing 3 white discs and 2 black discs.

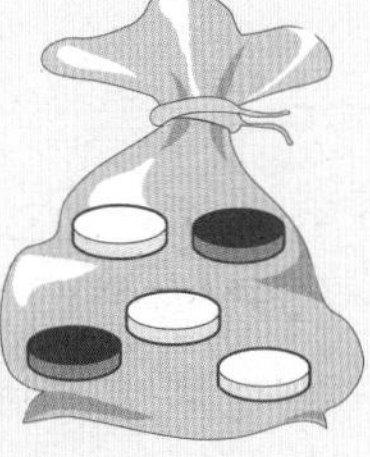

If one disc is taken from the bag it can be black or white. But these are not equally likely events: there are three ways of choosing a white disc and two ways of choosing a black disc, so

$$P(\text{choosing a white disc}) = \frac{3}{5}$$

and $$P(\text{choosing a black disc}) = \frac{2}{5}$$

Exercise 22c

A letter is chosen at random from the letters of the word DIFFICULT. How many ways are there of choosing the letter I? What is the probability that the letter I will be chosen?

There are 2 ways of choosing the letter I and there are 9 letters in DIFFICULT.

$$P(\text{choosing I}) = \frac{2}{9}$$

1 How many ways are there of choosing an even number from the first 10 whole numbers?

2 A prime number is picked at random from the set {4, 5, 6, 7, 8, 9, 10, 11}. How many ways are there of doing this?

3 A card is taken at random from an ordinary pack of 52 playing cards. How many ways are there of taking a black card?

4 An ordinary six-sided die is thrown. How many ways are there of getting a score that is greater than 4?

5 A lucky dip contains 50 boxes, only 10 of which contain a prize, the rest being empty. How many ways are there of choosing a box that contains a prize?

6 A number is chosen at random from the first 10 integers. What is the probability that it is

- **a** an even number
- **b** an odd number
- **c** a prime number
- **d** exactly divisible by 3?

7 One card is drawn at random from an ordinary pack of 52 playing cards. What is the probability that it is

- **a** an ace
- **b** a red card

- **c** a heart
- **d** a picture card (include the aces)?

8 One letter is chosen at random from the word DIFFICULT. What is the probability that it is

- **a** the letter F
- **b** the letter D
- **c** a vowel
- **d** one of the first five letters of the alphabet?

9 An ordinary unbiased six-sided die is thrown. What is the probability that the score is

Unbiased means that any possible score is equally likely.

- **a** greater than 3
- **b** at least 5
- **c** less than 3?

10 A book of 150 pages has a picture on each of 20 pages. If one page is chosen at random, what is the probability that it has a picture on it?

11 One counter is picked at random from a bag containing 15 red counters, 5 white counters and 5 yellow counters. What is the probability that the counter removed is

a red **b** yellow **c** not red?

12 If you bought 10 raffle tickets and a total of 400 were sold, what is the probability that you win first prize?

13 A number wheel is spun. What is the probability that when it stops it will be pointing to

a an even number

b an odd number

c a number less than 10 excluding zero?

(The numbers on the number wheel go from 0 to 36, and zero is counted as neither an even number nor an odd number.)

14 One letter is chosen at random from the letters of the alphabet. What is the probability that it is a consonant?

15 A number is chosen at random from the set of two-digit numbers (i.e. the numbers from 10 to 99). What is the probability that it is exactly divisible both by 3 and by 4?

16 A bag of sweets contains 4 caramels, 3 fruit centres and 5 mints. If one sweet is taken out, what is the probability that it is

a a mint **b** a caramel **c** not a fruit centre?

Certainty and impossibility

Consider a bag that contains 5 red discs only. If one disc is removed it is absolutely certain that it will be red. It is impossible to take a blue disc from that bag.

$$P(\text{disc is red}) = \frac{5}{5} = 1$$

$$P(\text{disc is blue}) = \frac{0}{5} = 0$$

In all cases

$$P(\text{an event that is certain}) = 1$$

$$P(\text{an event that is impossible}) = 0$$

Most events fall somewhere between the two, so

$$0 \leqslant P(\text{that an event happens}) \leqslant 1$$

Exercise 22d

Discuss the probability that the following events will happen. Try to class them as certain, impossible or somewhere in between.

1 You will swim the Atlantic Ocean.

2 You will weigh 80 kg.

3 You will be late home from school at least once this term.

4 You will grow to a height of 2 m.

5 The sun will not rise tomorrow.

6 You will run a mile in $3\frac{1}{2}$ minutes.

7 You will have a drink sometime today.

8 Guyana will win next year's Digicel Four Day Championship.

9 A card chosen from an ordinary pack of playing cards is either red or black.

10 A coin that is tossed lands on its edge.

11 Give some examples of events that are likely or unlikely to happen. For example: you will own a car; your home will burn down.

Probability that an event does not happen

If one card is drawn at random from an ordinary pack of playing cards, the probability that it is a club is given by

$$P(\text{a club}) = \frac{13}{52} = \frac{1}{4}$$

Now there are 39 cards that are not clubs so the probability that the card is not a club is given by

$$P(\text{not a club}) = \frac{39}{52} = \frac{3}{4}$$

i.e. $P(\text{not a club}) + P(\text{a club}) = \frac{3}{4} + \frac{1}{4} = 1$

Hence $P(\text{not a club}) = 1 - P(\text{a club})$

This relationship is true in any situation because

$$\left(\begin{array}{c}\text{the number of ways}\\ \text{in which an event, A,}\\ \text{can } \textit{not} \text{ happen}\end{array}\right) = \left(\begin{array}{c}\text{the total number of}\\ \text{possible outcomes}\end{array}\right) - \left(\begin{array}{c}\text{the number of ways}\\ \text{in which A can}\\ \text{happen}\end{array}\right)$$

i.e. $P(\text{A does not happen}) = 1 - P(\text{A does happen})$

'A does not happen' is shortened to $\bar{A}$, where $\bar{A}$ is read as 'not A'.

$\bar{A}$ is sometimes written as A′.

Therefore $$P(\bar{A}) = 1 - P(A)$$

Exercise 22e

A letter is chosen at random from the letters of the word PROBABILITY. What is the probability that it is not B?

Method 1: There are 11 letters and 2 of them are Bs

$$\therefore\ P(\text{letter is B}) = \frac{2}{11}$$

Hence $$P(\text{letter is not B}) = 1 - \frac{2}{11}$$
$$= \frac{9}{11}$$

Method 2: There are 11 letters and 9 of them are not Bs

$$\therefore\ P(\text{letter is not B}) = \frac{9}{11}$$

1 A number is chosen at random from the first 20 whole numbers. What is the probability that it is not a prime number?

2 A card is drawn at random from an ordinary pack of playing cards. What is the probability that it is not a two?

3 One letter is chosen at random from the letters of the alphabet. What is the probability that it is not a vowel?

4 A box of 60 coloured crayons contains a mixture of colours, 10 of which are red. If one crayon is removed at random, what is the probability that it is not red?

5 A number is chosen at random from the first 10 whole numbers. What is the probability that it is not exactly divisible by 3?

6 One letter is chosen at random from the letters of the word ALPHABET. What is the probability that it is not a vowel?

7 In a raffle, 500 tickets are sold. If you buy 20 tickets, what is the probability that you will not win first prize?

8 If you throw an ordinary fair six-sided die, what is the probability that you will not get a score of 5 or more?

9 There are 200 packets hidden in a lucky dip. Five packets contain \$1 and the rest contain 1 c. What is the probability that you will not draw out a packet containing \$1?

10 When an ordinary pack of playing cards is cut, what is the probability that the card showing is not a picture card? (The picture cards are the jacks, queens and kings.)

11 A letter is chosen at random from the letters of the word SUCCESSION. What is the probability that the letter is

a N
b S
c a vowel
d not S?

12 A card is drawn at random from an ordinary pack of playing cards. What is the probability that it is

a an ace
b a spade
c not a club
d not a seven or an eight?

13 A bag contains a set of snooker balls (i.e. 15 red and 1 each of the following colours: white, yellow, green, brown, blue, pink and black). What is the probability that one ball removed at random is

a red
b not red
c black
d not red or white?

14 There are 60 cars in the parking lot. Of the cars, 22 are British made, 24 are Japanese made and the rest are European but not British. What is the probability that the first car to leave is

a Japanese
b not British
c European but not British
d American?

The number of times an event is likely to happen

Sometimes it is useful to be able to estimate how often an event *might* happen.

For example, Sue is organising a game at a bazaar. The game involves rolling a die. When a six shows, you win a prize.
Sue needs to estimate the number of prizes that will be won.

On one turn, the probability of winning is $\frac{1}{6}$. So there will be about 1 win in every 6 turns.

Sue estimates that there will be about 300 turns. So there will be about $\frac{1}{6}$ of 300 wins.

Now $\frac{1}{6}$ of 300 = 300 ÷ 6 = 50, so Sue will need about 50 prizes.

$$\left(\begin{array}{c}\text{The number of times that an event}\\ \text{is likely to happen}\end{array}\right) = \left(\begin{array}{c}\text{probability that it}\\ \text{will happen once}\end{array}\right) \times \left(\begin{array}{c}\text{the number of times}\\ \text{it is tried}\end{array}\right)$$

When we flip a fair coin, the probability that it will show a head is $\frac{1}{2}$.

If we flip this coin 20 times, we expect to get about $\frac{1}{2} \times 20$ heads, i.e. 10 heads.

What we expect to get is an *estimate*. It is **not** the same as what we will get.

Suppose we flip a coin 20 times and get 15 heads. This is more than the 10 heads we expect. This can happen by chance, or it could be that the coin is *biased*. Biased means that some outcomes are more likely than others.

Exercise 22f

Fair means the same as unbiased, i.e. any outcome is as likely to happen as any other possible outcome.

1 A fair coin is flipped 100 times.

Write the number of heads expected.

2 A fair ordinary die is rolled 60 times.

Find the number of times you expect it to show 1.

3 This spinner is fair. It is spun 100 times.

Work out the number of times you expect it to show 4.

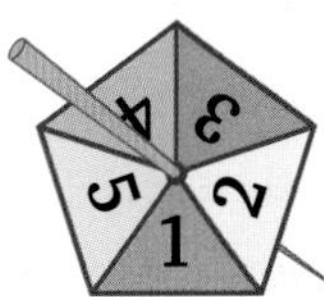

4 This spinner is fair. It is spun 40 times.

a Find the number of times you expect it will show 1.

b Work out the number of times you expect that it will show 3.

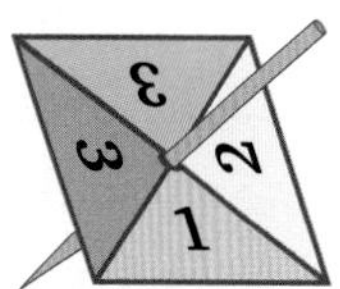

5 This fair spinner is spun 50 times.

How often do you expect it will show an even number?

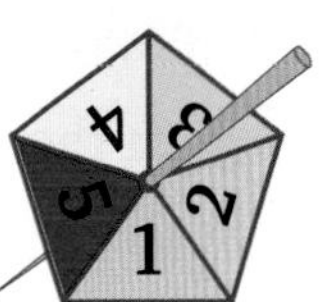

6 A ordinary fair die is rolled 90 times.

a Work out the number of times you expect it to show 6.

b Work out the number of times you expect it to show an odd number.

c Work out the number of times you expect it to show a number less than 3.

7 Jamestown Airport has 500 flights leaving each day.
The probability that a plane is delayed is $\frac{1}{25}$.
How many delayed flights are expected on one day?

8 Derek rolls two ordinary fair six-sided dice 360 times.
The probability that they show a double six is $\frac{1}{36}$.
Work out the number of double sixes Derek is likely to get.

9 The probability of winning a prize on a game of chance is $\frac{1}{50}$.
500 people have a go at this game. Find an estimate for the number of prizes that were won.

10 The probability that a lift will break down each time it is used is $\frac{1}{1000}$.
The lift is used about 5000 times each year. Estimate the number of times that it is likely to break down.

11 Sam goes to work by train. The probability that his train is late is $\frac{1}{8}$.
Sam works 200 days each year. Estimate the number of these days when Sam's train is late.

12 a One card is picked at random from an ordinary pack of playing cards. Write the probability that it is an ace.
b Joe has 40 packs of ordinary playing cards.
One card is picked at random from each pack.
Estimate the number of aces that are picked.

13 a Write the probability of getting a head on one flip of a fair coin.
b Work out the number of heads you expect to get if you flipped the coin 60 times.
c Angela said, 'If you flip a fair coin 10 times, you will get 5 heads.'
Is Angela correct? Give a reason for your answer.
d Sam tossed one coin 100 times. He got 10 heads.
Sam said, 'This coin is biased.'
Is Sam correct? Give a reason for your answer.

14 Harry plays a game of chance. The probability of winning is $\frac{1}{10}$.
Each go at the game costs 20 c and the prize is $1.
Harry plays this game 50 times.
a How much does Harry spend on the game?
b How many times is Harry likely to win?
c How much money is Harry likely to win?
d Is Harry likely to lose money or make money on this game?
Give a reason for your answer.

A game of chance means that any one outcome is as likely as any other. There is no skill involved.

15 The probability of winning a prize of \$25 from a scratch card is $\frac{1}{50}$.

Scratch cards cost \$1 each.

Tom buys100 cards.

a Work out how many times Tom is likely to win.

b Work out how much Tom is likely to win.

c Calculate the difference between the money Tom spends on scratch cards and his likely winnings.

Investigation

This investigation should be done as a class exercise.

A company runs the following promotional offer with tubes of sweets.

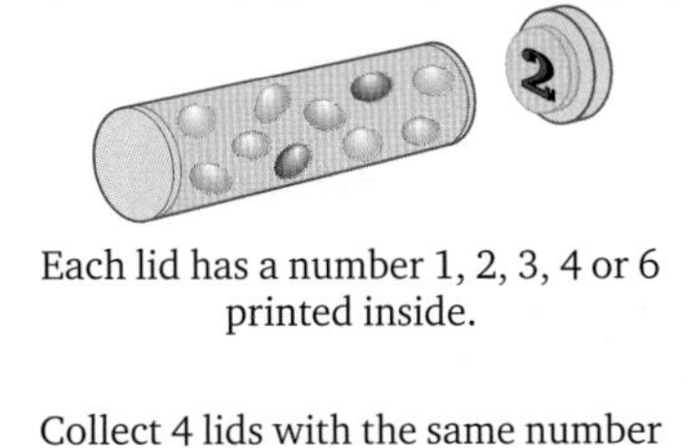

Each lid has a number 1, 2, 3, 4 or 6 printed inside.

Collect 4 lids with the same number and get a free T-shirt.

What are the chances of getting four numbers the same if you just buy four tubes?

What is the most likely number of tubes that you need to buy to collect enough lids?

1 We could answer the questions by collecting evidence, i.e. buying tubes of these sweets until we have four lids with the same number on them, and repeating this until we think we have reliable results.

What are the disadvantages of this?

2 We can avoid the disadvantages of having to buy tubes of these sweets by simulating the situation as follows:

First assume that any one of the numbers 1 to 6 is equally likely to be inside a lid.

Now throw a die to simulate the number we would get if we bought a tube, and carry on throwing it until you get four numbers the same. We will need several tally charts to keep a record of the number of throws needed on each occasion.

This shows the start of the simulation.

Score	Tally
1	/
2	///
3	/
4	//
5	////
6	/
Total	12

Number of throws needed to get 4 numbers the same	4	5	6	7	8	9	10	11	12	13	14	15	16	...
Tally									/					

Using probability to help decision making

There are many occasions when we have to choose between two or more options and probability can sometimes help us decide which option to take.

For example, suppose you want to have a barbeque on either Saturday or Sunday evening. The probability it will rain on Saturday evening is 20%. The probability it will rain on Sunday evening is 60%. Unless there are other reasons to choose Sunday, Saturday would be the better choice.

Exercise 22g

1 Jason visits a school bazaar. He cannot decide whether to spend money on the tombola or the lucky dip. The probability that he will win a prize in the tombola is 1 in 5. The probability that he will win a prize on the lucky dip is 1 in 8. Which one should he choose?

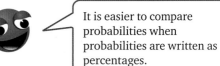

It is easier to compare probabilities when probabilities are written as percentages.

2 The chance of a hurricane occurring in August is 30%. The chance of a hurricane occurring in September is 44%.

Mr Khan wants to build a shed in his garden. Would he be wise to build it in September?

3 There are two medicines available to treat a particular virus. Medicine A has a 40% chance of curing an infection quickly.

Medicine B has a 70% chance of curing the infection quickly.

a Using just the information above, which medicine is the better choice?

b If the chance of serious side-effects with Medicine B is 1 in 10 and the chance of serious side-effects with Medicine A is 1 in 100, would this be likely to change the choice?

4 Angela needs to buy a new printer. Printer A costs $5000 and the probability that it will last for 10 years is 40%. Printer B costs $2000 and the probability it will last for 10 years is 15%.

Based on this information, which printer is it sensible to buy? Give reasons for your answer.

What other considerations could affect the decision?

5 Grace drives from home to her place of work every day. She can use two routes. If the roads are clear of traffic, using Route 1 takes 10 minutes less time than using Route 2. However, the probability of traffic congestion on Route 1 is $\frac{1}{3}$. The probability of traffic congestion on Route 2 is $\frac{2}{11}$. Which of these two routes is the better choice?

6 An engaged couple are choosing a date for their wedding. They would like a sunny day. Research shows the probability of sun on 10 June is $\frac{3}{7}$, the probability of sun on 17 June is $\frac{2}{5}$ and the probability of sun on 24 June is $\frac{5}{9}$. Based on just this information, which date should they choose? Give reasons for your answer.

Mixed exercise

Exercise 22h

Select the letter that gives the correct answer.

1 I roll an ordinary die. The probability that it shows an even number is

A $\frac{1}{6}$ B $\frac{1}{4}$ C $\frac{1}{3}$ D $\frac{1}{2}$

2 I choose a number from the first 10 whole numbers. The probability that it is a prime number is

A $\frac{1}{3}$ B $\frac{2}{5}$ C $\frac{1}{2}$ D $\frac{3}{5}$

3 A whole number is chosen from the first 10 whole numbers.

The probability that it is exactly divisible by 3 and 4 is

A 0 B $\frac{1}{10}$ C $\frac{1}{7}$ D $\frac{1}{5}$

4 An ordinary fair die is rolled 120 times. The number of times I expect it to show a 6 is

A 15 **B** 18 **C** 20 **D** 24

5 An ordinary fair die is rolled 60 times. The number of times I expect it to show a 2 or a 4 is

A 10 **B** 12 **C** 16 **D** 20

6 A letter is chosen at random from the letters in the word EXCELLENCE. The probability that it is an E is

A $\frac{1}{5}$ **B** $\frac{3}{10}$ **C** $\frac{2}{5}$ **D** $\frac{1}{2}$

In this chapter you have seen that...

✔ the probability that an event will happen $= \dfrac{\text{the number of ways that the event can happen}}{\text{the total number of equally likely outcomes}}$

✔ the probability that an event will happen lies between 0 and 1; it is 0 when the event is impossible and it is 1 when the event is certain

✔ the probability that an event will not happen is 1 – the probability that it will happen

✔ an estimate for the number of times an event will happen = (probability that it will happen once) × (the number of times it is tried).

REVIEW TEST 3: CHAPTERS 15–22

In questions **1** to **10**, choose the letter for the correct answer.

1 The equation of the straight line with gradient $\frac{1}{2}$ that passes through the point (2, –3) is

A $x + 2y + 8 = 0$ B $x + 2y = 8$ C $x - 2y = 8$ D $2x - y = 7$

2 The expansion of $(3 - 4x)^2$ is

A $9 - 12x + 16x^2$ B $9 - 12x + 4x^2$ C $9 - 24x + 16x^2$ D $9 - 16x^2$

3 $\frac{2a^3}{3} \times \frac{3a^{-3}}{2} =$

A 0 B 1 C a D $\frac{4}{9}a^6$

4

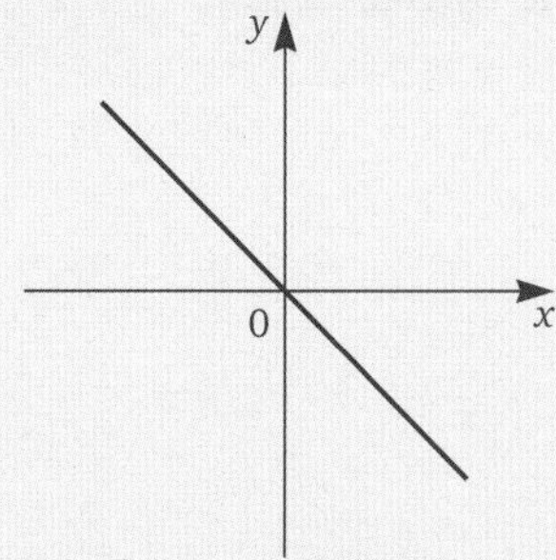

The most likely equation suggested for this straight line is

A $y = x$ B $y = -x$ C $y = 2x + 1$ D $y = -2x + 1$

5 Which of the following points does not lie on the line with equation $y = 2x - 3$?

A (2, 1) B (–1, –5) C (0, –3) D (–3, 0)

6 The solution of the inequality $8 < 3 - 5x$ is

A $x > -1$ B $x < 1$ C $x > 1$ D $x < -1$

7 What is the gradient of the line segment joining the points (–3, 2) and (5, 7)?

A $\frac{9}{2}$ B $\frac{5}{2}$ C $\frac{9}{8}$ D $\frac{5}{8}$

8 A line parallel to the x-axis at a distance k away from it has the equation

A $x = k$ B $y = k$ C $x + y = k$ D $y = x - k$

9 The point (11, –3) lies on the line $3x + 4y = 3n$. The value of n is

A 21 B 15 C 8 D 7

10 The factors of the expression $x^2 + x - 12$ are

A $(x-3)(x-4)$ B $(x+3)(x-4)$ C $(x-3)(x+4)$ D $(x+3)(x+4)$

11 A letter is chosen at random from the letters in the word CANADA. What is the probability that it is

a A b B c a vowel d not a vowel?

12 A letter is chosen at random from the letters in the word PARALLEL. What is the probability that it is

a A b L c S?

13 a What is the probability of choosing an integer that is exactly divisible by 6 from the set {8, 9, 10, 11, 12, 13, 14}?

b A whole number is chosen from the set of whole numbers from 10 to 30 inclusive. What is the probability that it is exactly divisible by 3 and 4?

14 Factorise: a $a^2 - 2ab + 2a - 4b$ b $27 - 12x + x^2$ c $4x^2 - 5x - 6$

15 Factorise: a $9x^2 - 16$ b $5a^2 - 45$ c $46^2 - 36^2$

16 a Find the value of t if $(-2, t)$ is on the line $y = 7 - 2x$.

b What is the gradient of the line $2x + 3y = 7$?

c Find the equation of the line with gradient 4 and y-intercept -5.

17 Simplify: a $\dfrac{x^2-4}{3x^2-5x-2}$ b $\dfrac{1-x^2}{4x^2+7x+3}$

18 Simplify: a $\dfrac{p^2}{3q} \div 3p$ b $\dfrac{a}{b} \div \dfrac{3a}{2b} \times \dfrac{2b}{3a}$

19 Simplify: a $\dfrac{2}{x} + \dfrac{3}{2y}$ b $\dfrac{4}{5x} - \dfrac{3}{10x}$ c $\dfrac{a^2}{b^2} + \dfrac{5a}{4b}$

20 Solve the equations:

a $x^2 - 6x + 8 = 0$ b $4x^2 - 9 = 0$ c $3x^2 - 7x = 0$

21 A card is chosen at random from a pack of 52 playing cards.
What is the probability that it is

a a queen **b** a black card **c** a club?

22 $U = \{\text{whole numbers less than } 16\}, A = \{\text{multiples of } 5\},$
$B = \{\text{even numbers}\}$
Show these on a Venn diagram and use it to find

a A' **c** $A \cup B$ **e** $A' \cup B'$

b B' **d** $(A \cup B)'$ **f** $A' \cap B'$

REVIEW TEST 4: CHAPTERS 1–22

Choose the letter for the correct answer.

1 The value of $6 + 12 \div 3$ is

A 4 B 6 C 10 D 12

2 $0.35 \qquad \frac{9}{25}$

The correct symbol to place between these two numbers is

A $<$ B $\leqslant$ C $=$ D $>$

3 The value of $\left(\frac{1}{6}\right)^{-1}$ is

A $-\frac{1}{6}$ B 0 C $\frac{1}{6}$ D 6

4 For the prime numbers between 1 and 30 the largest exceeds the smallest by

A 17 B 21 C 26 D 27

5 3^2 exceeds $\left(\frac{1}{2}\right)^{-2}$ by

A 2 B 5 C $5\frac{3}{4}$ D $8\frac{3}{4}$

6 The value of $4 - 3 - 5(-2)$ is

A -9 B -6 C 4 D 11

7 The value of x that satisfies the equation $x - 3(x - 2) = 5$ is

A $-\frac{1}{2}$ B $\frac{1}{2}$ C 2 D $5\frac{1}{2}$

8 Given that $a = \frac{3}{b-c}$ the value of a when $b = \frac{1}{2}$ and $c = \frac{1}{3}$ is

A $\frac{1}{2}$ B 3 C 9 D 18

9 The solution of the simultaneous equations $5x - y = 7$

$3x + 2y = -1$ is

A $x = 1, y = 2$ B $x = 2, y = 3$ C $x = -1, y = 2$ D $x = 1, y = -2$

10 For the equation $y = x^2 - x + 5$ the value of y when $x = -2$ is

A 3 B 5 C 7 D 11

11 If n is a positive integer, then $n + 7$ is always

A an integer that is positive
B an integer that is even
C an integer that is odd
D an integer that is prime

12 An item of jewellery appreciates by 10% each year. If its original cost was \$2000, then its value at the end of two years will be

A \$2020 B \$2200 C \$2400 D \$2420

13 30% of 30 exceeds 20% of 20 by

A 1 B 4 C 5 D 10

14 Which of the following points does not lie on the line with equation $y = 2x - 3$?

A (2, 1) B (–1, –5) C (0, –3) D (–3, 0)

15 The straight line $2y - 5x + 1 = 0$ has a gradient of

A 5 B $\frac{5}{2}$ C $\frac{2}{5}$ D -5

16 The point (–9, 2) lies on the line $2x + 3y + n = 0$. The value of n is

A 12 B 8 C 4 D 3

17 A car uses 6 litres of fuel at \$2 per litre, when a man drives to work from Monday to Friday. If he travels by bus the cost is \$1.75 per day. By travelling to work by bus instead of driving, the man would save

A \$1.50 B \$3.25 C \$3.50 D \$10.25

18 A circle of diameter 14 cm is inscribed in a square of side 14 cm. If $\pi = \frac{22}{7}$, the fraction that the area of the unshaded part of the diagram is of the area of the square is

A $\frac{1}{5}$ B $\frac{3}{14}$ C $\frac{3}{11}$ D $\frac{3}{10}$

19

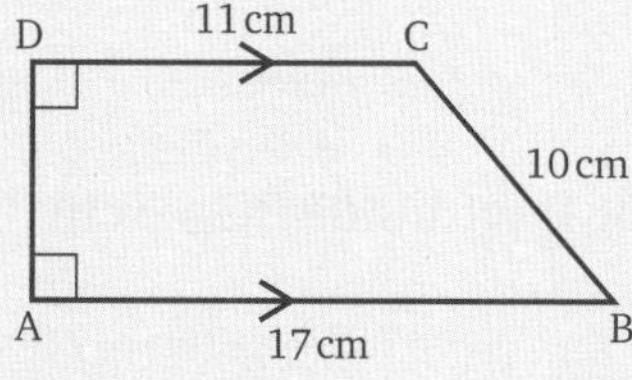

The area of trapezium ABCD, in cm^2, is

A 112 B 136 C 140 D 168

20

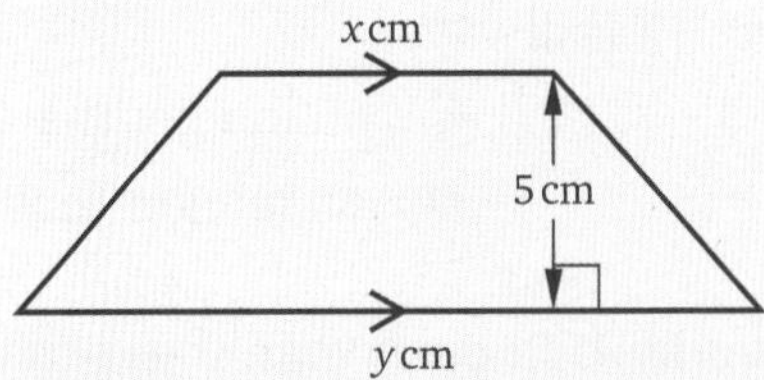

In this trapezium, the parallel sides are x cm and y cm. If the perpendicular distance between the parallel sides is 5 cm and the area of the trapezium is 30 cm^2 then $x + y =$

A 6 cm B 12 cm C 15 cm D 25 cm

21 $3(2x - 1) - 2(3x + 1) =$

A $12x - 1$ B $12x - 5$ C 0 D -5

22 $\frac{6x - 12y}{-3} =$

A $-2x + 4y$ B $2x - 4y$ C $-2x - 4y$ D $2x + 2y$

23 The interior angle of a regular polygon is twice its exterior angle. The number of sides of the polygon is

A 4 B 5 C 6 D 8

24 In a regular polygon, each exterior angle is 36°. The number of sides of the polygon is

A 12 B 10 C 8 D 5

25 The diagram shows a sector of a circle of radius 7 cm. Using $\pi = \frac{22}{7}$, the perimeter of the figure, in cm, is

A 47 B 44 C 40 D 33

26 The largest circle that may be inscribed in a rectangle of sides 8 cm by 12 cm will be of area, in cm^2,

A 8π B 10π C 12π D 16π

27 The diagram shows a rectangle ABCD with side BC = 5 cm and diagonal AC = 13 cm. The perimeter of the rectangle, in cm, is

A 34 B 30 C 26 D 17

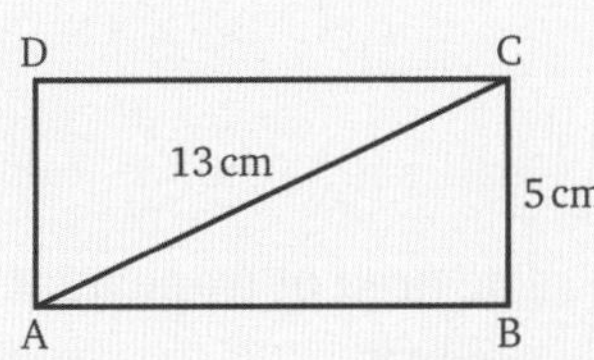

28 A ladder of length 13 m is placed with its foot on a horizontal floor and its top rests against a vertical wall, as shown in the above diagram. If the foot is 5 m from the wall, then the distance of the top from the floor, in m, is

A 18 B 12 C 9 D 8

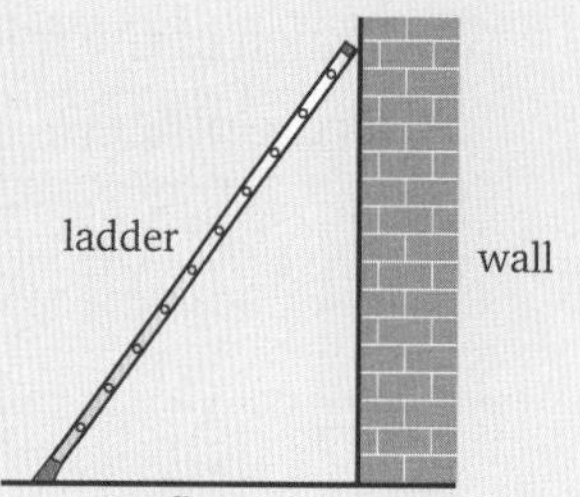

29 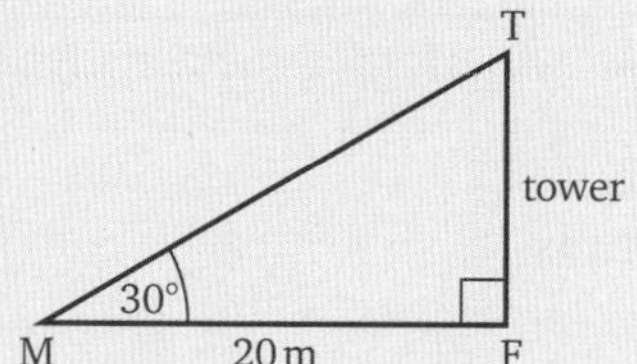

The angle of elevation of the top, T, of a vertical tower is 30° from a point M, 20 m from the base F. The height of the tower, in m, is

A $20\sqrt{3}$ B 20 C $\frac{20}{\sqrt{3}}$ D 10

30 Two finite sets X and Y are such that $n(X) = 8$, $n(Y) = 11$, $n(X \cap Y) = 2$ and $n(U) = 20$. Hence, $n(X \cup Y)' =$

A 7 B 5 C 3 D 1

Use this diagram for questions **31** and **32**.

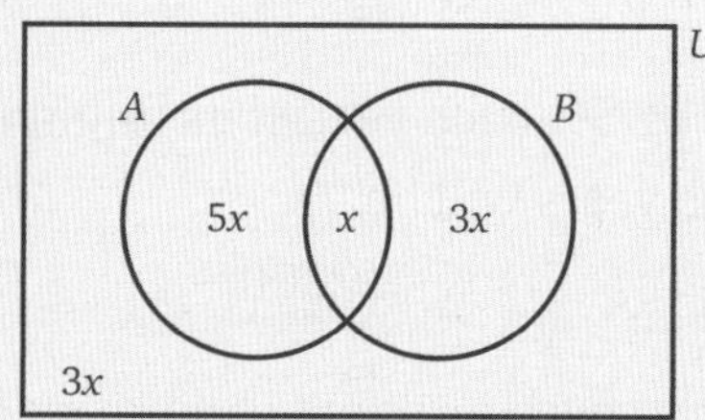

31 The probability that an element chosen at random from U does not belong to $A \cup B$ is

A $\frac{1}{6}$ B $\frac{1}{4}$ C $\frac{1}{3}$ D $\frac{1}{2}$

32 If $x \in A \cap B$ which of the following statements is true?

A $x \in A$ and $x \in B$

B $x \in A$ and $x \notin B$

C $x \notin A$ and $x \in B$

D $x \in A$ or $x \in B$

33 In the right-angled-triangle, PQR, PQ = 6 cm and angle P = 60°. The length of PR, in cm, is

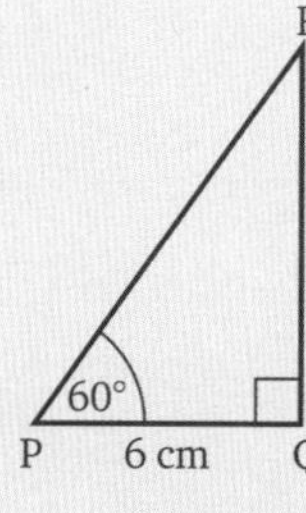

A 15 B 12 C 9 D 8

34 Which of the following computations does not have the same result as the others?

A $\sqrt{(2-1)^3}$ B $(2-1)^{-2}$ C $(1-2)^{-2}$ D $(1-2)^3$

35

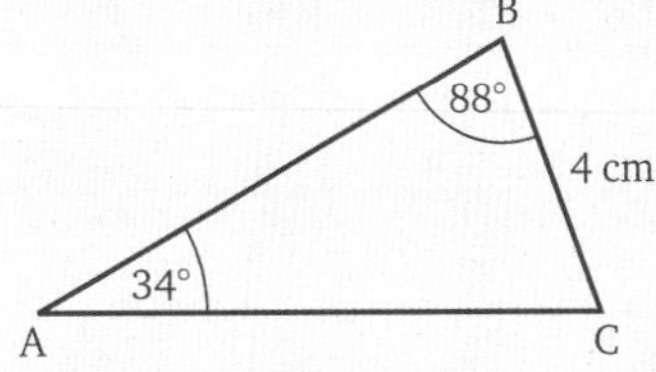

The condition that makes triangles ABC and DEF congruent is

A two sides and the included angle

B three sides

C two angles and a corresponding side

D right angle, hypotenuse and side

36 The equation of the straight line which passes through the point (0, 3) with gradient $\frac{1}{2}$ is

A $y = 2x + 3$ B $y = 2x + 6$ C $2y = x + 3$ D $2y = x + 6$

37 An item of jewellery appreciates by 5% each year. If its original cost was \$2000, its value at the end of two years will be

A \$2400 B \$2205 C \$2200 D \$2010

38 In a certain town of 12 000 people, two-thirds are children and one-half of the remainder are women. A person is chosen at random. The probability that this person is a woman is

A $\frac{2}{3}$ B $\frac{1}{2}$ C $\frac{1}{4}$ D $\frac{1}{6}$

39 The set of inequalities that describe the unshaded region are

A $x > -2,\ x < 3,\ y \leq 2$

B $x > -2,\ x < 3,\ y < 2$

C $x > 2,\quad x \leq 3\ \ y < 2$

D $x \geq -2,\ x < 3,\ y \leq 2$

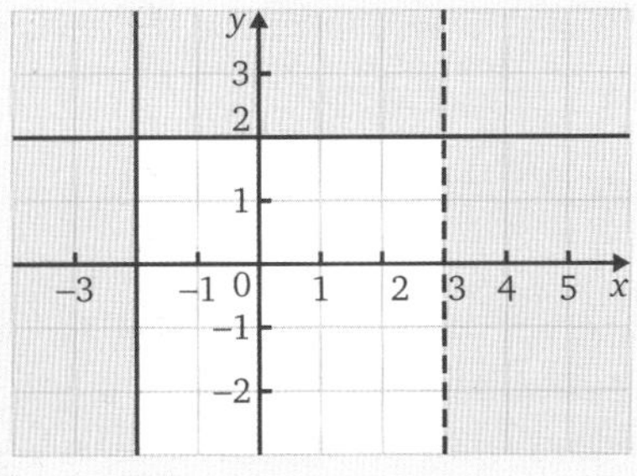

40 A box contains 9 bulbs of which 3 are defective. If one bulb is chosen at random then the probability that it is not defective is

A $\frac{1}{9}$ B $\frac{1}{3}$ C $\frac{2}{3}$ D $\frac{8}{9}$

41 $E = \{\text{equilateral triangles}\}$
$I = \{\text{isosceles triangles}\}$
The diagram illustrating R and I is

A
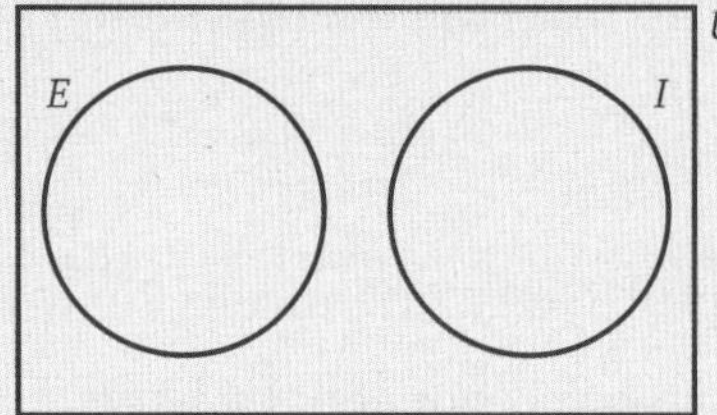

C
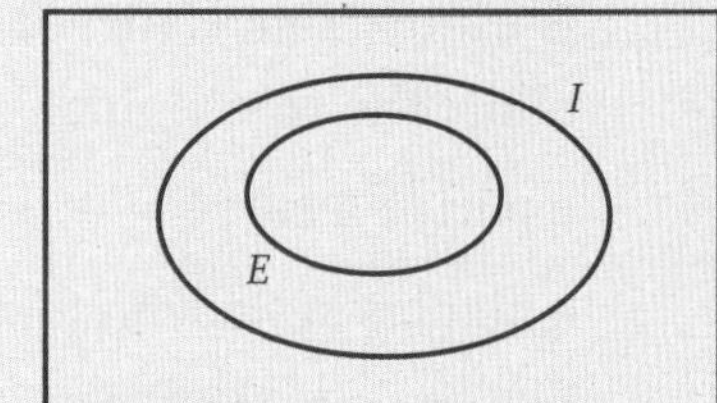

B
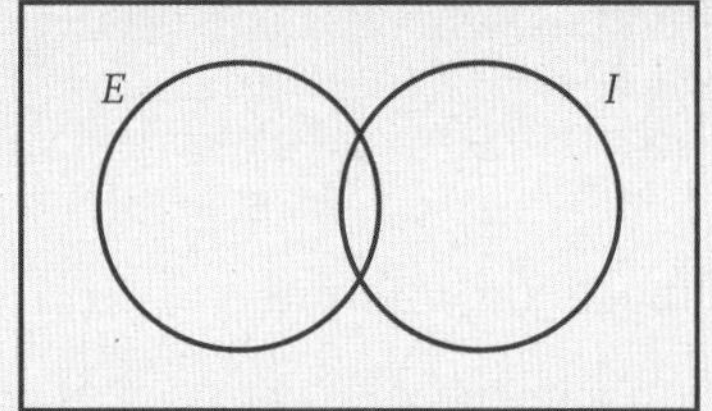

D
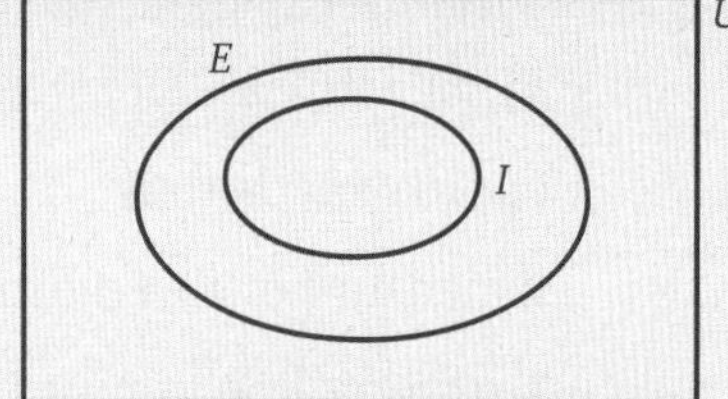

42 The probability that a particular car will break down when travelling one kilometre is $\frac{1}{10\,000}$.
The number of times the car is likely to break down in 200 000 kilometres is

A 2 B 20 C 200 D 2000

Glossary

adjacent side	next to an angle
alternate angles	equal angles on opposite sides of a transversal, e.g.
amount	sum of money
angle of depression	the angle that is turned through down from the horizontal to view an object below the view point
angle of elevation	the angle that is turned through up from the horizontal to view an object above the view point
arc	a part of a curve
base 3 numbers	a number system based on powers of 3, e.g. 212_3 means $2(3^2) + 1(3^1) + 2(3^0)$
biased	where each outcome of an experiment is not equally likely
binary numbers	a number system based on powers of 2, e.g. 1101_2 means $1(2^3) + 1(2^2) + 0(2^1) + 1(2^0)$
bisect	cut in exactly half
capacity	a measure of three-dimensional space, i.e. volume
chord	a straight line joining two points on a curve
circumcircle	a circle passing through the vertices of a polygon
circumference	the total distance round a circle
coefficient	the multiplier of an unknown, e.g. 3 is the coefficient of $3x$
commission	payment of a percentage of the value of sales
common denominator	a number that is a multiple of all the denominators of a set of fractions
common factor	a number that divides exactly into all the numbers in a set
common fraction	a fraction of the form $\frac{a}{b}$ where a and b are integers
complement of a set	the members of the universal set not included in the given set
compound interest	the interest accumulated over a given time when each successive interest is added to the principal before calculating the next interest payable
congruent	objects that are exactly the same shape and size
converse	the converse reverses the two objects in a relationship, e.g. the converse of 'a rectangle is a quadrilateral' is 'a quadrilateral is a rectangle'
coordinates	an ordered pair of numbers that specifies the position of a point
corresponding angles	equal angles on the same side of a transversal, e.g.
cosine	in a right-angled triangle, the cosine of an angle is equal to the length of the side adjacent to the angle divided by the length of the hypotenuse
cross-section	the shape formed by a plane cutting a solid

cuboid	a three-dimensional solid whose faces are rectangles
cylinder	a solid whose constant cross-section is a circle
decimal fraction	part of a unit expressed as tenths, hundredths,…, represented by numbers to the right of the decimal point
denary numbers	a number system based on powers of 10
denominator	the number on the bottom of a fraction
diameter	a chord of a circle that goes through the centre of the circle
digit	one of the figures 0, 1, 2, 3, 4, 5, 6, 7, 8, 9
directed number	a positive or negative number
dodecahedron	a twelve-sided solid whose faces are pentagons
element	a member of a set
enlargement	a transformation where an object is increased or reduced in size but retains its shape
equation	an equality between two expressions
equilateral	equal sided
equivalent fraction	a fraction equal in value to another fraction with a different denominator
even	an integer that is divisible by 2
event	the result of an experiment, e.g. tossing a coin
experiment	the action where the outcome is not certain
expression	a collection of algebraic terms
exterior angle	the angle between the extension of one side of a polygon and another side, e.g.
factor	a number that divides into another number exactly
factorise	express as a product
frustum	the part of a solid left when part of it is removed, e.g.
gradient of a line	the fraction given by the increase in y value over the increase in x value when moving from one point on the line to another
hexagon	a plane figure bounded by six straight lines
hypotenuse	the side opposite the right angle in a right-angled triangle
image	the result of a transformation or a mapping
improper fraction	a fraction whose numerator is larger than its denominator
index (indices)	the superscript of a number that tells you how many of them to multiply together
inequality	the relationship between two quantities that are not equal

infinite	without end
integer	a positive or negative whole number
intercept	the point at which a graph cuts the y-axis or the x-axis
interior angle	the angle inside a polygon between two adjacent sides
intersection of sets	the set of elements common to both sets
irrational number	a number that cannot be written as $\frac{a}{b}$ where a and b are integers, e.g. π
isosceles	having two equal sides
kilowatt-hour	a measure of energy equal to the use of 1 kilowatt in one hour
kite	a quadrilateral with two pairs of equal length adjacent sides, e.g.
like terms	terms in an algebraic expression that have the same combination of letters
linear equation	an equation containing one unknown to the power 1
lowest common multiple	the smallest number that is a multiple of every number in a set
member	an item that belongs to a set of items
mixed number	the sum of a whole number and a proper fraction
multiple	a product of a given number with an integer
$\mathbb{N}$	the set of natural numbers, i.e. $\{1, 2, 3, \ldots\}$
natural number	one of the numbers 1, 2, 3, 4,…
number line	a line on which points represent numbers
numerator	the number on the top of a fraction
octagon	a plane figure bounded by eight straight lines
odd	an integer that does not divide exactly by 2
opposite side	the side opposite a given angle in a right-angled triangle
parallel	a pair of lines that are always the same distance apart
parallelogram	a quadrilateral whose opposite sides are parallel
pentagon	a plane figure bounded by five straight lines
percentage	a fraction whose denominator is 100
percentage decrease	a decrease as a percentage of the original quantity
percentage increase	an increase as a percentage of the original quantity
perfect cube	a number whose cube root is exact
perfect square	a number whose square root is exact
perimeter	the distance round the edge of a plane figure
perpendicular bisector	a line at right angles to another line and cutting it exactly in half

perpendicular height	the length of the perpendicular line from a vertex to the base of an object
polygon	a plane figure drawn with three or more straight lines
polyhedron	a solid whose faces are polygons
positive number	a number greater than zero
prime number	a integer whose only factors are one and itself
principal	the sum of money invested or borrowed
probability	the likelihood of an event happening expressed as a fraction or as a decimal
product	the multiplication of two or more quantities
proper subset	a proper subset is a set of some, but not all, of the elements in another set
proportion	two quantities in the same ratio
pyramid	a solid with any polygon as the base, the other faces are triangles that meet in a common point
$\mathbb{Q}$	the set of rational numbers
quadratic	an expression such as $3x^2 - 2x + 6$
quadratic equation	an equation that can be written in the form $ax^2 + bx + c = 0$
quadrilateral	a plane figure bounded by four straight lines
$\mathbb{R}$	the set of real numbers
radius	the distance from the centre of a circle to its edge
random	selection where each member of a set has an equal chance of being chosen
ratio	a comparison of the size of two quantities
rational number	a number that can be written as $\frac{a}{b}$ where a and b are integers
real number	any rational or irrational number
reciprocal	the reciprocal of a number a is $\frac{1}{a}$
rectangle	a quadrilateral whose opposite sides are equal and whose angles are right angles
recurring decimal	the numbers in the decimal places form a repeating pattern
reflection	a transformation in which any two corresponding points in the object and the image are both the same distance from a fixed straight line
rhombus	a quadrilateral whose sides are all the same length
root	the numerical value of the solution of an equation
rotation	a transformation in which a figure is turned about a given point
salary	a yearly sum paid to employees usually in monthly amounts
scale factor	a number that enlarges or reduces the size of an object
sector	part of a circle between two radii

semicircle	half a circle
set	a collection of particular objects
significant figure	the first significant figure is the first non-zero digit, the second significant figure is the next digit (which may be zero) and so on
similar	objects that are the same shape but different sizes
simple interest	interest that is always calculated on the original principal
simultaneous equations	a set of equations with a common solution
sine	the sine of an angle in a right-angled triangle is the length of the side opposite the angle divided by the length of the hypotenuse
slant height	the length of a sloping edge or curved surface
standard form	a number expressed as the product of a number between 1 and 10 and a power of ten, e.g. 3.6×10^6
subset	a set of some and maybe all of the elements of another set
supplementary angles	two angles that add up to 180°
symmetry	having congruent parts each side of a line or point
tangent of an angle	the length of the side opposite the angle divided by the length of the side adjacent to the angle in a right-angled triangle
tessellate	cover a flat surface with shapes without gaps
tetrahedron	a solid with four triangular faces
transformation	a change in position and/or size
translation	a movement in one direction
trapezium	a quadrilateral with just one pair of opposite sides parallel
triangle	a plane figure bounded by three straight lines
unbiased	where each outcome of an experiment is equally likely
union of sets	the set of all the elements in two or more sets
universal set	a set large enough to include all the elements of defined sets
vector	a quantity with magnitude and direction
Venn diagram	a diagram used to represent sets
vertex	the point where two sides of a plane figure meet or where two or more edges of a solid meet
vertically opposite	the pair of angles opposite each other where two lines cross
volume	the amount of three-dimensional space occupied by a solid
$\mathbb{W}$	the set of whole numbers, i.e. $\{0, 1, 2, \ldots\}$
$\mathbb{Z}$	the set of integers, i.e. $\{\ldots, -2, -1, 0, 1, 2, \ldots\}$

Answers

CHAPTER 1

Exercise 1a page 2

1 2, 3, 5, 7
2 11, 13, 17, 19
3 5, 7, 11, 13
4 23
5 a 8, 16, 40, 206   b 40, 35, 515   c 81
6 1, 2, 3, 6
7 1, 2, 4, 8
8 1, 3, 9
9 1, 2, 3, 6, 9, 18
10 1, 3, 7, 21
11 1, 2, 13, 26

Exercise 1b page 4

1 2×5
2 3×7
3 5×7
4 $2\times2\times3$
5 $2\times2\times2$
6 $2\times2\times7$
7 $2\times2\times3\times5$
8 $2\times5\times5$
9 $2\times2\times3\times3$
10 $2\times3\times11$
11 $2\times3\times3\times7$
12 $2\times2\times3\times3\times3$

Exercise 1c page 4

1 a 2, 6, 8, 10, 12, 14, 16, 18, 20
  b 3, 6, 12, 15, 18
  c 8, 12, 16, 20
  d 5, 10, 15, 20
  e 6, 12, 18
  f 8, 16
2 54, 63, 72, 81, 90, 99
3 14, 21, 28, 35, 42, 49

Exercise 1d page 5

1 4, 9
2 16, 25, 36, 49, 64, 81, 100
3 4, 16   4 9, 81
5 $6 = 2\times3$; $8 = 2\times2\times2$; $25 = 5\times5$;
$64 = 2\times2\times2\times2\times2\times2$; $81 = 3\times3\times3\times3$;
$125 = 5\times5\times5$; 8, 64, 125

Exercise 1e page 6

1	24	8	96	15	7	22	16
2	30	9	105	16	1	23	6
3	40	10	4	17	12	24	5
4	30	11	6	18	10	25	8
5	60	12	6	19	13	26	9
6	36	13	11	20	1		
7	60	14	13	21	5		

Exercise 1f page 8

1 a yes, $5\in\mathbb{N}$ b yes, $6\in\mathbb{N}$
  c no, $\frac{3}{2}\notin\mathbb{N}$ d yes, $1\in\mathbb{N}$
  e no, $-1\notin\mathbb{N}$
2 a $\frac{3}{4}$ b -5 c 2   d π
3 set of negative integers
4 $\mathbb{N}$
5 set of irrational numbers

Exercise 1g page 9

1	21	9	$1\frac{13}{24}$	17	$\frac{7}{30}$
2	18	10	$\frac{9}{10}$	18	$\frac{1}{20}$
3	12	11	$1\frac{29}{40}$	19	$3\frac{29}{40}$
4	6	12	1	20	$\frac{7}{18}$
5	12	13	$1\frac{17}{48}$	21	$-\frac{9}{40}$
6	60	14	$\frac{11}{12}$	22	$3\frac{11}{12}$
7	18	15	$\frac{13}{36}$	23	$4\frac{7}{8}$
8	72	16	$\frac{1}{36}$	24	$\frac{17}{20}$

Exercise 1h page 11

1	$\frac{5}{9}$	4	$\frac{1}{10}$	7	2	10	$\frac{3}{2}$
2	$1\frac{1}{3}$	5	$\frac{10}{21}$	8	3	11	$\frac{4}{3}$
3	$1\frac{1}{2}$	6	$\frac{3}{10}$	9	3	12	$\frac{8}{7}$

Exercise 1i page 12

1	$\frac{1}{4}$	12	$1\frac{1}{3}$	23	$2\frac{1}{18}$
2	2	13	2	24	$5\frac{3}{10}$
3	$\frac{5}{2}$	14	$\frac{5}{8}$	25	$\frac{57}{110}$
4	$\frac{1}{10}$	15	$6\frac{1}{4}$	26	$4\frac{23}{42}$
5	$\frac{11}{3}$	16	$\frac{14}{81}$	27	7
6	$\frac{1}{100}$	17	$\frac{12}{49}$	28	$\frac{9}{50}$
7	$\frac{9}{2}$	18	$\frac{1}{18}$	29	$1\frac{2}{25}$
8	$\frac{4}{15}$	19	$4\frac{1}{2}$	30	$\frac{1}{14}$
9	$\frac{4}{9}$	20	$\frac{13}{30}$	31	$\frac{21}{68}$
10	$\frac{5}{17}$	21	$\frac{69}{112}$	32	$1\frac{1}{4}$
11	$\frac{7}{11}$	22	$\frac{8}{25}$	33	2

Exercise 1j page 14

1	$\frac{7}{20}$	6	$\frac{3}{250}$	11	0.6
2	$\frac{27}{125}$	7	$\frac{1}{200}$	12	0.24
3	$\frac{51}{250}$	8	$1\frac{1}{100}$	13	0.0625
4	$1\frac{9}{25}$	9	0.15	14	0.54
5	$\frac{3}{100}$	10	0.125	15	1.75
				16	0.15625

Exercise 1k **page 16**

1 $0.\dot{3}$
2 $0.\dot{2}$
3 $0.8\dot{3}$
4 $0.0\dot{6}$
5 $0.\dot{1}4285\dot{7}$
6 $0.08\dot{3}$
7 $0.\dot{0}\dot{9}$
8 $0.0\dot{5}$
9 $0.41\dot{6}$
10 $0.0\dot{7}1428\dot{5}$
11 $0.2\dot{3}$
12 $0.\dot{0}7692\dot{3}$

Exercise 1l **page 17**

1 5.01
2 19.1
3 6.17
4 8.8
5 1.82
6 26.36
7 4.832
8 1.106
9 0.00202
10 3.2
11 3.3
12 0.08
13 0.96
14 0.042
15 0.008
16 0.3
17 2.7
18 0.6
19 7.8
20 0.5
21 129
22 11.882
23 3.094
24 1
25 2
26 1.69
27 0.2

Exercise 1m **page 18**

1 $<$
2 $>$
3 $<$
4 $<$
5 $>$
6 $>$
7 $>$
8 $>$
9 $>$
10 $0.6, \frac{2}{3}, \frac{4}{5}$
11 $0.79, \frac{4}{5}, 0.85$
12 $\frac{1}{5}, \frac{2}{7}, 0.3$
13 $\frac{5}{7}, 0.75, \frac{7}{9}, 0.875$
14 $\frac{3}{20}, 0.16, 0.2, \frac{6}{25}$
15 $1\frac{1}{8}, 1\frac{1}{5}, 1.24, 1.3$

Exercise 1n **page 19**

1 25
2 81
3 125
4 64
5 144
6 1600
7 864
8 325
9 8010
10 2^7
11 3^7
12 not possible
13 2^5
14 a^5
15 not possible
16 2^2
17 7
18 4^3
19 3^3
20 a^4
21 not possible

Exercise 1p **page 20**

1 **a** 2^6 **b** 3^4 **c** 5^4
2 **a** $3t^{15}$ **b** $8d^{15}$ **c** $2a^6$ **d** $125p^9$
3 **a** 192 **b** 6400 **c** 810 **d** 50
4 **a** $3x^9y^3$ **b** $5a^4b^{12}$ **c** $64u^6v^3$ **d** $2p^8q^2$

Exercise 1q **page 22**

1 $\frac{1}{2}$
2 $\frac{1}{10}$
3 $\frac{1}{5}$
4 $\frac{1}{7}$
5 $\frac{1}{8}$
6 $\frac{1}{4}$
7 $\frac{1}{a}$
8 $\frac{1}{x}$
9 3
10 $1\frac{1}{2}$
11 4
12 $1\frac{1}{3}$
13 5
14 $1\frac{1}{4}$
15 a
16 $\frac{y}{x}$
17 $\frac{1}{8}$
18 $\frac{1}{25}$
19 $\frac{1}{1000}$
20 $\frac{1}{36}$
21 $\frac{1}{32}$
22 $\frac{1}{10000}$
23 $\frac{1}{100}$
24 $\frac{1}{64}$
25 125
26 16
27 32
28 81
29 512
30 10 000
31 8
32 36
33 $1\frac{7}{9}$
34 $3\frac{3}{8}$
35 $5\frac{1}{16}$
36 $12\frac{1}{4}$
37 $5\frac{1}{16}$
38 $2\frac{7}{9}$
39 $123\frac{37}{81}$
40 $2\frac{14}{25}$
41 8
42 $6\frac{1}{4}$
43 $\frac{1}{16}$
44 64
45 1
46 1
47 125
48 $\frac{1}{9}$
49 16
50 1
51 $2\frac{10}{27}$
52 $3\frac{1}{2}$
53 1
54 $2\frac{314}{343}$
55 $\frac{1}{4}$
56 $\frac{64}{125}$
57 $\frac{1}{12}$
58 729
59 64
60 1

Exercise 1r **page 24**

1 345
2 1200
3 0.0501
4 0.0047
5 280
6 0.73
7 902 000
8 0.000 637
9 8 720 000
10 2.65×10^2
11 1.8×10^{-1}
12 3.02×10^3
13 1.9×10^{-2}
14 7.67×10^4
15 3.9×10^5
16 8.5×10^{-4}
17 7×10^3
18 4×10^{-3}
19 5.87×10^4
20 2.6×10^3
21 4.5×10^5
22 7×10^{-6}
23 8×10^{-1}
24 5.6×10^{-4}
25 2.4×10^4
26 3.9×10^7
27 8×10^{-11}

Exercise 1s **page 26**

1 **a** 2.785 **b** 2.78
2 **a** 0.157 **b** 0.157
3 **a** 3.209 **b** 3.21
4 **a** 0.073 **b** 0.0733
5 **a** 0.151 **b** 0.151
6 **a** 0.020 **b** 0.0204
7 **a** 0.001 **b** 0.000 926
8 **a** 7.820 **b** 7.82
9 **a** 0.010 **b** 0.009 64
10 0.04; 0.0384
11 60 000; 47 500
12 0.05; 0.0447
13 80; 69.8
14 500 000; 665 000
15 2; 2.17
16 0.2: 0.217
17 9; 8.89
18 0.08; 0.0688
19 60; 56.0
20 0.04; 0.0390
21 80; 69.3
22 0.03; 0.0328
23 2; 1.74
24 0.06; 0.0403

Exercise 1t **page 28**

1 **a** 5 **b** 6 **c** 21 **d** 59
2 **a** 4 **b** 18 **c** 15 **d** 14 **e** 55 **f** 44
3 **a** 1000_2 **b** 10_2
4 **a** 1001_2 **b** 101_2
5 **a** 10100_2 **b** 110_2
6 **a** 1110_2 **b** 100_2
7 **a** 100010_2 **b** 1000_2
8 **a** 1010010_2 **b** 11000_2
9 **a** 110_3 **b** 2_3
10 **a** 101_3 **b** 20_3
11 **a** 210_3 **b** 102_3
12 **a** 1010_3 **b** 112_3
13 **a** 1222_3 **b** 120_3

Exercise 1u **page 29**

1 B
2 C
3 A
4 B
5 C
6 B
7 A

Exercise 1v page 30

1 a $\frac{3}{2}$ b $\frac{4}{9}$
2 $2\frac{3}{10}$
3 a 3.36 b 0.2943 c 109
4 a 16 b 1 c $\frac{1}{16}$
5 a 5^2 b 5^{12}
6 a 2.56×10^3 b 2.56×10^{-4}
7 a 24 b 30
8 a 5 b $\frac{2}{3}$
9 a $\frac{3}{4}$ b $1\frac{17}{20}$
10 $3\frac{1}{12}$
11 a 1.45 b 2.625 c 0.42
12 a $\frac{1}{4}$ b 1 c 4
13 a 5.7×10^5 b 5.7×10^{-2}
14 a 110_2 b 1101_3

CHAPTER 2

Exercise 2a page 34

1 $20\,cm^2$
2 $10\,cm^2$
3 $17\,cm^2$
4 $19.35\,cm^2$
5 12 sq. units
6 30 sq. units
7 12 sq. units
8 16 sq. units
9 $24\frac{1}{2}$ sq. units
10 4 cm
11 $450\,mm^2$
12 5 cm
13 5 m, $25\,m^2$
14 4 cm
15 a $17.5\,cm^2$ b 5.83 cm
16 a $12\,cm^2$ b 3.43 cm
17 a $40\,cm^2$ b 6.67 cm
18 a $7\,cm^2$ b 2 cm

Exercise 2b page 36

1 $60\,cm^2$
2 $40\,cm^2$
3 $30\,cm^2$
4 $45\,cm^2$
5 $135\,cm^2$
6 $27.75\,cm^2$

Exercise 2c page 38

1 $42\,cm^2$
2 $94.5\,cm^2$
3 $21\,cm^2$
4 $8.75\,cm^2$
5 30 sq. units
6 33 sq. units
7 56 sq. units
8 16 sq. units
9 84 sq. units
10 47 sq. units

Exercise 2d page 39

1 Area of each parallelogram is $35\,cm^2$.
2 Area of each triangle is $28\,cm^2$.
3 Each parallelogram has a base of length 4 units and height of 3 units. The areas are each equal to 12 sq. units.
4 Each base is 6 units long. Each height is 3 units. The areas are each equal to 9 sq. units.
8 Ratio of heights is 4 : 5 : 7 : 9. Ratio of areas is 4 : 5 : 7 : 9. The ratio of areas is equal to the ratio of heights.
9 The y-coordinate of D is 9 (or –7 if drawn below the x-axis).
10 The y-coordinate of E is 3 (or –1 if drawn below the x-axis).
11 a 4 : 5 : 3 : 9 b 4 : 5 : 3 : 9
The triangles have equal heights and the ratio of their areas is equal to the ratio of their bases.

Exercise 2e page 41

7 12 cm
8 2 : 1
9 14 cm
10 8 cm
11 30°
12 $\triangle BEC = 27\,cm^2$
$\triangle DEC = 12\,cm^2$
13 132°
14 6 cm
15 $36\,cm^2$

Exercise 2f page 45

1 C
2 B
3 B
4 B
5 D
6 C

CHAPTER 3

Exercise 3a page 47

1 $\frac{2\pi}{3}$ cm
2 $\frac{8\pi}{9}$ cm
3 4π cm
4 8π cm
5 2.55 cm
6 8.43 cm
7 43.8 cm
8 84.6 cm
9 138°
10 40°
11 13.0 cm
12 18 cm
13 11.9 cm
14 13.5 cm
15 26.3 cm
16 5.47 cm
17 19.1 cm
18 146°
19 115°
20 85.9°
21 30.5 m
22 10.6 cm
23 20.5 cm
24 28 cm
25 6.68 cm
26 27.1 m
27 178 mm
28 19.1°

Exercise 3b page 50

1 $262\,cm^2$
2 $151\,cm^2$
3 $118\,cm^2$
4 $31.2\,cm^2$
5 $21.6\,cm^2$
6 $4220\,mm^2$
7 $2260\,m^2$
8 $327\,m^2$
9 $4.19\,cm^2$
10 $75.4\,cm^2$
11 90°
12 55°
13 $131\,cm^2$
14 6 cm
15 6.93 cm
16 a 15° b $6\pi\,cm^2$
17 16°
18 a 6.78 m b $2.84\,m^2$
19 a 19.4 m b 9.05
20 $58.6\,mm^2$
21 blue by $9.43\,cm^2$
22 a 94.6 mm b $456\,mm^2$
23 a 12.0 m c $8.89\,m^2$
b \$390 d 498 g
24 A = $370\,cm^2$, B = C = $576\,cm^2$; total $1522\,cm^2$

Exercise 3c page 53

1 D 2 C 3 D 4 C 5 B

CHAPTER 4

Exercise 4a page 56

1 a HI b CD c L d B
3 yes
4 no
6
7

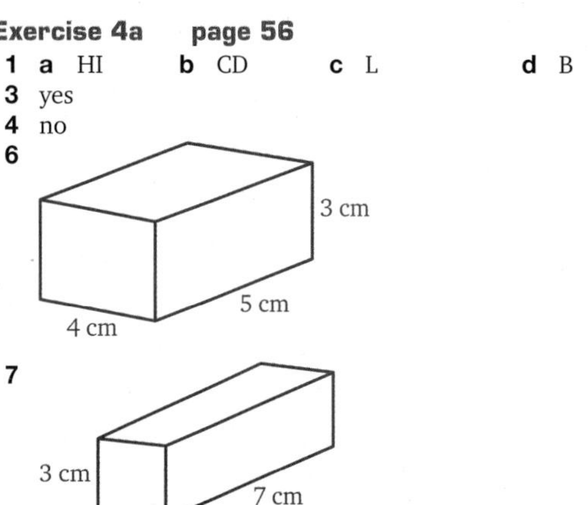

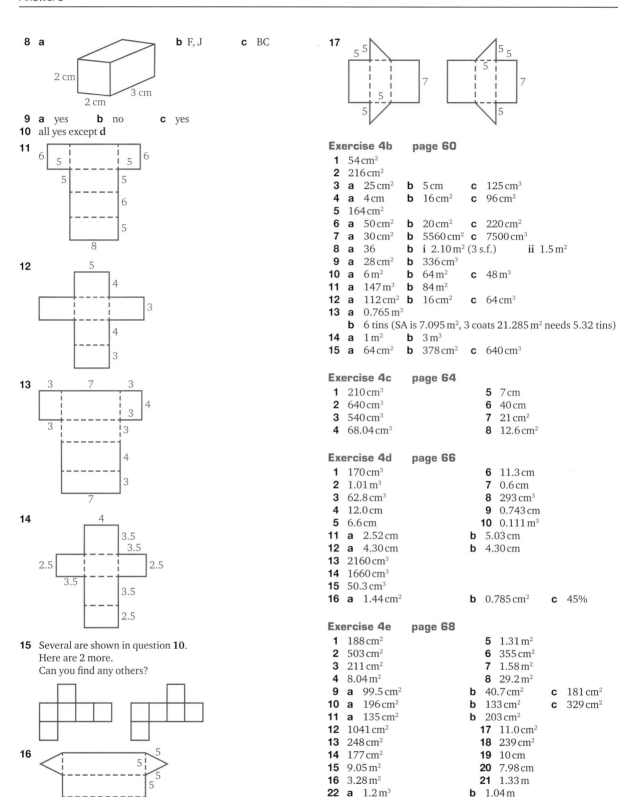

8 a 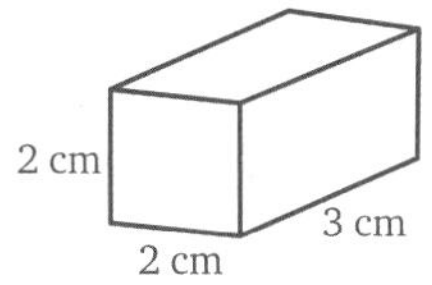

b F, J **c** BC

9 a yes **b** no **c** yes

10 all yes except **d**

11 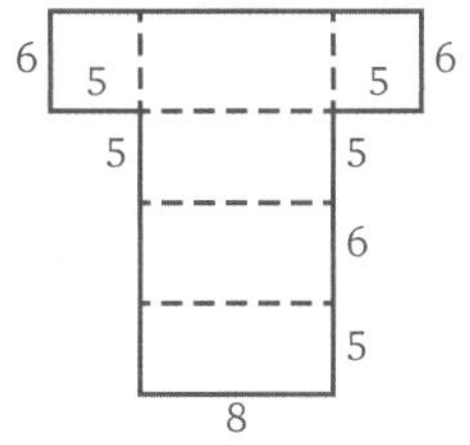

12 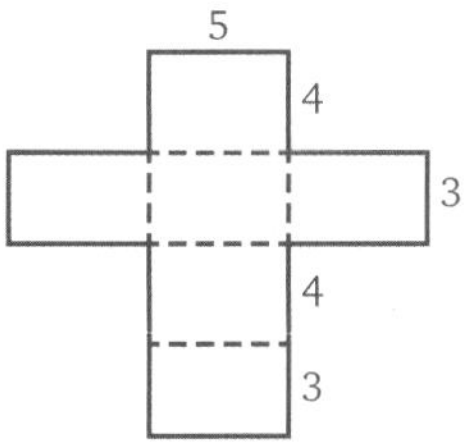

13 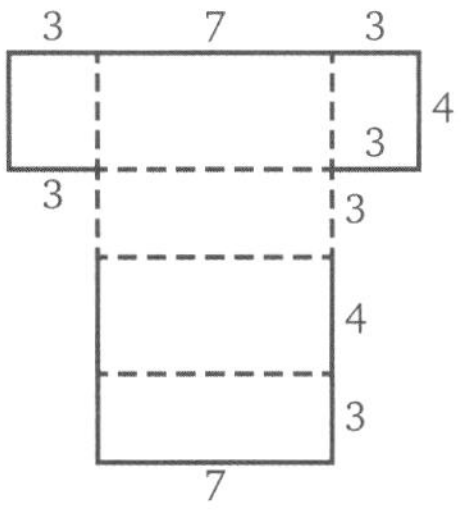

14 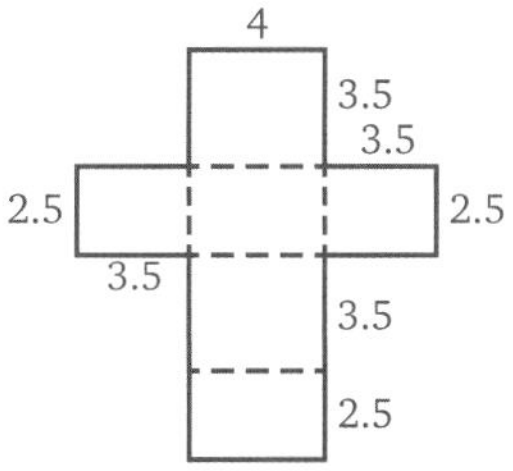

15 Several are shown in question **10**.
Here are 2 more.
Can you find any others?

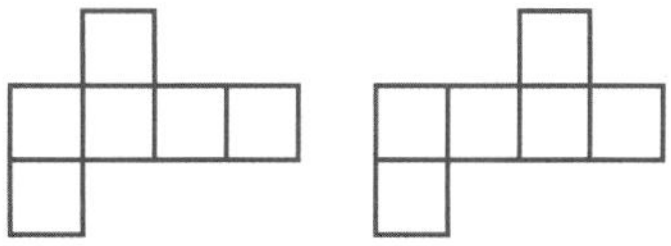

16 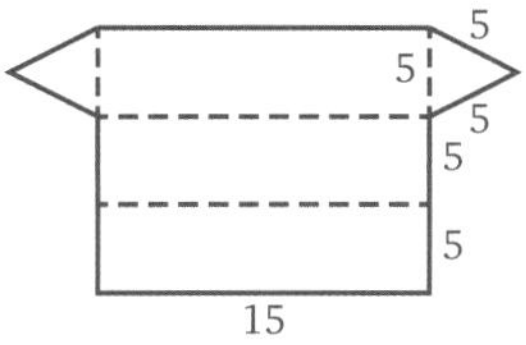

17 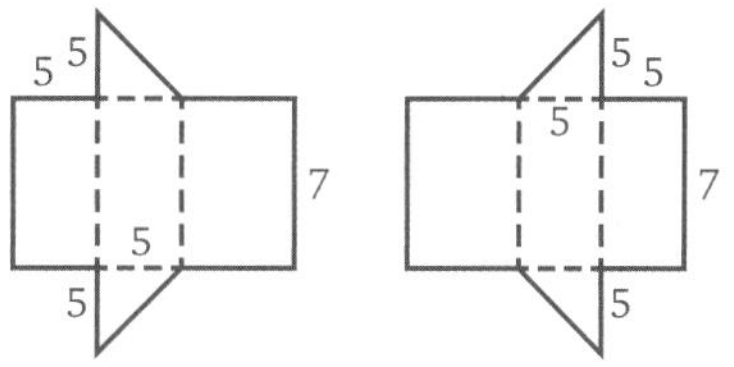

Exercise 4b page 60

1 54 cm²

2 216 cm²

3 a 25 cm² **b** 5 cm **c** 125 cm³

4 a 4 cm **b** 16 cm² **c** 96 cm²

5 164 cm²

6 a 50 cm² **b** 20 cm² **c** 220 cm²

7 a 30 cm² **b** 5560 cm² **c** 7500 cm³

8 a 36 **b** i 2.10 m² (3 s.f.) **ii** 1.5 m²

9 a 28 cm² **b** 336 cm³

10 a 6 m² **b** 64 m² **c** 48 m³

11 a 147 m³ **b** 84 m²

12 a 112 cm² **b** 16 cm² **c** 64 cm³

13 a 0.765 m³
b 6 tins (SA is 7.095 m², 3 coats 21.285 m² needs 5.32 tins)

14 a 1 m² **b** 3 m³

15 a 64 cm² **b** 378 cm² **c** 640 cm³

Exercise 4c page 64

1 210 cm³

2 640 cm³

3 540 cm³

4 68.04 cm³

5 7 cm

6 40 cm

7 21 cm²

8 12.6 cm²

Exercise 4d page 66

1 170 cm³

2 1.01 m³

3 62.8 cm³

4 12.0 cm

5 6.6 cm

6 11.3 cm

7 0.6 cm

8 293 cm³

9 0.743 cm

10 0.111 m³

11 a 2.52 cm **b** 5.03 cm

12 a 4.30 cm **b** 4.30 cm

13 2160 cm³

14 1660 cm³

15 50.3 cm³

16 a 1.44 cm² **b** 0.785 cm² **c** 45%

Exercise 4e page 68

1 188 cm²

2 503 cm²

3 211 cm²

4 8.04 m²

5 1.31 m²

6 355 cm²

7 1.58 m²

8 29.2 m²

9 a 99.5 cm² **b** 40.7 cm² **c** 181 cm²

10 a 196 cm² **b** 133 cm² **c** 329 cm²

11 a 135 cm² **b** 203 cm²

12 1041 cm²

13 248 cm²

14 177 cm²

15 9.05 m²

16 3.28 m²

17 11.0 cm²

18 239 cm²

19 10 cm

20 7.98 cm

21 1.33 m

22 a 1.2 m³ **b** 1.04 m

Exercise 4f page 70

1 804 cm³

2 29.0 cm³

3 26 300 cm³

4 325 cm³

5 334 cm³

6 0.259 m³

7 71.2 cm³

8 1257 cm³ (400π)

9 704 cm³ (224π)

10 509 cm³

Exercise 4g page 72

1 157 cm²

2 2.26 m²

3 76.3 cm²

4 326 cm²

5 81.2 cm²

6 253 cm²

7 283 cm²

8 1018 cm²

9 6.37 cm

10 4.72 cm

Exercise 4h page 72

1 D

2 C

3 B

4 C

5 C

6 D

7 D

CHAPTER 5

Exercise 5a page 75

1

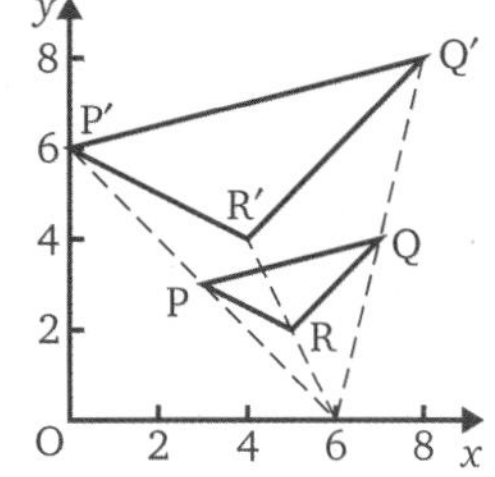

Centre of enlargement is (6, 0).

2

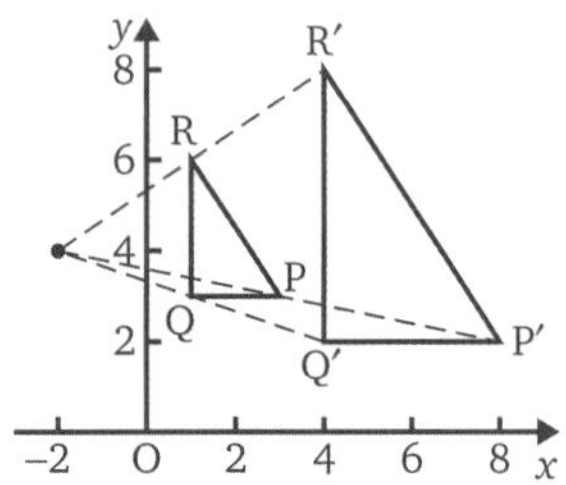

Centre of enlargement is (–2, 4).

3

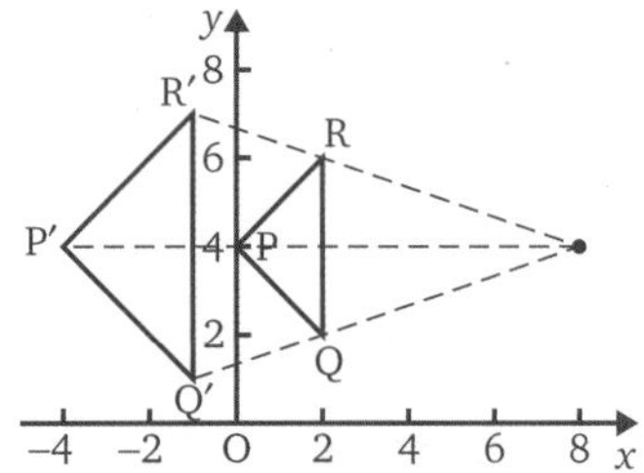

Centre of enlargement is (8, 4).

4 In 1 PQ||P′Q′, PR||P′R′, RQ||R′Q′
In 2 PQ||P′Q′, PR||P′R′, RQ||R′Q′
In 3 PQ||P′Q′, PR||P′R′, RQ||R′Q′

5

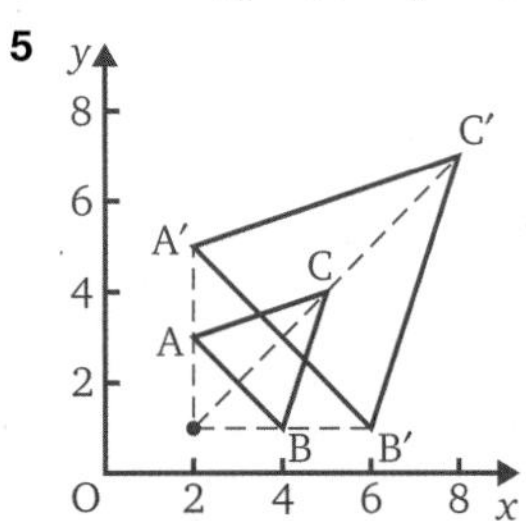

a Centre of enlargement is (2, 1).

6

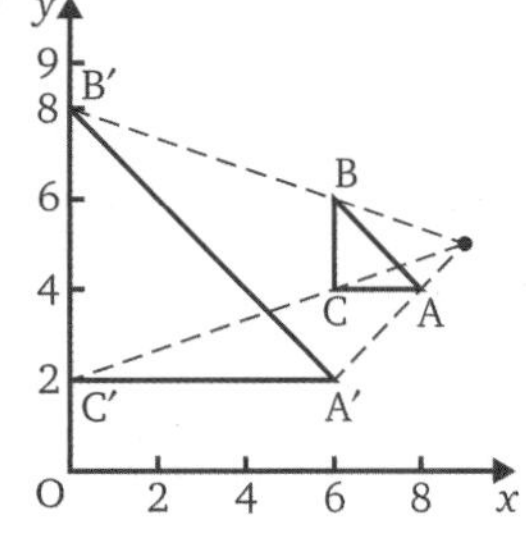

Centre of enlargement is (9, 5).

7

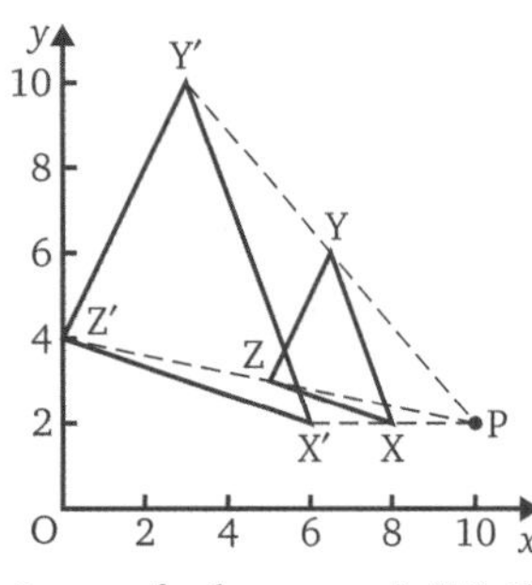

Centre of enlargement is (10, 2).

Exercise 5b page 77

1

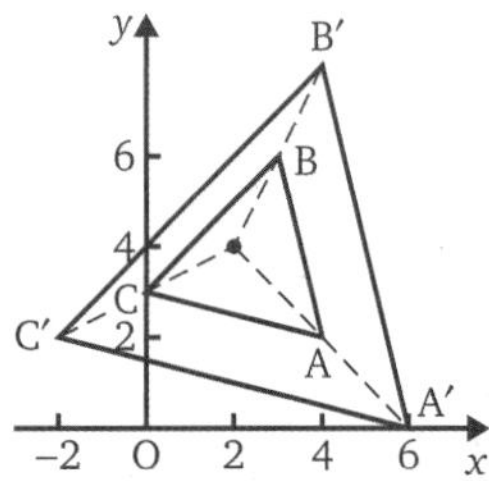

Centre of enlargement is (2, 4).

2 Centre of enlargement is (2, 2).

3

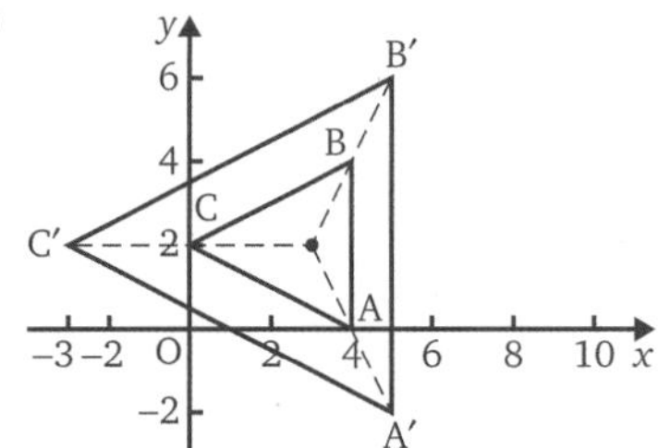

Centre of enlargement is (3, 2).

4

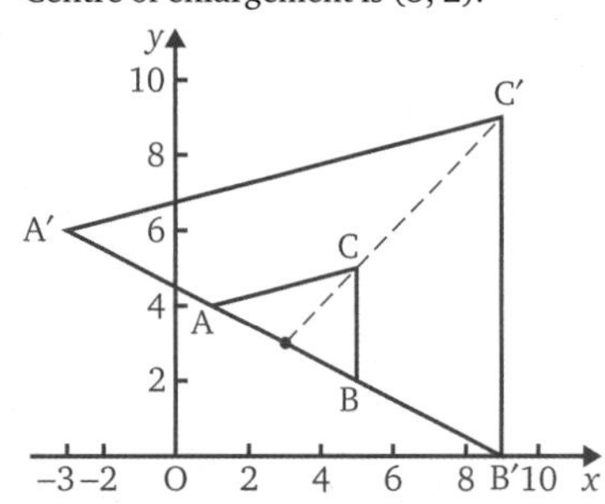

Centre of enlargement is (3, 3).

Exercise 5c page 79

1

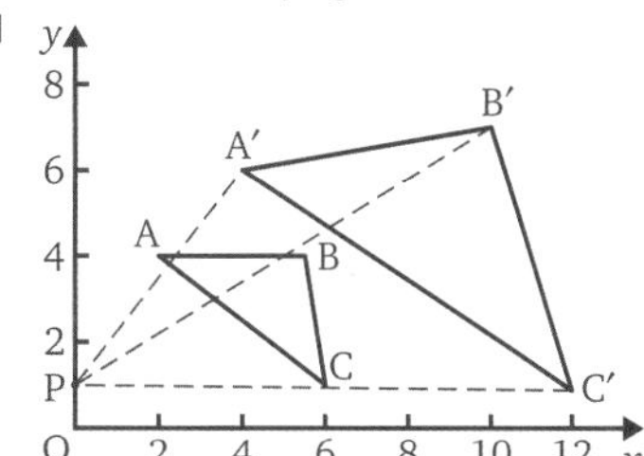

2

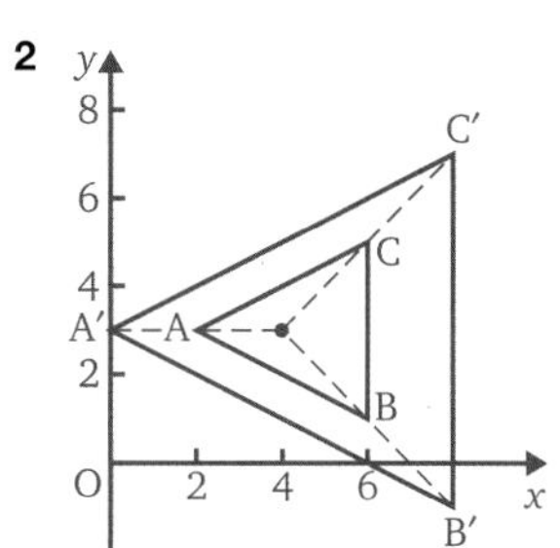

3

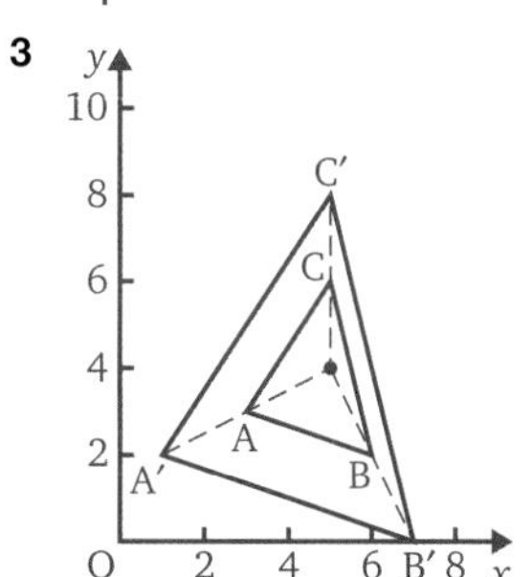

4

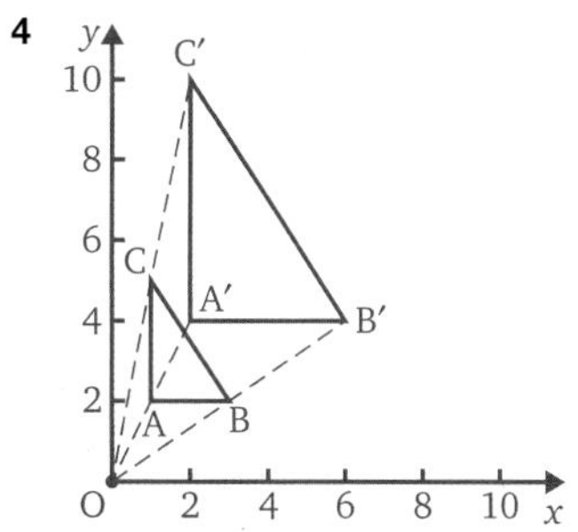

Coordinates of A′ are double the coordinates of A.

5

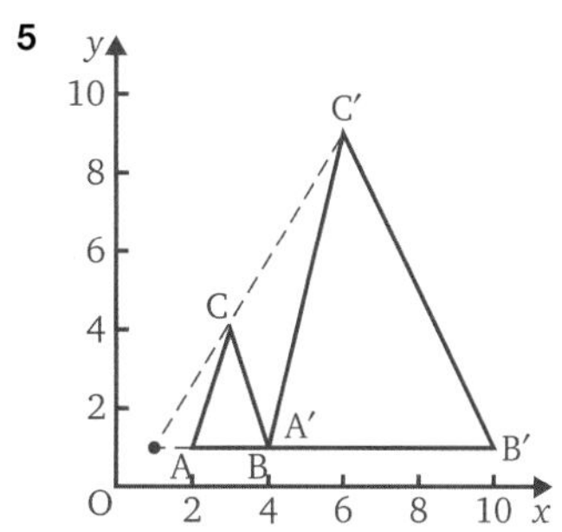

6

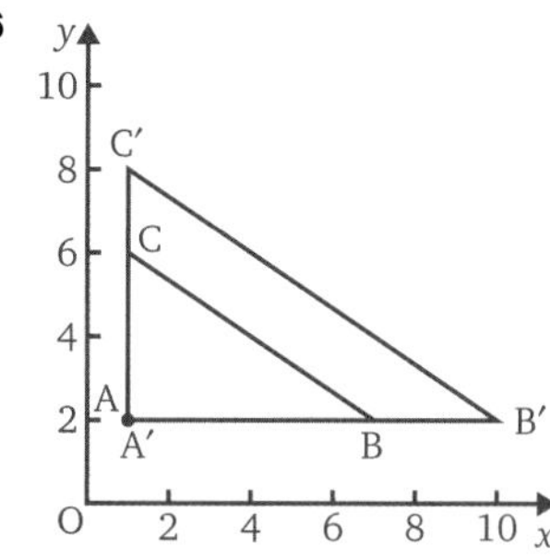

9

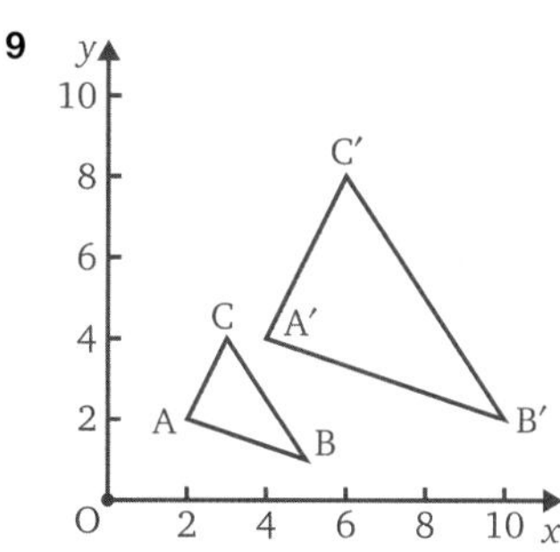

10

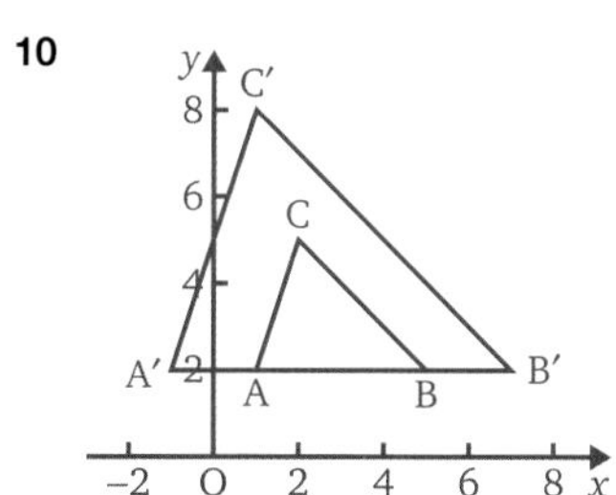

Exercise 5d page 81

1 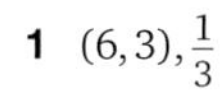 $(6,3), \frac{1}{3}$

2 $(-1,0), \frac{1}{2}$

3 $\left(3\frac{1}{2}, 4\right), \frac{1}{3}$

4 $(1,2), \frac{1}{2}$

5

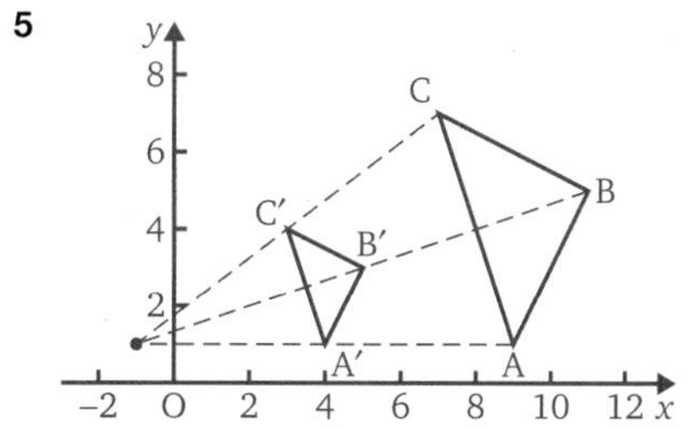

6

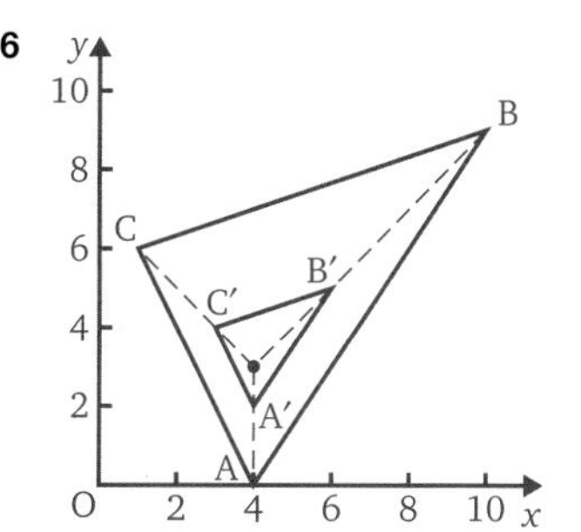

Exercise 5e page 82

1 D
2 C
3 B
4 C

CHAPTER 6

Exercise 6a page 86

11 500 m
12 2.29 m

Exercise 6b page 89

1 a 5.5 cm b 5.5 m
c 4 cm d 4 m
2 a 33 cm b 6 cm c 5 cm
3 a i 6 cm ii 4.5 cm b i 24 ft ii 18 ft
c soccer 6 ft, rugby 10 ft d 30 ft
4 a 15 cm b 9.6 cm
5 a i 5 m by 4 m ii 4 m by 3.5 m
b 2.5 m c 20 m^2 d $2600
6 a i 236 mm ii 188 mm iii 208 mm iv 34 mm
b i 32 mm ii 26 mm
c yes, going + twice the rise = 584 mm d yes

Exercise 6c page 94

1 a $\frac{3}{2\,000\,000}$ b $21\frac{1}{3}$ km c $35\frac{1}{3}$ km d 34 km
e 38 km
2 72 000 m^2 = 7.2 hectares
3 a 7.5 km b 100 cm^2
4 a 2.4 km b 2.8 km^2
5 a 1 : 3000 b 192 m c $\frac{16}{9}$ cm^2 or 1.78 cm^2 (3 s.f.)

Exercise 6d page 96

1 23 m
2 22 m
3 50 m
4 38 m
5 70 m
6 32 m
7 55 m
8 58 m
9 9 m
10 46 m
11 91 m

Exercise 6e page 98

1 86 m
2 60 m
3 71 m
4 100 m
5 339 m
6 824 m
7 112 m
8 923 m
9 528 m
10 54 m
11 1099 m
12 8660 m
13 433 m
14 134 m
15 582 m
16 280 m

Exercise 6f page 100

1 a $\frac{1}{4}$ b $\frac{3}{4}$
2 a 2 b $\frac{3}{2}$
3 a $\frac{1}{3}$ b $\frac{2}{3}$ c $\frac{4}{3}$
4 $\frac{3}{4}$
5 $\frac{5}{3}$
6 $\frac{2}{3}$
7 $\frac{5}{8}$

Exercise 6g page 102

1 $\frac{3}{2}$
2 $\frac{4}{3}$
3 $\frac{6}{5}$
4 $\frac{3}{4}$
5 $\frac{1}{2}$
6 $\frac{5}{4}$
7 $\frac{2}{3}$
8 $\frac{7}{5}$

Exercise 6h page 103

1 a i 5 cm ii 8 cm
b i 16 cm^2 ii 48 cm^2
c i 72 cm^3 ii 160 cm^3
2 a i 2 cm ii 2.8 cm
b i 2 cm^2 ii 12 cm^2
c i 2 cm^3 ii 5 cm^3
3 a i 9 cm ii 60 mm
b i 18 cm^2 ii 108 cm^2
c i 27 cm^3 ii 135 cm^3
4 a i 2.25 cm ii 9 mm
b i 2 cm^2 ii 6 cm^2
c i 2 cm^3 ii 2.5 cm^3
5 a 18 cm b 16 cm c 45 cm^2 d 63 cm^2
6 a i 80 cm^2 ii 128 cm^2 b i 128 cm^3 ii $\frac{64}{3}$ m^3 or $21\frac{1}{3}$ m^3
7 525 cm^2
8 $a = \frac{3}{2}$
9 a $\frac{5}{4}$ b $\frac{4}{5}$
10 $\frac{2}{3}$

Exercise 6i page 105

1 860 cm
2
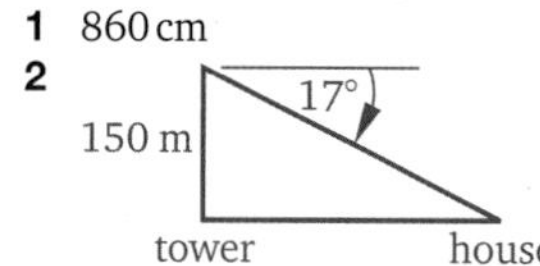

3
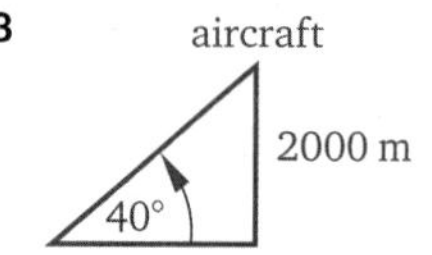

4
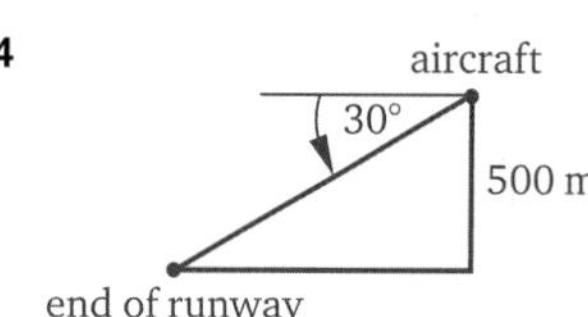

Exercise 6j page 106

1 94 m
2
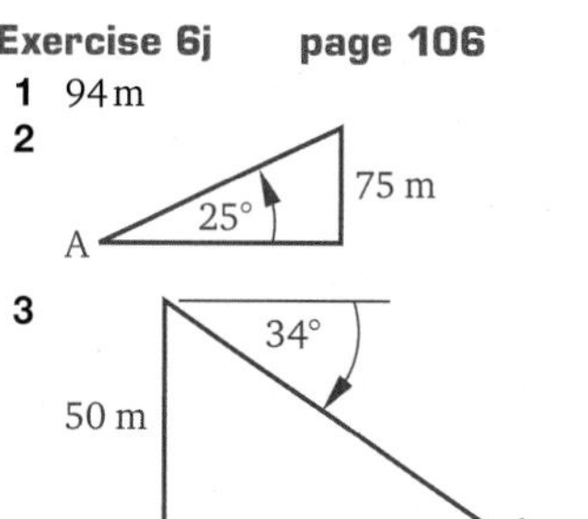

3
4 30 m, 500 m^2

Exercise 6k page 107

1 C	**3** D	**5** A	**7** A
2 B	**4** B	**6** D	**8** C

CHAPTER 7

Exercise 7a page 111

1 70°	**3** 60°	**5** 45°
2 110°	**4** 70°	**6** 66°

Exercise 7b page 113

1 yes	**3** yes	**5** no	**7** yes
2 no	**4** no	**6** yes	**8** yes

Exercise 7c page 115

1 reflection in x-axis; yes
2 enlargement, scale factor 2, centre (–4, 0); no
3 translation $\begin{pmatrix}-2\\-2\end{pmatrix}$; yes
4 reflection in y-axis; yes
5 enlargement, scale factor $\frac{1}{2}$, centre (0, 0); no
6 rotation; yes

Exercise 7d page 116

1 $B\hat{A}C = 38.7°$, $A\hat{B}C = 51.3°$, $A\hat{C}B = 90°$; no
2 yes
3 $B\hat{A}C = 106°$, $A\hat{B}C = 39.9°$, $A\hat{C}B = 34.1°$; no
4 yes
5 the length of one side

Exercise 7e page 117

1 yes; SSS
2 no
3 no
4 no
5 yes
6 △ABC and △ADC
7 yes
8 yes

Exercise 7f page 119

5 two are: △ABC and △LMN
6 two

Exercise 7g page 120

1 yes; AAS	**6** yes; AAS
2 no; similar	**7** yes; AAS
3 yes; AAS	**8** no
4 yes; AAS	**9** yes
5 no	**10** yes

Exercise 7h page 121

1 yes; AC = 4.4 cm, $\hat{A} = 34.3°$, $\hat{C} = 115.7°$
2 no
3 yes; PR = 7.2 cm, $\hat{R} = 46°$, $\hat{P} = 74°$
4 no
5 yes; DF = 7.8 cm, $\hat{D} = 50°$, $\hat{F} = 40°$

Exercise 7i page 122

1 yes
2 no; there are two possibilities
3 yes
4 no; there are two possibilities
5 yes
6 yes

Exercise 7j page 122

1 yes; SAS
2 not necessarily
3 yes; RHS
4 yes; SAS
5 yes; SAS
6 not necessarily
7 yes; RHS
8 not necessarily
9 yes; RHS
10 yes

Exercise 7k page 124

1 no
2 yes; AAS
3 yes; SSS
4 Yes; AAS
5 no
6 yes; SAS
7 not necessarily
8 yes; AAS
9 yes; RHS
10 yes; SSS
11 yes; ASS
12 yes; SAS

Exercise 7l page 126

9 △BDF and △CDE

Exercise 7n page 132

1 AC bisects both angles; yes
2 both are right angles
3 no
4 they are equal
5 yes; no; yes, of AC; they are all right angles
6 no
7 they are equal

Exercise 7p page 134

1 5 cm
2 60°

Exercise 7q page 136

1 A	**3** C	**5** C
2 B	**4** A	

REVIEW TEST 1 page 139

1 C	**7** A
2 A	**8** B
3 D	**9** C
4 D	**10** C
5 B	**11** D
6 D	

12 a i 47.976 **ii** 48.0
b i 0.457 **ii** 0.457
c i 263.006 **ii** 263
13 a 2 **b** $25\frac{1}{5}$
14 proof

15 yes, AAS
16 $a = 80°$ $c = 25°$ $e = 105°$
$b = 75°$ $d = 75°$ $f = 100°$
17 **a** $a = 83°$ **b** 24.4 cm^2
18 **a** 21 cm^3 **b** 160 cm^2
19 **a** 700 m **b** 8.5 ha
20 centre (0, 2), scale factor 2
21 49.82 cm^2

CHAPTER 8

Exercise 8a page 143

1 yes
2 no
3 yes
4 no
5 yes
6 yes
7 yes
8 no
9 no
10 no
11 A and D

Exercise 8b page 145

1 **a** yes
b AC = 4.1 cm, CB = 3.2 cm, A′C′ = 8.2 cm, C′B′ = 6.4 cm
c each is 2
d all equal to 2
2 **a** yes
b AC = 8.6 cm, CB = 7.7 cm, A′C′ = 5.7 cm, C′B′ = 5.1 cm
c each is 0.67 or $\frac{2}{3}$
d all equal to 0.67
3 **a** yes
b AC = 7.9 cm, CB = 6.4 cm, A′C′ = 3.9 cm, C′B′ = 3.2 cm
c each is 0.5 or $\frac{1}{2}$
d all equal to 0.5
4 **a** yes
b AC = 10.1 cm, CB = 6.6 cm, A′C′ = 7.6 cm, C′B′ = 4.9 cm
c each is 0.75 or $\frac{3}{4}$
d all equal to 0.75
5 **a** yes
b AC = 6.1 cm, CB = 9.2 cm, A′C′ = 9.2 cm, C′B′ = 13.8 cm
c each is 1.5 cm or $\frac{3}{2}$
d all equal to 1.5
6 80°, 52°, yes
7 72°, 72°, yes
8 70°, 70°, yes
9 93°, 52°, no

Exercise 8c page 147

1 yes, $\frac{AB}{PQ} = \frac{BC}{QR} = \frac{AC}{PR}$
2 yes, $\frac{AB}{PR} = \frac{BC}{RQ} = \frac{AC}{PQ}$
3 no
4 yes, $\frac{AC}{QP} = \frac{CB}{PR} = \frac{AB}{QR}$

Exercise 8d page 150

1 8 cm
2 6 cm
3 10 cm
4 30 cm
5 24 cm
6 yes, 2.5 cm
7 yes, 7.2 cm
8 no
9 yes, 6.3 cm
10 7.5 cm
11 7.5 cm
12 $8\frac{1}{3}$ cm
13 $4\frac{1}{2}$ cm
14 **b** 4 cm
15 **b** CD = 9 cm, DE = 10.5 cm
16 **b** 5 cm
17 **b** DE = 18 cm, AE = 13.5 cm, CE = 4.5 cm

Exercise 8e page 155

1 yes, $\hat{P}$
2 yes, $\hat{Q}$
3 no
4 yes, $\hat{P}$
5 no
6 yes, $\hat{P}$
7 yes, $\hat{B} = \hat{D}$, $\hat{C} = \hat{E}$, they are parallel

Exercise 8f page 157

1 yes, CB = 3.6 cm
2 no
3 yes, RQ = 35 cm
4 yes, RQ = 7.2 cm
5 yes, AC = $10\frac{2}{3}$ cm
6 5.1 cm
7 3 cm

Exercise 8g page 160

1 yes, 4 cm
2 yes, 2.4 cm
3 yes, 83°
4 no
5 yes, 34°
6 yes, 32°
7 yes, $3\frac{1}{2}$ cm
8 yes, 18 cm
9 **b** AC = 3.15 cm, CE = 1.05 cm
10 **b** 143 cm
11 **c** yes
12 10 m
13 19.2 m
14 60 cm

CHAPTER 9

Exercise 9a page 165

1 38.44
2 187.69
3 58 564
4 7 728 400
5 0.5041
6 0.003 481
7 0.000 002 89
8 973 44
9 9.7344
10 0.000 973 44
11 84.64
12 8464
13 27 140 000
14 2714
15 0.2714
16 0.002 714
17 3.142
18 4.461
19 11.14
20 311.1
21 0.2195
22 0.069 43
23 9.798
24 17.92
25 1.619
26 0.2490
27 0.027 93
28 0.7071
29 0.6790
30 2.147
31 21.47
32 0.021 47

Exercise 9b page 166

1 10 cm
2 11.7 cm
3 9.43 cm
4 13 cm
5 11.4 cm
6 13.9 cm
7 The square of the third side is equal to the sum of the squares of the other two.

Exercise 9c page 168

1 10 cm
2 13 cm
3 20 cm
4 9.85 cm
5 10.8 cm
6 10.6 cm
7 11.7 cm
8 12.6 cm
9 12.1 cm
10 10.4 cm
11 3.61 cm
12 11.4 cm
13 6.40 m
14 11.4 m
15 12.2 cm
16 5.40 cm
17 121 cm
18 3.31 cm
19 9.57 cm
20 44.7 m
21 0.361 cm
22 8.64 cm
23 17.4 m
24 2.61 cm
25 35.0 cm
26 13.0 cm
27 12.0 cm

Exercise 9d page 171

1 30 cm
2 18.4 cm
3 130 mm
4 7.5 cm
5 26 m
6 32.0 cm
7 $2\frac{1}{2}$ cm
8 12.8 cm

Exercise 9e page 172

1	12 cm	6	2.65 cm	11	6.24 cm
2	48 cm	7	1.73 m	12	16.0 cm
3	24 cm	8	4.58 cm	13	6.71 cm
4	10 m	9	7.48 m	14	13.7 m
5	4.90 cm	10	7.94 cm		

Exercise 9f page 174

1	6.71 cm	7	3.46 cm	13	9.27 cm
2	8.87 cm	8	8.15 m	14	2.5 cm
3	55 cm	9	88.5 cm	15	6.8 m
4	5.66 cm	10	7, 24	16	89.6 cm
5	11.5 cm	11	4.9 cm	17	3.51 cm
6	9 cm	12	265 cm		

Exercise 9g page 176

1	12.5 cm	3	15.0 cm, 30 cm	5	11.3 cm
2	10 cm	4	4.25 m		

Exercise 9h page 178

1	2.71 cm	3	10.4 cm	5	12.7 cm
2	4.69 cm	4	16.2 m		

Exercise 9i page 179

1 2.60 m
2 7.81 cm
3 14.1 cm
4 105 m
5 7.55 m
6 74.3 cm
7 83.1 m
8 1.63 m
9 14.1 cm
10 6.22 km
11 8.94 units
12 38.8 n.m.
13 5.52 m
14 0.589 m
15 21.2 cm
16 **a** 39.4 cm
17 **a** 2.4 cm **b** 4.64 cm
no; $AC^2 \neq AB^2 + BC^2$
18 **c** AC = 7.07 cm
AD = 8.66 cm
AE = 10 cm
19 use 7 cm and 4 cm
or 8 cm and 1 cm
$\sqrt{65} = 8.06$

Exercise 9j page 182

1	yes	3	no	5	yes
2	yes	4	no	6	no

Exercise 9k page 183

1	18.9 cm	8	130 cm
2	6.52 cm	9	3.58 cm
3	2.02 cm	10	64.5 cm
4	0.0265 cm	11	yes
5	20.5 cm	12	3.13 cm
6	4.16 cm	13	26.2 cm
7	0.05 cm	14	yes, $\widehat{M} = 90°$

Exercise 9l page 184

1 C **2** A **3** C **4** B **5** C **6** C

CHAPTER 10

Exercise 10a page 188

7	$\frac{5}{12}$, 0.4167	9	$\frac{3}{4}$, 0.75	11	$\frac{12}{5}$, 2.4
8	$\frac{8}{15}$, 0.5333	10	$\frac{3}{4}$, 0.75	12	$\frac{35}{12}$, 2.917

Exercise 10b page 190

1	1.8807	7	4.8716	13	10.1°	19	42.7°
2	0.2493	8	1	14	19.6°	20	38.7°
3	0.5890	9	0.5774	15	55.0°	21	17.8°
4	0.3019	10	1.1184	16	23.4°	22	69.6°
5	0.0805	11	0.0524	17	53.7°	23	42.7°
6	3.0777	12	0.5635	18	32.3°	24	0.1°

Exercise 10c page 190

1	32.0°	4	35.8°	7	48.4°
2	63.4°	5	31.0°	8	47.7°
3	23.2°	6	51.3°	9	34.2°

Exercise 10d page 191

1	2.44 cm	8	22.2 cm	15	46.6 cm
2	5.40 cm	9	2.82 cm	16	10.4 cm
3	2.56 cm	10	7.54 cm	17	4.69 cm
4	6.72 cm	11	3.60 cm	18	366 cm
5	17.0 cm	12	11.4 cm	19	0.976 cm
6	81.8 cm	13	2.42 cm	20	69.5 cm
7	5.62 cm	14	1.76 cm		

Exercise 10e page 194

1	0.8862	8	0.5	15	31.6°
2	0.9397	9	0.9903	16	65.4°
3	0.2470	10	0.4664	17	41.8°
4	0.1564	11	0.2723	18	21.8°
5	0.2622	12	0.9988	19	37.9°
6	0.6088	13	15.7°	20	46.7°
7	0.8625	14	26.2°	21	7.1°

Exercise 10f page 194

1	30°	6	62.7°	11	4.38 cm	16	23.2 cm
2	17.5°	7	44.4°	12	10.6 cm	17	6.31 cm
3	48.6°	8	41.8°	13	1.46 cm	18	21.9 m
4	44.4°	9	23.6°	14	4.57 cm	19	3.34 cm
5	14.5°	10	19.5°	15	11.7 cm	20	45.7 cm

Exercise 10g page 196

1	0.8480	7	0.6143	13	51.1°
2	0.7455	8	0.6561	14	71.6°
3	0.1392	9	69.7°	15	30.1°
4	0.6717	10	20.6°	16	89.2°
5	0.5	11	44.0°		
6	0.9632	12	69.6°		

Exercise 10h page 197

1	34.9°	8	66.4°	15	11.6 cm
2	36.9°	9	81.4°	16	38.2 cm
3	45.6°	10	25.8°	17	2.90 cm
4	48.2°	11	34.0°	18	17.1 cm
5	48.2°	12	3.50 cm	19	2.23 cm
6	53.1°	13	26.9 cm	20	4.12 cm
7	50.2°	14	1.96 cm	21	13.5 cm

Exercise 10i page 199

1	40.0°	13	56.9°	25	6.04 cm
2	33.6°	14	37.8°	26	3.50 cm
3	51.3°	15	39.3°	27	13.7 cm
4	42.8°	16	55.6°	28	3.08 cm
5	35.5°	17	42.1°	29	113 cm
6	33.7°	18	66.2°	30	2.59 cm
7	39.8°	19	6.69 cm	31	9.99 cm
8	33.7°	20	19.3 cm	32	7.45 cm
9	37.7°	21	8.03 cm	33	14.5 cm
10	53.1°	22	4.86 cm	34	21.4 cm
11	68.5°	23	4.48 cm	35	74.5 cm
12	14.5°	24	80.5 cm	36	60.6 cm

Exercise 10j page 202

1 4.13 cm
2 8.72 cm
3 23.3 cm
4 4.67 cm
5 14.9 cm
6 17.0 cm
7 4.40 cm
8 14.9 cm
9 33.1 cm
10 42.6 cm

Exercise 10k page 203

1 8.99 cm
2 47.7 m
3 143 m
4 39.8°
5 61.6°
6 56.3°
7 48.2°
8 11.3°
9 a 5.30 cm b 6.25 cm
10 a 5.20 cm b 15.6 cm^2
11 4.66 m

Exercise 10l page 205

1 C 2 D 3 C 4 A 5 B 6 C

CHAPTER 11

Exercise 11a page 207

1 36°
2 45°
3 30°
4 60°
5 24°
6 20°
7 40°
8 22.5°
9 18°

Exercise 11b page 208

1 720°
2 540°
3 1440°
4 360°
5 900°
6 1800°
7 2880°
8 1260°
9 2340°

Exercise 11c page 209

1 a 3240° b 2520° c 1620°
2 80°
3 120°
4 110°
5 105°
6 85°
7 110°
8 108°
9 120°
10 135°
11 144°
12 150°
13 162°
14 a 18 b 24
15 a 12 b 20
16 a yes, 12
b yes, 9
c no
d yes, 6
e no
f yes, 4
17 a yes, 4
b yes, 6
c no
d yes, 72
e yes, 36
f yes, 8

Exercise 11d page 211

1 54°
2 45°
3 150°
4 72°
5 60°
6 50°
7 80°
8 135°
9 100°
10 60°
11 72°
12 45°
13 60°
14 36°
15 a 36° b 36°
16 a 128.6° b 25.7°
17 77.1°
18 a 22.5° b 22.5°
19 22.5°
20 45°

Exercise 11e page 214

1 B 2 A 3 B 4 A 5 B 6 C

Exercise 11f page 215

1 a the interior angles (135°) do not divide exactly into 360°
b a square
2 a no
b a regular ten-sided polygon
4 square, equilateral triangle

CHAPTER 12

Exercise 12a page 219

1 a 70° b isosceles
2 a DF = 11.1 cm, EF = 6.5 cm b 45°
3 ∠G = 36.9°, ∠H = 53.1°, ∠I = 90°, a right angle
4–7 constructions
8 PQ and SR are parallel
9 105°
10 BC = 6 cm, angle BCA = 45°
11 75°

Exercise 12b page 221

1 EF = $\frac{1}{2}$AB
2 d RU = SU e QT = RS f parallelogram
3 trapezium

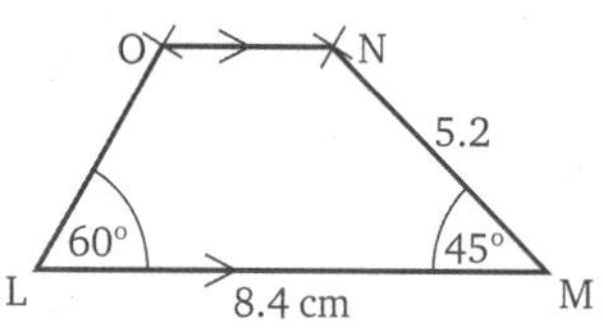

Exercise 12c page 221

2 they are equal
3 AC and BD
4 coincident
5 coincident
6 at the midpoint of AC
7 at the midpoint of BD
8 90°
9 each is 90°
10 BD = 7.2 cm
11 8 cm
12 5 cm
13 9.5 cm
14 6 cm
15 5.7 cm

Exercise 12d page 224

2 5.83 cm
3 a 10.9 cm b 6.3 cm
4 O is the midpoint of AB
$A\hat{C}B$ = 90° since it is in a semicircle
5 a they all pass through one point
b it is outside the triangle
6 Yes; it passes through D.
This happens because the trapezium is symmetrical about the perpendicular bisector of AB.
No
7 4.5 cm 8 5 cm
9 OP = OQ = OR = 4 cm, 4 cm
10 Yes; the perpendicular bisectors intersect at the centre of the circle, O.

Exercise 12e page 226

1 a 72° b 45° c 36° d 24°
2 yes, a square
3 a equal b equal c twice the length of a side
4 a equal b equal c twice the length of a side (8 cm)

5 3.83 cm
6 4.34 cm
7 **a** 5.88 cm **b** midpoint of DC **c** identical
8 **a** 7.05 cm

Exercise 12f page 227

1 4.8 cm **2** 5.56 cm **3** congruent **4** no
5 bisects PQ and passes through O
6 yes, it is the circumcircle of triangle ABC
7 yes, it is the circumcircle of the square ABCD
8 the lengths of the side equal the radius of the circle
9 **a** regular polygon, all the angles at the centre are equal
b AOB is an isosceles triangle
10 yes
11 yes, all 90°
12

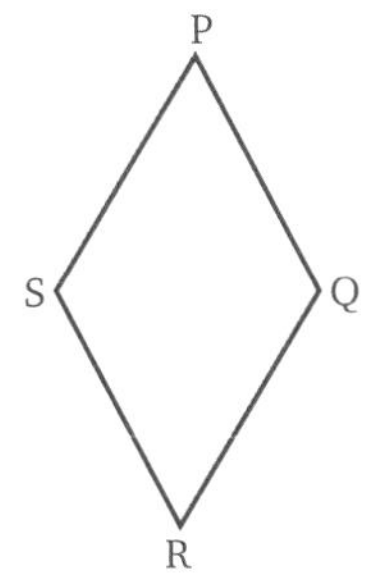

13

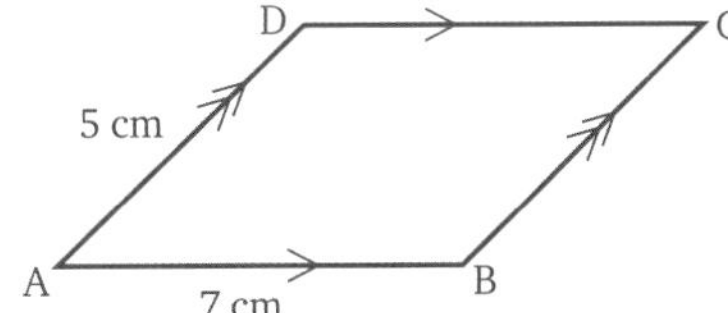

14 4.46 cm
15 **a** SR **b** total 360° **c** total 180°
16 7.81 cm and 4.58 cm
17 rhombus; its diagonals bisect each other at right angles
18 4.82 cm and 11.64 cm
19

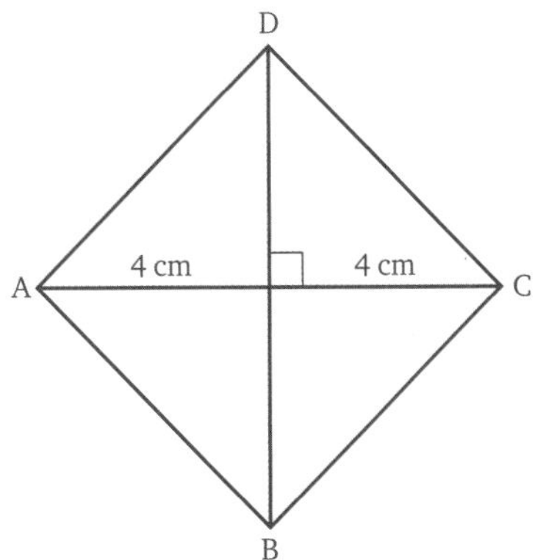

20 **a** yes **b** their sum is 180°

Exercise 12g page 229

1 4.2 cm
2 11.6 cm by 3.1 cm
3 angle C = 70°, isosceles
4 **a** **i** 11.14 cm **ii** 6.49 cm
b 45°
5 5.2 cm

6 PS = 5.4 cm, SR = 3.4 cm
7 4.24 cm
8 7.05 cm

CHAPTER 13

Exercise 13a page 232

1 **a** 140% **c** 125% **e** $105\frac{1}{2}\%$
b 160% **d** 250%
2 **a** 70% **c** 95% **e** $96\frac{1}{2}\%$
b 40% **d** $66\frac{2}{3}\%$
3 **a** 130 **b** 3888 **c** 621.3 **d** 2136.9
4 **a** 30 **b** 1815 **c** 1098.75 **d** 145.6
5 **a** 192 **b** 82
6 $3808 **7** 1140 **8** 83.60 kg
9 **a** $280 **b** $238 **10** $3.25

Exercise 13b page 233

1 Singh $640, Edwards $577.60, Smith $777, Pierre $631.40
2 $610.50, $41\frac{1}{4}$
3 **a** $7\frac{1}{4}$ **b** $36\frac{1}{4}$, $475.60
4 **a** $8\frac{1}{4}$ **b** $775.50
5 $577.20
6 **a** $37\frac{1}{2}$ **b** $412.50 **c** $11\frac{1}{2}$ hours **d** $602.25
7 $502.86
8 $603
9 $782.36
10 $778
11 **a** $814 **b** $716.32
12 **a** 13 **b** $4480 **c** $58 240

Exercise 13c page 234

1 **a** $3000 **b** $17 000
2 **a** $6300 **b** **i** $28 700 **ii** $551.92
3

M Davis	$164	$1476
P Evans	$295.20	$2164.80
G Brown	$635.40	$2894.60
A Khan	$1091	$3273

4 **a** $9.12 **b** $85.12
5 $3760
6 $47
7 $49 350
8 $1506.50
9 $752, $780.80
10 **a** $2530 **b** no
c The manager added $2\frac{1}{2}\%$ to the original sale price. The manager should have added $17\frac{1}{2}\%$ to the pre-sales tax price, giving a new price of £2585.

Exercise 13d page 236

1 **a** $636 **b** $954 **c** $1457.50
2 **a** $656 **b** $721.60
3 **a** **i** $660 **ii** $792 **b** $23 100 **c** $11 748
4 **a** **i** $480 000 **ii** $4 560 000
b **i** 35 c **ii** 55 c

Exercise 13e page 237

1 **a** \$126 **b** \$201.60 **c** \$375.30 **d** \$500 **e** \$163.35
2 \$440
3 7 years
4 6.5%
5 \$300
6 4%
7 \$406
8 \$42
9 \$76.32
10 \$103.88
11 \$191.77
12 \$143.99
13 \$229.40
14 \$48 400
15 \$6272
16 \$76.04
17 \$1093.50
18 \$12 800
19 **a** \$1041.86 **b** \$1148.65 (both 2 d.p.)
20 **a** \$324 000 **b** \$262 440, \$262 000 (3 s.f.)

Exercise 13f page 239

1 **a** \$4280 **b** no; cost is \$4536, i.e. \$256 more
2 **a** \$153.60 **b** yes, by \$8.60
3 \$86
4 \$130.95
5 \$127.53
6 \$99.09
7 \$243.10
8 \$138.44

Exercise 13g page 240

1 **a** 2 **b** 0.04 **c** 6
2 **a** 4 **b** 1.68 **c** 3.6
3 **a** $8\frac{1}{3}$ h **b** $2\frac{6}{7}$ h **c** 200 h **d** $\frac{1}{2}$ h
4 **a** 8 c **b** 12 c **c** 6.72 c
5 \$45
6 \$95.80
7 \$129.80
8 \$146.22
9 \$107.38
10 \$144
11 \$180
12 \$162
13 \$146.38
14 \$114.80

Exercise 13h page 241

1 C **2** B **5** D **4** C **5** D **6** C

CHAPTER 14

Exercise 14a page 245

1 3, 2
2 2, 4
3 3, 5
4 1, 7
5 4, –3
6 2, 5
7 –2, 1
8 5, 1
9 3, $1\frac{1}{2}$
10 6, 0
11 –1, –2
12 0, 9

Exercise 14b page 246

1 3, 1
2 4, 2
3 3, 4
4 2, –4
5 3, $\frac{1}{2}$
6 9, 1
7 4, –2
8 1, 0
9 0, 6
10 2, 3
11 4, –1
12 6, 2
13 5, $1\frac{1}{2}$
14 4, 3
15 $\frac{1}{2}$, 4
16 4, –2
17 –3, 1
18 2, $\frac{1}{3}$
19 3, 2
20 4, 5
21 3, 0
22 $1\frac{1}{2}$, 2
23 –3, 2
24 4, –2
25 6, 2
26 4, 3
27 –1, 4
28 –1, –2
29 5, 4
30 2, –4

Exercise 14c page 248

1 3, 1
2 1, 2
3 $\frac{1}{3}$, 1
4 –12, 27
5 0, 1
6 4, 3
7 1, 2
8 2, 1
9 3, –1
10 0, 3
11 1, –1
12 3, $\frac{1}{2}$

Exercise 14d page 249

1 3, 2
2 1, 5
3 3, 1
4 $1\frac{1}{2}$, 0
5 0, 6
6 3, –1
7 1, 4
8 1, 1
9 2, 2
10 3, –1
11 4, 2
12 –3, 0
13 2, $\frac{2}{3}$
14 –1, 2
15 3, –2
16 2, –2
17 0, 4
18 –1, –2
19 1, 1
20 3, 1
21 2, –1
22 8, 4
23 –3, 4
24 3, $-3\frac{1}{2}$
25 3, 4
26 2, 5
27 3, 2
28 –1, –3

Exercise 14e page 250

1 1, 4
2 –1, 5
3 3, –2
4 6, 28
5 2, 3
6 –1, –1
7 $3\frac{1}{2}, 2\frac{1}{2}$
8 1, –2
9 5, 0
10 0, 4
11 3, 1
12 –4, –5

Exercise 14f page 250

1 2, 4
2 5, 3
3 1, 1
4 –2, 7
5 4, 6
6 1, 1
7 1, 10
8 $2\frac{1}{3}, -\frac{2}{3}$
9 –1, 5
10 –12, –4
11 2, 6
12 $4\frac{1}{2}, 7\frac{1}{2}$

Exercise 14h page 253

1 1, 2
2 $1\frac{4}{7}, 1\frac{6}{7}$
3 2, –2
4 $\frac{1}{2}$, 1
5 3, 4
6 –2, –1
7 1, 10
8 $2\frac{1}{3}, -\frac{2}{3}$
9 –1, 5
10 –12, –4
11 2, 6
12 $4\frac{1}{2}, 7\frac{1}{2}$

Exercise 14i page 253

1 12, 8
2 11, 5
3 8, 2
4 10, 3
5 10, 6
6 11, 5
7 3 choc ices, 7 orange ices
8 54, 36
9 cup \$1.80, saucer \$1.35
10 patties \$1.40 each, roti \$2.10 each
11 Harry 32, Adam 10, Sam 20
12 3, 5
13 AB = $9\frac{1}{2}$ cm, BC = 6 cm
14 $m = 2, c = 4, y = 2x + 4$

Exercise 14j page 256

1 $1\frac{1}{2}, 4\frac{1}{2}$
2 $1\frac{1}{3}, 3\frac{2}{3}$
3 $1\frac{1}{2}, 5\frac{1}{2}$
4 $-\frac{1}{2}, 1\frac{1}{2}$
5 $\frac{1}{2}$, 2
6 $1\frac{1}{2}, 3\frac{1}{2}$
7 $2\frac{2}{5}, 1\frac{4}{5}$
8 $-\frac{2}{5}, 1\frac{3}{5}$
9 $2\frac{2}{5}, \frac{9}{10}$
10 $\frac{1}{3}, 1\frac{2}{3}$

Exercise 14k page 257

1 A **2** A **3** D **4** D **5** C

REVIEW TEST 2 page 258

1 B
2 D
3 C
4 C
5 C
6 B
7 C
8 D
9 D
10 C
11 C
12 C
13 yes, 3.6 cm
14 15 cm
15 1.5 cm
16 **a** \$2820 **b** \$1440
17 **a** 25 h **b** 4 c
18 $x = 2, y = -3$
19 $a = 48°$ $b = 48°$ $c = 84°$ $d = 84°$ $e = 96°$
20 $x = 95°$, other angles are 132°, 83°, 121° and 109°, 49°
21 **a** 22.6 cm **b** 37.6 cm
23 **a** yes, $\frac{AB}{AD} = \frac{AC}{AE}$, ∠A is common
b ∠B = ∠D, ∠C = ∠E
c they are parallel

CHAPTER 15

Exercise 15a page 262

1 **a** infinite **b**, **c** and **d** finite
2 **a** **i** 21 **ii** 11
b **i** 4 **ii** 11, 13, 17, 19; no
iii ∅ or { } null or empty set
3 $A = \{11, 13, 17, 19, 23, 29\}$, $B = \{12, 18, 24\}$, $C = \{18\}$
4 {1, 2, 3,..., 10}
5 **a** {2, 4, 6, 8, 10, 12, 14, 16, 18, 20}
b infinite
6 {−1, 0, 1, 2}
7 {(−1, −3), (0, 0), (1, 3)}
8 $n(A) = 4$
9 $P = \{3, 6, 9, 12\}$, $Q = \{2, 4, 6, 8, 10, 12, 14\}$,
$R = \{5, 10\}$
10 $A = \{-6, -4, -2, 0, 2, 4\}$,
$B = \{-6, -5, -4, -3, -2, -1\}$,
$C = \{2, 3, 5\}$
11 $A' = \{1, 3, 5, 7, 8\}$
12 **a**

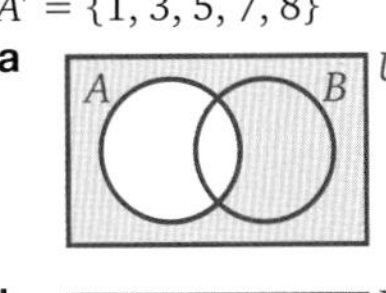

c

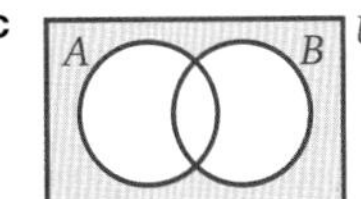

b

Exercise 15b page 263

1

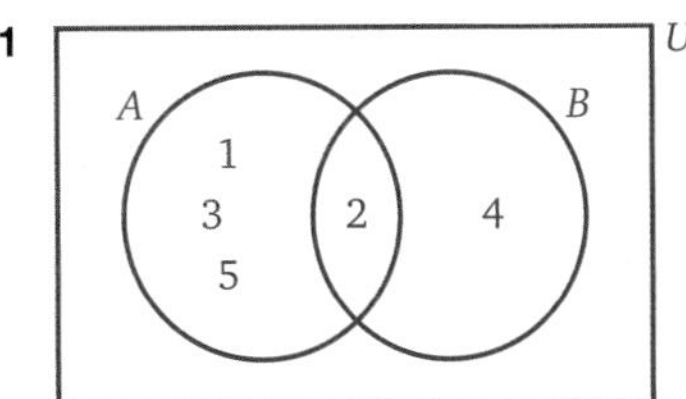

a $A' = \{4\}$
b $B' = \{1, 3, 5\}$
c $A \cup B = \{1, 2, 3, 4, 5\}$
d $(A \cup B)' = \{ \}$ or ∅
e $A' \cap B' = \{ \}$ or ∅

2

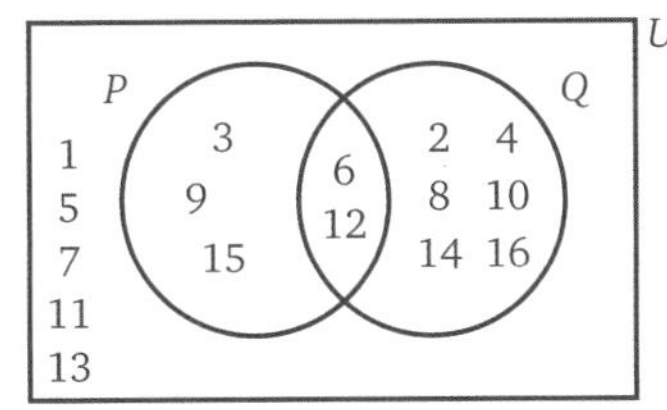

a $P' = \{1, 2, 4, 5, 7, 8, 10, 11, 13, 14, 16\}$
b $Q' = \{1, 3, 5, 7, 9, 11, 13, 15\}$
c $P \cup Q = \{2, 3, 4, 6, 8, 9, 10, 12, 14, 15, 16\}$
d $(P \cup Q)' = \{1, 5, 7, 11, 13\}$
e $P' \cap B' = \{1, 5, 7, 11, 13\}$

3

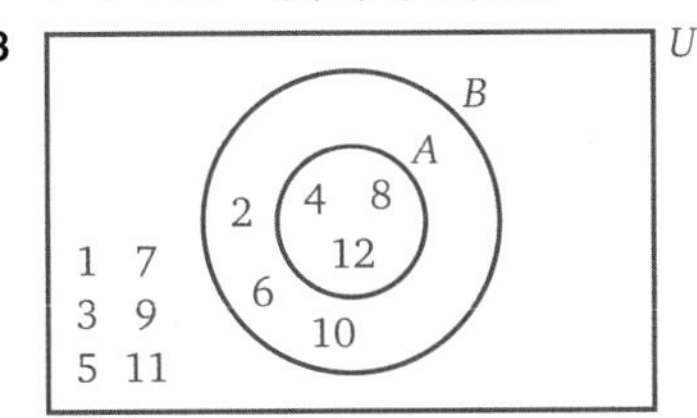

a $A' = \{1, 2, 3, 5, 6, 7, 9, 10, 11\}$
b $B' = \{1, 3, 5, 7, 9, 11\}$
c $A \cup B = \{2, 4, 6, 8, 10, 12\}$
d $(A \cup B)' = \{1, 3, 5, 7, 9, 11\}$
e $A' \cap B' = \{1, 3, 5, 7, 9, 11\}$

4

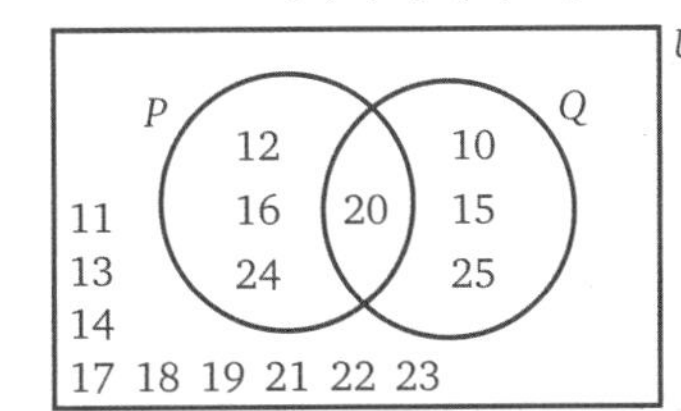

a $P' = \{10, 11, 13, 14, 15, 17, 18, 19, 21, 22, 23, 25\}$
b $Q' = \{11, 12, 13, 14, 16, 17, 18, 19, 21, 22, 23, 24\}$
c $P \cup Q = \{10, 12, 15, 16, 20, 24, 25\}$
d $(P \cup Q)' = \{11, 13, 14, 17, 18, 19, 21, 22, 23\}$
e $P' \cap Q' = \{11, 13, 14, 17, 18, 19, 21, 22, 23\}$

5

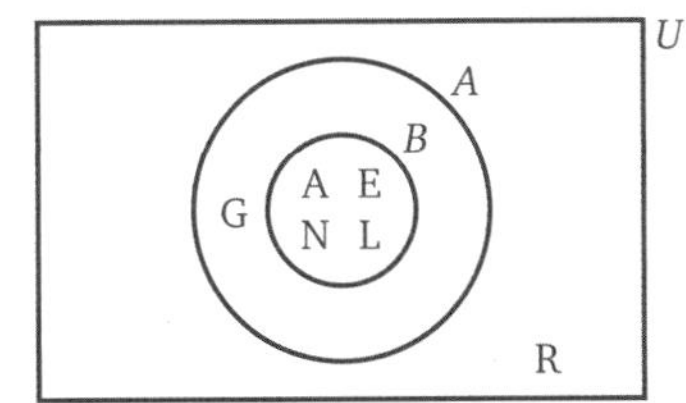

a $A' = \{R\}$
b $B' = \{G, R\}$
c $A \cap B = \{A, E, L, N\}$
d $A \cup B = \{A, E, G, L, N\}$
e $(A \cap B)' = \{G, R\}$
f $A' \cap B' = \{R\}$

6

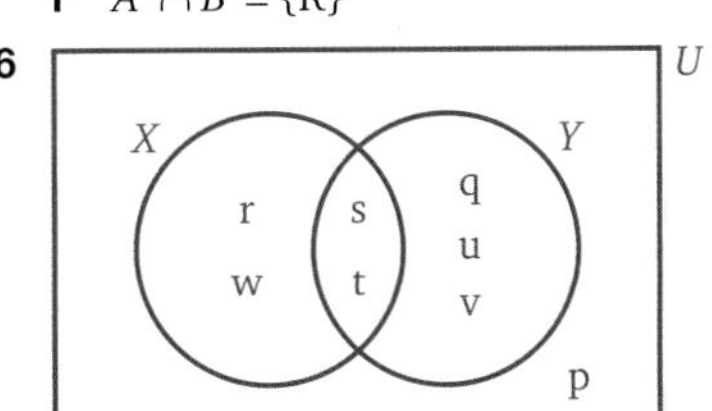

a $X' = \{p, q, u, v\}$
b $Y' = \{p, r, w\}$
c $X' \cap Y' = \{p\}$
d $X \cup Y' = \{p, r, w\}$
e $(X \cup Y)' = \{p\}$
$X' \cap Y'$ and $(X \cup Y)'$ are equal

7

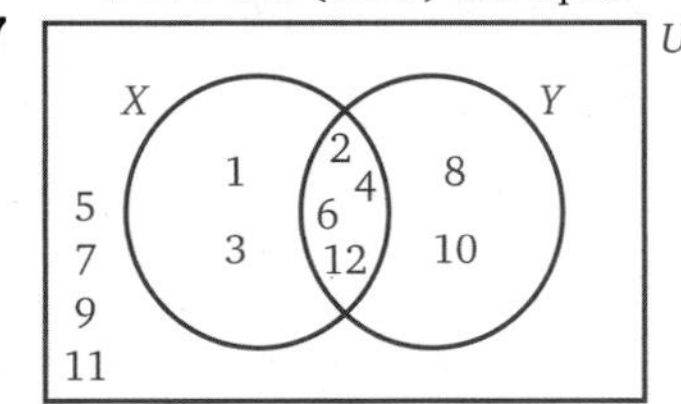

a $X' = \{5, 7, 8, 9, 10, 11\}$
b $Y' = \{1, 3, 5, 7, 9, 11\}$
c $X' \cap Y' = \{5, 7, 9, 11\}$
d $X' \cup Y' = \{1, 3, 5, 7, 8, 9, 10, 11\}$
e $X \cup Y = \{1, 2, 3, 4, 6, 8, 10, 12\}$
f $(X \cup Y)' = \{5, 7, 9, 11\}$
$X' \cap Y'$ and $(X \cup Y)'$ are equal

8 **a** **b** **c**

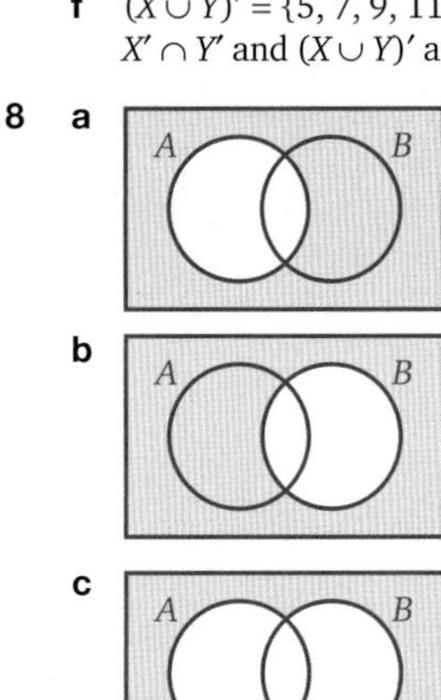

d

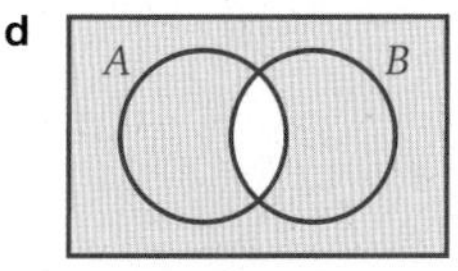

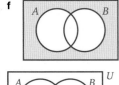

e **f**

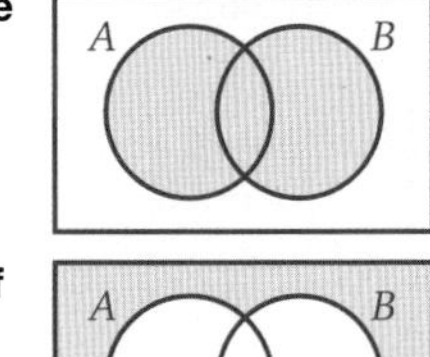

9

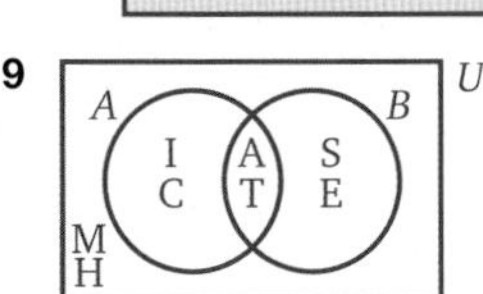

a $A' = \{E, H, M, S\}$
b $B' = \{C, H, I, M\}$
c $A \cup B = \{A, C, E, I, S, T\}$
d $(A \cup B)' = \{H, M\}$
e $A' \cup B' = \{C, E, H, I, M, S\}$
f $A' \cap B' = \{H, M\}$

10 **a** P' = {pupils in my class without compasses}
b Q' = {pupils in my class without protractors}
c $P' \cap Q'$ = {pupils in my class with neither compasses nor protractors}
d $(P \cup Q)'$ = {pupils in my class with neither compasses nor protractors}
e $P \cup Q$ = {pupils in my class with either compasses and/or a protractor}

11 **a** $A' = \{1, 2, 4, 5, 7, 8, 10, 11\}$
b $B' = \{1, 3, 5, 7, 9, 11\}$
c $A' \cap B' = \{1, 5, 7, 11\}$
d $(A \cup B)' = \{1, 5, 7, 11\}$

12 **a** $P' = \{-6, -4, -2, 0, 2, 4, 6\}$
b $Q' = \{-6, -4, -1, 0, 1, 4, 6\}$
c $P' \cap Q' = \{-6, -4, 0, 4, 6\}$
d $P' \cup Q' = \{-6, -4, -2, -1, 0, 1, 2, 4, 6\}$
e $(P \cup Q)' = \{-6, -4, 0, 4, 6\}$

13 **a** $A' = \{10, 11, 13, 14, 15, 17, 18, 19, 21, 22, 23\}$
b $B' = \{10, 11, 13, 14, 16, 17, 19, 20, 22, 23,\}$
c $A' \cap B' = \{10, 11, 13, 14, 16, 17, 19, 22, 23\}$
d $(A \cup B)' = \{10, 11, 13, 14, 17, 19, 22, 23\}$

Exercise 15c page 266

	$n(A)$	$n(B)$	$n(A \cup B)$	$n(A \cap B)$
1	5	7	9	3
2	4	5	7	2
3	3	6	7	2
4	6	4	8	2
	$n(X)$	$n(Y)$	$n(X \cup Y)$	$n(X \cap Y)$
5	9	7	12	4
6	5	2	7	0
7	13	10	16	7
8	12	12	20	4

	9	**10**	**11**	**12**	**13**	**14**	**15**	**16**
$n(A)$	3	3	6	11	8	9	8	4
$n(B)$	5	1	5	13	5	5	2	5
$n(A')$	9	5	4	15	6	6	4	8
$n(B')$	7	7	5	13	9	10	10	7
$n(A \cup B)$	7	4	8	18	10	12	8	9
$n(A \cap B)$	1	0	3	6	3	2	2	0
$n(A' \cup B')$	11	8	7	20	11	13	10	12
$n[(A \cap B)']$	11	8	7	20	11	13	10	12

Exercise 15d page 269

1 **a** 3	**b** 4	**c** 12	**d** 13
2 **a** 27	**b** 14	**c** 8	**d** 19
3 **a** 11	**b** 13	**c** 19	
4 **a** 41	**b** 20	**c** 29	
5 23			
6 **a** 19	**b** 9	**c** 23	
7 3			
8 **a** 8	**b** 11	**c** 23	
9 **a** 32	**b** 20	**c** 17	
10 **a** 28	**b** 20		
11 **a** 15	**b** 37	**c** 22	
12 **a** 15	**b** 21	**c** 7	
13 **a** 13	**b** 18		

Exercise 15e page 272

1 a $x+8$

b $2x+3+x+5+x-5=43$, i.e. $4x=40$

c 20 **d** 10

2 a

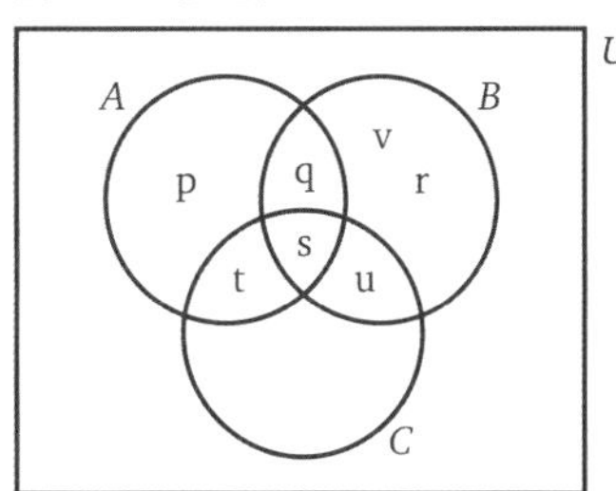

b p, q, s, t, u **c** 6

3

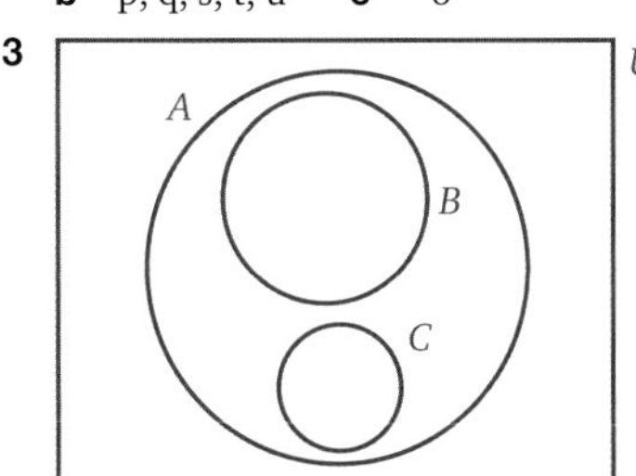

4

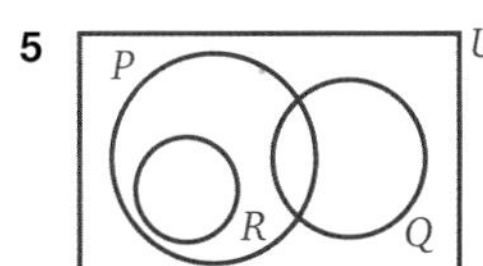

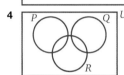

5

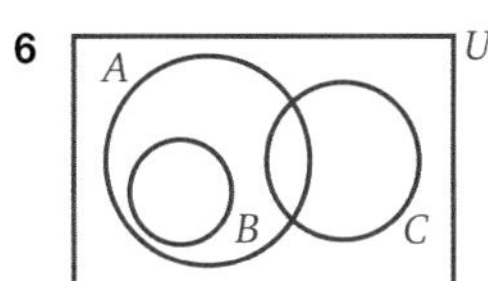

6

7 a $A \cup B = \{1, 2, 3, 4, 5, 6\}$,
$B \cup C = \{1, 2, 4, 5, 6, 8, 10\}$
$(A \cup B) \cup C = \{1, 2, 3, 4, 5, 6, 8, 10\}$
$A \cup (B \cup C) = \{1, 2, 3, 4, 5, 6, 8, 10\}$

b $A \cap B = \{1, 2\}$ $B \cap C = \{2, 6\}$
$(A \cap B) \cap C = \{2\}$ $A \cap (B \cap C) = \{2\}$

8

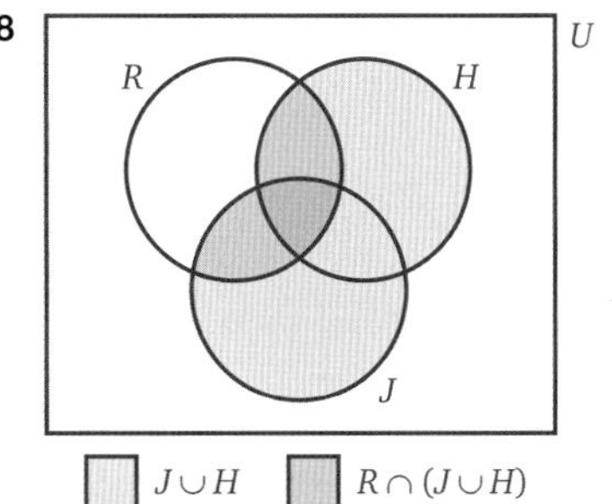

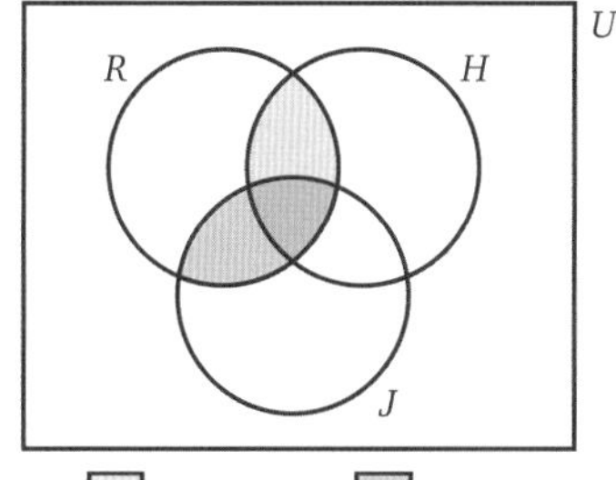

9

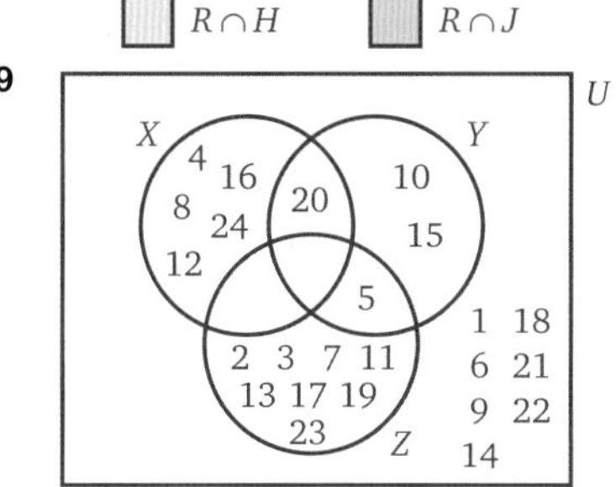

a {4, 5, 8, 10, 12, 15, 16, 20, 24}

b {2, 3, 5, 7, 11, 13, 17, 19, 23}

c {1, 6, 9, 14, 18, 21, 22}

d {5, 10, 15, 20}

10 a {E, G, M, R, T} **b** 11

11

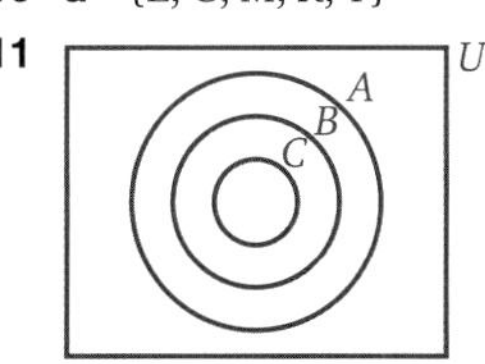

12

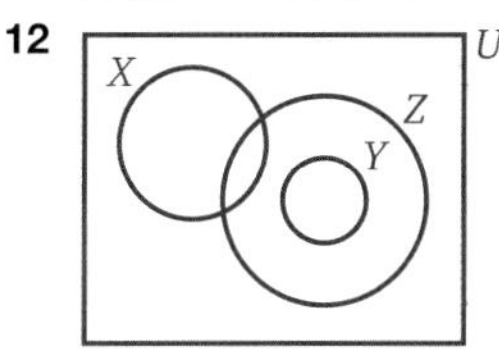

a isosceles right-angled triangles

b equilateral triangles

c equilateral triangles and right-angled triangles

13

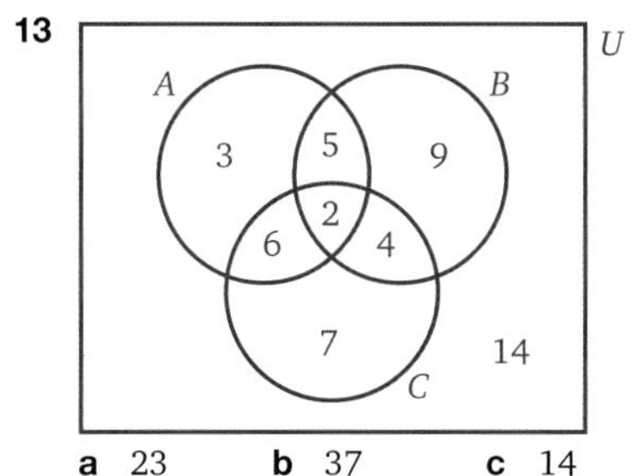

a 23 **b** 37 **c** 14

14

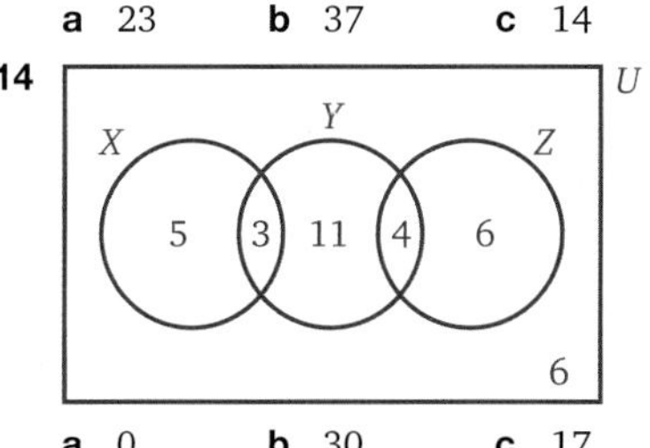

a 0 **b** 30 **c** 17

15 a 5 **b** 16 **c** 11 **d** 0

Exercise 15f page 276

1 A **2** A **3** D **4** C **5** D **6** A

CHAPTER 16

Exercise 16a page 279

1 $x = 4$
2 $y = 5$
3 $y = -3$
4 $x = -2$
5

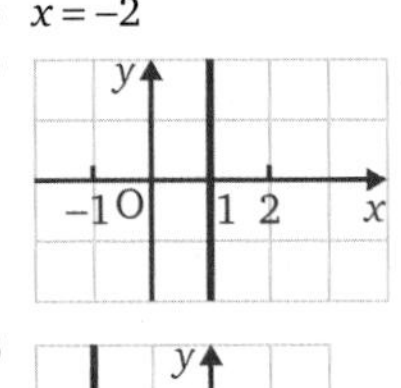

6

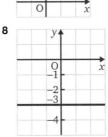

7

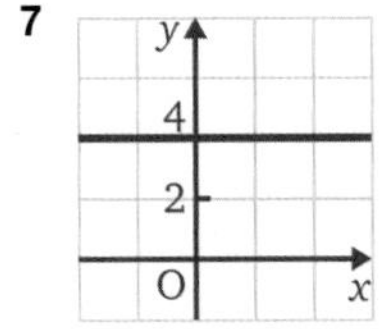

8

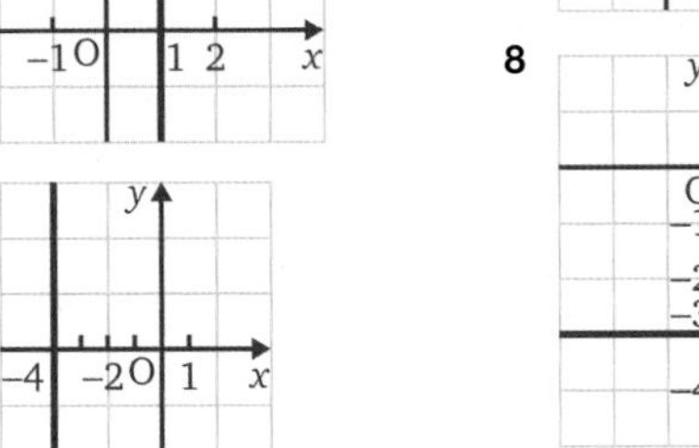

Exercise 16b page 281

1

x	−2	0	4
y	2	4	8

2

x	−2	0	3
y	−3	1	7

3

x	−3	0	3
y	7	4	1

4

x	−2	0	4
y	8	2	−10

13 a $1\frac{1}{2}$ **b** 0.4 **c** −1.6
14 a 0 **b** −0.8 **c** −3.4
15 a −2.6 **b** −1.8 **c** 1.2
16 a 3.6 **b** 0.6 **c** 1.2
17 a $-2\frac{1}{2}$ **b** 4.4 **c** 2.4
18 a 4.8 **b** 1.2 **c** −11.2
19 a −1.4 **b** 1.4 **c** 3.5
20 a 8.6 **b** 2.8 **c** 3

Exercise 16c page 283

1 yes, no **3** no, no **5** yes, yes
2 yes, yes **4** no, yes **6** no, yes

Exercise 16d page 284

1 lines are parallel; coefficient of x is 2 in each equation
2 lines are parallel; coefficient of x is −3 in each equation
3 lines are parallel; coefficient of x is $\frac{1}{2}$ in each equation
4 lines are parallel; coefficient of x is 1 in each equation
5 lines **a** and **c** are parallel
6 lines are parallel; coefficient of x is −1 in each equation

Exercise 16e page 286

1 4 **3** 1 **5** $-\frac{9}{5}$ **7** 0
2 −2 **4** $-\frac{3}{4}$ **6** $\frac{2}{3}$

8 y-axis; you find yourself dividing by zero
9 a parallel to the y-axis
b zero gradient
c zero gradient
d parallel to the y-axis

Exercise 16f page 288

1 2 **3** 2 **5** 4
2 1 **4** −2
6 a 4 **b** −3 **c** 1 **d** $\frac{1}{2}$

Exercise 16g page 289

1 2, 4 **7** 5, 2 **13** −0.4, 9
2 5, 3 **8** $\frac{1}{2}$, −1 **14** 5, 4
3 3, −4 **9** $-\frac{1}{3}$, 4 **15** 2, $2\frac{1}{2}$
4 1, −6 **10** 3, −7 **16** $\frac{1}{3}$, −2
5 −2, 3 **11** −3, 7 **17** $\frac{2}{5}$, 1
6 −4, 2 **12** $\frac{1}{3}$, 7 **18** $-\frac{3}{4}$, 2
19 $y = 2x + 7$ **23** $y = \frac{1}{2}x + 6$
20 $y = 3x + 1$ **24** $y = -2x + 1$
21 $y = x + 3$ **25** $y = x - 2$
22 $y = 2x - 5$ **26** $y = -\frac{1}{2}x + 4$

Exercise 16h page 291

1 $y = 3x + 1$, $y = 5 + 3x$, $y = 3x - 4$
2 $y = 2 - x$, $y = 4 - x$, $2y = 3 - 2x$, $y = -x + 1$, $y = -x$
3 $3y = x$, $y = \frac{1}{3}x + 2$, $y = \frac{1}{3} + \frac{1}{3}x$, $y = \frac{1}{3}x - 4$
4 $y = \frac{1}{2}x + 2$ and $y = \frac{1}{2}x - 1$; $y = 2 - \frac{1}{2}x$ and $2y = 3 - x$
5 2; $y = 2x + 3$
6 −3; $y = -3x + 1$
7 $y = 4x$
8 e.g. $y = 6 - x$, $y = -x$, $y = -2 - x$
9 a $y = 4x + 4$ **c** $y = \frac{1}{2}x + 4$
b $y = -3x + 4$
10 a $y = \frac{1}{3}x + 6$ **c** $y = \frac{1}{3}x - 3$
b $y = \frac{1}{3}x$
11 a $y = 2x + 2$ **c** $y = 2x - 4$
b $y = 2x + 10$
12 $y = 3 + 2x$ and $y = 2x - 3$
13 −3, 4; 4, −3; $y = -3x - 3$
14 a $y = -4x$ **b** $y = -4x - 7$

Exercise 16i page 293

1 $-\frac{3}{5}$ **4** −1 **7** $\frac{1}{3}$
2 $-\frac{1}{3}$ **5** −2 **8** 2
3 $\frac{1}{4}$ **6** $-\frac{1}{3}$ **9** −1 in each case

Exercise 16j page 294

1 $-\frac{3}{4}$ **3** $\frac{1}{2}$ **5** 2
2 $-\frac{3}{5}$ **4** −2 **6** $\frac{3}{4}$

7 a (2, 0), (0, 4) b (12, 0), (0, −9)

8 a $\frac{x}{6}+\frac{y}{5}=1$ b $\frac{x}{4}-\frac{y}{3}=1$

9 $-\frac{1}{3}$

Exercise 16k page 295

1 $-\frac{3}{5}, 3$
2 $-\frac{1}{3}, 2$
3 $\frac{1}{4}, -2$
4 $\frac{1}{3}, -2$
5 3, 6
6 $-\frac{1}{3}, 2$
7 $-\frac{3}{4}, 3$
8 $-\frac{3}{5}, 3$
9 $\frac{1}{2}, -2$
10 −3, 6
11 $-\frac{4}{3}, 4$
12 $\frac{4}{3}, -4$
13 4, 2
14 −1, 4
15 −2, 4
16 $-\frac{2}{5}, 3$
17 $-\frac{1}{2}, 5$
18 $2, \frac{5}{2}$
19 2, −4
20 −1, −3
21 $-\frac{3}{4}, 3$

Exercise 16l page 296

1 $-\frac{4}{3}, 4; y=-\frac{4}{3}x+4$
2 $-2, 7; y=-2x+7$
3 $\frac{3}{5}, 1; y=\frac{3}{5}x+1$
4 $-\frac{4}{3}, 2; y=-\frac{4}{3}x+2$
5 $\frac{7}{2}, -4; y=\frac{7}{2}x-4$
6 $\frac{1}{3}, -1; y=\frac{1}{3}x-1$
7 $\frac{1}{6}, 1; y=\frac{1}{6}x+1$
8 $\frac{4}{5}, -3; y=\frac{4}{5}x-3$
9 $\frac{5}{3}, -4; y=\frac{5}{3}x-4$
10 $-1, -5; y=-x-5$
11 $2, 12; y=2x+12$
12 $\frac{5}{6}, 6; y=\frac{5}{6}x+6$
13 AB, $5y=2x+20$; AC, $5x+3y=12$
14 $3, y=3x-11$
15 $-3, y=-3x+7$
16 $\frac{5}{2}, y=\frac{5}{2}x-\frac{1}{2}$
17 $2, y=2x+7$
18 $5, y=5x-21$
19 $-1, y=-x+3$
20 $-1, y=-x+1$
21 $2, y=2x-11$
22 $\frac{1}{5}, y=\frac{1}{5}x-\frac{6}{5}$
23 $-\frac{5}{4}, \frac{x}{4}+\frac{y}{5}=1$ or $y=-\frac{5}{4}x+5$
24 $-\frac{2}{3}, \frac{x}{3}+\frac{y}{5}=1$ or $y=-\frac{2}{3}x+2$
25 $\frac{2}{3}, \frac{x}{3}+\frac{y}{2}=1$ or $y=\frac{2}{3}x-2$
26 $-3, \frac{x}{2}+\frac{y}{6}=1$ or $y=-3x+6$
27 $3, y=3x-10$
28 $-1, y=-x+4$
29 $\frac{7}{2}, y=\frac{7}{2}x-6$
30 $-1, y=-x+3$
31 $\frac{5}{2}, -\frac{x}{2}+\frac{y}{5}=1$ or $y=\frac{5}{2}x+5$
32 $\frac{2}{11}, y=\frac{2}{11}x+\frac{45}{11}$
33 $1, y=x-1$
34 $-\frac{1}{4}, y=-\frac{1}{4}x+\frac{11}{4}$

Exercise 16m page 298

1 $y=3x-16$
2 square
3 rhombus
4 $\left(\frac{1}{2}, 3\right)$
5 midpoint is (5, 3); $y=-2x+13$
6 $2y=-x+4$
7 square

Exercise 16n page 298

1 2
2 (0, 4)
3 (4, 0)
4 12
5 $y=5x$
6 (12, 0)
7 yes
8 $\frac{3}{5}$

Exercise 16p page 299

1 −3
2 no
3 $y=-4x$
4 (0, 4)
5 (0, 6), (6, 0)
6 $-\frac{3}{2}$
7 $y=\frac{1}{2}x$
8 (2, 0), (0, 3)

CHAPTER 17

Exercise 17a page 302

1 $x=4$
2 $x=3$
3 $x=3$
4 $x=6$
5 $x=2$
6 $x=2$
7 $x=4$
8 $x=3$
9 $5x+17$
10 $6x+6$
11 $31x+24$
12 $x+26$
13 $8x+19$
14 $3x+42$
15 $19x-5$
16 $33x-15$
17 $x=4$
18 $x=7$
19 $x=3$
20 $x=-2\frac{2}{3}$
21 $x=3$
22 $x=5$
23 $x=\frac{1}{3}$
24 $x=17$
25 $x=2$
26 $x=8$
27 $x=1$
28 $x=-1\frac{1}{10}$
29 $x=\frac{3}{4}$
30 $x=\frac{3}{11}$

Exercise 17b page 303

1 $\frac{x}{2}$
2 $\frac{x}{6}$
3 $\frac{3x}{2}$
4 $\frac{2x}{3}$
5 $\frac{4x}{5}$
6 $2x$
7 $\frac{3x}{10}$
8 $\frac{3x}{2}$
9 $6x$
10 $\frac{x^2}{6}$
11 $\frac{5x}{8}$
12 $\frac{x}{18}$
13 $2x$
14 $\frac{x}{2}$
15 $\frac{4x}{5}$
16 $\frac{3x}{10}$
17 $\frac{2x}{3}$
18 $9x$
19 $9x$
20 $\frac{2x^2}{3}$

Exercise 17c page 304

1 15
2 8
3 48
4 12
5 $3\frac{5}{9}$
6 $22\frac{1}{2}$
7 14
8 $8\frac{1}{3}$
9 $\frac{1}{6}$
10 $\frac{3}{20}$
11 $\frac{3}{2}$
12 $\frac{5}{9}$
13 $1\frac{1}{3}$
14 $1\frac{1}{20}$
15 $\frac{5}{12}$
16 $\frac{7}{10}$
17 $2\frac{1}{4}$
18 $13\frac{3}{4}$
19 $3\frac{6}{13}$
20 $1\frac{11}{17}$
21 $6\frac{3}{4}$
22 $3\frac{1}{2}$
23 $12\frac{2}{3}$
24 20
25 $-1\frac{1}{4}$
26 $1\frac{5}{7}$
27 $\frac{3}{4}$
28 $1\frac{1}{3}$
29 11
30 $\frac{1}{14}$
31 $1\frac{6}{7}$
32 $\frac{23}{27}$
33 $\frac{18}{23}$
34 $\frac{1}{2}$
35 $1\frac{1}{7}$
36 $1\frac{2}{3}$
37 $1\frac{1}{6}$
38 $5\frac{5}{6}$
39 $1\frac{1}{22}$
40 $1\frac{18}{23}$
41 $\frac{1}{30}$
42 7
43 $2\frac{17}{26}$
44 2
45 $-\frac{1}{4}$
46 $\frac{28}{33}$

Exercise 17d page 306

1	\$150	**3**	30 cm	**5**	24 cm	**7**	9	**9**	12
2	40	**4**	12	**6**	5 cm	**8**	3	**10**	\$1000

Exercise 17e page 307

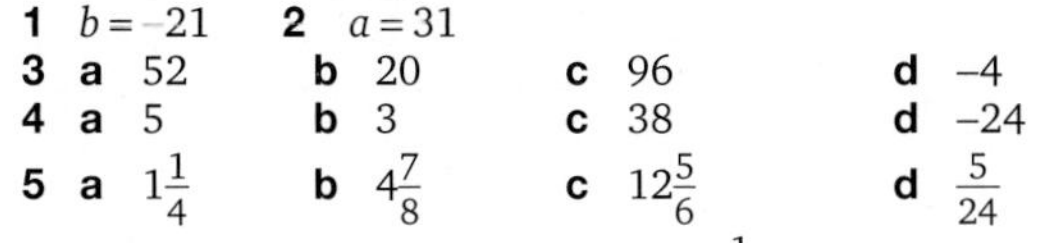

1 $b = -21$ **2** $a = 31$

3 **a** 52 **b** 20 **c** 96 **d** –4

4 **a** 5 **b** 3 **c** 38 **d** –24

5 **a** $1\frac{1}{4}$ **b** $4\frac{7}{8}$ **c** $12\frac{5}{6}$ **d** $\frac{5}{24}$

6 **a** $P = 10$ **b** $s = -5\frac{1}{2}$

7 **a** $A = 2$ **b** $C = 5$

Exercise 17f page 308

1 $x < 6$ **5** $x < 7$ **9** $x > 36$

2 $x > 6$ **6** $x \leqslant 6$ **10** $x \geqslant 5$

3 $x \geqslant -3$ **7** $x < 5$

4 $x \leqslant 5$ **8** $x \geqslant -3$

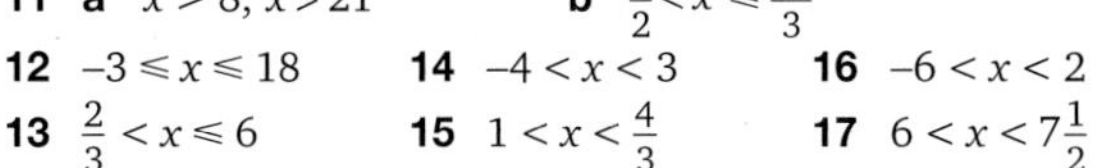

11 **a** $x > 8, x > 21$ **b** $\frac{5}{2} < x \leqslant \frac{10}{3}$

12 $-3 \leqslant x \leqslant 18$ **14** $-4 < x < 3$ **16** $-6 < x < 2$

13 $\frac{2}{3} < x \leqslant 6$ **15** $1 < x < \frac{4}{3}$ **17** $6 < x < 7\frac{1}{2}$

Exercise 17g page 310

1

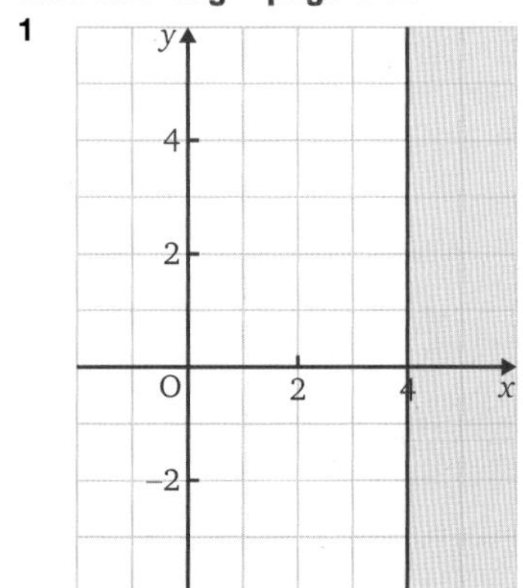

2

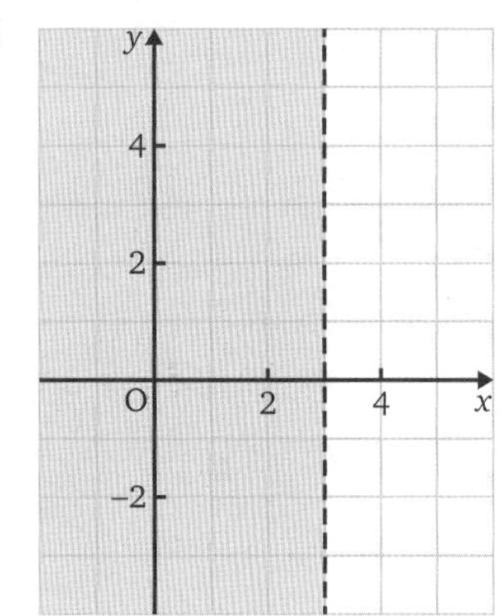

3

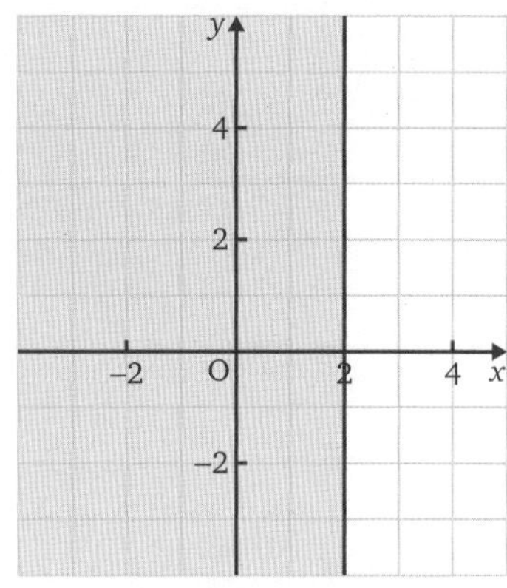

4

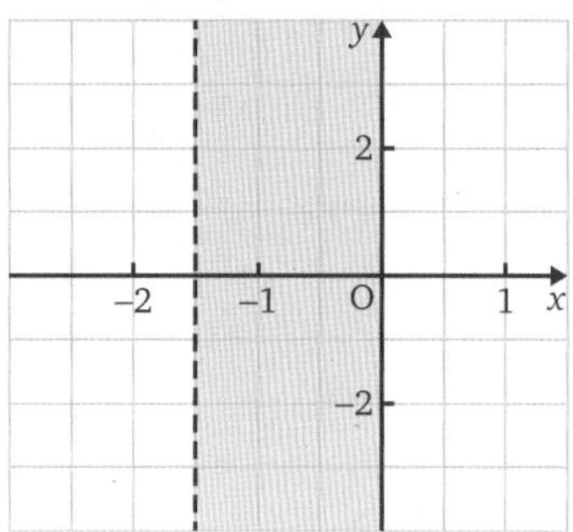

5

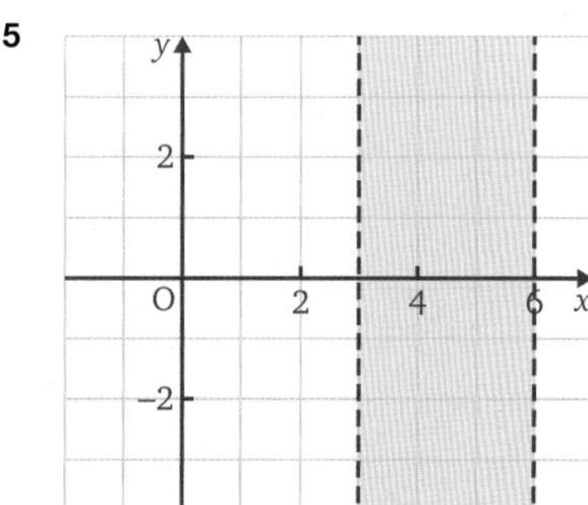

6

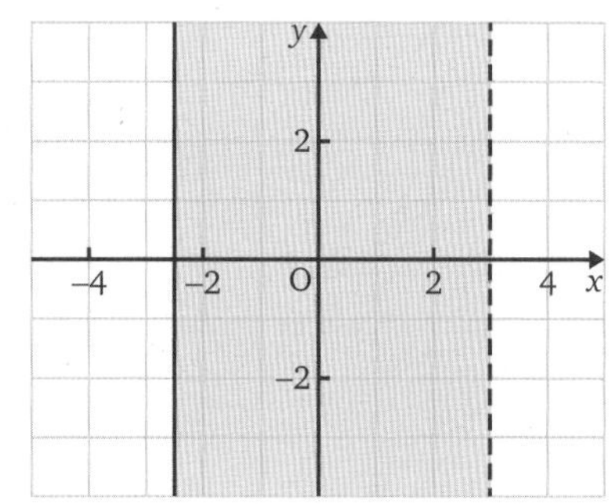

7

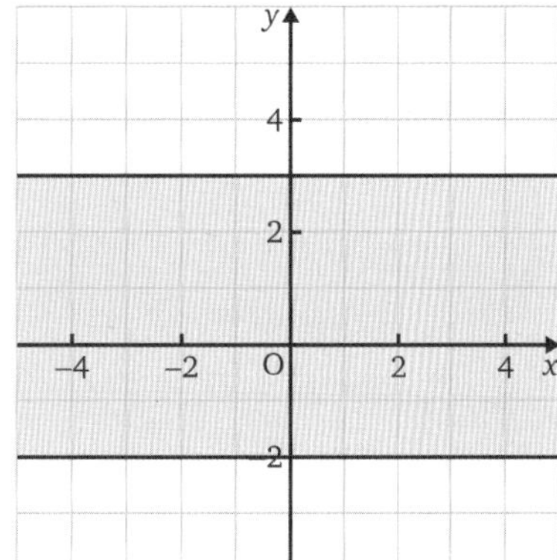

8

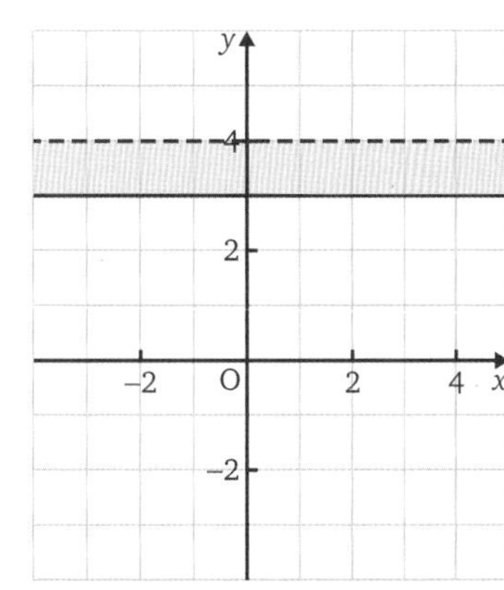

For the point (2, –3), yes for **5**, **7** and **8**; no for **6**

9 $x < -3$

10 $y < 2$

11 $-\frac{3}{2} < y \leqslant \frac{1}{2}$

12 $-1 < x \leqslant 3$

13 $-\frac{3}{4} < x < \frac{3}{2}$

14 yes, **10**; no **9**, **11**, **12** and **13**

Exercise 17h page 312

1

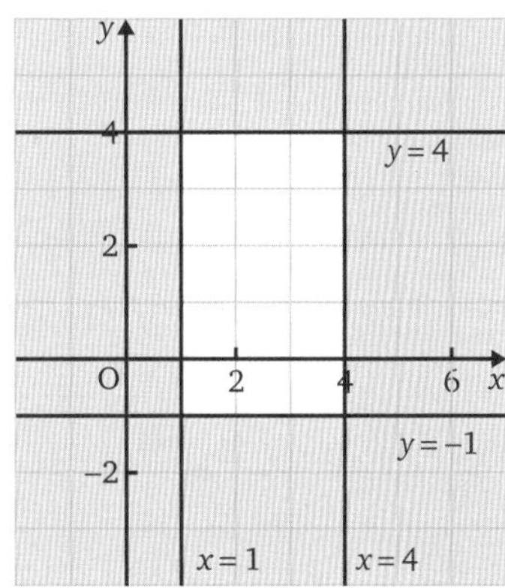

2

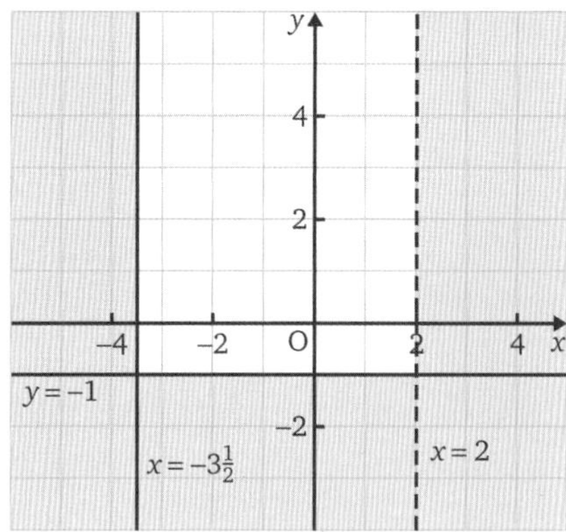

3

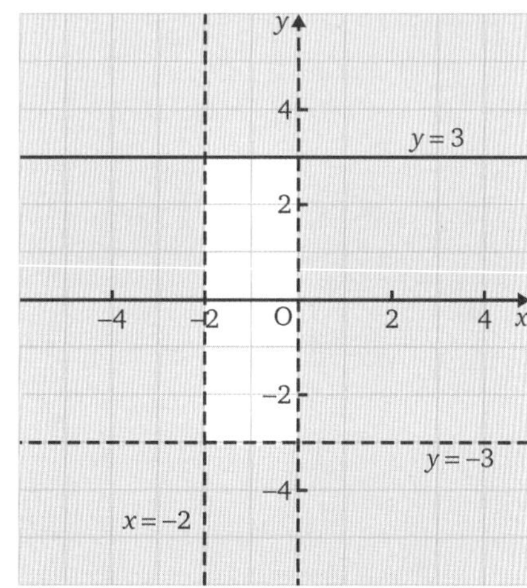

4

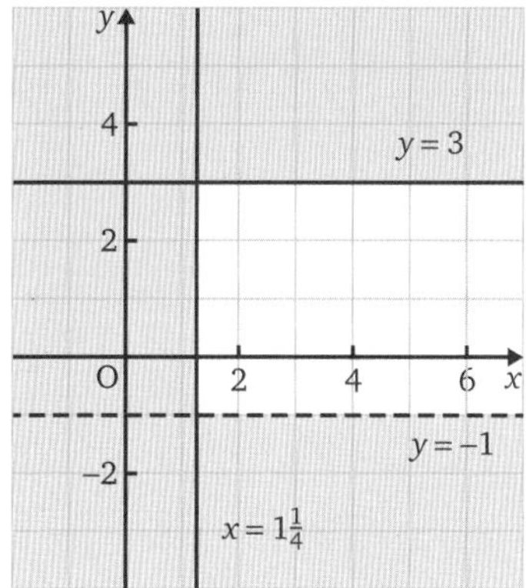

5 $-3\frac{1}{2} < x \leqslant 2\frac{1}{2}$, $-3 \leqslant y < 4\frac{1}{2}$

6 $-1\frac{1}{2} \leqslant x < 1\frac{1}{2}$

Exercise 17i page 313

1 C **2** A **3** D **4** C **5** A

CHAPTER 18

Exercise 18a page 315

1 $2x+2$
2 $3x-3$
3 $4x+12$
4 $5a+20$
5 $3b+21$
6 $3-3a$
7 $5-5b$
8 $6a-2$
9 $8+12b$
10 $5ab-5ac$
11 $4ab-8ac$
12 $6a^2+3ab$
13 $15xy+5xz$
14 $16xy+12yz$
15 $6np-10nq$
16 $16rt-8rs$
17 $3ab-15ac$
18 $12xy+8xz$

Exercise 18b page 316

1 $ac+ad+bc+bd$
2 $ps+pt+qs+qt$
3 $2ac+4ad+bc+2bd$
4 $5xz+15x+2yz+6y$
5 $xz-4x+yz-4y$
6 $ac+ad-bc-bd$
7 $xy+xz+y^2+yz$
8 $6ac+2ad+3bc+bd$
9 $5xz+10x+4yz+8y$
10 $15x-3xz-10y+2yz$
11 $2ps-3pt+2qs-3qt$
12 $ac-ad-2bc+2bd$
13 $6uw-30ur-5vw+25vr$
14 $6ac-9ad+8bc-12bd$
15 $9xz+6x+6yz+4y$
16 $12pr-9ps-4qr+3qs$
17 $9ac+12ad-12bc-16bd$
18 $21x-14xz-6y+4yz$

Exercise 18c page 316

1 $x^2+7x+12$
2 x^2+6x+8
3 x^2+7x+6
4 $x^2+7x+10$
5 $x^2+11x+24$
6 $a^2+9a+20$
7 $b^2+9b+14$
8 $c^2+10c+24$
9 $p^2+15p+36$
10 x^2-5x+6
11 $x^2-12x+35$
12 $a^2-10a+16$
13 $x^2-13x+30$
14 $b^2-10b+25$
15 $x^2-7x+12$
16 $x^2-12x+32$
17 b^2-6b+8
18 $a^2-8a+16$
19 x^2+x-6
20 x^2+x-20
21 $x^2-3x-28$
22 $a^2-7a-30$
23 p^2-25
24 $x^2+5x-14$
25 x^2+x-30
26 $x^2+9x-10$
27 $b^2-15b+56$

Exercise 18d page 318

1 $x^2+9x+20$
2 $a^2+7a+10$
3 $x^2-9x+20$
4 $a^2-7a+10$
5 $x^2+14x+48$
6 $a^2+17a+70$
7 $x^2-14x+48$
8 $a^2-17a+70$
9 $a^2-3a-10$
10 $y^2-3y-18$
11 $z^2-6z-40$
12 $p^2-3p-40$
13 $a^2-3a-70$
14 $y^2+8y-20$
15 $z^2-11z-12$
16 $p^2-11p-26$
17 x^2-6x+5
18 $b^2+16b+63$
19 a^2-16
20 $r^2-12r-28$
21 $p^2+14p+24$
22 $t^2-7t-60$
23 $c^2+3c-40$
24 x^2-25

Exercise 18e page 319

1 $2x^2+3x+1$
2 $5x^2+12x+4$
3 $5x^2+17x+6$
4 $3x^2+19x+20$
5 $3x^2+5x+2$
6 $3x^2+11x+6$
7 $4x^2+7x+3$
8 $7x^2+23x+6$
9 $6x^2+13x+6$
10 $12x^2-25x+12$
11 $10x^2-3x-18$
12 $21a^2-58a+21$
13 $10x^2+31x+15$
14 $21x^2-20x+4$
15 $12x^2-5x-2$
16 $6b^2-5b-25$
17 $4a^2-9$
18 $9b^2-49$
19 $49y^2-25$
20 $20a^2+a-12$
21 $16x^2-9$
22 $25y^2-4$
23 $9x^2-1$
24 $16x^2-8x-35$
25 $6x^2+5x+1$
26 $-5x^2+8x+4$
27 $-6x^2+19x-3$
28 $-35a^2+29a-6$
29 $8+10x-3x^2$
30 $4x^2+7x-15$
31 $15x^2+26x+8$
32 $-14x^2+13x+12$
33 $-20x^2+27x-9$
34 $12-p-p^2$
35 $x^2-3x-10$
36 $4x^2+9x-9$

Exercise 18f page 321

1 x^2+2x+1
2 x^2+4x+4
3 a^2+6a+9
4 $b^2+8b+16$
5 $t^2+20t+100$
6 $x^2+24x+144$
7 $x^2+16x+64$
8 $p^2+14p+49$
9 $x^2+2xy+y^2$
10 $y^2+2yz+z^2$
11 $c^2+2cd+d^2$
12 $m^2+2mn+n^2$
13 $p^2+2pq+q^2$
14 $a^2+2ab+b^2$
15 $e^2+2ef+f^2$
16 $u^2+2uv+v^2$
17 $4x^2+4x+1$
18 $16b^2+8b+1$
19 $25x^2+20x+4$
20 $36c^2+12c+1$
21 $9a^2+6a+1$
22 $4x^2+20x+25$
23 $9a^2+24a+16$
24 $16y^2+24y+9$
25 $x^2+4xy+4y^2$
26 $9x^2+6xy+y^2$
27 $4x^2+20xy+25y^2$
28 $9a^2+12ab+4b^2$
29 $9a^2+6ab+b^2$
30 $p^2+8pq+16q^2$
31 $49x^2+28xy+4y^2$
32 $9s^2+24st+16t^2$
33 x^2-4x+4
34 $x^2-12x+36$
35 $a^2-20a+100$
36 $x^2-2xy+y^2$
37 x^2-6x+9
38 $x^2-14x+49$
39 $a^2-2ab+b^2$
40 $u^2-2uv+v^2$
41 $9x^2-6x+1$
42 $25z^2-10z+1$
43 $100a^2-180a+81$
44 $16x^2-24x+9$
45 $4a^2-4a+1$
46 $16y^2-8y+1$
47 $49b^2-28b+4$
48 $25x^2-30x+9$
49 $4y^2-4yx+x^2$
50 $25x^2-10xy+y^2$
51 $9m^2-12mn+4n^2$
52 $49x^2-42xy+9y^2$
53 $a^2-6ab+9b^2$
54 $m^2-16mn+64n^2$
55 $25a^2-20ab+4b^2$
56 $9p^2-30pq+25q^2$

Exercise 18g page 322

1 x^2-16
2 b^2-36
3 c^2-9
4 x^2-144
5 x^2-25
6 a^2-49
7 q^2-100
8 x^2-64
9 $4x^2-1$
10 $9x^2-1$
11 $49a^2-4$
12 $25a^2-16$
13 $25x^2-1$
14 $4a^2-9$
15 $100m^2-1$
16 $9x^2-16y^2$
17 $4a^2-25b^2$
18 $1-4a^2$
19 $49y^2-9z^2$
20 $100a^2-81b^2$
21 $25a^2-16b^2$
22 $1-9x^2$
23 $9-25x^2$
24 $25m^2-64n^2$

Exercise 18h page 323

1 $2x^2+9x+12$
2 $2x^2+9x+2$
3 $x^2+15x+32$
4 $a^2-9a+36$
5 $2a^2-10a-3$
6 $x^2+13x+25$
7 $x^2-2x-21$
8 $x^2-2x-23$
9 $16x^2+6x-10$
10 $12x^2+8x-20$
11 $x^2y^2-6xy+9$
12 $25-10yz+y^2z^2$
13 $x^2y^2+8xy+16$
14 $9p^2q^2+48pq+64$
15 $a^2-2abc+b^2c^2$
16 $a^2b^2-4ab+4$
17 $36-12pq+p^2q^2$
18 $m^2n^2+6mn+9$
19 $u^2v^2-4uvw+4w^2$

Exercise 18i page 325

1 $5x+10$
2 $24pq-16pr$
3 $6a^2-13ab-5b^2$
4 $12x^2-17x-5$
5 $x^2+16x+60$
6 $x^2-20x+96$
7 $16y^2-16y-21$
8 $16y^2-81$
9 $25x^2+20x+4$
10 $4a^2-28ab+49b^2$

Exercise 18j page 325

1 $8-20x$
2 $16a-24a^2$
3 $12a^2-35a-33$
4 $x^2+2x-99$
5 $-20x^2-48x+5$
6 $y^2+4yz+4z^2$
7 $36y^2+24yz-5z^2$
8 $16a^2+8a+1$
9 $25a^2-70a+49$
10 $36z^2-156zy+169y^2$

Exercise 18k page 325

1 B 2 D 3 B 4 A 5 D 6 B

CHAPTER 19

Exercise 19a page 328

1 $4(x+1)$
2 $3(4x-1)$
3 $2(3a+1)$
4 $5(a-2b)$
5 $3(t-3)$
6 $5(2a-1)$
7 $4(3a+1)$
8 $2(a+2b)$
9 $7(2x-1)$
10 $x(x+2)$
11 $x(x-7)$
12 $a(a+6)$
13 $x(2x+1)$
14 $2t(2-t)$
15 $x(x+5)$
16 $x(x-4)$
17 $b(b+4)$
18 $a(4a-1)$
19 $2x(x-3)$
20 $2z(z^2+2)$
21 $5a(5a-1)$
22 $4x(3x+4)$
23 $5b(a-2c)$
24 $3y(y+9)$
25 $2a(a-6)$
26 $2p(3p+1)$
27 $3y(3y-2)$
28 $2(x^2+2x+3)$
29 $5(2a^2-a+4)$
30 $b(a+4c-3d)$
31 $4(2x-y+3z)$
32 $3a(3b-2c-d)$
33 $3(x^2-2x+3)$
34 $4(a^2+2a-1)$
35 $x(5y+4z+3)$
36 $5b(a+2c+d)$
37 $2y(x-2z+4w)$
38 $x^2(x+1)$
39 $x^2(1-x)$
40 $5a^2(4-a)$
41 $4x^2(3x-4)$
42 $4x^2(x^2+3)$
43 $a^2(1+a)$
44 $b^2(b-1)$
45 $2x^2(2x-1)$
46 $9a^2(3-2a)$
47 $5x^2(2-3x^2)$
48 $4(3x+2)$
49 $4x(2x+3)$
50 $3(3x^2-2x+4)$
51 $5x(x^2-2)$
52 $4q(2p+r)$
53 $x(x-8)$
54 $3(4+3y^2)$
55 $4x(3y+4z+2)$
56 $2x(3x^2+3)$
57 $\frac{1}{2}h(a+b)$
58 $m(g-a)$
59 $\frac{1}{2}m(v^2+u^2)$
60 $P\left(1+\frac{RT}{100}\right)$
61 $\pi r(2r+h)$
62 $\pi(R^2+r^2)$
63 $2g(h_1-h_2)$
64 $m\left(\frac{1}{2}v^2-gh\right)$
65 $\frac{\pi r^2}{3}(4r-h)$
66 $\pi r(3r+2h)$
67 $\frac{1}{2}mu(u+1)$
68 $\frac{1}{4}c(2b-a)$

Exercise 19b page 330

1 $(x+3)(y+3)$
2 $(a+2b)(1+b)$
3 $(a+b)(a+c)$
4 $(x-3)(y+2)$
5 $(x+1)(y+z)$
6 $(x+2)(y+4)$
7 $(a+b)(c+4)$
8 $(x+4)(y-2)$
9 $(p+q)(r+s)$
10 $(y+4)(x-3)$
11 $(x+2)(y-5)$
12 $(p+q)(r-s)$
13 $(a+2)(b-3)$
14 $(p-q)(r+s)$
15 $(p+4)(q+2)$
16 $(2+a)(3+b)$
17 $(p-q)(r-s)$
18 $(3a-b)(3-b)$
19 $(2a-b)(1-b)$
20 $(a-2)(a+2b)$
21 $(2-x)(3-y)$
22 $(a-2)(4a-b)$
23 $(3a-b)(2a-3)$
24 $(2m-3n)(1-n)$
25 $(t+r)(t+s)$
26 $(x-1)(x+y)$
27 $2(1-a)(2a+b)$
28 $(x+y)(1-y)$
29 $(2a+3b)(2-3a)$
30 $(a+b)(2a+c)$
31 $2(2x+y)(1-y)$
32 $(x+y)(y+z)$
33 $(x-2)(5-y)$
34 $(a+4)(b-3)$
35 $(x+3)(y-z)$
36 $(p-4)(2-q)$
37 $(a-2)(b-3)$
38 $(a-4)(3-b)$
39 $(m+n)(m+1)$
40 $(a+1)(a-b)$
41 $(2p+1)(p-2q)$
42 $(x+1)(1-y)$
43 $(a+b)(a+1)$
44 $(a-b)(a+1)$
45 $(x+y)(x-1)$
46 $(a-1)(2a+b)$
47 $(x+2y)(5x-1)$
48 $(n-1)(m-1)$
49 $(x-1)(3x+y)$
50 $(2p-1)(p+2q)$
51 $(1-a)(3a+b)$
52 $(1-z)(2x+y)$

Exercise 19c page 333

1 $(x+1)(x+2)$
2 $(x+1)(x+5)$
3 $(x+3)(x+4)$
4 $(x+3)(x+5)$
5 $(x+1)(x+20)$
6 $(x+1)(x+7)$
7 $(x+6)(x+2)$
8 $(x+1)(x+12)$
9 $(x+1)(x+15)$
10 $(x+2)(x+10)$
11 $(x+4)(x+4)$
12 $(x+3)(x+12)$
13 $(x+1)(x+18)$
14 $(x+2)(x+20)$
15 $(x+1)(x+8)$
16 $(x+3)(x+3)$
17 $(x+2)(x+18)$
18 $(x+3)(x+6)$
19 $(x+5)(x+6)$
20 $(x+4)(x+10)$

Exercise 19d page 333

1 $(x-1)(x-8)$
2 $(x-3)(x-4)$
3 $(x-2)(x-15)$
4 $(x-4)(x-7)$
5 $(x-6)(x-7)$
6 $(x-2)(x-3)$
7 $(x-1)(x-15)$
8 $(x-3)(x-3)$
9 $(x-2)(x-16)$

Exercise 19e page 334

1 $(x+2)(x-3)$
2 $(x+5)(x-4)$
3 $(x-4)(x+3)$
4 $(x-4)(x+7)$
5 $(x+5)(x-3)$
6 $(x-6)(x+4)$
7 $(x-3)(x+9)$
8 $(x-11)(x+2)$
9 $(x-7)(x+5)$

Exercise 19f page 335

1 $(x+2)(x+7)$
2 $(x-3)(x-7)$
3 $(x+7)(x-2)$
4 $(x+6)(x-5)$
5 $(x+1)(x+8)$
6 $(x-5)(x-5)$
7 $(x+9)(x-1)$
8 $(x-13)(x-2)$
9 $(x+8)(x-7)$
10 $(x+2)(x+30)$
11 $(x+3)(x-9)$
12 $(x+20)(x-4)$
13 $(x+1)(x+13)$
14 $(x-2)(x+14)$
15 $(x+10)(x-8)$
16 $(x-5)(x-6)$
17 $(x-4)(x+12)$
18 $(x+6)(x+12)$
19 $(x+4)(x+13)$
20 $(x+2)(x-14)$
21 $(x+3)(x+8)$
22 $(x+3)(x-14)$
23 $(x-2)(x-16)$
24 $(x+12)(x-5)$

Exercise 19g page 335

1 $(x+1)(x+8)$
2 $(x-3)(x-3)$
3 $(x+4)(x+7)$
4 $(x-5)(x+4)$
5 $(x+3)(x+3)$
6 $(x-1)(x-8)$
7 $(x+2)(x+15)$
8 $(x-3)(x-9)$
9 $(x+2)(x+11)$
10 $(x-13)(x+2)$

11 $(x-1)(x-7)$
12 $(x-6)(x+7)$
13 $(x-8)(x+3)$
14 $(x-2)(x-7)$
15 $(x+1)(x+27)$
16 $(x-7)(x+9)$
17 $(x+5)^2$
18 $(x-5)^2$
19 $(x+2)^2$
20 $(x-7)^2$
21 $(x+6)^2$
22 $(x-6)^2$
23 $(x-2)^2$
24 $(x+8)^2$

Exercise 19h page 335

1 $(2+x)(1-x)$
2 $(3-x)(2+x)$
3 $(1-x)(4+x)$
4 $(4-x)(2+x)$
5 $(3+x)(2-x)$
6 $(2-x)(1+x)$
7 $(4+x)(2-x)$
8 $(5+x)(1-x)$
9 $(5+x)(2-x)$
10 $(6-x)(2+x)$
11 $(5-x)(1+x)$
12 $(7+x)(2-x)$
13 $(6-x)(1+x)$
14 $(5+x)(4-x)$
15 $(5+x)(3-x)$
16 $(4-x)(3+x)$

Exercise 19i page 336

1 $(x+5)(x-5)$
2 $(x+2)(x-2)$
3 $(x+10)(x-10)$
4 $(x+1)(x-1)$
5 $(x+8)(x-8)$
6 $(x+4)(x-4)$
7 $(x+6)(x-6)$
8 $(x+9)(x-9)$
9 $(3+x)(3-x)$
10 $(6+x)(6-x)$
11 $(10+x)(10-x)$
12 $(a+b)(a-b)$
13 $(3y+z)(3y-z)$
14 $(4+x)(4-x)$
15 $(5+x)(5-x)$
16 $(9+x)(9-x)$
17 $(x+y)(x-y)$

Exercise 19j page 337

1 7.5
2 18.5
3 17.7
4 35.04
5 31.2
6 20.4
7 12.9
8 1000
9 336
10 53.2
11 5.336
12 8
13 140
14 75.8
15 0.526

Exercise 19k page 338

1 $(x+5)(x+8)$
2 $(x+6)(x-6)$
3 does not factorise
4 $(x-2)(x-6)$
5 $(x+7)(x-1)$
6 $(x-3)(x-8)$
7 $(x+15)(x-1)$
8 $(x+2)(x+6)$
9 $(x+7)(x-7)$
10 does not factorise
11 $(x+6)(x+7)$
12 $(2x+3y)(2x-3y)$
13 $(x+13)(x-2)$
14 $(x+2)(x+9)$
15 $(x-4)(x-6)$
16 $4(x+2y)(x-2y)$
17 does not factorise
18 $(x-2)(x+15)$
19 $(a-7)(a-9)$
20 $(1+2x)(1+4x^2)$
21 $(x+17)(x-4)$
22 $(p+1)(p^2+1)$
23 $(a+16)(a+7)$

Exercise 19l page 338

1 a $7a+21$
b $3x-6y$
2 a $x^2+14x+40$
b $6x^2-19x+15$
3 a $25+10x+x^2$
b $25-10x+x^2$
c $25-x^2$
4 a $10(a+2)$
b $5p(3p-2)$
5 a $(a+1)(a^2+1)$
b $(k+l)(2m-n)$
6 a $(x-3)(x+9)$
b $\left(a+\frac{b}{2}\right)\left(a-\frac{b}{2}\right)$

Exercise 19m page 338

1 a $4a+28$
b $6x^2-9xy$
2 a $x^2+12x+27$
b $15x^2-x-2$
3 a $25x^2+20x+4$
b $25x^2-4$
c $25x^2-20x+4$
4 a $6z(2z-1)$
b $4y(2x-3z)$
5 a $(z+2)(z^2+1)$
b $(3a+b)(c+2)$
6 a $(x-6)(x+4)$
b $\left(3m+\frac{n}{3}\right)\left(3m-\frac{n}{3}\right)$
7 a *Hint*: rewrite $100a+10b+c$ as $98a+2a+2b+7b+b+c$
b *Hint*: rewrite $100a+10b+c$ as $91a+9a+9b+b+c$

Exercise 19n page 339

1 C 2 C 3 A 4 D 5 A

CHAPTER 20

Exercise 20a page 342

1 $\frac{x}{4}$
2 $\frac{a}{2}$
3 $\frac{p}{q}$
4 $\frac{a}{b}$
5 $\frac{x}{y}$
6 $\frac{1}{2a}$
7 $\frac{a}{2c}$
8 $\frac{2}{q}$
9 $\frac{pq}{2}$
10 $\frac{a}{c}$
11 $\frac{a}{2}$
12 $\frac{z}{2}$
13 $\frac{b}{d}$
14 $\frac{1}{3x}$
15 $\frac{q}{2}$
16 $\frac{2}{3y}$
17 $\frac{m}{k}$
18 $\frac{s}{4t}$

Exercise 20b page 343

1 $\frac{1}{x}$
2 $\frac{t}{s-t}$
3 not possible
4 not possible
5 $\frac{x}{2(x-y)}$
6 $\frac{(a+b)}{2ab}$
7 $p-q$
8 $\frac{1}{(4-a)}$
9 not possible
10 $\frac{1}{v}$
11 $\frac{y}{x+y}$
12 $\frac{1}{2}$
13 $\frac{2a}{3(a-b)}$
14 $\frac{2(x-y)}{3xy}$
15 not possible
16 $u-v$
17 not possible
18 $\frac{1}{(s-6)}$

Exercise 20c page 344

1 $\frac{2a}{4a-b}$
2 $\frac{2q}{p-q}$
3 $\frac{1}{a}$
4 $\frac{3}{5}$
5 $\frac{2-x}{3y}$
6 $\frac{a}{3-b}$
7 $\frac{1}{3a}$
8 s
9 $\frac{3}{a}$
10 $\frac{2x}{3x-y}$
11 $\frac{3a}{a+b}$
12 $\frac{p+q}{5}$
13 $\frac{1}{3}$
14 $\frac{3+a}{4b}$
15 $\frac{2-y}{x}$
16 $\frac{1}{3y}$
17 a
18 $\frac{p}{2}$
19 $\frac{1}{a-2}$
20 $\frac{1}{x-4}$
21 $\frac{1}{y+2}$
22 $\frac{2}{a+3}$
23 $\frac{3}{x+3}$
24 $\frac{9}{y+2}$
25 $\frac{y}{x-2}$
26 $\frac{q}{p+2}$
27 $\frac{t}{s-7}$
28 $\frac{1}{p+3}$
29 $\frac{1}{x+6}$
30 $\frac{2}{x-4}$
31 $\frac{3}{x-4}$
32 $\frac{v}{u+6}$
33 $\frac{y}{x-2}$

Exercise 20d page 345

1 $\frac{4}{x+2}$
2 $\frac{1}{2-x}$
3 $\frac{a+b}{a-b}$
4 $\frac{2-x}{y}$
5 $-a$
6 $\frac{x-3y}{x}$
7 $\frac{-1}{1+a}$
8 $a+b$
9 $\frac{x-2y}{y}$
10 $\frac{1+y}{x+y}$

Exercise 20e page 346

1 $\frac{ac}{bd}$
2 $\frac{ad}{bc}$
3 $\frac{5(x-y)}{2x}$
4 $\frac{x(x-y)}{10}$
5 $\frac{a}{bc}$
6 $\frac{ac}{b}$
7 $\frac{3(a-b)}{4(a+b)}$
8 $\frac{(x-2)(x+3)}{3}$
9 $\frac{x-2}{3(x+3)}$
10 $\frac{pr}{q}$
11 $\frac{6b}{a}$
12 $\frac{q}{2p}$
13 $\frac{12y}{x}$
14 $\frac{2b^2}{5}$
15 $\frac{pq}{6}$
16 $\frac{x}{2y}$
17 $\frac{1}{2b}$
18 $\frac{2}{3p}$
19 $\frac{a}{4b}$
20 $\frac{a^3}{b^3}$
21 $\frac{1}{4(b-2)}$
22 $2(x-2)$
23 $2(a+3)$
24 6
25 $x-3$
26 $x-3$
27 $\frac{1}{x-2}$
28 $\frac{2}{x+4}$
29 $\frac{3(x-2)}{5(x+6)}$
30 $\frac{2(2x-3)}{9}$
31 a
32 $\frac{-c(a+b)}{b}$
33 $(x-4)(x-2)$

Exercise 20f page 349

1 pq
2 rst
3 30
4 abc
5 $wxyz$
6 ad
7 uvw
8 168
9 xy
10 $2x^2$
11 $3pq$
12 $2x^2y$
13 abc
14 st
15 $3p^2$
16 $5ab$
17 $3pq^2$
18 $6x$
19 $8x$
20 $18a$
21 60
22 a^2b
23 $30x$
24 $12x$
25 $15y$
26 $12x$

Exercise 20g page 350

1 $\frac{x+y}{xy}$
2 $\frac{3q+2p}{pq}$
3 $\frac{2t-s}{st}$
4 $\frac{6b+a}{2ab}$
5 $\frac{5y-6x}{15xy}$
6 $\frac{2b+5a}{2ab}$
7 $\frac{2y-3x}{xy}$
8 $\frac{4q+6p}{3pq}$
9 $\frac{3y-2x}{xy}$
10 $\frac{20b+21a}{28ab}$
11 $\frac{5}{6x}$
12 $-\frac{1}{35x}$
13 $\frac{5}{4y}$
14 $\frac{1}{8p}$
15 $\frac{13}{8a}$
16 $\frac{4}{21x}$
17 $\frac{6}{35x}$
18 $\frac{1}{3y}$
19 $\frac{3a+2b}{4ab}$
20 $\frac{ab-2a^2}{2b^2}$
21 $\frac{3y-4}{xy}$
22 $\frac{4-3p}{2p^2}$
23 $\frac{9a^2+2b^2}{12ab}$
24 $\frac{10q-3p}{4pq}$
25 $\frac{2s+ts^2}{2t^2}$
26 $\frac{15b+4}{6ab}$
27 $\frac{3+2x}{3x^2}$
28 $\frac{4y^2-9x^2}{6xy}$
29 $\frac{5y+4x}{8xy}$
30 $\frac{pq+3p^2}{3q^2}$
31 $\frac{10y-3}{14xy}$
32 $\frac{18b-3a}{2a^2b}$
33 $\frac{3x^2-3y^2}{2xy}$
34 $\frac{14q-15p}{18pq}$
35 $\frac{5a^2+4ab}{5b^2}$
36 $\frac{21+8p}{15pq}$

Exercise 20h page 351

1 $\frac{9x+3}{20}$
2 $\frac{5-x}{12}$
3 $\frac{13x+1}{15}$
4 $\frac{4x+13}{12}$
5 $\frac{1-2x}{35}$
6 $\frac{7x+3}{10}$
7 $\frac{3x+9}{35}$
8 $\frac{5x-3}{42}$
9 $\frac{5-22x}{21}$
10 $\frac{7x+9}{12}$
11 $\frac{22-13x}{6}$
12 $\frac{11-7x}{12}$
13 $\frac{20-17x}{24}$
14 $\frac{22-7x}{20}$
15 $\frac{10-5x}{6}$
16 $\frac{31x-6}{24}$
17 $\frac{11-7x}{10}$
18 $\frac{2-11x}{18}$
19 $\frac{26x+34}{15}$
20 $\frac{17x-1}{12}$
21 $\frac{5x-19}{21}$
22 $\frac{42x-49}{10}$
23 $\frac{27x+3}{14}$
24 $\frac{19x-73}{9}$
25 $\frac{26x-18}{15}$
26 $\frac{-17x+104}{30}$
27 $\frac{3a+6}{a(a+3)}$
28 $\frac{6x+4}{x(x+2)}$
29 $\frac{7x-4}{2x(x-4)}$
30 $\frac{2x-3}{4x(2x+1)}$
31 $\frac{5a+12}{a(a+4)}$
32 $\frac{7x-4}{x(x-1)}$
33 $\frac{11x+1}{3x(2x+1)}$
34 $\frac{21x-6}{5x(2x+3)}$

Exercise 20i page 354

1 $\frac{2c-ab}{ac}$
2 $\frac{qr^2}{p}$
3 $\frac{7x-14}{12}$
4 $\frac{a}{a-b}$
5 $\frac{1}{12x}$
6 $\frac{1}{x+2}$
7 $\frac{-p}{p+q}$
8 $\frac{12-2x}{3x^2}$
9 $\frac{1-2x}{x(x+1)}$
10 $\frac{ab}{c}$
11 $\frac{8}{15}$
12 $\frac{23}{20x}$
13 $\frac{3}{10x^2}$
14 $\frac{4x+7}{10}$
15 $\frac{(x+4)(2x-1)}{50}$
16 $\frac{25}{12x}$
17 $\frac{25}{24x^2}$
18 $\frac{3}{2}$
19 $\frac{19x-1}{3x(x-1)}$
20 $\frac{2}{x(x-1)}$
21 $\frac{-a-3}{2a(a-1)}$
22 $\frac{3}{a(a-1)}$
23 $\frac{3}{y}$
24 -1

Exercise 20j page 355

1 8
2 –5
3 6
4 $1\frac{1}{3}$
5 10
6 5
7 $9\frac{3}{5}$
8 $5\frac{1}{4}$
9 –1
10 $8\frac{3}{4}$
11 2
12 –18
13 3
14 –1
15 21
16 $\frac{4}{9}$
17 $-2\frac{1}{2}$
18 –17
19 2
20 4
21 1
22 $-2\frac{1}{19}$

Exercise 20k page 356

1 a $\frac{b}{2}$ b a c $a-b$
2 a $\frac{4}{3x}$ b $\frac{1}{3x^2}$ c 3
3 –13
4 a $\frac{5x-7}{6}$ b $1\frac{7}{10}$

Exercise 20l page 356

1 a $\frac{v}{uw}$ b $\frac{1}{2a-b}$ c $\frac{x}{3-x}$
2 a $18s^2$ b $2(x-2)$ c $\frac{2-5x}{x(4x-1)}$
3 4
4 a $\frac{x}{6}$ b 30
5 a $x = 40$ b $x = 21$ c $x = 66$
x equals the LCM
6 $x = ab$

Exercise 20m page 357

1 C 2 C 3 A 4 C 5 D 6 B

CHAPTER 21

Exercise 21a page 359

1 a 8 b 0 c 0
2 a 0 b 5 c 0
3 a 0 b 7 c 0
4 a 0 b 0 c 3
5 a 33 b 0 c 0
6 a –24 b 0 c 0
7 a 70 b 0 c 0

Exercise 21b page 361

1 0
2 0
3 0
4 any value
5 4
6 1
7 0
8 2
9 0
10 7
11 any value
12 0
13 a 0 b 0
14 a 0 b 0
15 a 0 b 0
16 a 0 b any value
17 $a = 0$ or $b = 1$
18 $a = 0$ or $b = 5$
19 $a = 0$ or $b = 2$
20 $a = 3$ or $b = 0$
21 $a = 9$ or $b = 0$
22 $a = 0$ or $b = 4$
23 $a = 0$ or $b = 10$
24 $a = 1$ or $b = 0$
25 $a = 7$ or $b = 0$

Exercise 21c page 362

1 0 or 3
2 0 or 5
3 0 or 3
4 0 or –4
5 0 or –5
6 0 or 6
7 0 or 10
8 0 or 7
9 0 or –7
10 1, 2
11 5 or 9
12 7 or 10
13 4 or 7
14 1 or 6
15 8 or –11
16 3 or –5
17 –7 or 2
18 –2 0r –3
19 –4 or –9
20 –1 or –8
21 p or q
22 $-a$ or $-b$
23 4 or –1
24 –9 or 8
25 –6 or –7
26 –10 or –11
27 a or b

Exercise 21d page 363

1 1 or $2\frac{1}{2}$
2 4 or $\frac{2}{3}$
3 $\frac{4}{5}$ or $\frac{3}{4}$
4 0 or $1\frac{1}{4}$
5 0 or $\frac{3}{10}$
6 $-\frac{2}{5}$ or 7
7 $-\frac{5}{6}$ or $\frac{2}{3}$
8 $\frac{3}{8}$ or $-2\frac{1}{2}$
9 $1\frac{1}{7}$ or $-3\frac{3}{4}$
10 $-\frac{3}{4}$ or $-1\frac{1}{2}$
11 $2\frac{1}{3}$ or 2
12 $1\frac{2}{3}$ or $\frac{1}{2}$
13 0 or $\frac{1}{3}$
14 0 or $\frac{3}{7}$
15 $-1\frac{1}{2}$ or 3
16 $-\frac{3}{4}$ or $2\frac{1}{2}$
17 $-\frac{9}{10}$ or $\frac{4}{5}$
18 $\frac{2}{3}$ or $-2\frac{1}{4}$
19 $2\frac{2}{5}$ or $-3\frac{1}{2}$
20 $-1\frac{3}{5}$ or $-\frac{3}{4}$

Exercise 21e page 363

1 1 or 2
2 1 or 7
3 2 or 3
4 2 or 5
5 3 or 4
6 1 or 5
7 1 or 11
8 2 or 4
9 2 or 6
10 1 or 12
11 1 or –7
12 4 or –2
13 3 or –4
14 5 or –3
15 2 or –9
16 –1 or 13
17 2 or –3
18 –2 or 6
19 4 or –5
20 –3 or 8
21 –1 or –2
22 –1 or –7
23 –3 or –5
24 –2 or –6
25 –2 or –9
26 –1 or –6
27 –2 or –5
28 –1 or –13
29 –1 or –15
30 –3 or –6
31 ± 1
32 ± 3
33 ± 4
34 ± 9
35 ± 13
36 ±2
37 ± 5
38 ± 10
39 ± 12
40 ± 6

Exercise 21f page 365

1 0 or 2
2 0 or 10
3 0 or –8
4 0 or $\frac{1}{2}$
5 0 or $\frac{5}{4}$
6 0 or 5
7 0 or –3
8 0 or –1
9 0 or $\frac{5}{3}$
10 0 or $\frac{7}{5}$
11 0 or $-\frac{3}{2}$
12 0 or $-\frac{5}{8}$
13 0 or 7
14 0 or $-\frac{5}{3}$
15 0 or $\frac{12}{7}$
16 0 or $-\frac{7}{6}$
17 0 or $-\frac{7}{12}$
18 0 or –4
19 0 or $\frac{2}{7}$
20 0 or $-\frac{3}{14}$

Exercise 21g page 365

1 1 (twice)
2 5 (twice)
3 10 (twice)
4 –4 (twice)
5 –3 (twice)
6 3(twice)
7 4 (twice)
8 9 (twice)
9 –1 (twice)
10 –10 (twice)
11 –9 (twice)
12 7 (twice)

13 11 (twice)
14 −6 (twice)
15 $\frac{1}{2}$ (twice)
16 −5 (twice)
17 6 (twice)
18 20 (twice)
19 8 (twice)
20 $-\frac{2}{3}$ (twice)

Exercise 21h page 366

1 −5 and 6
2 −2 and 8
3 3 and −12
4 3 and −2
5 1 and −7
6 3 or −1
7 −4 and 6
8 5 and 7
9 −2 and 5
10 2 and 4
11 2 and 5
12 1 and 7
13 2 and 4
14 3 and 7
15 2 and 6
16 4 and 5
17 5 and 7
18 3 and 5

Exercise 21i page 367

1 −4 and 5
2 2 (twice)
3 $\pm\frac{1}{3}$
4 0 and $-3\frac{1}{2}$
5 −1 and −12
6 $\pm\frac{1}{4}$
7 0 and 6
8 −5 and 7
9 1 and −7
10 $\pm\frac{2}{5}$
11 $\pm 2\frac{1}{2}$
12 −2 and −9
13 0 and $2\frac{1}{2}$
14 0 and $1\frac{3}{4}$
15 3 and −4
16 3 and −1
17 −3 and 8
18 5 and 7
19 5 and −10
20 −11 and 8
21 5 and −9
22 −2 and 7
23 7 and −4
24 5 and −11
25 −4 and−5
26 −4 and −5
27 −2, −1
28 3, 2
29 −2, −2
30 −3, −3
31 1, −4
32 −3, −3
33 $\frac{2}{3}$, 1
34 −2, −1

Exercise 21j page 368

1 −2 or 8
2 −2 or 7
3 −7 or 6
4 $x + (x^2 - 6) = 66$; $x = -9$ or 8; 8 marbles
5 $x + x^2 = 56$; $x = -8$ or 7; Ahmed is 7 and his father is 49
6 $x + (x^2 + 2) = 44$; $x = -7$ or 6; Kathryn is 6 and her mother is 38
7 $x(x + 5) = 84$; $x = 7$ or −12; Peter is 7
8 $x(x - 4) = 140$; $x = 14$ or −10; Ann is 10
9 $x(x + 3) = 28$; $x = 4$ or −7; 4 cm by 7 cm
10 $x(x + 5) = 66$; $x = -11$ or 6; 6 cm by 11 cm
11 $\frac{1}{2}x \times \frac{1}{2}x = 25$; $x = \pm 10$; 5 cm
12 **a** $A = 20x\text{ m}^2$, $B = x^2\text{ m}^2$, $C = 30x\text{ m}^2$
b $x^2 + 50x = 104$; $x = 2$ or −52; path is 2m wide

Exercise 21k page 370

1 **a** −10 **b** 0 **c** 8
2 **a** −2 **b** 0 **c** 12 **d** 0
3 **a** −11 **b** 0 **c** 0
4 **a** 0 or −7 **b** 0 or $\frac{1}{2}$
5 **a** 0 or 2 **b** 0 or $-\frac{3}{7}$
6 **a** 0 or −7 **b** 0 or $\frac{3}{4}$
7 **a** 3 or 8 **b** 2 or $-\frac{3}{5}$
8 **a** 2 or −5 **b** $1\frac{1}{3}$ or −2 **c** $1\frac{1}{2}$ or $-1\frac{1}{2}$
9 **a** −4 or 5 **b** $1\frac{3}{4}$ or −3 **c** $\frac{3}{5}$ or $-\frac{3}{5}$
10 **a** 7 or −5 **b** 5 or 8
11 **a** −3 or 2 **b** −5 or −6
12 **a** 5 or −3 **b** −4 or −8
13 **a** 5 or −9 **b** 5 or −6
14 **a** −5 or 2 **b** −10 or 3

Exercise 21l page 370

1 B **2** D **3** B **4** A **5** B **6** C

CHAPTER 22

Exercise 22a page 373

1 2, {H, T}
2 3, {R, B, Y}
3 10, {1, 2, 3, 4, 5, 6, 7, 8, 9, 10}
4 6, {R, Y, B, Brown, Black, G}
5 3, {chewing gum, boiled sweets, bar of chocolate}
6 4, {1 c, 10 c, 20 c, 50 c}
7 13,{A, 2, 3, 4, 5, 6, 7, 8, 9, 10, J, Q, K}
8 5, {a, e, i, o, u}
9 5, {2, 3, 5, 7, 11}
10 10, {2, 4, 6, 8, 10, 12, 14, 16, 18, 20}

Exercise 22b page 374

1 $\frac{1}{4}$
2 $\frac{1}{10}$
3 $\frac{1}{5}$
4 $\frac{1}{6}$
5 $\frac{1}{7}$
6 $\frac{1}{200}$
7 $\frac{1}{52}$
8 $\frac{1}{7}$
9 $\frac{1}{15}$

Exercise 22c page 376

1 5 **2** 3 **3** 26 **4** 2 **5** 10
6 **a** $\frac{1}{2}$ **b** $\frac{1}{2}$ **c** $\frac{2}{5}$ **d** $\frac{3}{10}$
7 **a** $\frac{1}{13}$ **b** $\frac{1}{2}$ **c** $\frac{1}{4}$ **d** $\frac{4}{13}$
8 **a** $\frac{2}{9}$ **b** $\frac{1}{9}$ **c** $\frac{1}{3}$ **d** $\frac{2}{9}$
9 **a** $\frac{1}{2}$ **b** $\frac{1}{3}$ **c** $\frac{1}{3}$
10 $\frac{2}{15}$
11 **a** $\frac{3}{5}$ **b** $\frac{1}{5}$ **c** $\frac{2}{5}$
12 $\frac{1}{40}$
13 **a** $\frac{18}{37}$ **b** $\frac{18}{37}$ **c** $\frac{9}{37}$
14 $\frac{21}{26}$
15 $\frac{4}{45}$
16 **a** $\frac{5}{12}$ **b** $\frac{1}{3}$ **c** $\frac{3}{4}$

Exercise 22d page 378

1 0, impossible
2 0.3, unlikely to be this heavy
3 1, almost certain
4 0.001, possible but unlikely
5 0, most unlikely!

6 0, impossible
7 1, certain
8 0, virtually impossible
9 1, it must be
10 0, almost impossible
11 Likely: you will watch TV this week, you will get maths homework this week.
Unlikely: you will be a millionaire, it will snow in Britain on mid-summer's day.

Exercise 22e page 379

1 $\frac{3}{5}$ 3 $\frac{21}{26}$ 5 $\frac{7}{10}$ 7 $\frac{24}{25}$ 9 $\frac{39}{40}$
2 $\frac{12}{13}$ 4 $\frac{5}{6}$ 6 $\frac{5}{8}$ 8 $\frac{2}{3}$ 10 $\frac{10}{13}$

11 a $\frac{1}{10}$ b $\frac{3}{10}$ c $\frac{2}{5}$ d $\frac{7}{10}$
12 a $\frac{1}{13}$ b $\frac{1}{4}$ c $\frac{3}{4}$ d $\frac{11}{13}$
13 a $\frac{15}{22}$ b $\frac{7}{22}$ c $\frac{1}{22}$ d $\frac{3}{11}$
14 a $\frac{2}{5}$ b $\frac{19}{30}$ c $\frac{7}{30}$ d 0

Exercise 22f page 381

1 about 50
2 10
3 20
4 a 10 b 20
5 20
6 a 15 b 45 c 30
7 20
8 10
9 10
10 5
11 25
12 a $\frac{1}{13}$ b 3
13 a $\frac{1}{2}$ b 30
c no, possible but not certain
d probably, you'd expect about 50
14 a \$10 b 5 c \$5
d lose, spending greater than likely winnings
15 a 2 b \$50
c spends \$50 more than winnings.

Exercise 22g page 384

1 the tombola (1 in 5 = 20% and is greater than 1 in 8 = 13%)
2 no, August is the better choice
3 a Medicine B
b probably, because the chance of serious side effects is lot lower with Medicine A
4 a Printer A as it is likely to last longer
b the size of the printers; the advance in technology over the life span of the printers; any other sensible answers
5 $\frac{2}{11}$ is less than $\frac{1}{3}$ so route 2 is the better choice
6 $\frac{5}{9} > \frac{3}{7}$ and $\frac{2}{5}$ so 24 June is the best choice

Exercise 22h page 385

1 D 2 B 3 A 4 C 5 D 6 C

REVIEW TEST 3 page 387

1 C 3 B 5 D 7 D 9 D
2 C 4 B 6 D 8 B 10 C

11 a $\frac{1}{2}$ b 0 c $\frac{1}{2}$ d $\frac{1}{2}$
12 a $\frac{1}{4}$ b $\frac{3}{8}$ c 0
13 a $\frac{1}{7}$ b $\frac{2}{21}$
14 a $(a+2)(a-2b)$
b $(x-3)(x-9)$
c $(4x+3)(x-2)$
15 a $(3x+4)(3x-4)$
b $5(a+3)(a-3)$
c 820
16 a 11 b $-\frac{2}{3}$ c $y=4x-5$
17 a $\frac{x+2}{3x+1}$ b $\frac{1-x}{4x+3}$
18 a $\frac{p}{9q}$ b $\frac{4b}{9a}$
19 a $\frac{3x+4y}{2xy}$ b $\frac{1}{2x}$ c $\frac{a(4a+5b)}{4b^2}$
20 a 2, 4 b $\frac{3}{2}, -\frac{3}{2}$ c $0, \frac{7}{3}$
21 a $\frac{1}{13}$ b $\frac{1}{2}$ c $\frac{1}{4}$
22

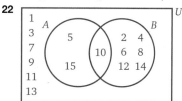

a {1, 2, 3, 4, 6, 7, 8, 9, 11, 12, 13, 14}
b {1, 3, 5, 7, 9, 11, 13, 15}
c {2, 4, 5, 6, 8, 10, 12, 14, 15}
d {1, 3, 7, 9, 11, 13}
e {1, 2, 3, 4, 5, 6, 7, 8, 9, 11, 12, 13, 14, 15}
f {1, 3, 7, 9, 11, 13}

REVIEW TEST 4 page 390

1 C 15 B 29 C
2 A 16 A 30 C
3 D 17 B 31 B
4 D 18 B 32 A
5 B 19 A 33 B
6 D 20 B 34 D
7 B 21 D 35 C
8 D 22 A 36 D
9 D 23 C 37 B
10 D 24 B 38 D
11 A 25 A 39 D
12 D 26 D 40 C
13 C 27 A 41 C
14 D 28 B 42 B

Index